TABLE OF CONTENTS

COLLECTOR'S EDITION

Fruits Basket 11

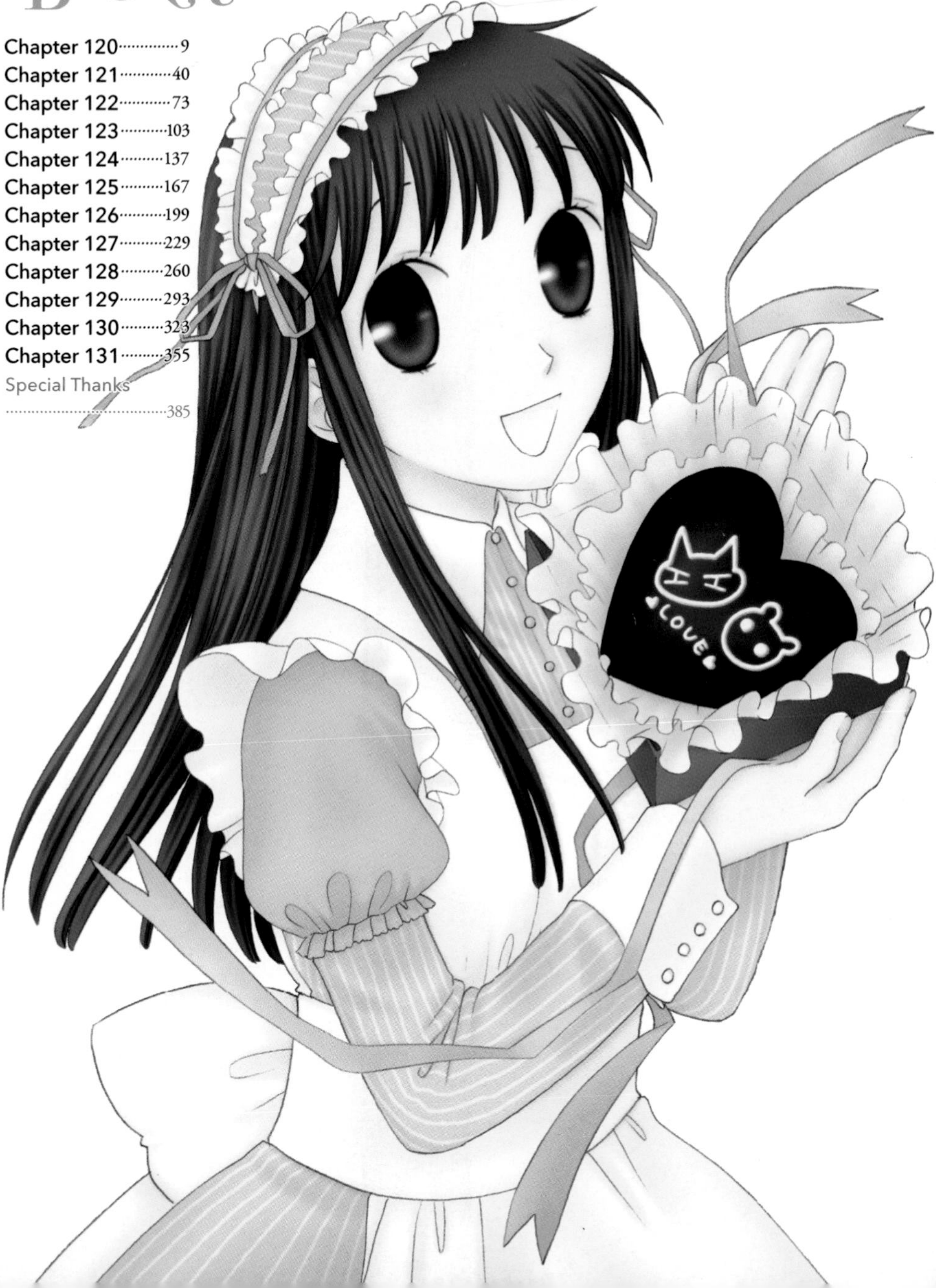
LOVE

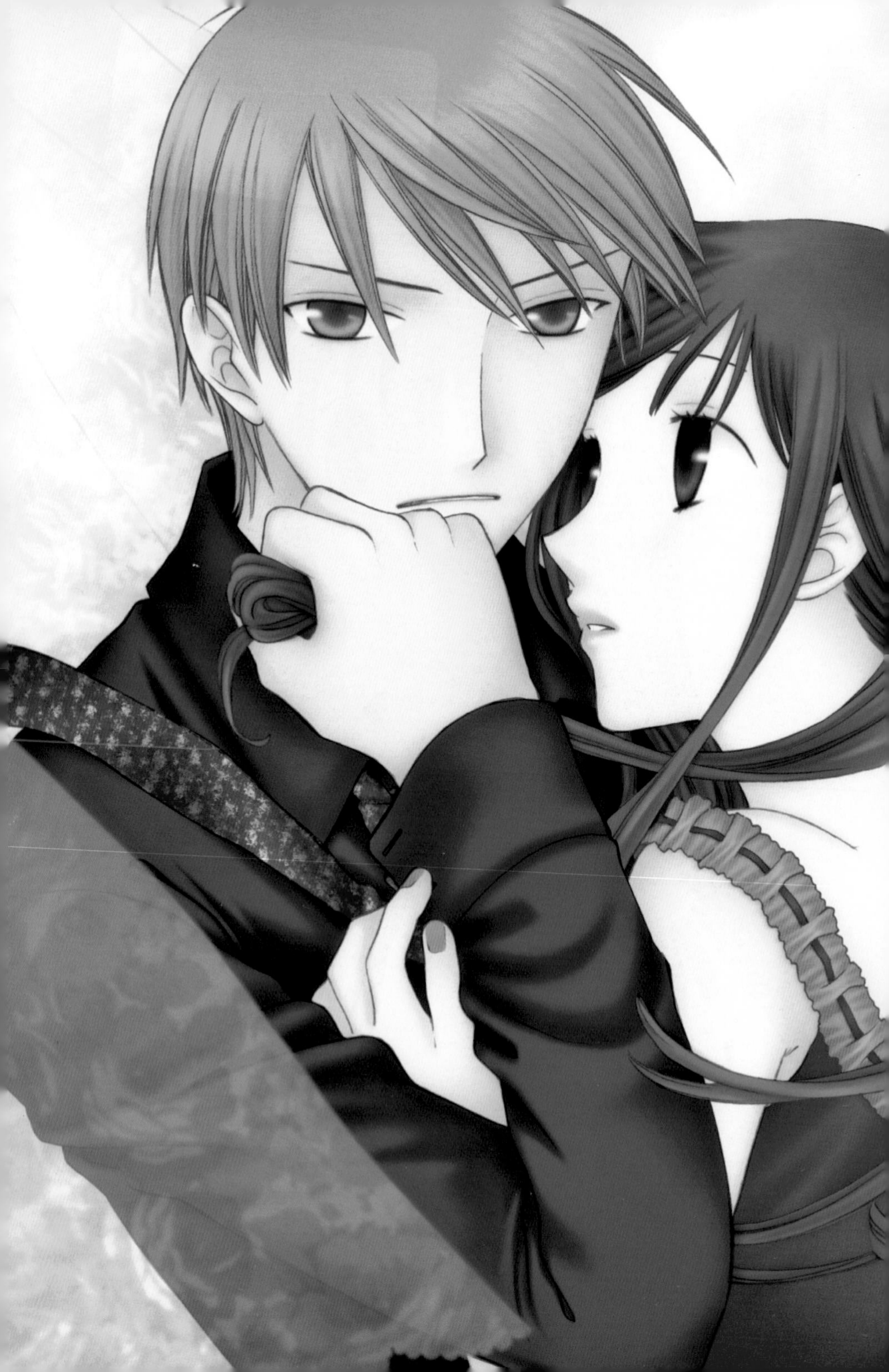

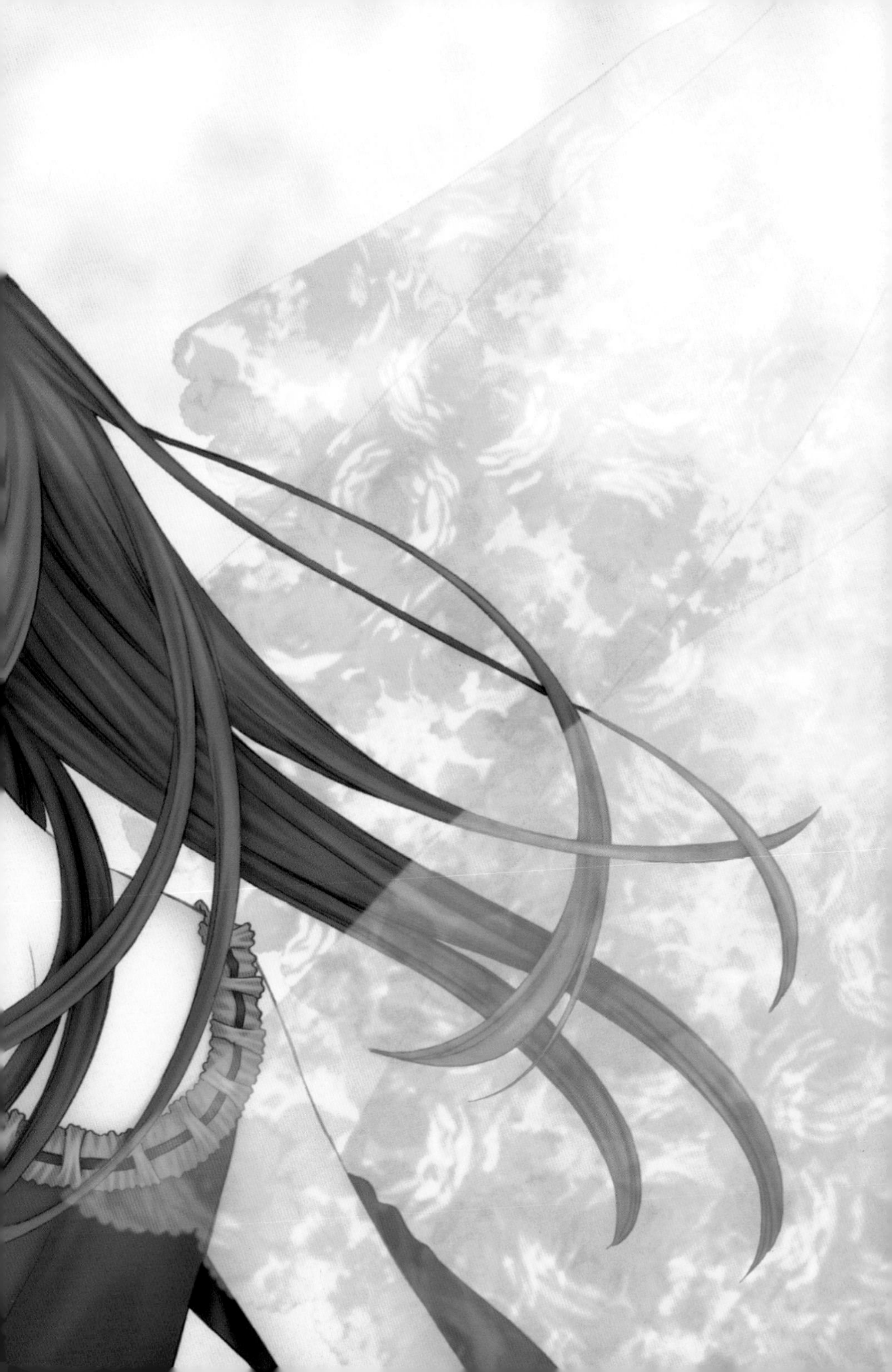

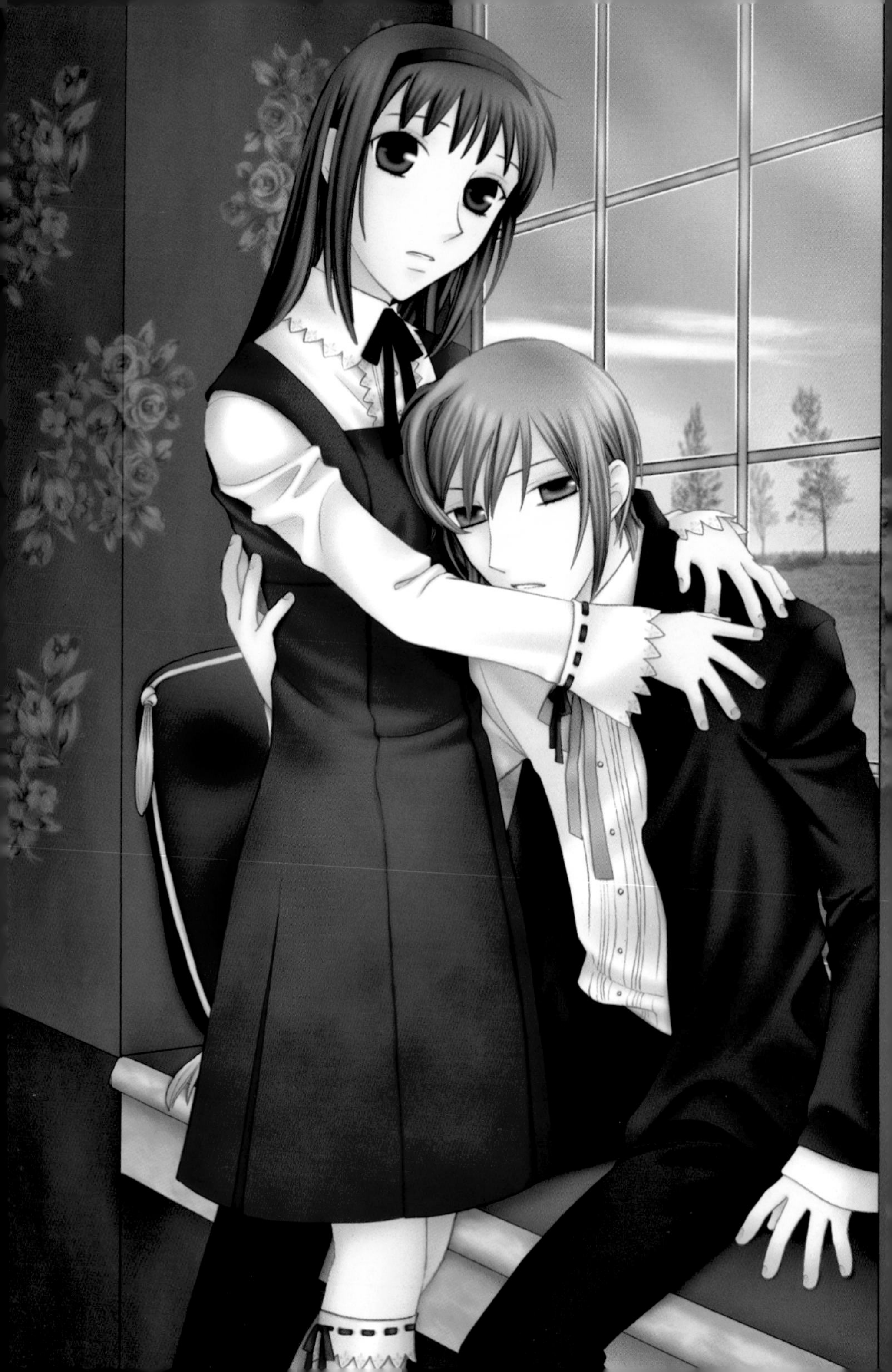

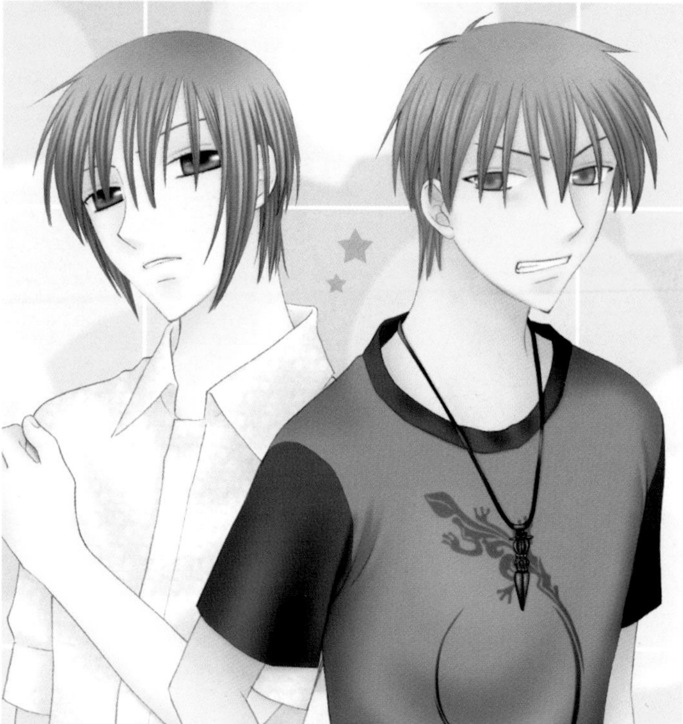

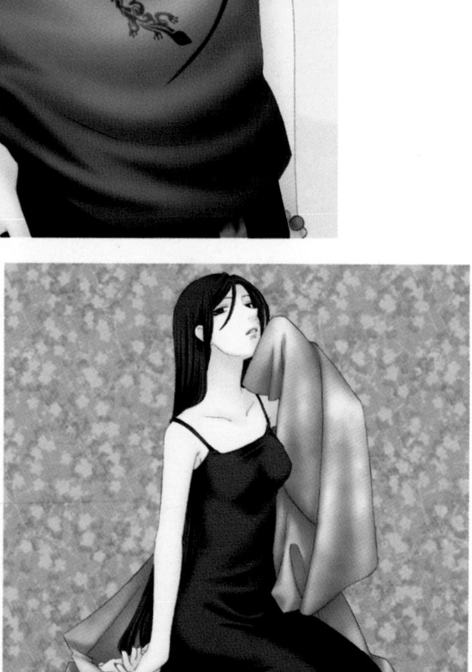

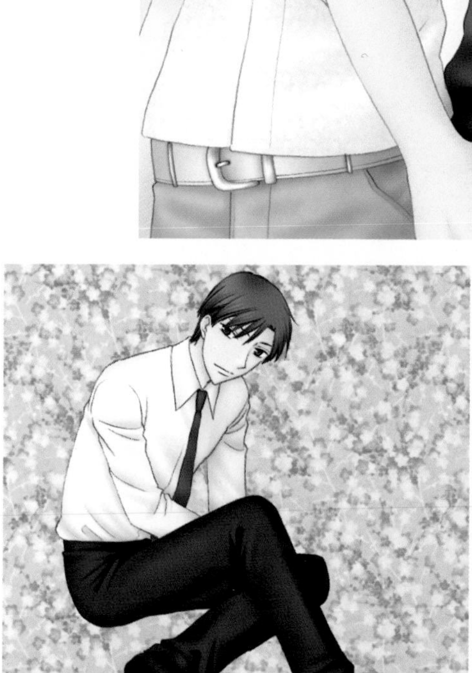

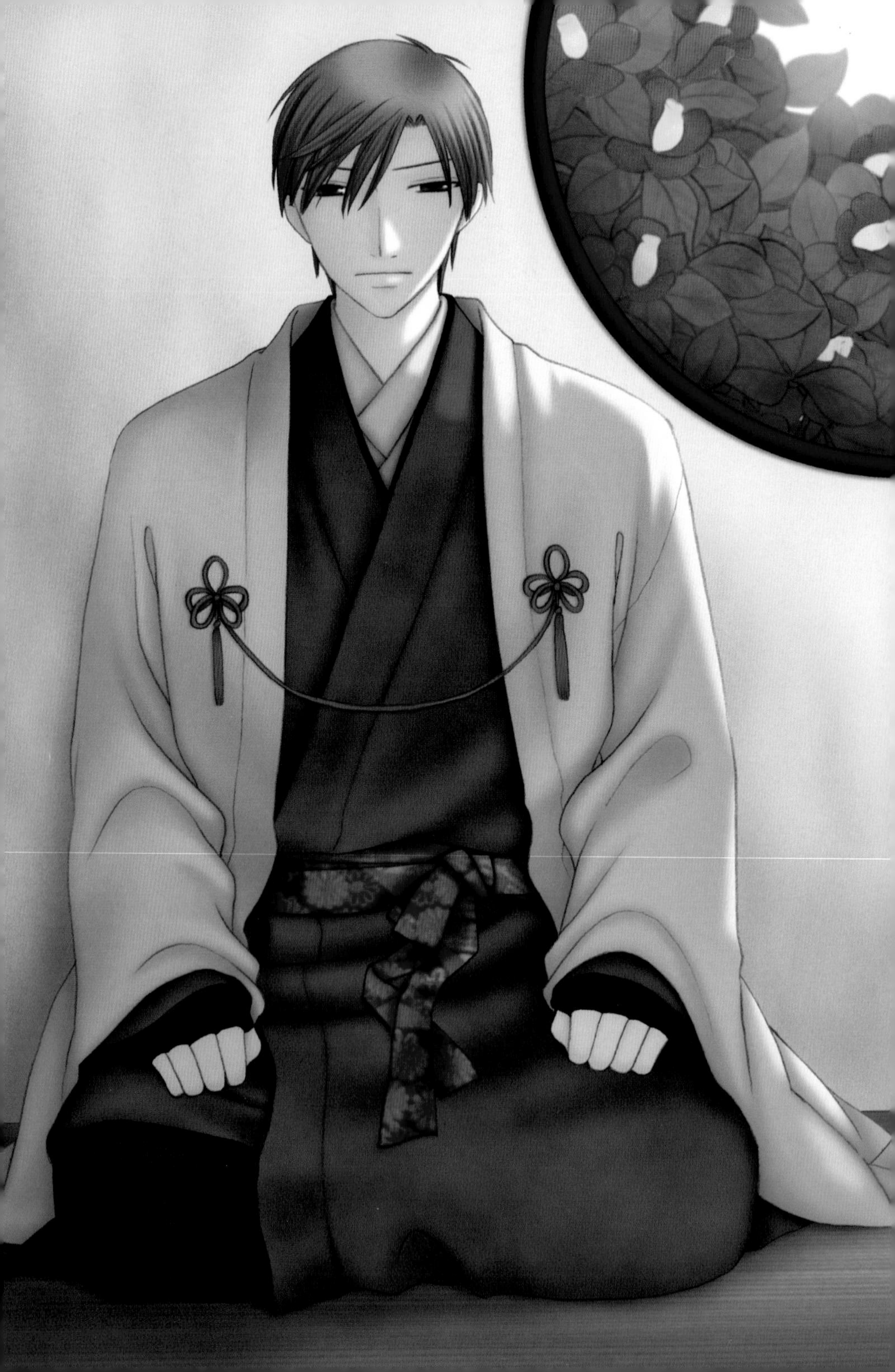

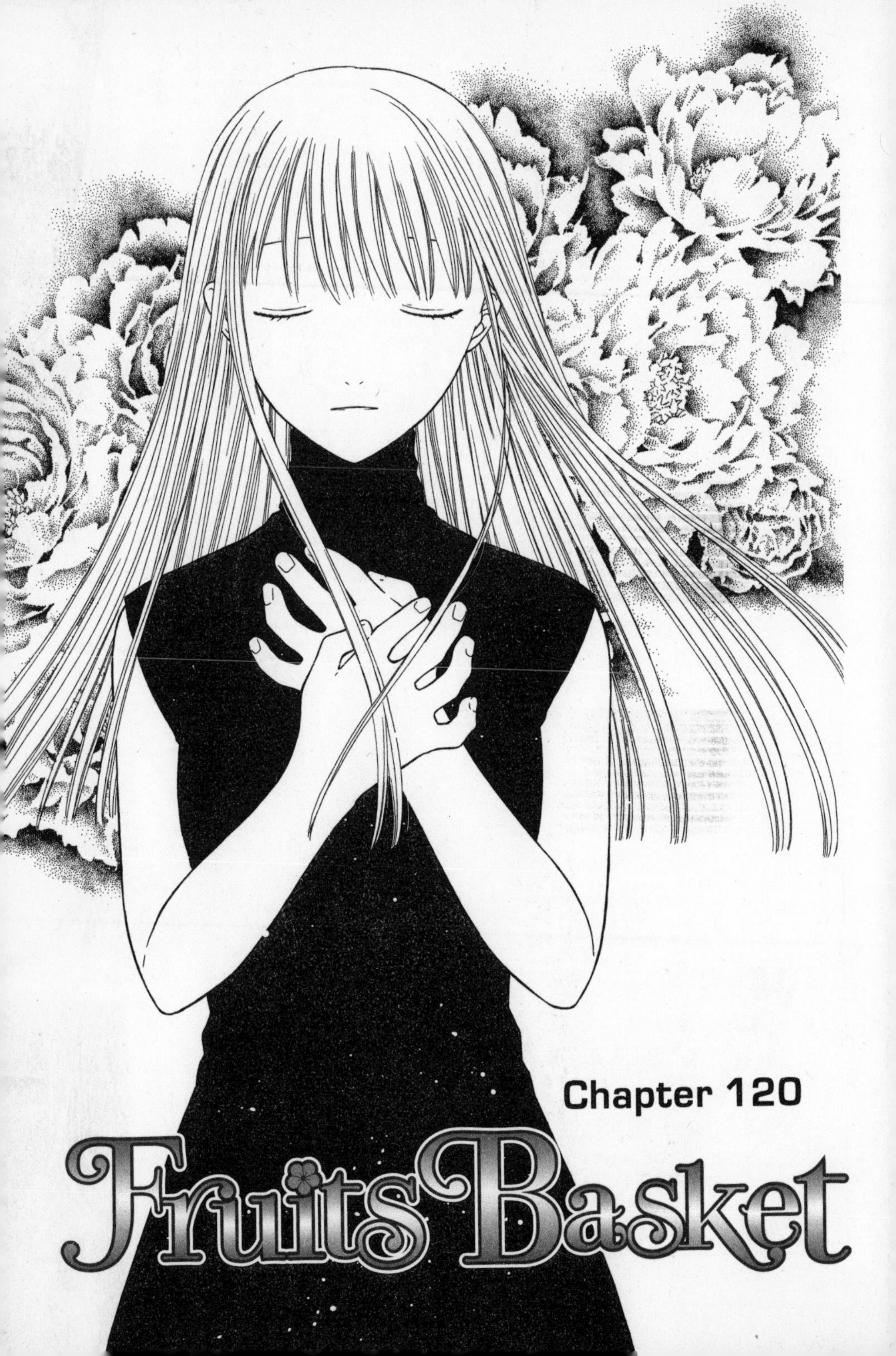
Chapter 120
Fruits Basket

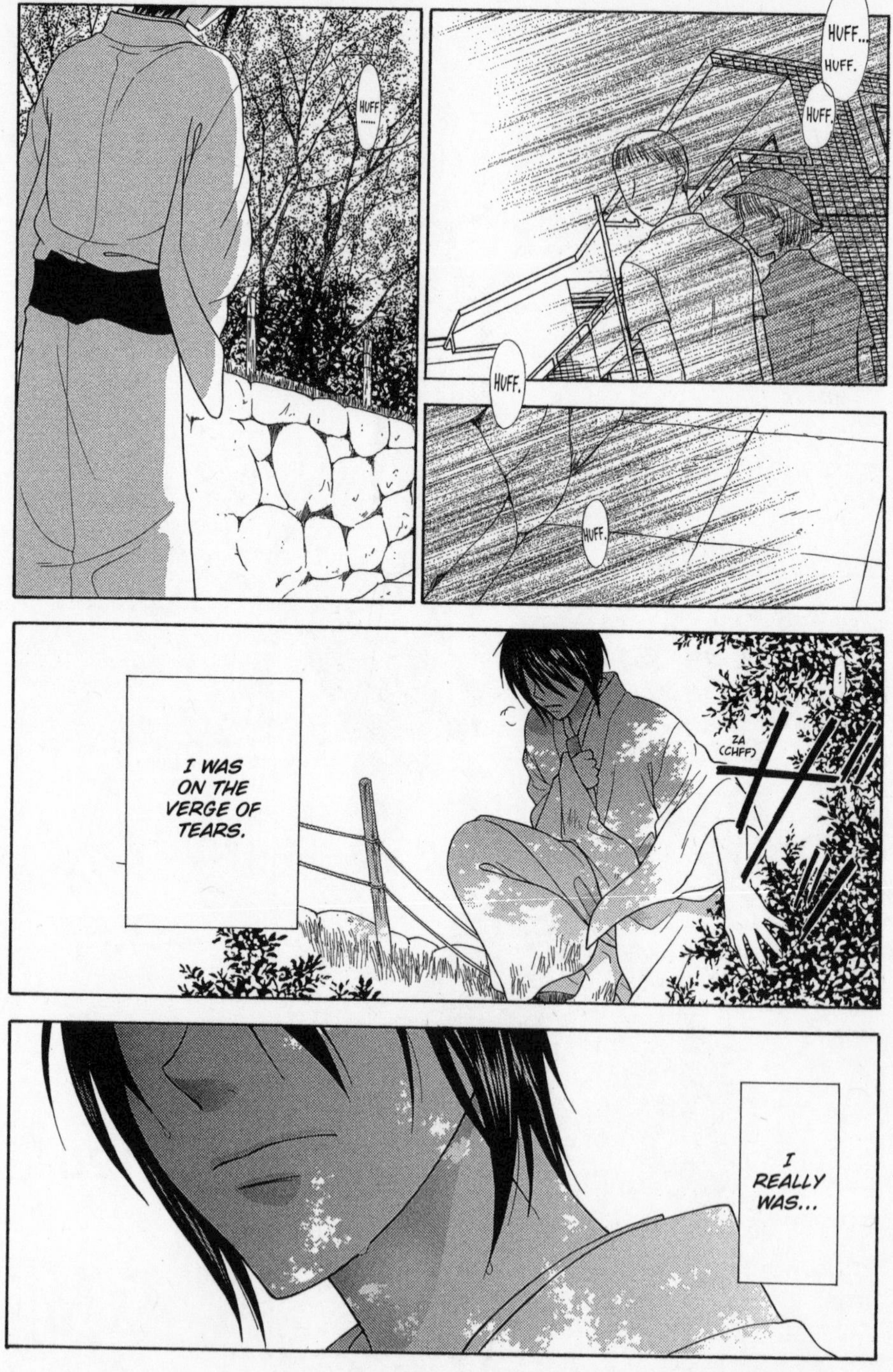
HUFF...
HUFF.
HUFF.
HUFF.
HUFF.
HUFF......
...
ZA (CHFF)
I WAS ON THE VERGE OF TEARS.
I REALLY WAS...

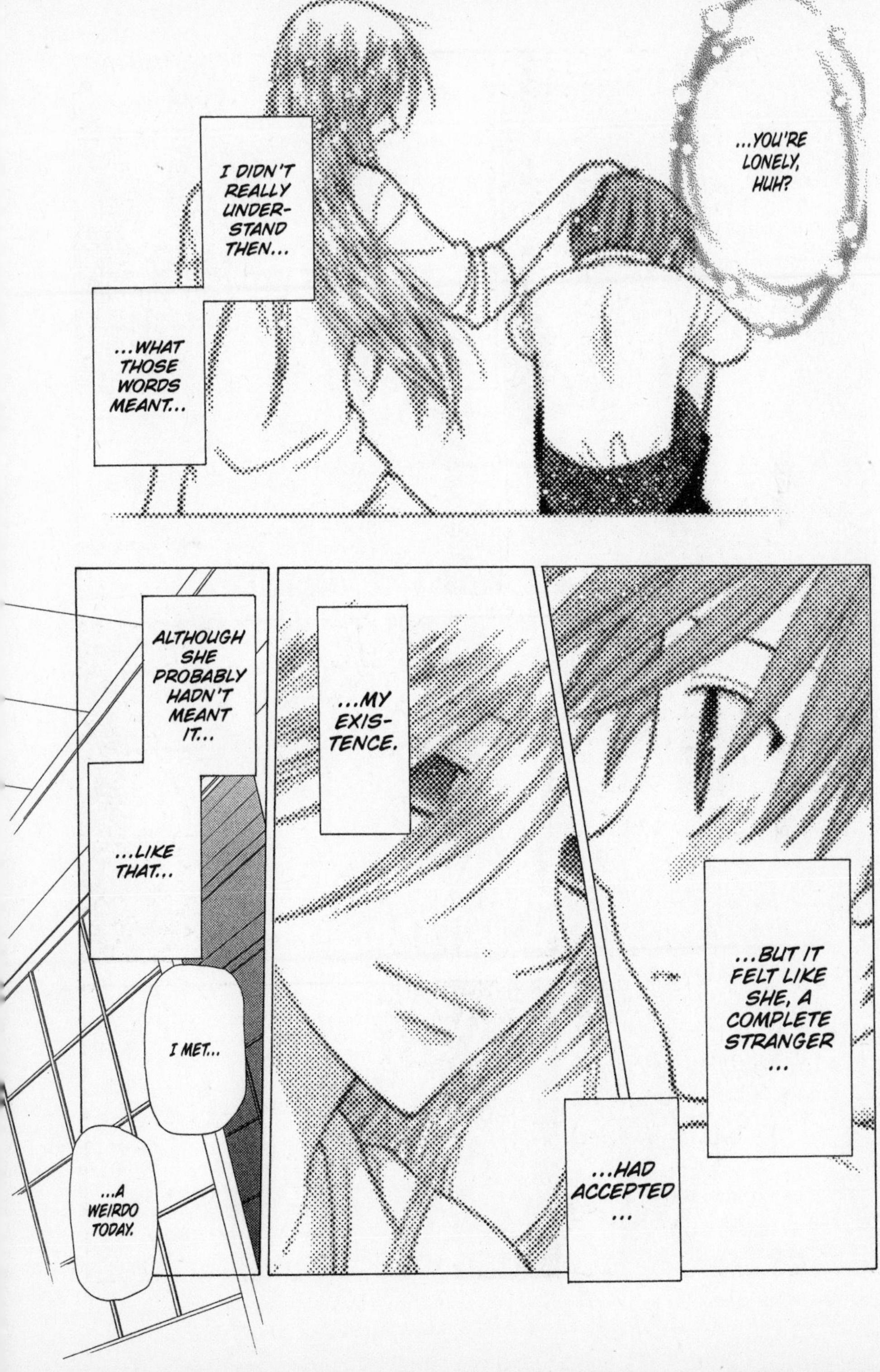
...YOU'RE LONELY, HUH?
I DIDN'T REALLY UNDER-STAND THEN...
...WHAT THOSE WORDS MEANT...
...BUT IT FELT LIKE SHE, A COMPLETE STRANGER...
...HAD ACCEPTED...
...MY EXIS-TENCE.
ALTHOUGH SHE PROBABLY HADN'T MEANT IT...
...LIKE THAT...
I MET...
...A WEIRDO TODAY.

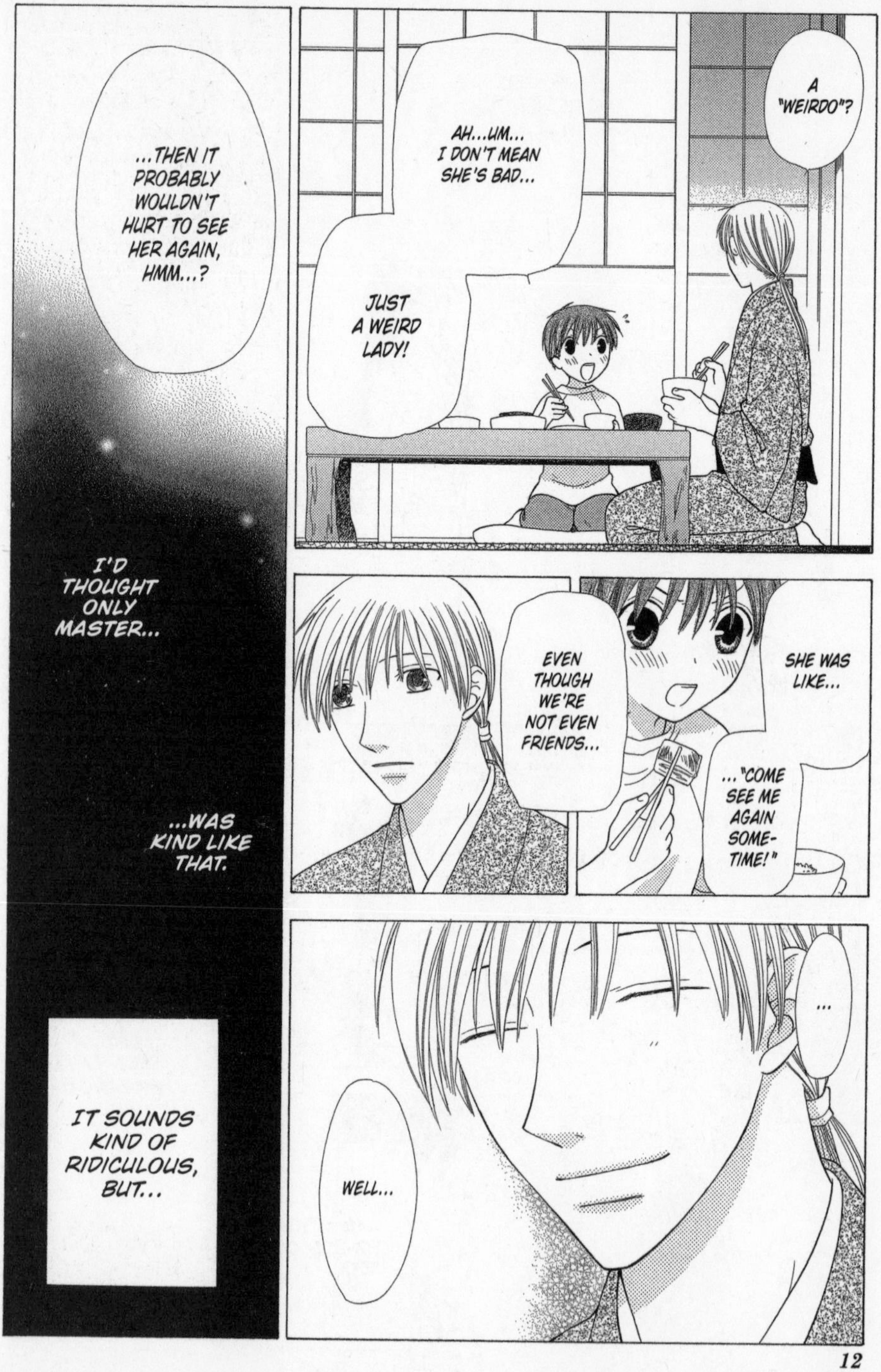
A "WEIRDO"?
AH...UM... I DON'T MEAN SHE'S BAD...
JUST A WEIRD LADY!
SHE WAS LIKE...
..."COME SEE ME AGAIN SOME-TIME!"
EVEN THOUGH WE'RE NOT EVEN FRIENDS...
...
WELL...
...THEN IT PROBABLY WOULDN'T HURT TO SEE HER AGAIN, HMM...?
I'D THOUGHT ONLY MASTER...
...WAS KIND LIKE THAT.
IT SOUNDS KIND OF RIDICULOUS, BUT...

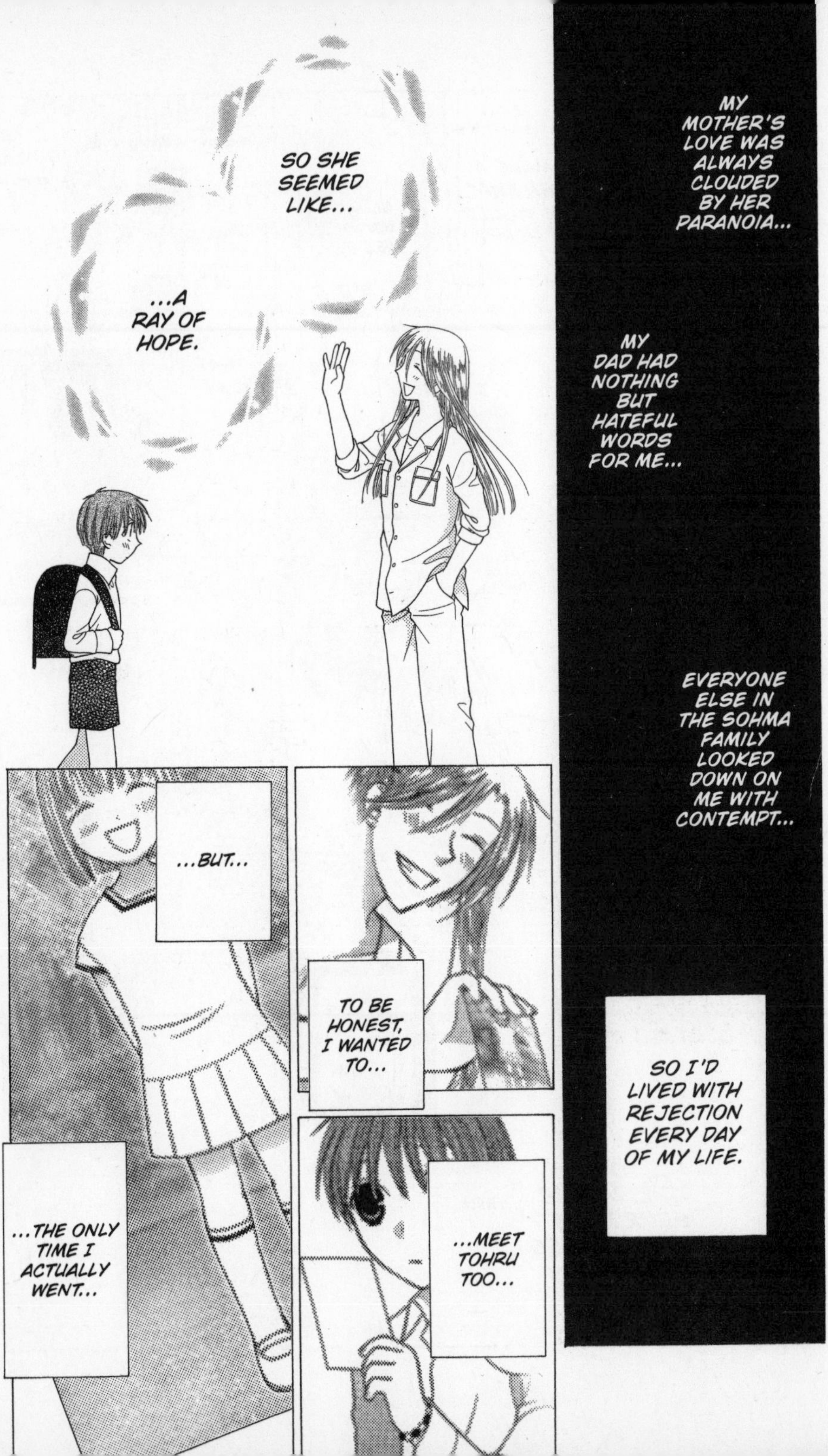
MY MOTHER'S LOVE WAS ALWAYS CLOUDED BY HER PARANOIA...
MY DAD HAD NOTHING BUT HATEFUL WORDS FOR ME...
EVERYONE ELSE IN THE SOHMA FAMILY LOOKED DOWN ON ME WITH CONTEMPT...
SO I'D LIVED WITH REJECTION EVERY DAY OF MY LIFE.
SO SHE SEEMED LIKE...
...A RAY OF HOPE.
TO BE HONEST, I WANTED TO...
...MEET TOHRU TOO...
...BUT...
...THE ONLY TIME I ACTUALLY WENT...

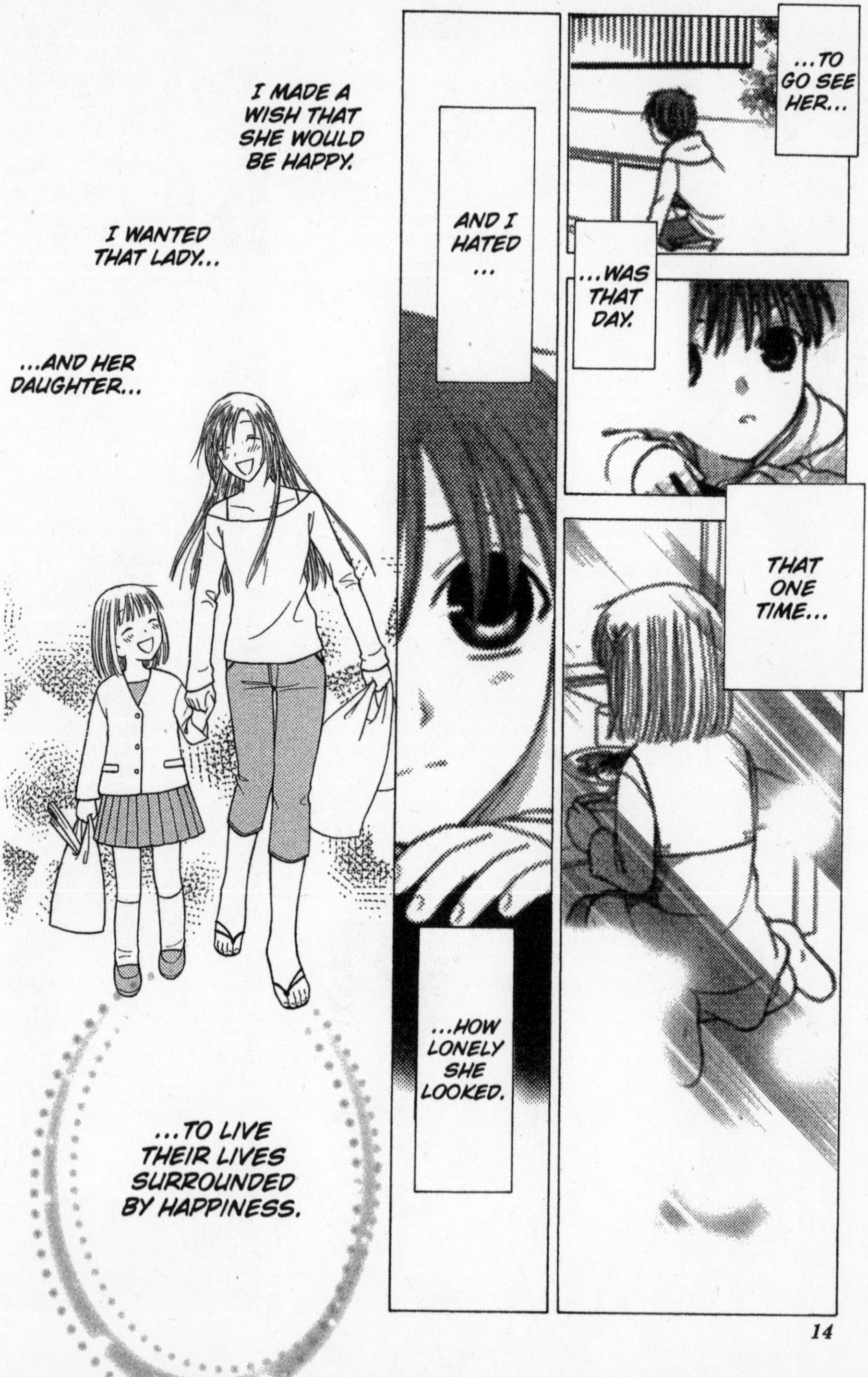
...TO GO SEE HER...
...WAS THAT DAY.
THAT ONE TIME...
AND I HATED...
...HOW LONELY SHE LOOKED.
I MADE A WISH THAT SHE WOULD BE HAPPY.
I WANTED THAT LADY...
...AND HER DAUGHTER...
...TO LIVE THEIR LIVES SURROUNDED BY HAPPINESS.

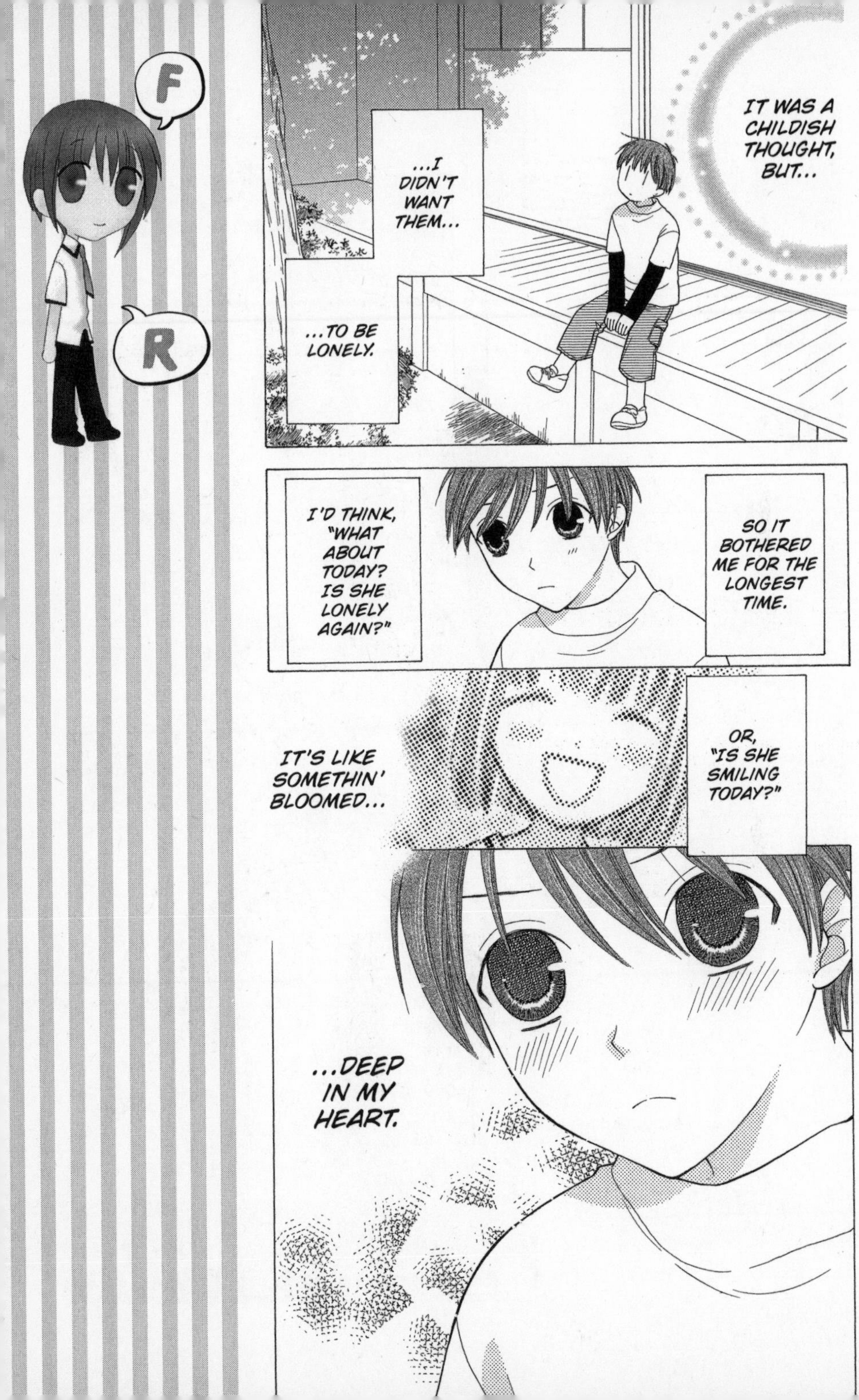

IT WAS A CHILDISH THOUGHT, BUT...
...I DIDN'T WANT THEM...
...TO BE LONELY.
SO IT BOTHERED ME FOR THE LONGEST TIME.
I'D THINK, "WHAT ABOUT TODAY? IS SHE LONELY AGAIN?"
OR, "IS SHE SMILING TODAY?"
IT'S LIKE SOMETHIN' BLOOMED...
...DEEP IN MY HEART.
F
R

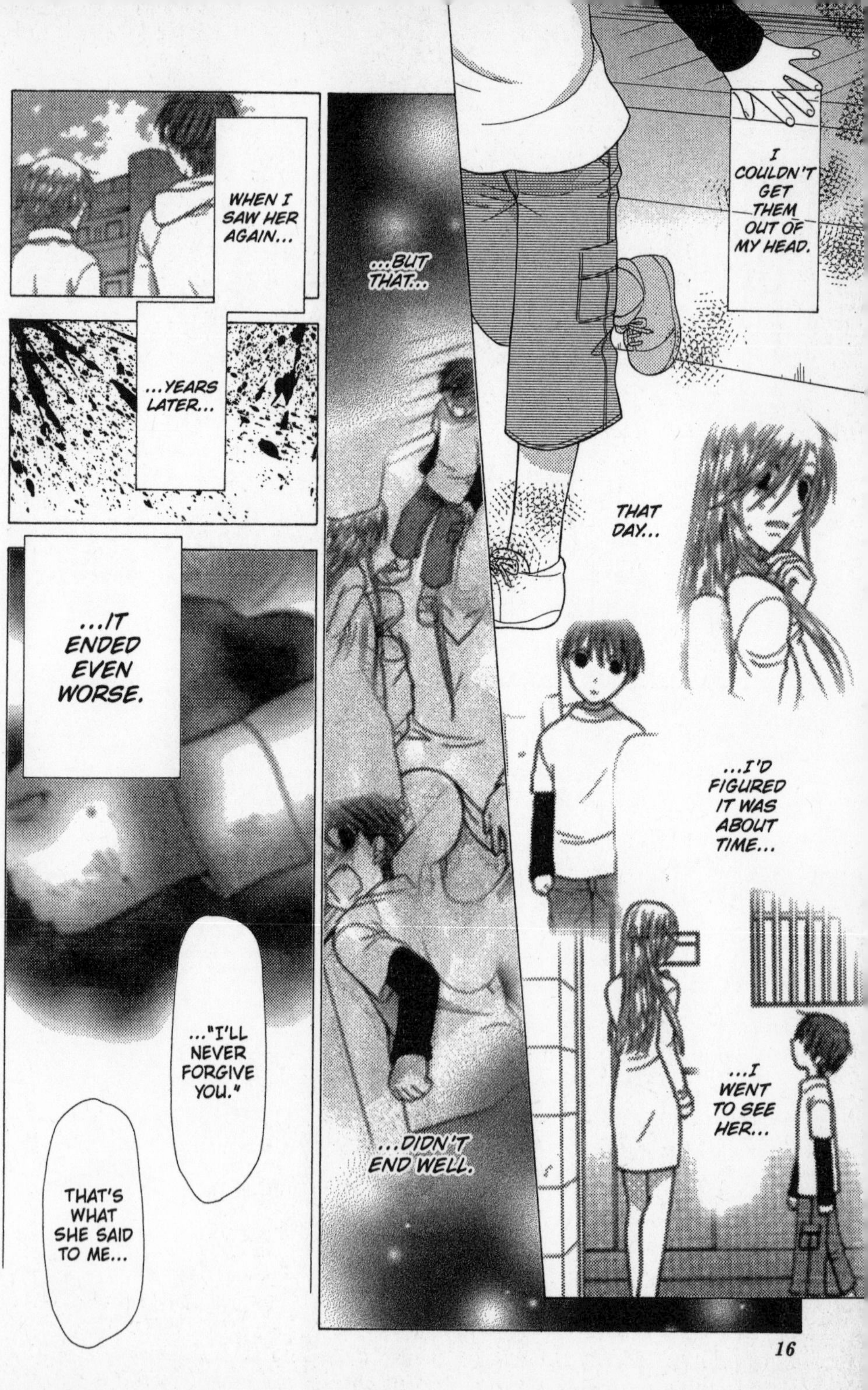
I COULDN'T GET THEM OUT OF MY HEAD.
THAT DAY...
...I'D FIGURED IT WAS ABOUT TIME...
...I WENT TO SEE HER...
...BUT THAT...
...DIDN'T END WELL.
WHEN I SAW HER AGAIN...
...YEARS LATER...
...IT ENDED EVEN WORSE.
..."I'LL NEVER FORGIVE YOU."
THAT'S WHAT SHE SAID TO ME...

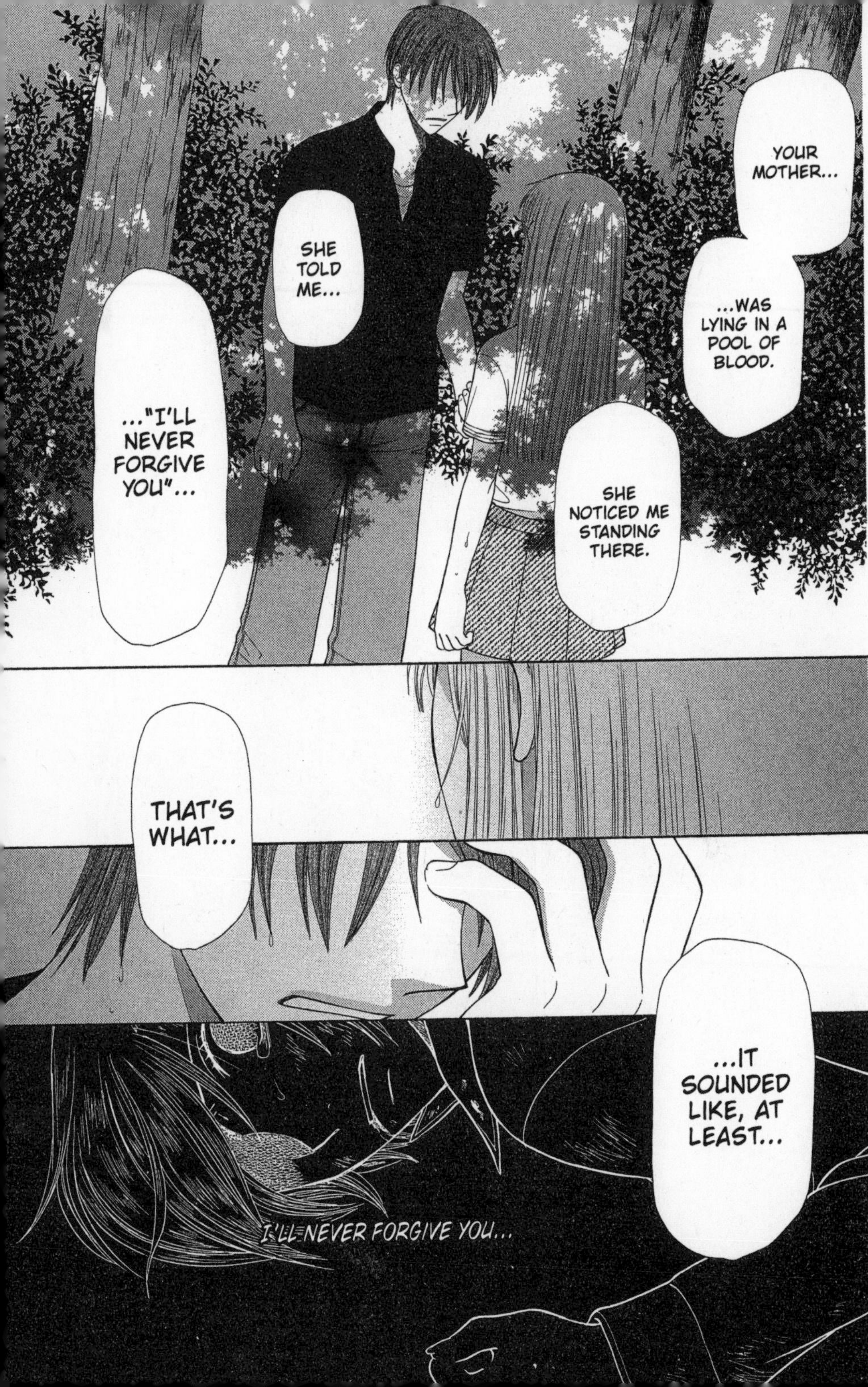
YOUR MOTHER...
...WAS LYING IN A POOL OF BLOOD.
SHE NOTICED ME STANDING THERE.
SHE TOLD ME...
..."I'LL NEVER FORGIVE YOU"...
THAT'S WHAT...
...IT SOUNDED LIKE, AT LEAST...
I'LL NEVER FORGIVE YOU...

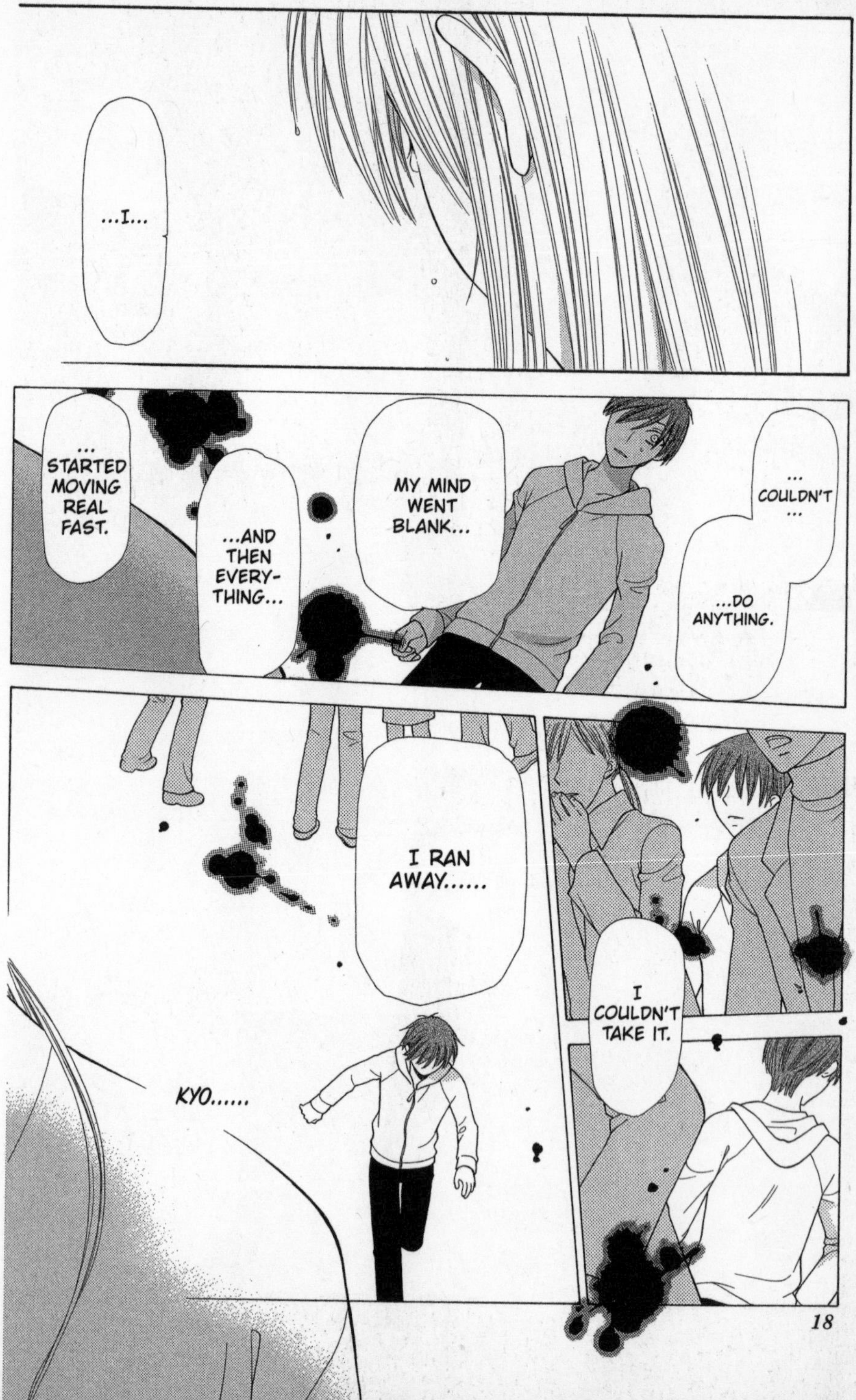
...I...
... COULDN'T ...
...DO ANYTHING.
MY MIND WENT BLANK...
...AND THEN EVERY- THING...
... STARTED MOVING REAL FAST.
I COULDN'T TAKE IT.
I RAN AWAY......
KYO......

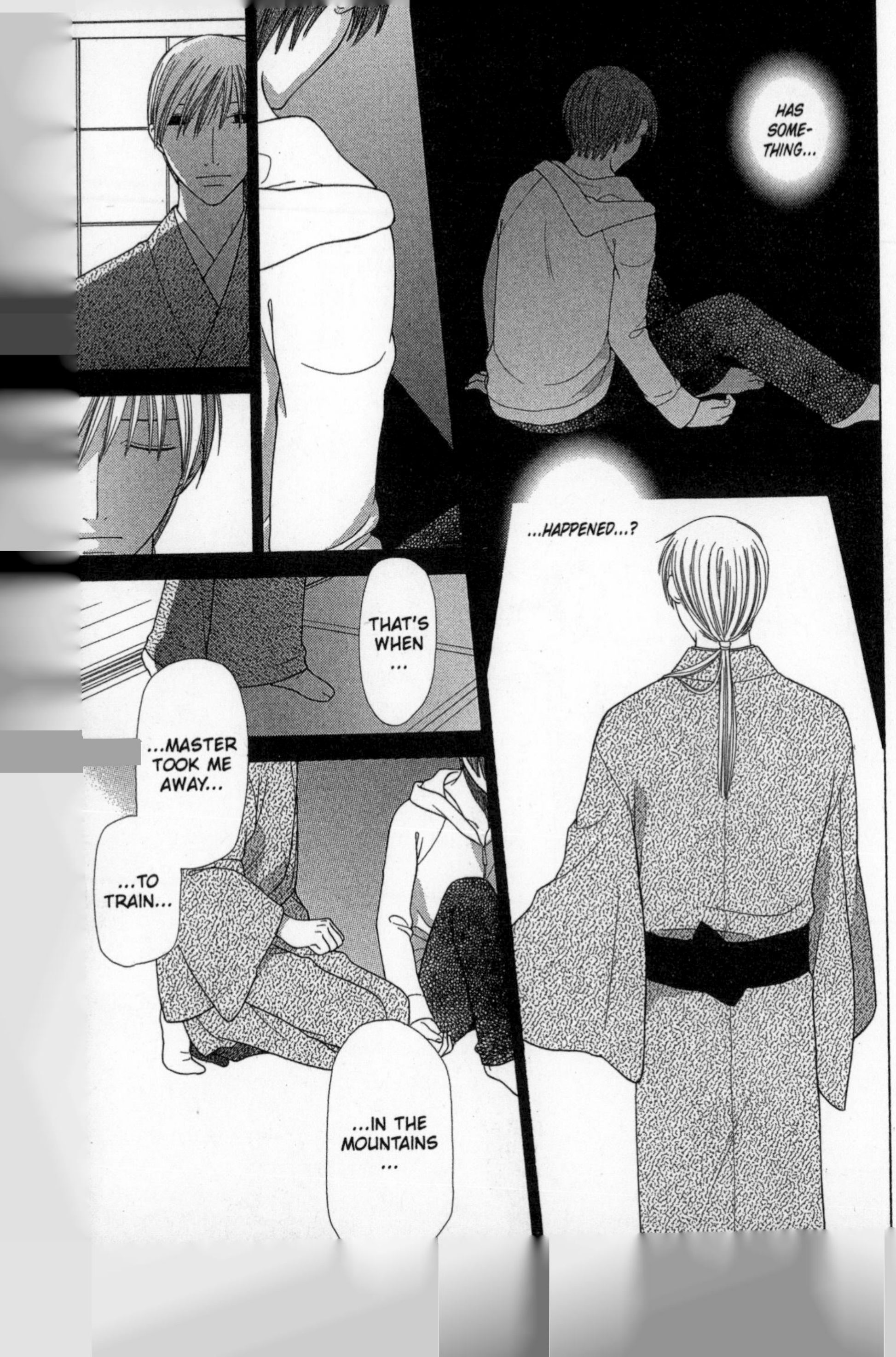
HAS SOMETHING...
...HAPPENED...?
THAT'S WHEN...
...MASTER TOOK ME AWAY...
...TO TRAIN...
...IN THE MOUNTAINS...

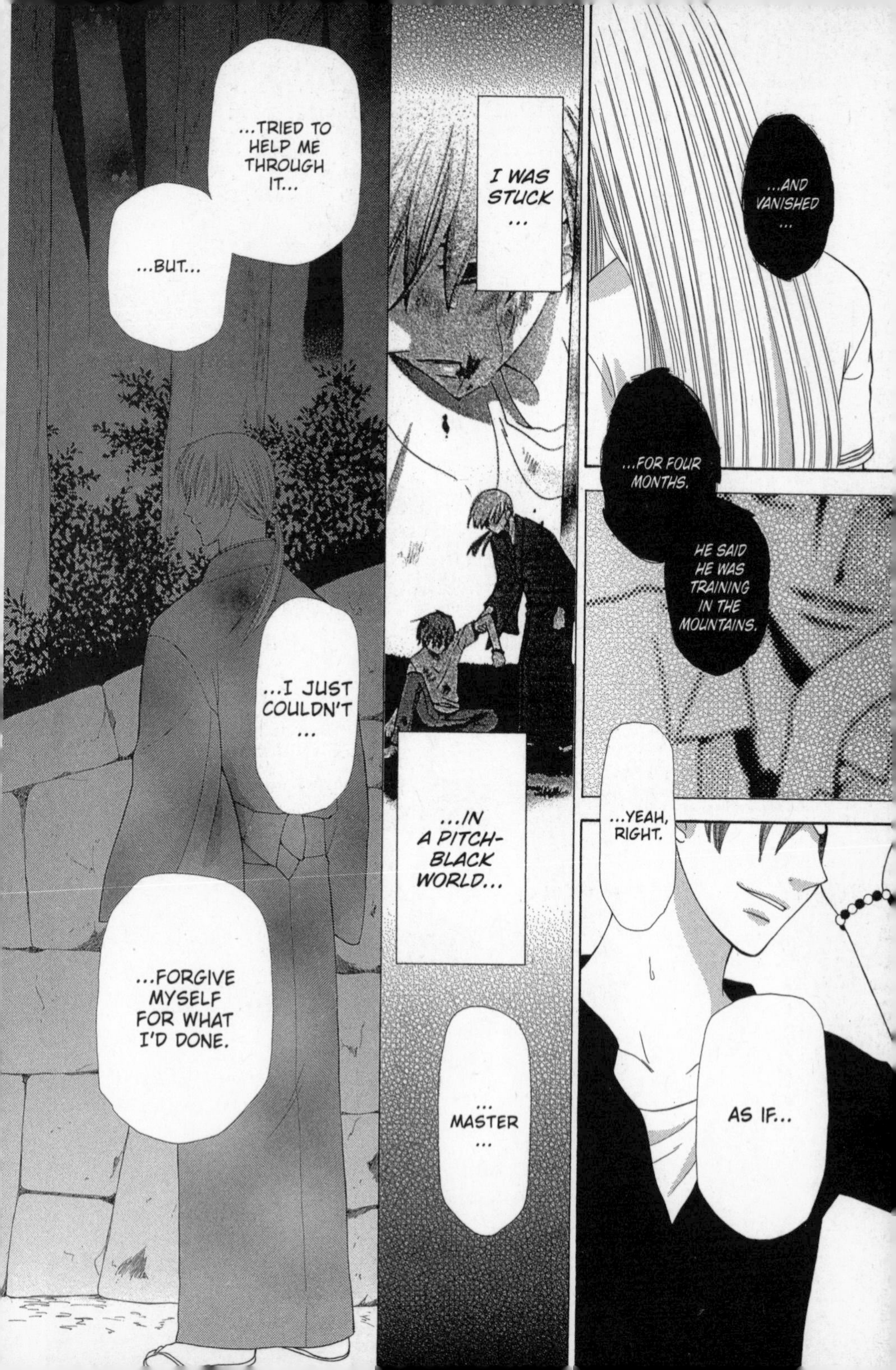
...AND VANISHED...
...FOR FOUR MONTHS.
HE SAID HE WAS TRAINING IN THE MOUNTAINS.
...YEAH, RIGHT.
AS IF...
I WAS STUCK...
...IN A PITCH-BLACK WORLD...
...MASTER...
...TRIED TO HELP ME THROUGH IT...
...BUT...
...I JUST COULDN'T...
...FORGIVE MYSELF FOR WHAT I'D DONE.

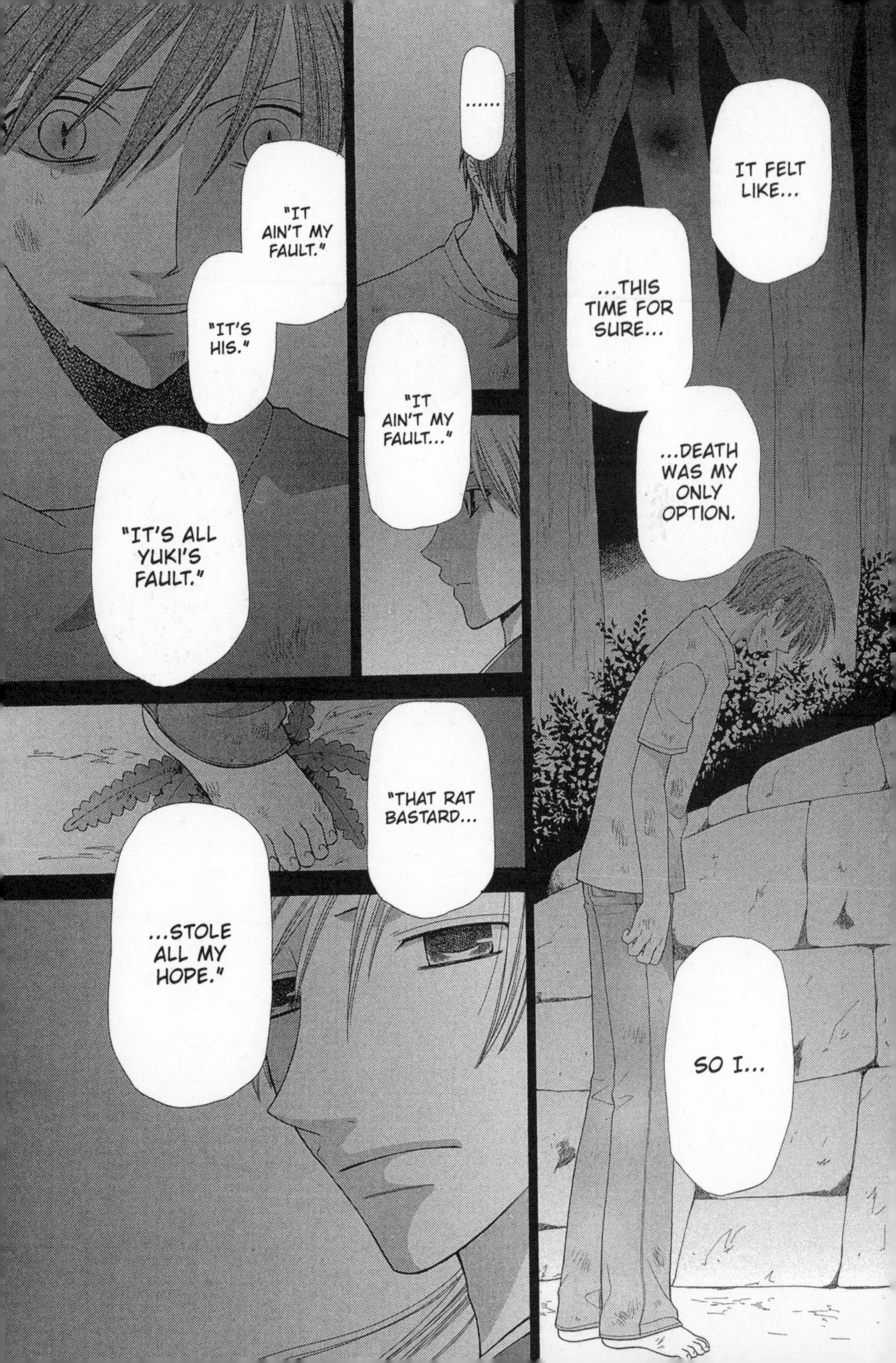
IT FELT LIKE...
...THIS TIME FOR SURE...
...DEATH WAS MY ONLY OPTION.
SO I...
......
"IT AIN'T MY FAULT..."
"IT AIN'T MY FAULT."
"IT'S HIS."
"IT'S ALL YUKI'S FAULT."
"THAT RAT BASTARD...
...STOLE ALL MY HOPE."

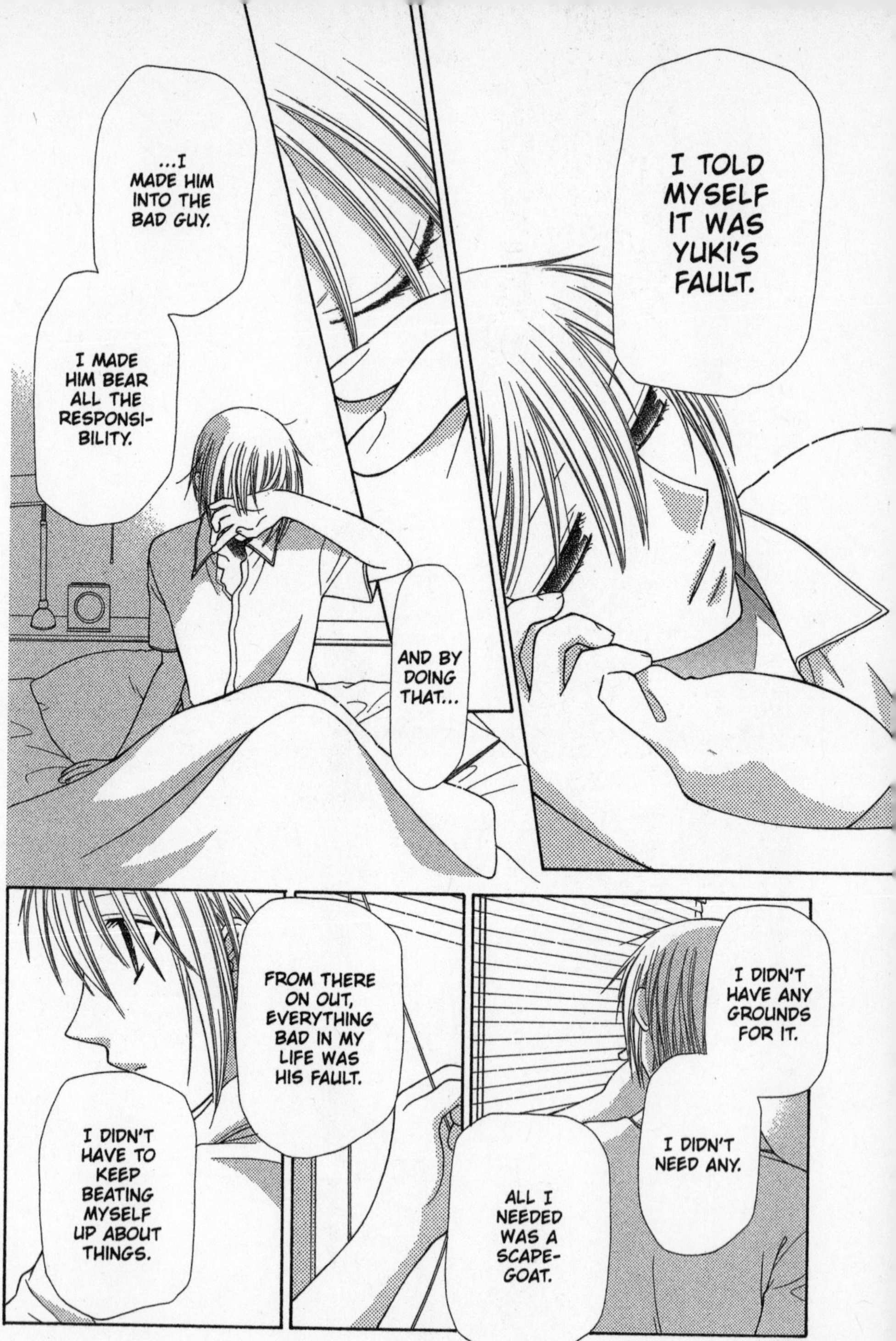
I TOLD MYSELF IT WAS YUKI'S FAULT.
...I MADE HIM INTO THE BAD GUY.
I MADE HIM BEAR ALL THE RESPONSIBILITY.
AND BY DOING THAT...
I DIDN'T HAVE ANY GROUNDS FOR IT.
I DIDN'T NEED ANY.
ALL I NEEDED WAS A SCAPEGOAT.
FROM THERE ON OUT, EVERYTHING BAD IN MY LIFE WAS HIS FAULT.
I DIDN'T HAVE TO KEEP BEATING MYSELF UP ABOUT THINGS.

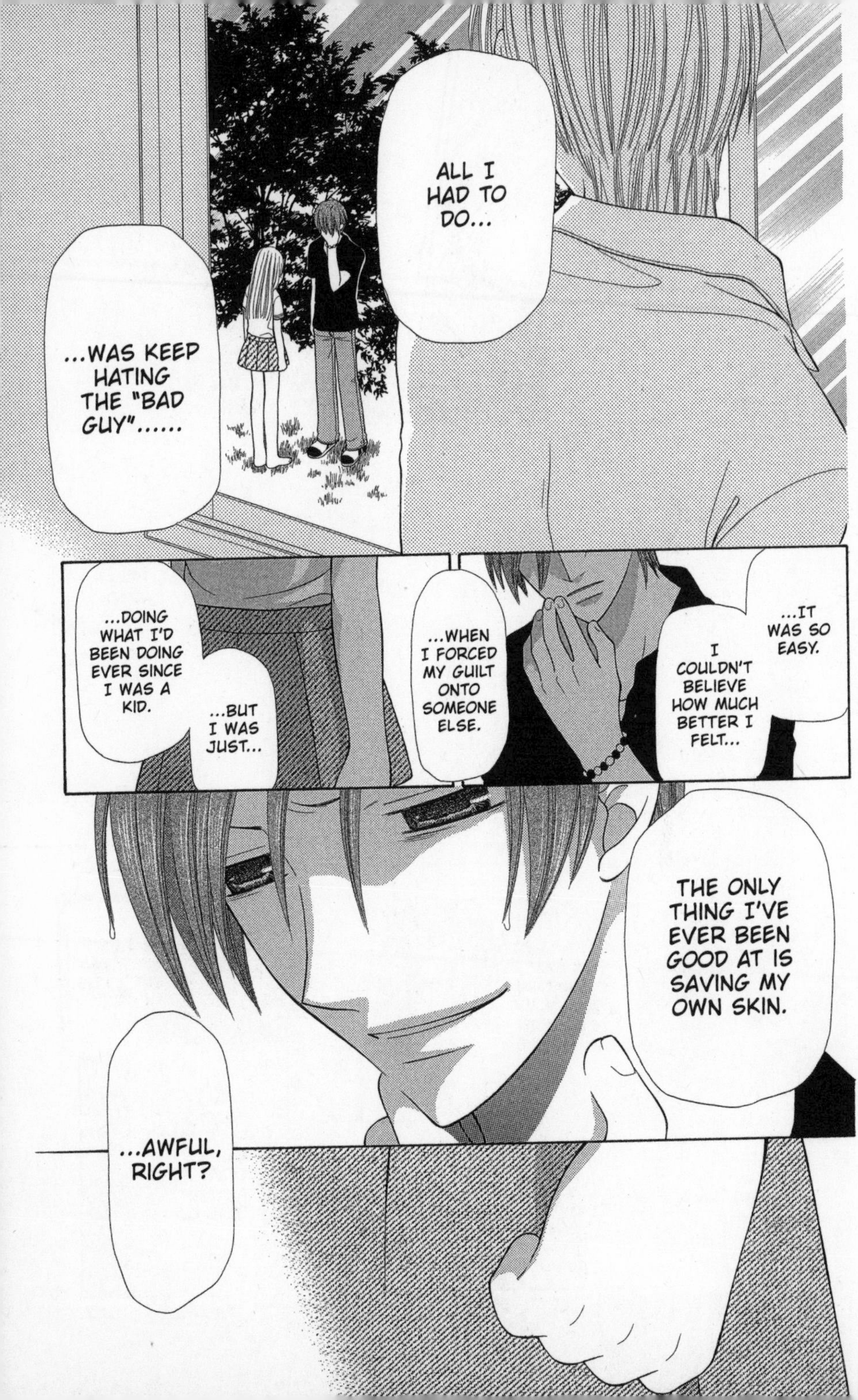
ALL I HAD TO DO...
...WAS KEEP HATING THE "BAD GUY"......
...IT WAS SO EASY.
I COULDN'T BELIEVE HOW MUCH BETTER I FELT...
...WHEN I FORCED MY GUILT ONTO SOMEONE ELSE.
...BUT I WAS JUST...
...DOING WHAT I'D BEEN DOING EVER SINCE I WAS A KID.
THE ONLY THING I'VE EVER BEEN GOOD AT IS SAVING MY OWN SKIN.
...AWFUL, RIGHT?

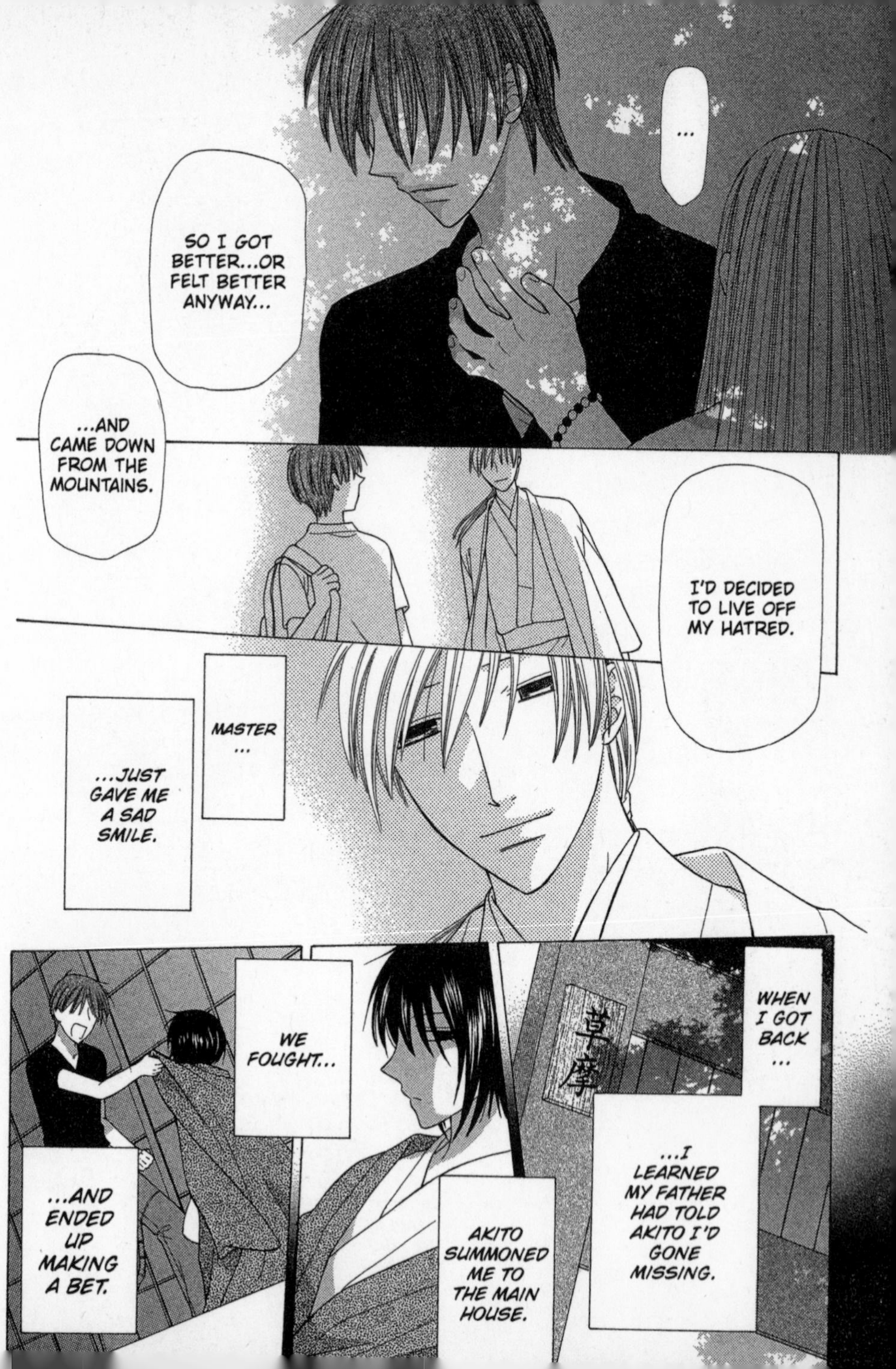
...
SO I GOT BETTER...OR FELT BETTER ANYWAY...
...AND CAME DOWN FROM THE MOUNTAINS.
I'D DECIDED TO LIVE OFF MY HATRED.
MASTER...
...JUST GAVE ME A SAD SMILE.
WHEN I GOT BACK...
...I LEARNED MY FATHER HAD TOLD AKITO I'D GONE MISSING.
草摩
AKITO SUMMONED ME TO THE MAIN HOUSE.
WE FOUGHT...
...AND ENDED UP MAKING A BET.

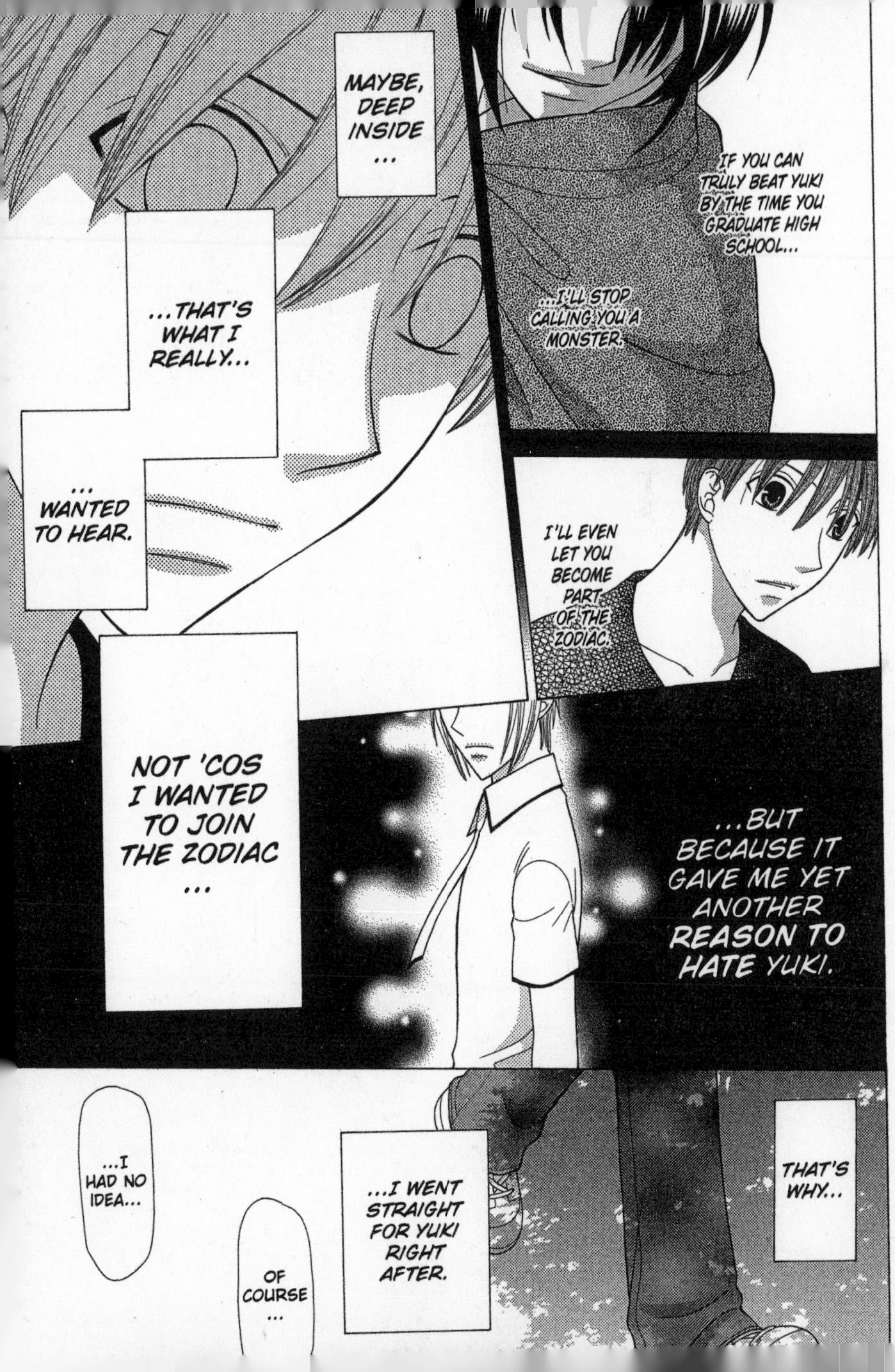
IF YOU CAN TRULY BEAT YUKI BY THE TIME YOU GRADUATE HIGH SCHOOL...
...I'LL STOP CALLING YOU A MONSTER.
I'LL EVEN LET YOU BECOME PART OF THE ZODIAC.
MAYBE, DEEP INSIDE...
...THAT'S WHAT I REALLY...
...WANTED TO HEAR.
NOT 'COS I WANTED TO JOIN THE ZODIAC...
...BUT BECAUSE IT GAVE ME YET ANOTHER REASON TO HATE YUKI.
THAT'S WHY...
...I WENT STRAIGHT FOR YUKI RIGHT AFTER.
OF COURSE...
...I HAD NO IDEA...

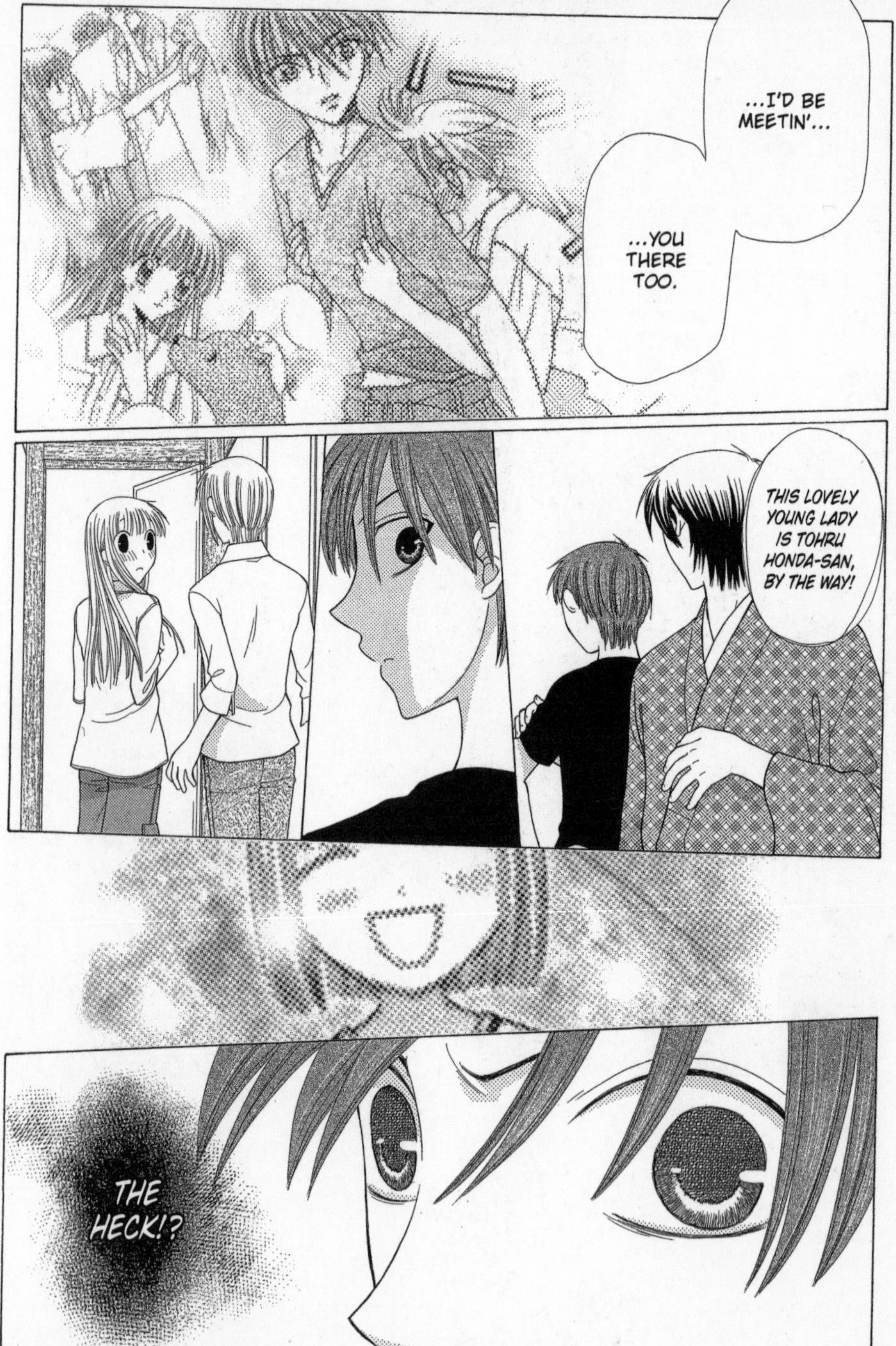
...I'D BE MEETIN'...
...YOU THERE TOO.
THIS LOVELY YOUNG LADY IS TOHRU HONDA-SAN, BY THE WAY!
THE HECK!?

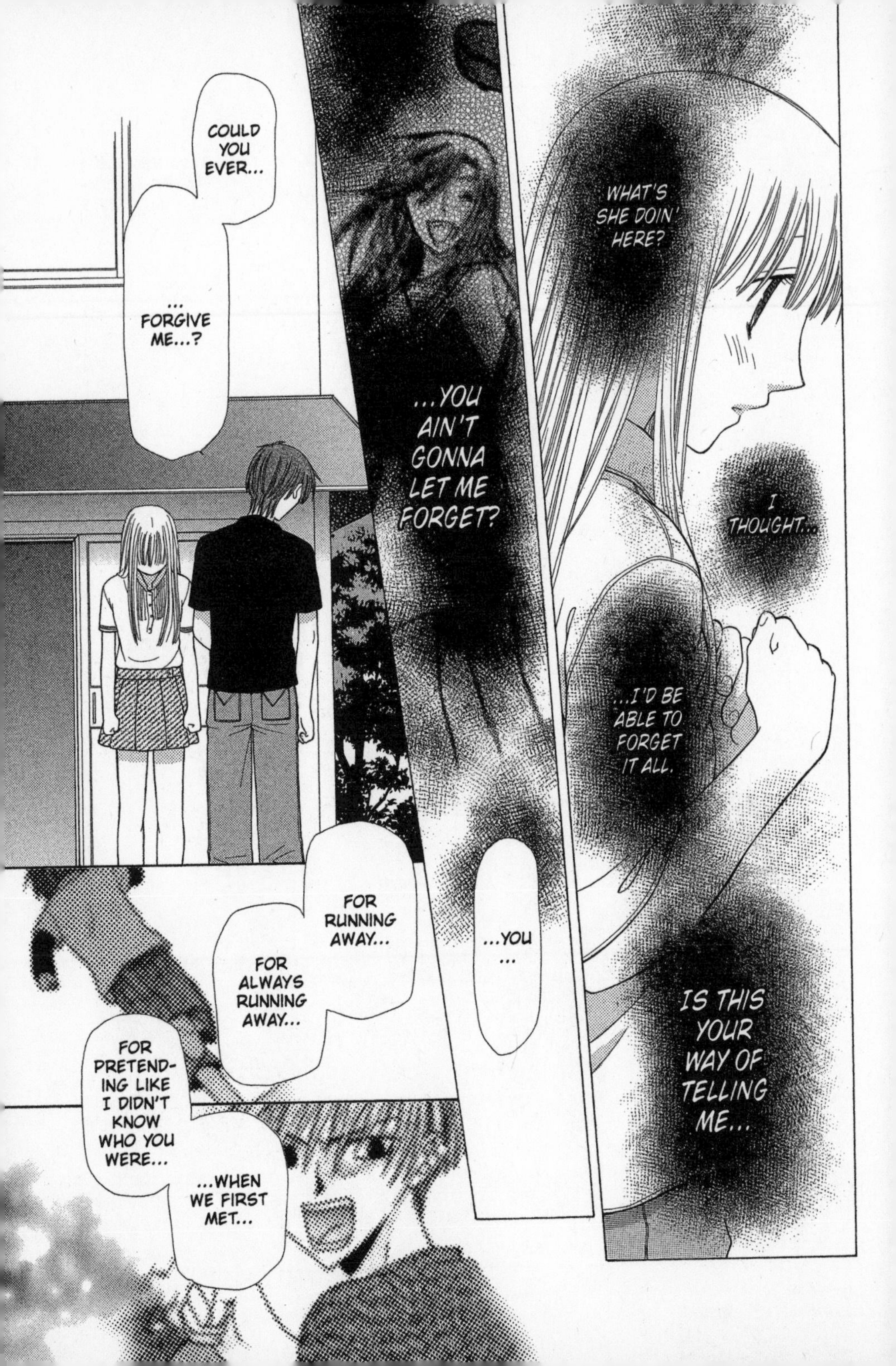
WHAT'S SHE DOIN' HERE?
I THOUGHT...
...I'D BE ABLE TO FORGET IT ALL.
IS THIS YOUR WAY OF TELLING ME...
...YOU AIN'T GONNA LET ME FORGET?
...YOU ...
COULD YOU EVER...
...FORGIVE ME...?
FOR RUNNING AWAY...
FOR ALWAYS RUNNING AWAY...
FOR PRETENDING LIKE I DIDN'T KNOW WHO YOU WERE...
...WHEN WE FIRST MET...

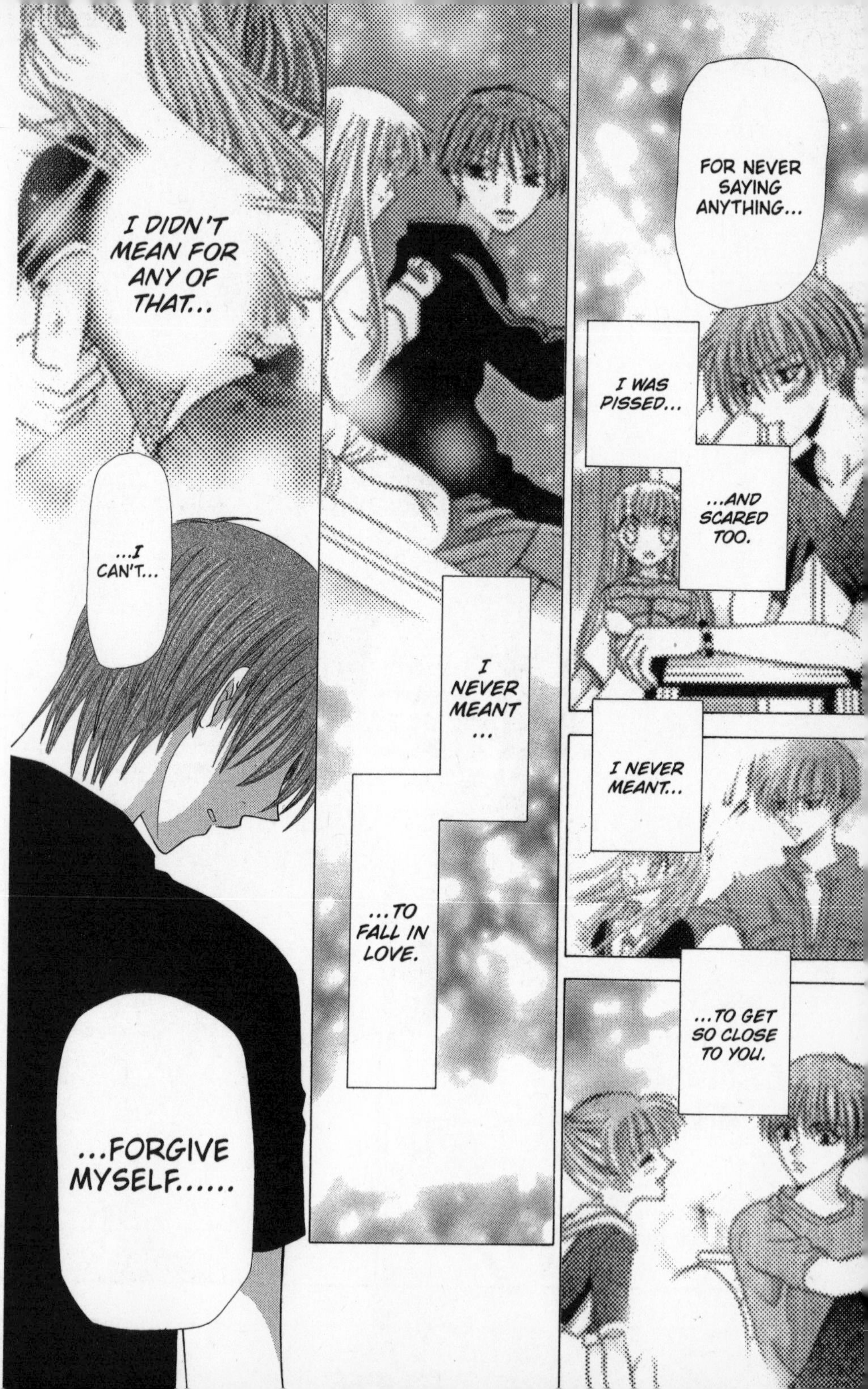
FOR NEVER SAYING ANYTHING...
I WAS PISSED...
...AND SCARED TOO.
I NEVER MEANT...
...TO GET SO CLOSE TO YOU.
I NEVER MEANT...
...TO FALL IN LOVE.
I DIDN'T MEAN FOR ANY OF THAT...
...I CAN'T...
...FORGIVE MYSELF......

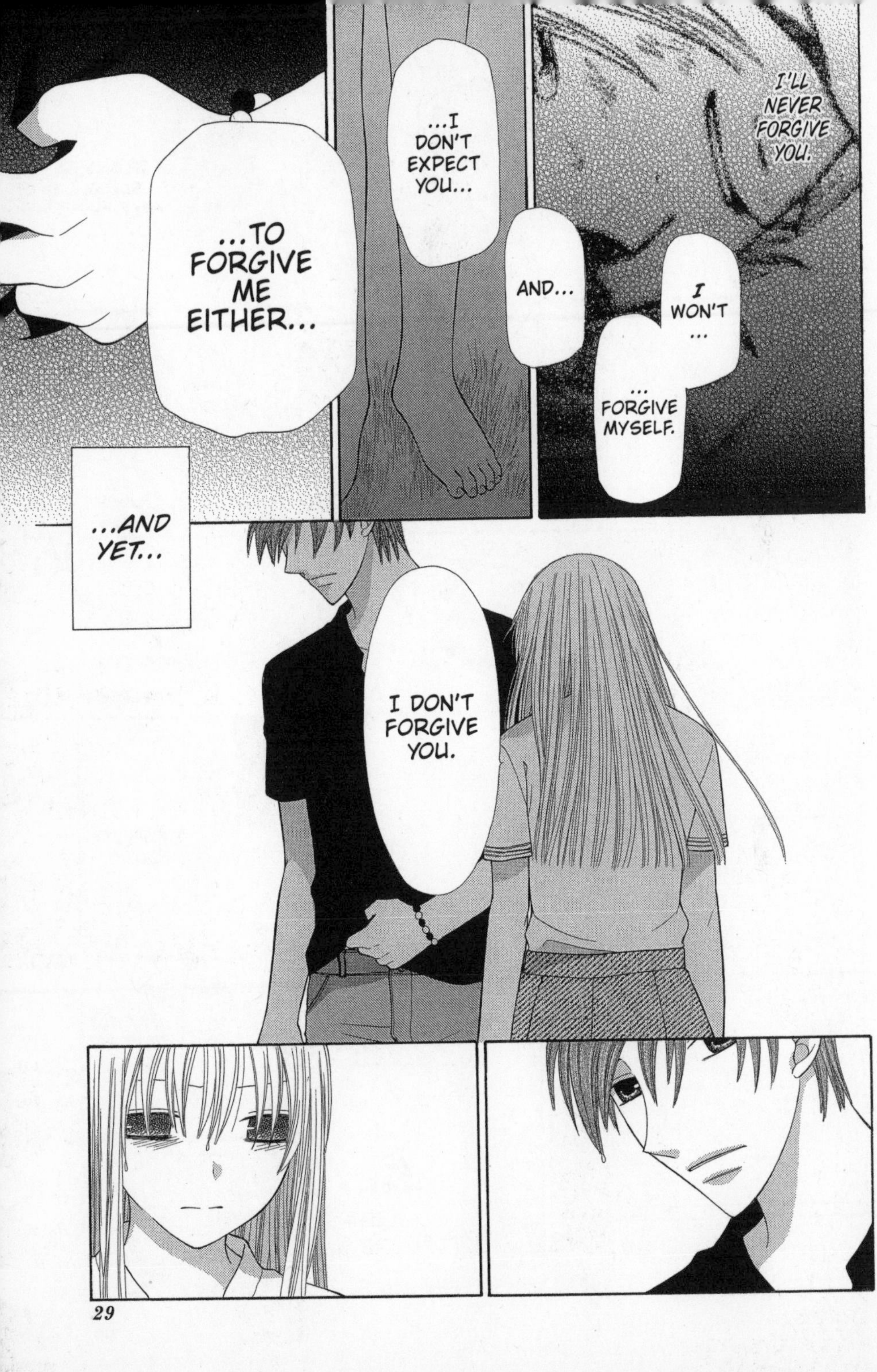
I'LL NEVER FORGIVE YOU.
AND...
I WON'T ...
... FORGIVE MYSELF.
...I DON'T EXPECT YOU...
...TO FORGIVE ME EITHER...
...AND YET...
I DON'T FORGIVE YOU.

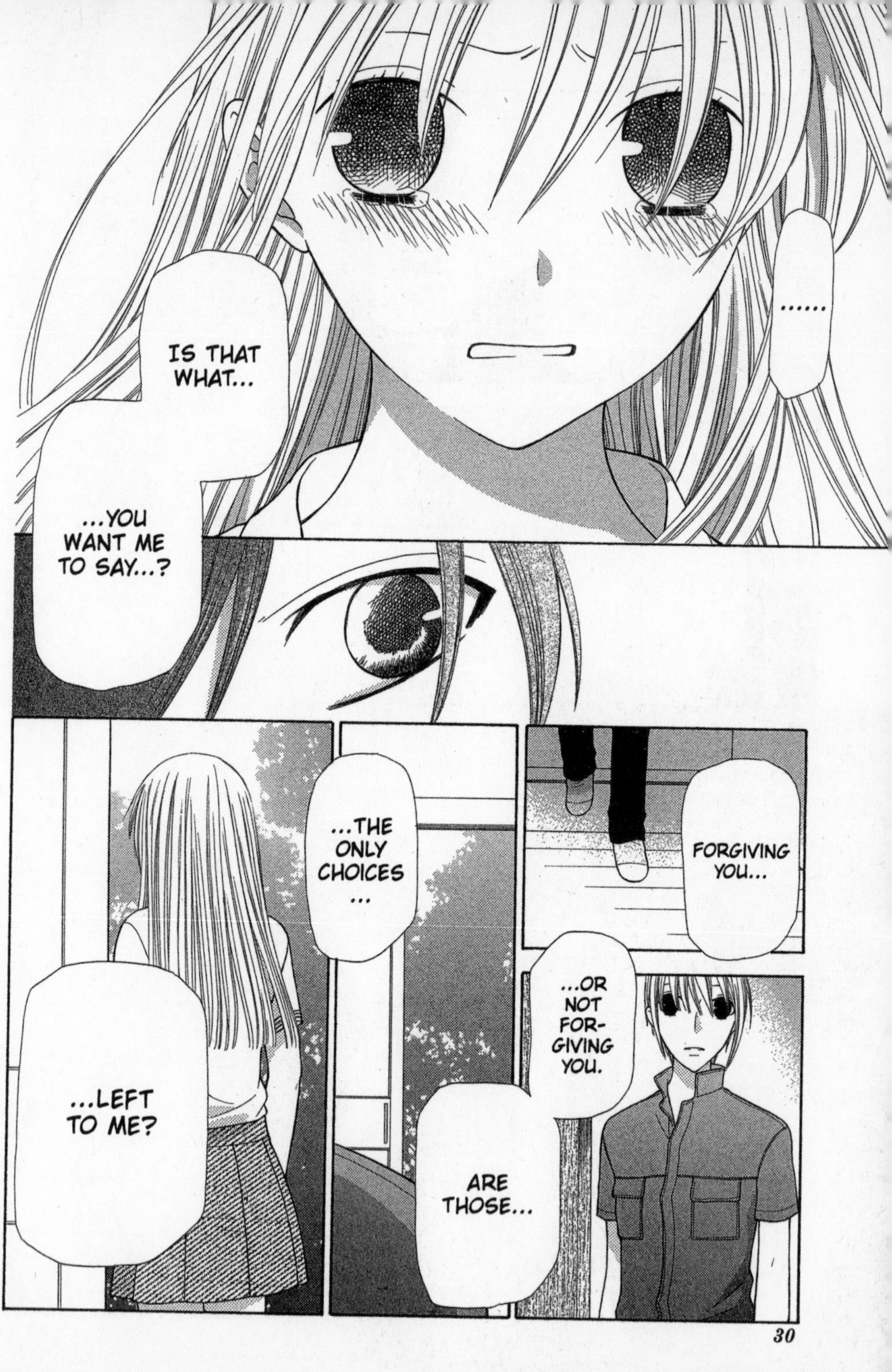
......
IS THAT WHAT...
...YOU WANT ME TO SAY...?
FORGIVING YOU...
...OR NOT FOR-GIVING YOU.
ARE THOSE...
...THE ONLY CHOICES...
...LEFT TO ME?

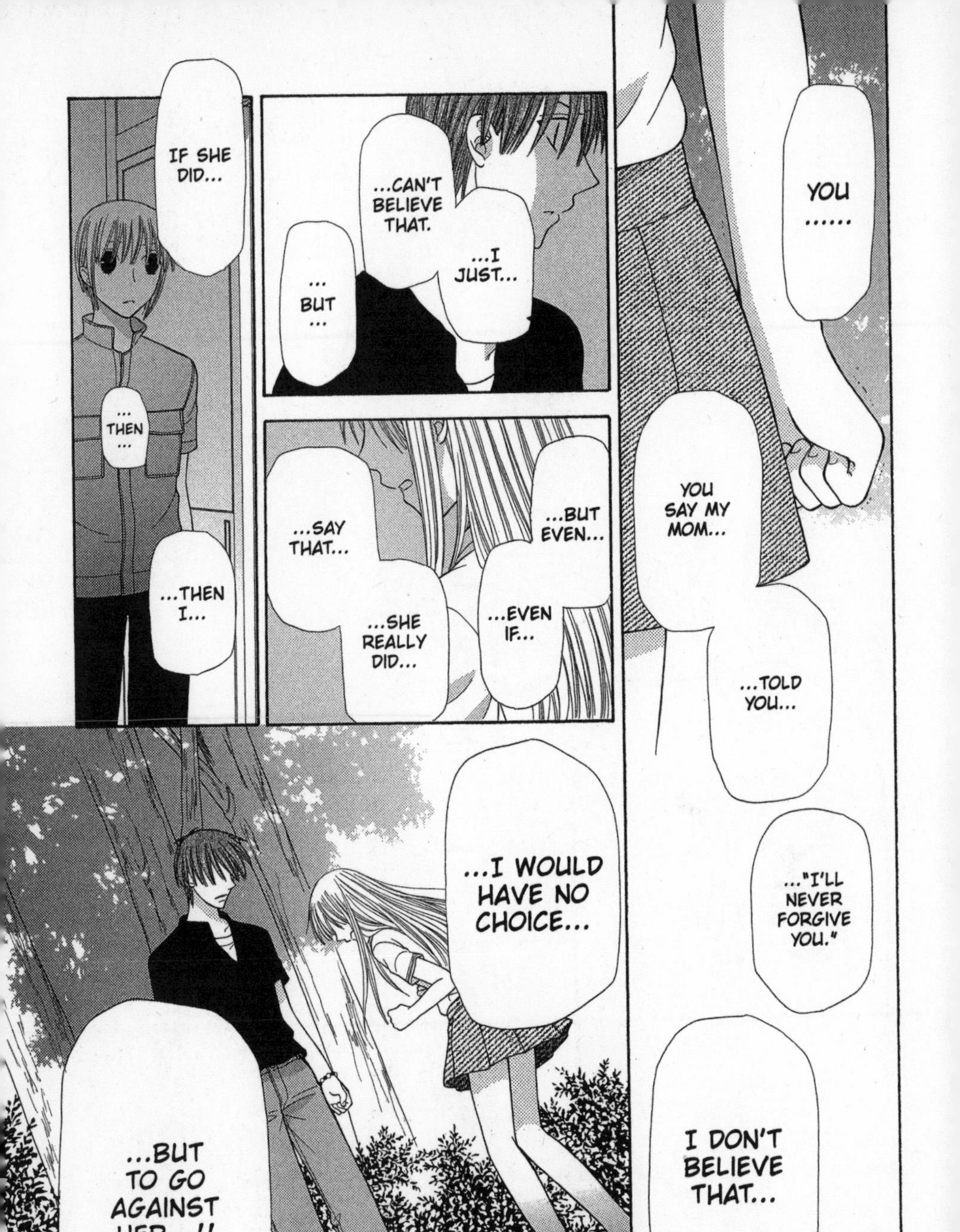
YOU......
YOU SAY MY MOM...
...TOLD YOU...
..."I'LL NEVER FORGIVE YOU."
I DON'T BELIEVE THAT...
...I JUST...
...CAN'T BELIEVE THAT.
...BUT...
...BUT EVEN...
...SAY THAT...
...EVEN IF...
...SHE REALLY DID...
IF SHE DID...
...THEN...
...THEN I...
...I WOULD HAVE NO CHOICE...
...BUT TO GO AGAINST HER...!!

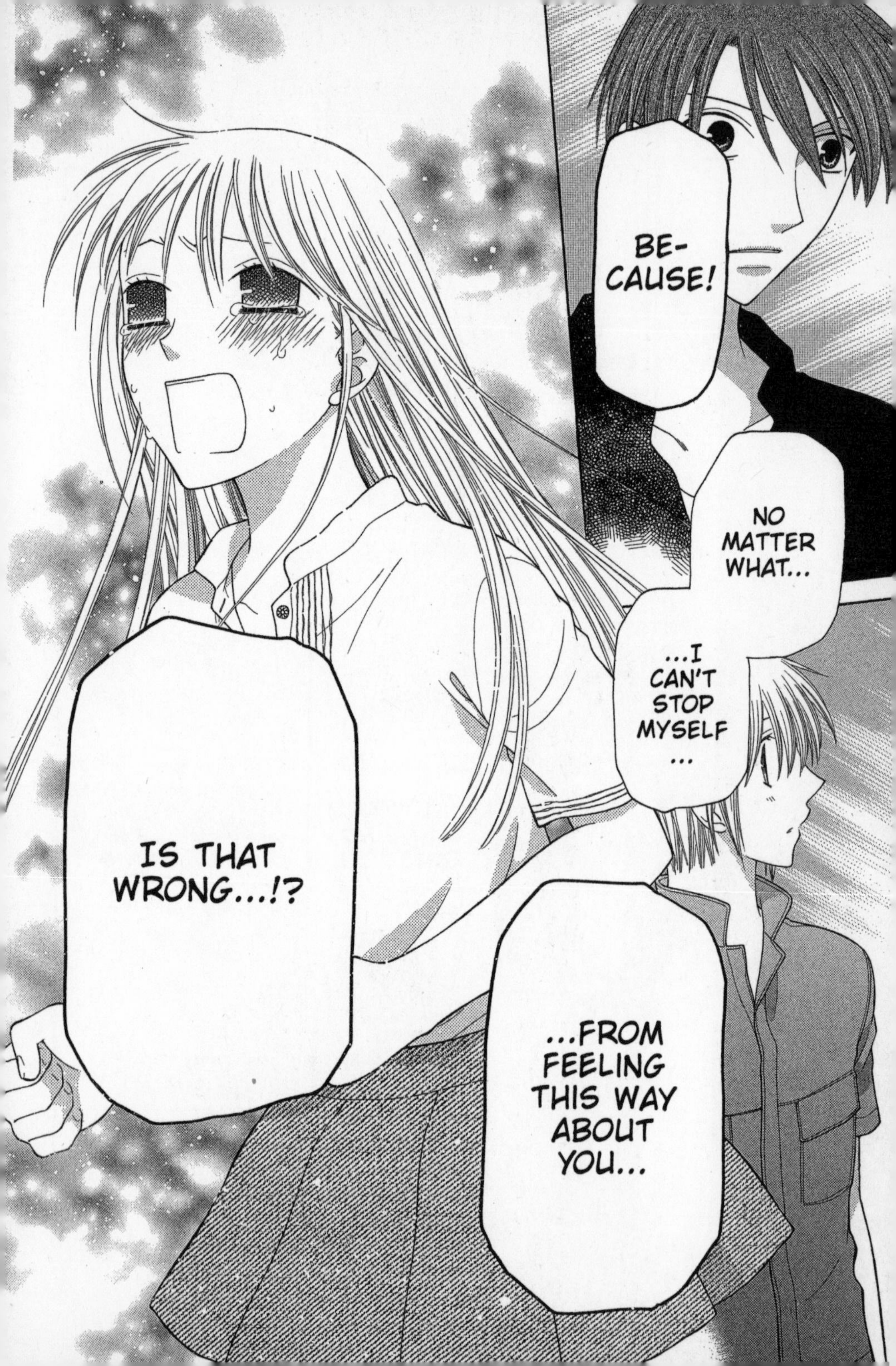
BE-CAUSE!
NO MATTER WHAT...
...I CAN'T STOP MYSELF ...
...FROM FEELING THIS WAY ABOUT YOU...
IS THAT WRONG...!?

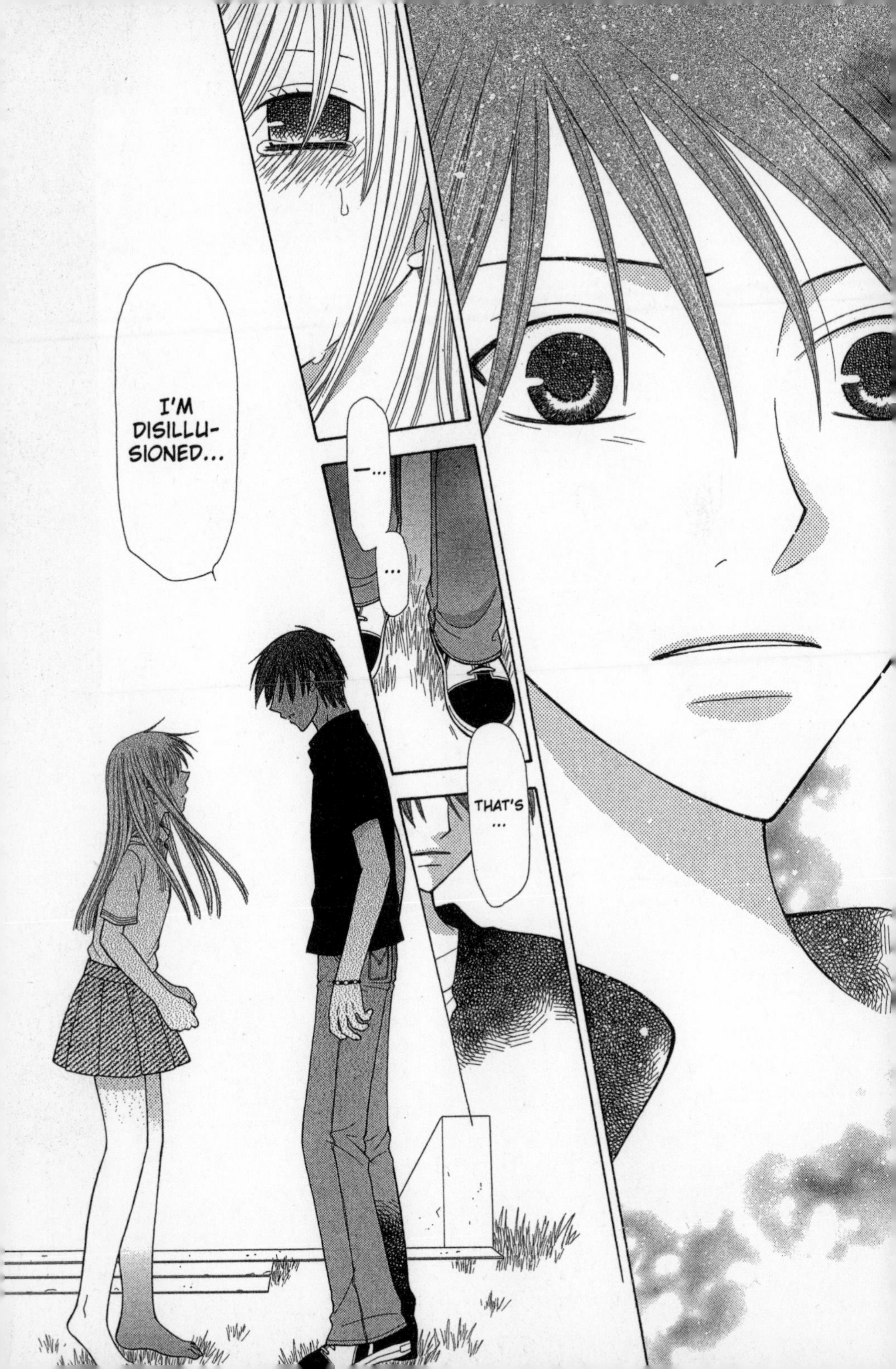
—...
...
THAT'S ...
I'M DISILLU-SIONED...

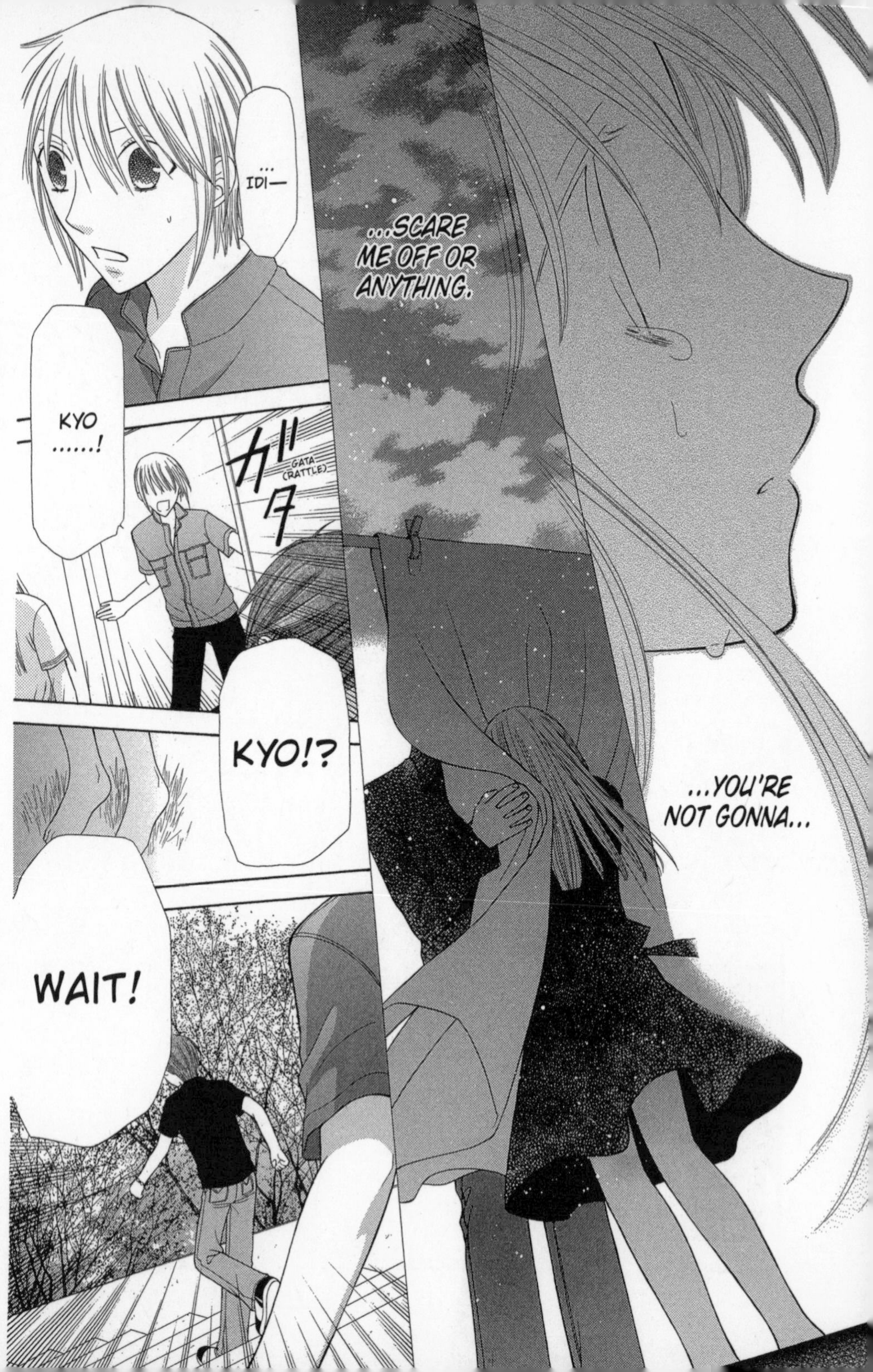
...YOU'RE NOT GONNA...
...SCARE ME OFF OR ANYTHING.
...IDI—
KYO......!
GATA (RATTLE)
KYO!?
WAIT!

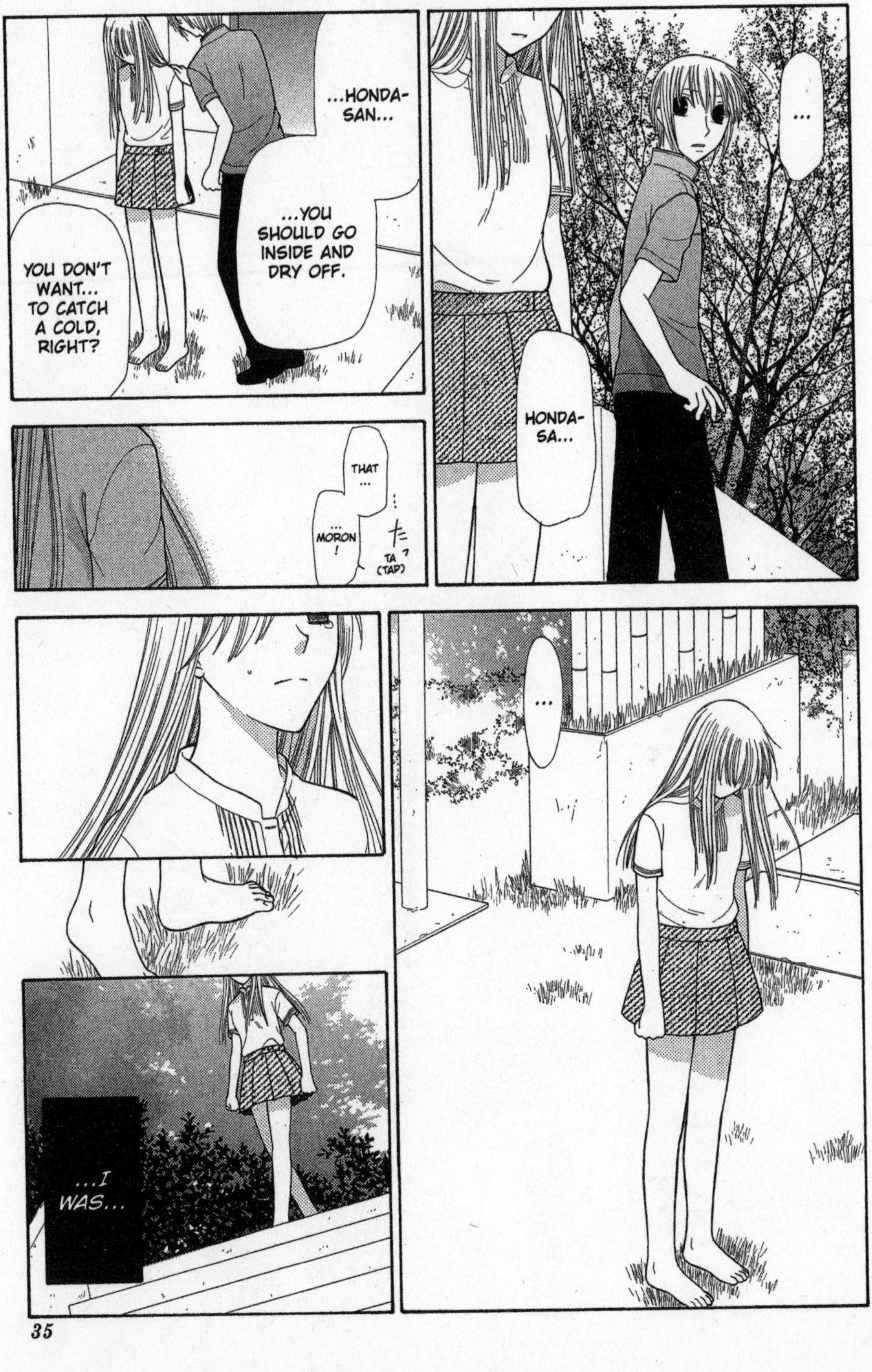
...
HONDA-SA...
...HONDA-SAN...
...YOU SHOULD GO INSIDE AND DRY OFF.
YOU DON'T WANT... TO CATCH A COLD, RIGHT?
THAT...
...MORON!
TA (TAP)
...
...I WAS...

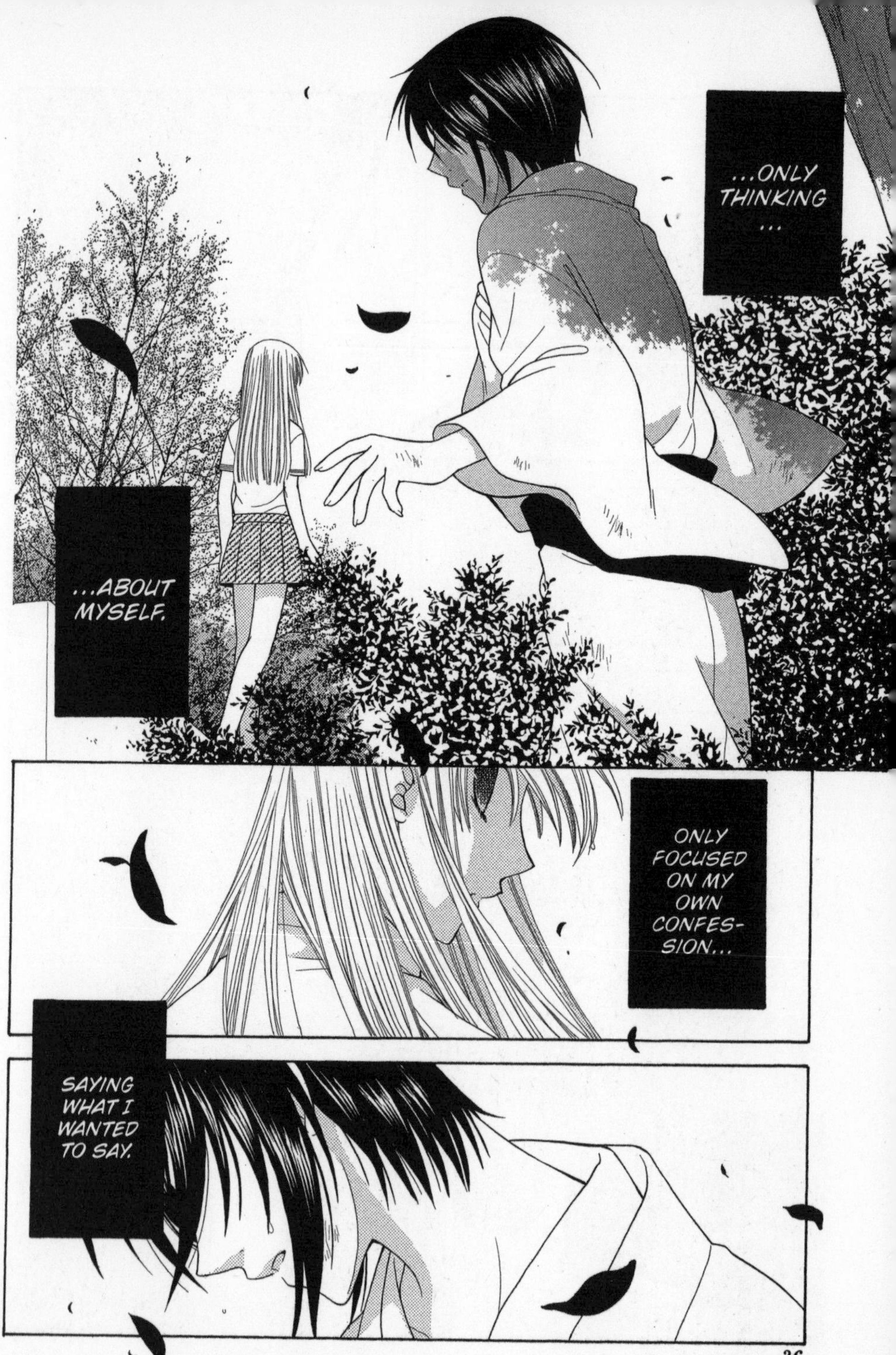
...ONLY THINKING ...
...ABOUT MYSELF.
ONLY FOCUSED ON MY OWN CONFES-SION...
SAYING WHAT I WANTED TO SAY.

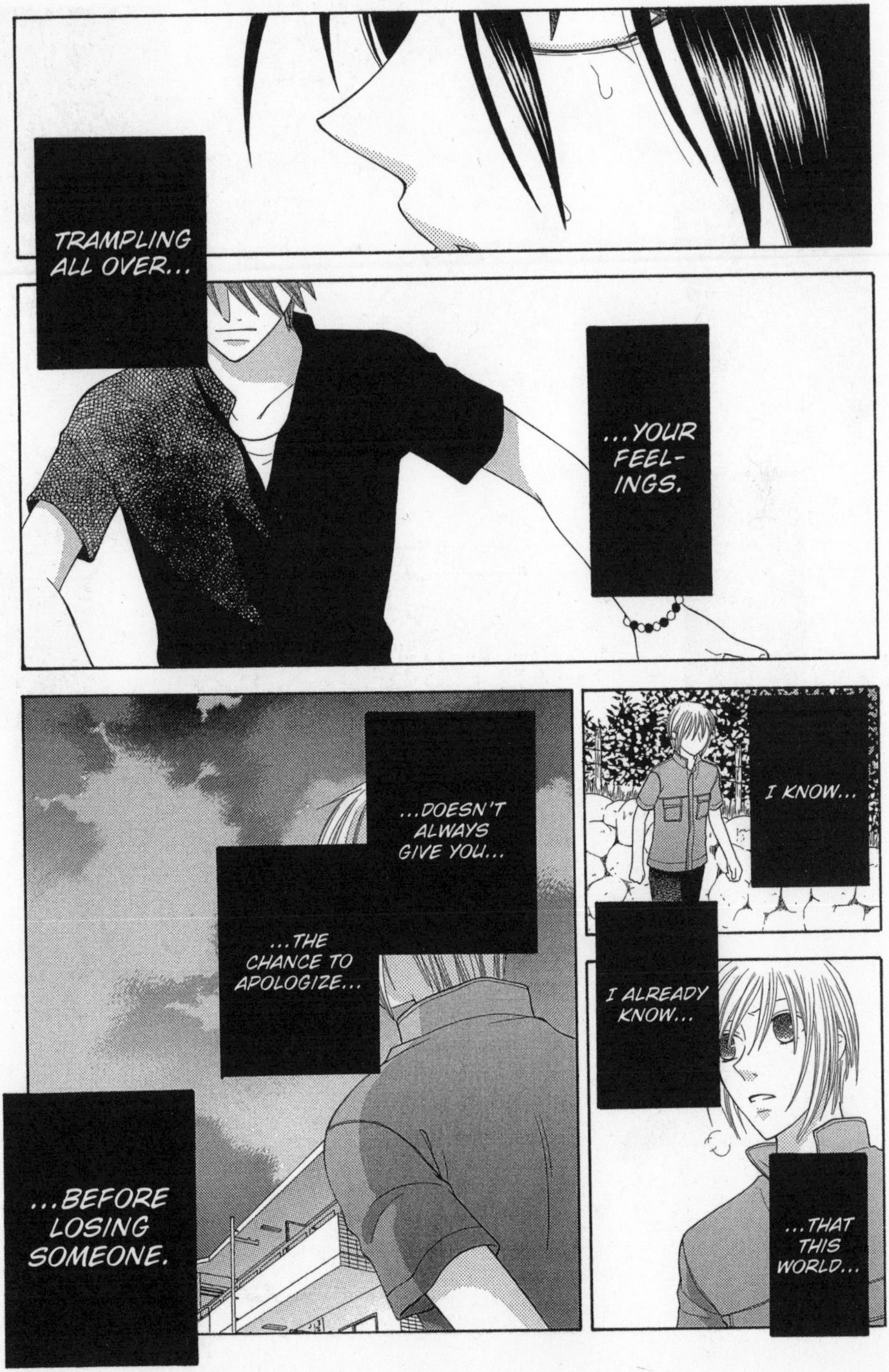
TRAMPLING ALL OVER...
...YOUR FEELINGS.
I KNOW...
I ALREADY KNOW...
...THAT THIS WORLD...
...DOESN'T ALWAYS GIVE YOU...
...THE CHANCE TO APOLOGIZE...
...BEFORE LOSING SOMEONE.

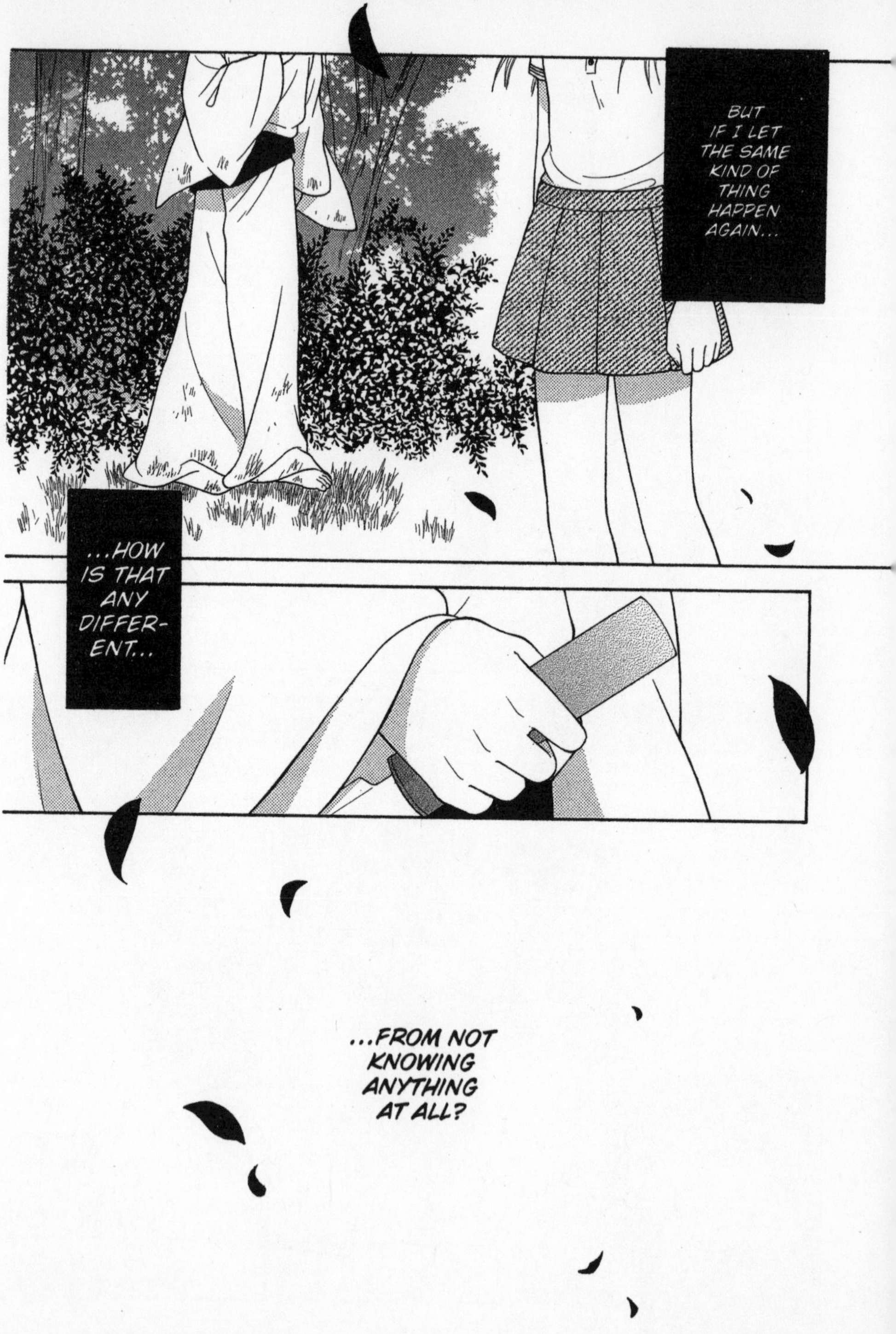
BUT IF I LET THE SAME KIND OF THING HAPPEN AGAIN...
...HOW IS THAT ANY DIFFER-ENT...
...FROM NOT KNOWING ANYTHING AT ALL?

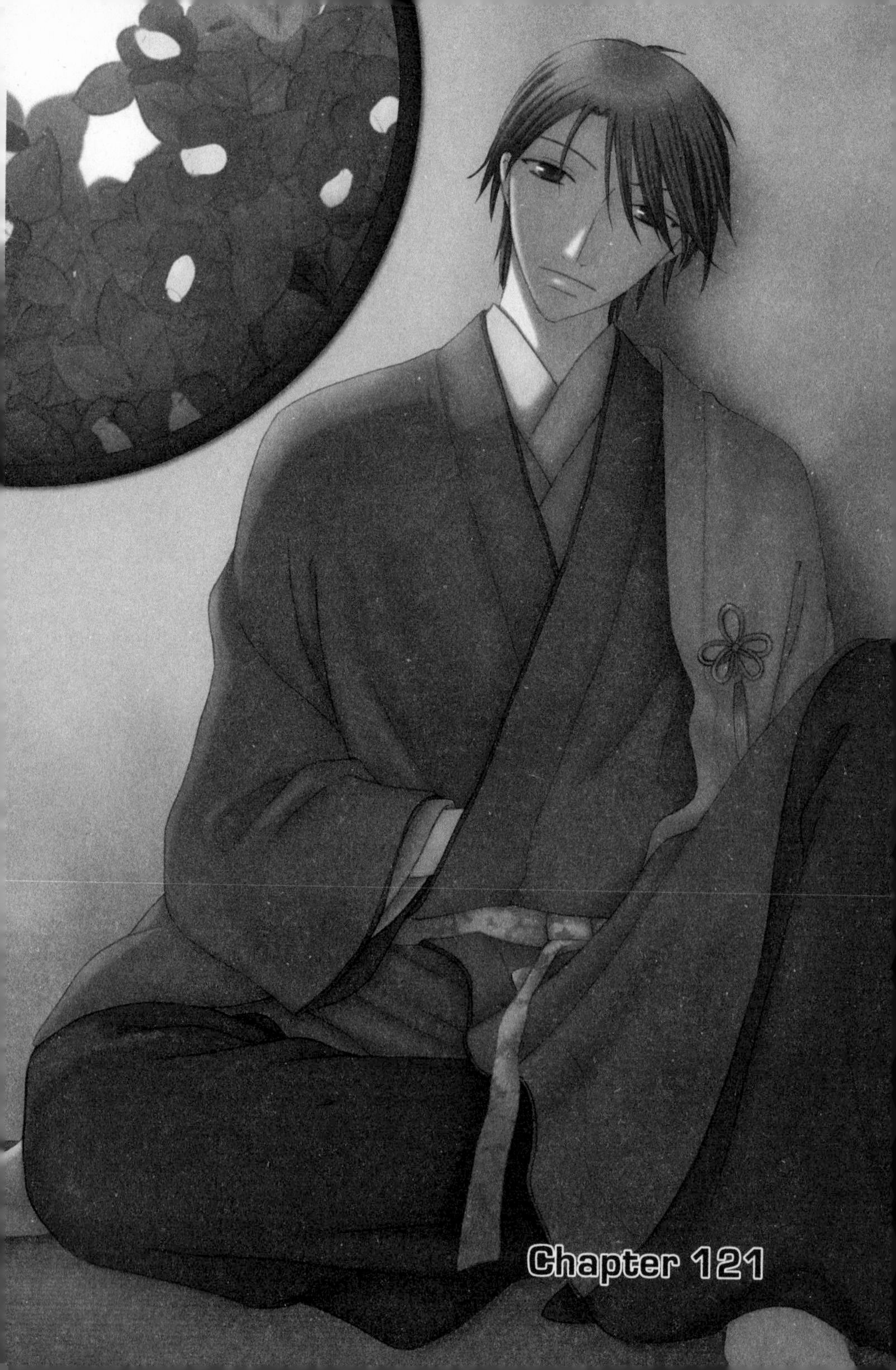
Chapter 121

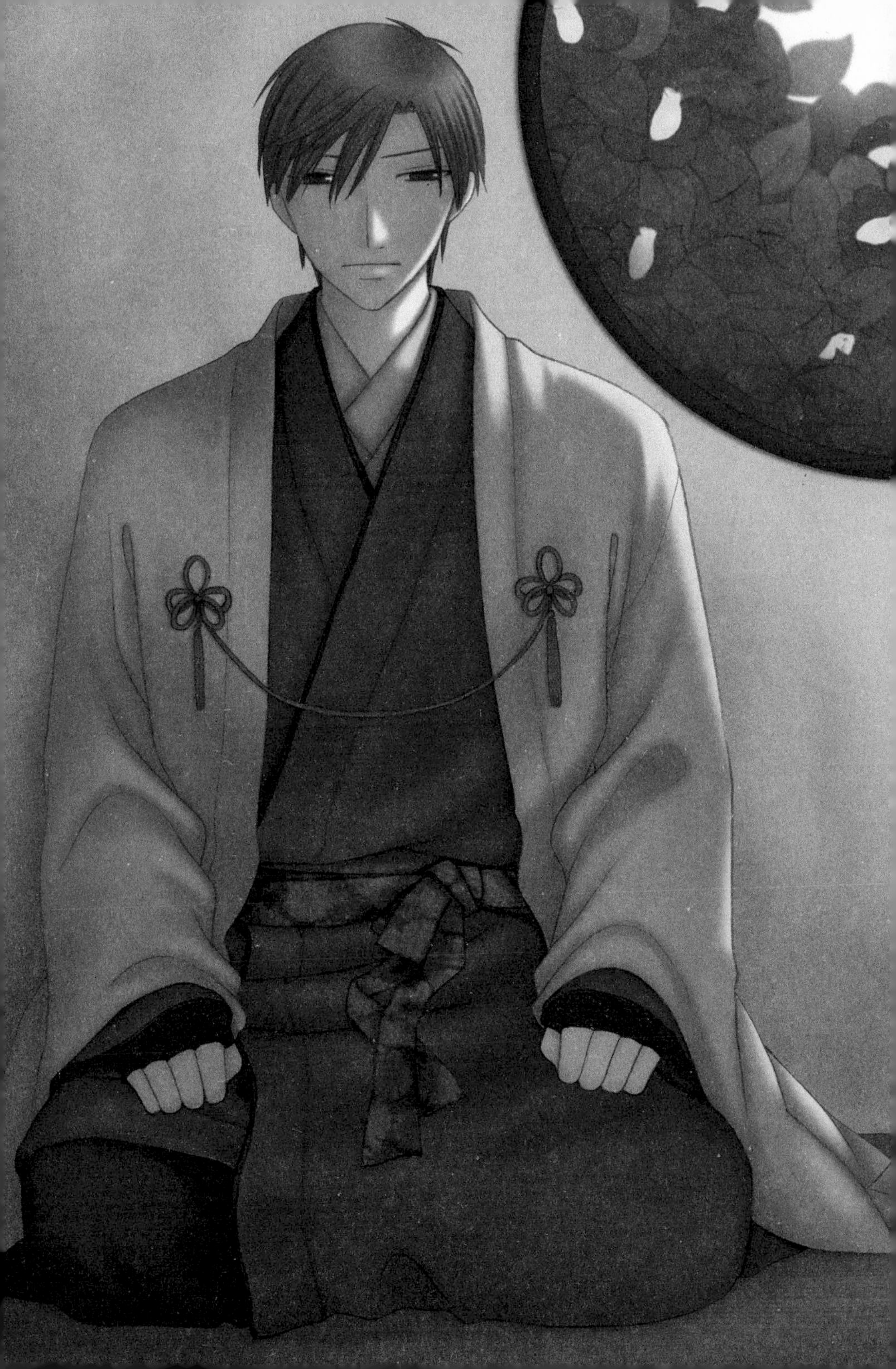

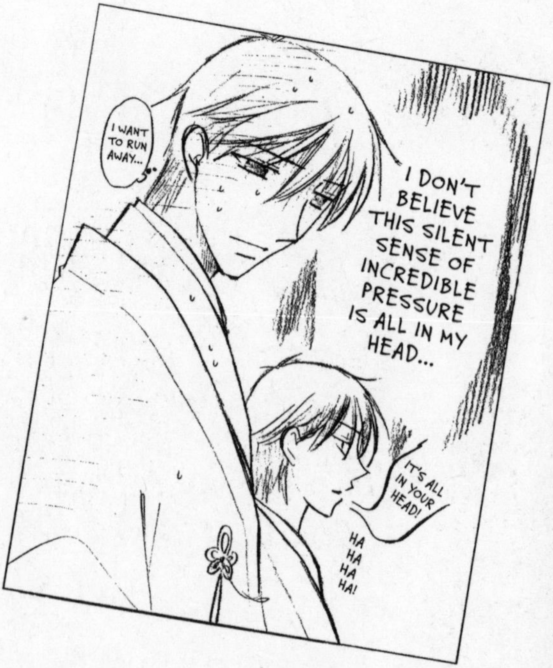
I DON'T BELIEVE THIS SILENT SENSE OF INCREDIBLE PRESSURE IS ALL IN MY HEAD...
I WANT TO RUN AWAY...
IT'S ALL IN YOUR HEAD!
HA HA HA HA!

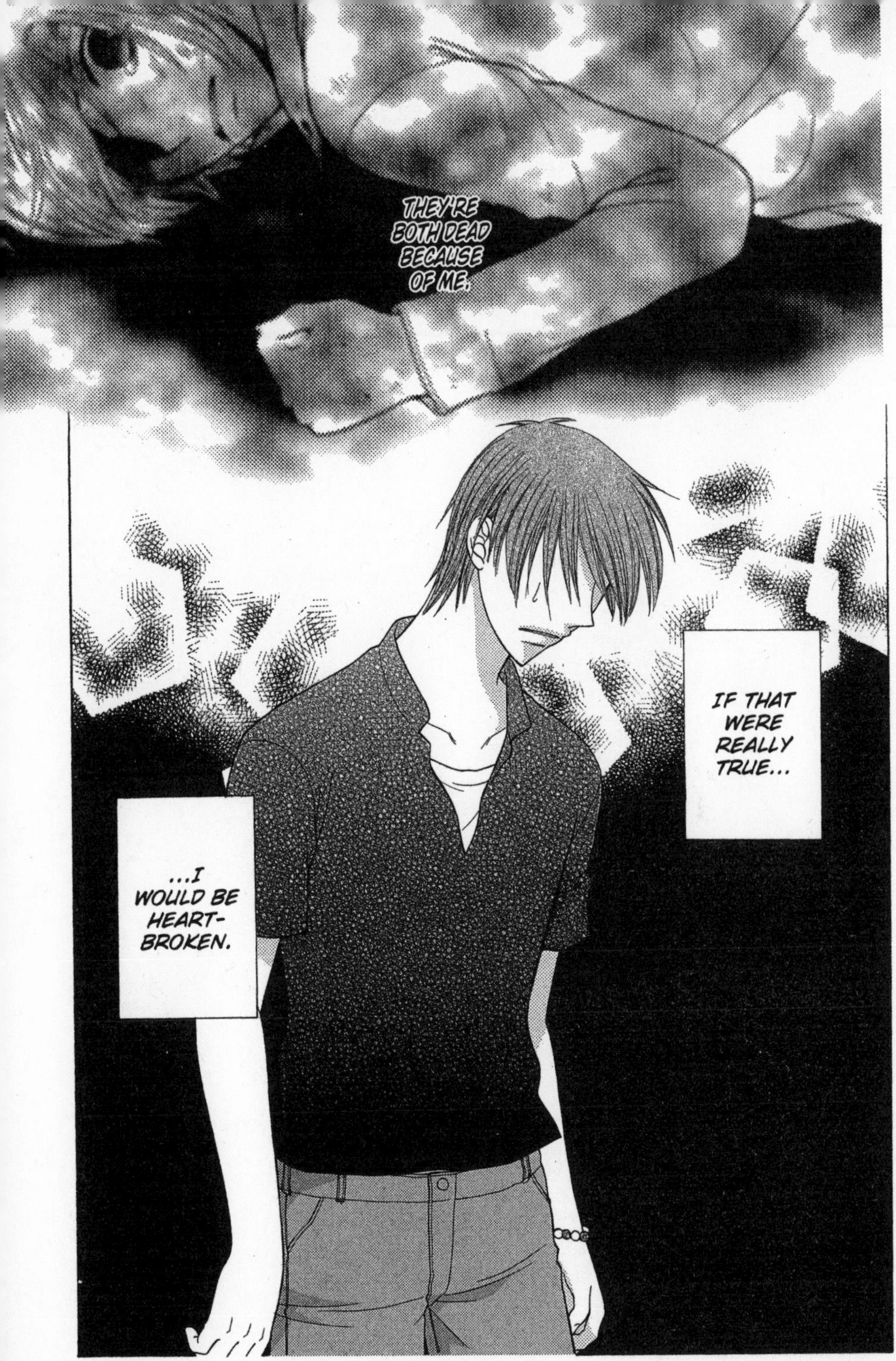
THEY'RE BOTH DEAD BECAUSE OF ME.
IF THAT WERE REALLY TRUE...
...I WOULD BE HEART-BROKEN.

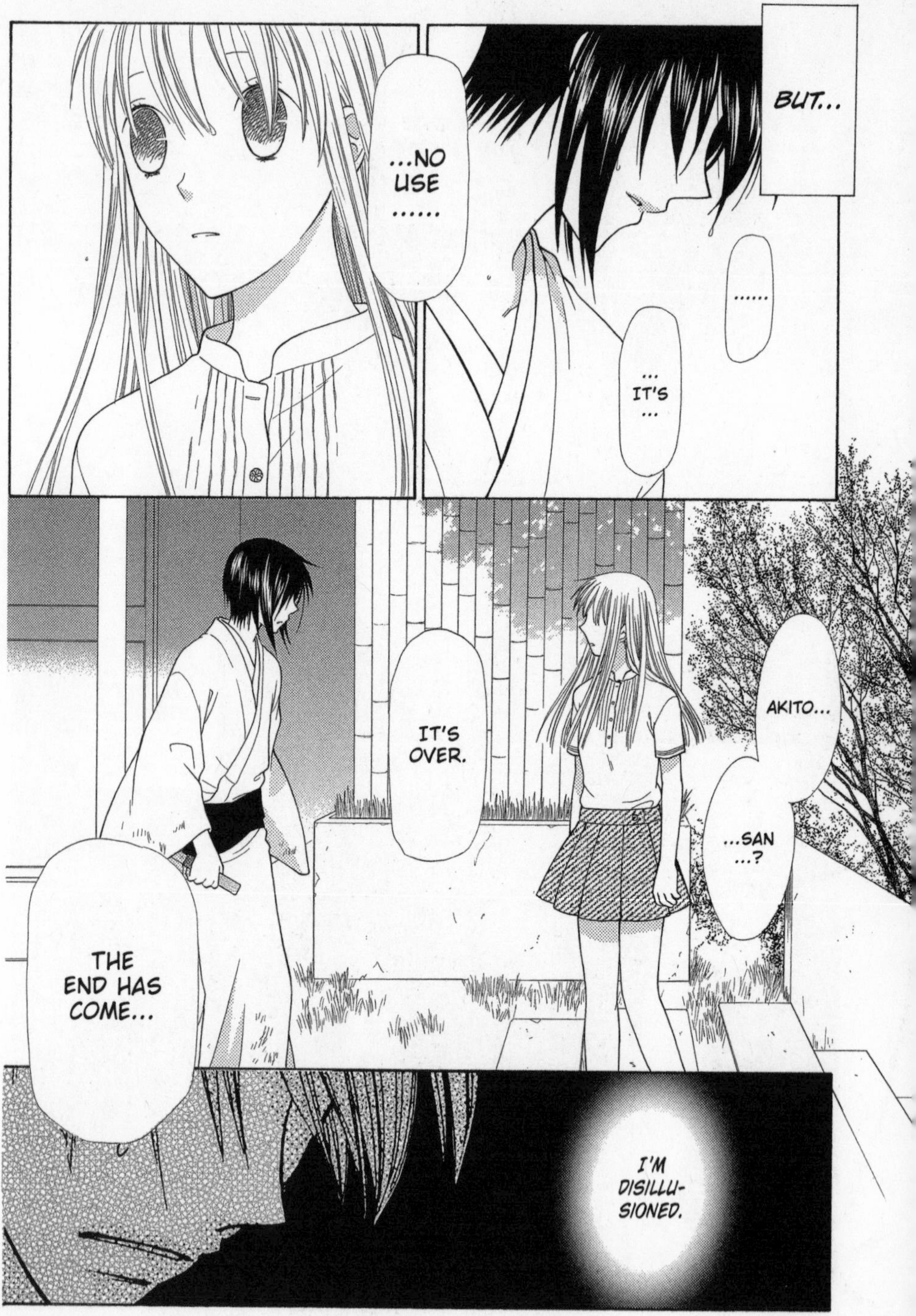
BUT...
......
...IT'S...
...NO USE......
AKITO...
...SAN...?
IT'S OVER.
THE END HAS COME...
I'M DISILLUSIONED.

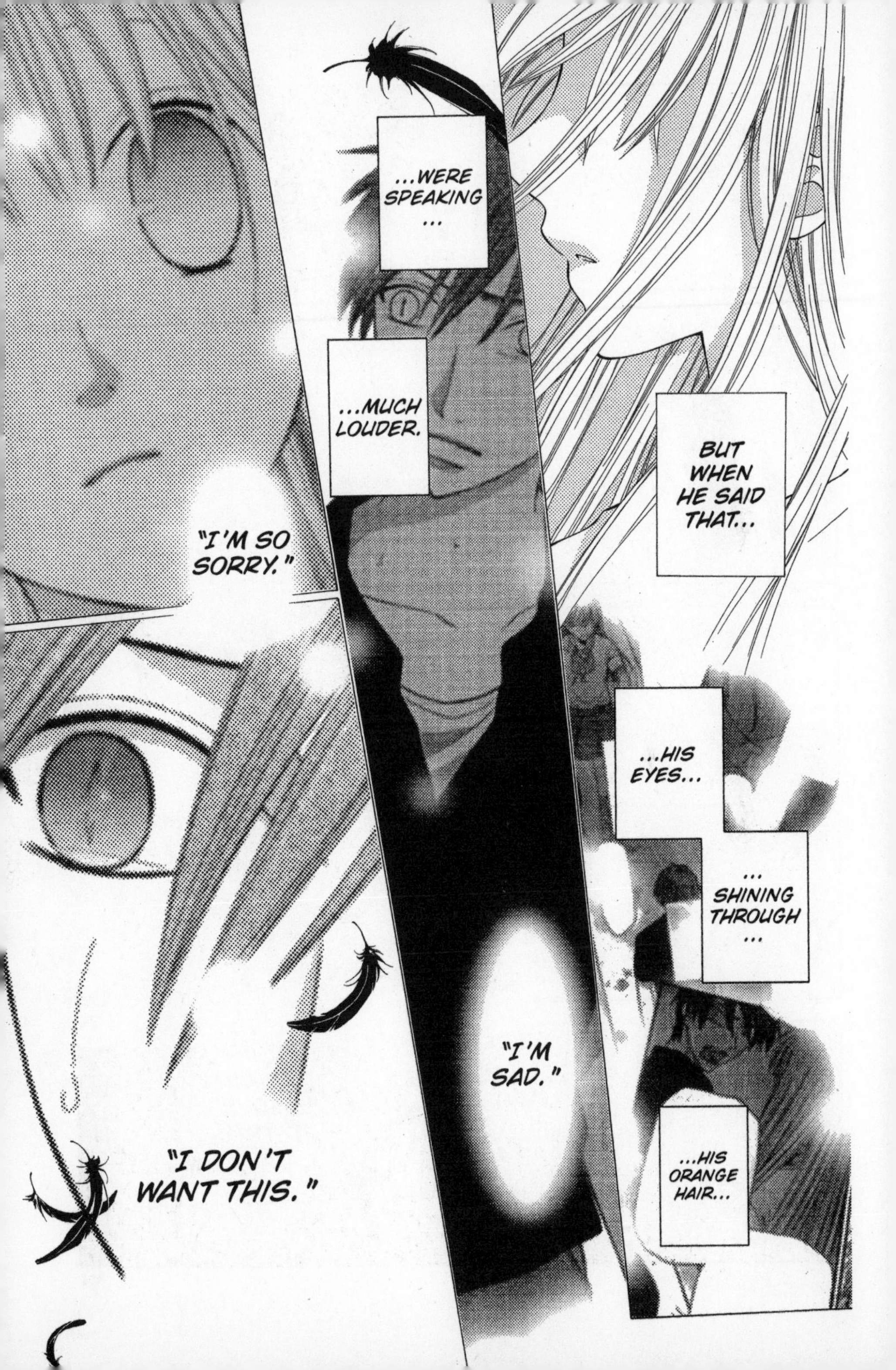
BUT WHEN HE SAID THAT...
...HIS EYES...
...SHINING THROUGH...
...HIS ORANGE HAIR...
...WERE SPEAKING...
...MUCH LOUDER.
"I'M SAD."
"I'M SO SORRY."
"I DON'T WANT THIS."

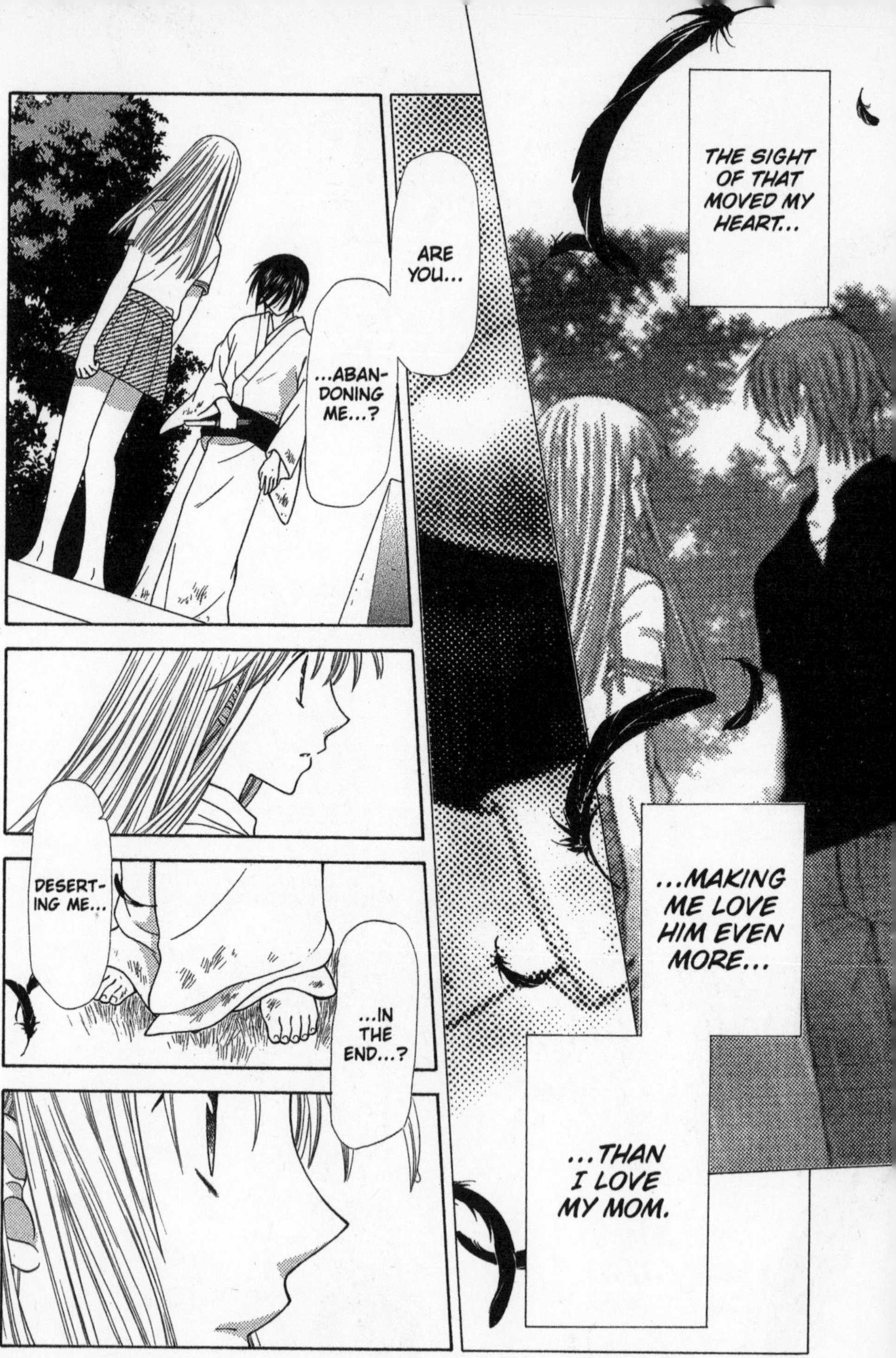
THE SIGHT OF THAT MOVED MY HEART...
...MAKING ME LOVE HIM EVEN MORE...
...THAN I LOVE MY MOM.
ARE YOU...
...ABAN-DONING ME...?
DESERT-ING ME...
...IN THE END...?

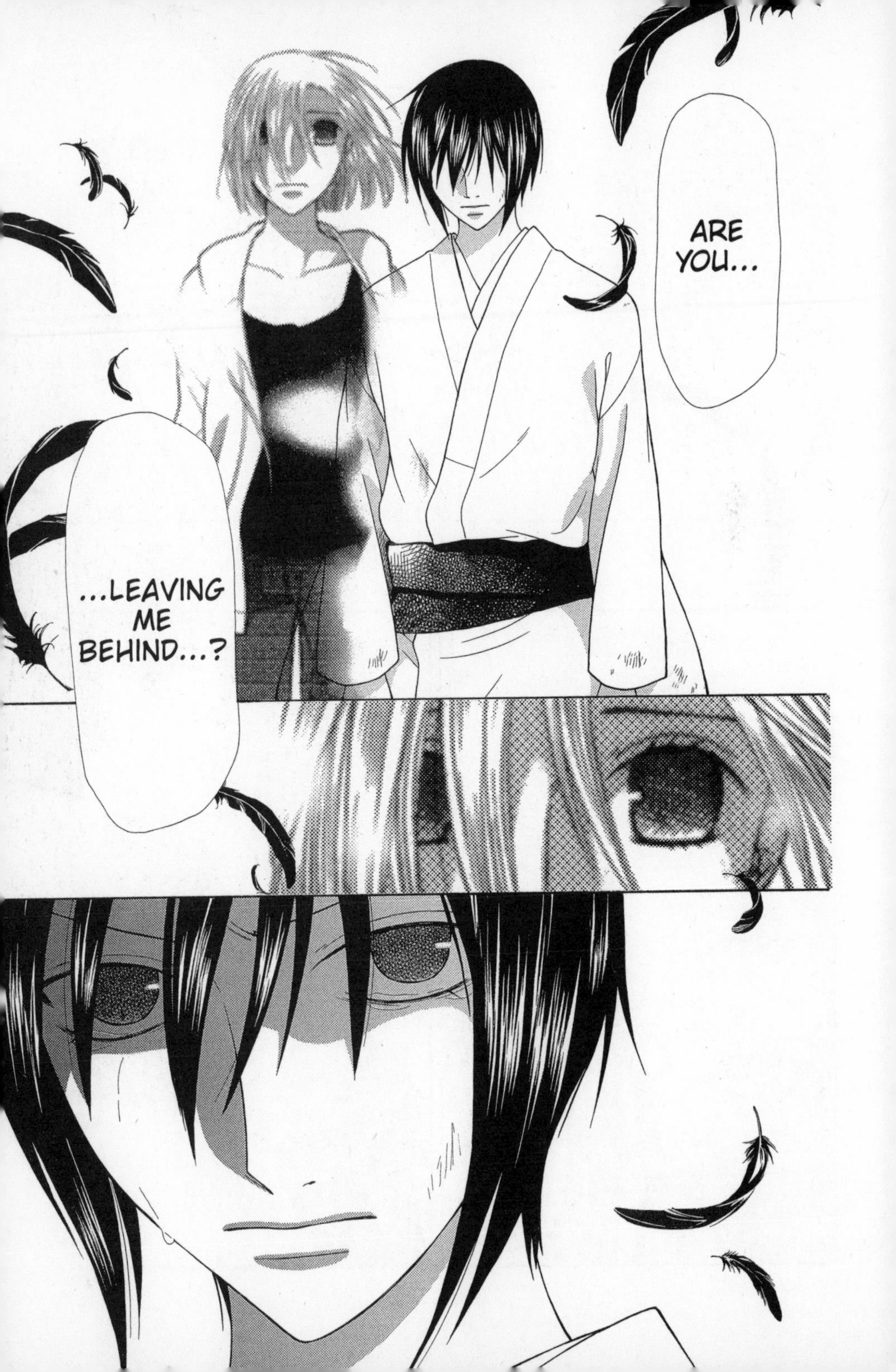
ARE YOU...
...LEAVING ME BEHIND...?

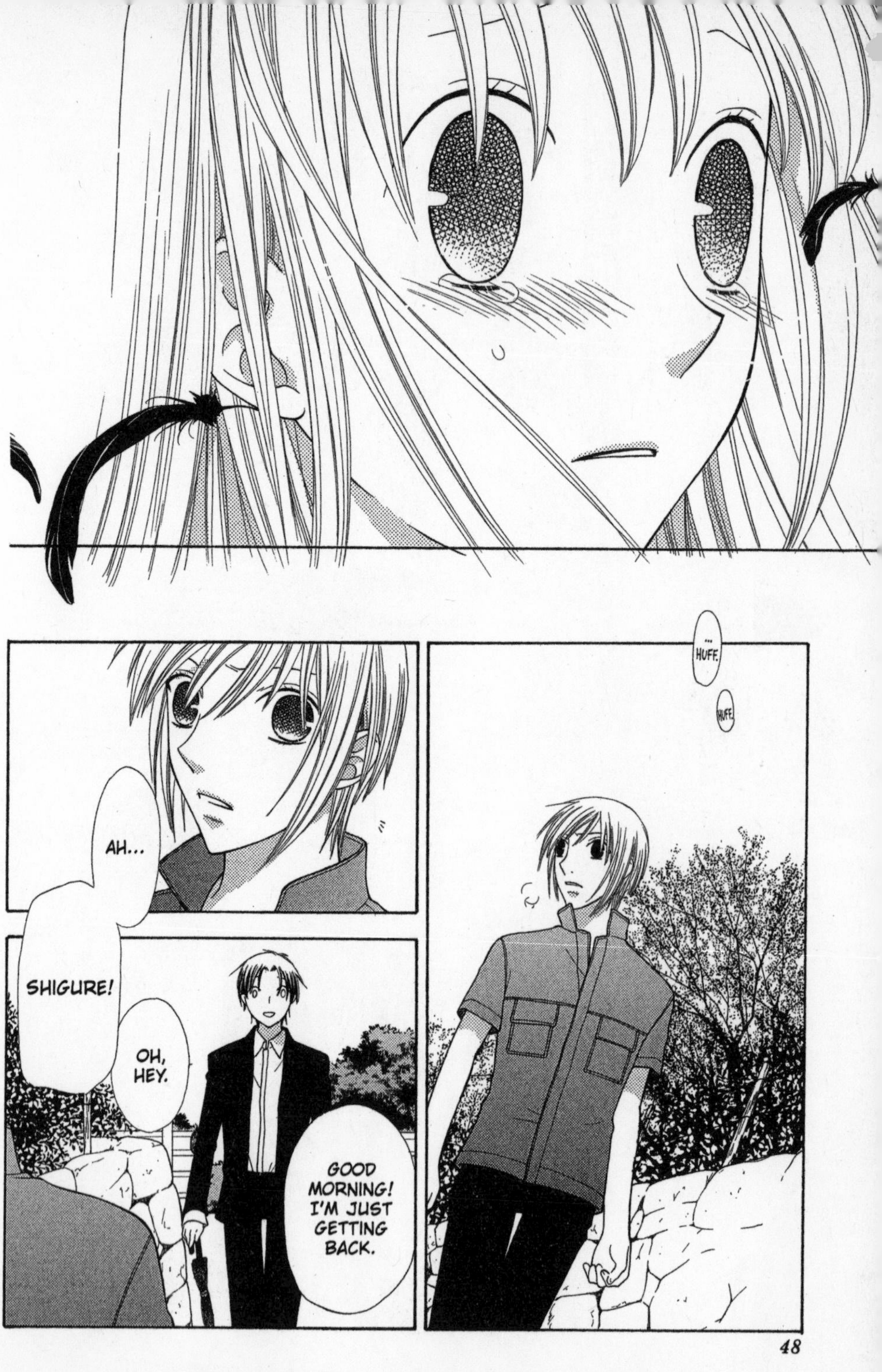

...HUFF.
HUFF.
AH...
SHIGURE!
OH, HEY.
GOOD MORNING! I'M JUST GETTING BACK.

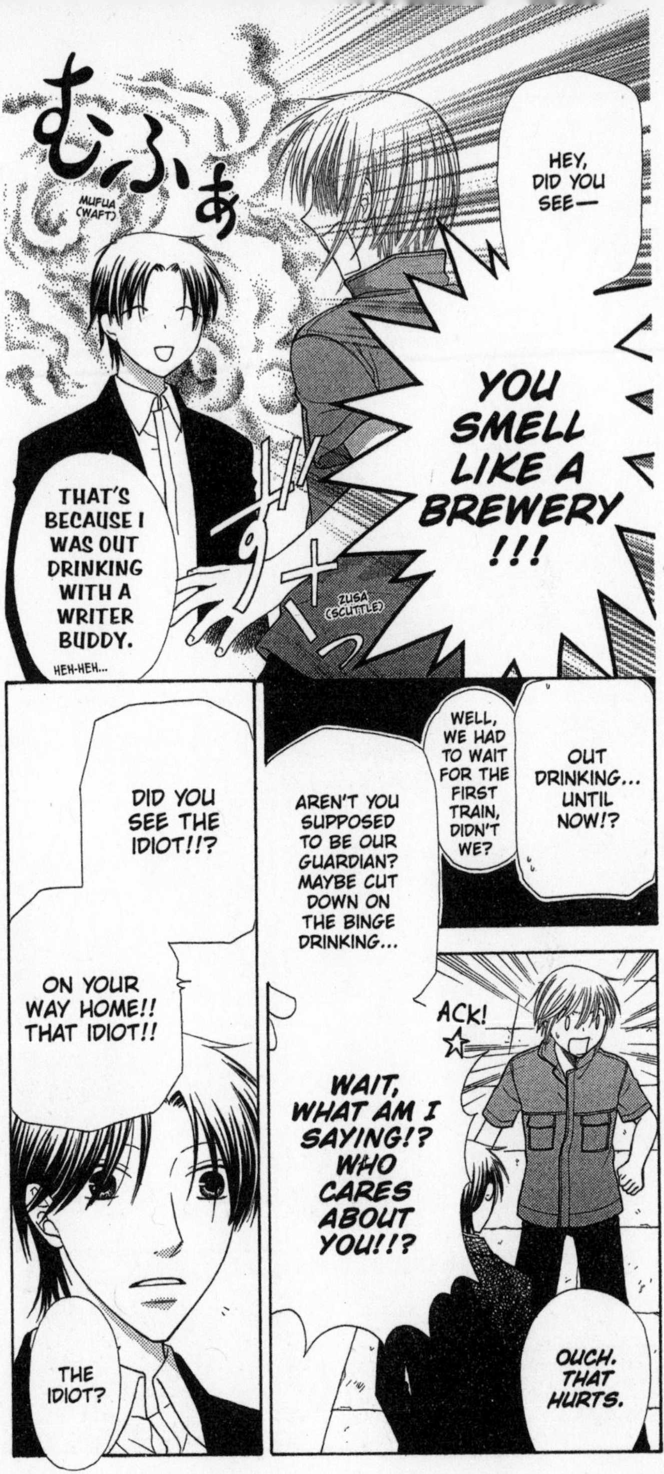

HEY, DID YOU SEE—
YOU SMELL LIKE A BREWERY!!!
むふぁ
MUFUA (WAFT)
ZUSA (SCUTTLE)
THAT'S BECAUSE I WAS OUT DRINKING WITH A WRITER BUDDY.
HEH-HEH...
OUT DRINKING... UNTIL NOW!?
WELL, WE HAD TO WAIT FOR THE FIRST TRAIN, DIDN'T WE?
AREN'T YOU SUPPOSED TO BE OUR GUARDIAN? MAYBE CUT DOWN ON THE BINGE DRINKING...
ACK!
WAIT, WHAT AM I SAYING!? WHO CARES ABOUT YOU!!?
OUCH. THAT HURTS.
DID YOU SEE THE IDIOT!!?
ON YOUR WAY HOME!! THAT IDIOT!!
THE IDIOT?

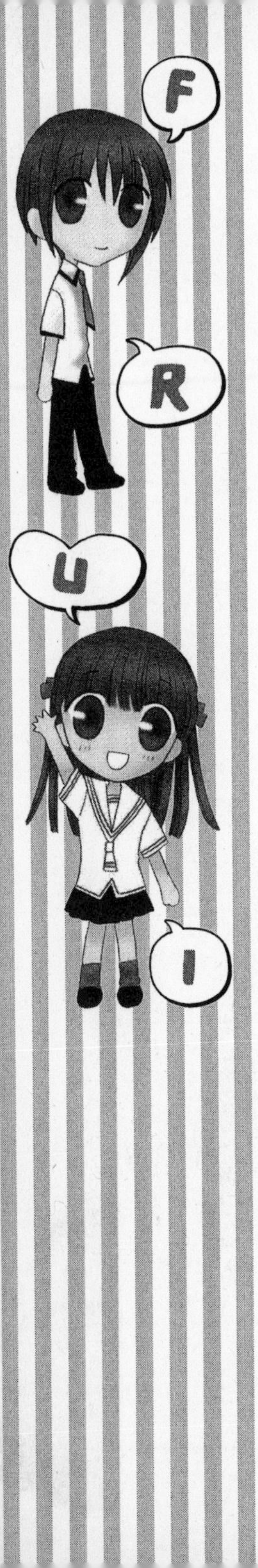

F
R
U
I

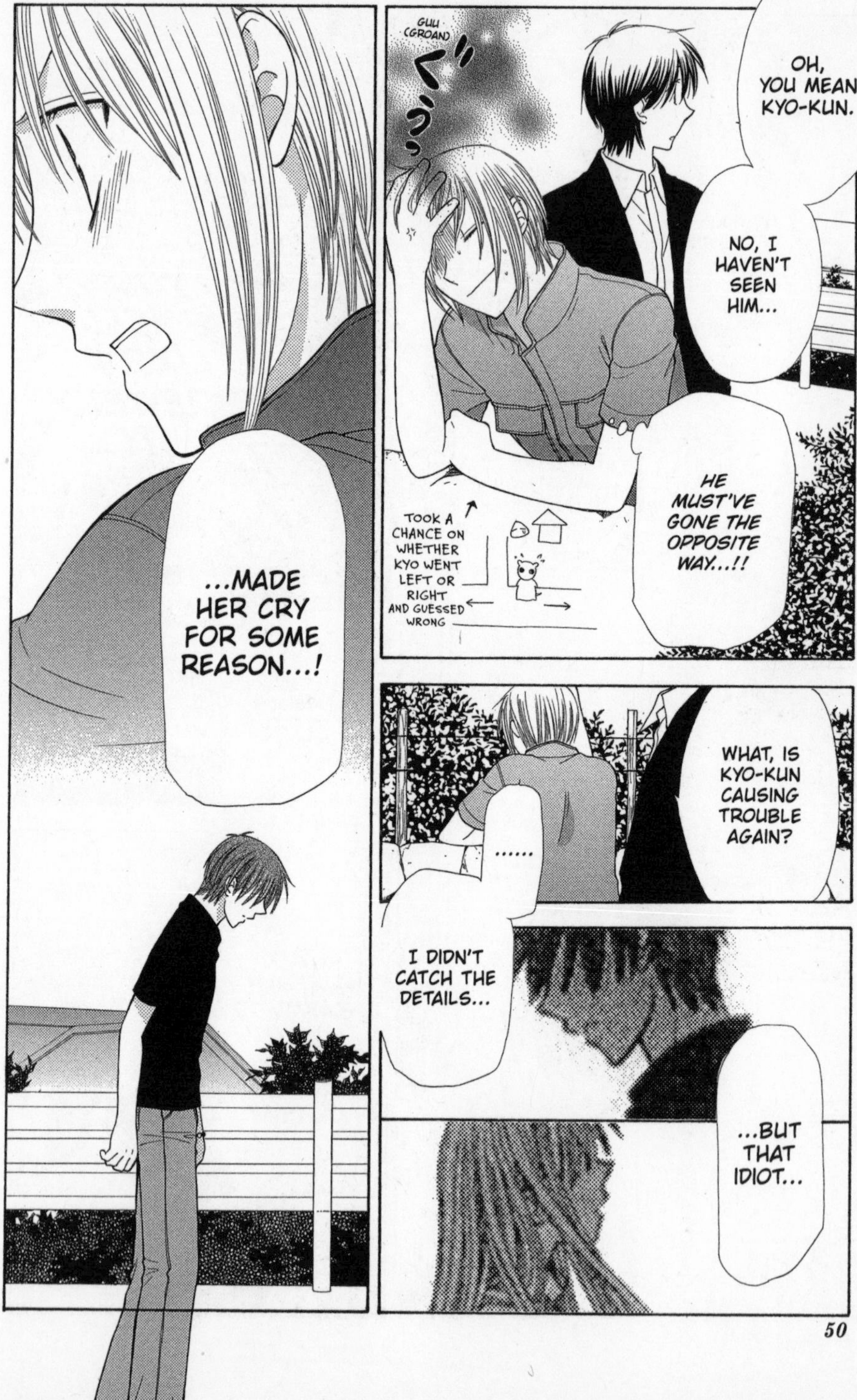
OH, YOU MEAN KYO-KUN.
NO, I HAVEN'T SEEN HIM...
GUU (GROAN)
HE MUST'VE GONE THE OPPOSITE WAY...!!
TOOK A CHANCE ON WHETHER KYO WENT LEFT OR RIGHT AND GUESSED WRONG
WHAT, IS KYO-KUN CAUSING TROUBLE AGAIN?
......
I DIDN'T CATCH THE DETAILS...
...BUT THAT IDIOT...
...MADE HER CRY FOR SOME REASON...!

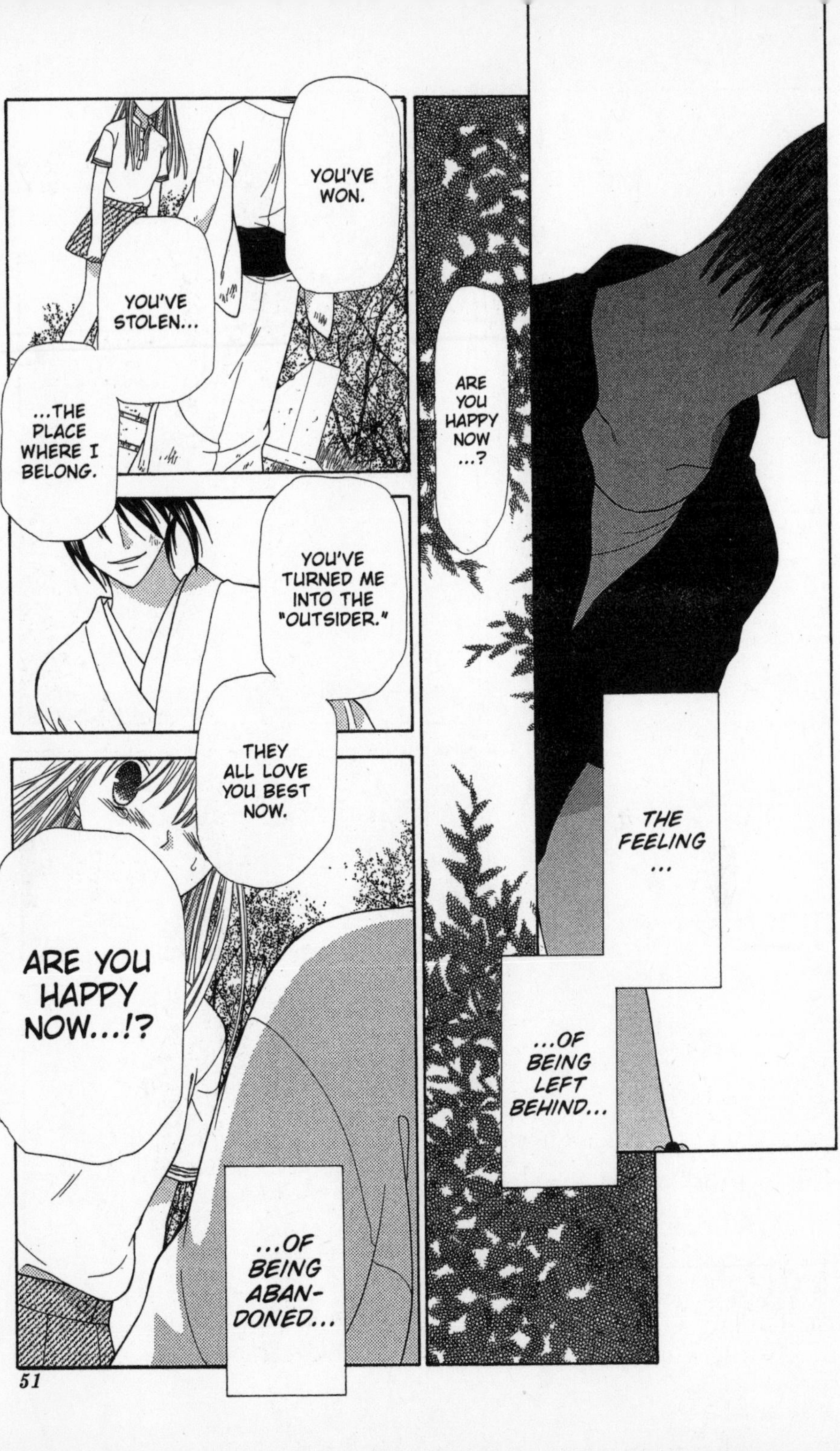
THE FEELING ...
...OF BEING LEFT BEHIND...
ARE YOU HAPPY NOW ...?
YOU'VE WON.
YOU'VE STOLEN...
...THE PLACE WHERE I BELONG.
YOU'VE TURNED ME INTO THE "OUTSIDER."
THEY ALL LOVE YOU BEST NOW.
ARE YOU HAPPY NOW...!?
...OF BEING ABAN-DONED...

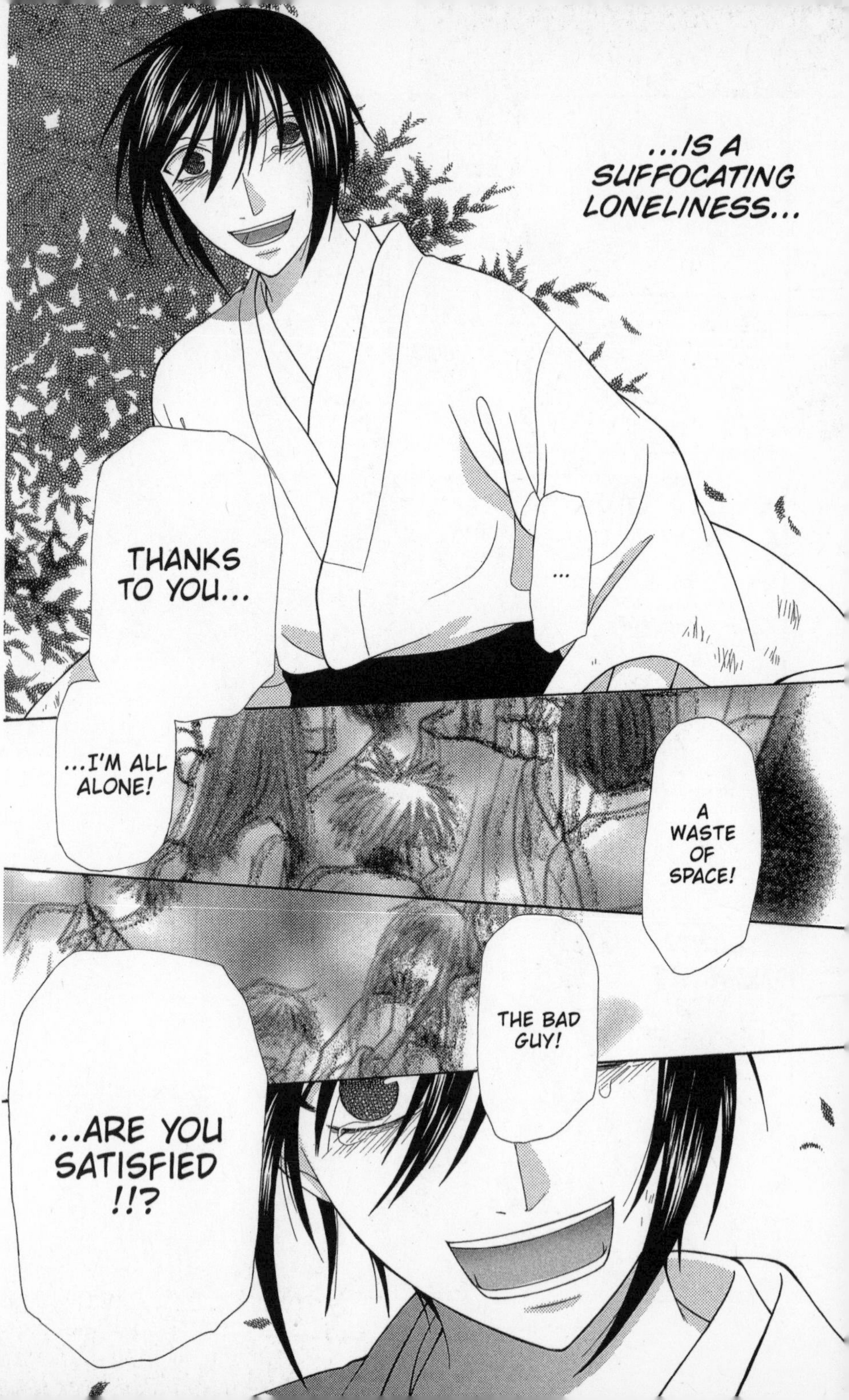
...IS A SUFFOCATING LONELINESS...
...
THANKS TO YOU...
...I'M ALL ALONE!
A WASTE OF SPACE!
THE BAD GUY!
...ARE YOU SATISFIED !!?

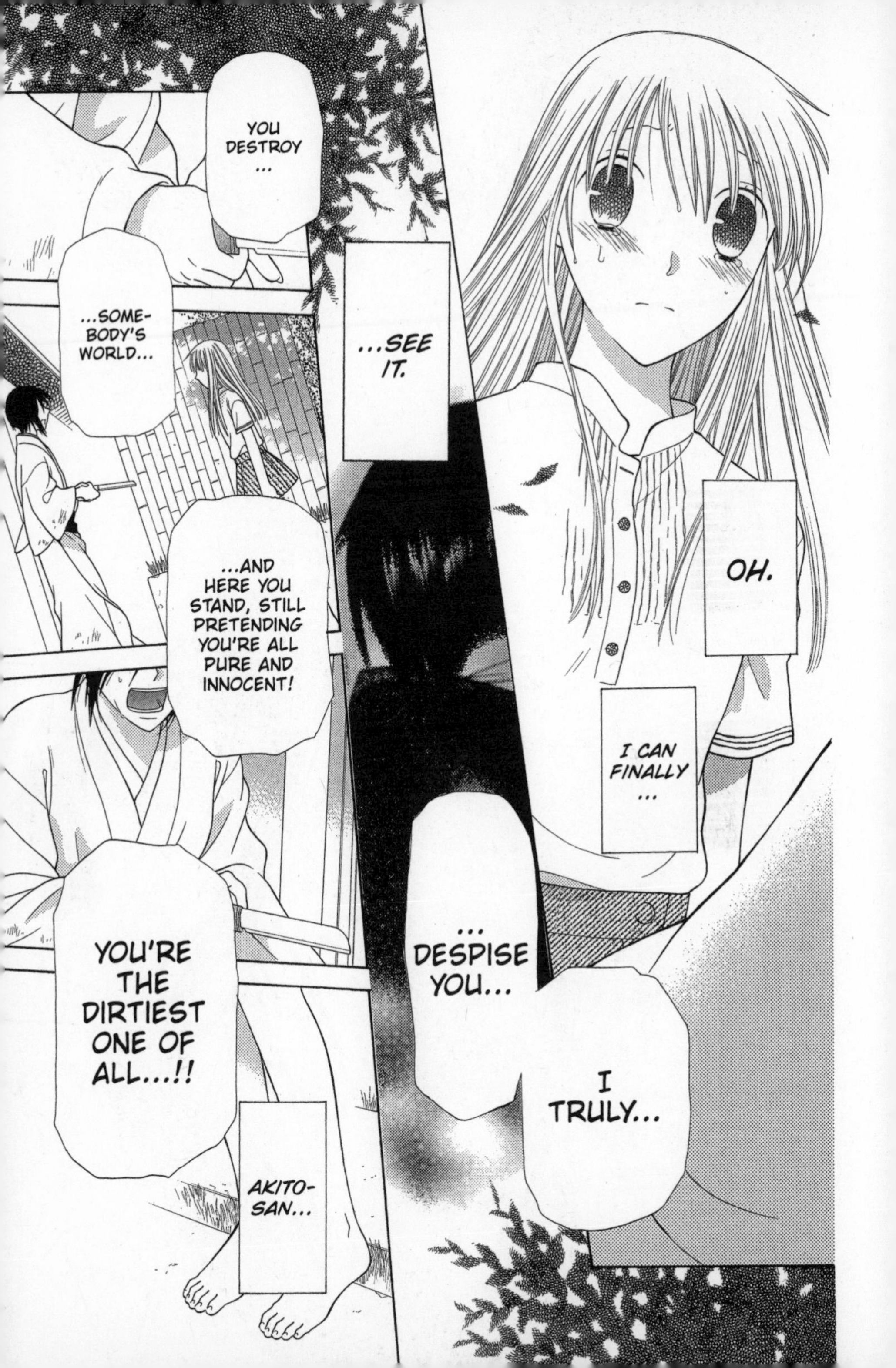
OH.
I CAN FINALLY ...
...SEE IT.
I TRULY...
... DESPISE YOU...
YOU DESTROY ...
...SOME-BODY'S WORLD...
...AND HERE YOU STAND, STILL PRETENDING YOU'RE ALL PURE AND INNOCENT!
YOU'RE THE DIRTIEST ONE OF ALL...!!
AKITO-SAN...

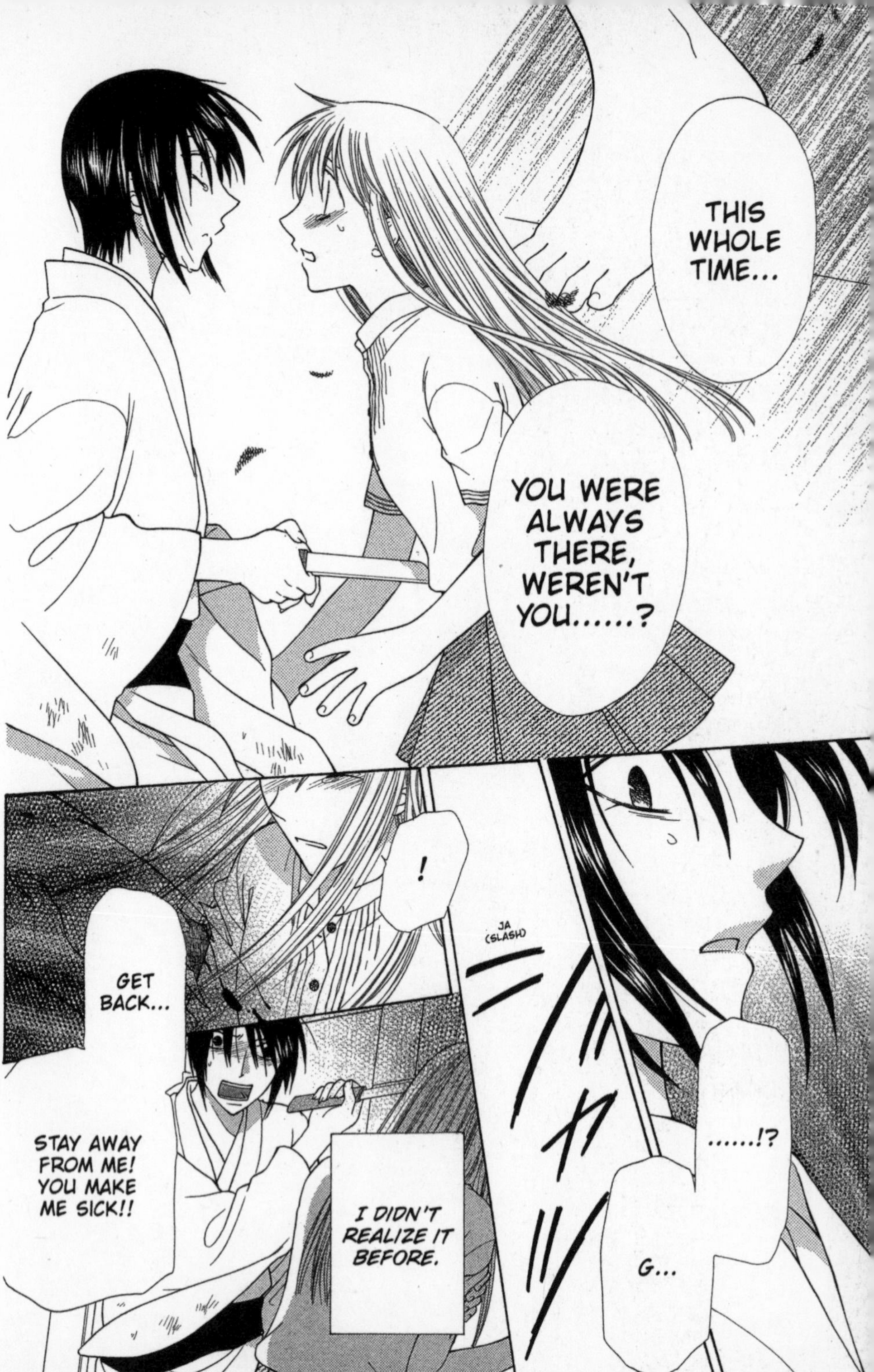
THIS WHOLE TIME...
YOU WERE ALWAYS THERE, WEREN'T YOU......?
JA (SLASH)
......!?
G...
!
GET BACK...
I DIDN'T REALIZE IT BEFORE.
STAY AWAY FROM ME! YOU MAKE ME SICK!!

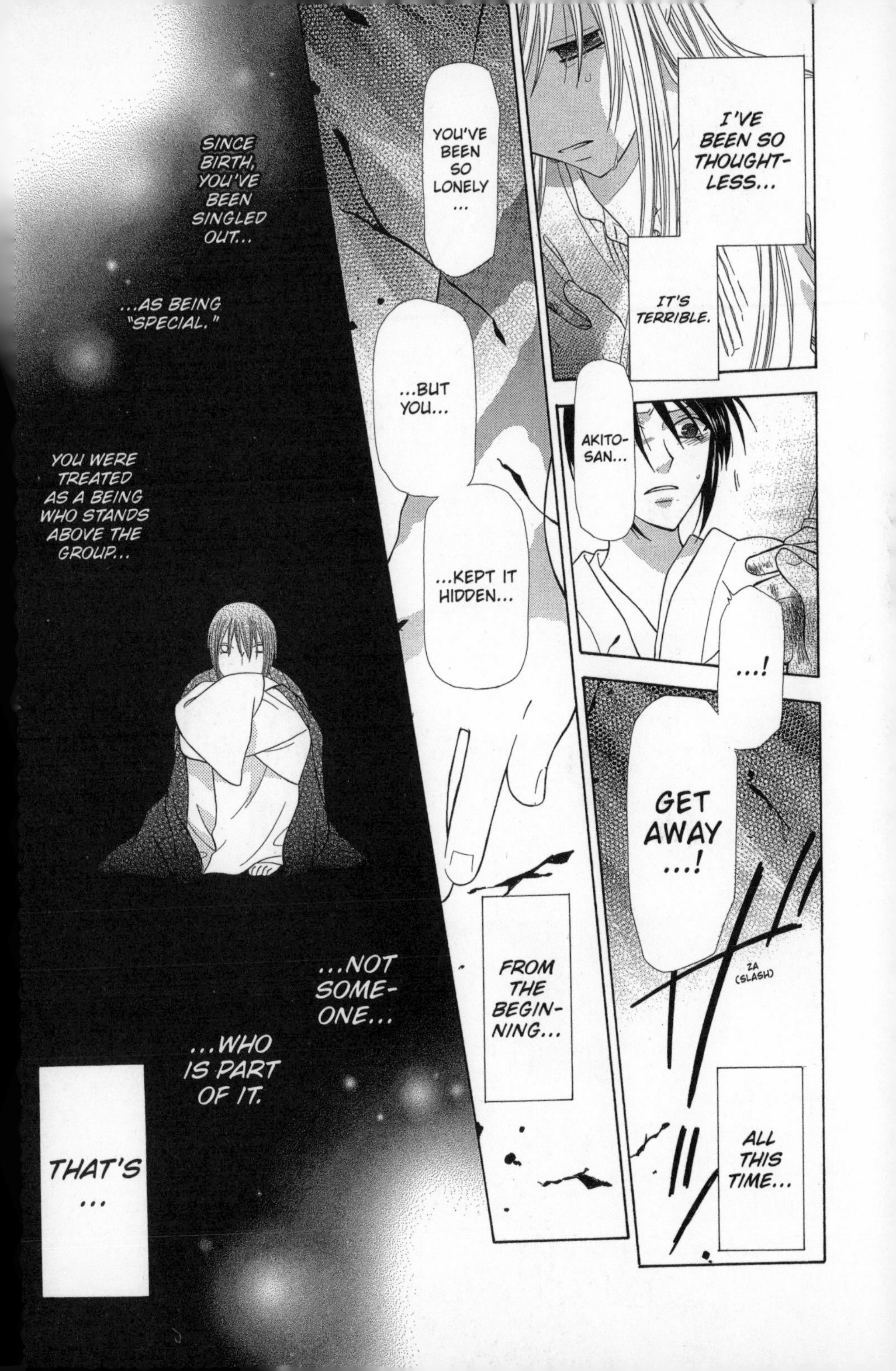
I'VE BEEN SO THOUGHTLESS...
IT'S TERRIBLE.
AKITO-SAN...
...!
GET AWAY...!
ZA (SLASH)
ALL THIS TIME...
YOU'VE BEEN SO LONELY...
...BUT YOU...
...KEPT IT HIDDEN...
FROM THE BEGINNING...
SINCE BIRTH, YOU'VE BEEN SINGLED OUT...
...AS BEING "SPECIAL."
YOU WERE TREATED AS A BEING WHO STANDS ABOVE THE GROUP...
...NOT SOMEONE...
...WHO IS PART OF IT.
THAT'S...

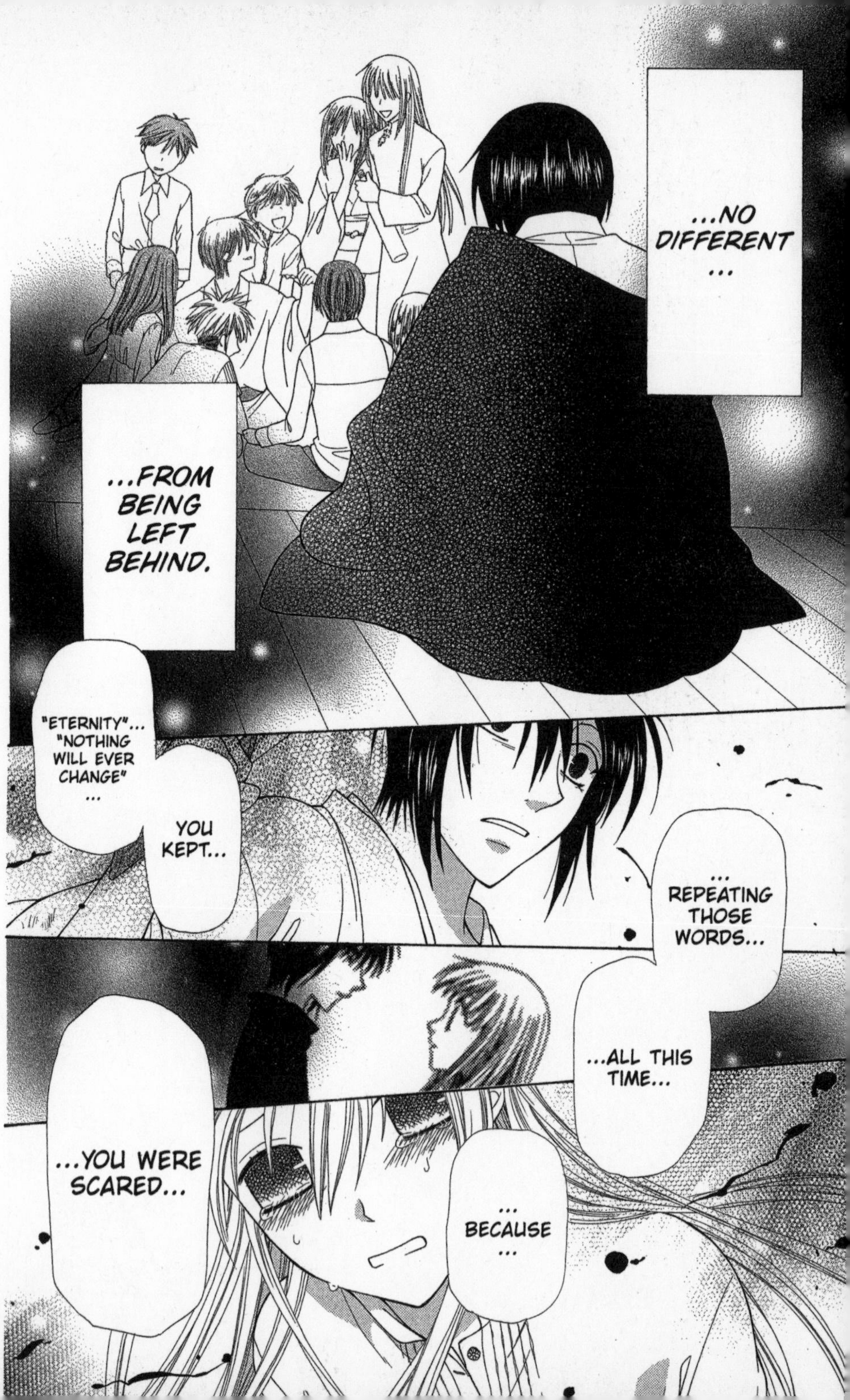
...NO DIFFERENT ...
...FROM BEING LEFT BEHIND.
"ETERNITY"... "NOTHING WILL EVER CHANGE" ...
YOU KEPT...
... REPEATING THOSE WORDS...
...ALL THIS TIME...
... BECAUSE ...
...YOU WERE SCARED...

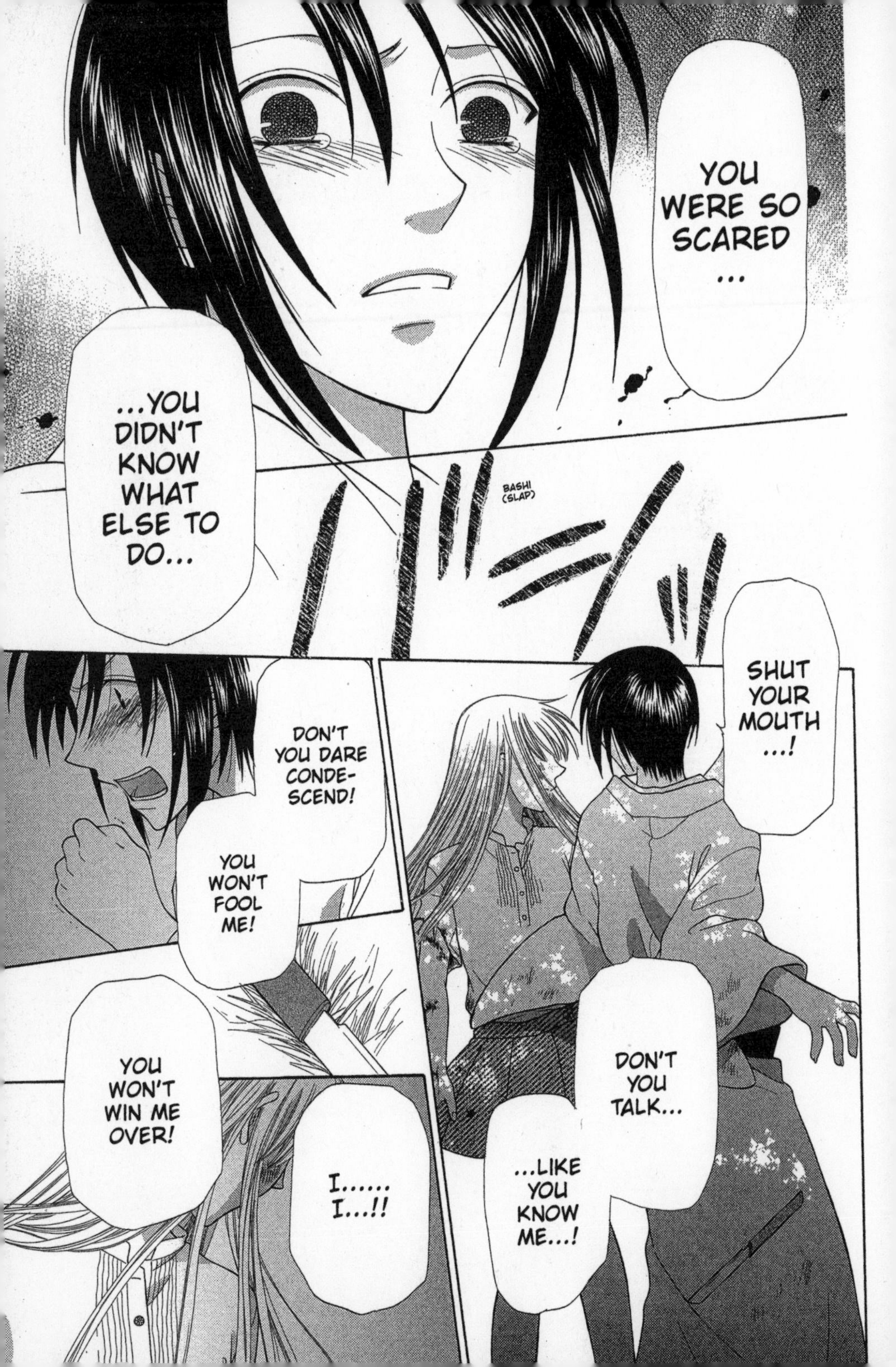
YOU WERE SO SCARED ...
...YOU DIDN'T KNOW WHAT ELSE TO DO...
BASHI (SLAP)
SHUT YOUR MOUTH ...!
DON'T YOU TALK...
...LIKE YOU KNOW ME...!
DON'T YOU DARE CONDE-SCEND!
YOU WON'T FOOL ME!
YOU WON'T WIN ME OVER!
I...... I...!!

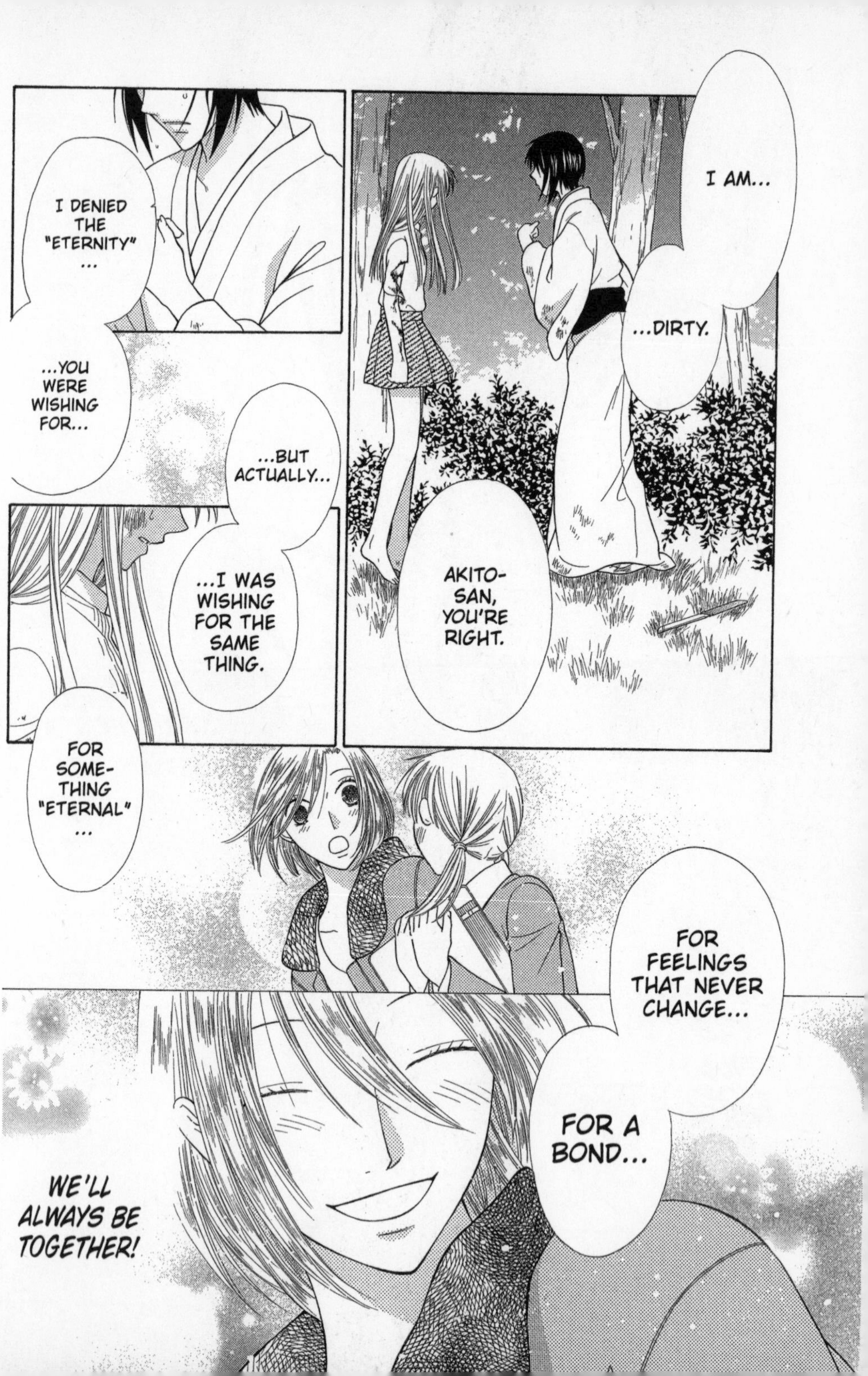
I AM...
...DIRTY.
AKITO-SAN, YOU'RE RIGHT.
I DENIED THE "ETERNITY"...
...YOU WERE WISHING FOR...
...BUT ACTUALLY...
...I WAS WISHING FOR THE SAME THING.
FOR SOMETHING "ETERNAL"...
FOR FEELINGS THAT NEVER CHANGE...
FOR A BOND...
WE'LL ALWAYS BE TOGETHER!

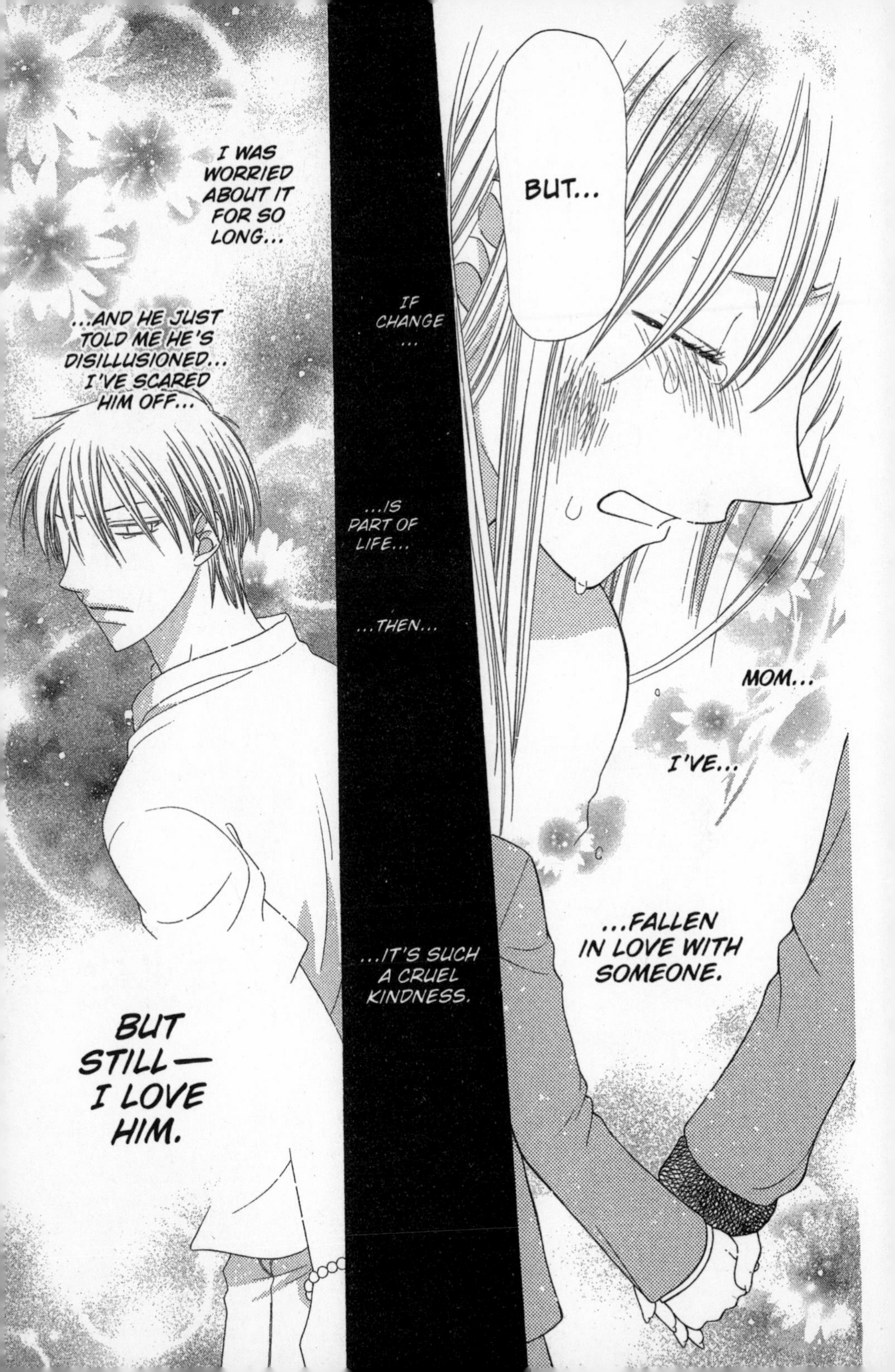
BUT...
MOM...
I'VE...
...FALLEN IN LOVE WITH SOMEONE.
IF CHANGE ...
...IS PART OF LIFE...
...THEN...
...IT'S SUCH A CRUEL KINDNESS.
I WAS WORRIED ABOUT IT FOR SO LONG...
...AND HE JUST TOLD ME HE'S DISILLUSIONED... I'VE SCARED HIM OFF...
BUT STILL— I LOVE HIM.

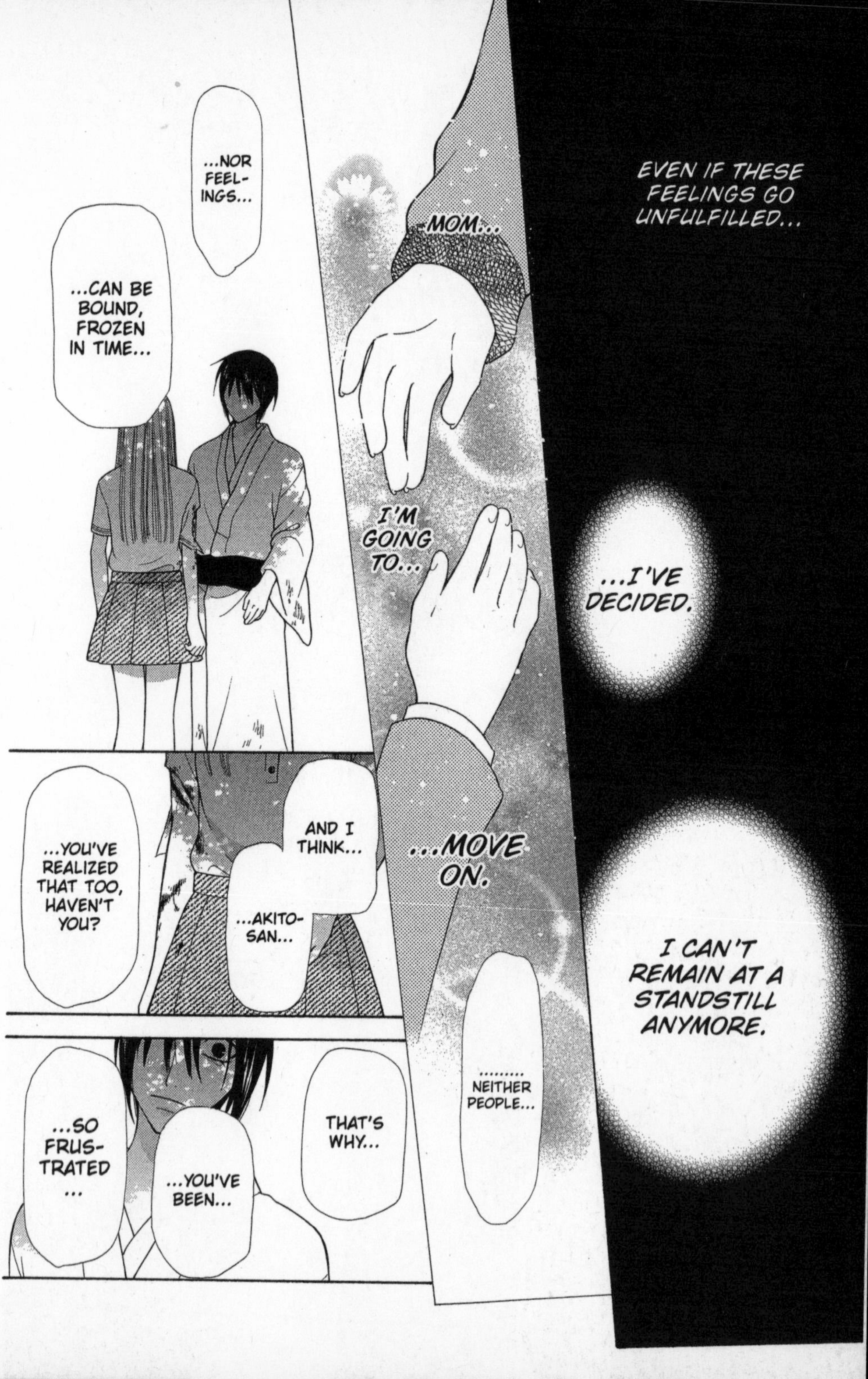
EVEN IF THESE FEELINGS GO UNFULFILLED...
...I'VE DECIDED.
I CAN'T REMAIN AT A STANDSTILL ANYMORE.
MOM...
I'M GOING TO...
...MOVE ON.
.... NEITHER PEOPLE...
...NOR FEEL-INGS...
...CAN BE BOUND, FROZEN IN TIME...
AND I THINK...
...AKITO-SAN...
...YOU'VE REALIZED THAT TOO, HAVEN'T YOU?
THAT'S WHY...
...YOU'VE BEEN...
...SO FRUS-TRATED ...

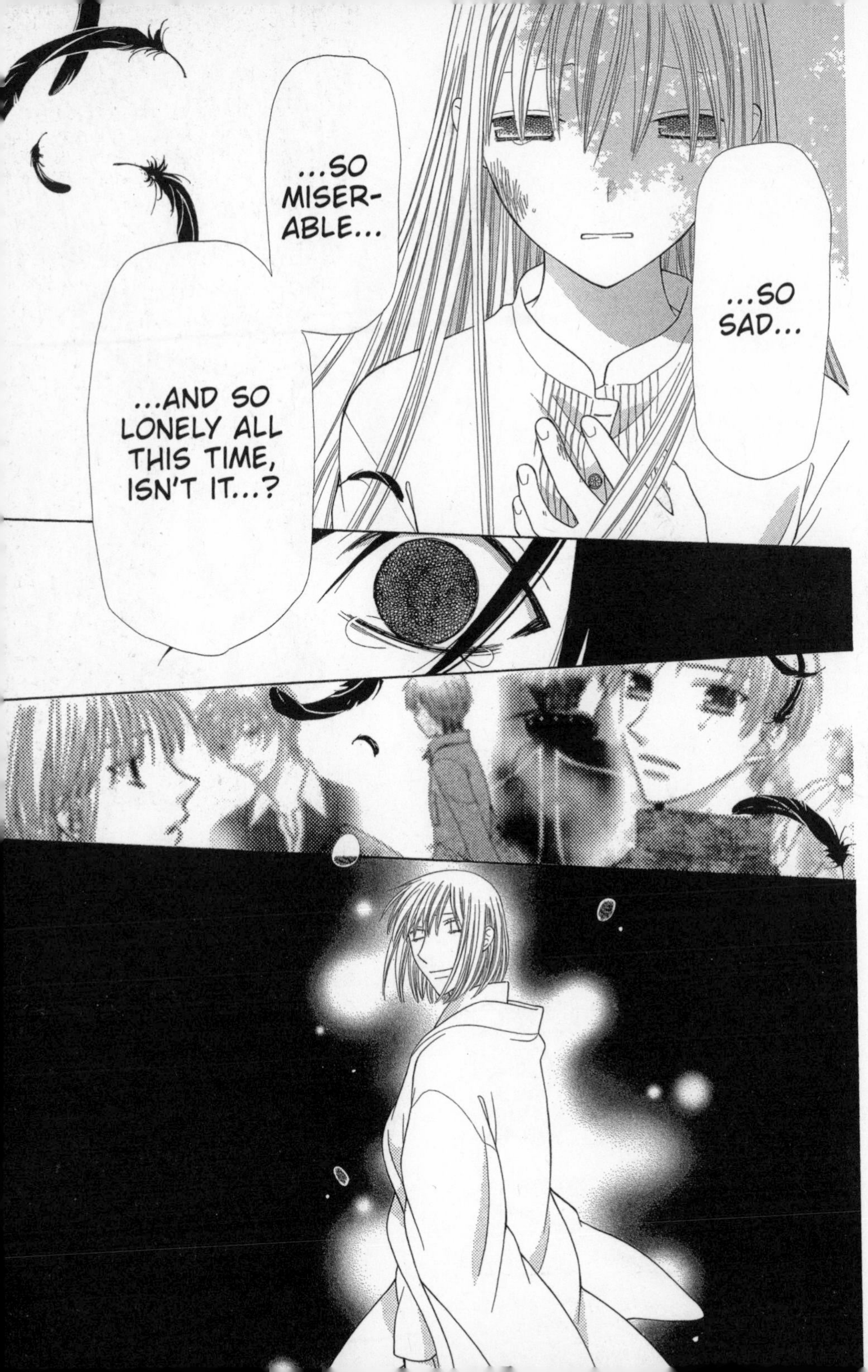
...SO SAD...
...SO MISER-ABLE...
...AND SO LONELY ALL THIS TIME, ISN'T IT...?

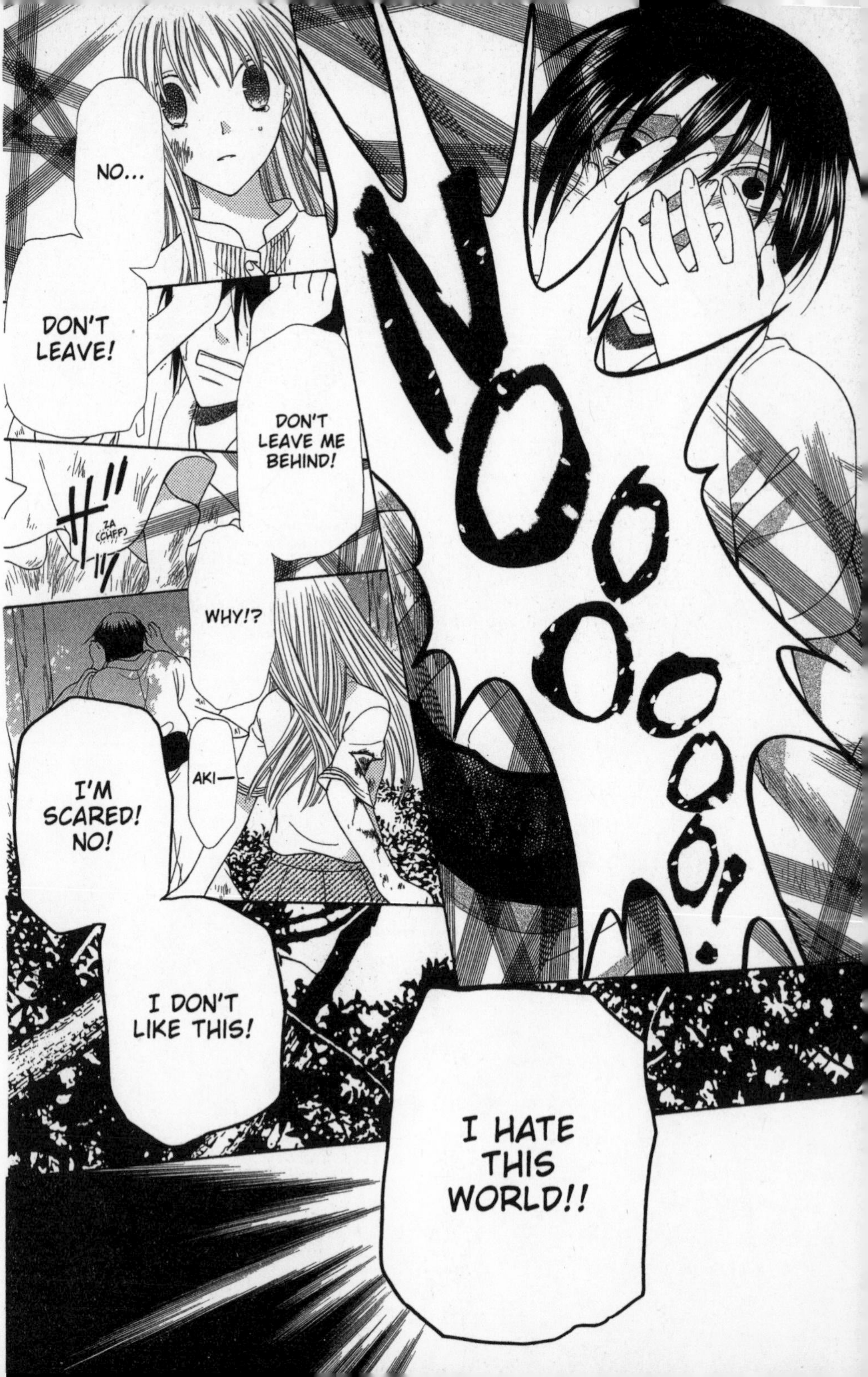
NOOOOOOO!
NO...
DON'T LEAVE!
DON'T LEAVE ME BEHIND!
ZA (CHFF)
WHY!?
AKI—
I'M SCARED! NO!
I DON'T LIKE THIS!
I HATE THIS WORLD!!

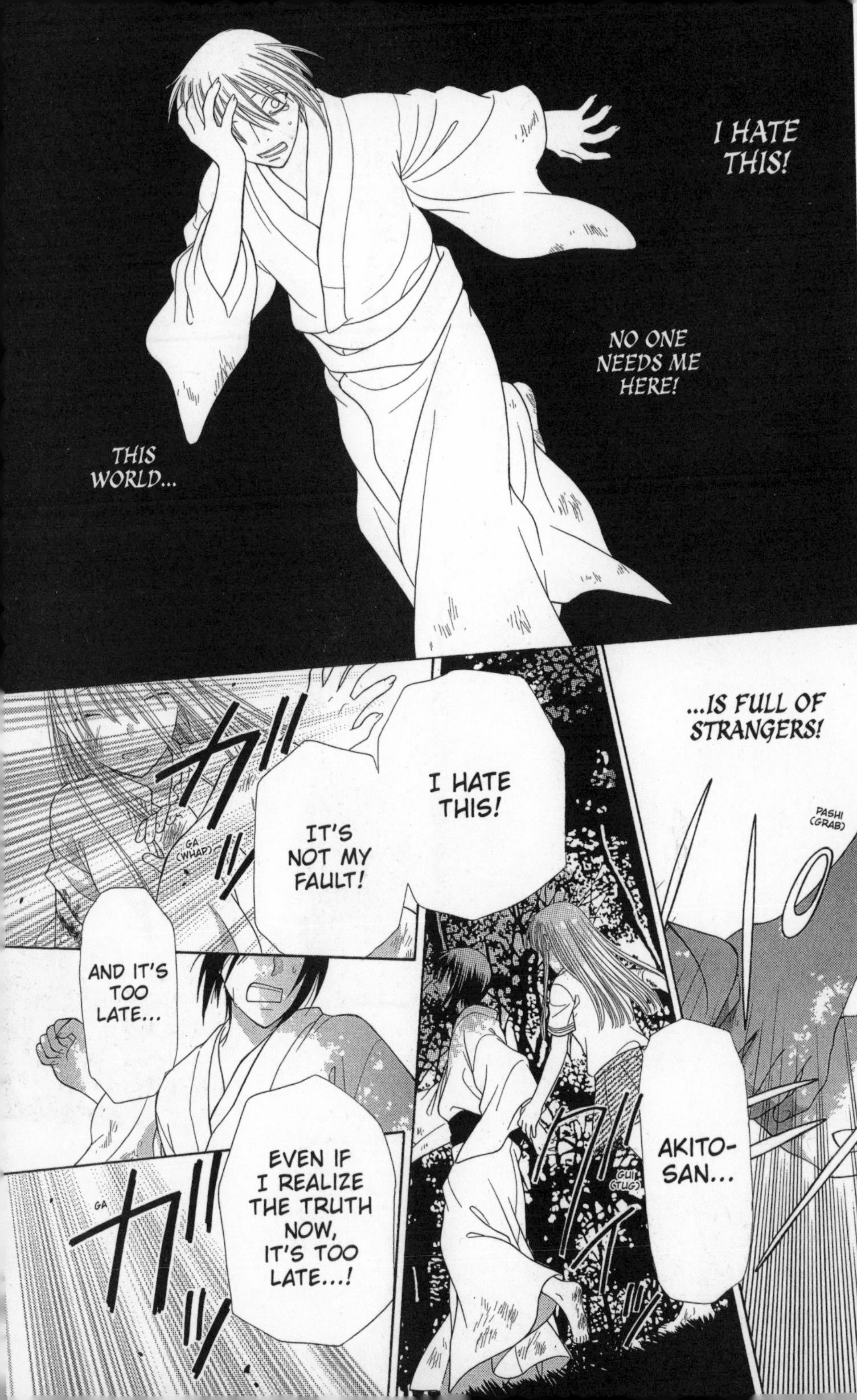
I HATE THIS!
NO ONE NEEDS ME HERE!
THIS WORLD...
...IS FULL OF STRANGERS!
PASHI (GRAB)
AKITO-SAN...
GUI (TUG)
I HATE THIS!
IT'S NOT MY FAULT!
GA (WHAP)
AND IT'S TOO LATE...
EVEN IF I REALIZE THE TRUTH NOW, IT'S TOO LATE...!
GA

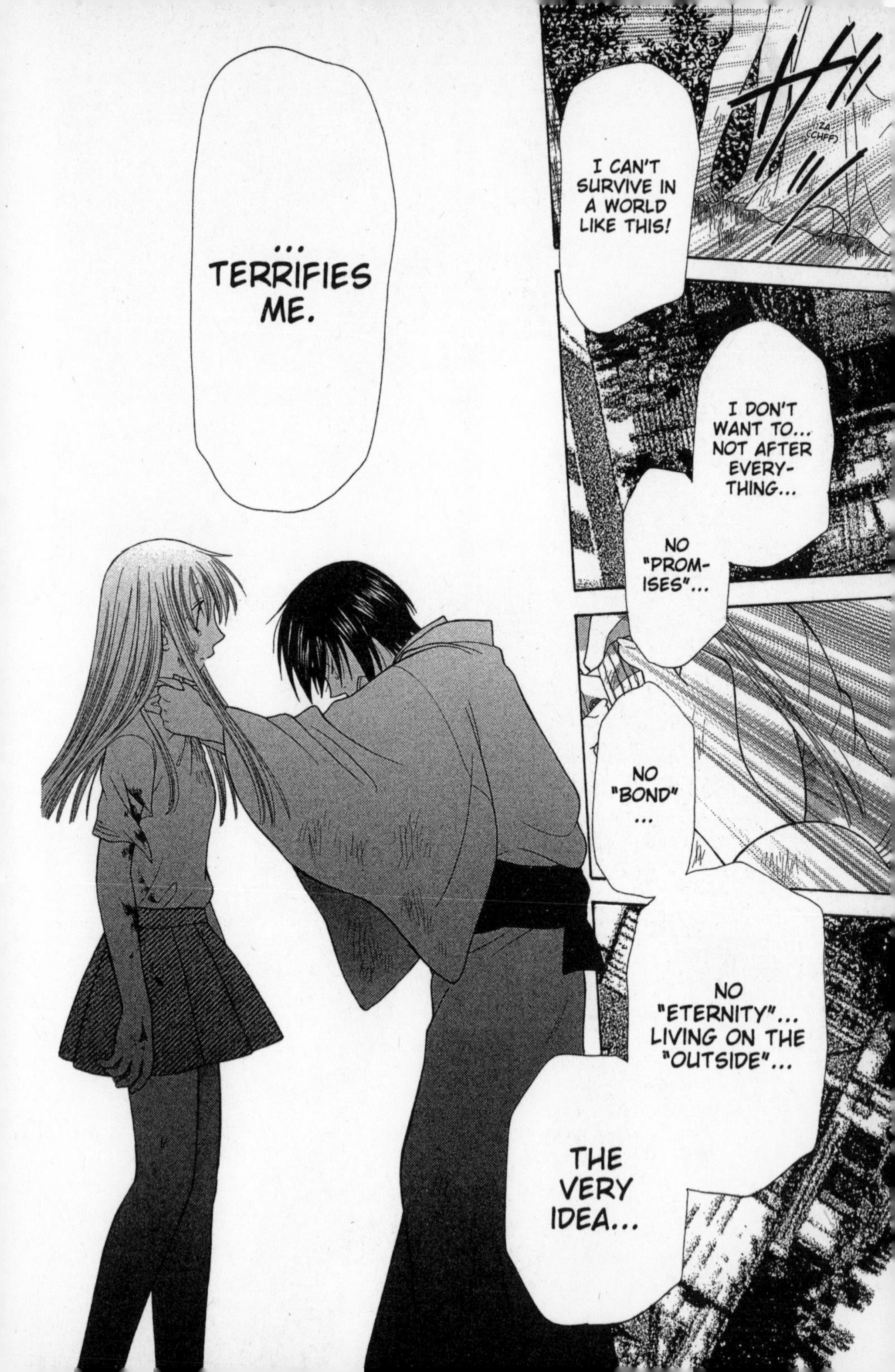
ZA (CHFF)
I CAN'T SURVIVE IN A WORLD LIKE THIS!
I DON'T WANT TO... NOT AFTER EVERYTHING...
NO "PROMISES"...
NO "BOND" ...
NO "ETERNITY"... LIVING ON THE "OUTSIDE"...
THE VERY IDEA...
... TERRIFIES ME.

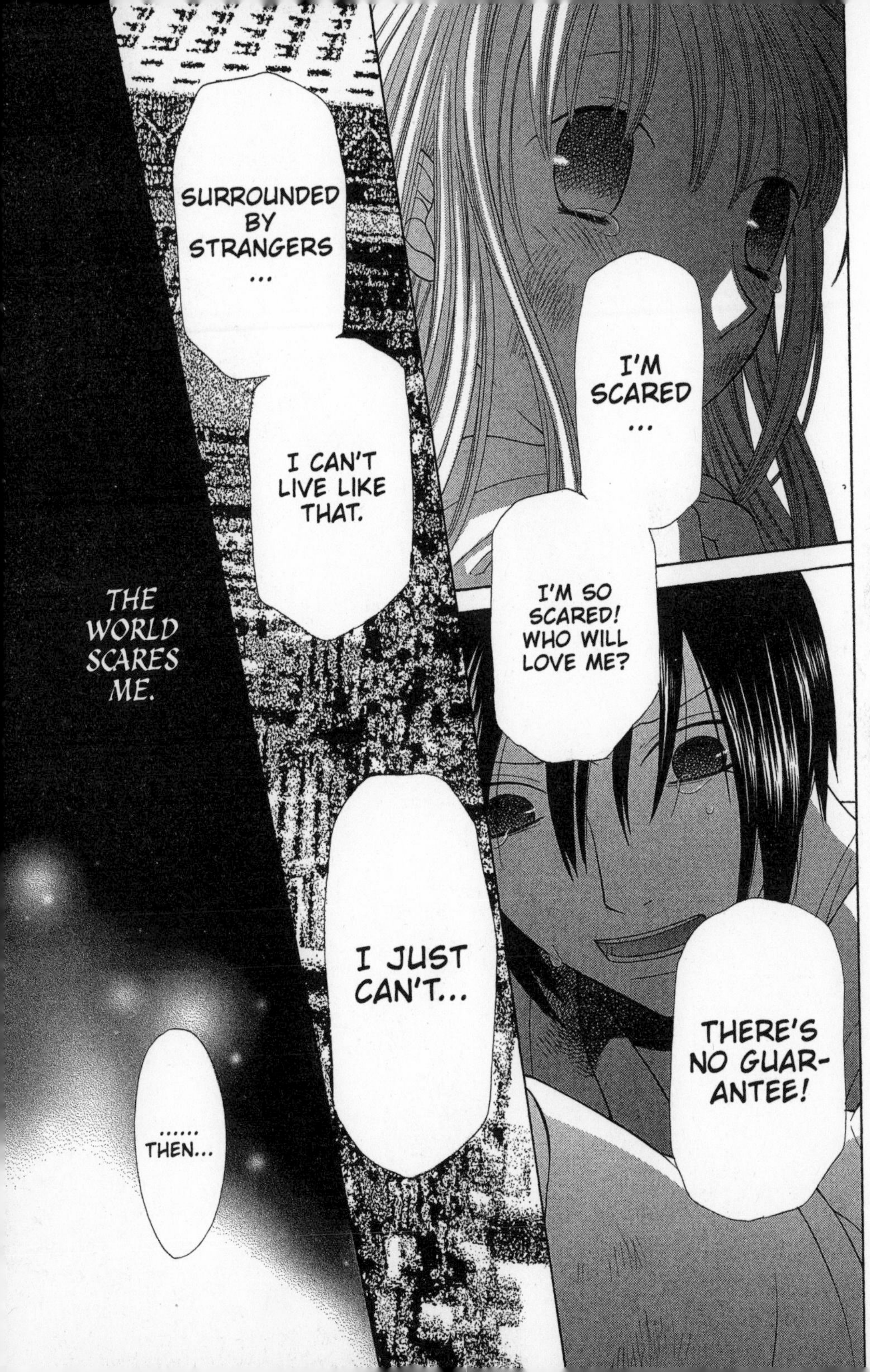
I'M SCARED...
I'M SO SCARED! WHO WILL LOVE ME?
THERE'S NO GUARANTEE!
SURROUNDED BY STRANGERS...
I CAN'T LIVE LIKE THAT.
I JUST CAN'T...
THE WORLD SCARES ME.
......THEN...

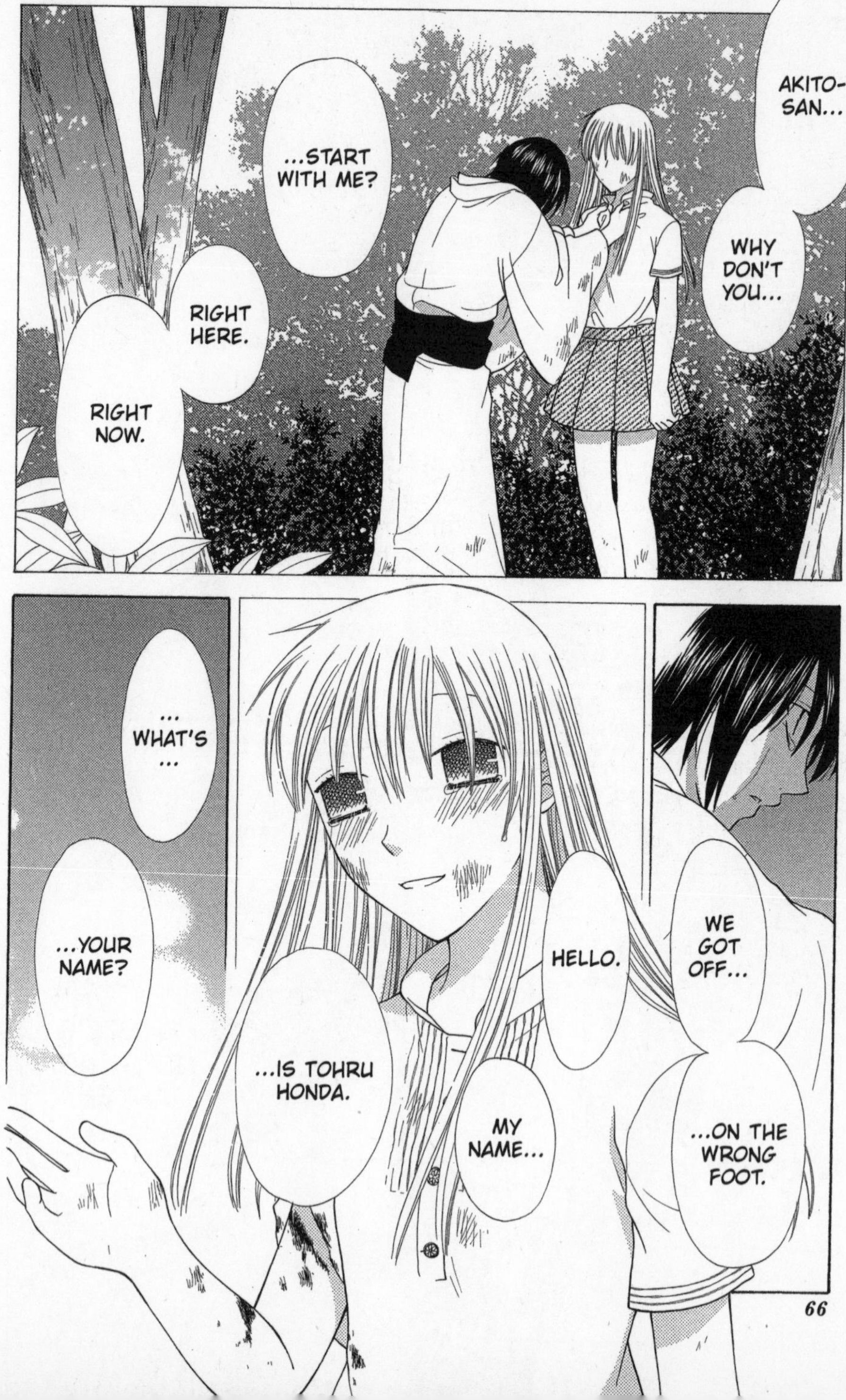
AKITO-SAN...
WHY DON'T YOU...
...START WITH ME?
RIGHT HERE.
RIGHT NOW.
WE GOT OFF...
...ON THE WRONG FOOT.
HELLO.
MY NAME...
...IS TOHRU HONDA.
... WHAT'S ...
...YOUR NAME?

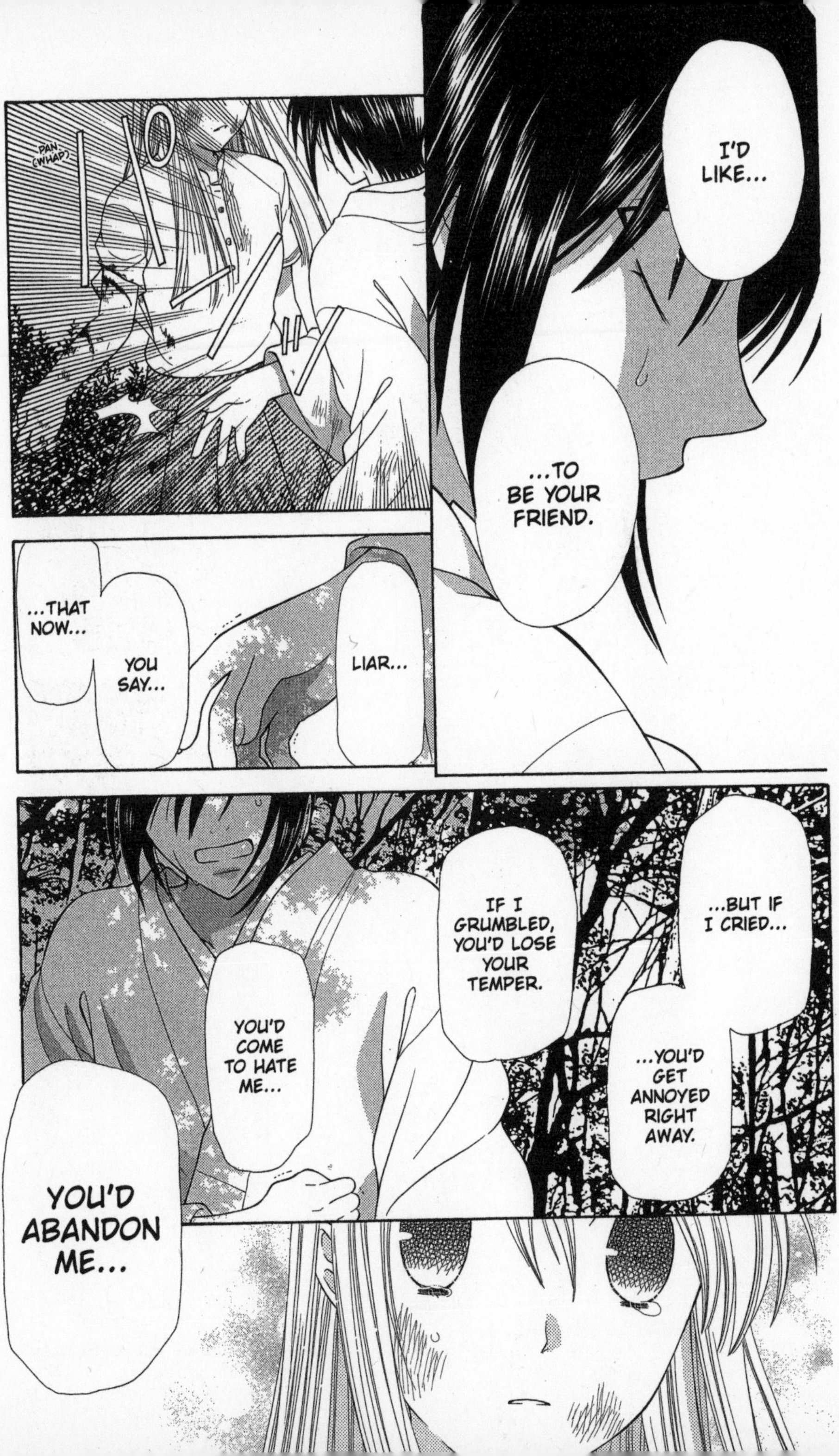
I'D LIKE...
...TO BE YOUR FRIEND.
PAN (WHAP)
LIAR...
YOU SAY...
...THAT NOW...
...BUT IF I CRIED...
...YOU'D GET ANNOYED RIGHT AWAY.
IF I GRUMBLED, YOU'D LOSE YOUR TEMPER.
YOU'D COME TO HATE ME...
YOU'D ABANDON ME...

...ALWAYS
THERE,
WEREN'T
YOU?

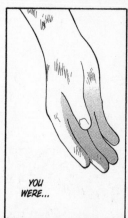

YOU
WERE...

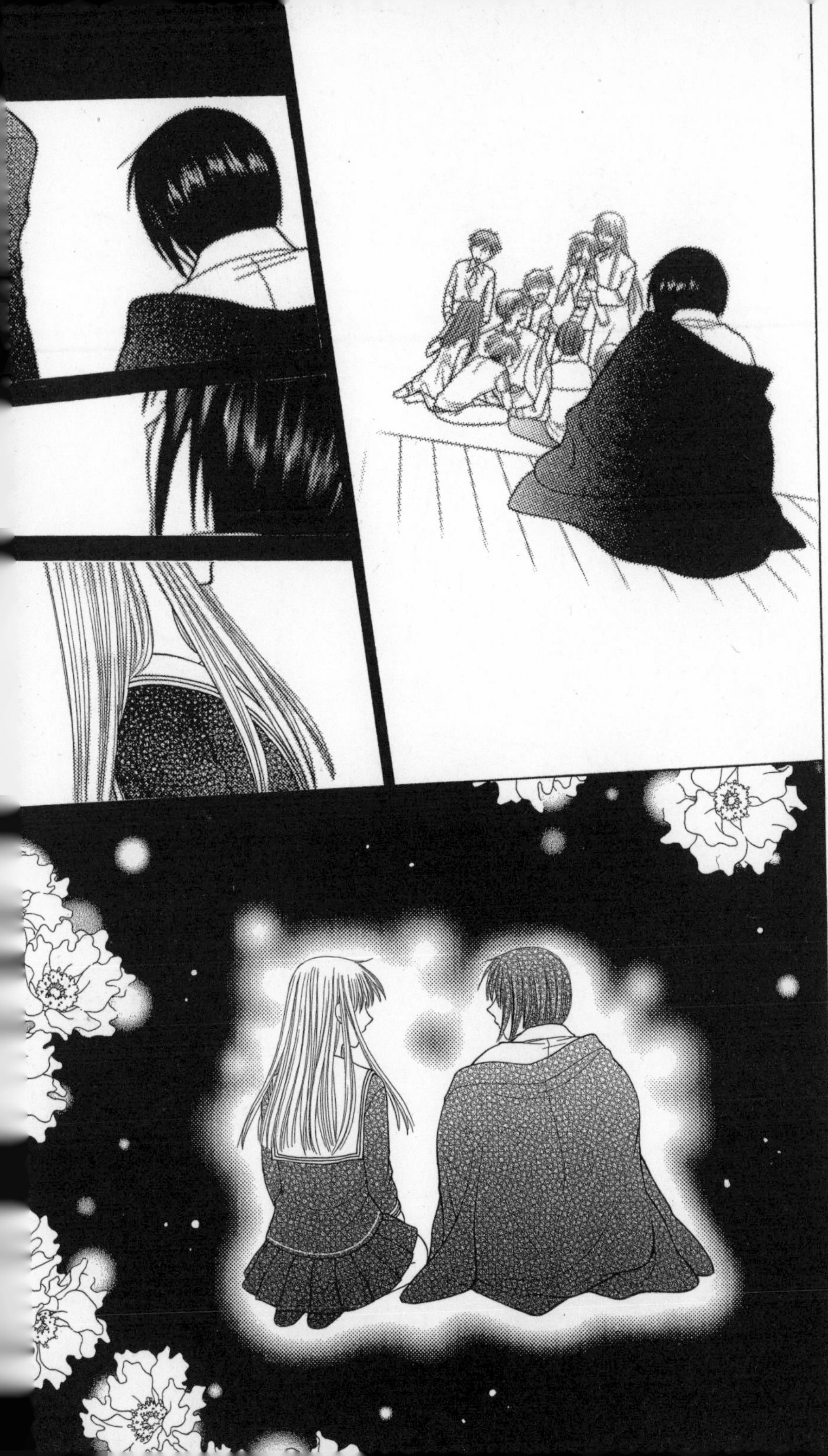

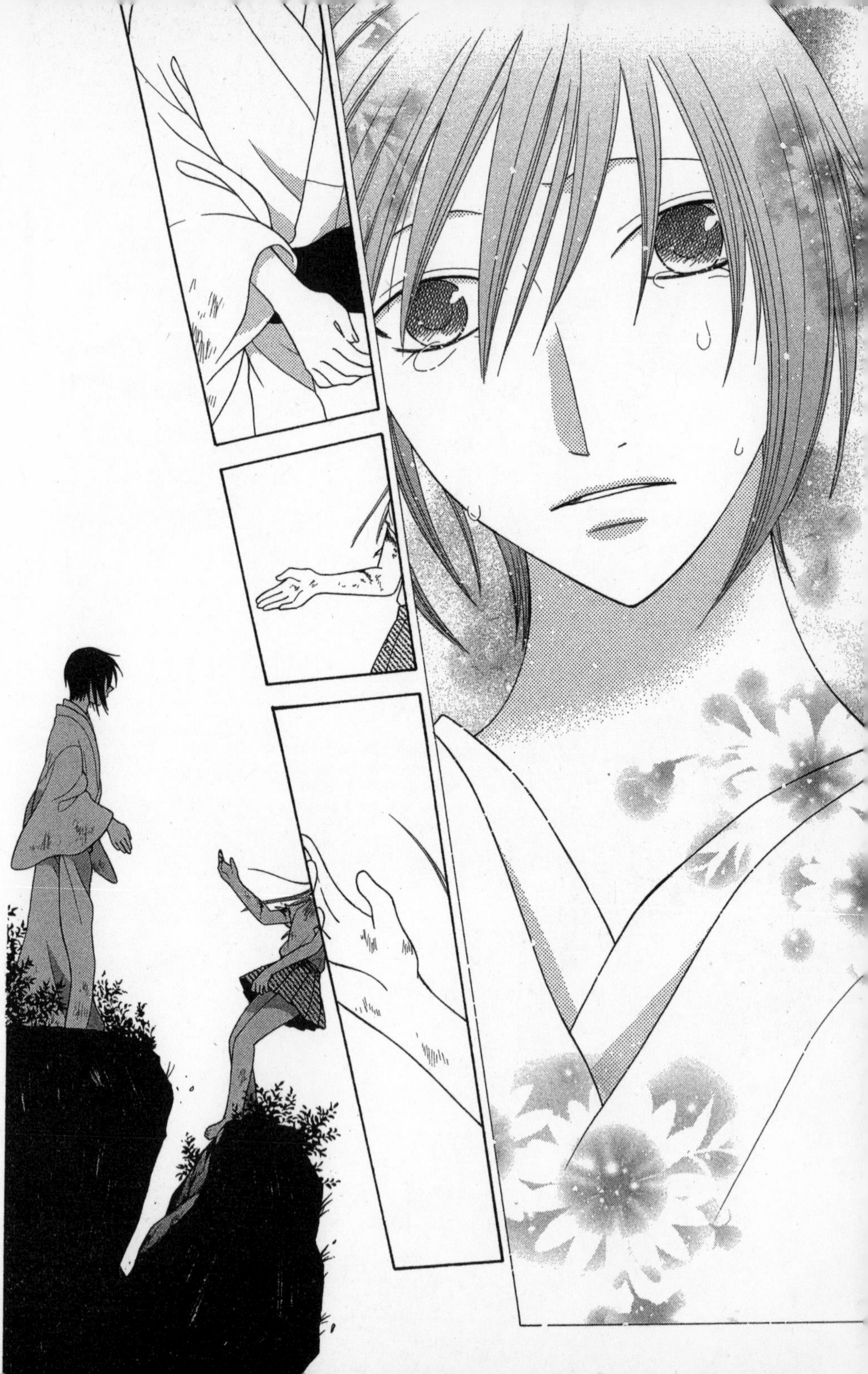

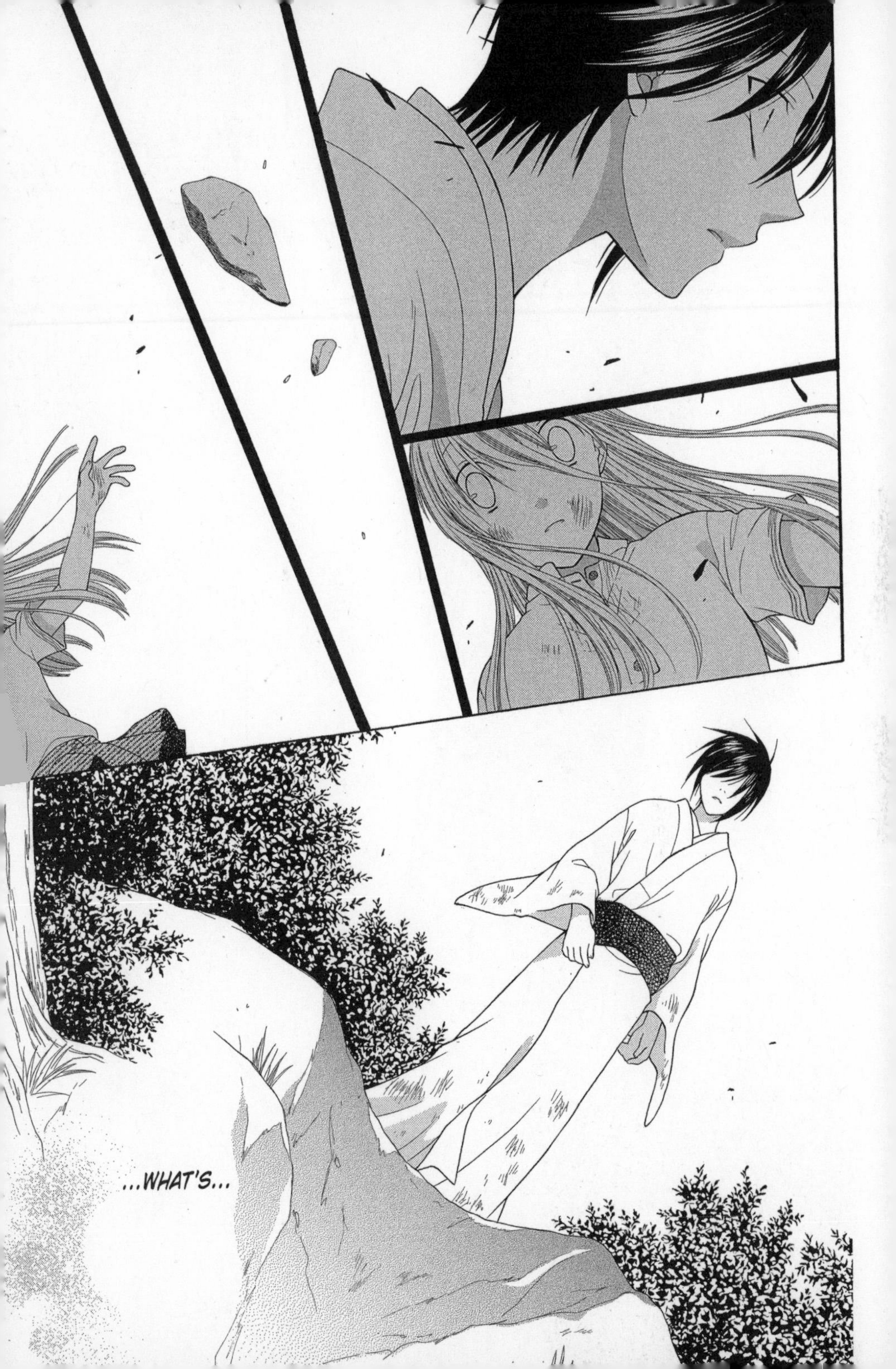
...WHAT'S...

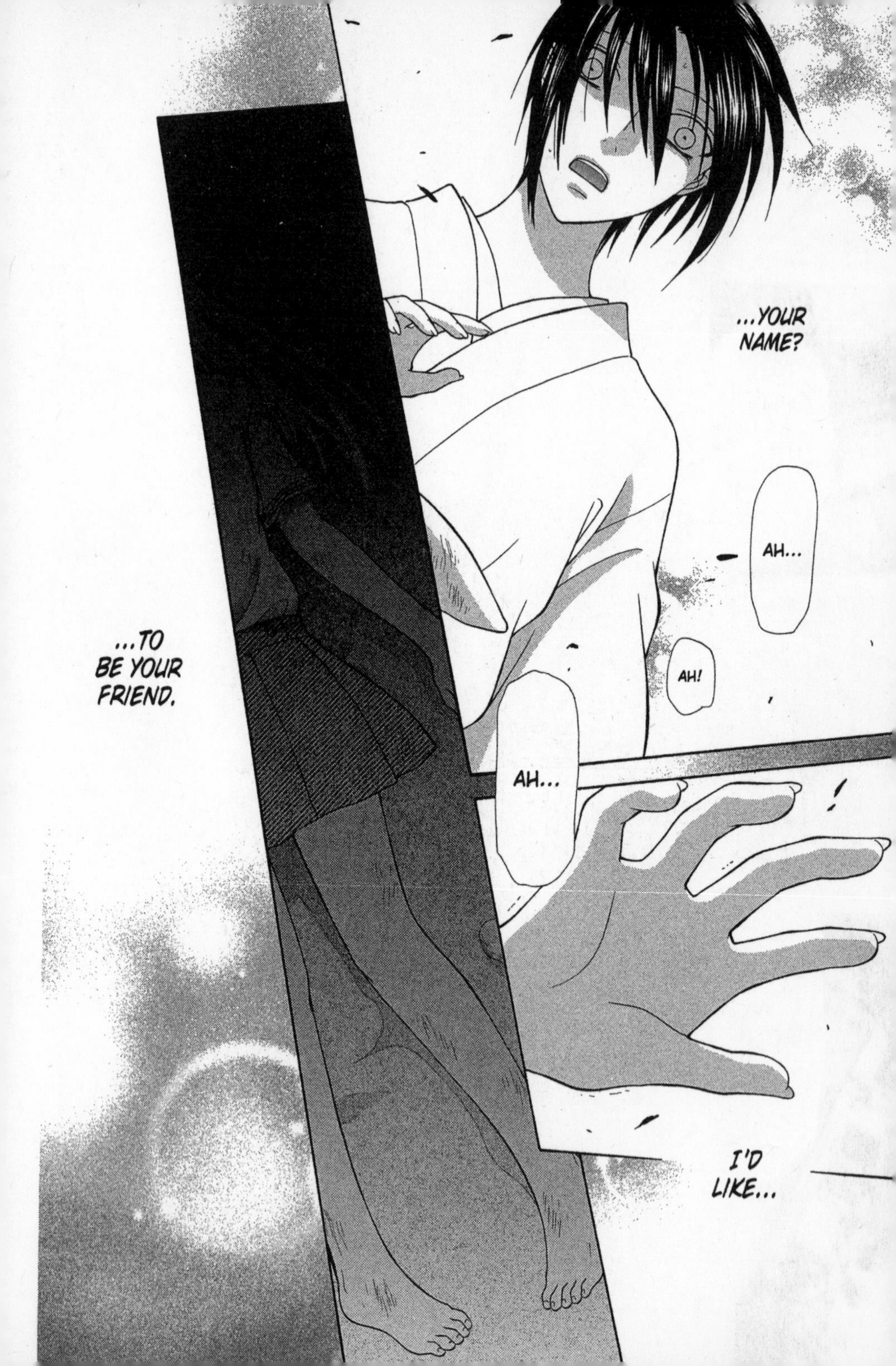
...YOUR NAME?
AH...
AH!
AH...
I'D LIKE...
...TO BE YOUR FRIEND.

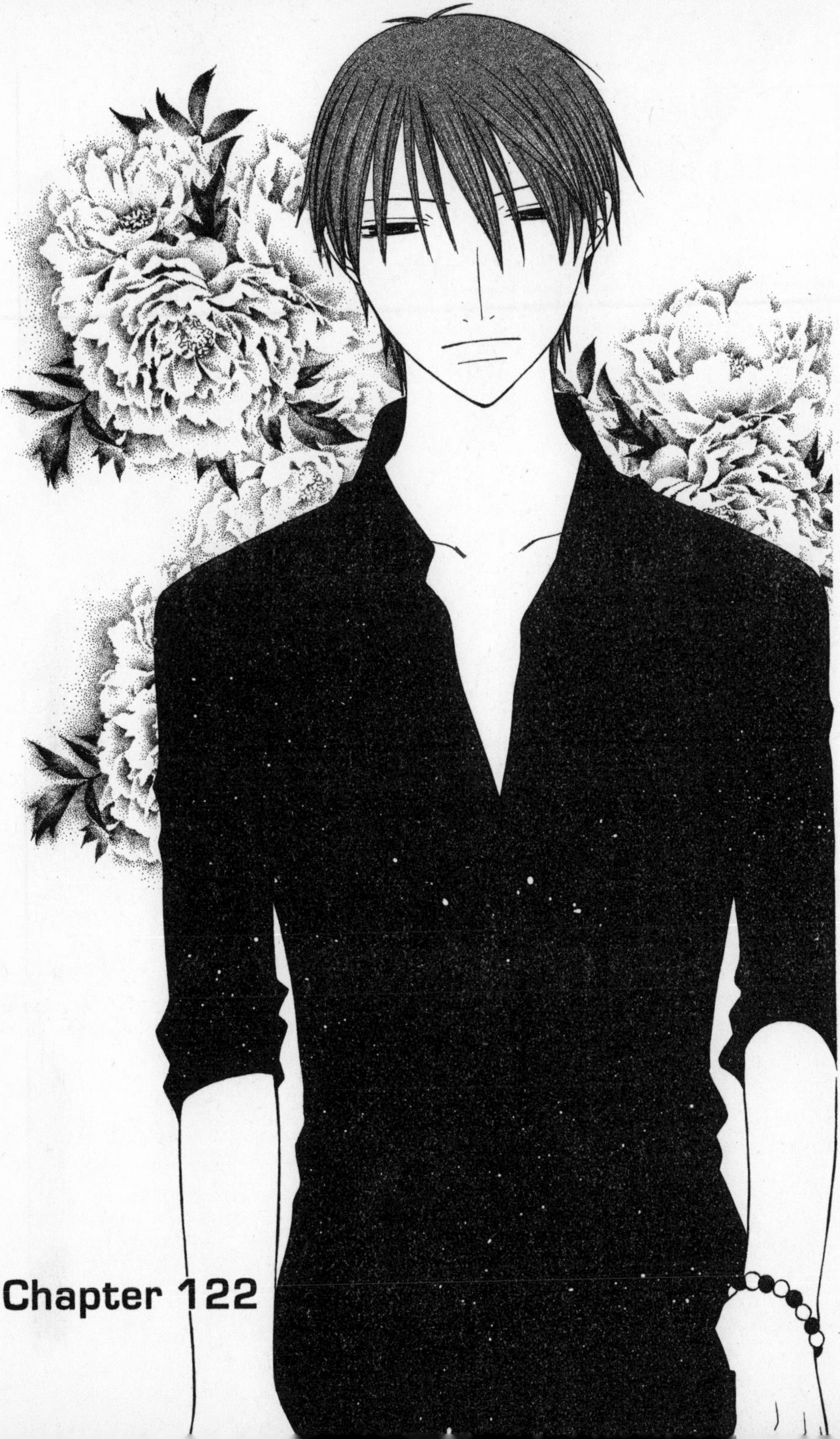

Chapter 122

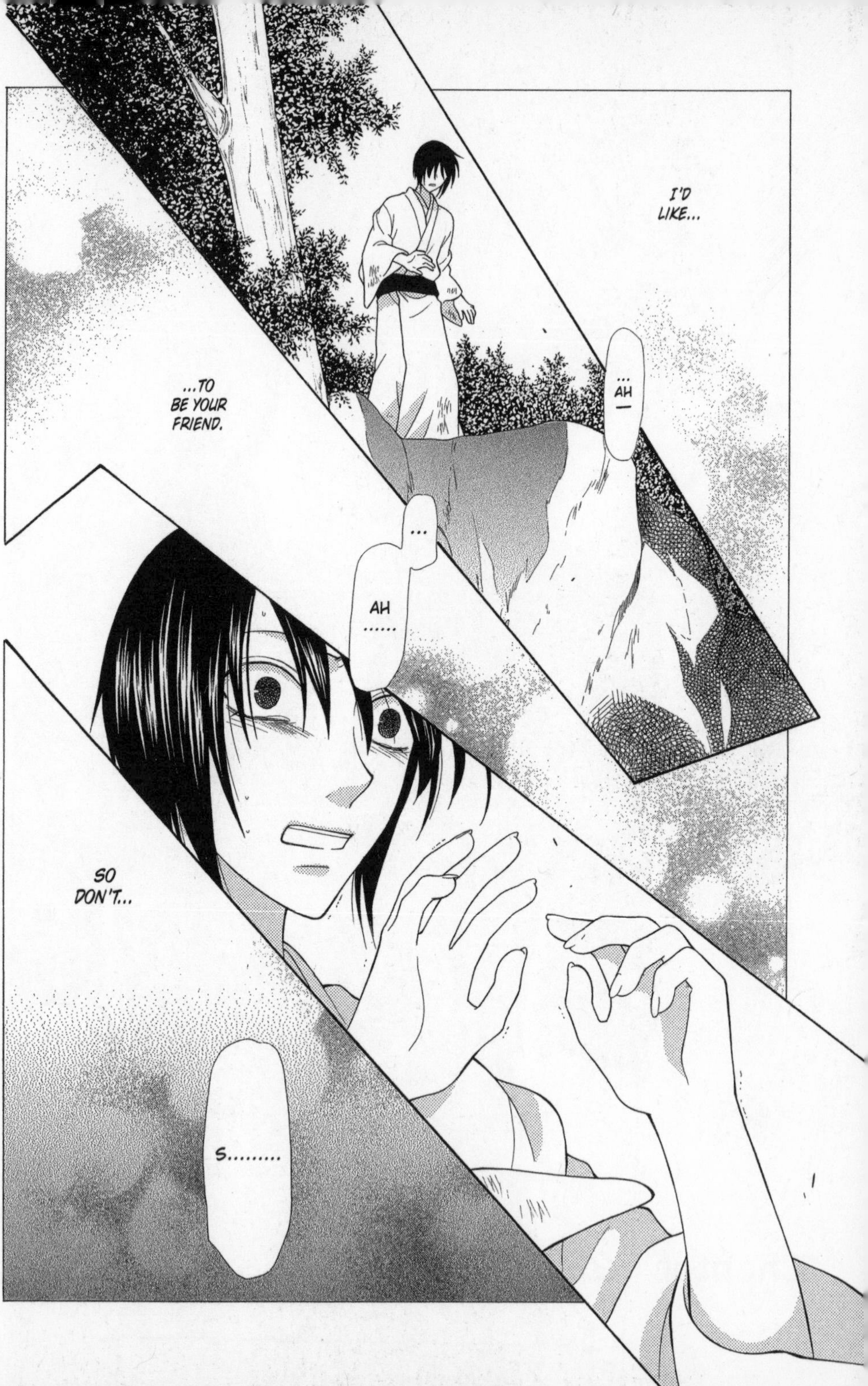
I'D LIKE...
...AH—
...TO BE YOUR FRIEND.
...
AH ......
SO DON'T...
S.........

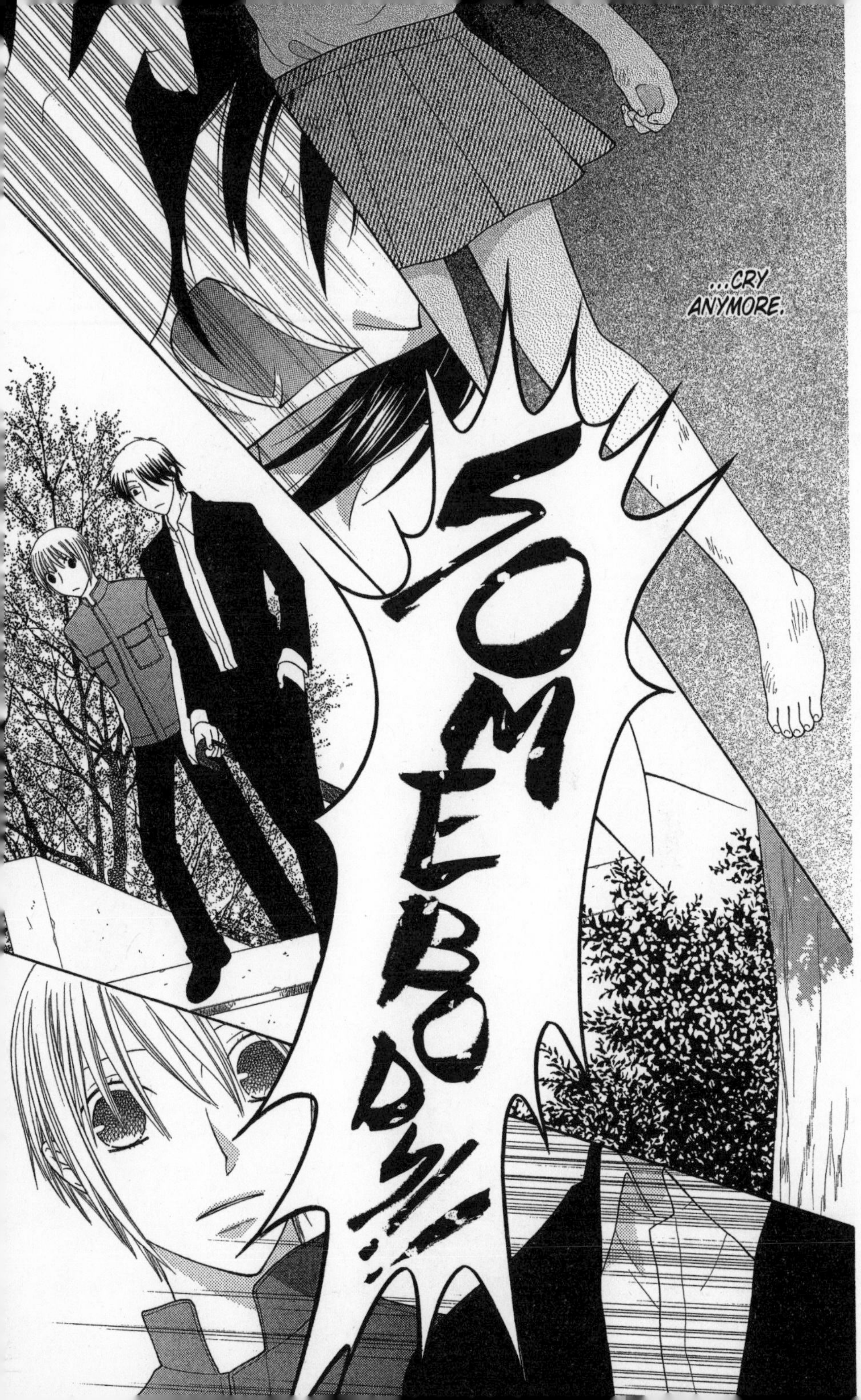
...CRY ANYMORE.
SOMEBODY!!

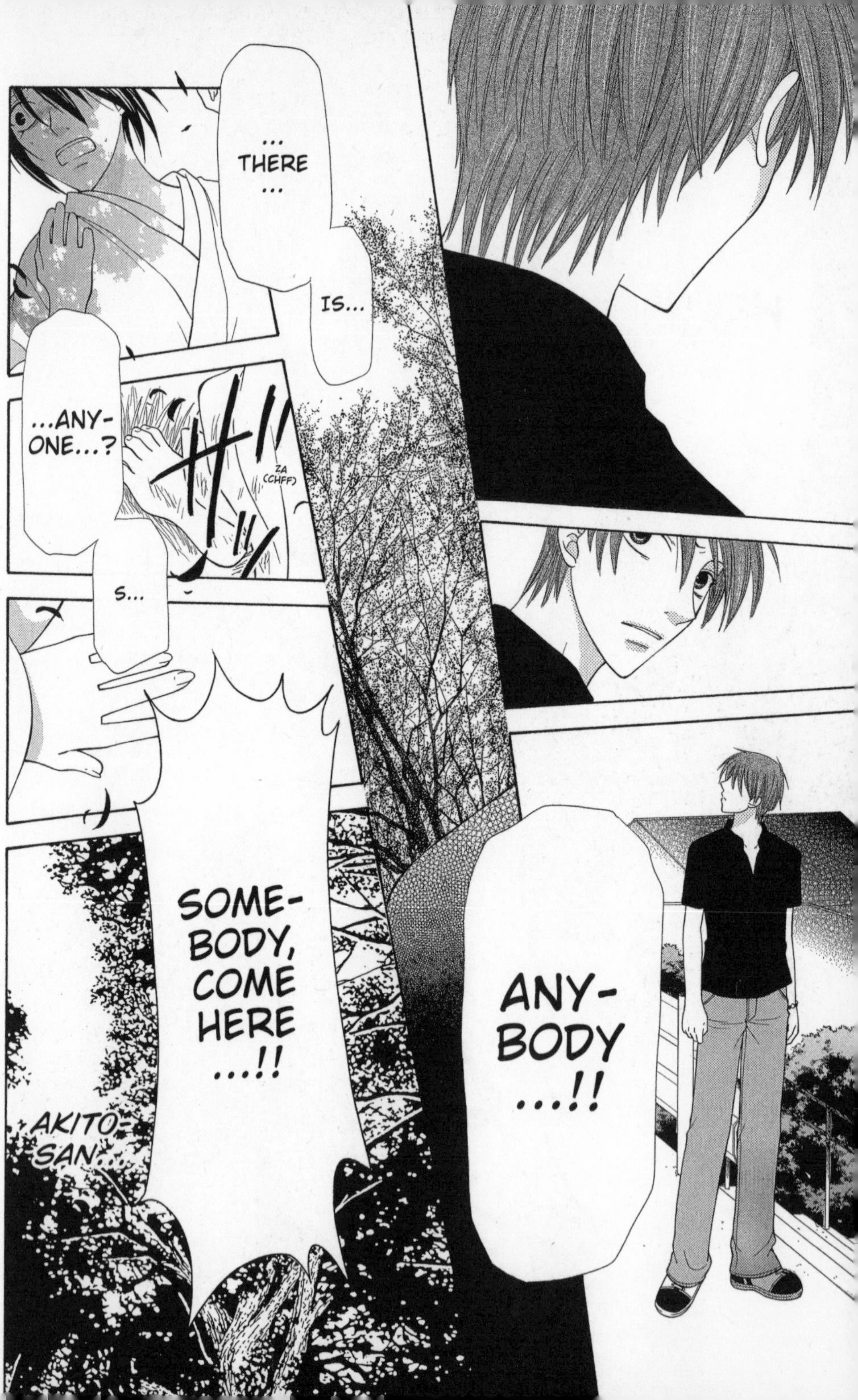
ANY-BODY...!!
...THERE... IS...
...ANY-ONE...?
ZA (CHFF)
S...
SOME-BODY, COME HERE...!!
AKITO-SAN...

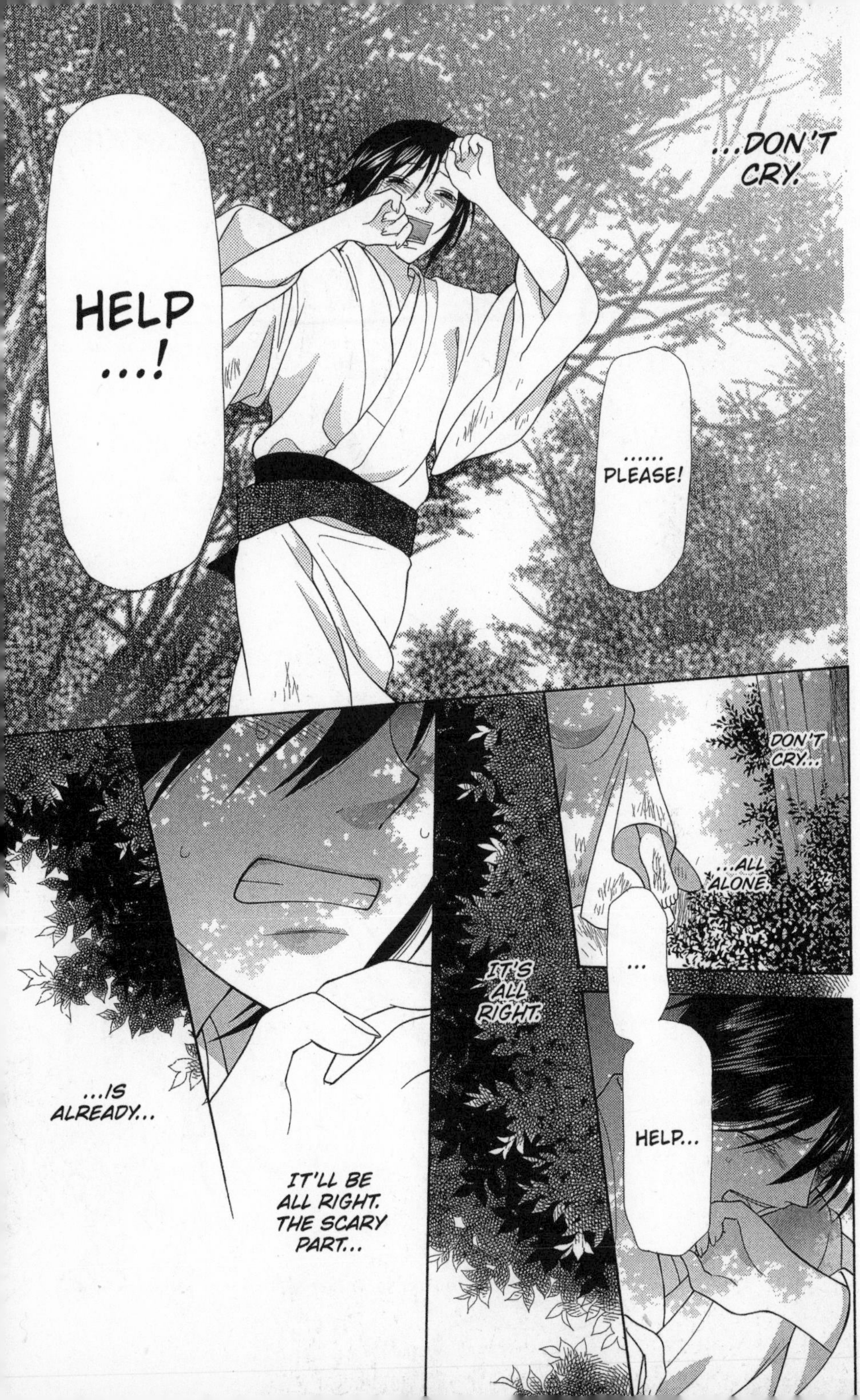
...DON'T CRY.
...... PLEASE!
HELP ...!
DON'T CRY...
...ALL ALONE.
...
HELP...
IT'S ALL RIGHT.
IT'LL BE ALL RIGHT. THE SCARY PART...
...IS ALREADY...

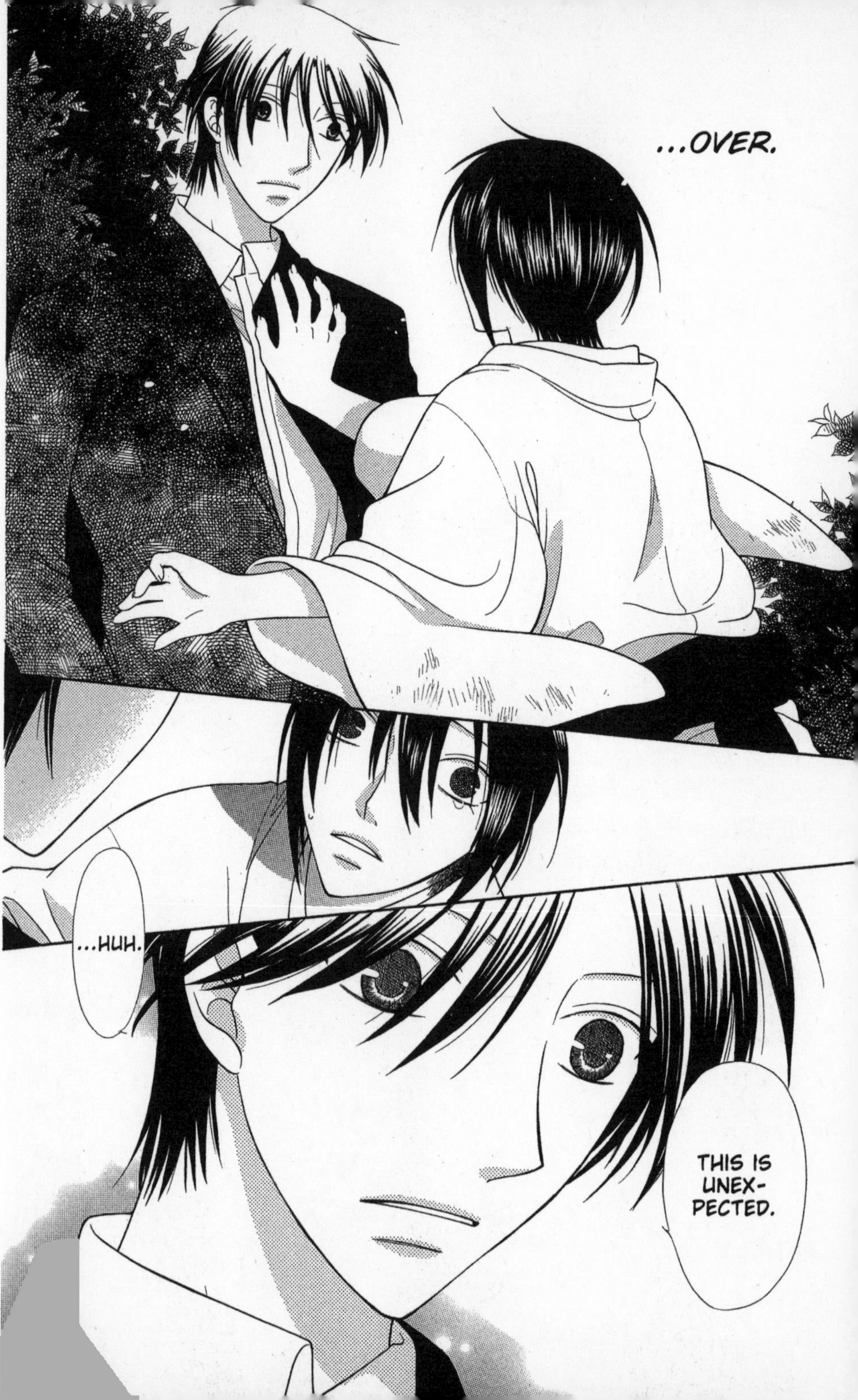

...OVER.
...HUH.
THIS IS UNEXPECTED.

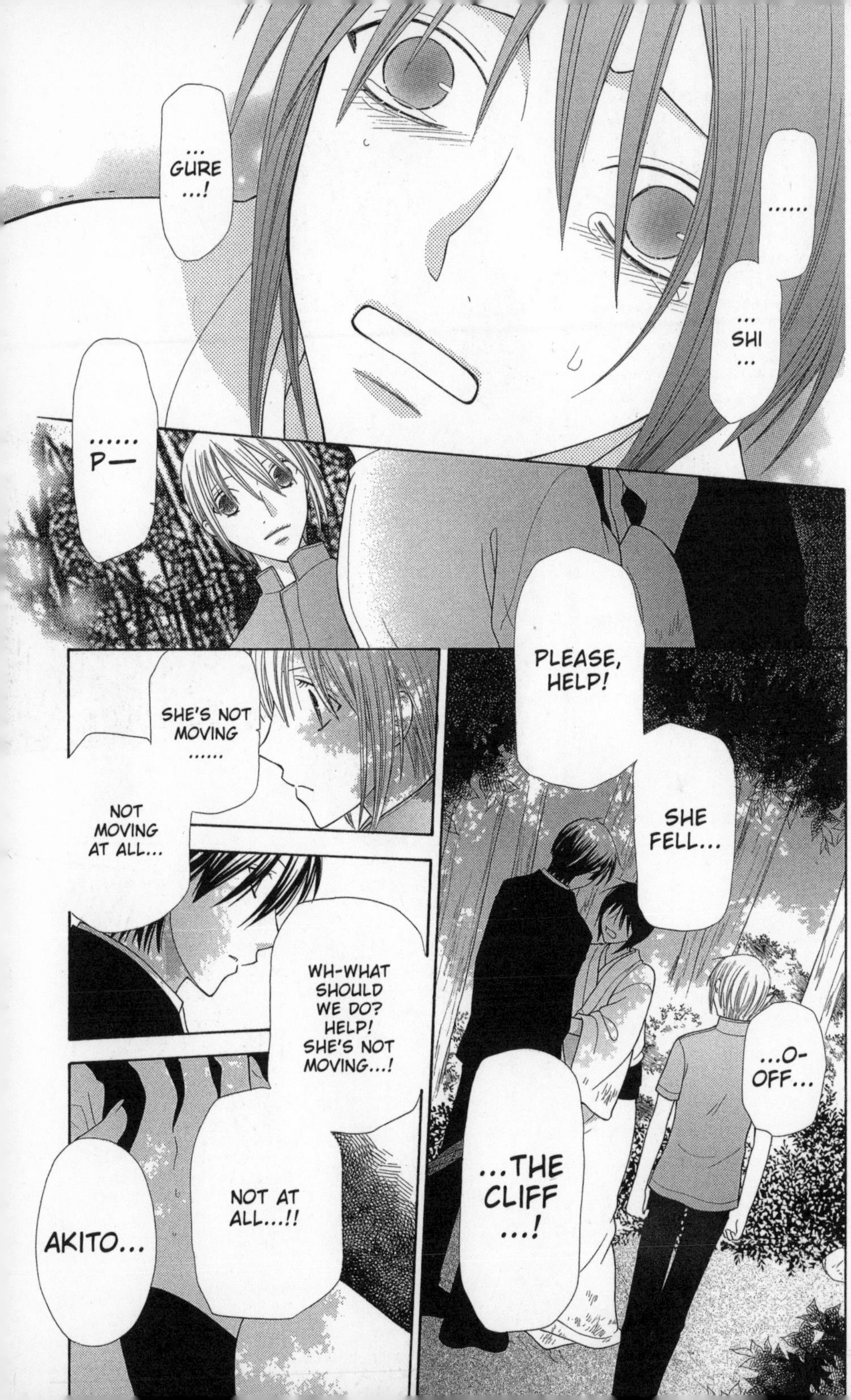
......
...
SHI
...
...
GURE
...!
......
P—
PLEASE, HELP!
SHE FELL...
...O-
OFF...
...THE CLIFF
...!
SHE'S NOT MOVING
......
NOT MOVING AT ALL...
WH-WHAT SHOULD WE DO? HELP! SHE'S NOT MOVING...!
NOT AT ALL...!!
AKITO...

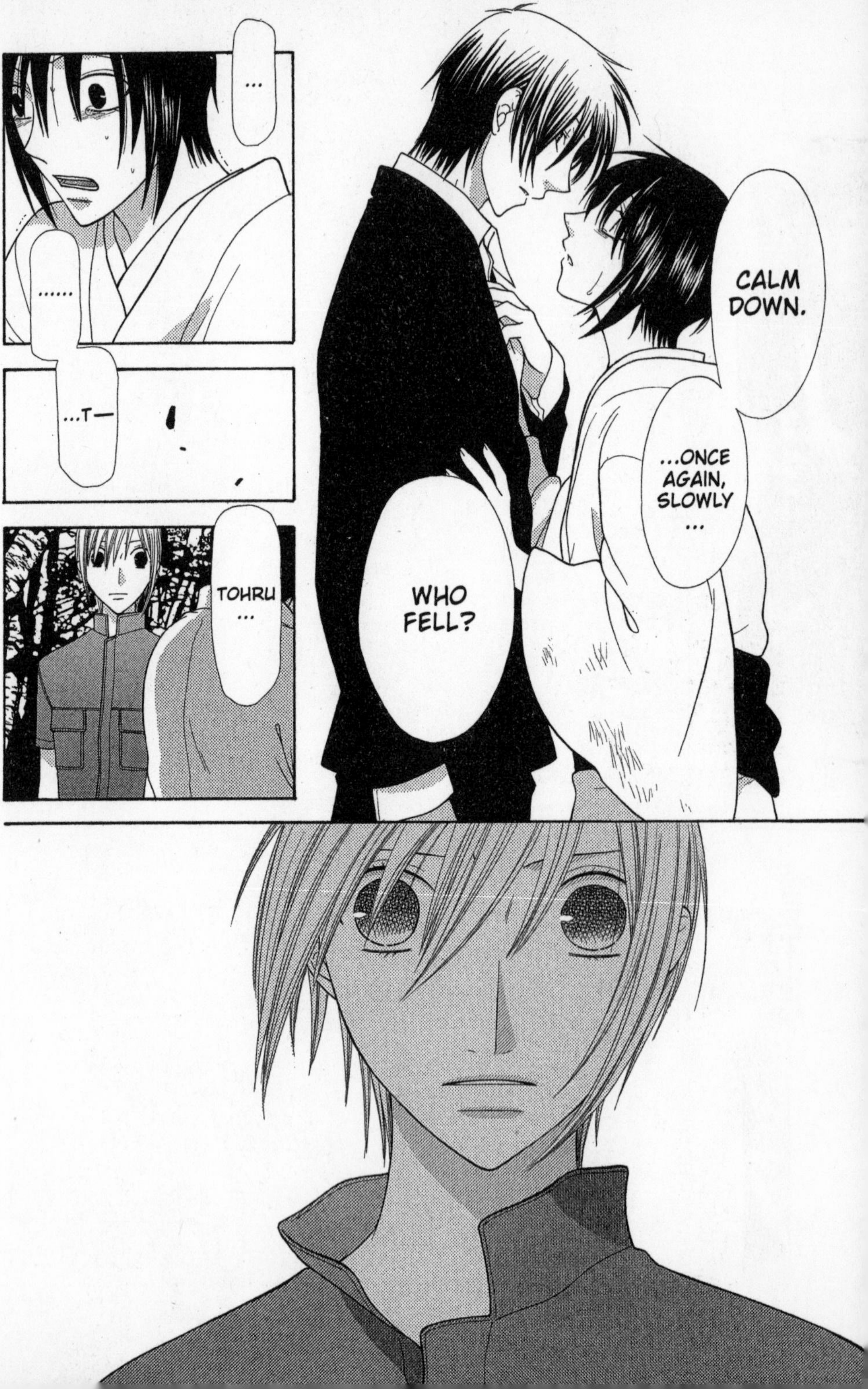
CALM DOWN.
...ONCE AGAIN, SLOWLY ...
WHO FELL?
...
......
...T—
TOHRU ...

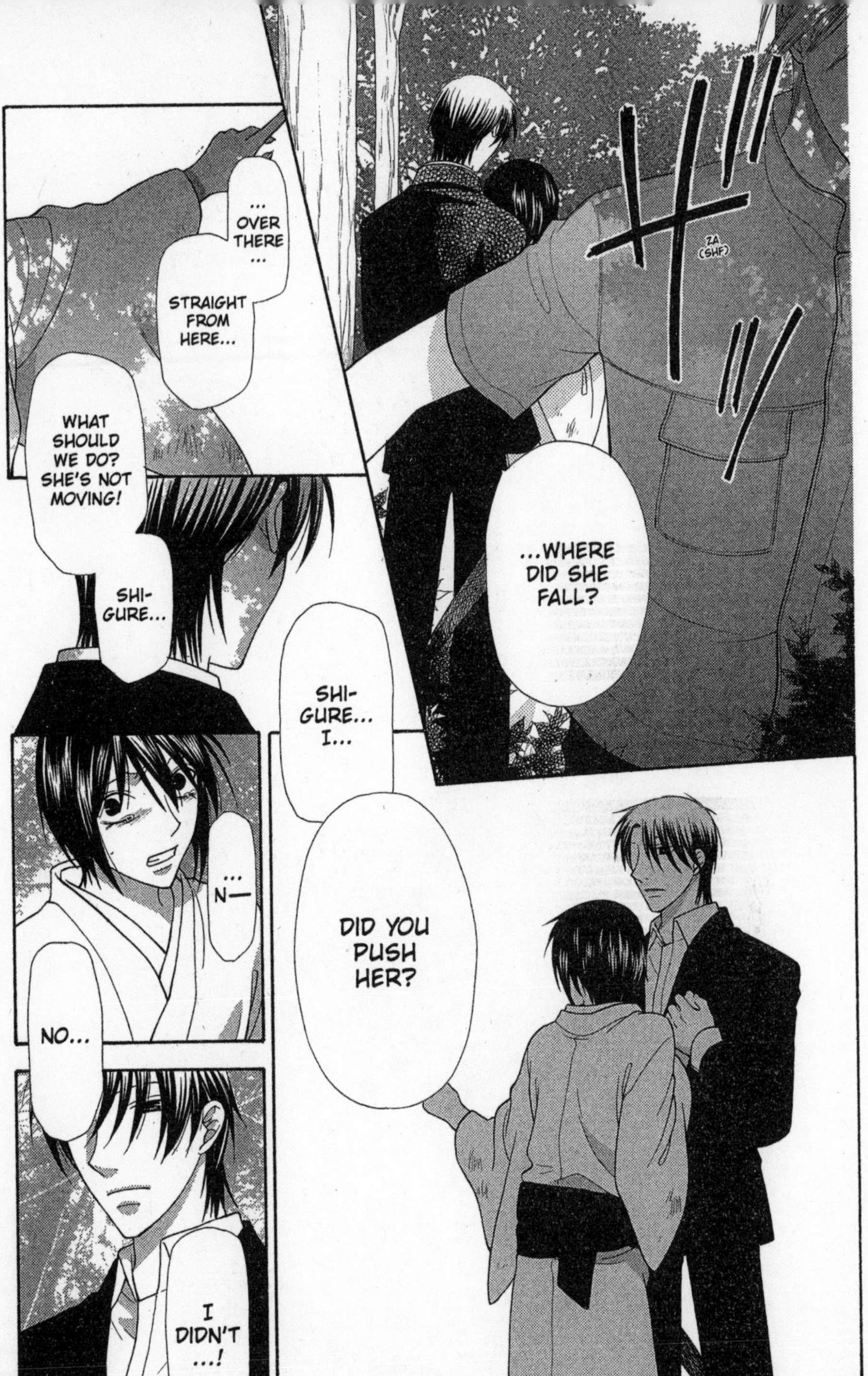
ZA (SHF)
...WHERE DID SHE FALL?
... OVER THERE ...
STRAIGHT FROM HERE...
WHAT SHOULD WE DO? SHE'S NOT MOVING!
SHI-GURE...
SHI-GURE... I...
DID YOU PUSH HER?
... N—
NO...
I DIDN'T ...!

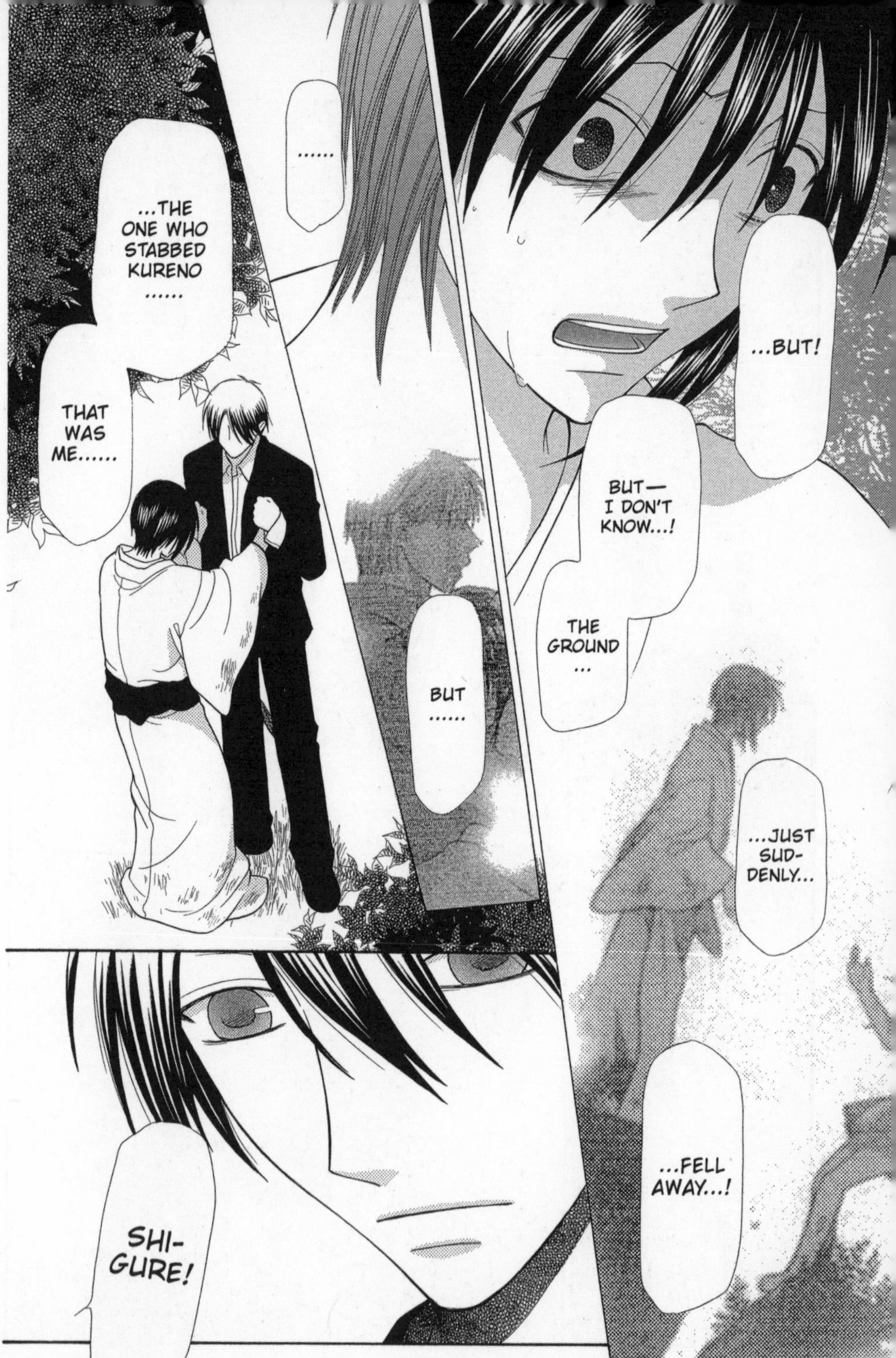
...BUT!
BUT— I DON'T KNOW...!
THE GROUND ...
...JUST SUD-DENLY...
...FELL AWAY...!
......
BUT ......
...THE ONE WHO STABBED KURENO ......
THAT WAS ME......
SHI-GURE!

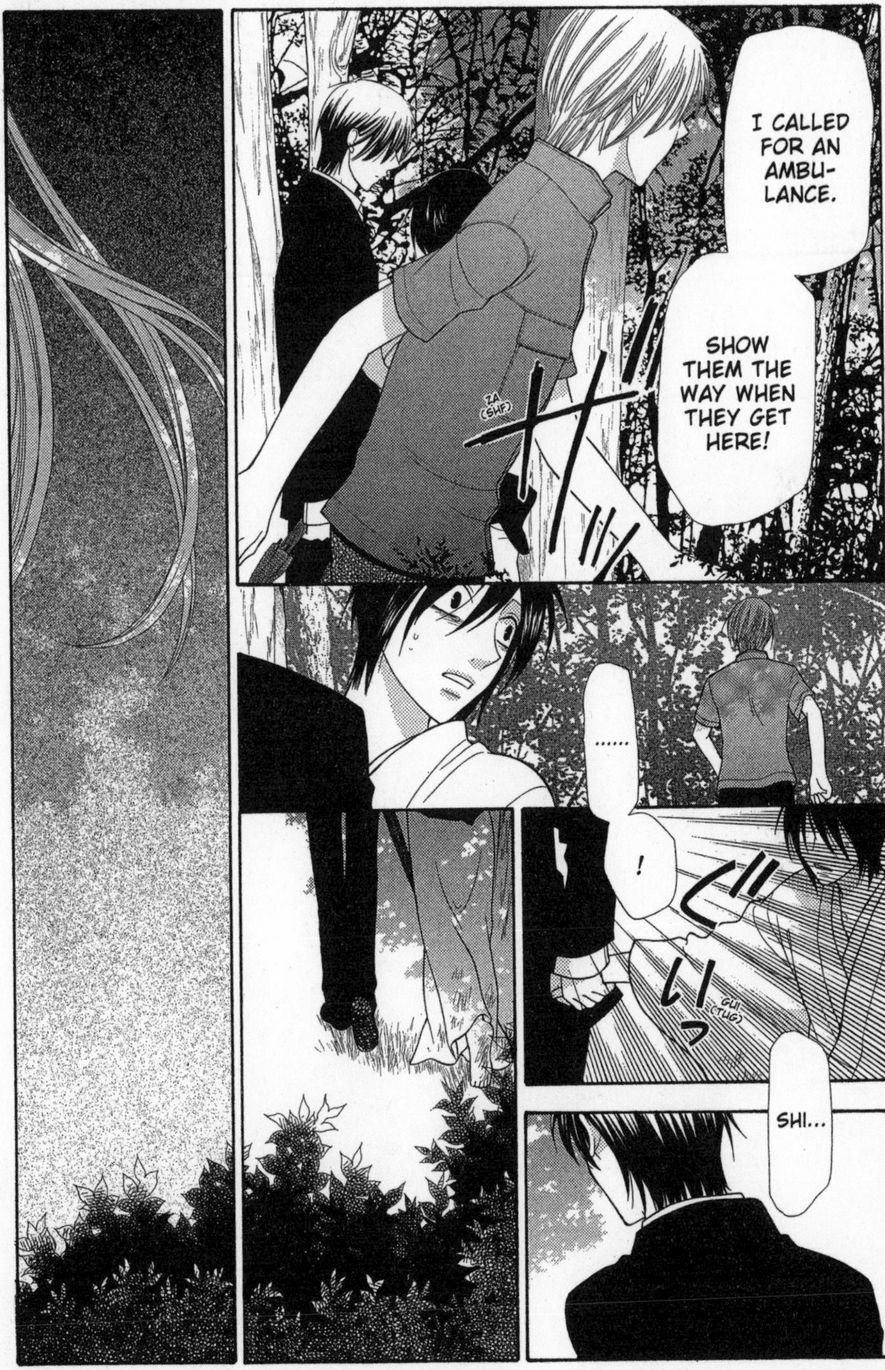
I CALLED FOR AN AMBULANCE.
SHOW THEM THE WAY WHEN THEY GET HERE!
ZA (SHF)
......
!
ぐいっ
GUI (TUG)
SHI...

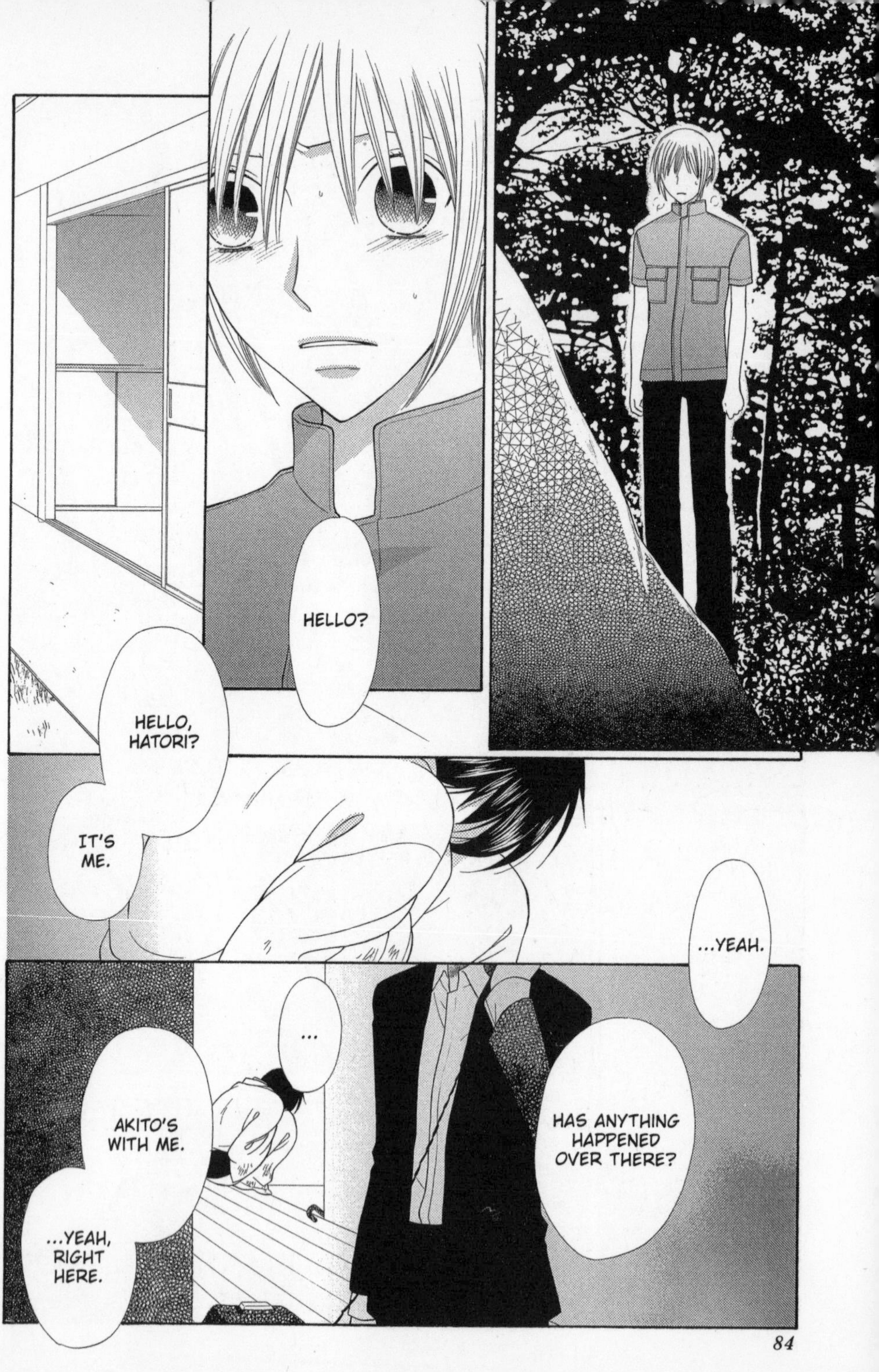
HELLO?
HELLO, HATORI?
IT'S ME.
...YEAH.
HAS ANYTHING HAPPENED OVER THERE?
...
AKITO'S WITH ME.
...YEAH, RIGHT HERE.

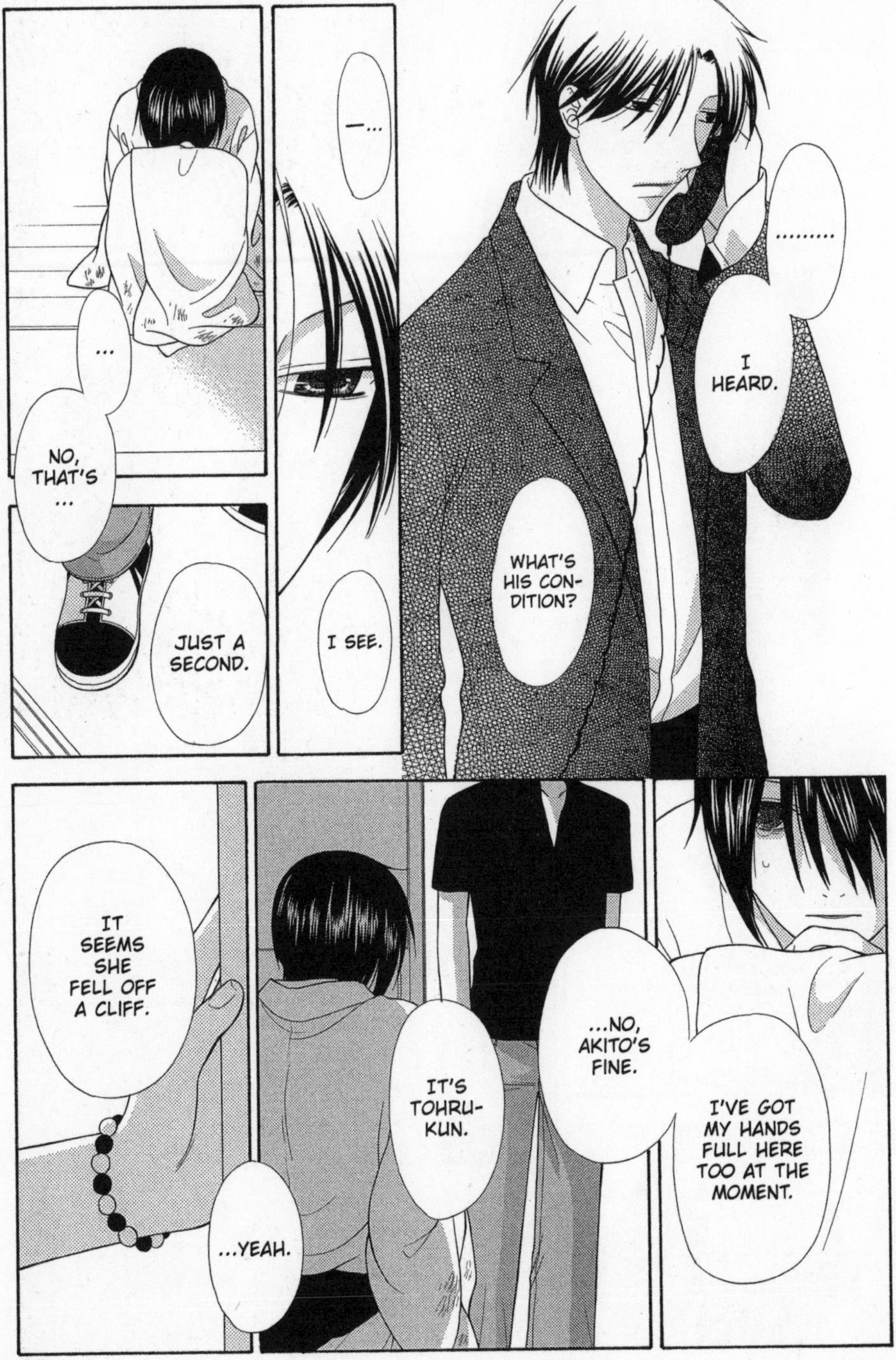
....
I HEARD.
WHAT'S HIS CON-DITION?
—...
I SEE.
...
NO, THAT'S ...
JUST A SECOND.
...NO, AKITO'S FINE.
I'VE GOT MY HANDS FULL HERE TOO AT THE MOMENT.
IT'S TOHRU-KUN.
...YEAH.
IT SEEMS SHE FELL OFF A CLIFF.

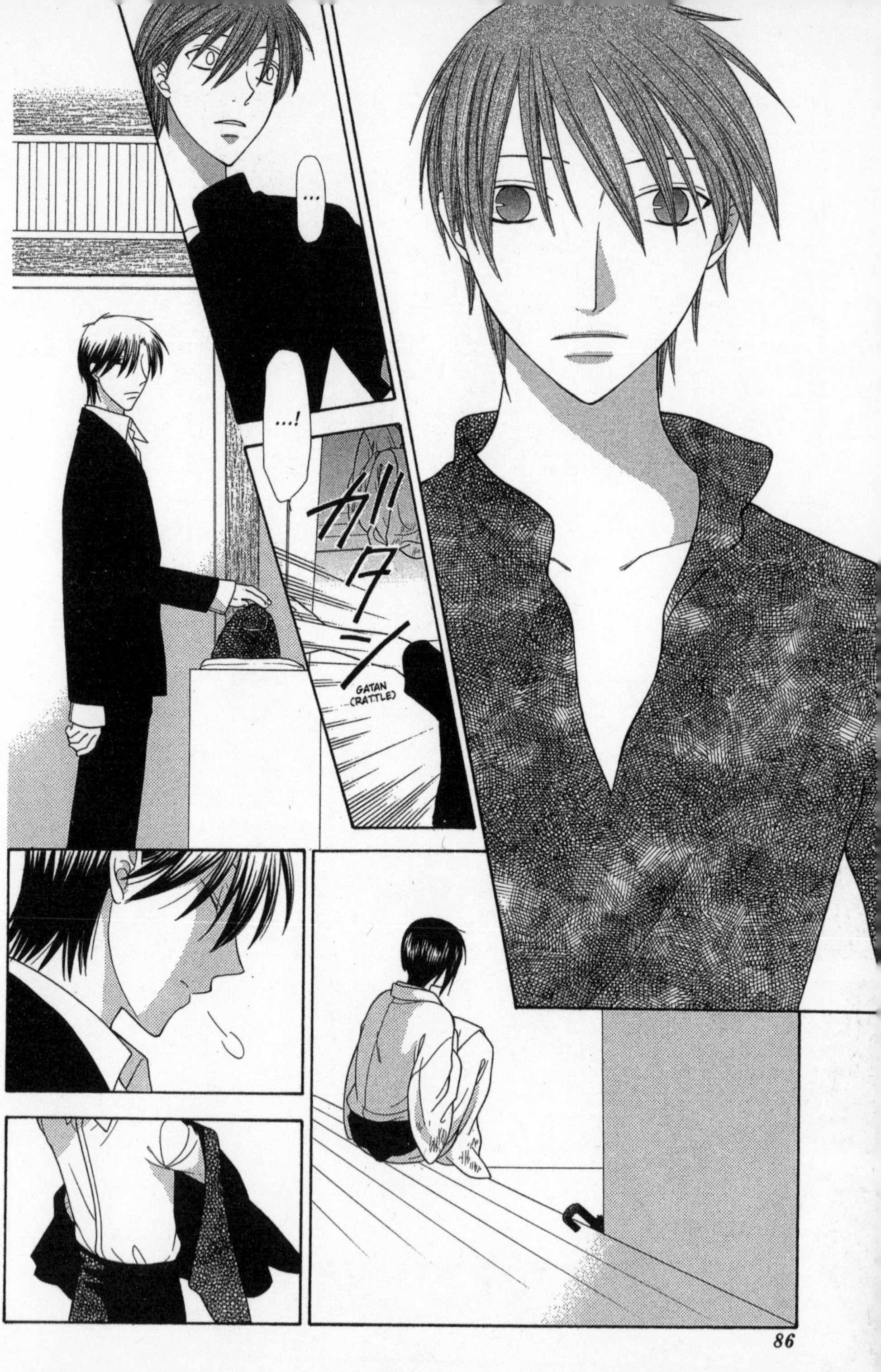
...
...!
ガタン
GATAN (RATTLE)

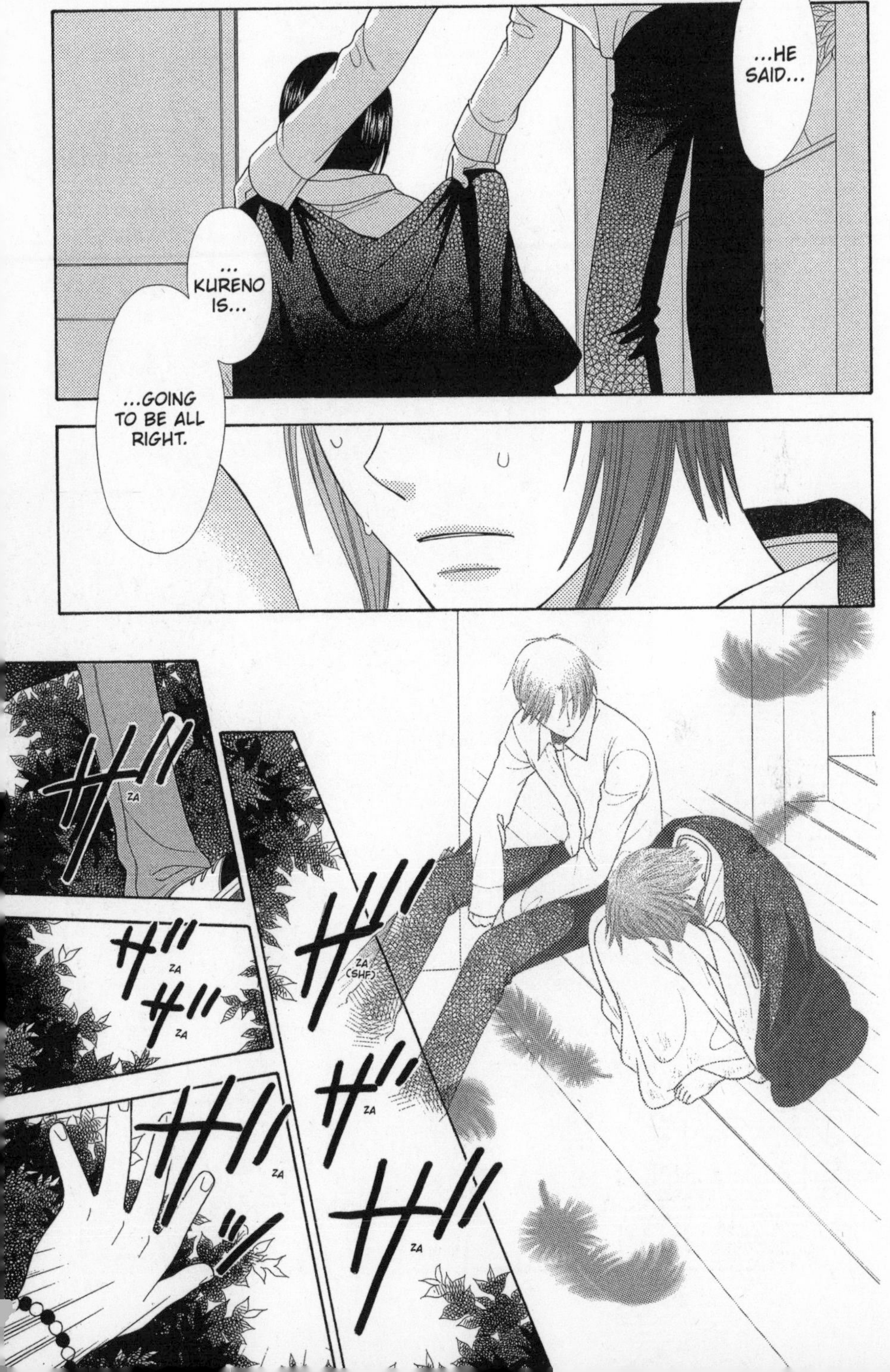
...HE SAID...
...KURENO IS...
...GOING TO BE ALL RIGHT.
ZA (SHF)
ZA
ZA
ZA
ZA
ZA
ZA

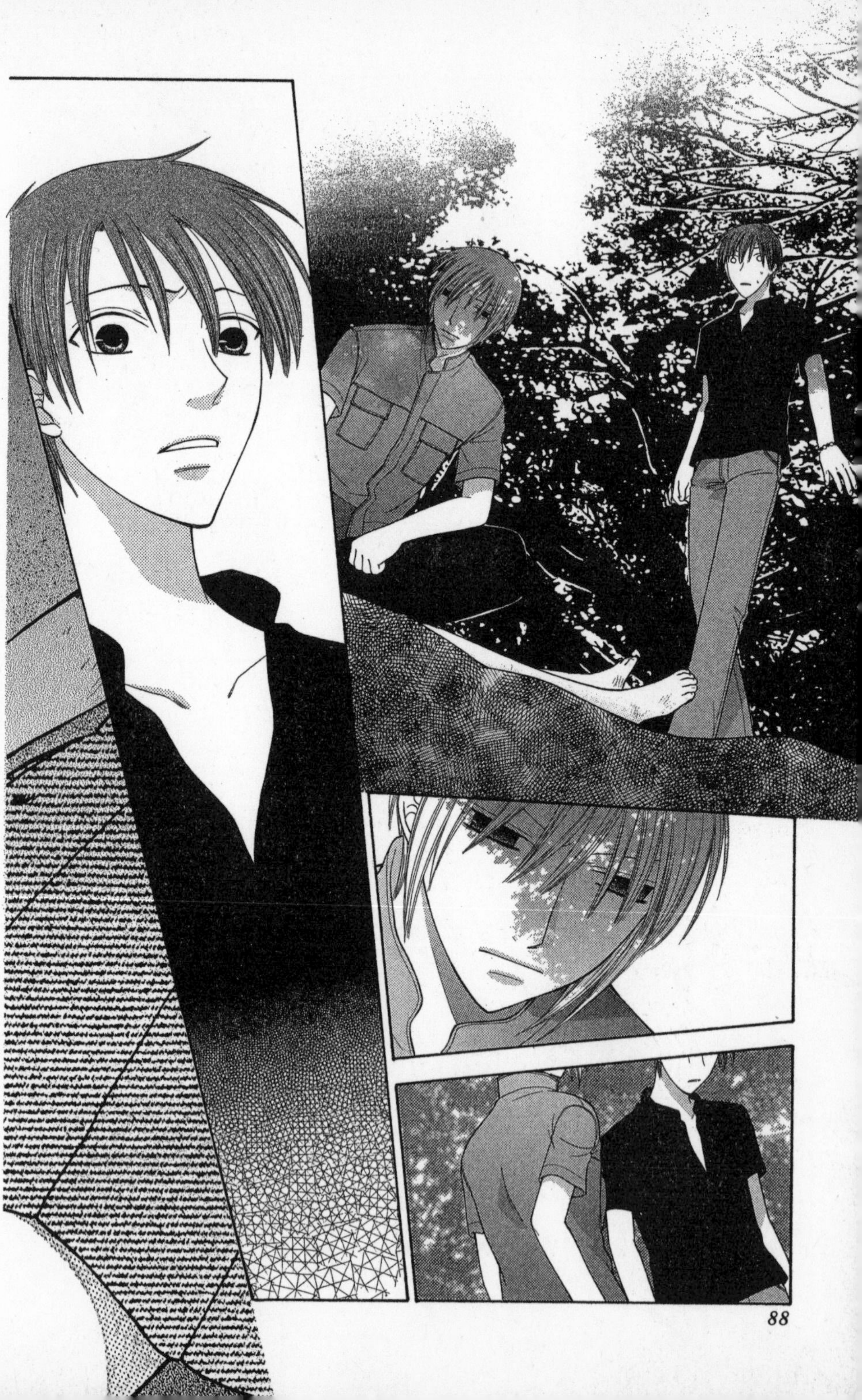

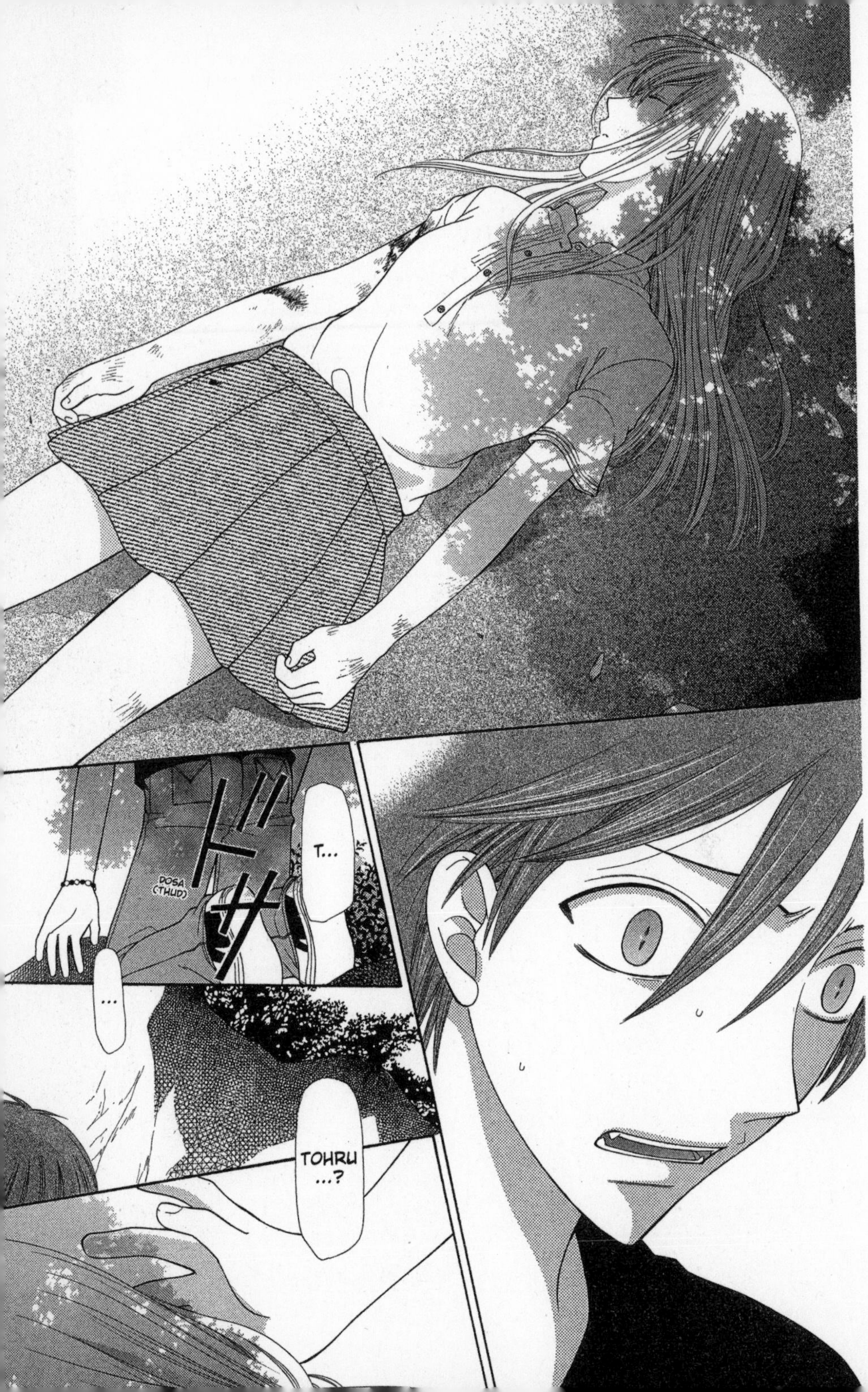
T...
DOSA (THUD)
...
TOHRU ...?

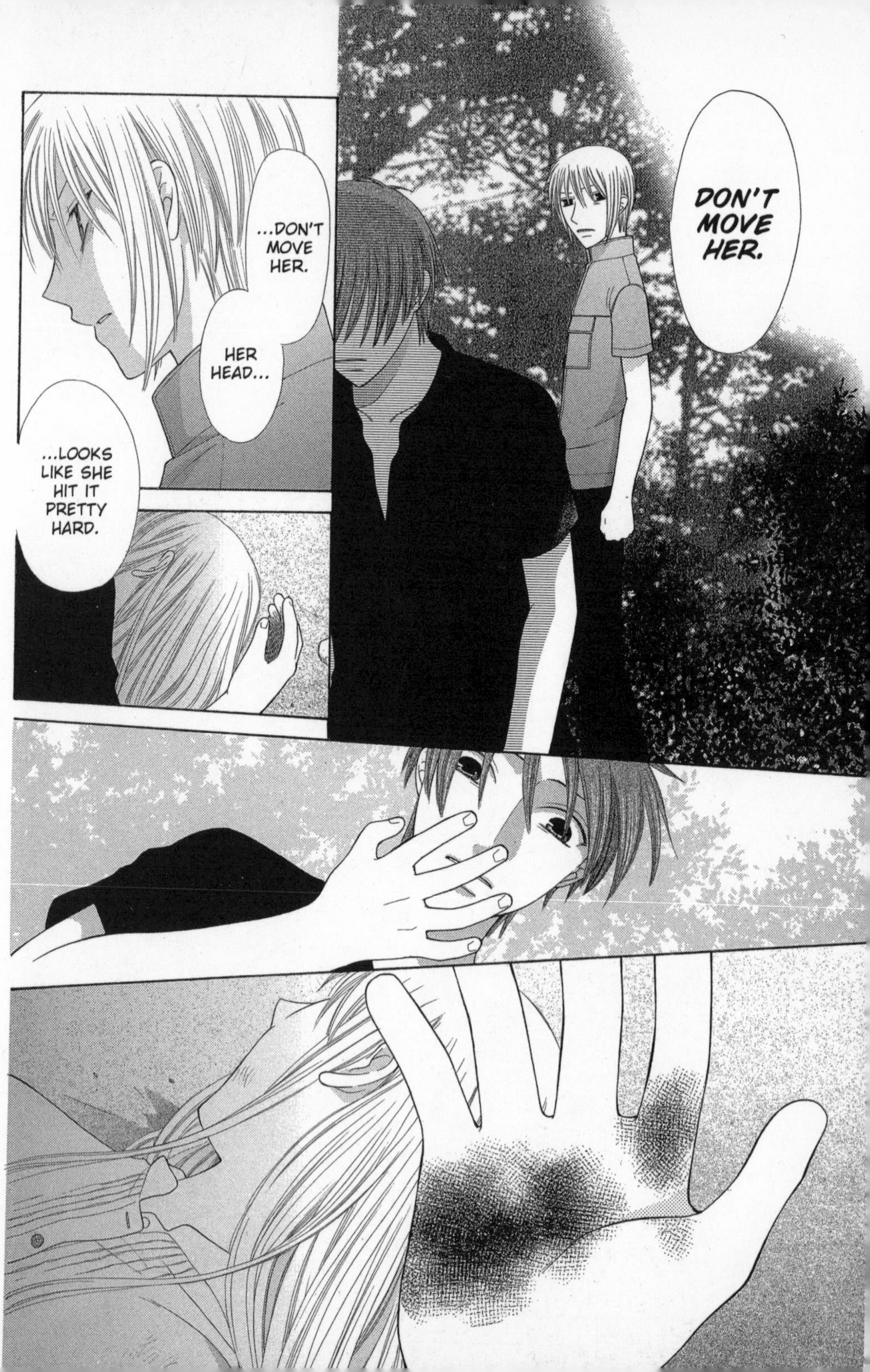
DON'T MOVE HER.
...DON'T MOVE HER.
HER HEAD...
...LOOKS LIKE SHE HIT IT PRETTY HARD.

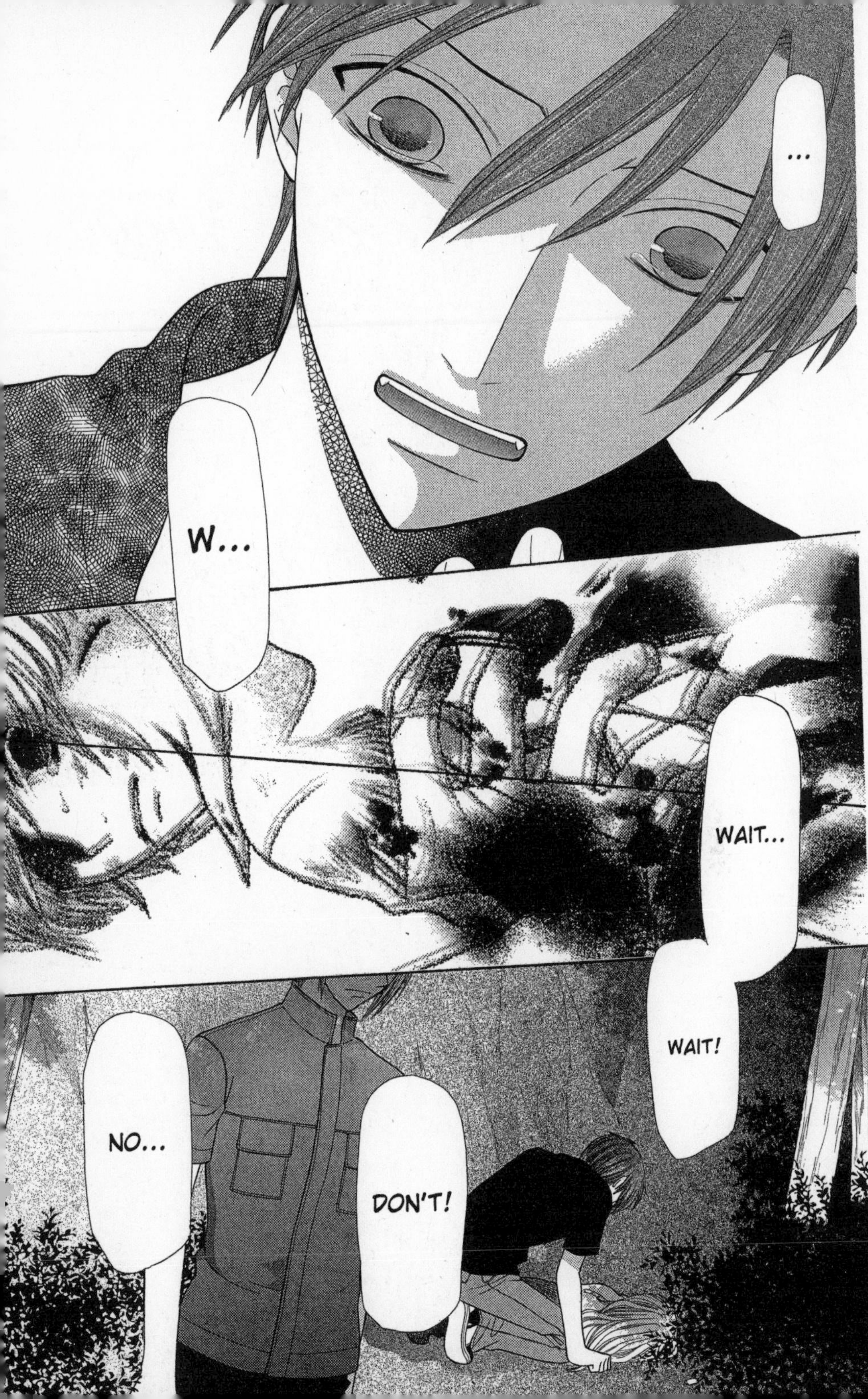
...
W...
WAIT...
WAIT!
DON'T!
NO...

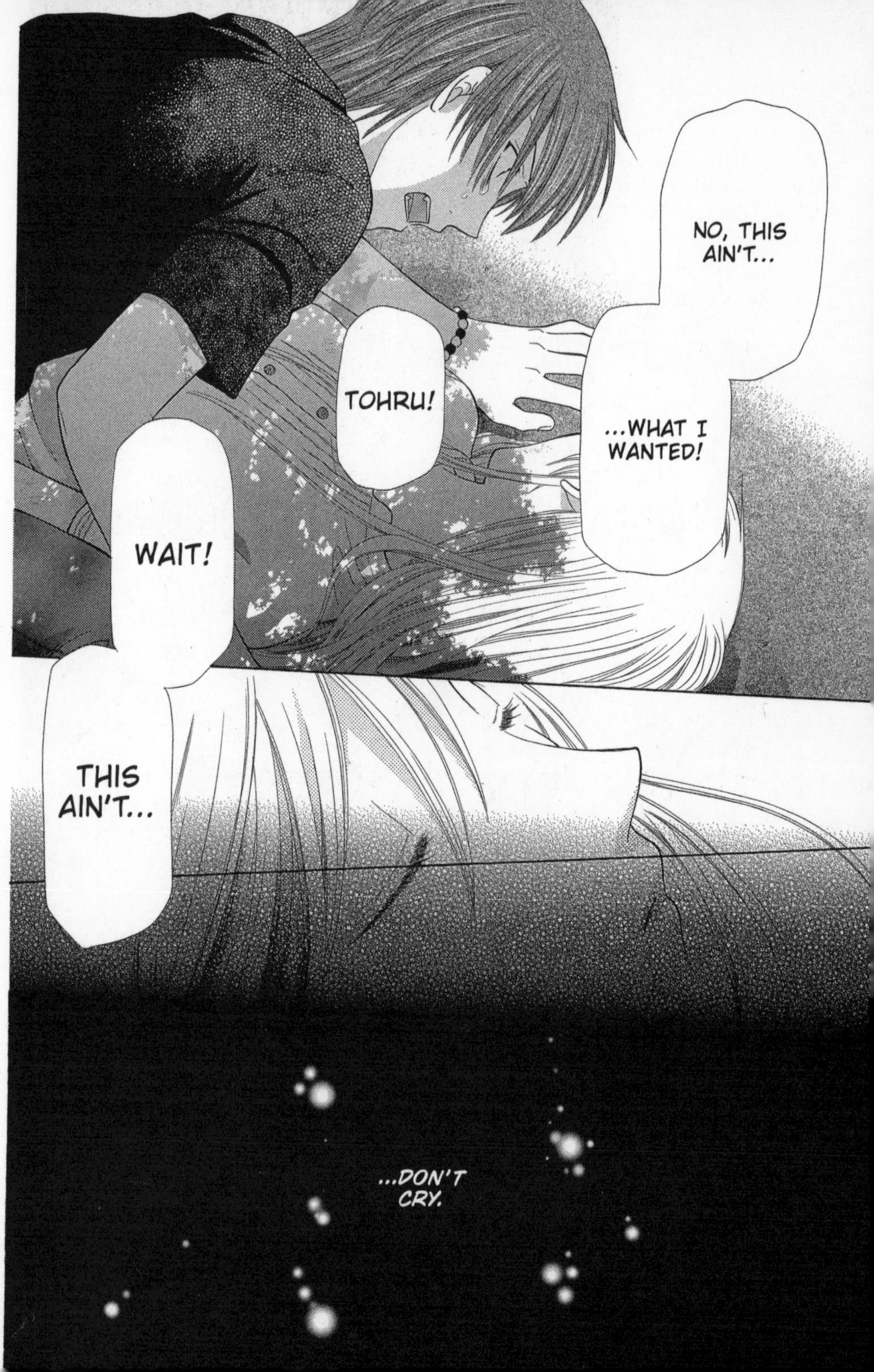
NO, THIS AIN'T...
...WHAT I WANTED!
TOHRU!
WAIT!
THIS AIN'T...
...DON'T CRY.

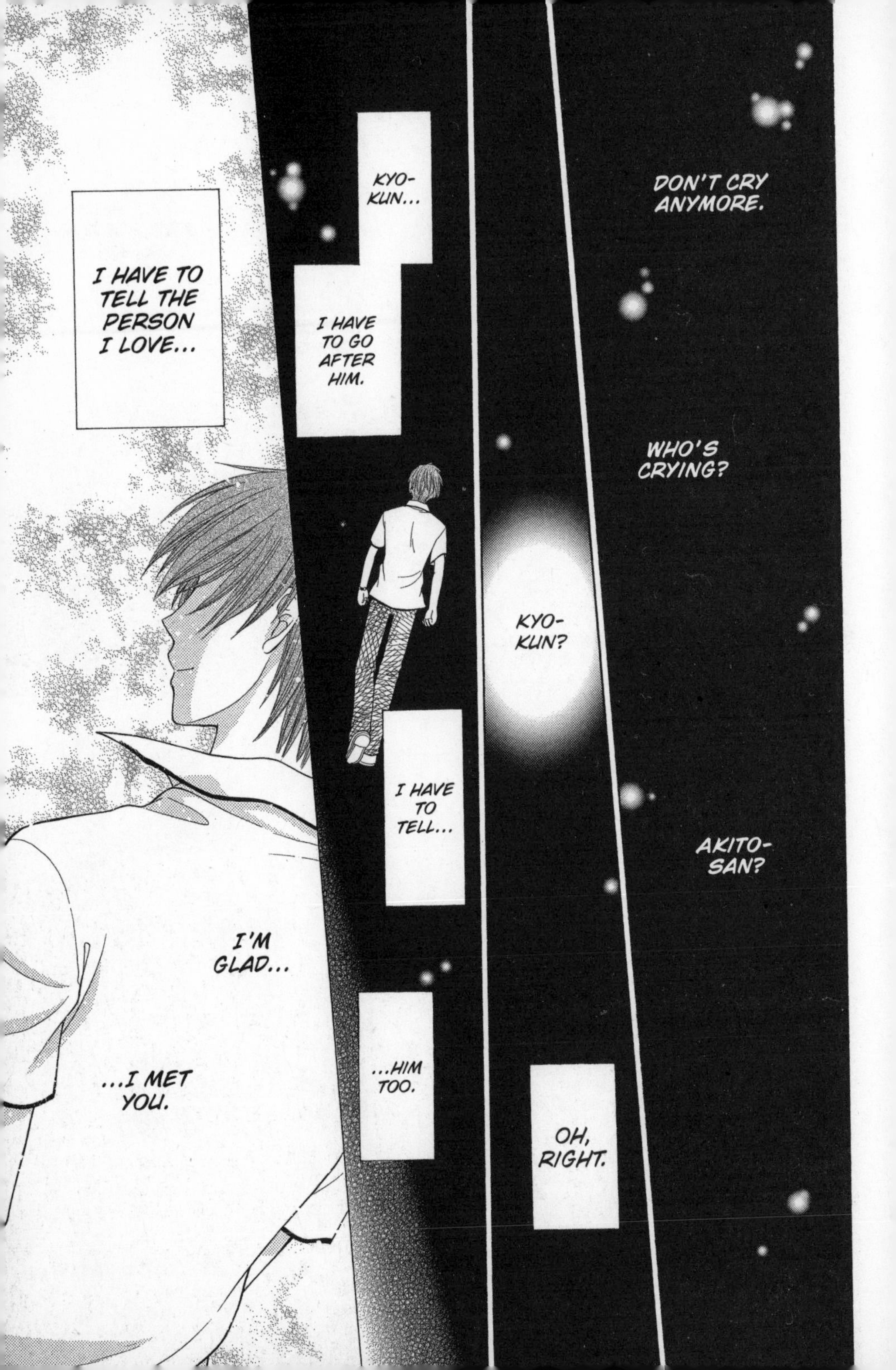
DON'T CRY ANYMORE.
WHO'S CRYING?
AKITO-SAN?
KYO-KUN?
OH, RIGHT.
KYO-KUN...
I HAVE TO GO AFTER HIM.
I HAVE TO TELL...
...HIM TOO.
I HAVE TO TELL THE PERSON I LOVE...
I'M GLAD...
...I MET YOU.

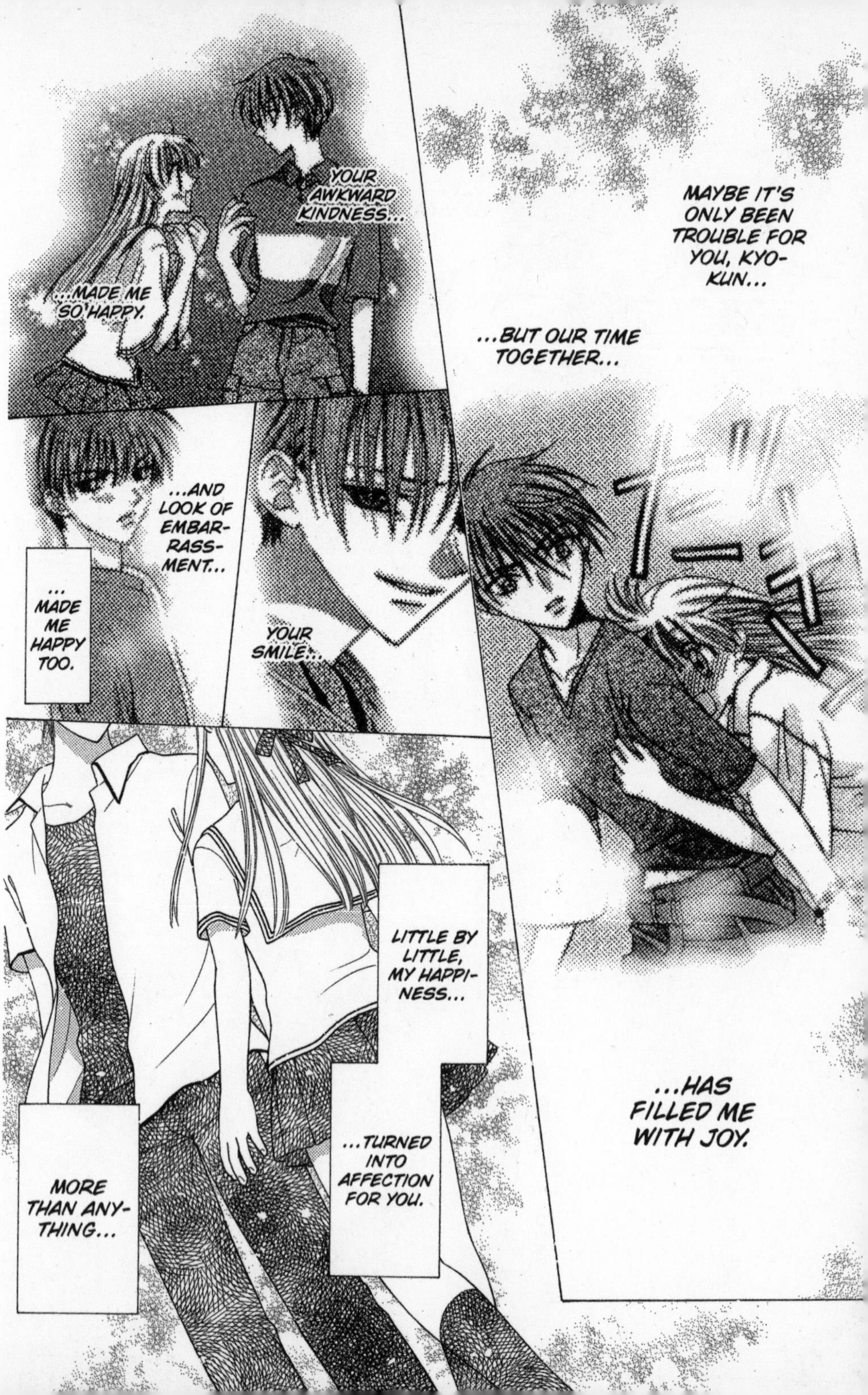
MAYBE IT'S ONLY BEEN TROUBLE FOR YOU, KYO-KUN...
...BUT OUR TIME TOGETHER...
...HAS FILLED ME WITH JOY.
YOUR AWKWARD KINDNESS...
...MADE ME SO HAPPY.
YOUR SMILE...
...AND LOOK OF EMBAR-RASS-MENT...
...MADE ME HAPPY TOO.
LITTLE BY LITTLE, MY HAPPI-NESS...
...TURNED INTO AFFECTION FOR YOU.
MORE THAN ANY-THING...

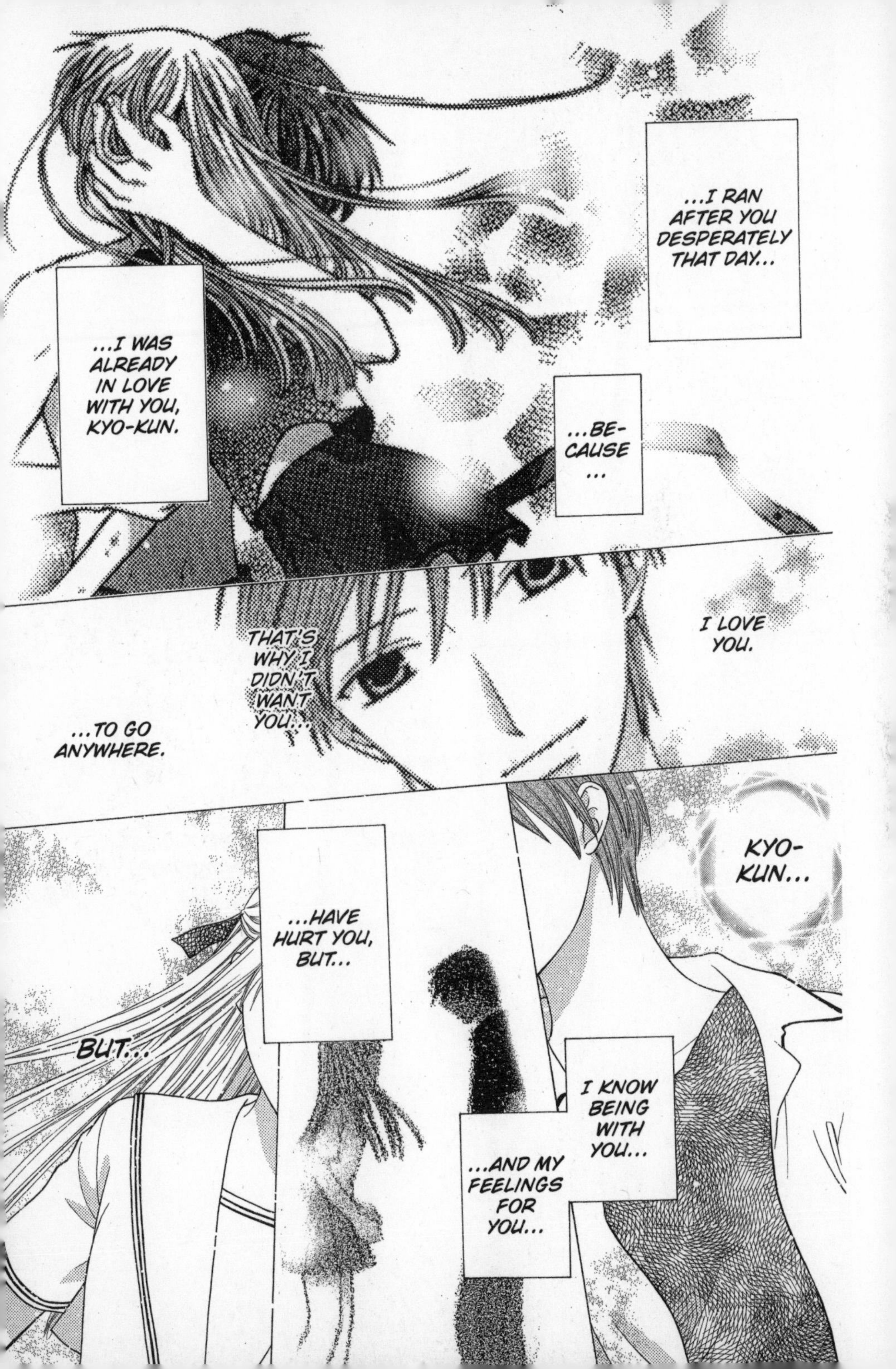
...I RAN AFTER YOU DESPERATELY THAT DAY...
...BE-CAUSE...
...I WAS ALREADY IN LOVE WITH YOU, KYO-KUN.
I LOVE YOU.
THAT'S WHY I DIDN'T WANT YOU...
...TO GO ANYWHERE.
KYO-KUN...
I KNOW BEING WITH YOU...
...AND MY FEELINGS FOR YOU...
...HAVE HURT YOU, BUT...
BUT...

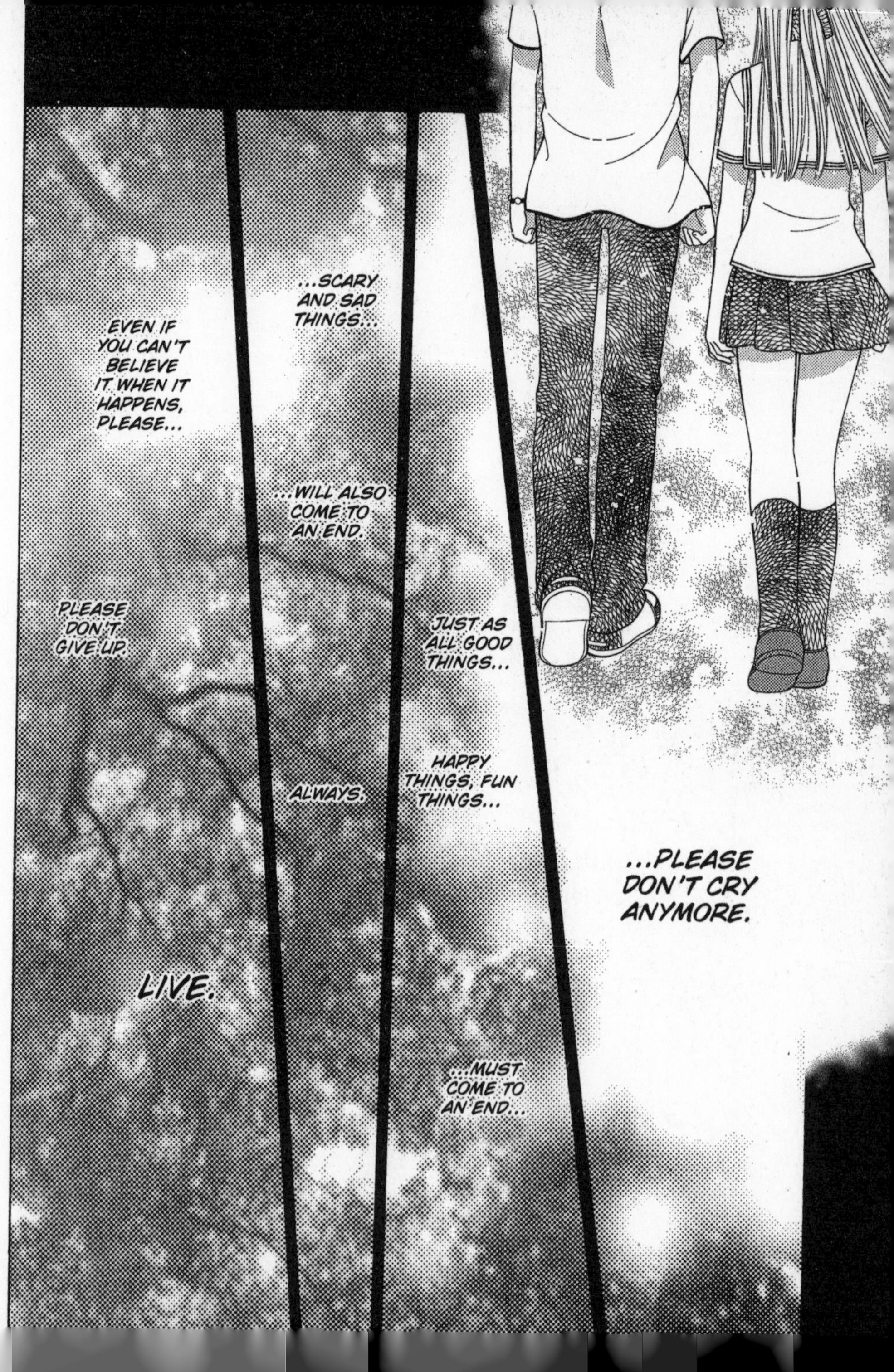
...PLEASE DON'T CRY ANYMORE.
JUST AS ALL GOOD THINGS...
HAPPY THINGS, FUN THINGS...
...MUST COME TO AN END...
...SCARY AND SAD THINGS...
...WILL ALSO COME TO AN END.
ALWAYS.
EVEN IF YOU CAN'T BELIEVE IT WHEN IT HAPPENS, PLEASE...
PLEASE DON'T GIVE UP.
LIVE.

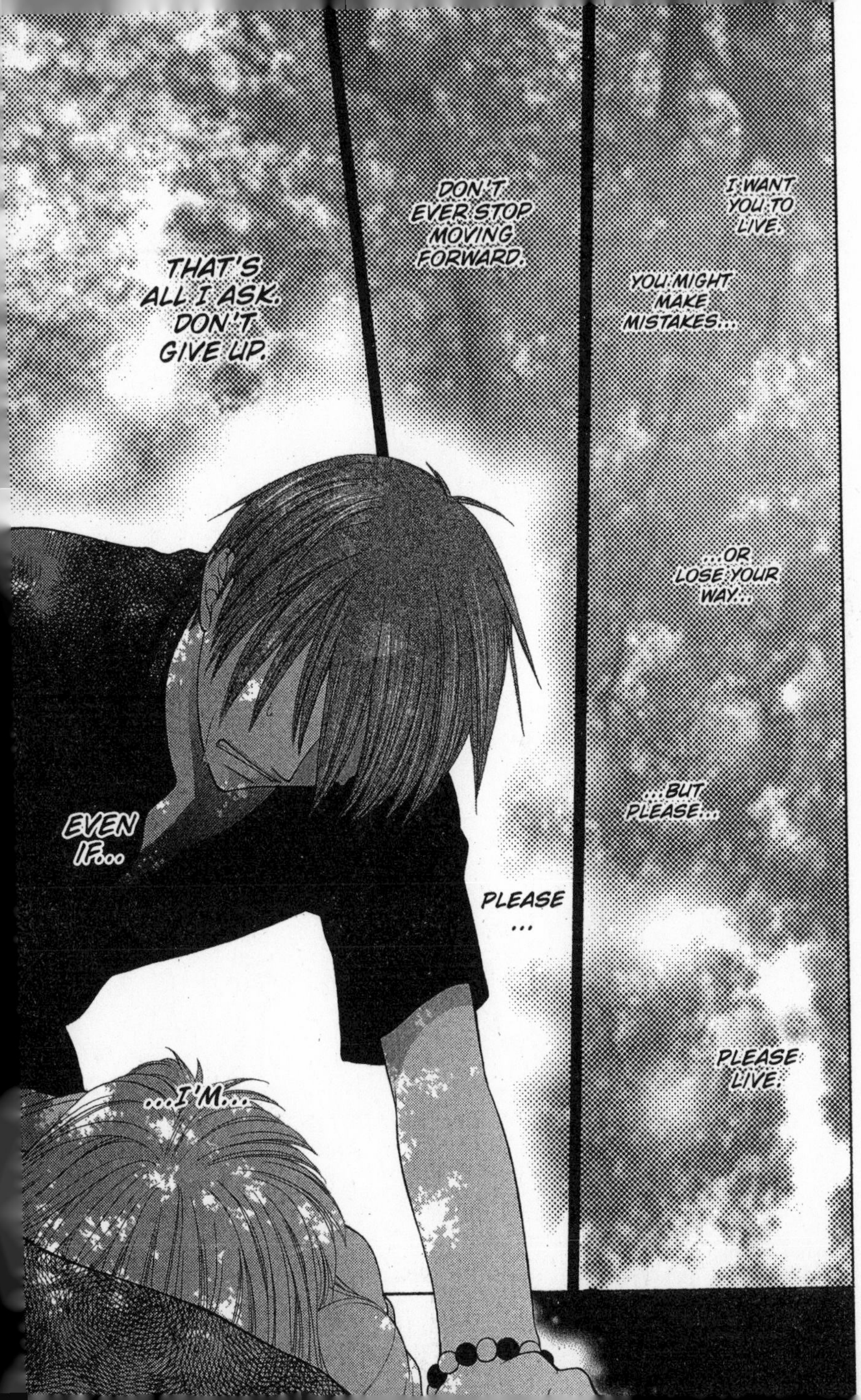
I WANT YOU TO LIVE.
YOU MIGHT MAKE MISTAKES...
...OR LOSE YOUR WAY...
...BUT PLEASE...
PLEASE LIVE.
DON'T EVER STOP MOVING FORWARD.
THAT'S ALL I ASK. DON'T GIVE UP.
PLEASE ...
EVEN IF...
...I'M...

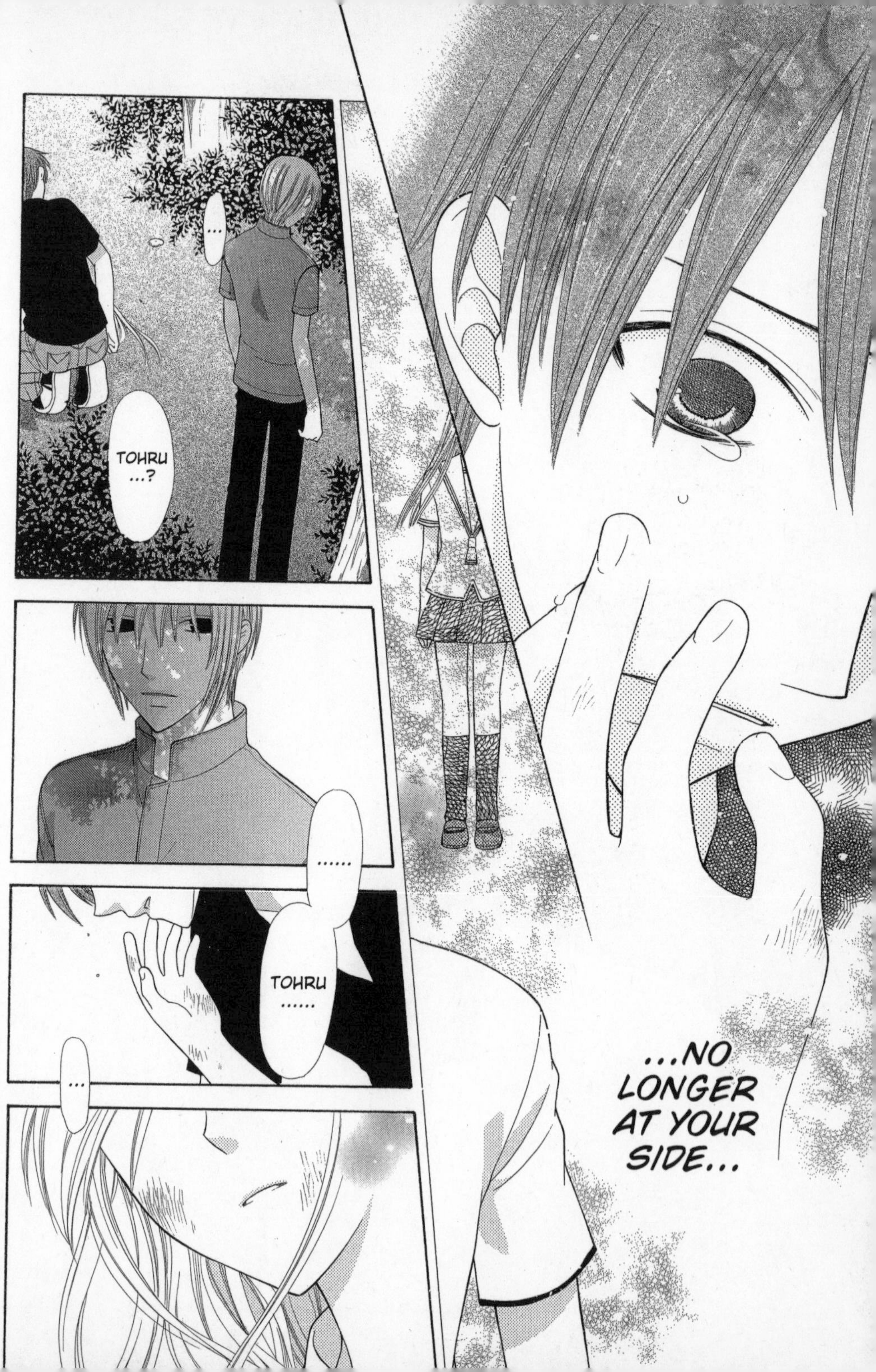
...NO LONGER AT YOUR SIDE...
...
TOHRU ...?
......
TOHRU ......
...

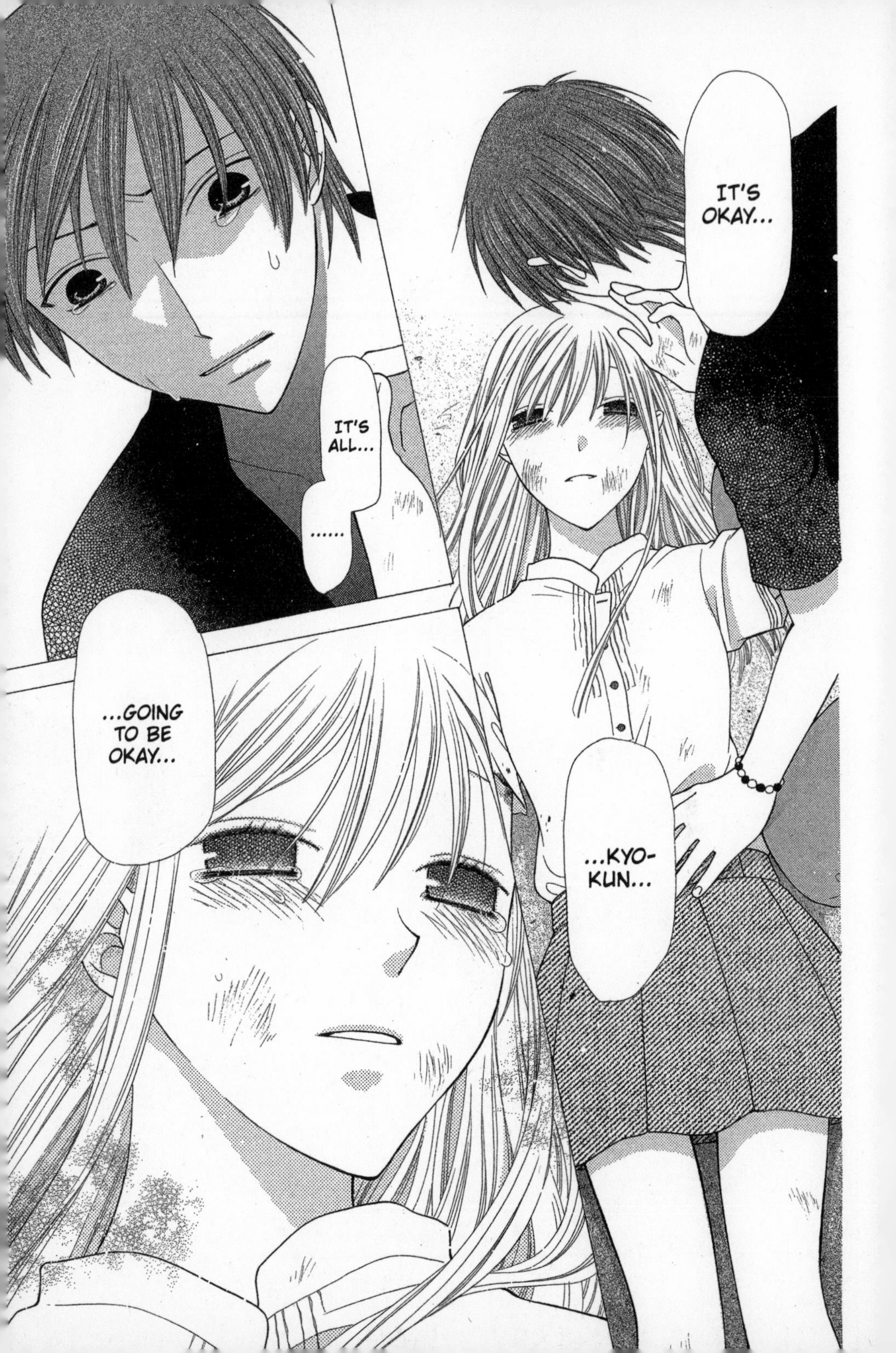
IT'S OKAY...
...KYO-KUN...
IT'S ALL...
......
...GOING TO BE OKAY...

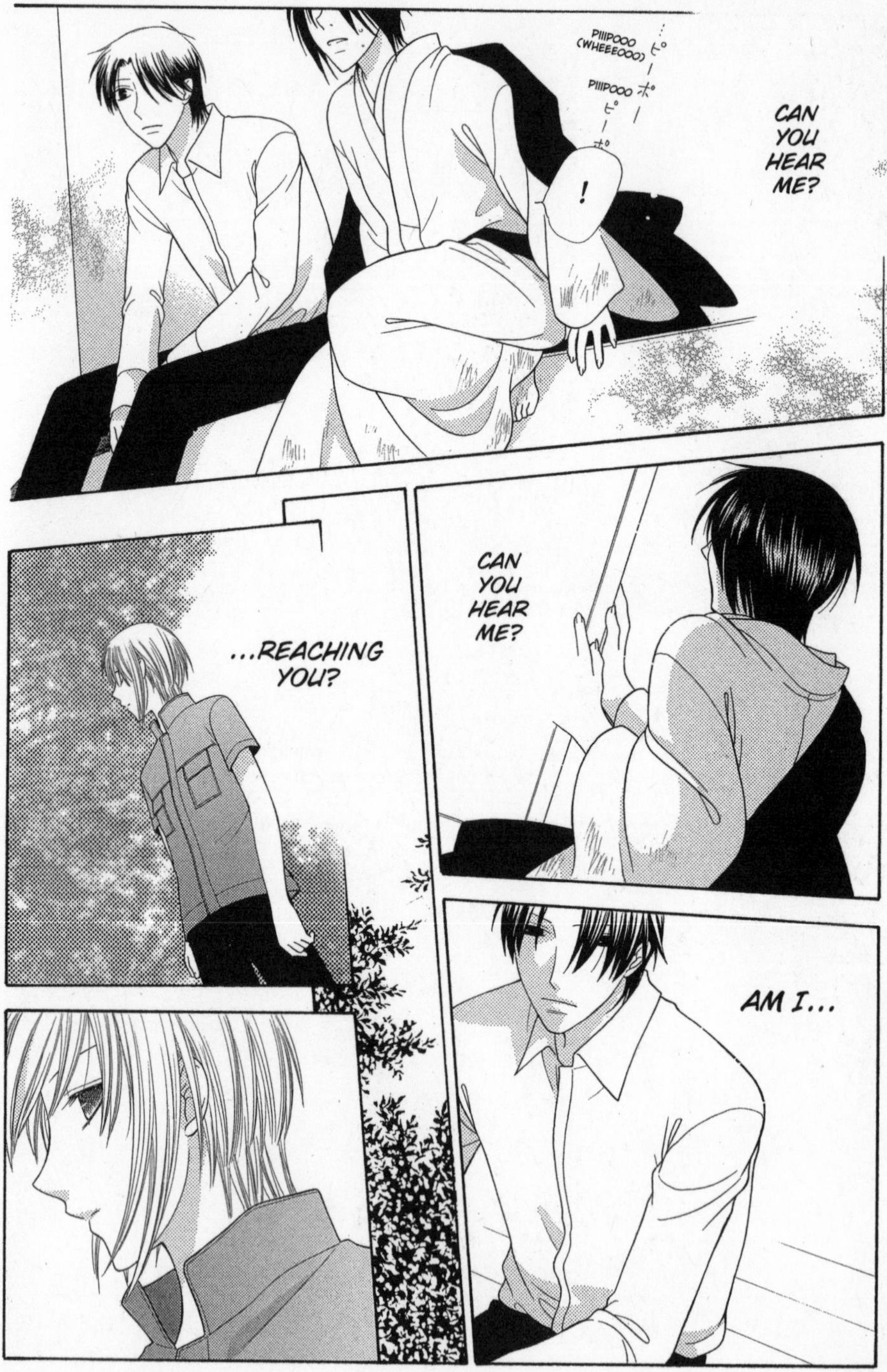
PIIIPOOO (WHEEEOOO)
…ピーポー
PIIIPOOO
ピーポ
!
CAN YOU HEAR ME?
CAN YOU HEAR ME?
AM I…
…REACHING YOU?

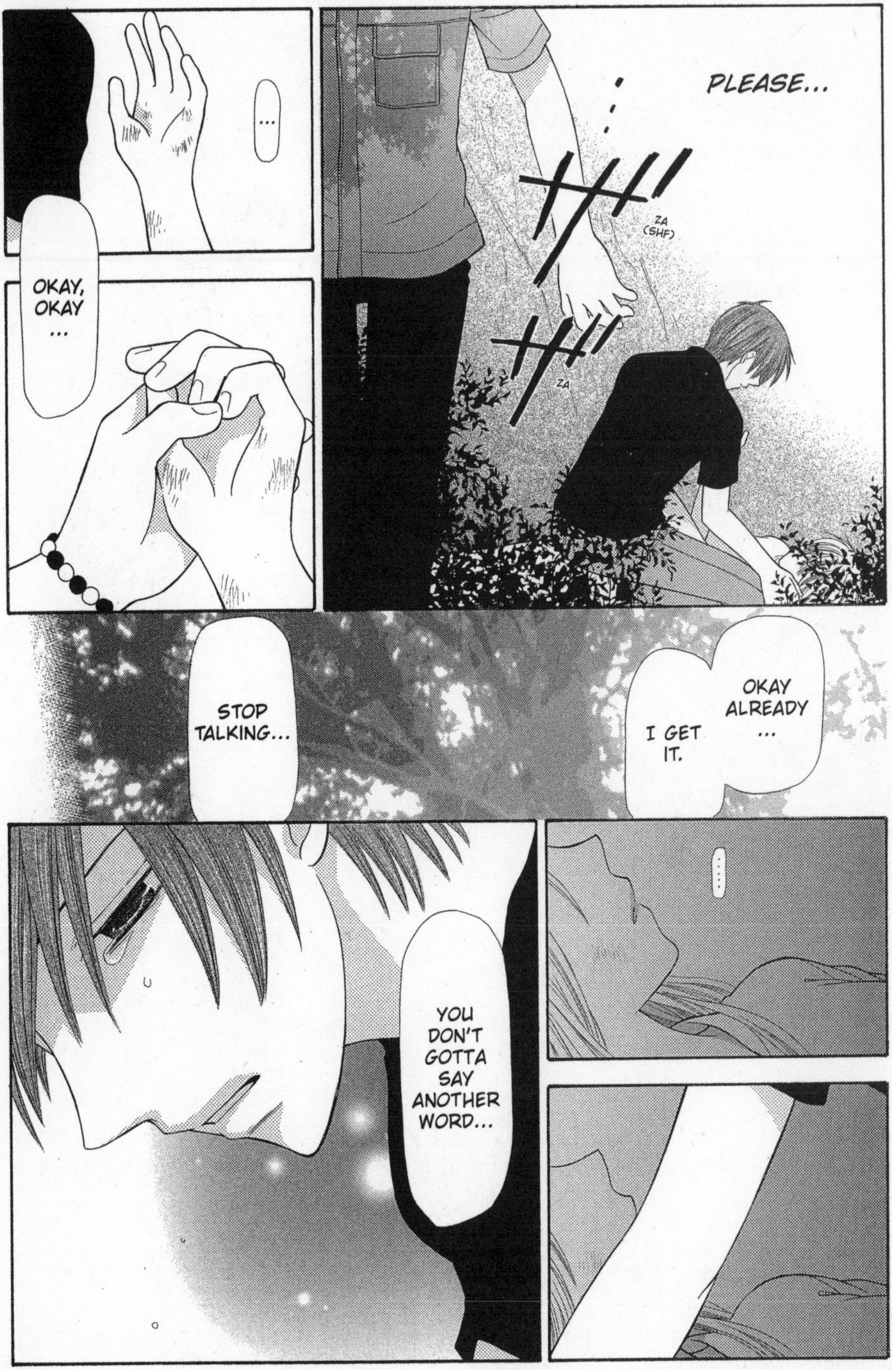
PLEASE...
...
ZA (SHF)
ZA
...
OKAY, OKAY ...
OKAY ALREADY ...
I GET IT.
STOP TALKING...
......
YOU DON'T GOTTA SAY ANOTHER WORD...

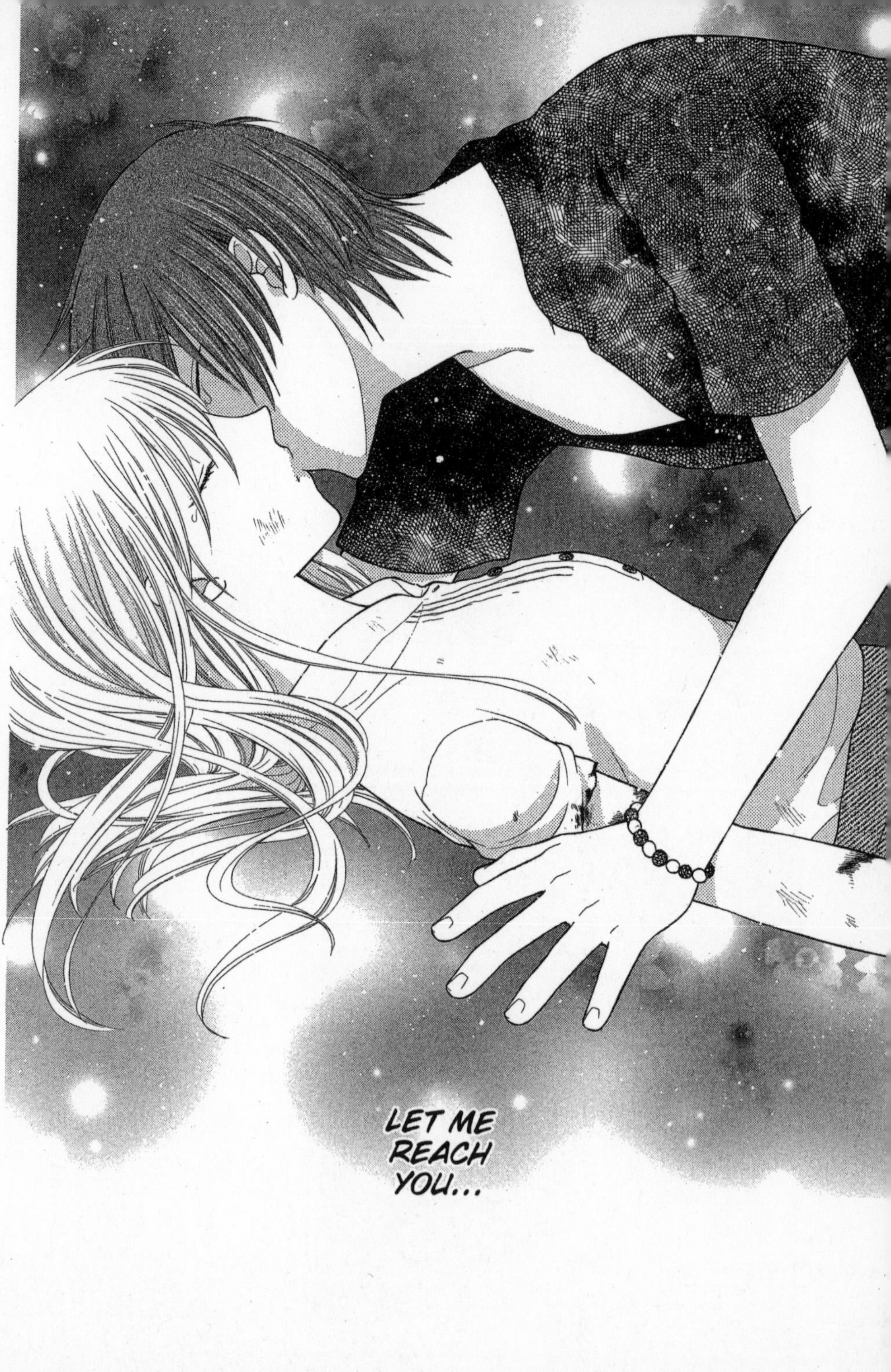
LET ME REACH YOU...

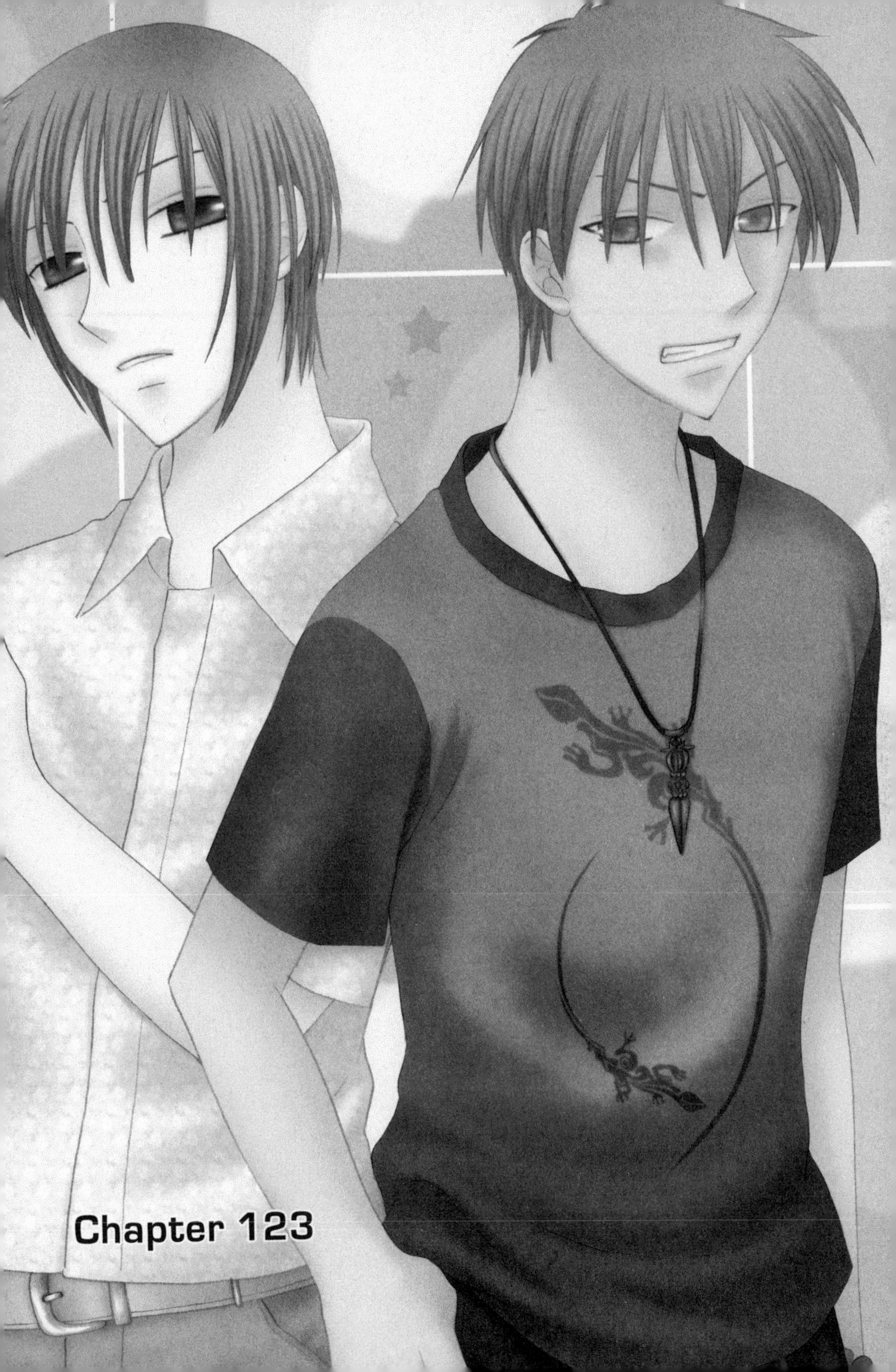

Chapter 123

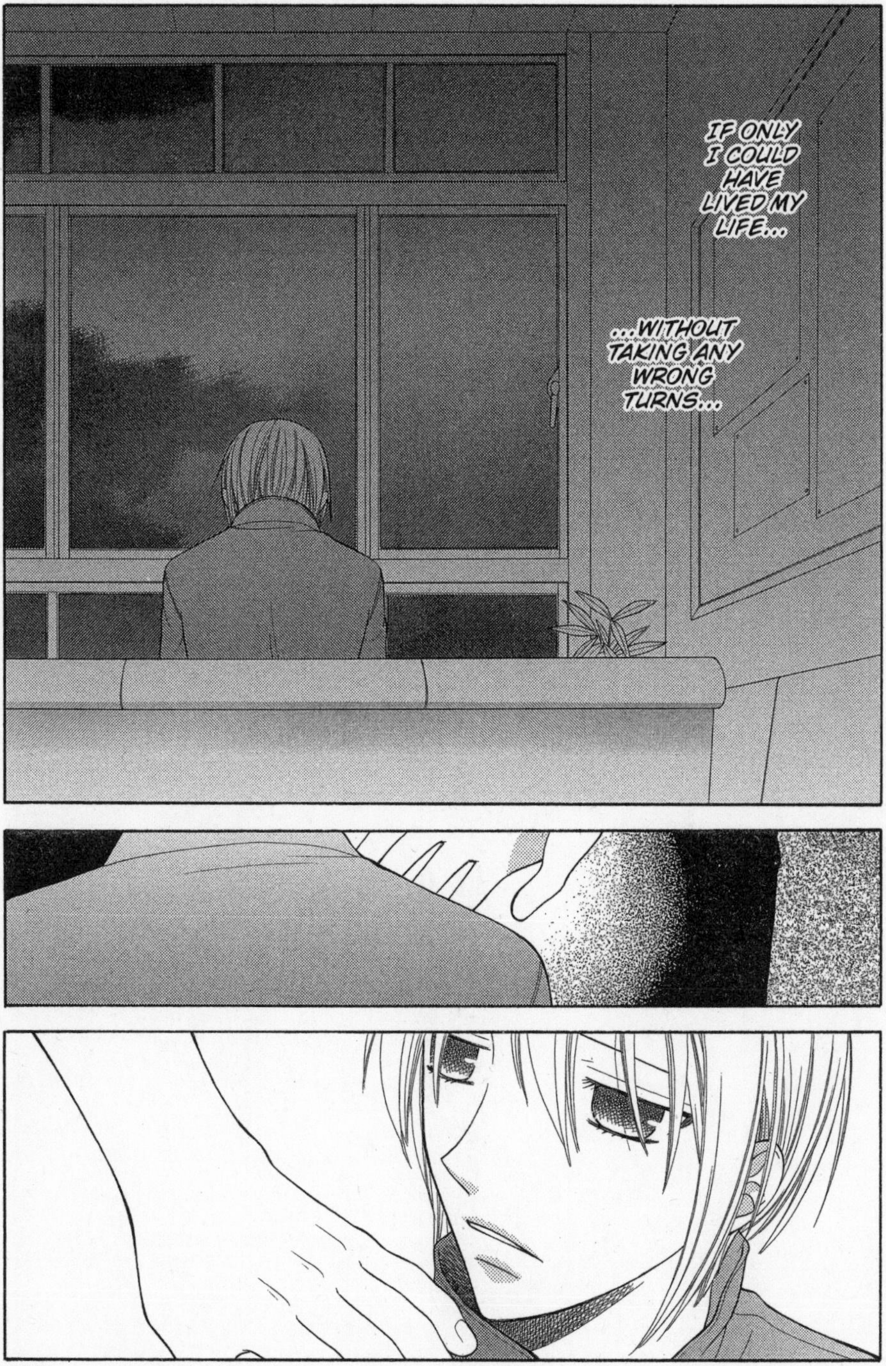
IF ONLY I COULD HAVE LIVED MY LIFE...
...WITHOUT TAKING ANY WRONG TURNS...

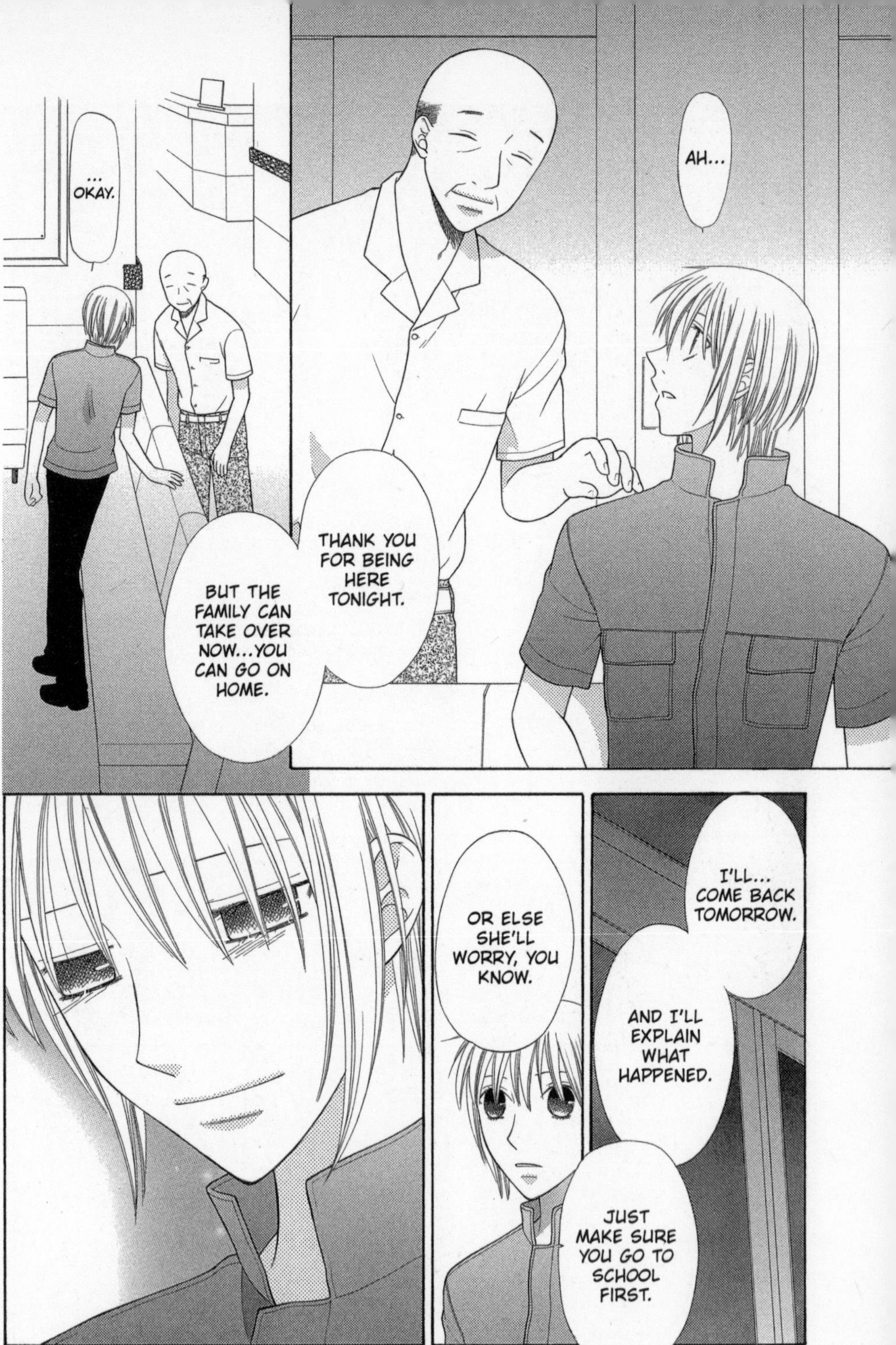
AH...
THANK YOU FOR BEING HERE TONIGHT.
BUT THE FAMILY CAN TAKE OVER NOW...YOU CAN GO ON HOME.
...OKAY.
I'LL... COME BACK TOMORROW.
AND I'LL EXPLAIN WHAT HAPPENED.
JUST MAKE SURE YOU GO TO SCHOOL FIRST.
OR ELSE SHE'LL WORRY, YOU KNOW.

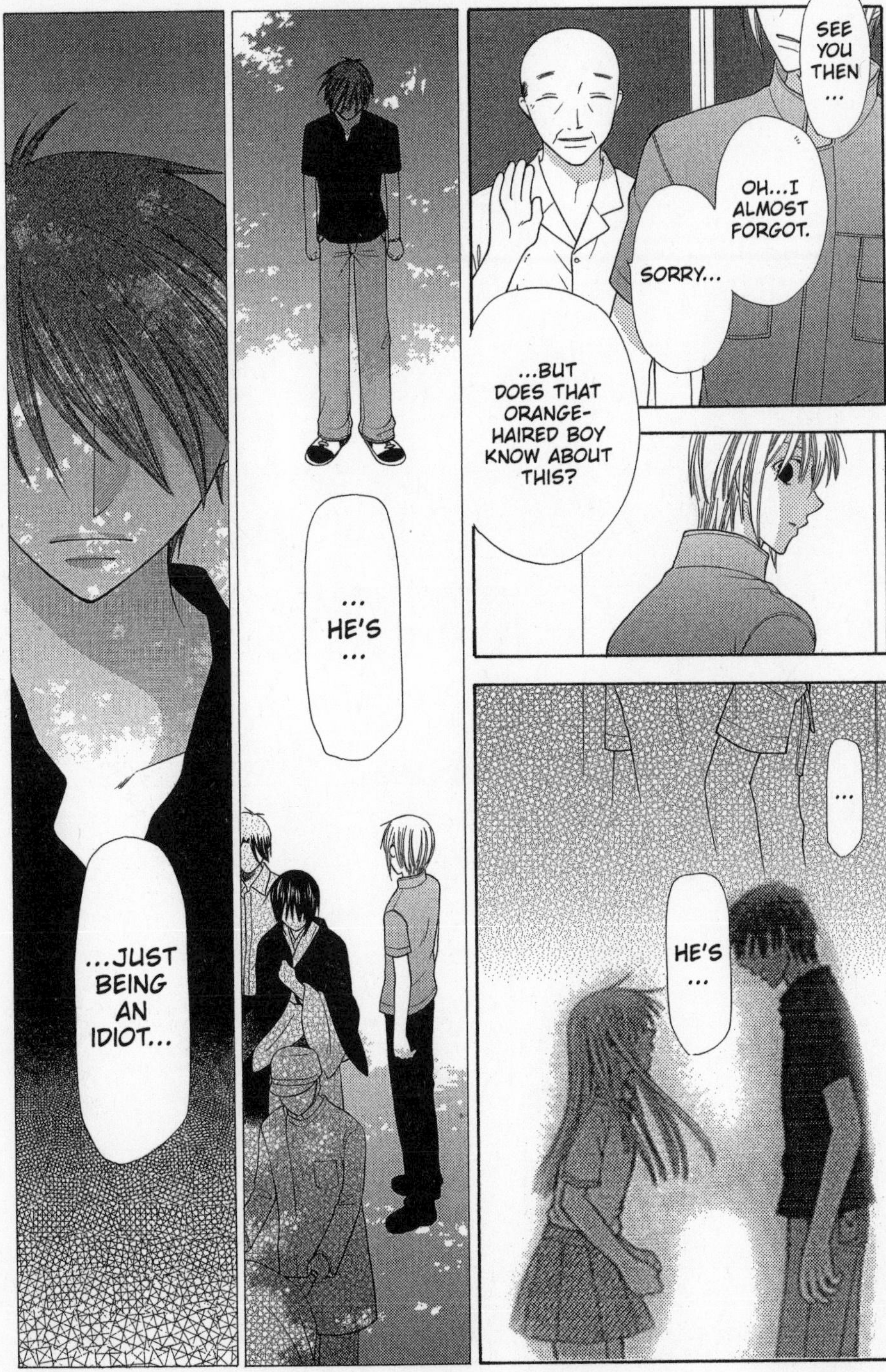
SEE YOU THEN ...
OH...I ALMOST FORGOT.
SORRY...
...BUT DOES THAT ORANGE-HAIRED BOY KNOW ABOUT THIS?
...
HE'S ...
... HE'S ...
...JUST BEING AN IDIOT...

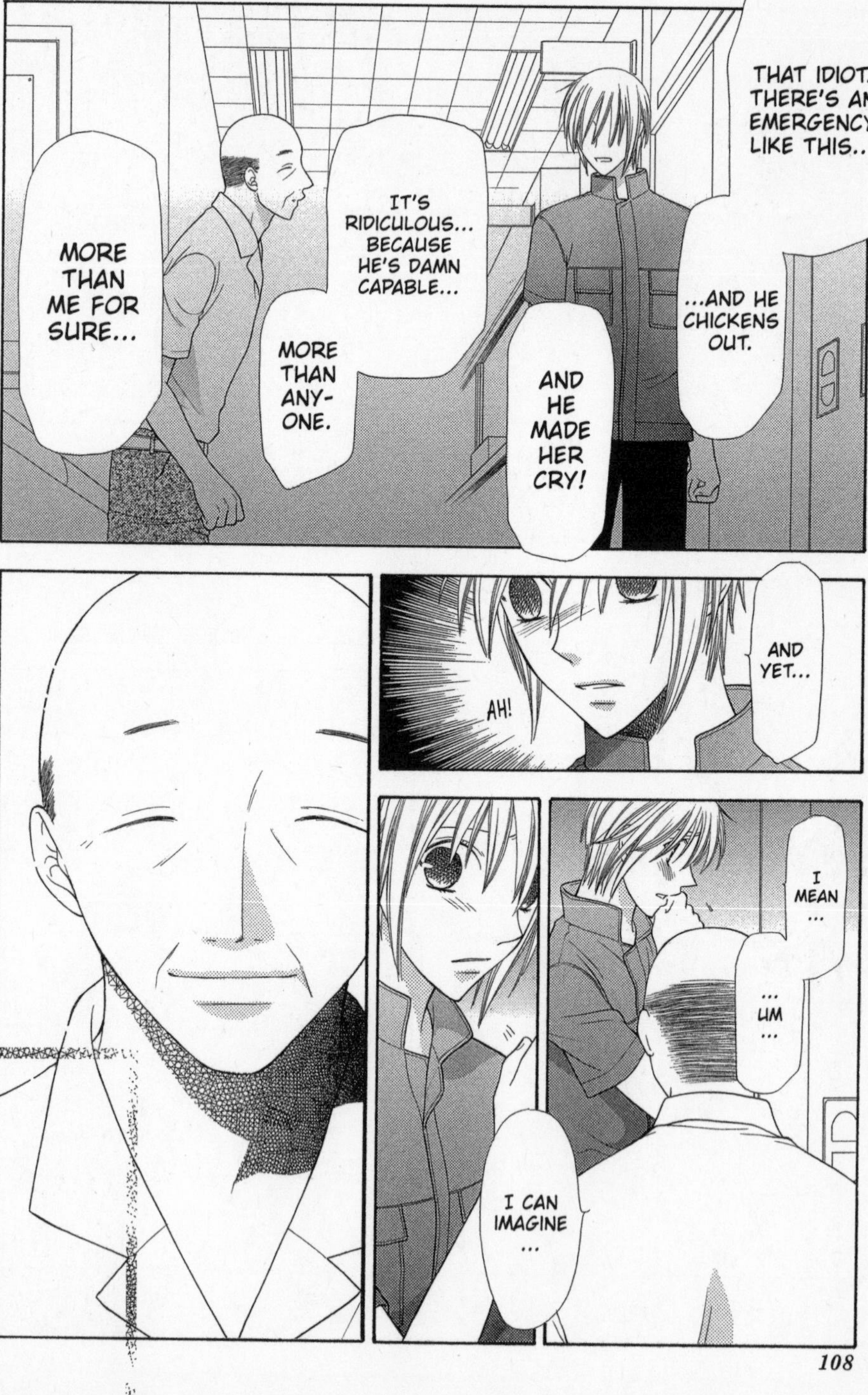
THAT IDIOT. THERE'S AN EMERGENCY LIKE THIS...
...AND HE CHICKENS OUT.
AND HE MADE HER CRY!
IT'S RIDICULOUS... BECAUSE HE'S DAMN CAPABLE...
MORE THAN ANYONE.
MORE THAN ME FOR SURE...
AND YET...
AH!
I MEAN ...
... UM ...
I CAN IMAGINE ...

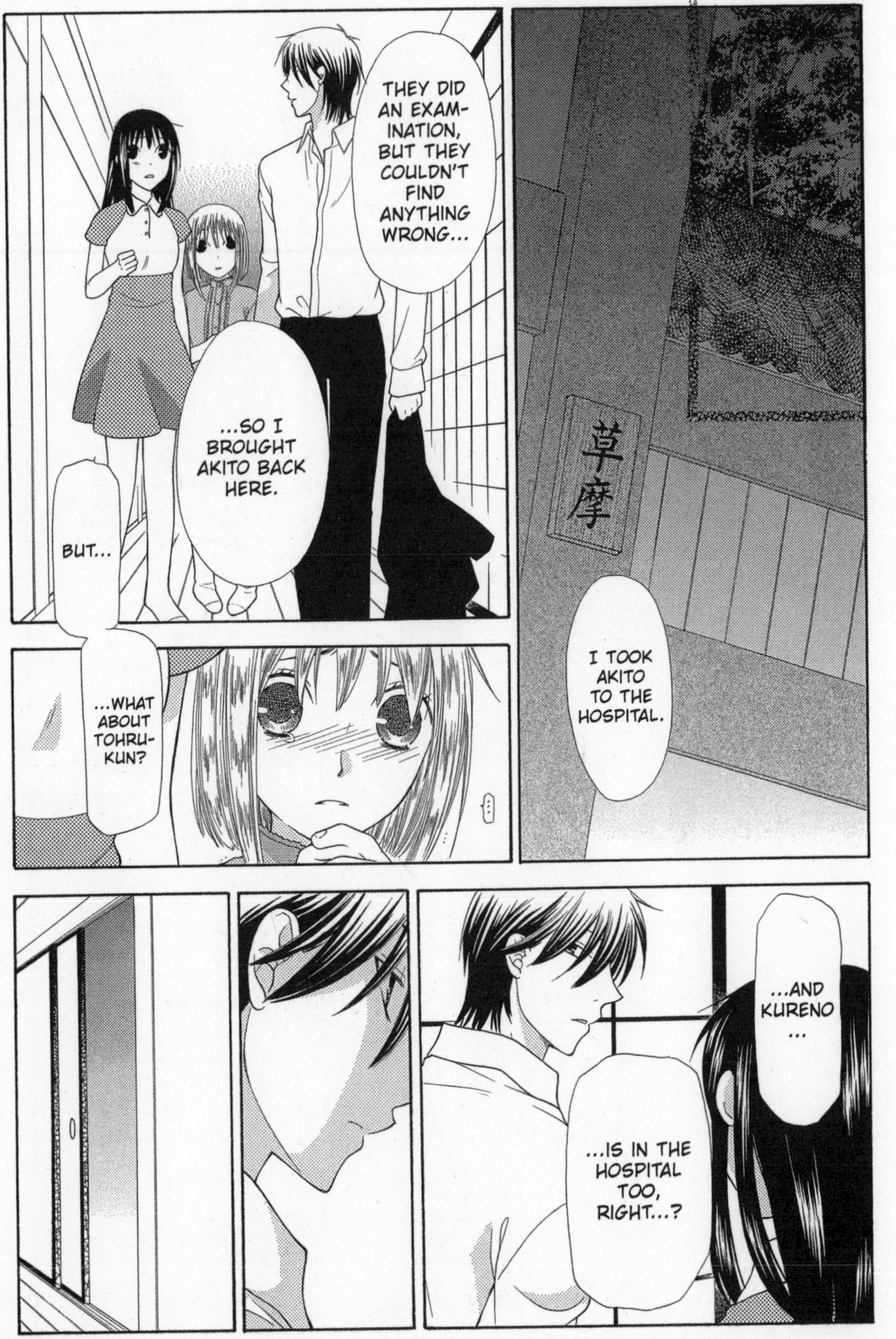

草摩
I TOOK AKITO TO THE HOSPITAL.
THEY DID AN EXAMINATION, BUT THEY COULDN'T FIND ANYTHING WRONG...
...SO I BROUGHT AKITO BACK HERE.
BUT...
...WHAT ABOUT TOHRU-KUN?
...
...AND KURENO...
...IS IN THE HOSPITAL TOO, RIGHT...?

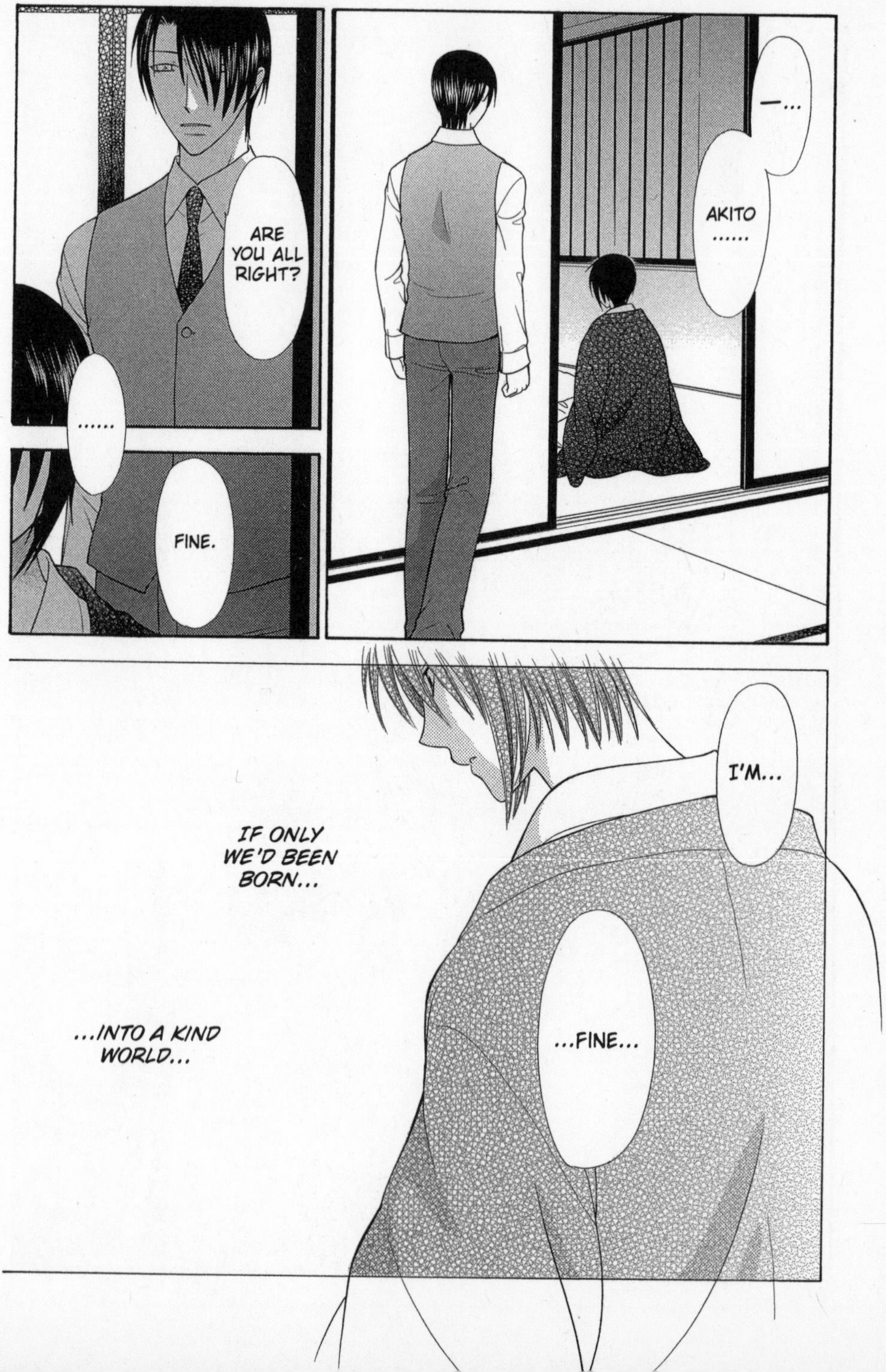

—...
AKITO ......
ARE YOU ALL RIGHT?
......
FINE.
I'M...
IF ONLY WE'D BEEN BORN...
...FINE...
...INTO A KIND WORLD...

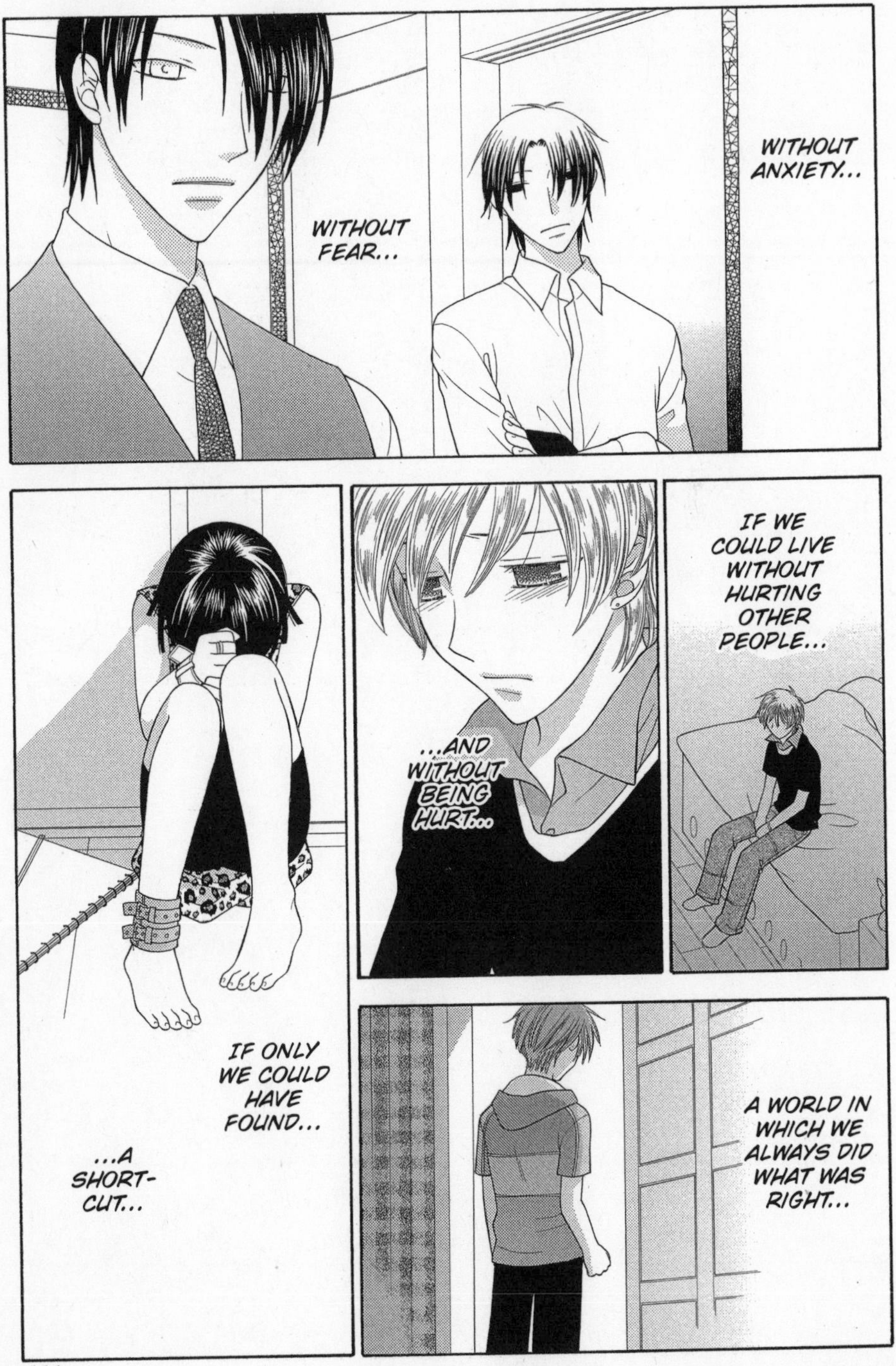
WITHOUT ANXIETY...
WITHOUT FEAR...
IF WE COULD LIVE WITHOUT HURTING OTHER PEOPLE...
...AND WITHOUT BEING HURT...
A WORLD IN WHICH WE ALWAYS DID WHAT WAS RIGHT...
IF ONLY WE COULD HAVE FOUND...
...A SHORT-CUT...

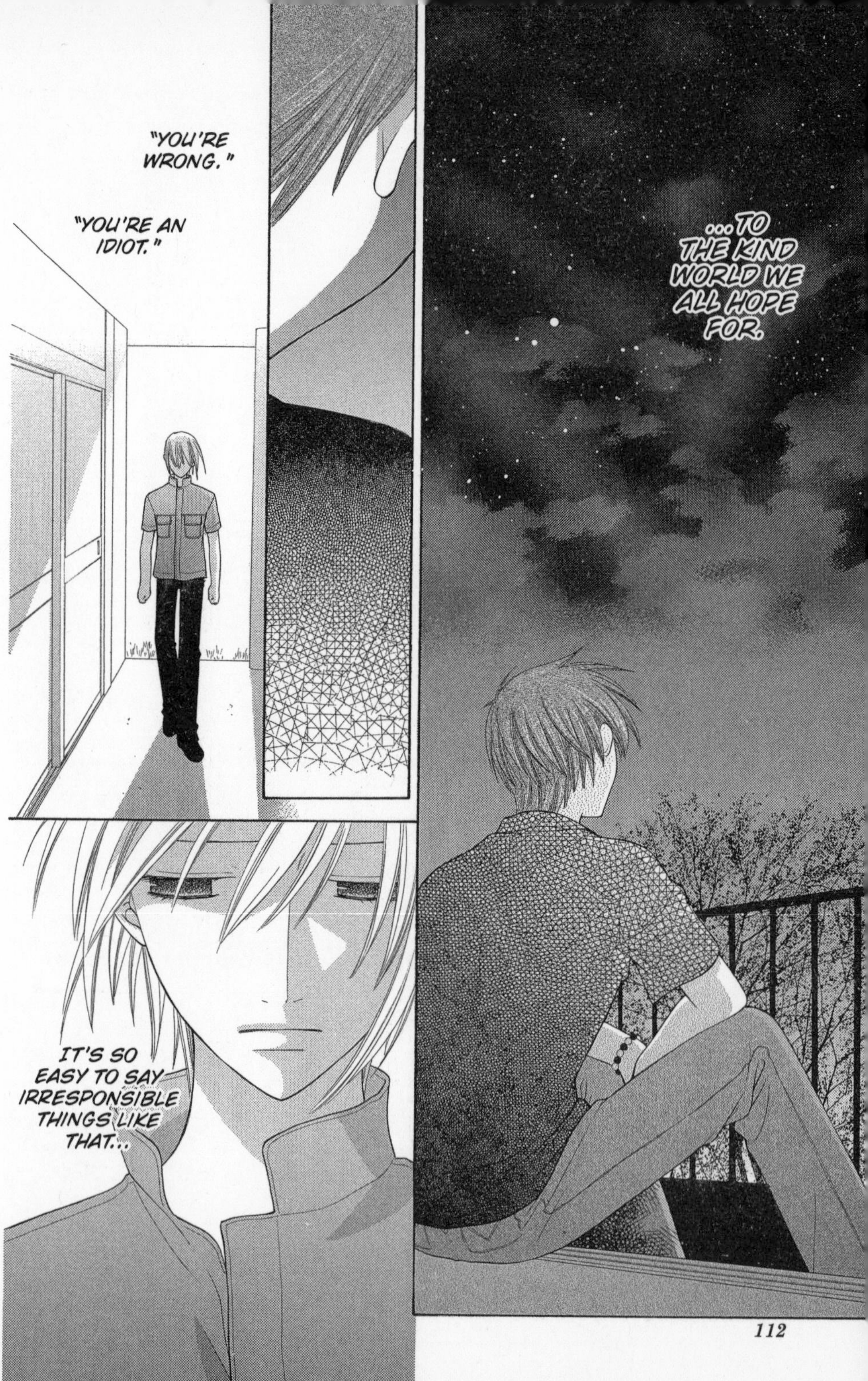
...TO THE KIND WORLD WE ALL HOPE FOR.
"YOU'RE WRONG."
"YOU'RE AN IDIOT."
IT'S SO EASY TO SAY IRRESPONSIBLE THINGS LIKE THAT...

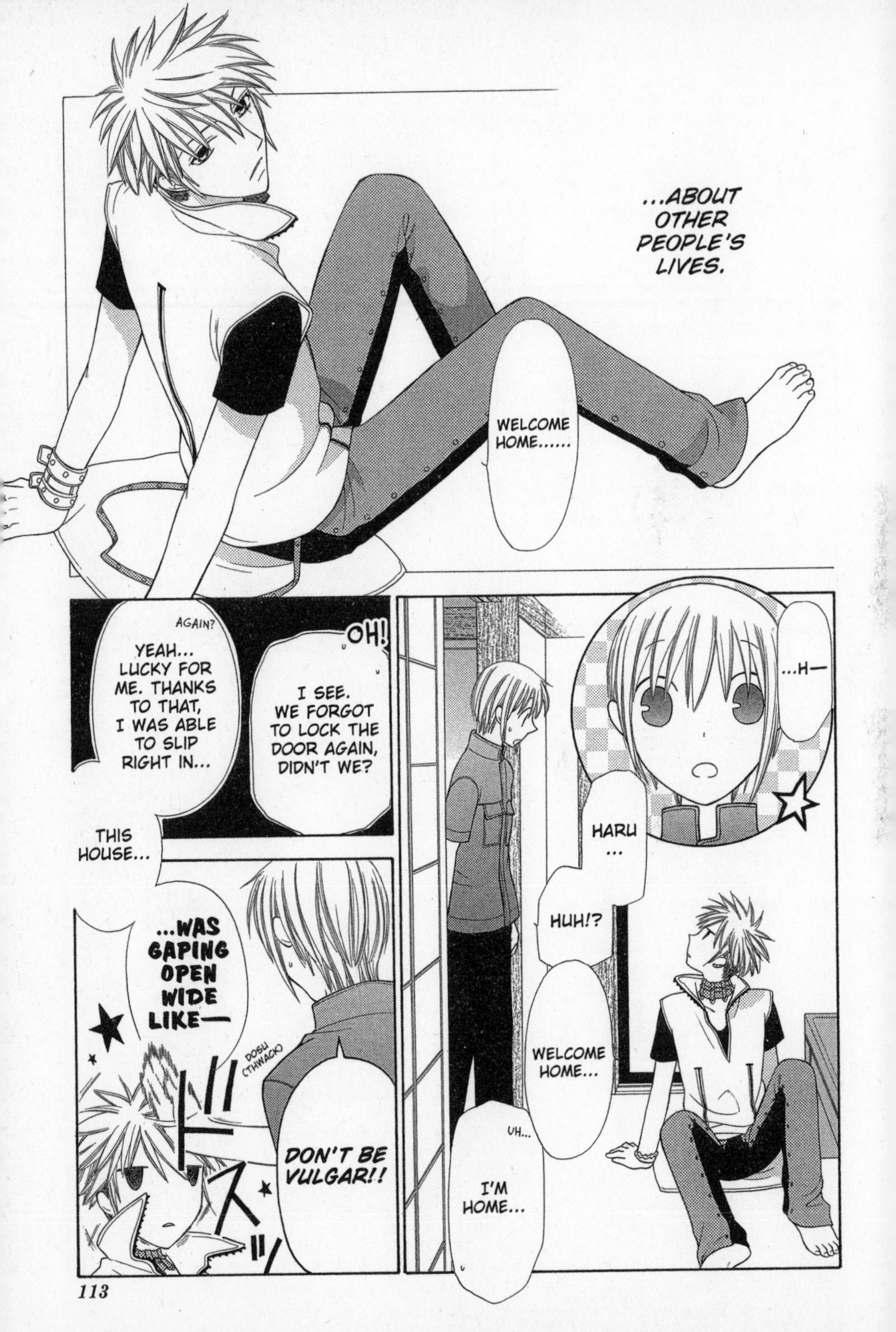
...ABOUT OTHER PEOPLE'S LIVES.
WELCOME HOME......
...H—
HARU ...
HUH!?
WELCOME HOME...
UH...
I'M HOME...
OH!
I SEE. WE FORGOT TO LOCK THE DOOR AGAIN, DIDN'T WE?
AGAIN?
YEAH... LUCKY FOR ME. THANKS TO THAT, I WAS ABLE TO SLIP RIGHT IN...
THIS HOUSE...
...WAS GAPING OPEN WIDE LIKE—
DON'T BE VULGAR!!
DOSU (THWACK)

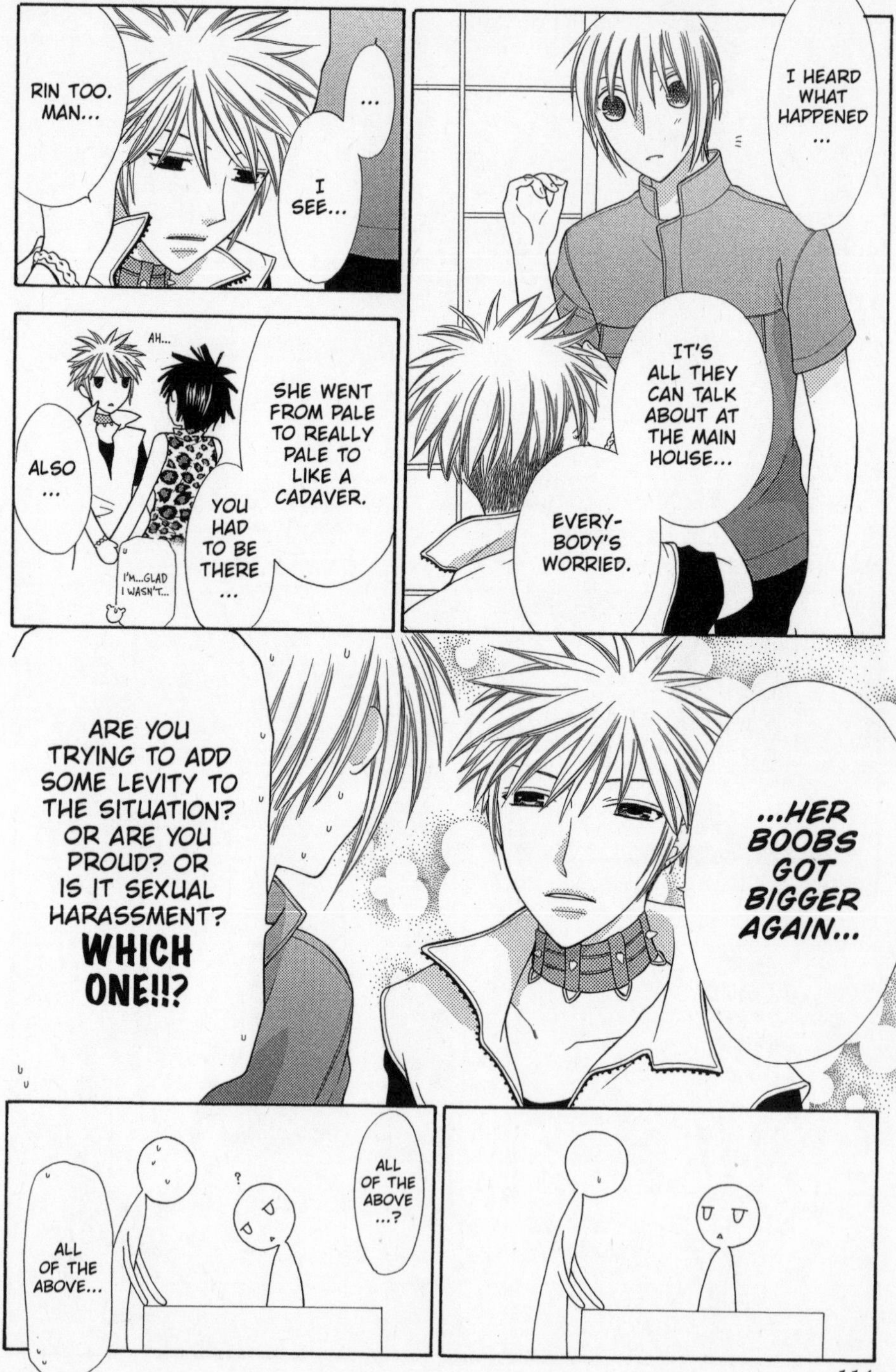
I HEARD WHAT HAPPENED ...
IT'S ALL THEY CAN TALK ABOUT AT THE MAIN HOUSE...
EVERY-BODY'S WORRIED.
...
I SEE...
RIN TOO. MAN...
SHE WENT FROM PALE TO REALLY PALE TO LIKE A CADAVER.
YOU HAD TO BE THERE ...
AH...
ALSO ...
I'M...GLAD I WASN'T...
...HER BOOBS GOT BIGGER AGAIN...
ARE YOU TRYING TO ADD SOME LEVITY TO THE SITUATION? OR ARE YOU PROUD? OR IS IT SEXUAL HARASSMENT? WHICH ONE!!?
ALL OF THE ABOVE ...?
ALL OF THE ABOVE...

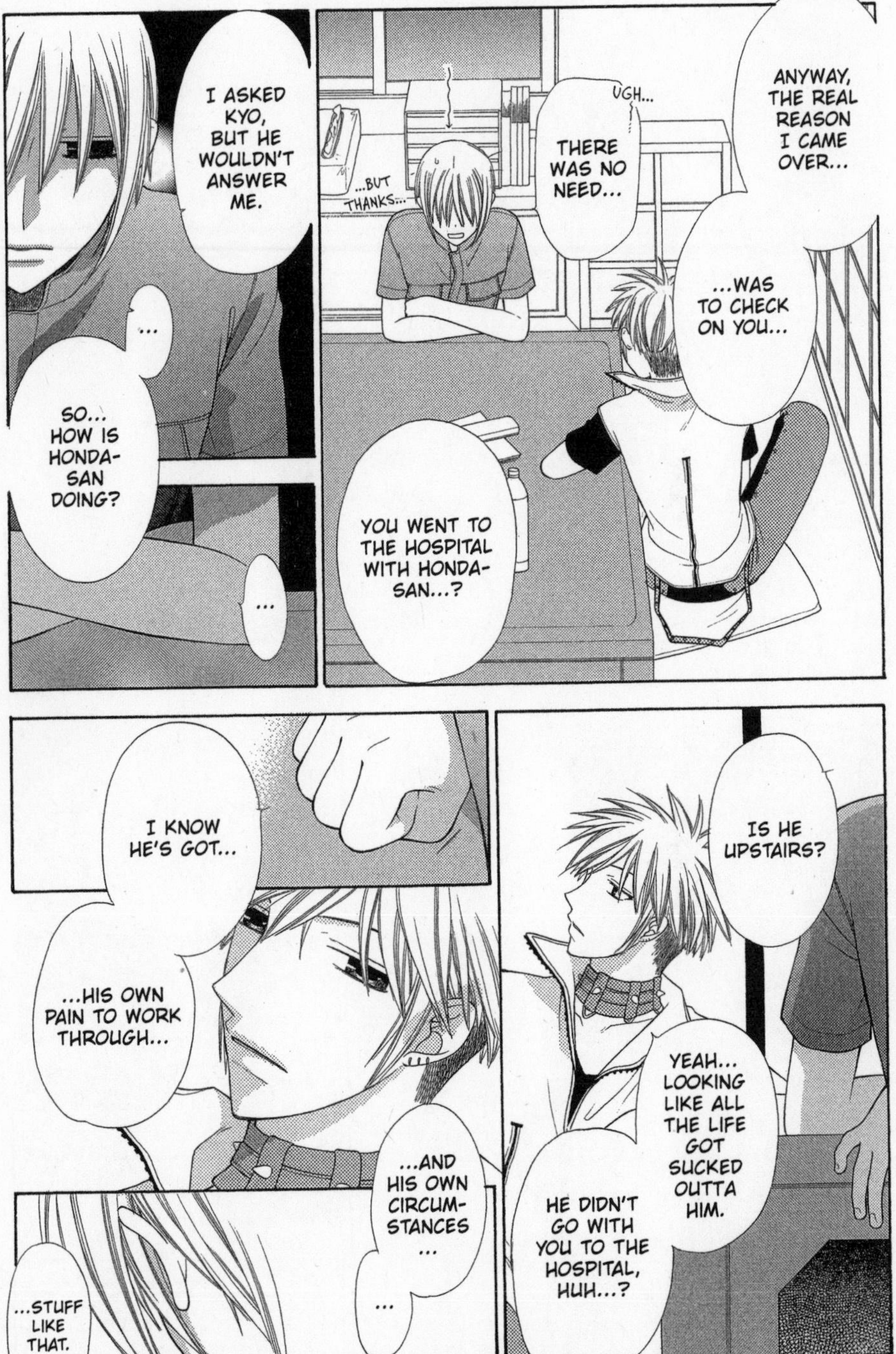
ANYWAY, THE REAL REASON I CAME OVER...
...WAS TO CHECK ON YOU...
UGH...
THERE WAS NO NEED...
...BUT THANKS...
YOU WENT TO THE HOSPITAL WITH HONDA-SAN...?
I ASKED KYO, BUT HE WOULDN'T ANSWER ME.
...
SO... HOW IS HONDA-SAN DOING?
...
IS HE UPSTAIRS?
YEAH... LOOKING LIKE ALL THE LIFE GOT SUCKED OUTTA HIM.
HE DIDN'T GO WITH YOU TO THE HOSPITAL, HUH...?
I KNOW HE'S GOT...
...HIS OWN PAIN TO WORK THROUGH...
...AND HIS OWN CIRCUM-STANCES...
...
...STUFF LIKE THAT.

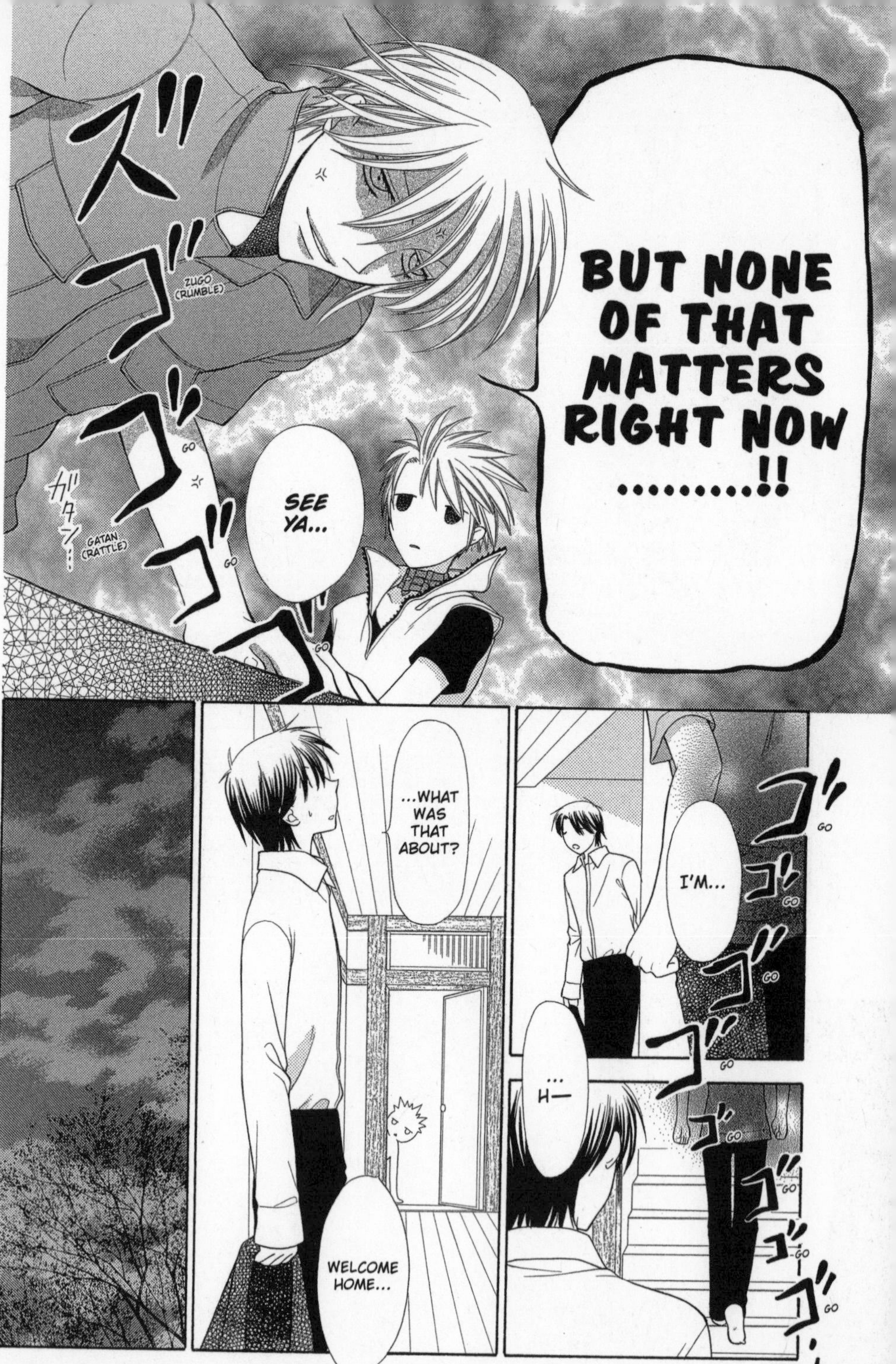
BUT NONE OF THAT MATTERS RIGHT NOW ....!!
ZUGO (RUMBLE)
GO
SEE YA...
GATAN (RATTLE)
GO
GO
GO
I'M...
GO
GO
GO
GO
GO
GO
GO
... H—
...WHAT WAS THAT ABOUT?
WELCOME HOME...

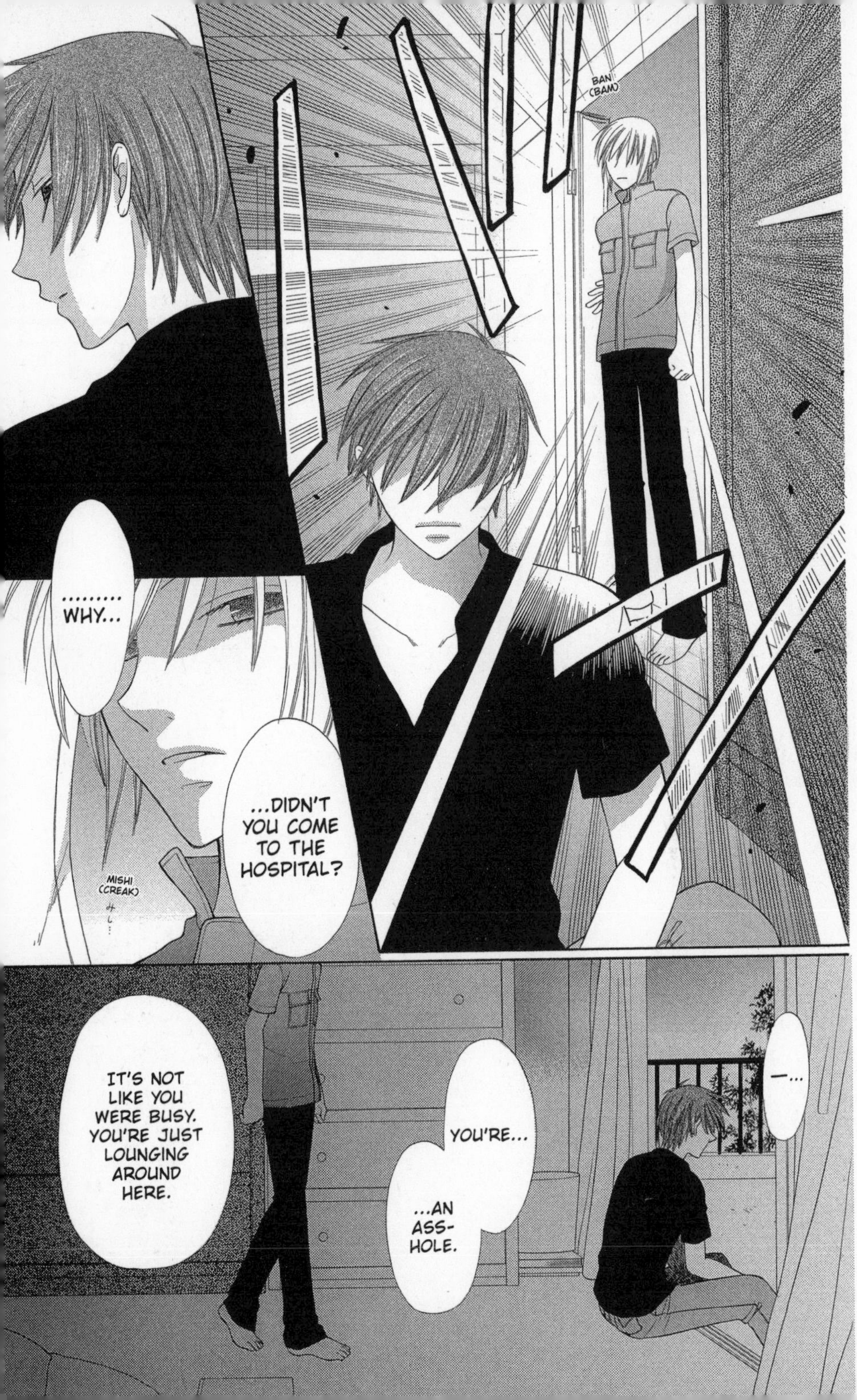
BAN (BAM)
....
WHY...
...DIDN'T YOU COME TO THE HOSPITAL?
MISHI (CREAK)
みし…
—...
YOU'RE...
...AN ASS-HOLE.
IT'S NOT LIKE YOU WERE BUSY. YOU'RE JUST LOUNGING AROUND HERE.

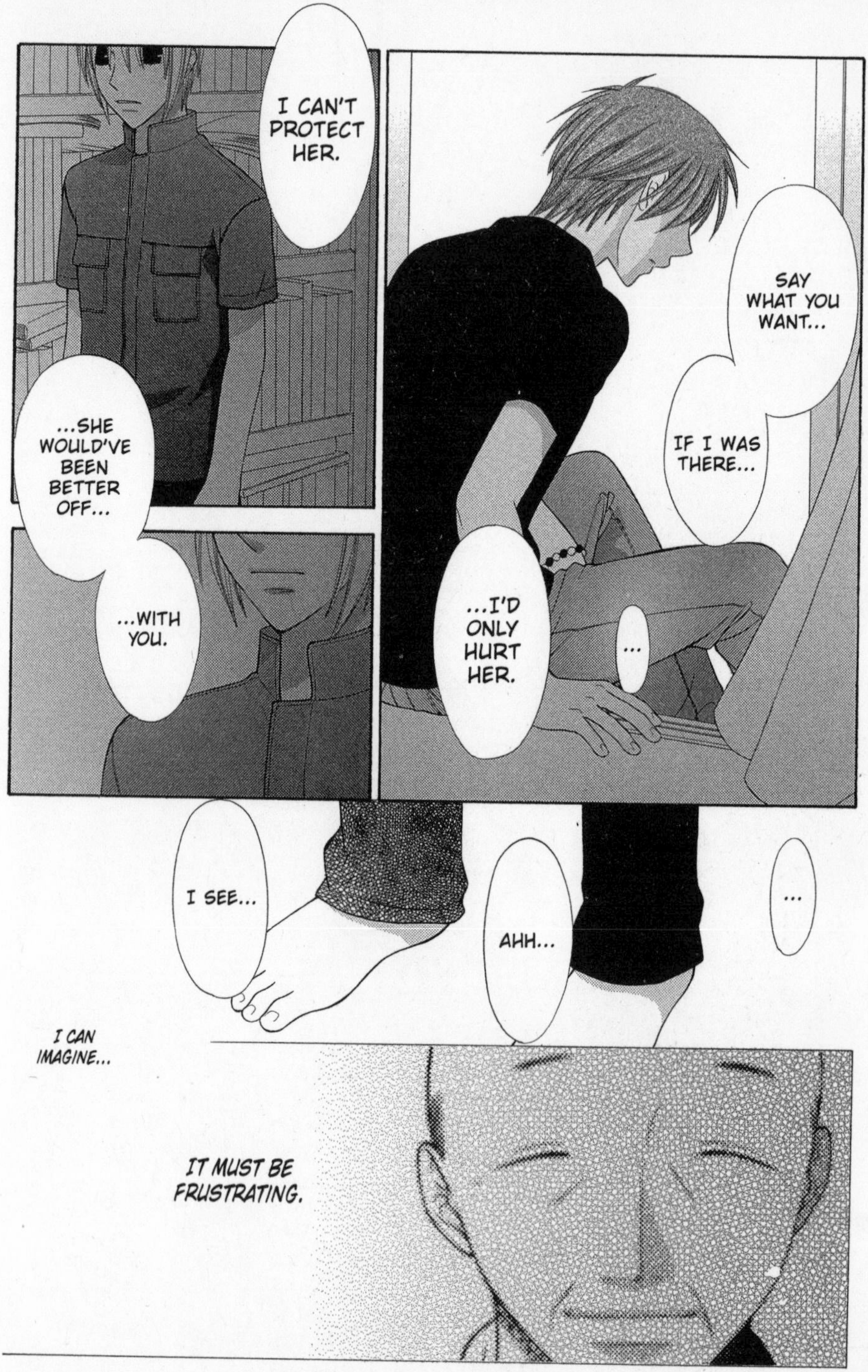
SAY WHAT YOU WANT...
IF I WAS THERE...
...I'D ONLY HURT HER.
...
I CAN'T PROTECT HER.
...SHE WOULD'VE BEEN BETTER OFF...
...WITH YOU.
...
AHH...
I SEE...
I CAN IMAGINE...
IT MUST BE FRUSTRATING.

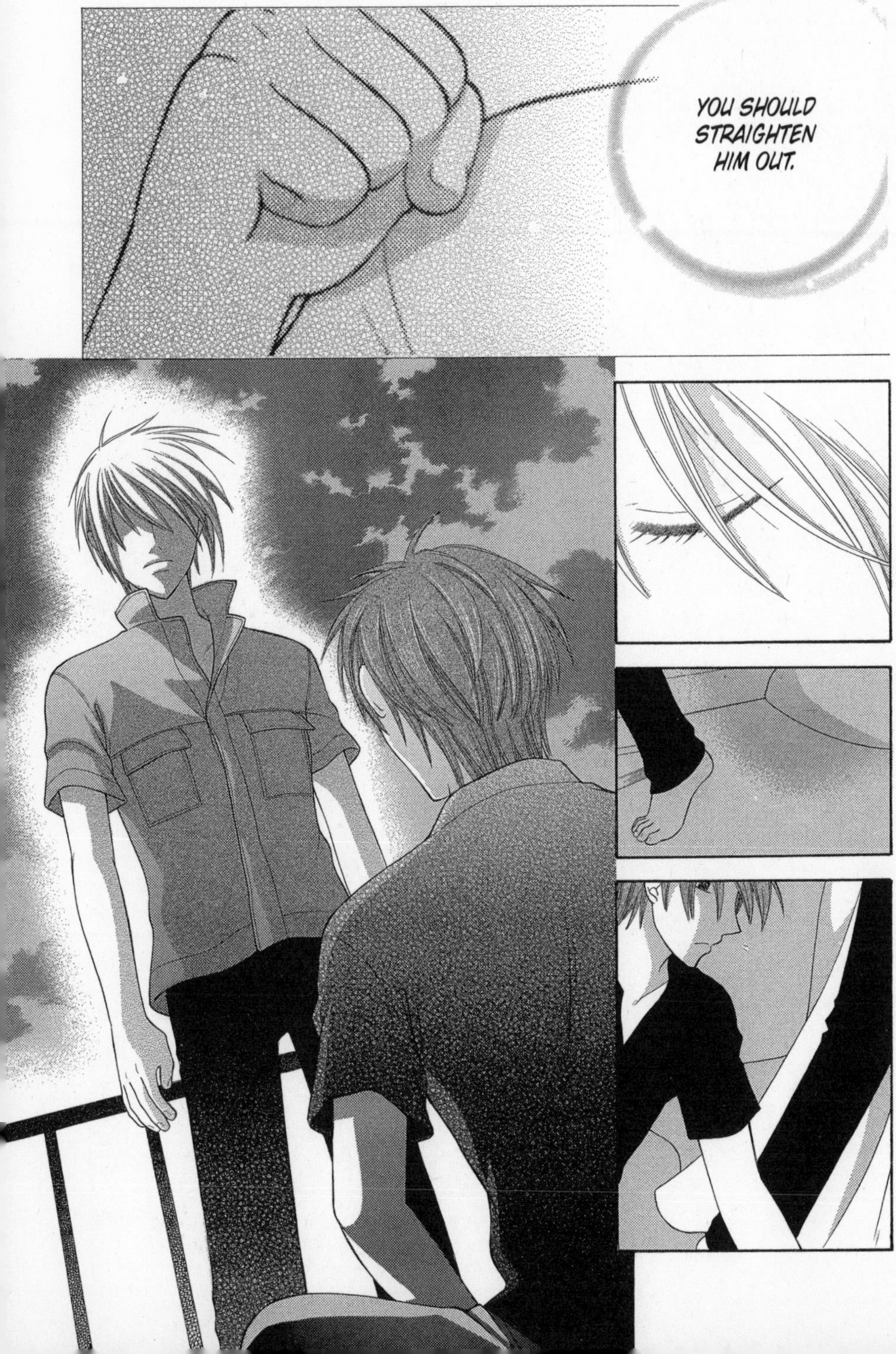
YOU SHOULD STRAIGHTEN HIM OUT.

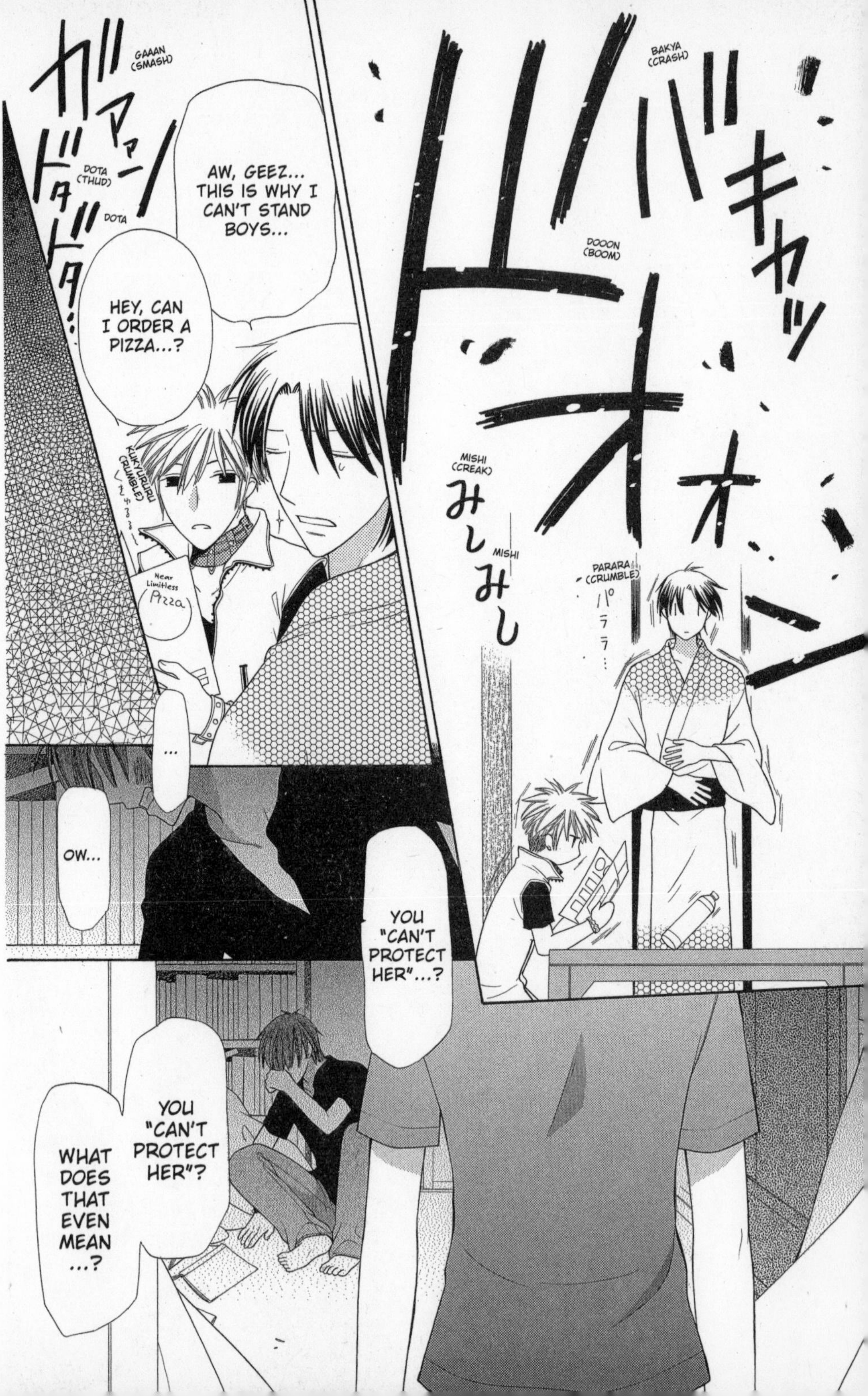
BAKYA (CRASH)
バキャッ
DOOON (BOOM)
ドオォン
MISHI (CREAK)
みし
MISHI
みし
PARARA (CRUMBLE)
パラ ラ…
GAAAN (SMASH)
ガァァーン
DOTA (THUD)
ドタ
DOTA
ドタ
AW, GEEZ... THIS IS WHY I CAN'T STAND BOYS...
HEY, CAN I ORDER A PIZZA...?
KUKYURURU (CRUMBLE)
Near Limitless Pizza
...
OW...
YOU "CAN'T PROTECT HER"...?
YOU "CAN'T PROTECT HER"?
WHAT DOES THAT EVEN MEAN ...?

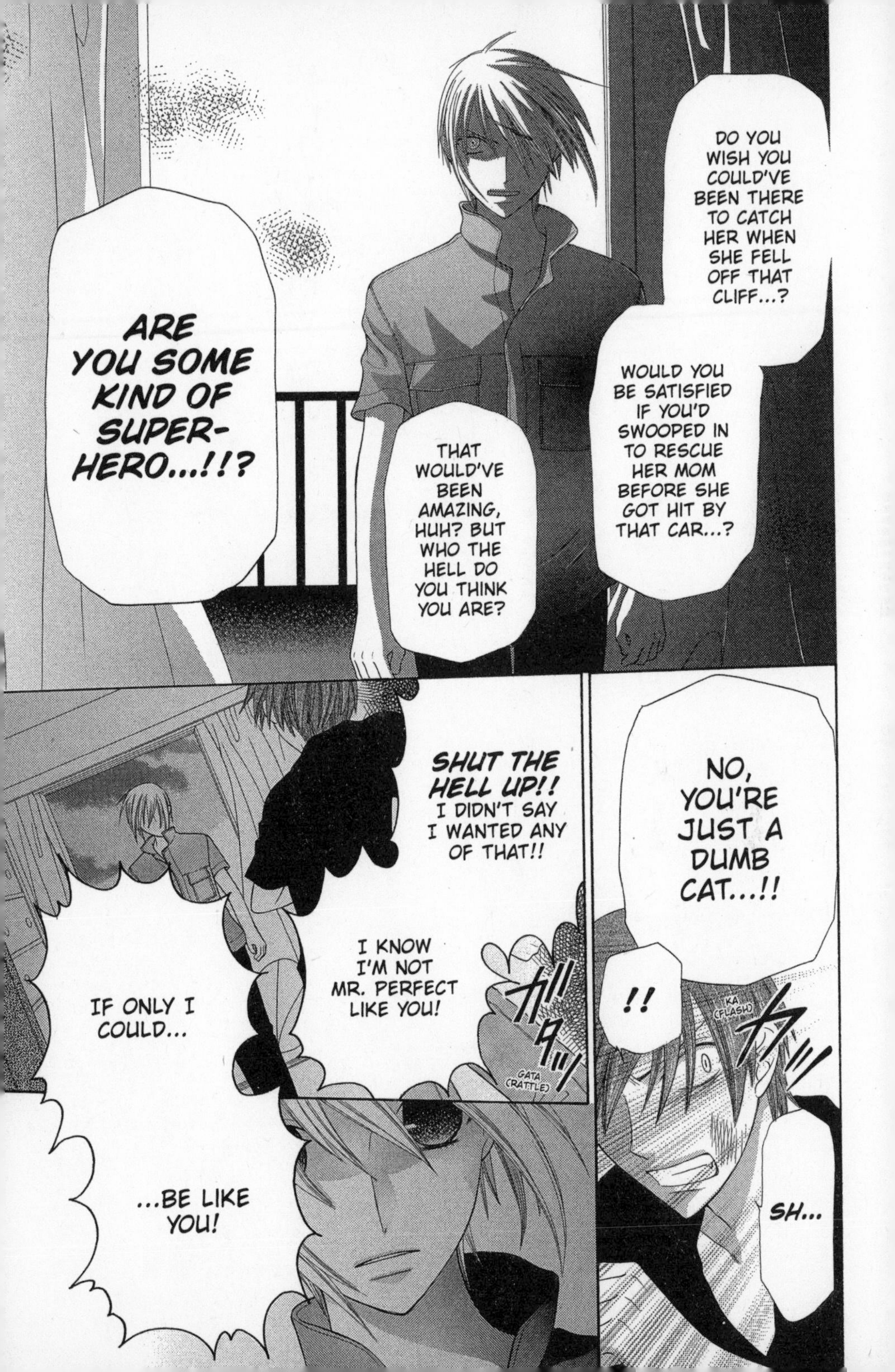
DO YOU WISH YOU COULD'VE BEEN THERE TO CATCH HER WHEN SHE FELL OFF THAT CLIFF...?
WOULD YOU BE SATISFIED IF YOU'D SWOOPED IN TO RESCUE HER MOM BEFORE SHE GOT HIT BY THAT CAR...?
THAT WOULD'VE BEEN AMAZING, HUH? BUT WHO THE HELL DO YOU THINK YOU ARE?
ARE YOU SOME KIND OF SUPER-HERO...!!?
NO, YOU'RE JUST A DUMB CAT...!!
!!
KA (FLASH)
SH...
SHUT THE HELL UP!! I DIDN'T SAY I WANTED ANY OF THAT!!
I KNOW I'M NOT MR. PERFECT LIKE YOU!
GATA (RATTLE)
IF ONLY I COULD...
...BE LIKE YOU!

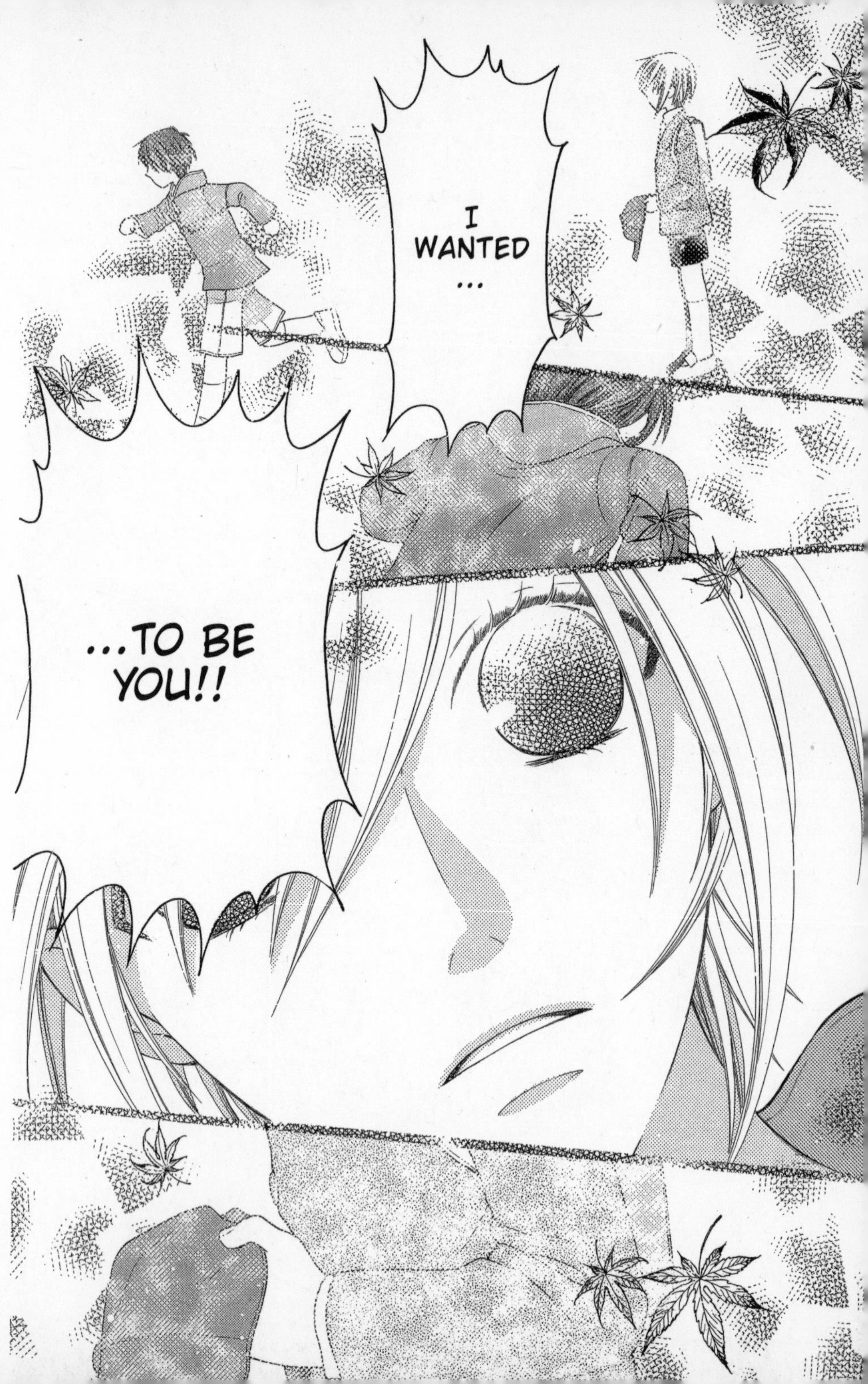
I WANTED ...
...TO BE YOU!!

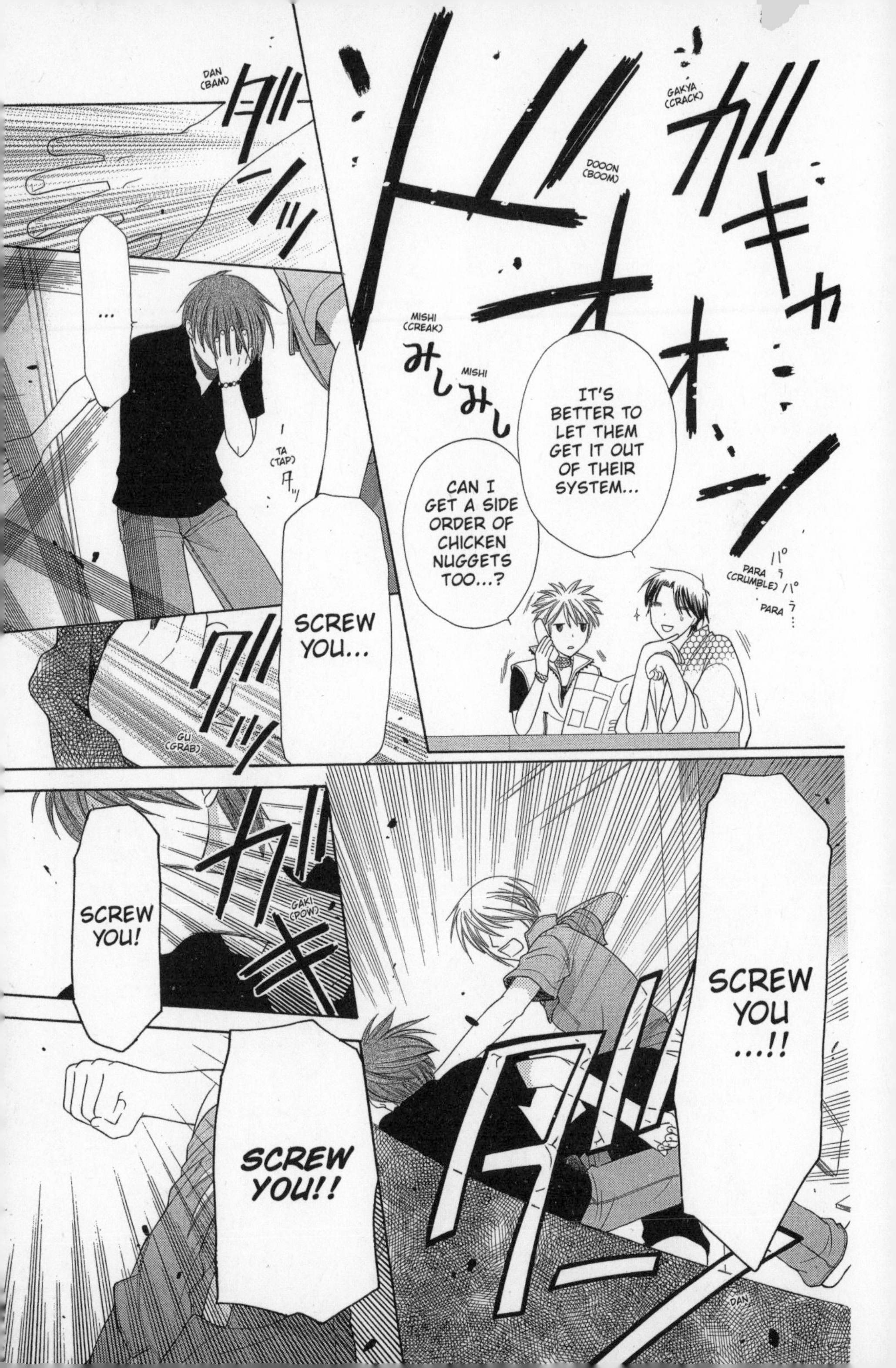
GAKYA (CRACK)
DOOON (BOOM)
MISHI (CREAK)
みしみし
MISHI
IT'S BETTER TO LET THEM GET IT OUT OF THEIR SYSTEM...
CAN I GET A SIDE ORDER OF CHICKEN NUGGETS TOO...?
PARA (CRUMBLE)
PARA
DAN (BAM)
...
TA (TAP)
GU (GRAB)
SCREW YOU...
SCREW YOU...!!
DAN
GAKI (POW)
SCREW YOU!
SCREW YOU!!

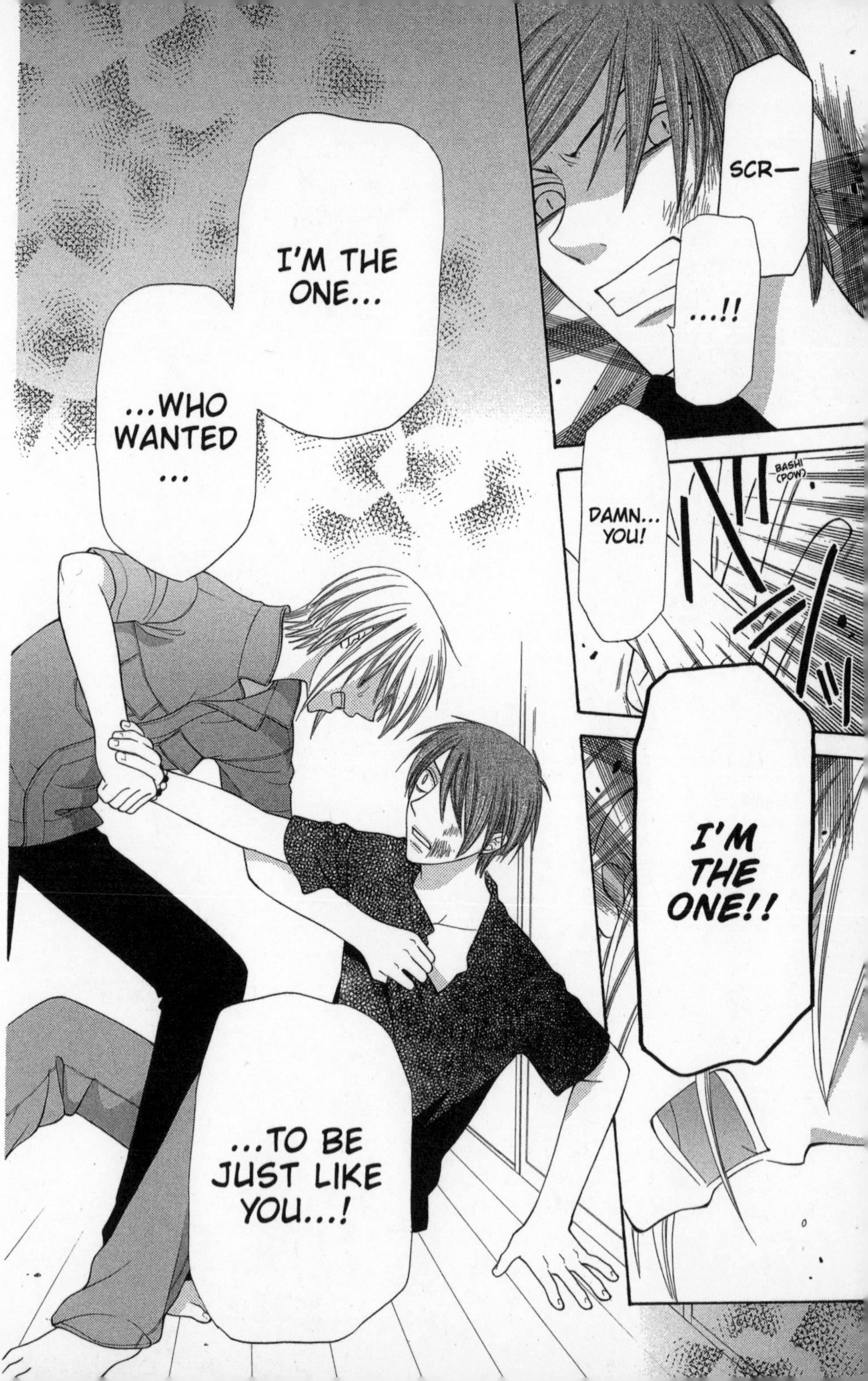
SCR—
...!!
BASHI (POW)
DAMN... YOU!
I'M THE ONE!!
I'M THE ONE...
...WHO WANTED ...
...TO BE JUST LIKE YOU...!

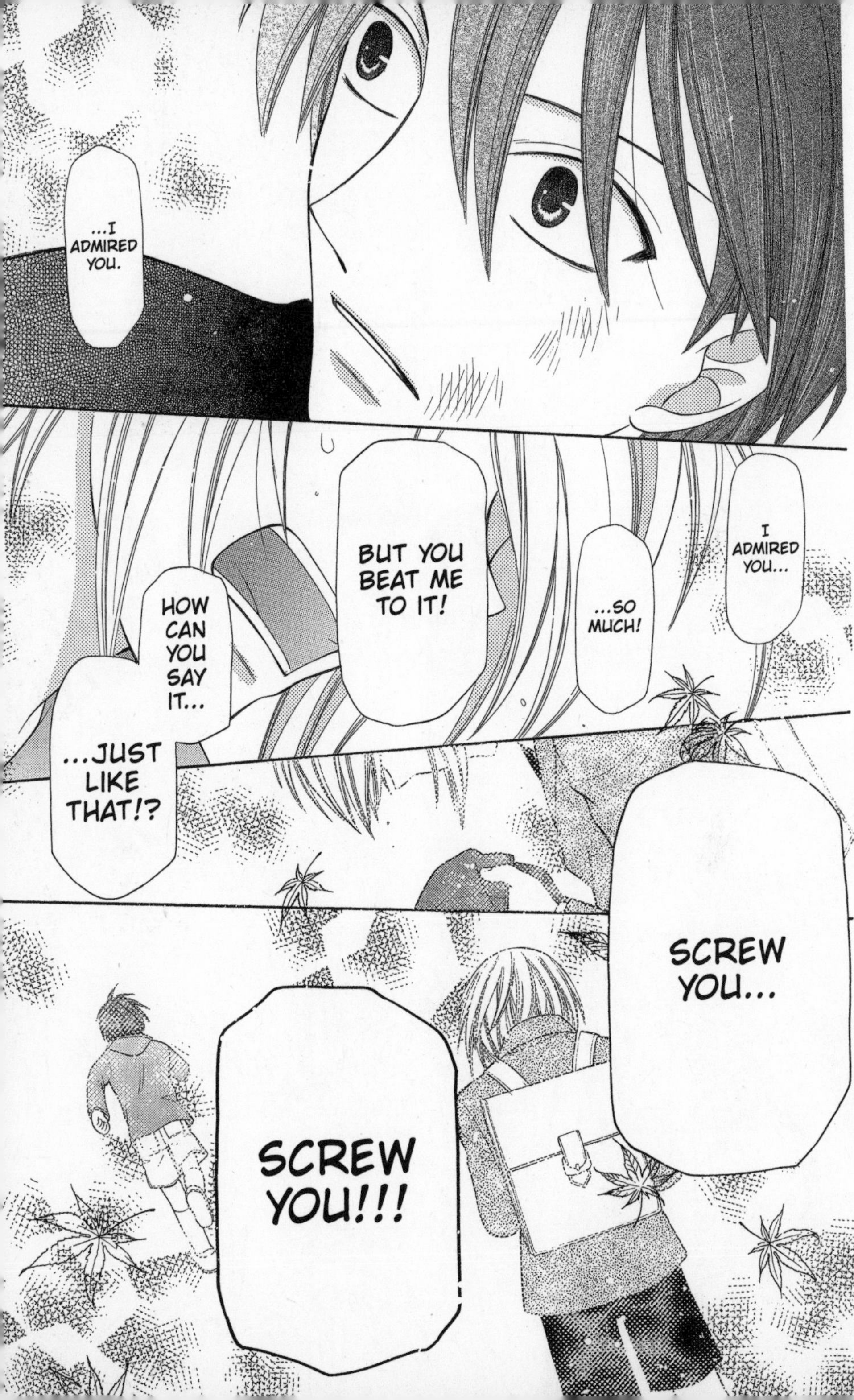
...I ADMIRED YOU.
I ADMIRED YOU...
...SO MUCH!
BUT YOU BEAT ME TO IT!
HOW CAN YOU SAY IT...
...JUST LIKE THAT!?
SCREW YOU...
SCREW YOU!!!

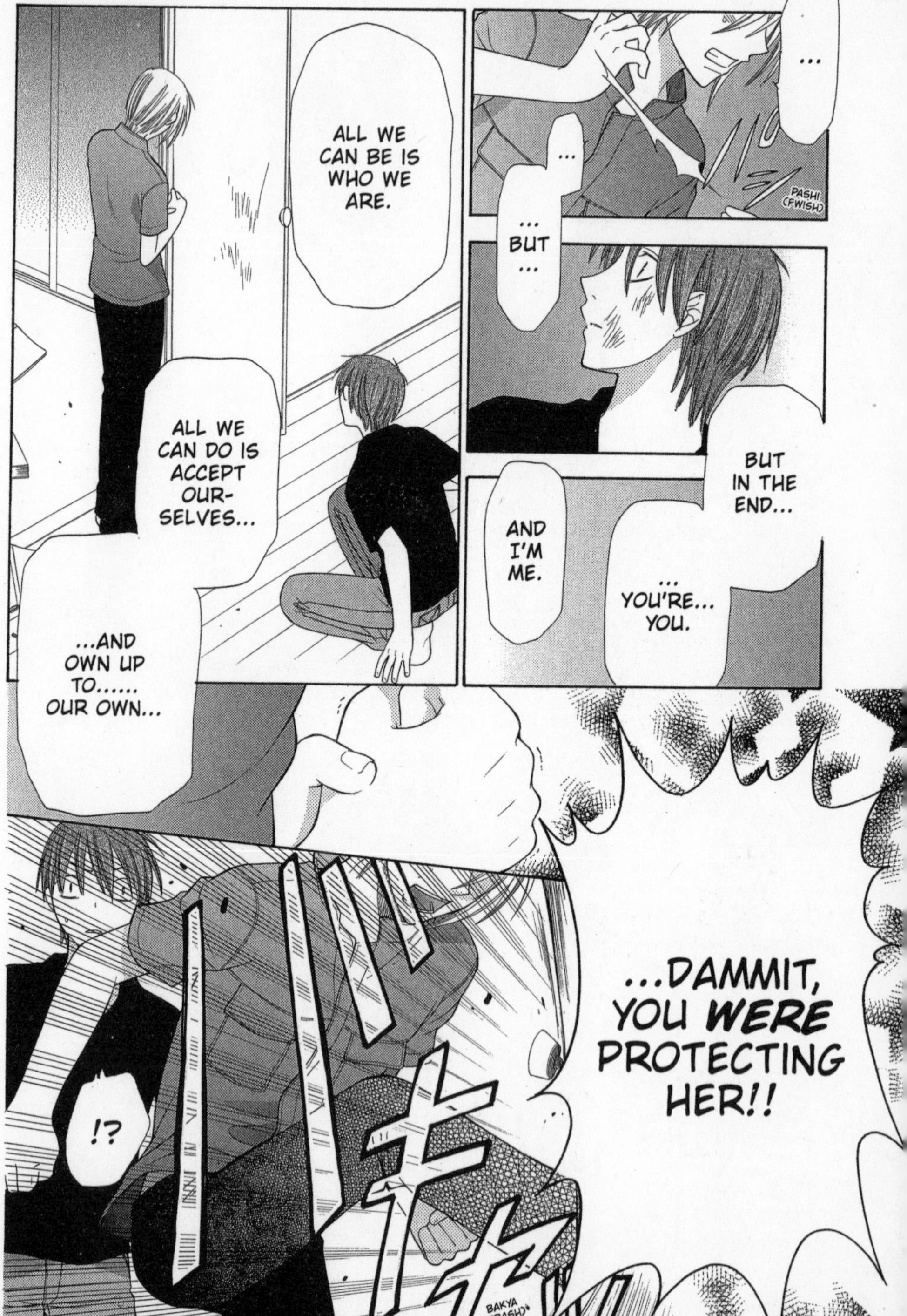
...
...
PASHI (FWISH)
... BUT ...
BUT IN THE END...
... YOU'RE... YOU.
AND I'M ME.
ALL WE CAN BE IS WHO WE ARE.
ALL WE CAN DO IS ACCEPT OUR-SELVES...
...AND OWN UP TO...... OUR OWN...
...DAMMIT, YOU *WERE* PROTECTING HER!!
!?
BAKYA (CRASH)

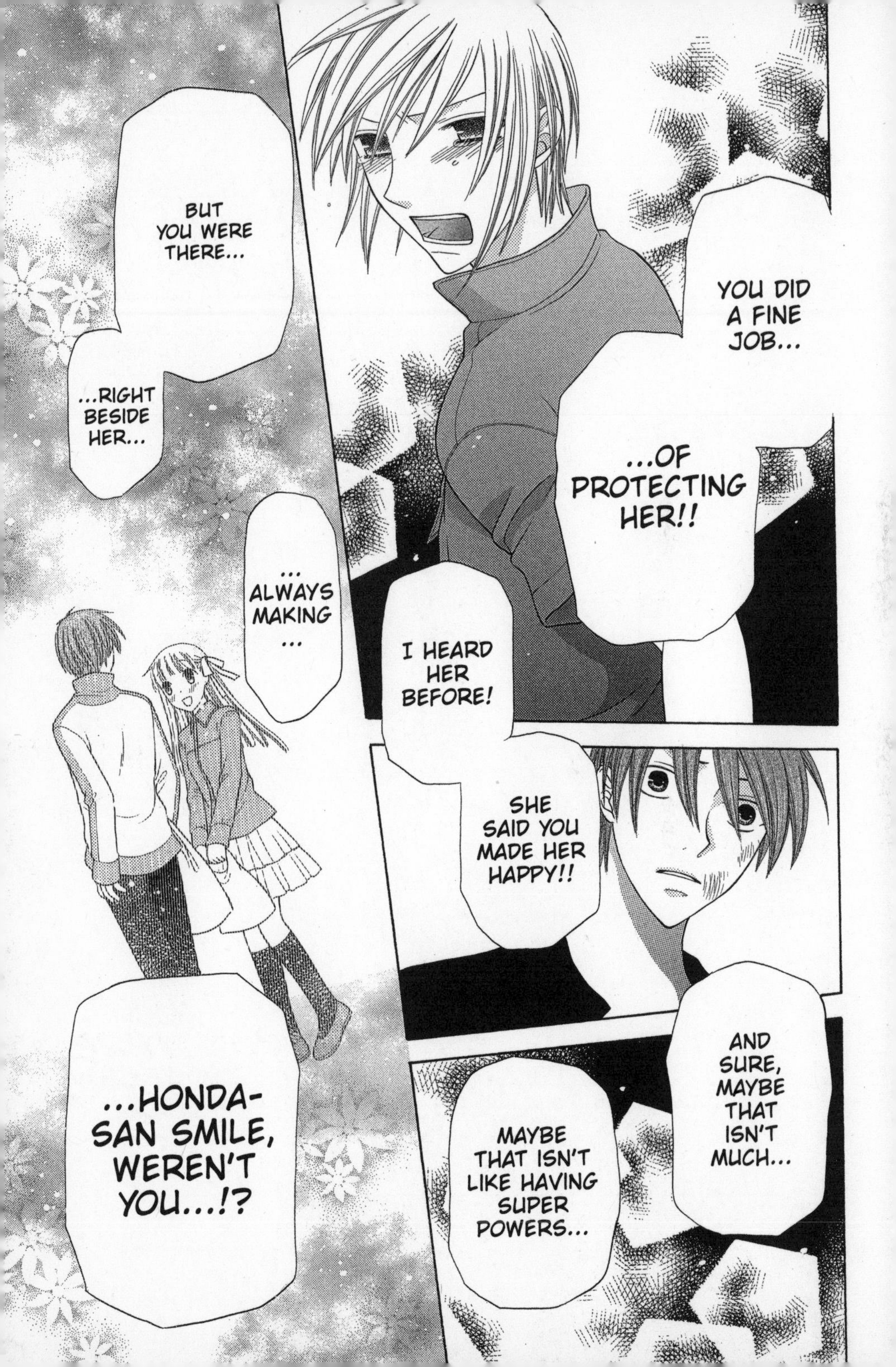
YOU DID A FINE JOB...
...OF PROTECTING HER!!
I HEARD HER BEFORE!
SHE SAID YOU MADE HER HAPPY!!
AND SURE, MAYBE THAT ISN'T MUCH...
MAYBE THAT ISN'T LIKE HAVING SUPER POWERS...
BUT YOU WERE THERE...
...RIGHT BESIDE HER...
...ALWAYS MAKING...
...HONDA-SAN SMILE, WEREN'T YOU...!?

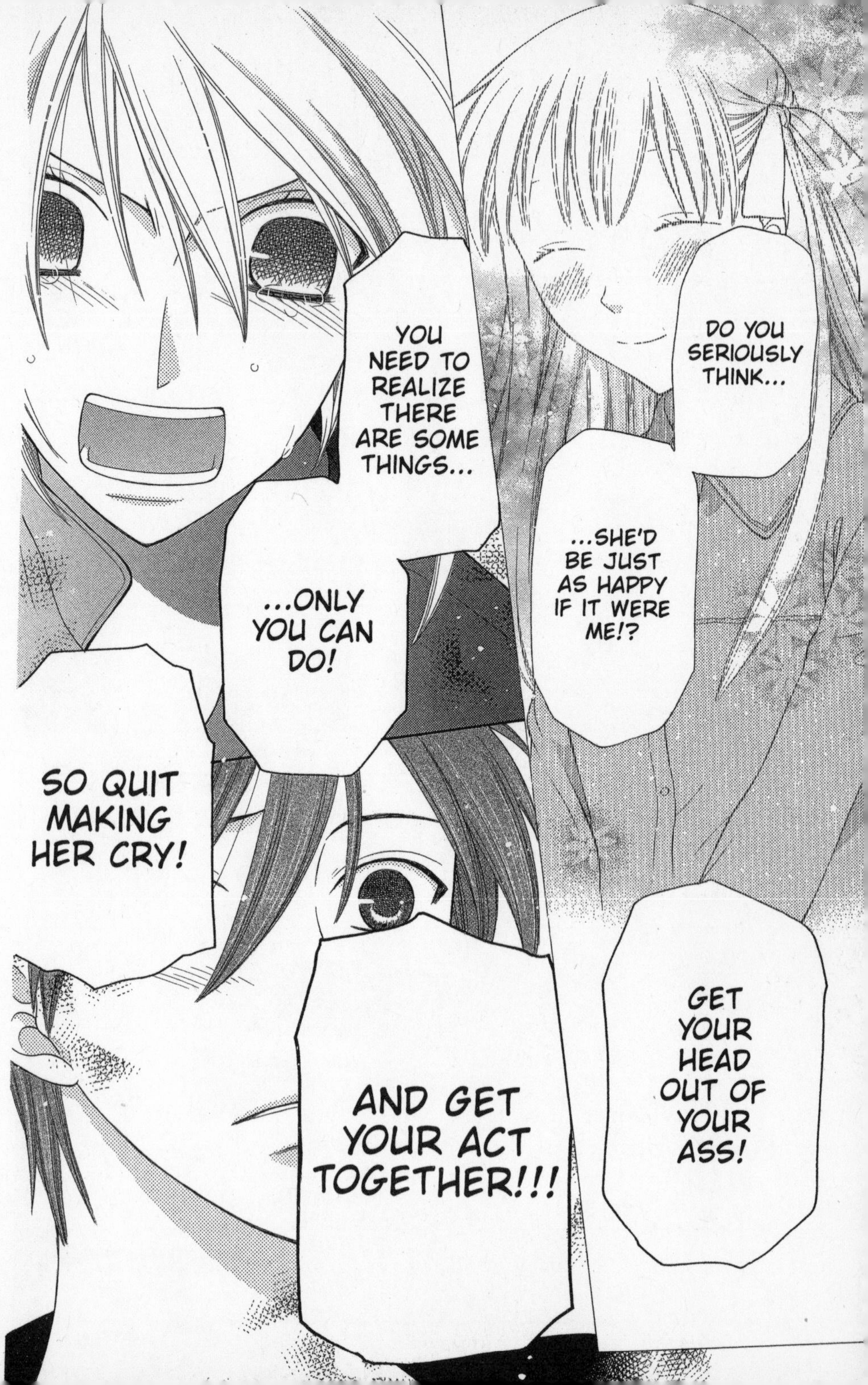
DO YOU SERIOUSLY THINK...
...SHE'D BE JUST AS HAPPY IF IT WERE ME!?
YOU NEED TO REALIZE THERE ARE SOME THINGS...
...ONLY YOU CAN DO!
SO QUIT MAKING HER CRY!
AND GET YOUR ACT TOGETHER!!!
GET YOUR HEAD OUT OF YOUR ASS!

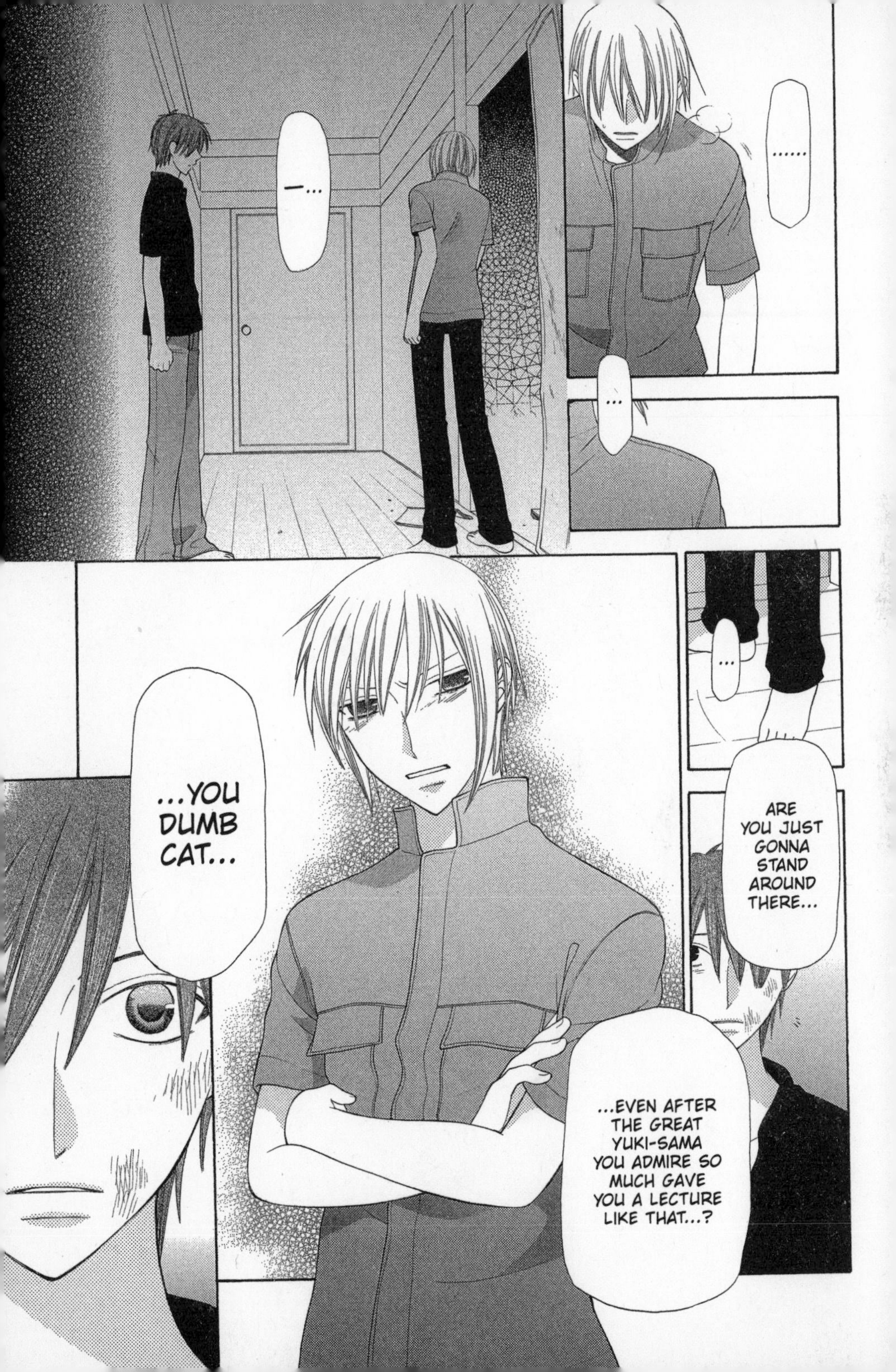
......
...
—...
...
ARE YOU JUST GONNA STAND AROUND THERE...
...EVEN AFTER THE GREAT YUKI-SAMA YOU ADMIRE SO MUCH GAVE YOU A LECTURE LIKE THAT...?
...YOU DUMB CAT...

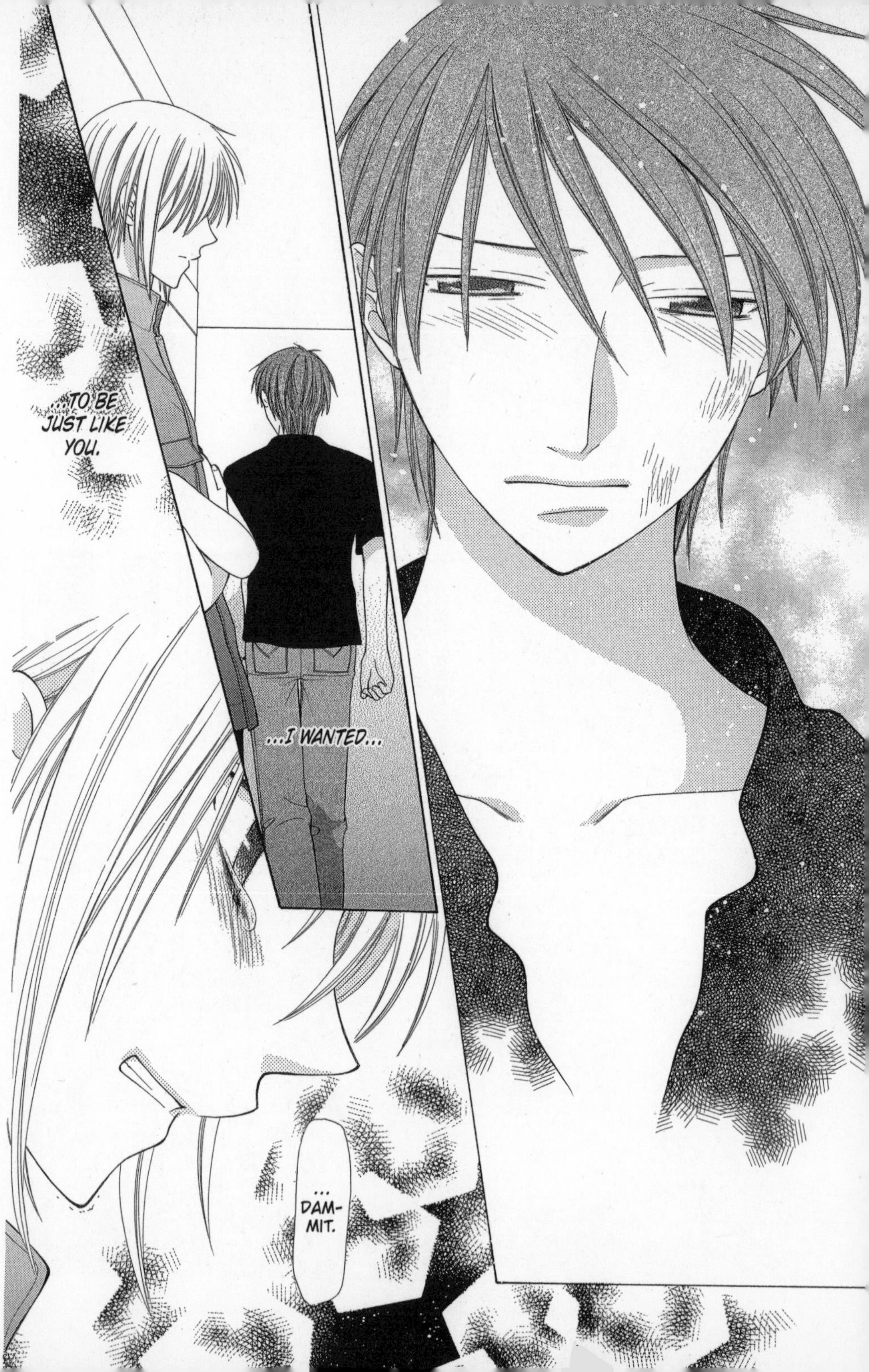
...I WANTED...
...TO BE JUST LIKE YOU.
... DAM-MIT.

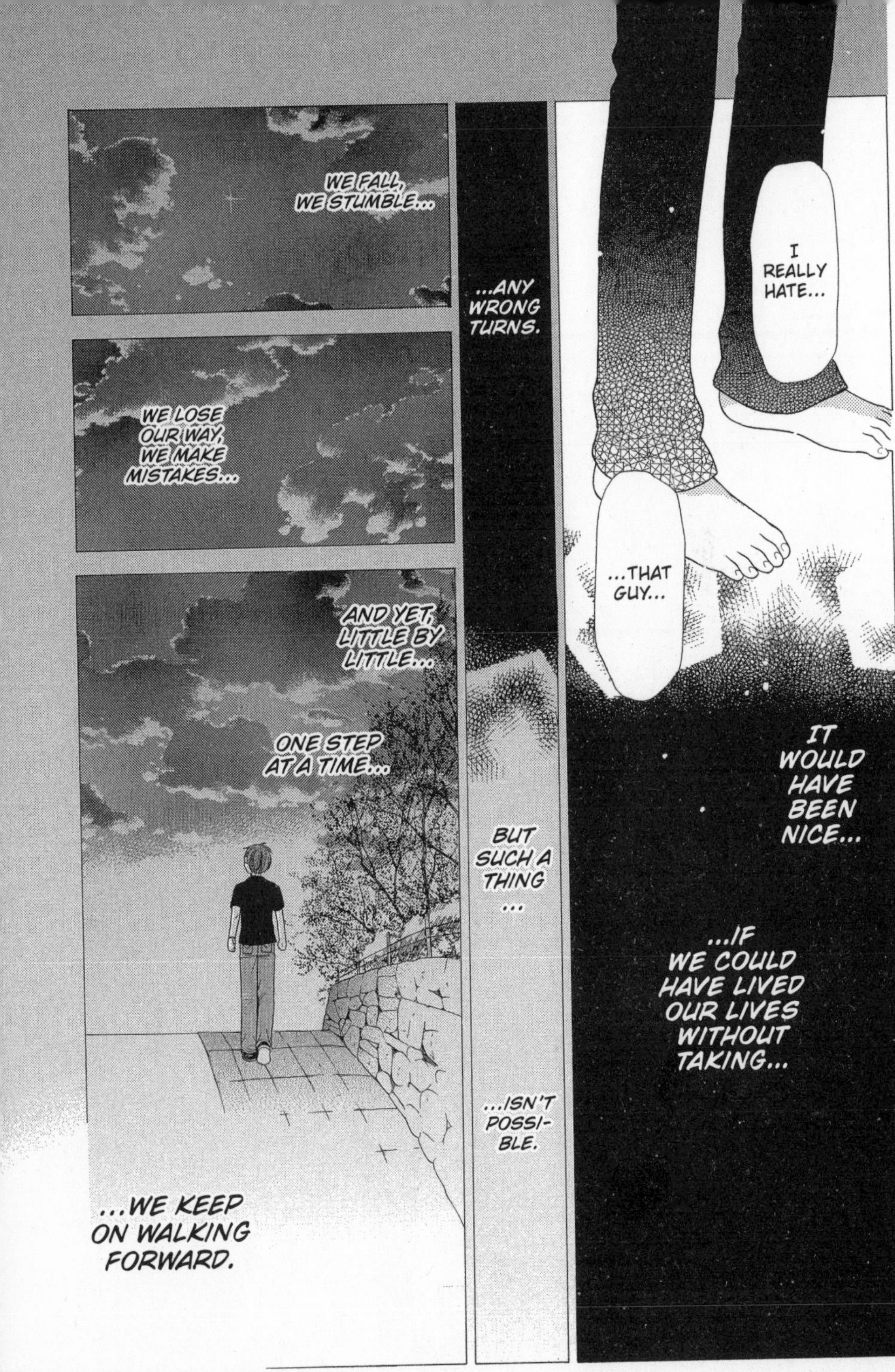
I REALLY HATE...
...THAT GUY...
IT WOULD HAVE BEEN NICE...
...IF WE COULD HAVE LIVED OUR LIVES WITHOUT TAKING...
...ANY WRONG TURNS.
BUT SUCH A THING...
...ISN'T POSSI-BLE.
WE FALL, WE STUMBLE...
WE LOSE OUR WAY, WE MAKE MISTAKES...
AND YET, LITTLE BY LITTLE...
ONE STEP AT A TIME...
...WE KEEP ON WALKING FORWARD.

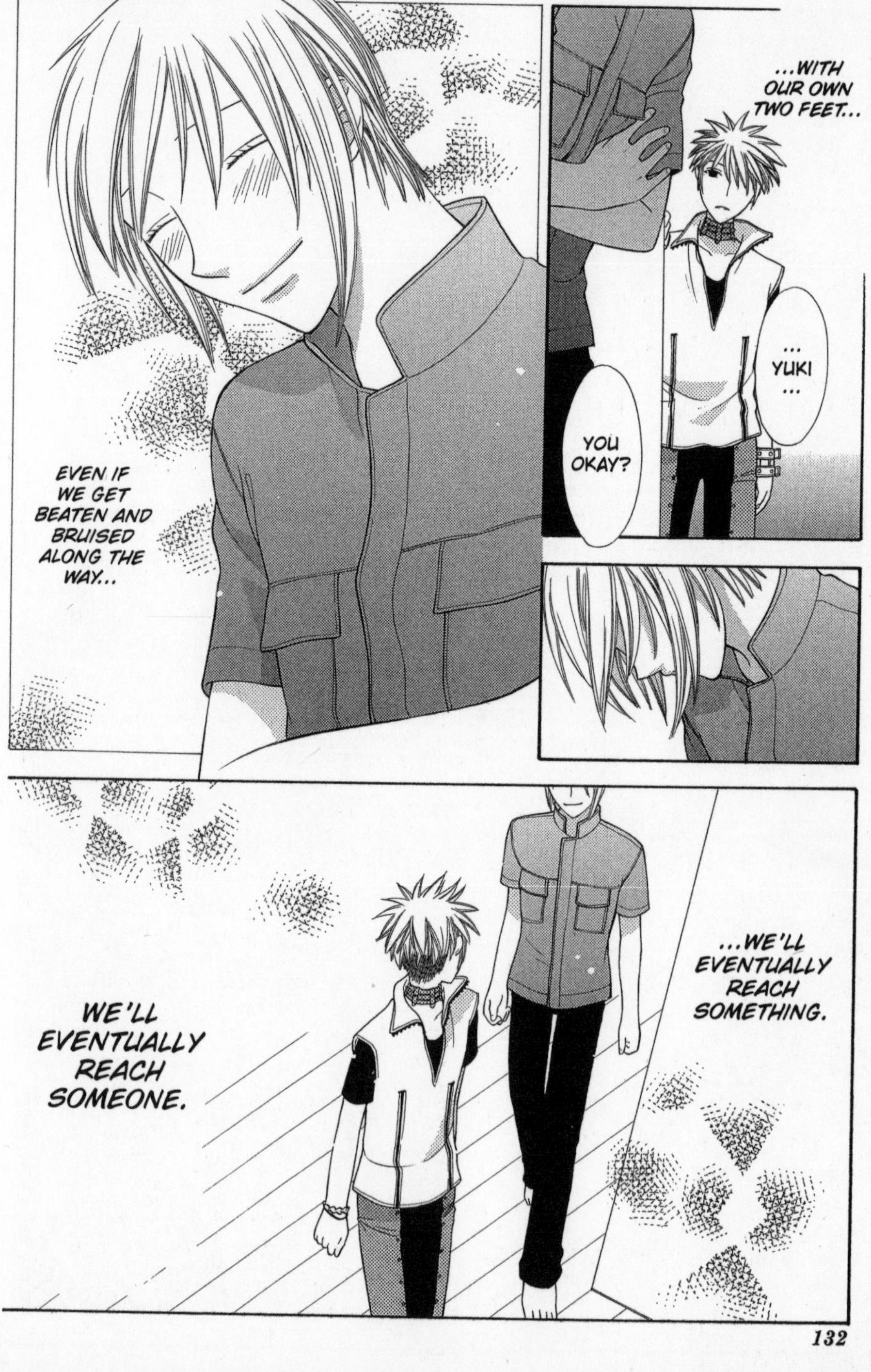
...WITH OUR OWN TWO FEET...
...YUKI...
YOU OKAY?
EVEN IF WE GET BEATEN AND BRUISED ALONG THE WAY...
...WE'LL EVENTUALLY REACH SOMETHING.
WE'LL EVENTUALLY REACH SOMEONE.

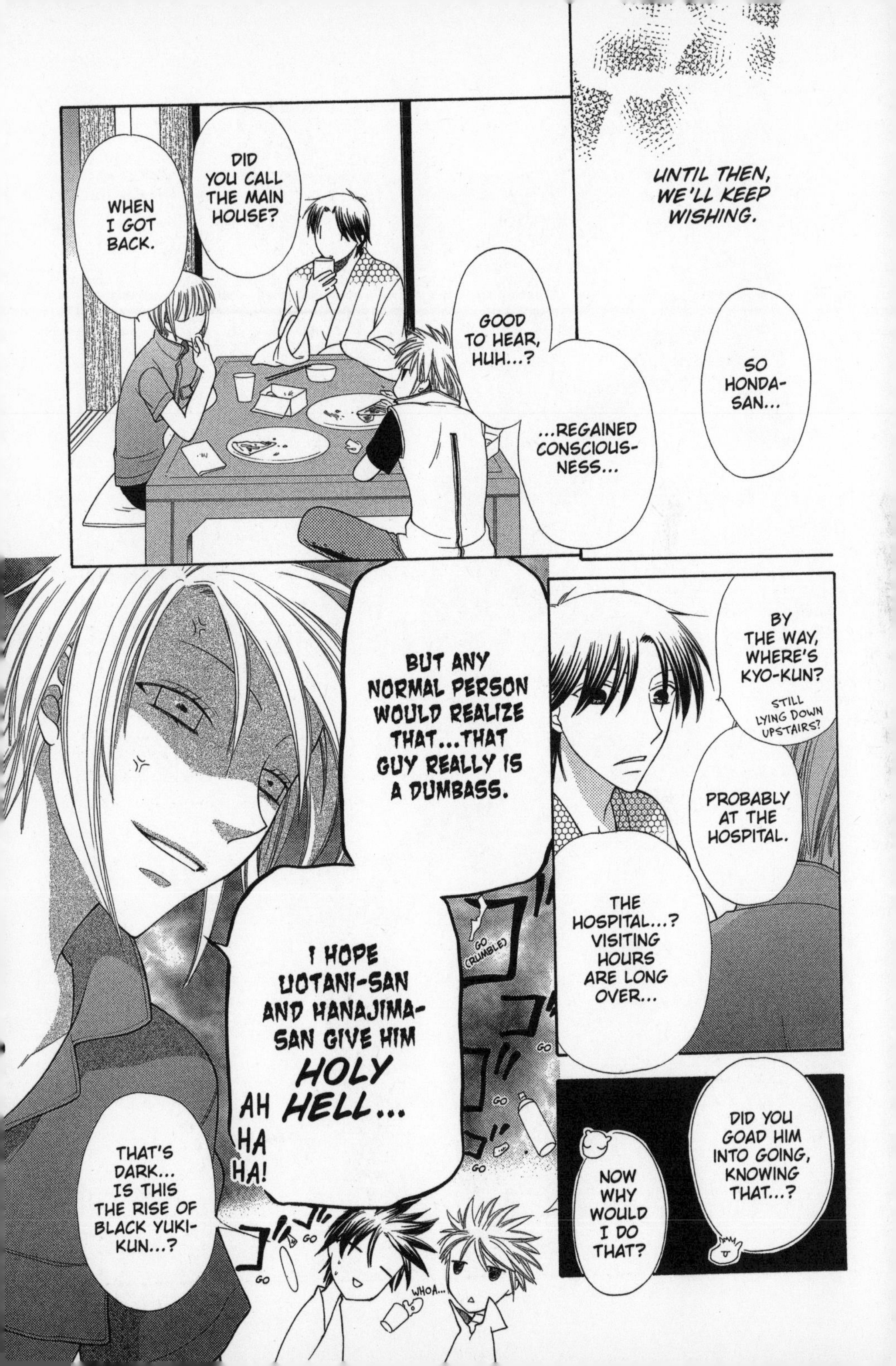
UNTIL THEN, WE'LL KEEP WISHING.
SO HONDA-SAN...
...REGAINED CONSCIOUSNESS...
GOOD TO HEAR, HUH...?
DID YOU CALL THE MAIN HOUSE?
WHEN I GOT BACK.
BY THE WAY, WHERE'S KYO-KUN?
STILL LYING DOWN UPSTAIRS?
PROBABLY AT THE HOSPITAL.
THE HOSPITAL...? VISITING HOURS ARE LONG OVER...
DID YOU GOAD HIM INTO GOING, KNOWING THAT...?
NOW WHY WOULD I DO THAT?
BUT ANY NORMAL PERSON WOULD REALIZE THAT...THAT GUY REALLY IS A DUMBASS.
I HOPE UOTANI-SAN AND HANAJIMA-SAN GIVE HIM HOLY HELL...
AH HA HA!
GO (RUMBLE)
GO
GO
GO
GO
GO
THAT'S DARK... IS THIS THE RISE OF BLACK YUKI-KUN...?
WHOA...

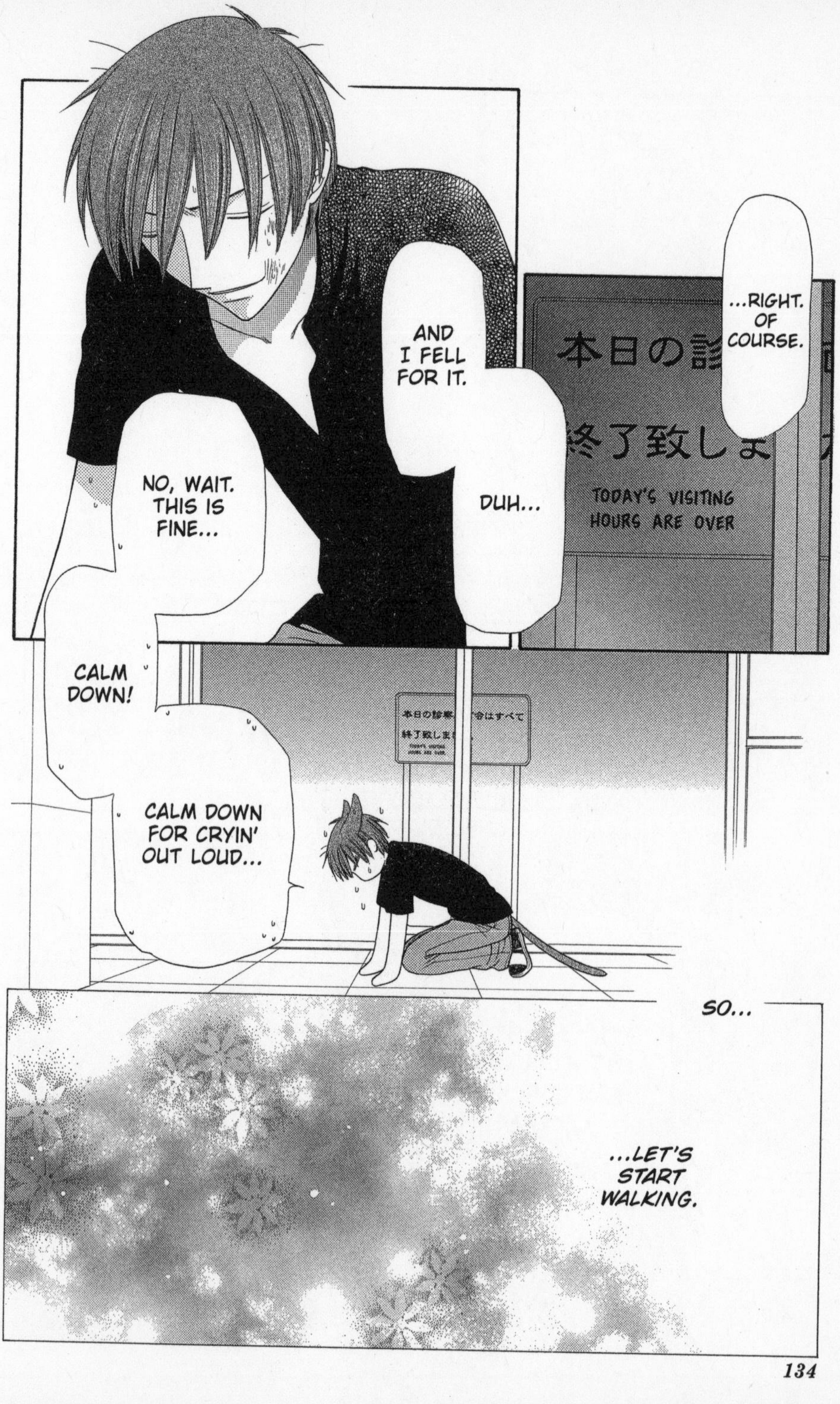
...RIGHT. OF COURSE.
TODAY'S VISITING HOURS ARE OVER
AND I FELL FOR IT.
DUH...
NO, WAIT. THIS IS FINE...
CALM DOWN!
CALM DOWN FOR CRYIN' OUT LOUD...
SO...
...LET'S START WALKING.

COLLECTOR'S EDITION

Fruits Basket

COLLECTOR'S EDITION

Fruits Basket

Chapter 124

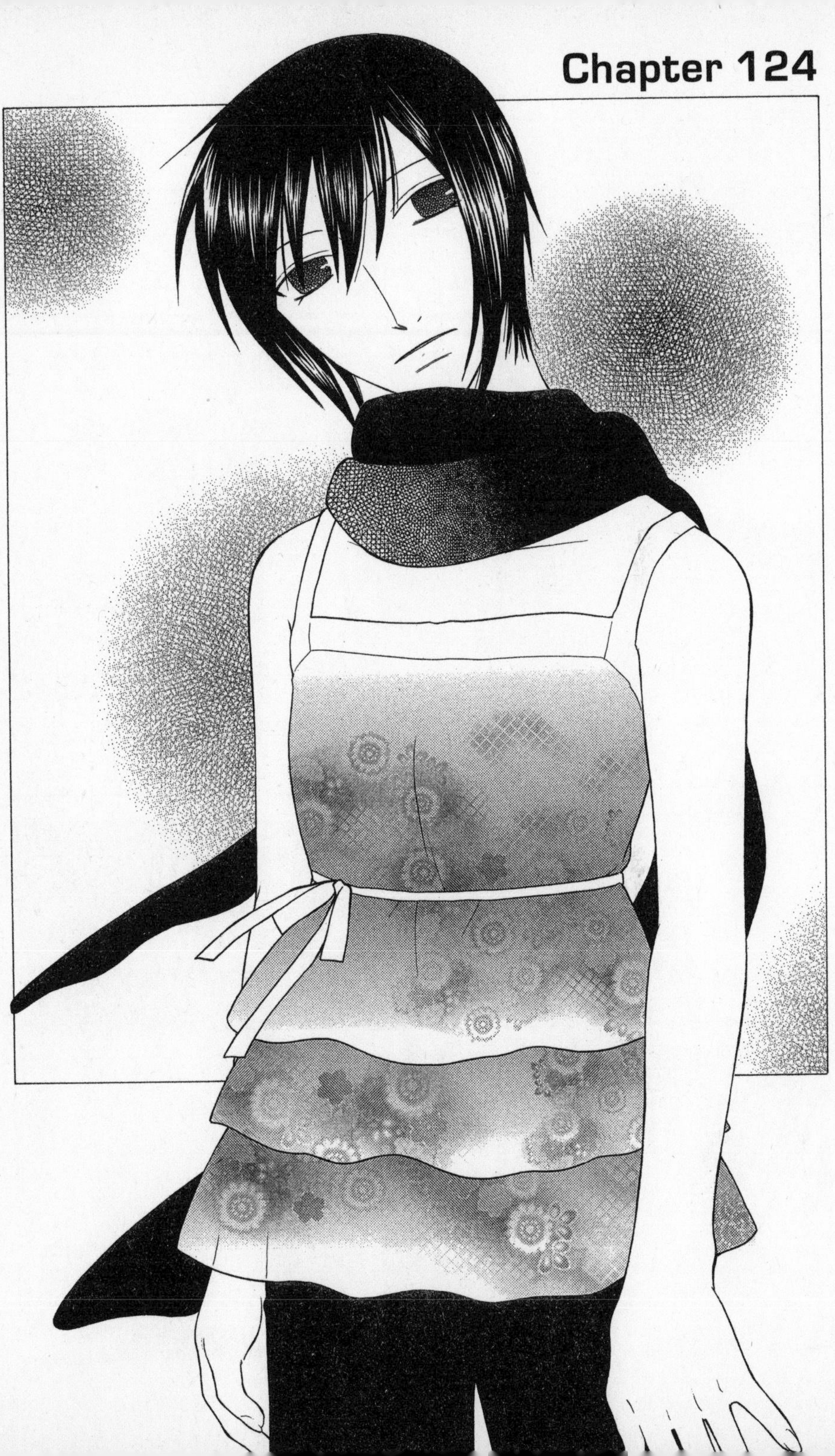

Kureno Sohma

草摩 紅野

KARA
カラ
カラ
KARA

カラ
カラ... KARA

KARA
(RATTLE)

KARA

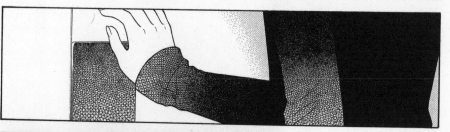

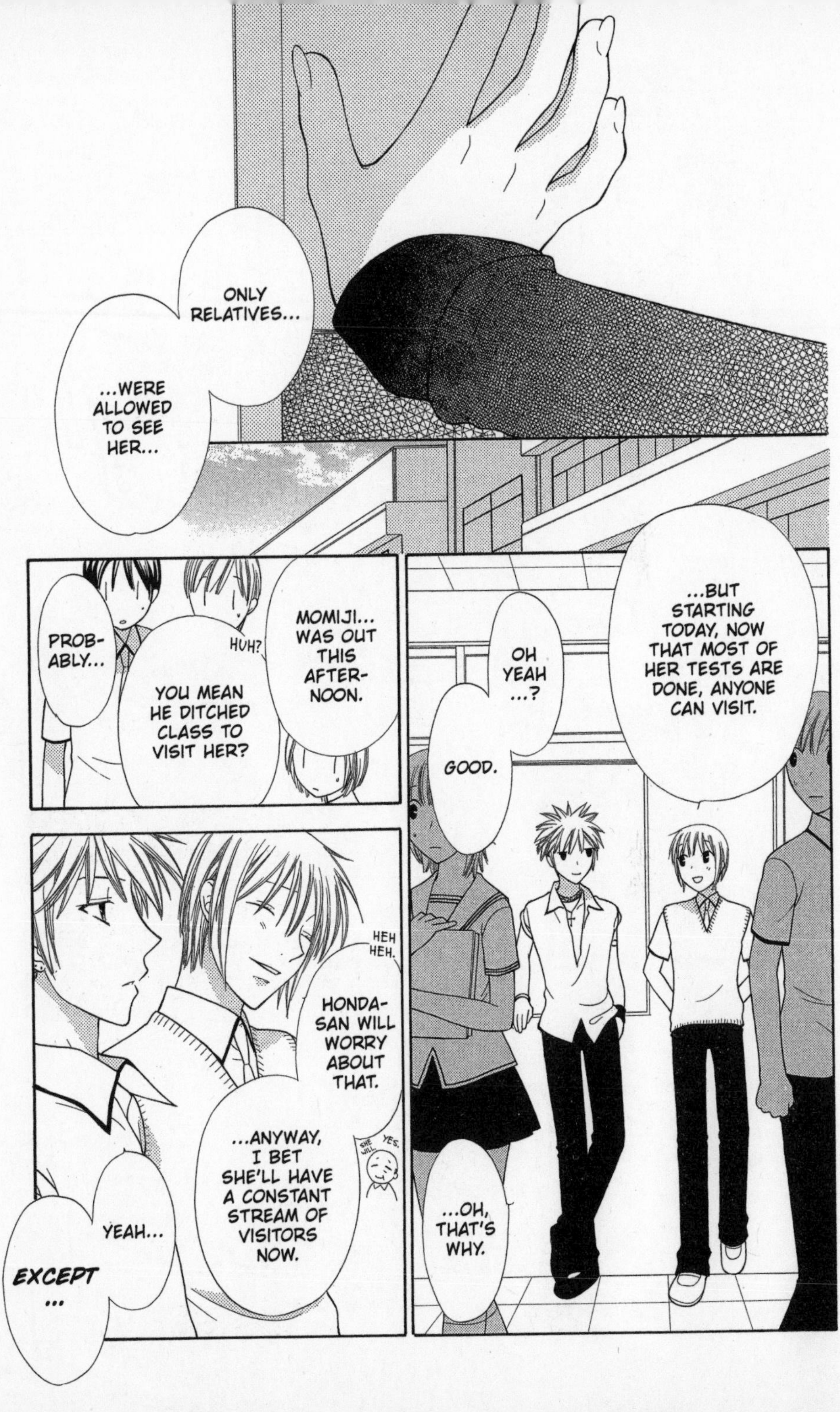
ONLY RELATIVES...
...WERE ALLOWED TO SEE HER...
...BUT STARTING TODAY, NOW THAT MOST OF HER TESTS ARE DONE, ANYONE CAN VISIT.
OH YEAH ...?
GOOD.
...OH, THAT'S WHY.
MOMIJI... WAS OUT THIS AFTERNOON.
HUH?
YOU MEAN HE DITCHED CLASS TO VISIT HER?
PROB-ABLY...
HEH HEH.
HONDA-SAN WILL WORRY ABOUT THAT.
SHE WILL.
YES.
...ANYWAY, I BET SHE'LL HAVE A CONSTANT STREAM OF VISITORS NOW.
YEAH...
EXCEPT ...

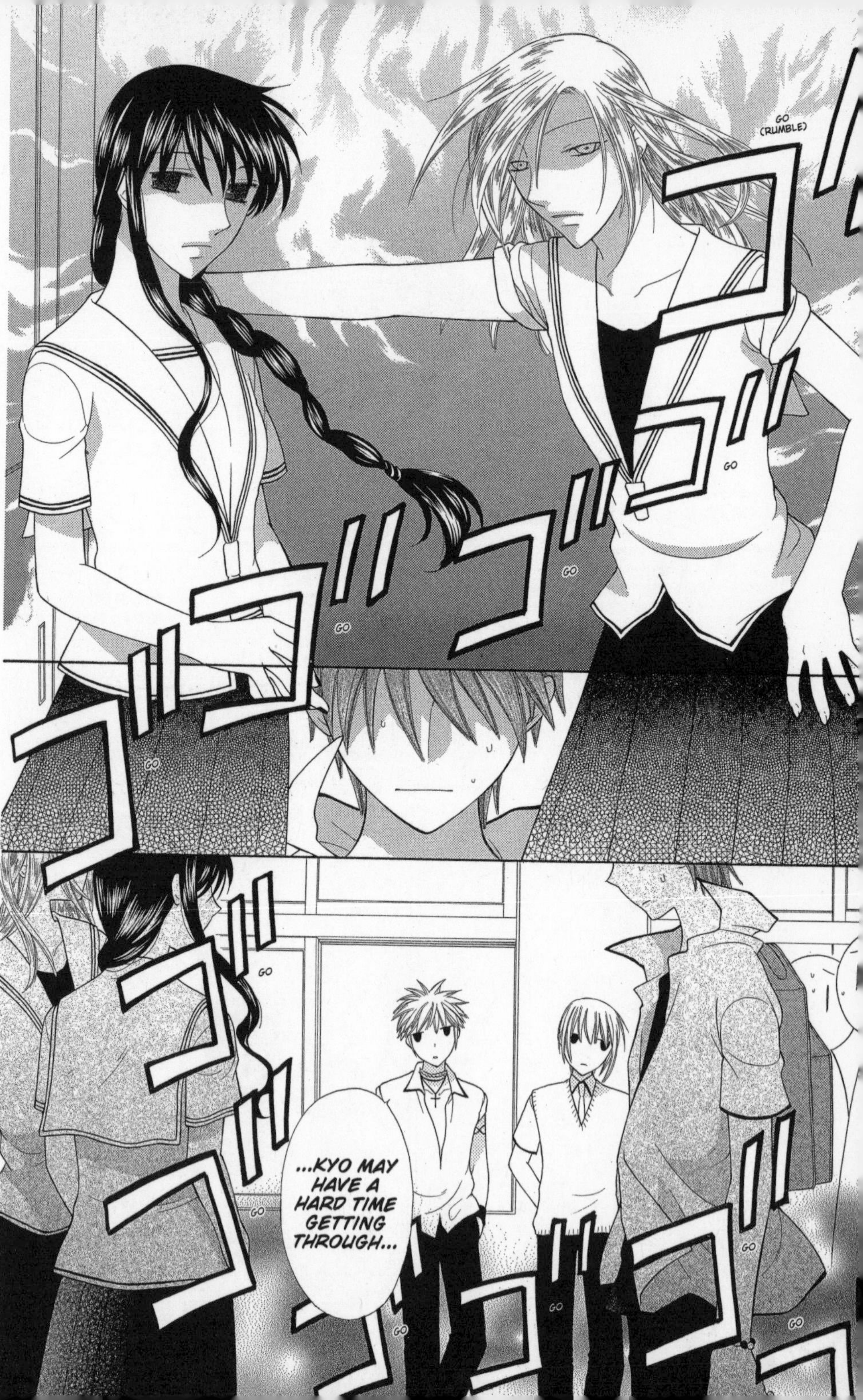
GO (RUMBLE)
GO
GO
GO
GO
GO
GO
GO
...KYO MAY HAVE A HARD TIME GETTING THROUGH...
GO
GO
GO

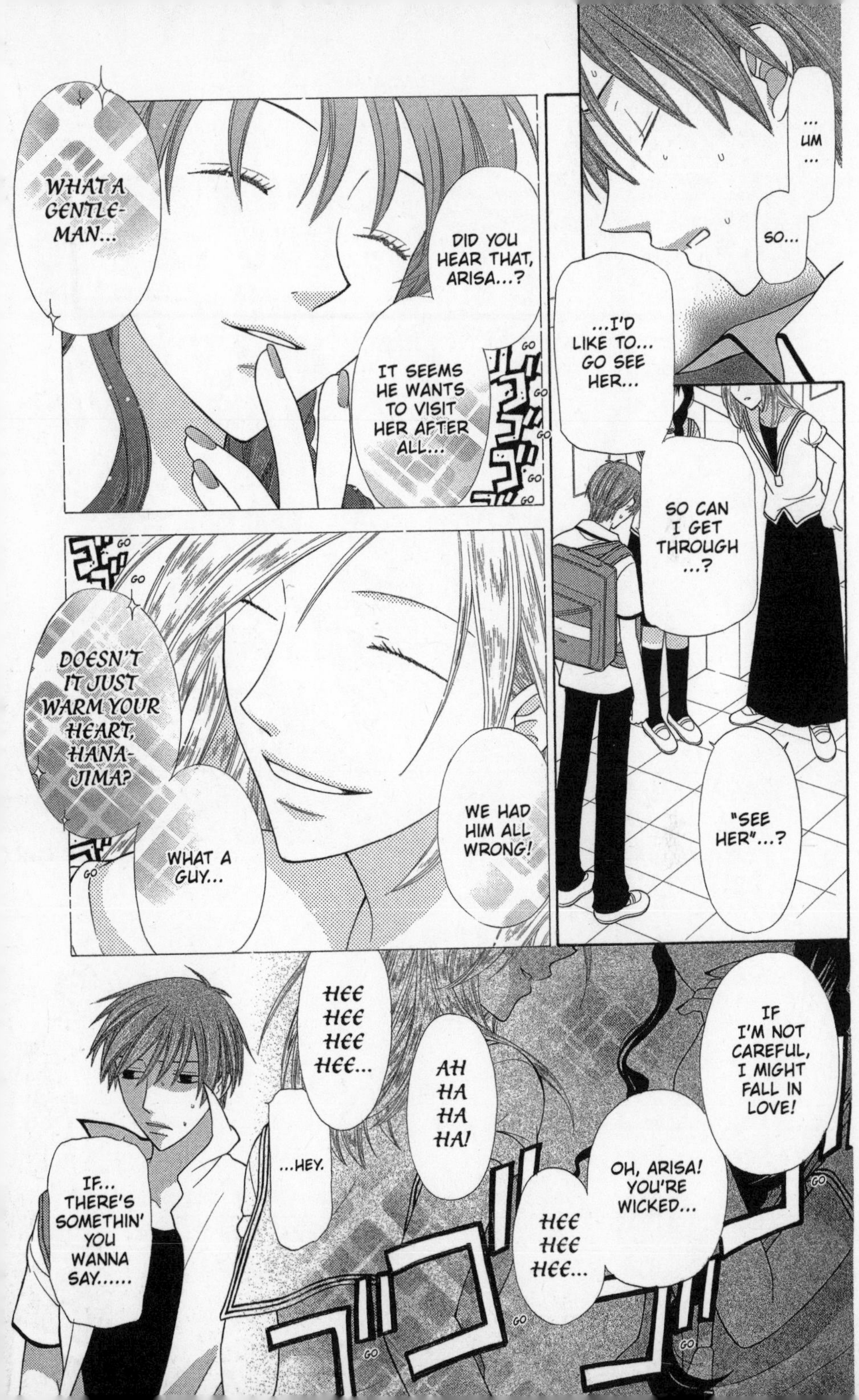

... UM ...
SO...
...I'D LIKE TO... GO SEE HER...
SO CAN I GET THROUGH ...?
"SEE HER"...?
DID YOU HEAR THAT, ARISA...?
WHAT A GENTLE-MAN...
IT SEEMS HE WANTS TO VISIT HER AFTER ALL...
GO GO GO GO GO
GO GO
WE HAD HIM ALL WRONG!
DOESN'T IT JUST WARM YOUR HEART, HANA-JIMA?
WHAT A GUY...
GO
IF I'M NOT CAREFUL, I MIGHT FALL IN LOVE!
HEE HEE HEE HEE...
AH HA HA HA!
OH, ARISA! YOU'RE WICKED...
HEE HEE HEE...
GO GO GO
...HEY.
IF... THERE'S SOMETHIN' YOU WANNA SAY......

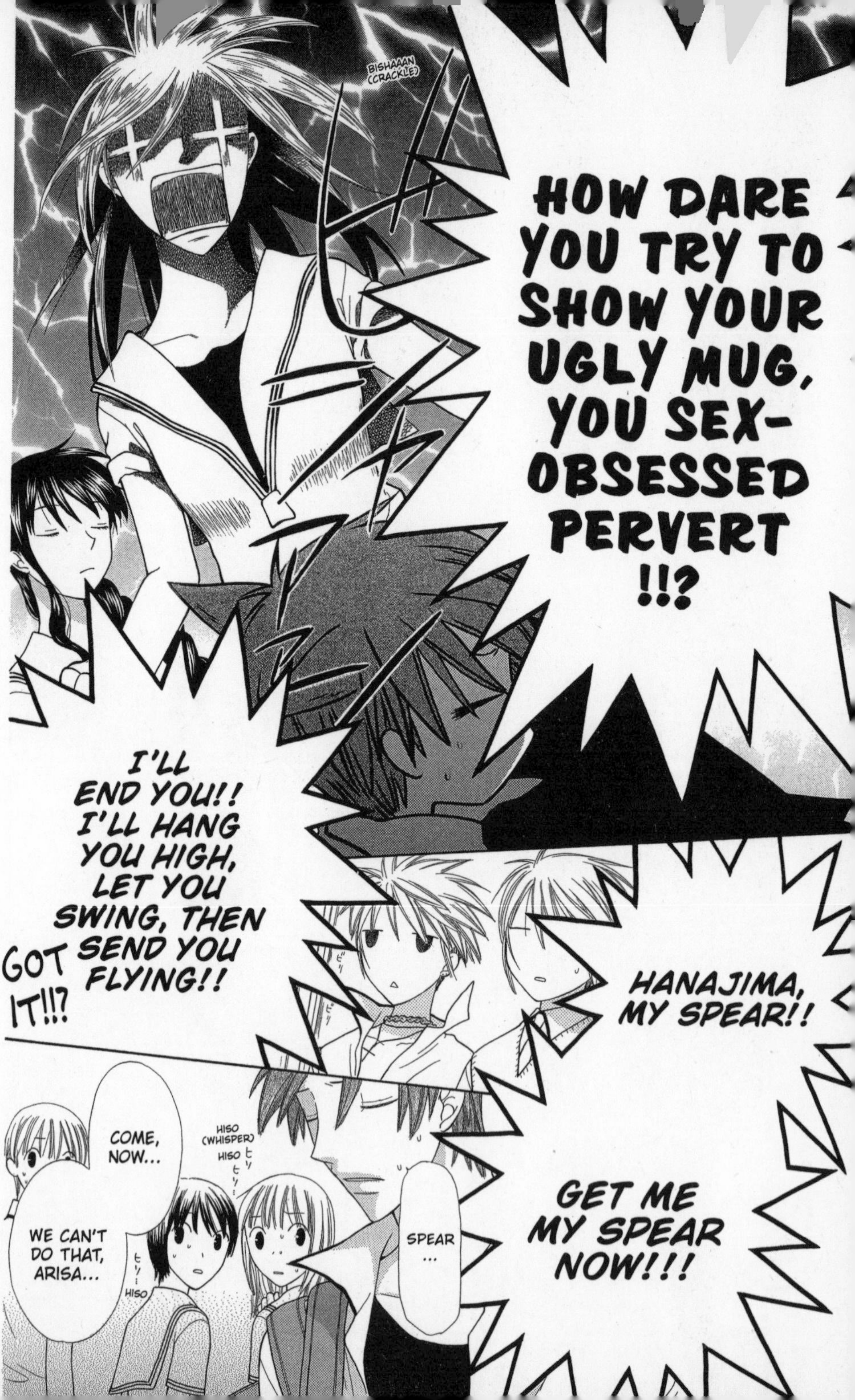
BISHAAAN (CRACKLE)
HOW DARE YOU TRY TO SHOW YOUR UGLY MUG, YOU SEX-OBSESSED PERVERT !!?
HANAJIMA, MY SPEAR!!
I'LL END YOU!! I'LL HANG YOU HIGH, LET YOU SWING, THEN SEND YOU FLYING!!
GOT IT!!?
GET ME MY SPEAR NOW!!!
SPEAR ...
HISO (WHISPER) HISO
COME, NOW...
WE CAN'T DO THAT, ARISA...
HISO

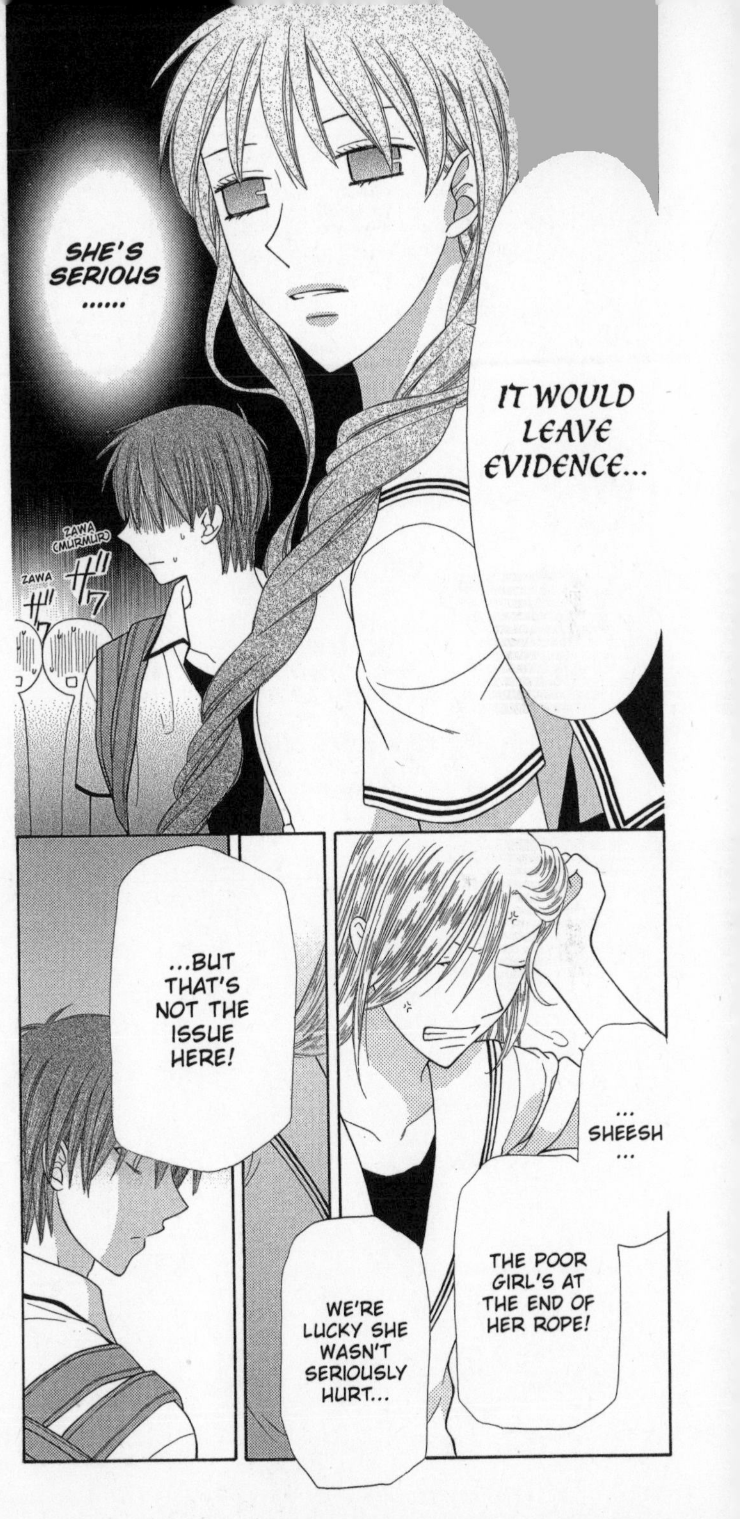
IT WOULD LEAVE EVIDENCE...
SHE'S SERIOUS ......
ZAWA (MURMUR)
ZAWA
... SHEESH ...
THE POOR GIRL'S AT THE END OF HER ROPE!
WE'RE LUCKY SHE WASN'T SERIOUSLY HURT...
...BUT THAT'S NOT THE ISSUE HERE!
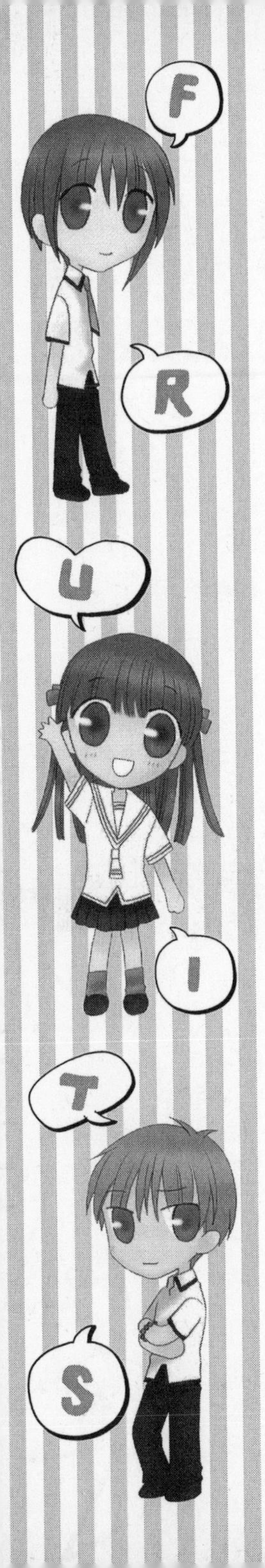
F
R
U
I
T
S

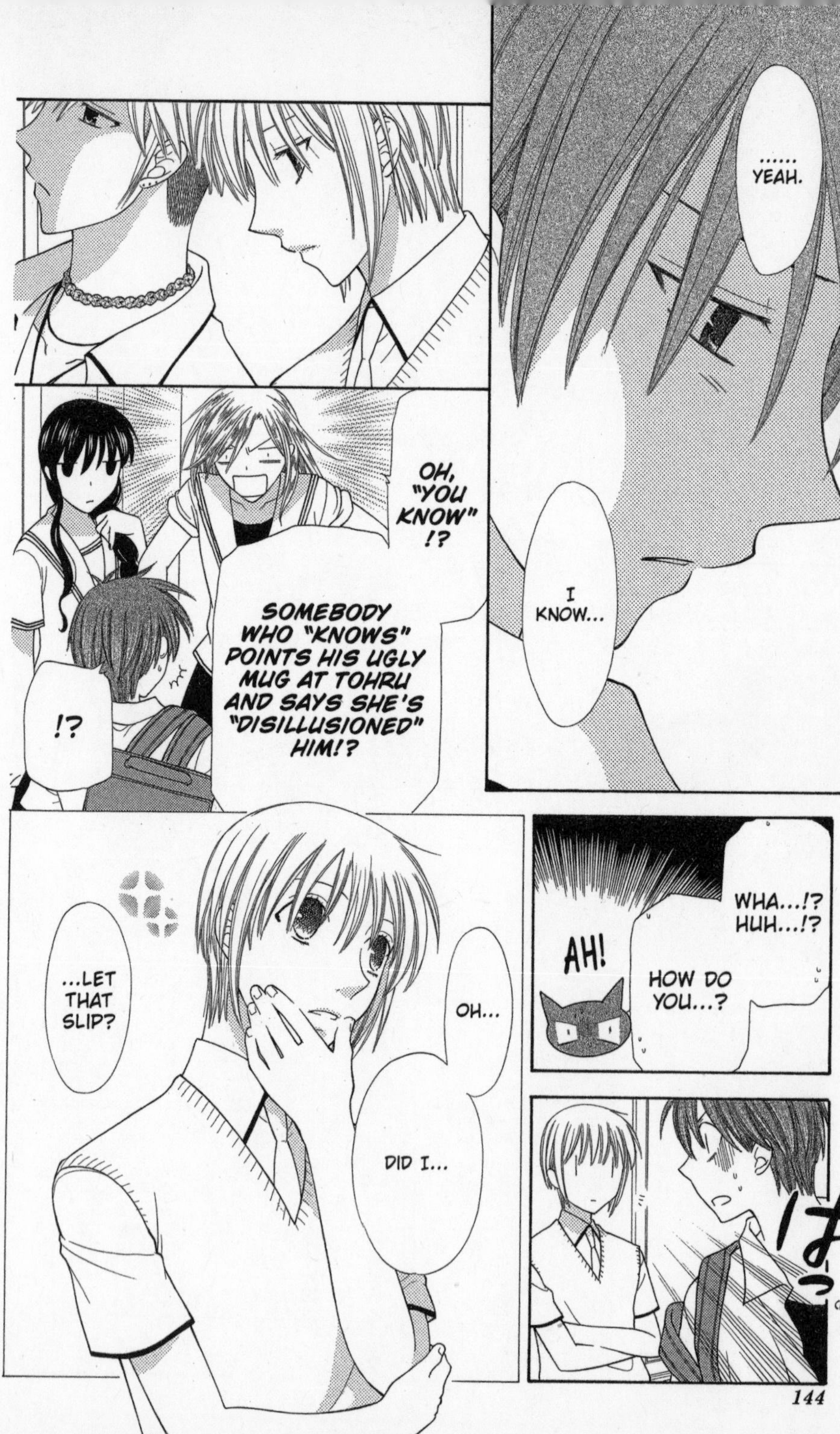
......YEAH.
I KNOW...
OH, "YOU KNOW"!?
SOMEBODY WHO "KNOWS" POINTS HIS UGLY MUG AT TOHRU AND SAYS SHE'S "DISILLUSIONED" HIM!?
!?
WHA...!? HUH...!?
AH!
HOW DO YOU...?
ばっ
BA (FWIP)
OH...
DID I...
...LET THAT SLIP?

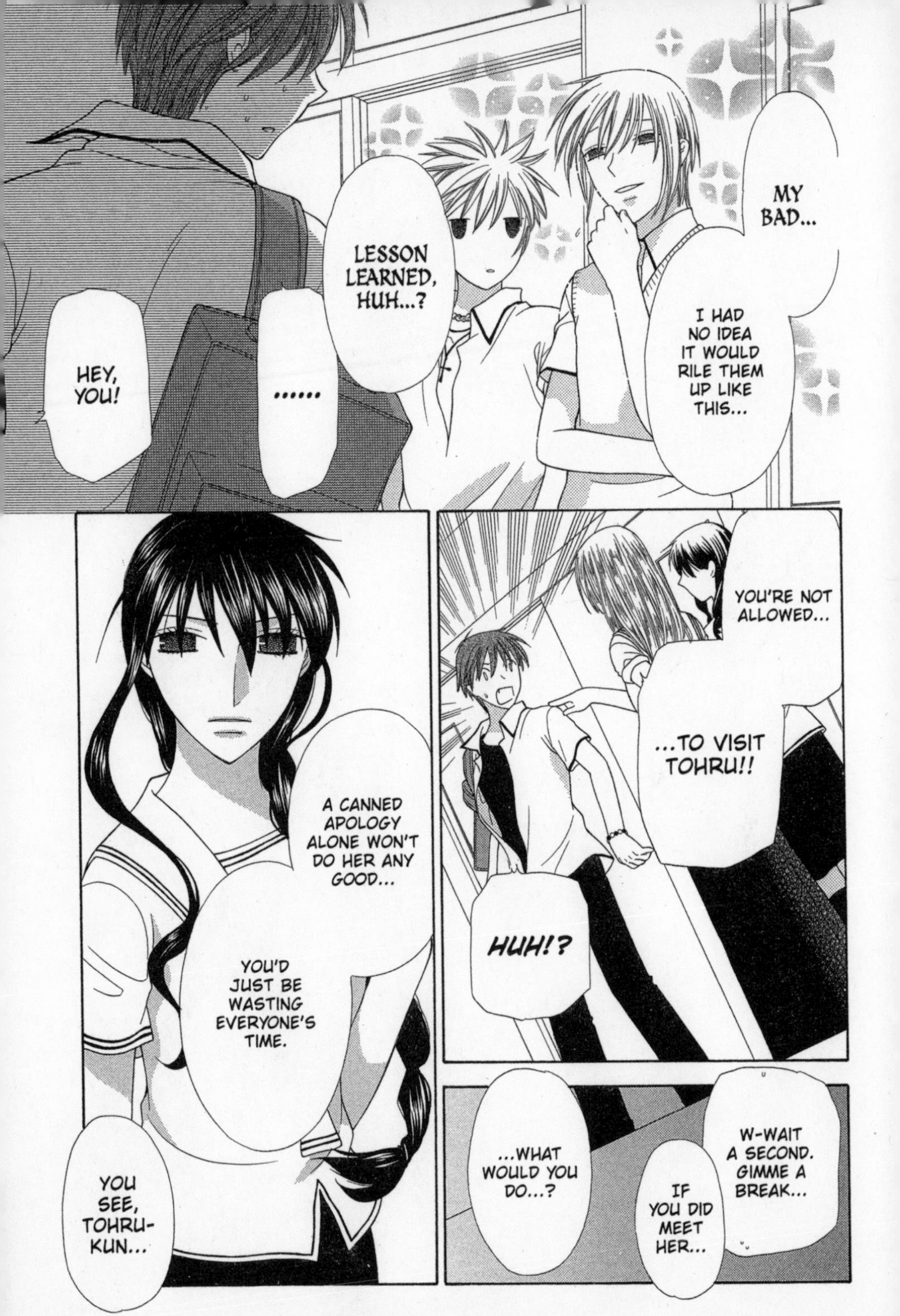
MY BAD...
I HAD NO IDEA IT WOULD RILE THEM UP LIKE THIS...
LESSON LEARNED, HUH...?
......
HEY, YOU!
YOU'RE NOT ALLOWED...
...TO VISIT TOHRU!!
HUH!?
W-WAIT A SECOND. GIMME A BREAK...
IF YOU DID MEET HER...
...WHAT WOULD YOU DO...?
A CANNED APOLOGY ALONE WON'T DO HER ANY GOOD...
YOU'D JUST BE WASTING EVERYONE'S TIME.
YOU SEE, TOHRU-KUN...

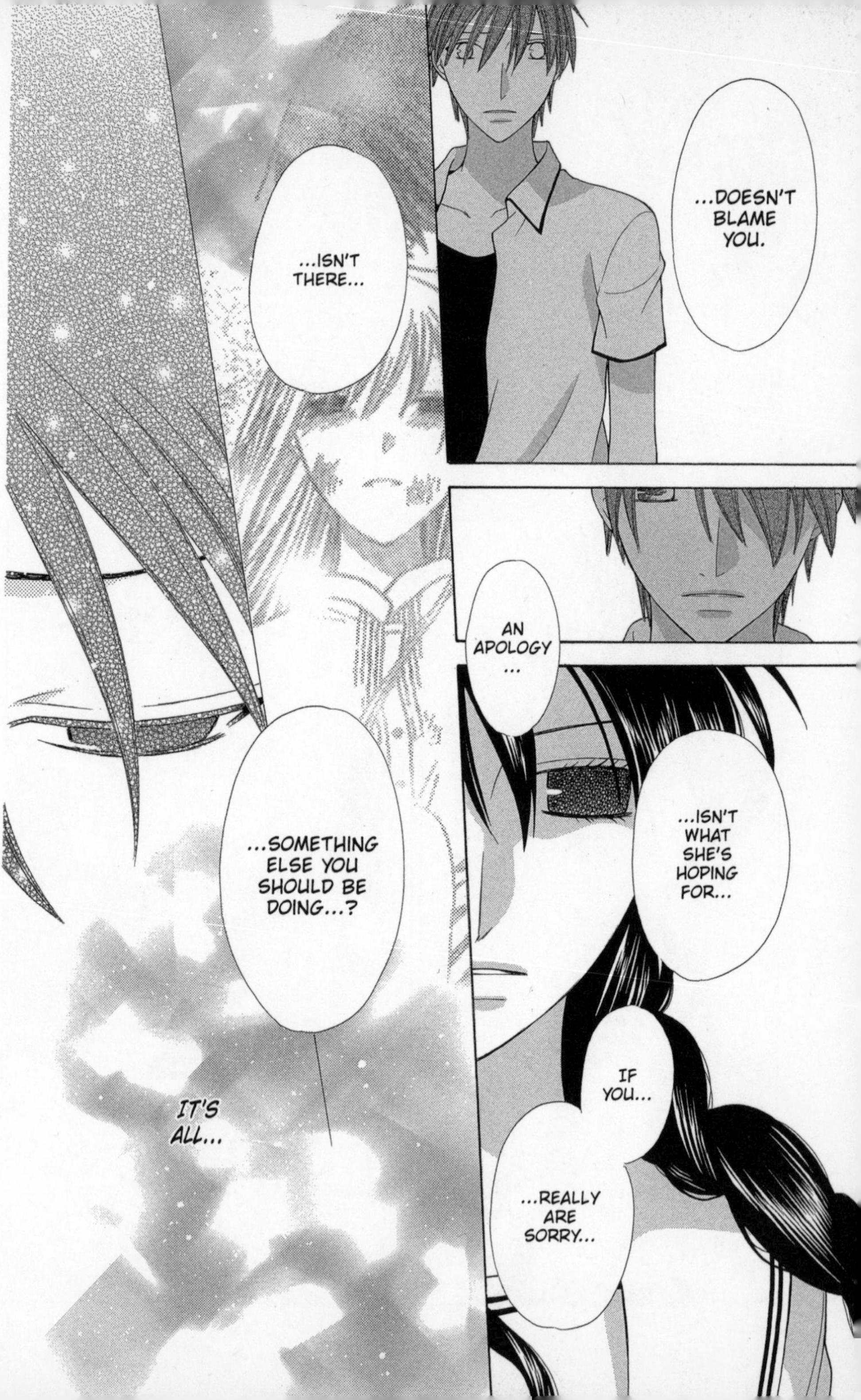
...DOESN'T BLAME YOU.
AN APOLOGY ...
...ISN'T WHAT SHE'S HOPING FOR...
IF YOU...
...REALLY ARE SORRY...
...ISN'T THERE...
...SOMETHING ELSE YOU SHOULD BE DOING...?
IT'S ALL...

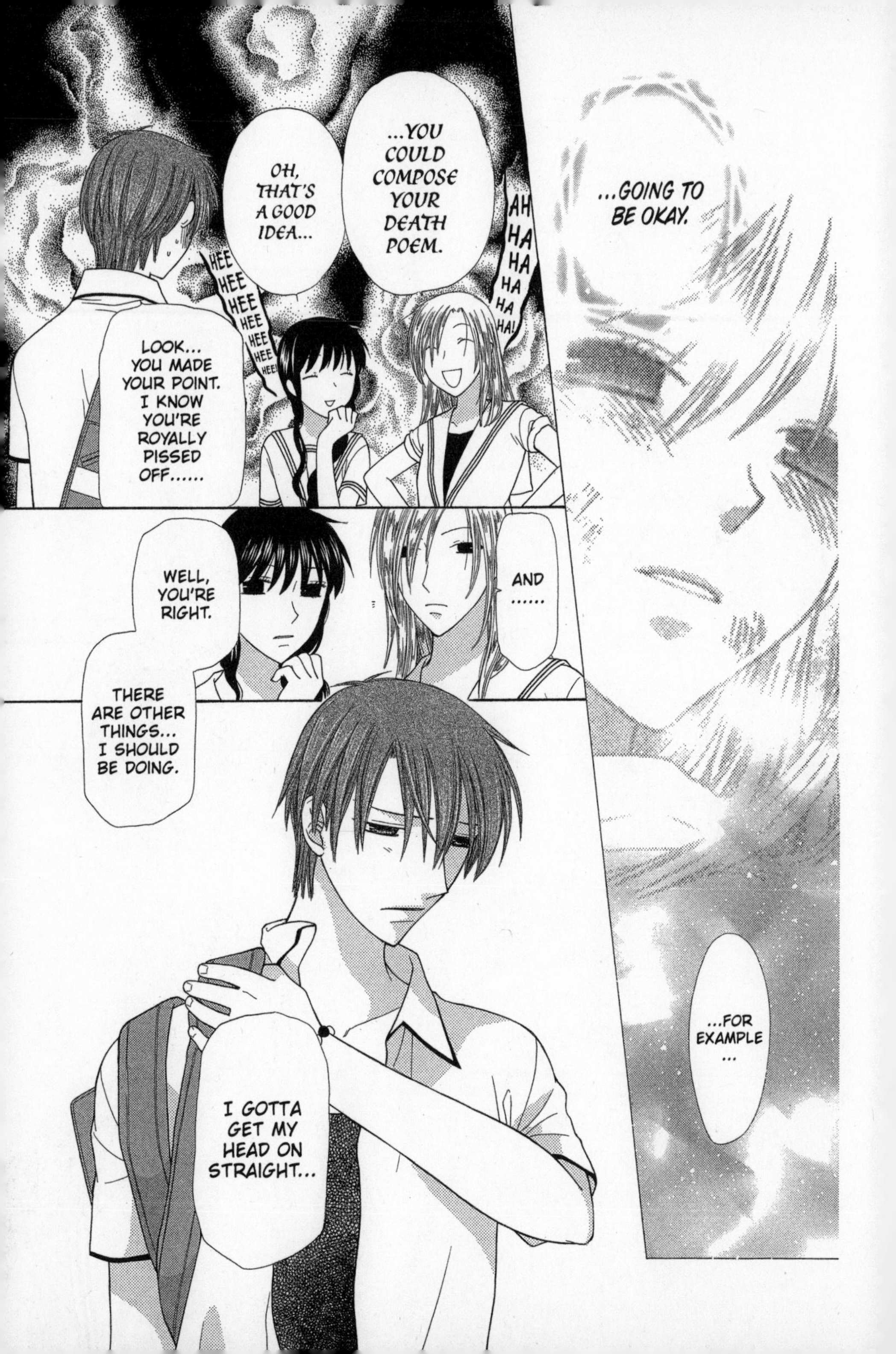
...GOING TO BE OKAY.
...FOR EXAMPLE ...
AH HA HA HA HA HA!
...YOU COULD COMPOSE YOUR DEATH POEM.
OH, THAT'S A GOOD IDEA...
HEE HEE HEE HEE HEE HEE HEE!
LOOK... YOU MADE YOUR POINT. I KNOW YOU'RE ROYALLY PISSED OFF......
AND ......
WELL, YOU'RE RIGHT.
THERE ARE OTHER THINGS... I SHOULD BE DOING.
I GOTTA GET MY HEAD ON STRAIGHT...

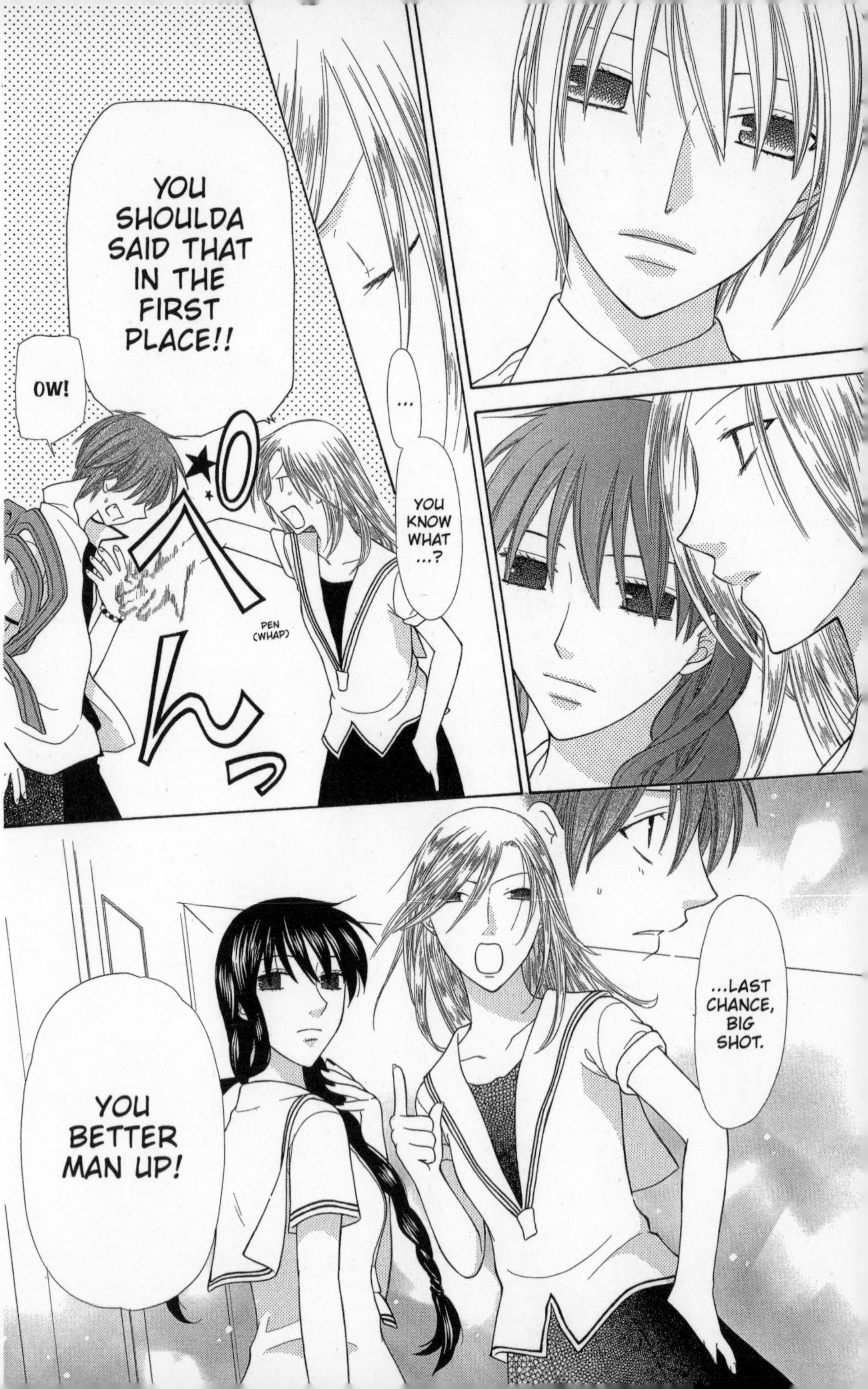
...
YOU KNOW WHAT ...?
YOU SHOULDA SAID THAT IN THE FIRST PLACE!!
OW!
PEN (WHAP)
...LAST CHANCE, BIG SHOT.
YOU BETTER MAN UP!

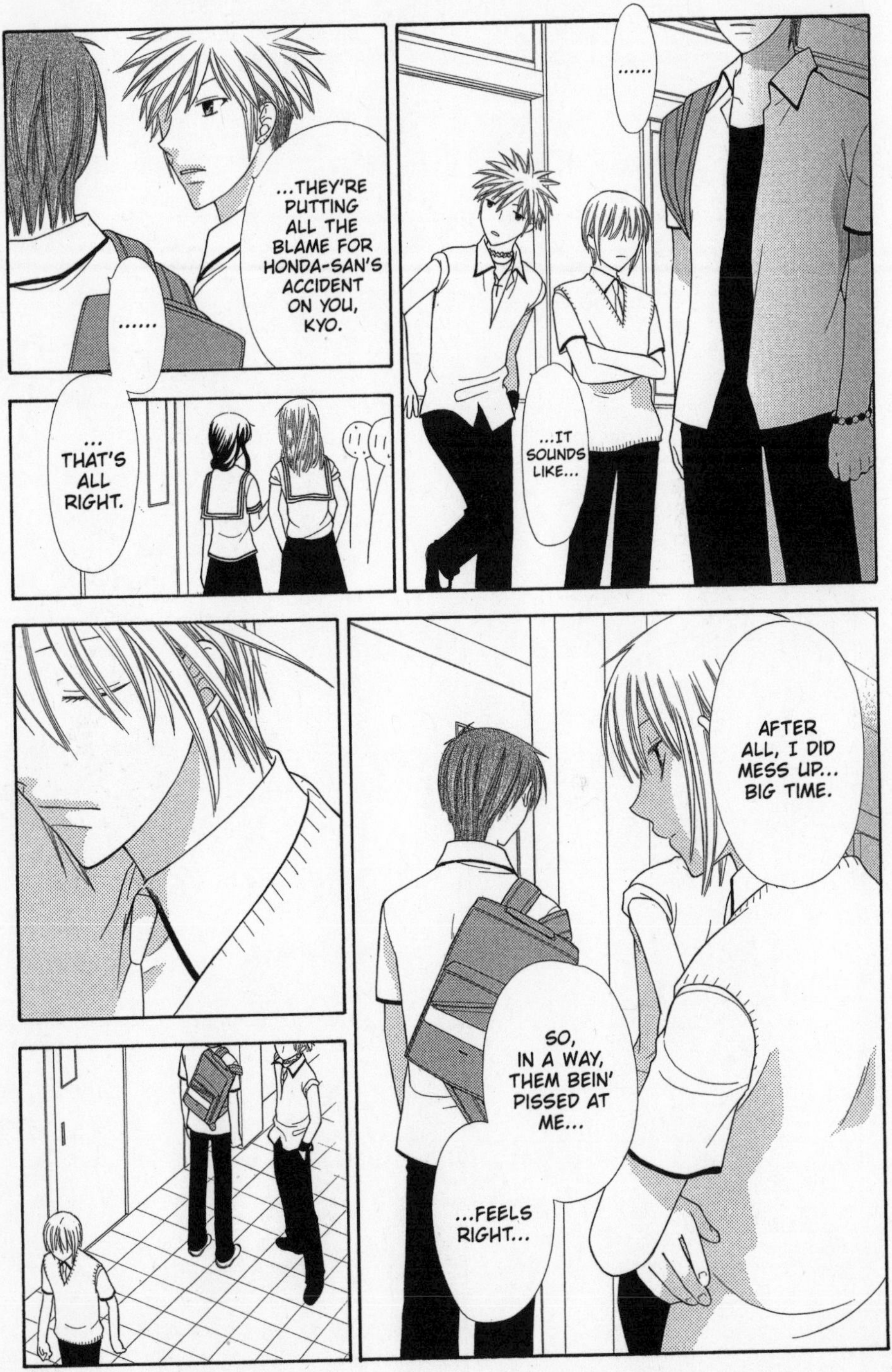
......
...IT SOUNDS LIKE...
...THEY'RE PUTTING ALL THE BLAME FOR HONDA-SAN'S ACCIDENT ON YOU, KYO.
......
... THAT'S ALL RIGHT.
AFTER ALL, I DID MESS UP... BIG TIME.
SO, IN A WAY, THEM BEIN' PISSED AT ME...
...FEELS RIGHT...

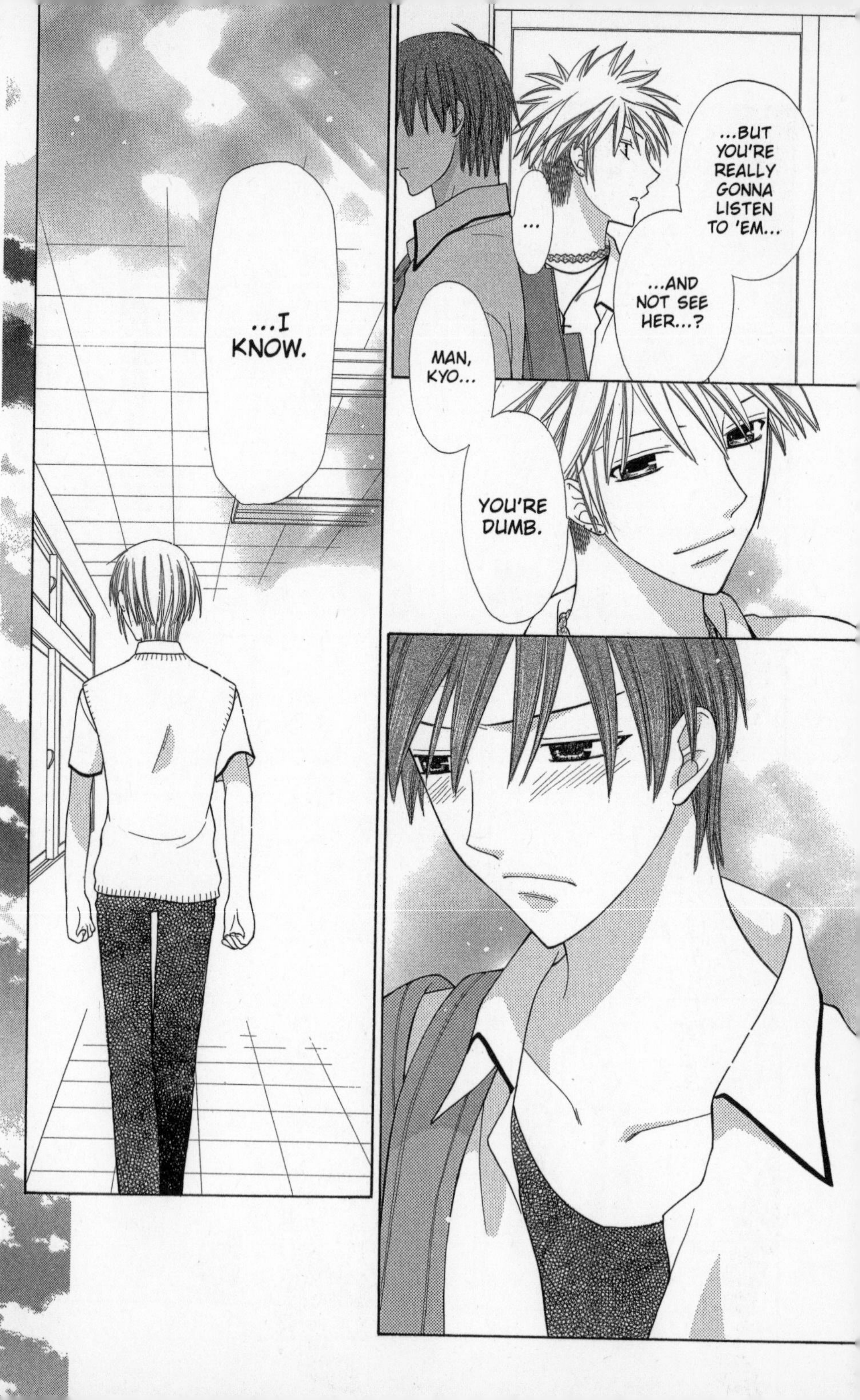
...BUT YOU'RE REALLY GONNA LISTEN TO 'EM...
...
...AND NOT SEE HER...?
MAN, KYO...
YOU'RE DUMB.
...I KNOW.

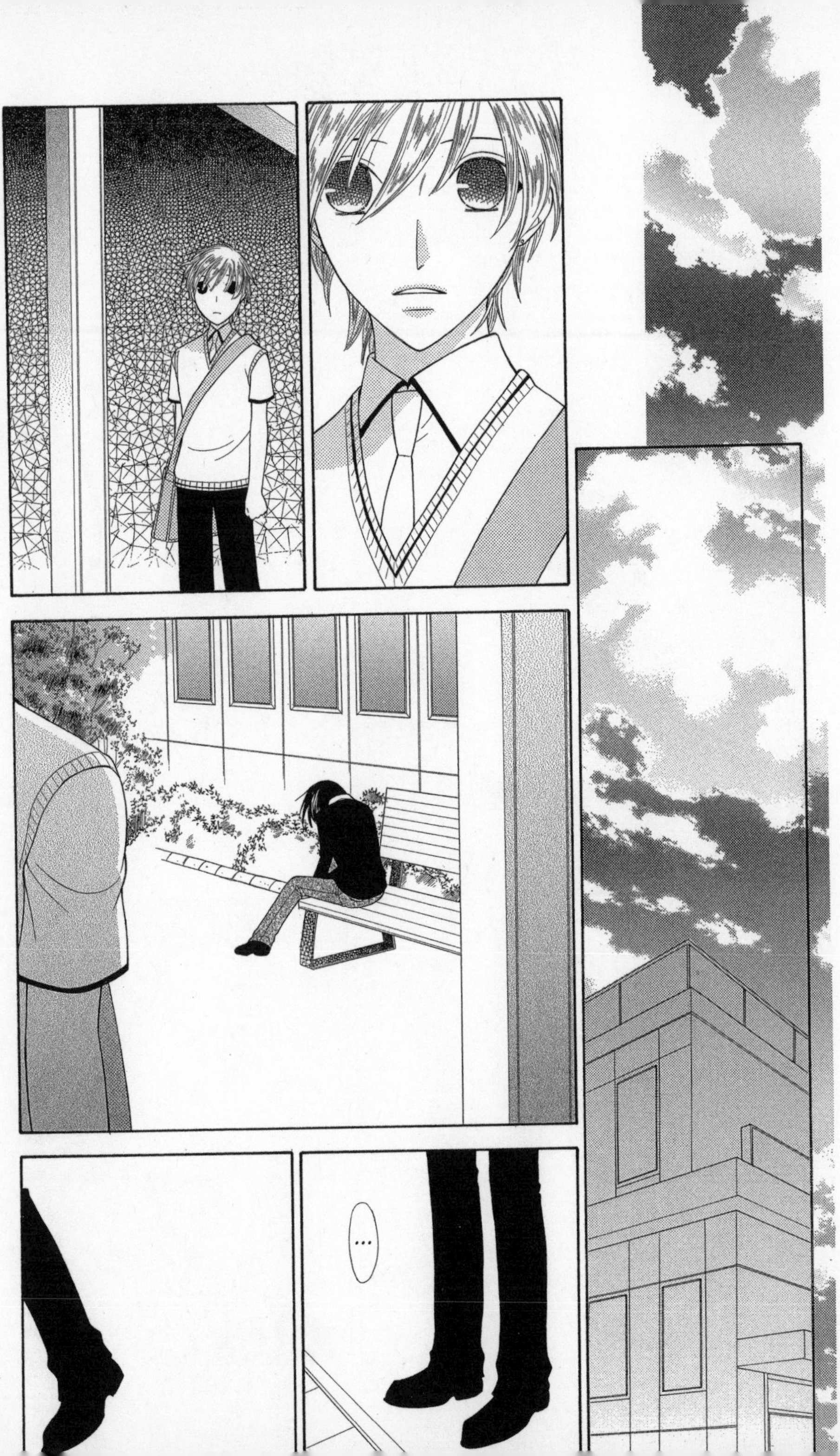
...

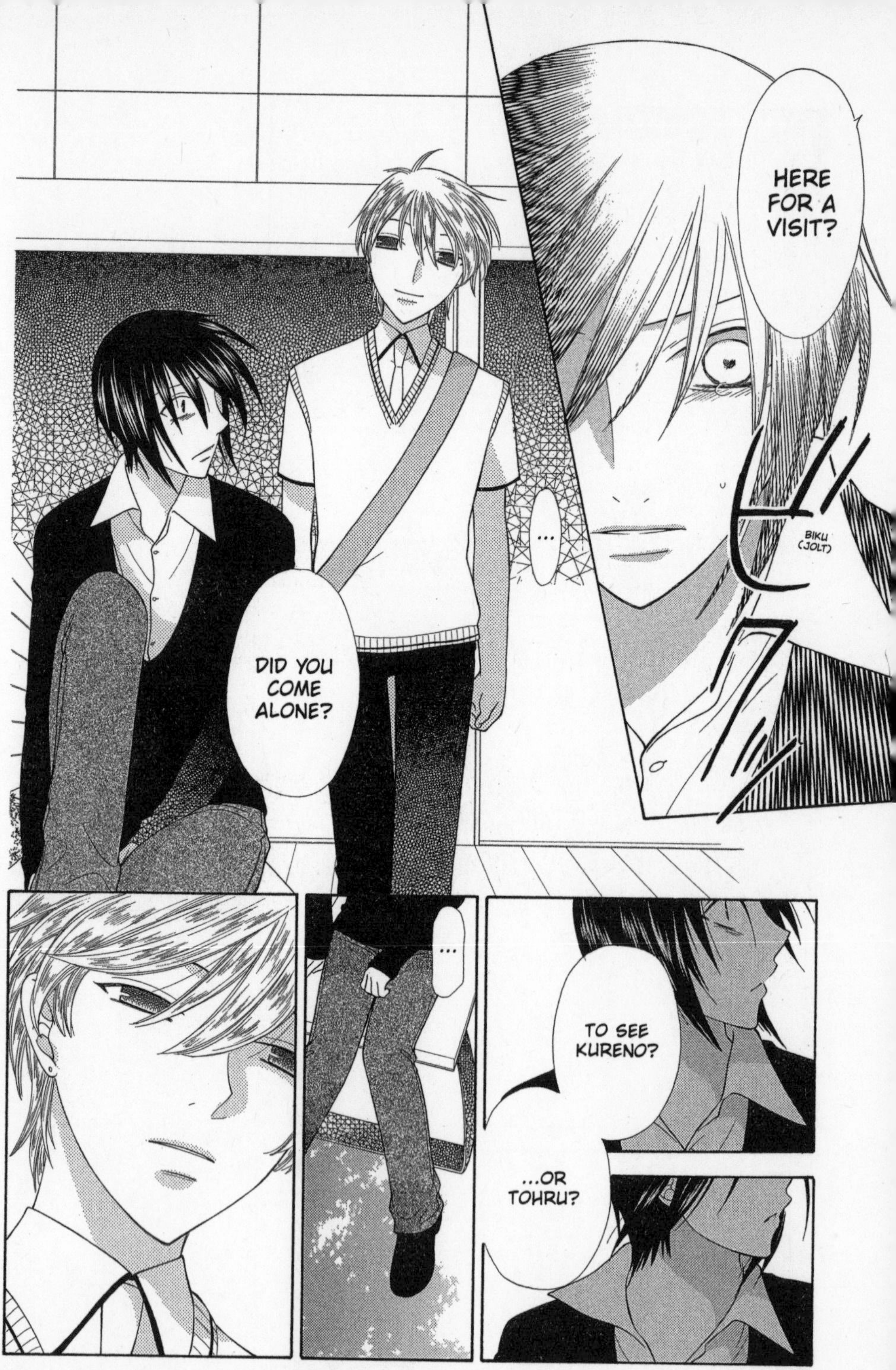
HERE FOR A VISIT?
BIKU (JOLT)
...
DID YOU COME ALONE?
TO SEE KURENO?
...OR TOHRU?
...

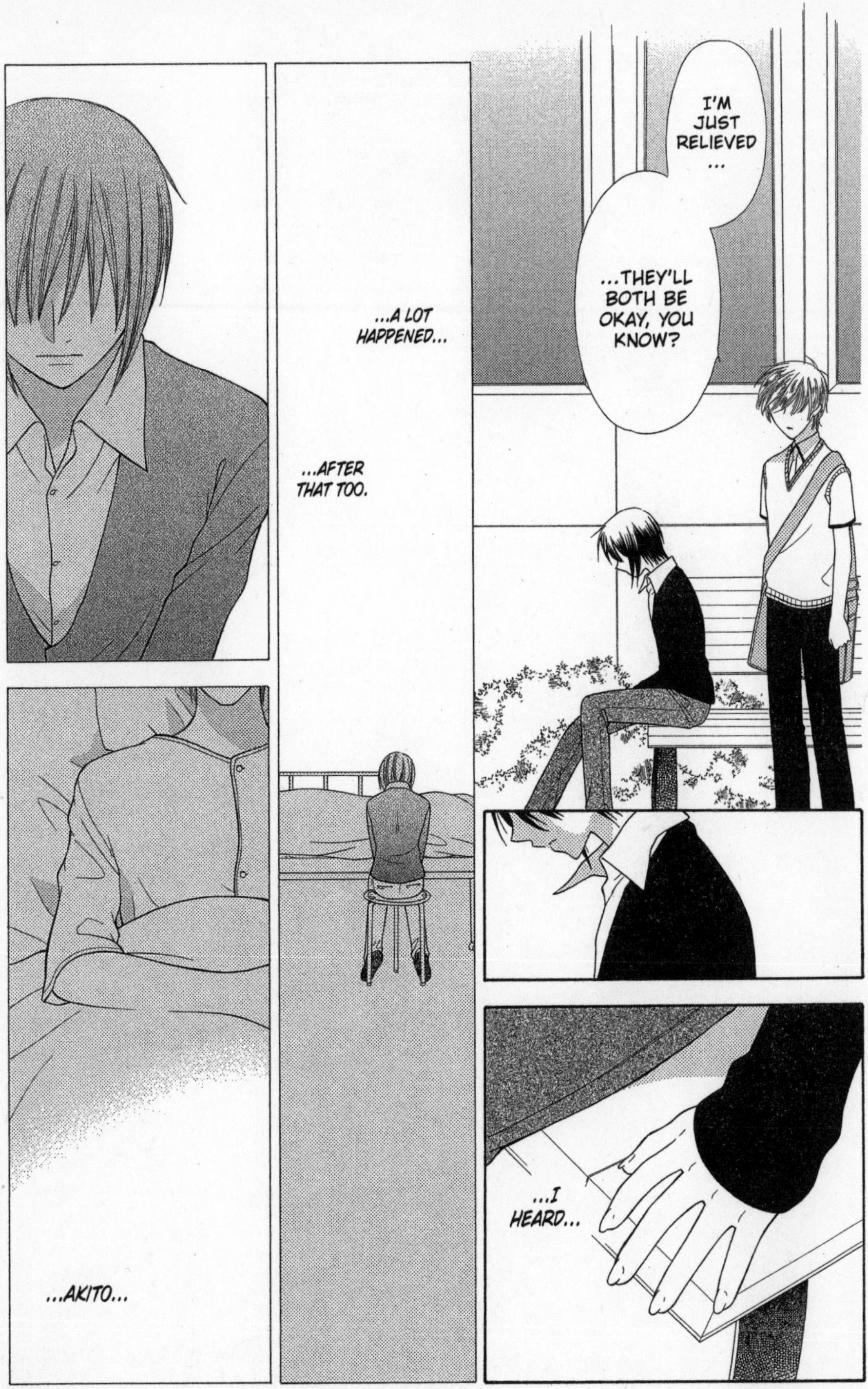
I'M JUST RELIEVED...
...THEY'LL BOTH BE OKAY, YOU KNOW?
...I HEARD...
...A LOT HAPPENED...
...AFTER THAT TOO.
...AKITO...

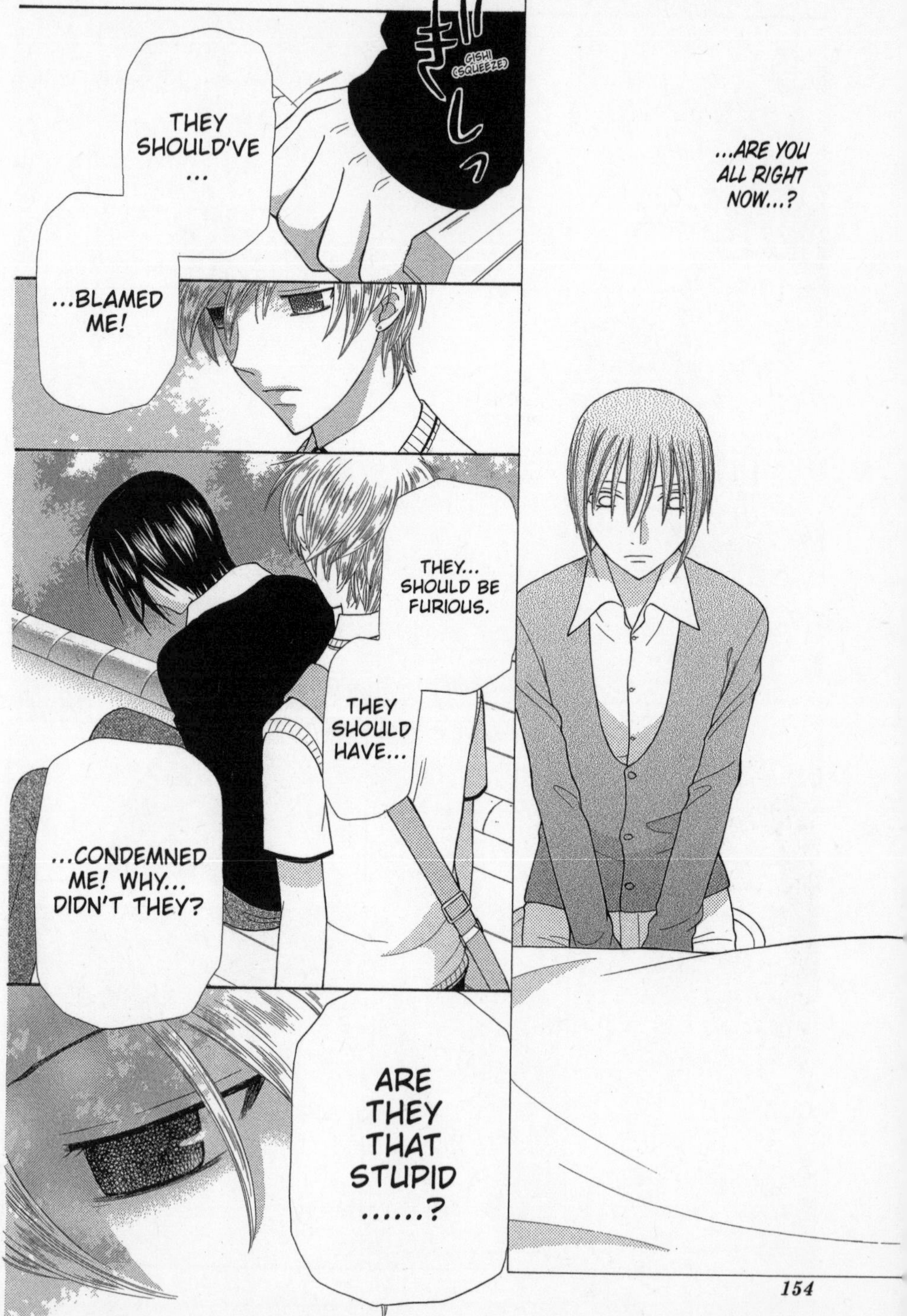
...ARE YOU ALL RIGHT NOW...?
GISHI (SQUEEZE)
THEY SHOULD'VE ...
...BLAMED ME!
THEY... SHOULD BE FURIOUS.
THEY SHOULD HAVE...
...CONDEMNED ME! WHY... DIDN'T THEY?
ARE THEY THAT STUPID ......?

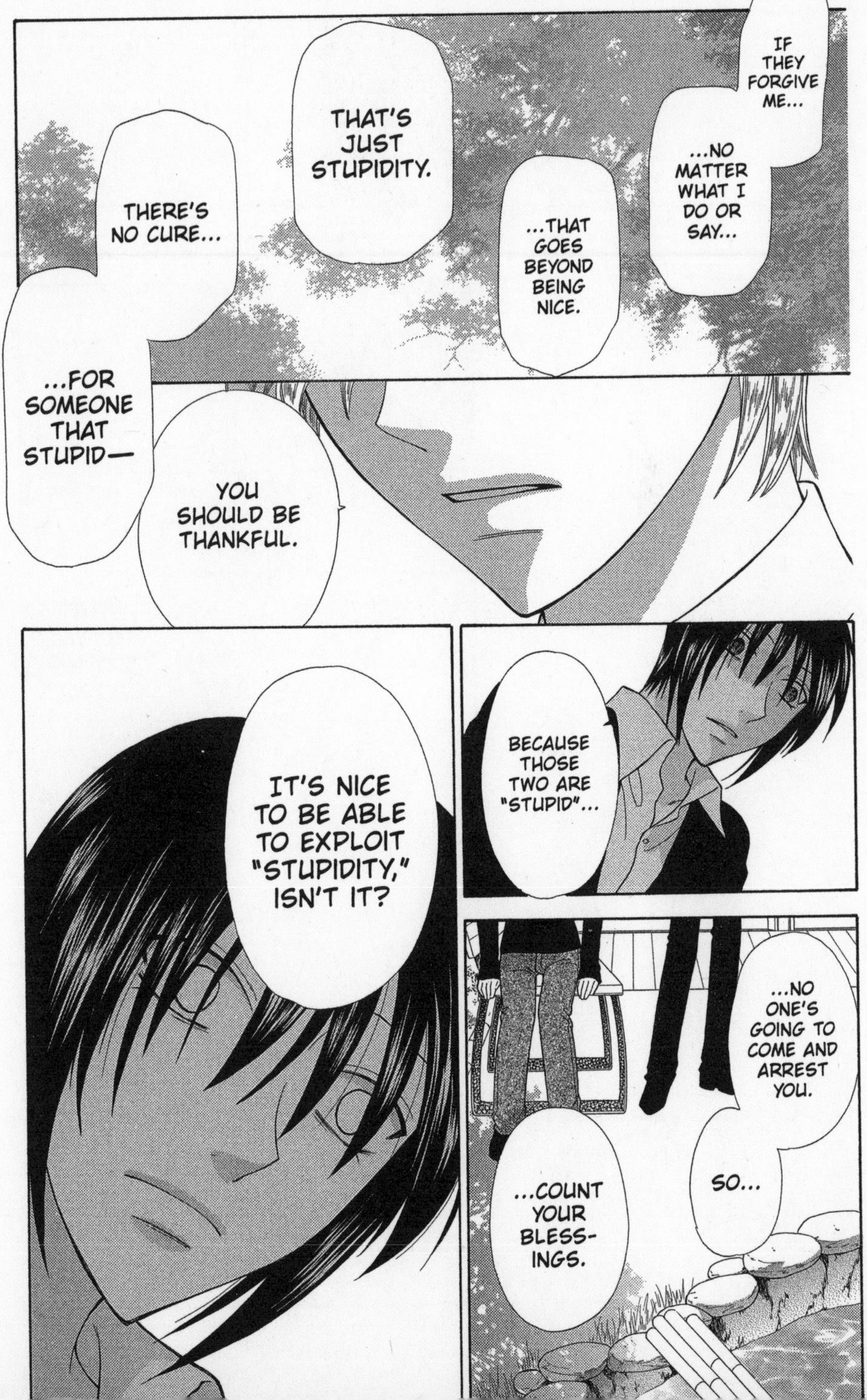
IF THEY FORGIVE ME...
...NO MATTER WHAT I DO OR SAY...
...THAT GOES BEYOND BEING NICE.
THAT'S JUST STUPIDITY.
THERE'S NO CURE...
...FOR SOMEONE THAT STUPID—
YOU SHOULD BE THANKFUL.
BECAUSE THOSE TWO ARE "STUPID"...
...NO ONE'S GOING TO COME AND ARREST YOU.
SO...
...COUNT YOUR BLESS-INGS.
IT'S NICE TO BE ABLE TO EXPLOIT "STUPIDITY," ISN'T IT?

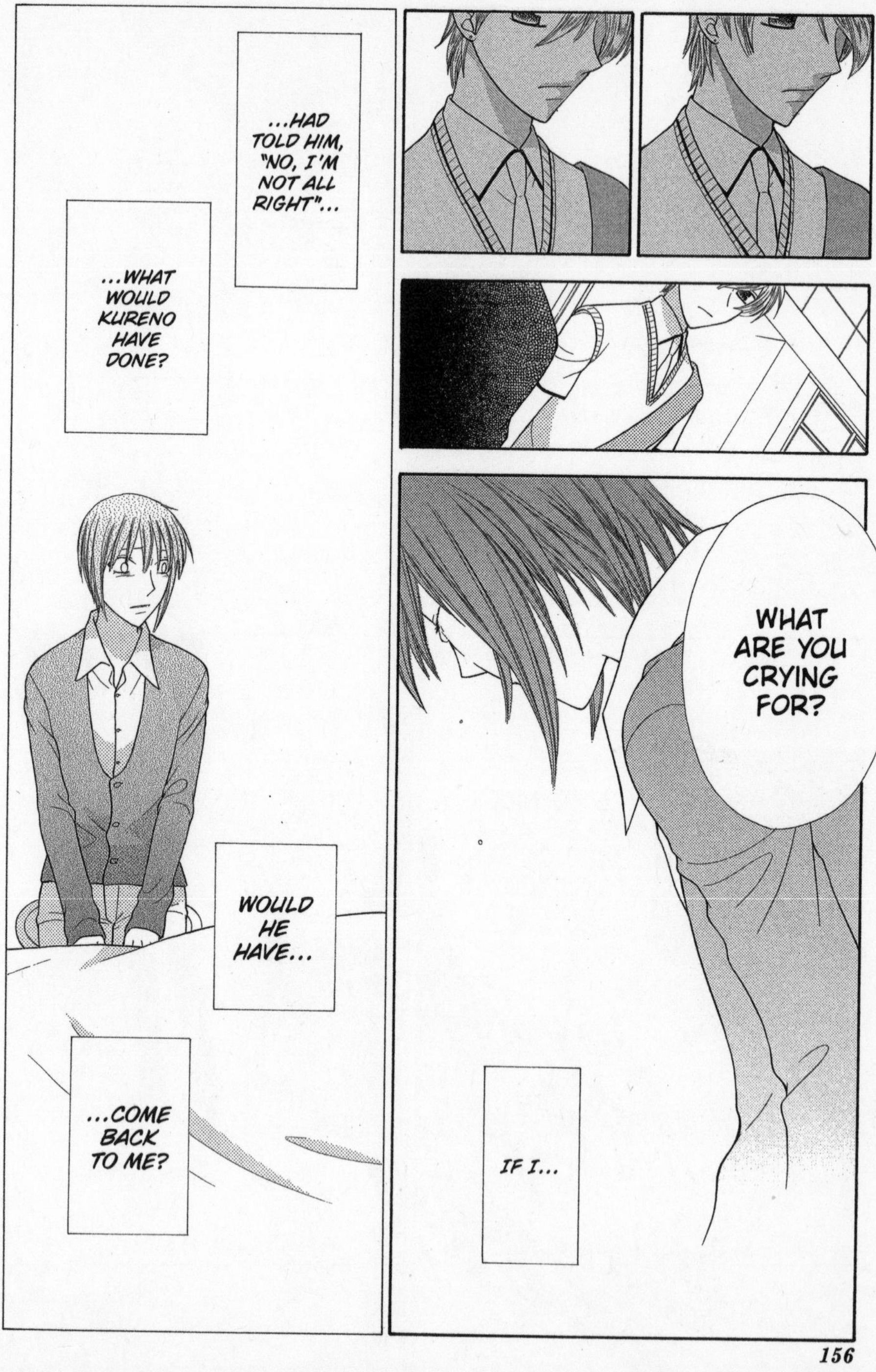
WHAT ARE YOU CRYING FOR?
IF I...
...HAD TOLD HIM, "NO, I'M NOT ALL RIGHT"...
...WHAT WOULD KURENO HAVE DONE?
WOULD HE HAVE...
...COME BACK TO ME?

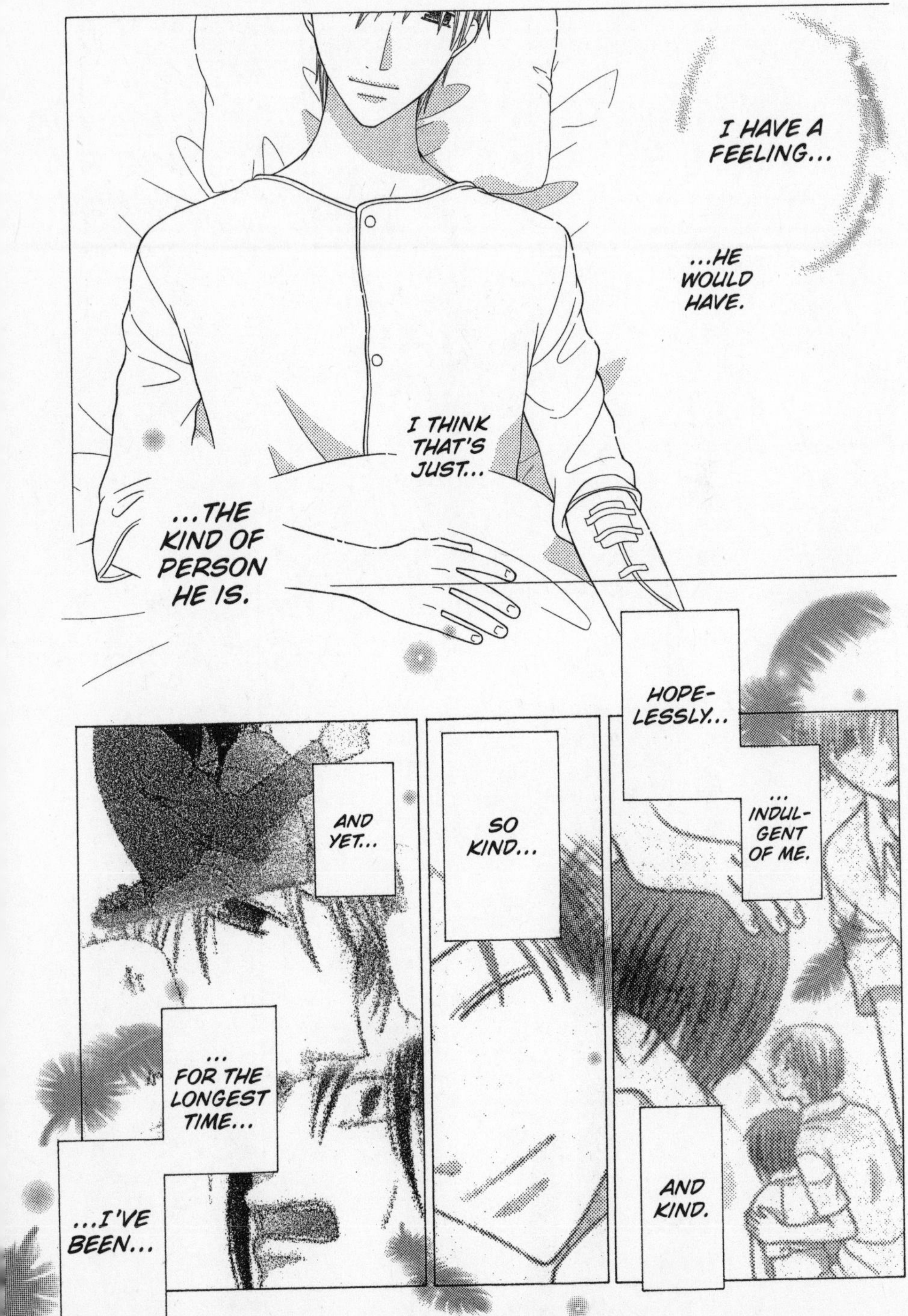
I HAVE A FEELING...
...HE WOULD HAVE.
I THINK THAT'S JUST...
...THE KIND OF PERSON HE IS.
HOPE-LESSLY...
...INDUL-GENT OF ME.
AND KIND.
SO KIND...
AND YET...
...FOR THE LONGEST TIME...
...I'VE BEEN...

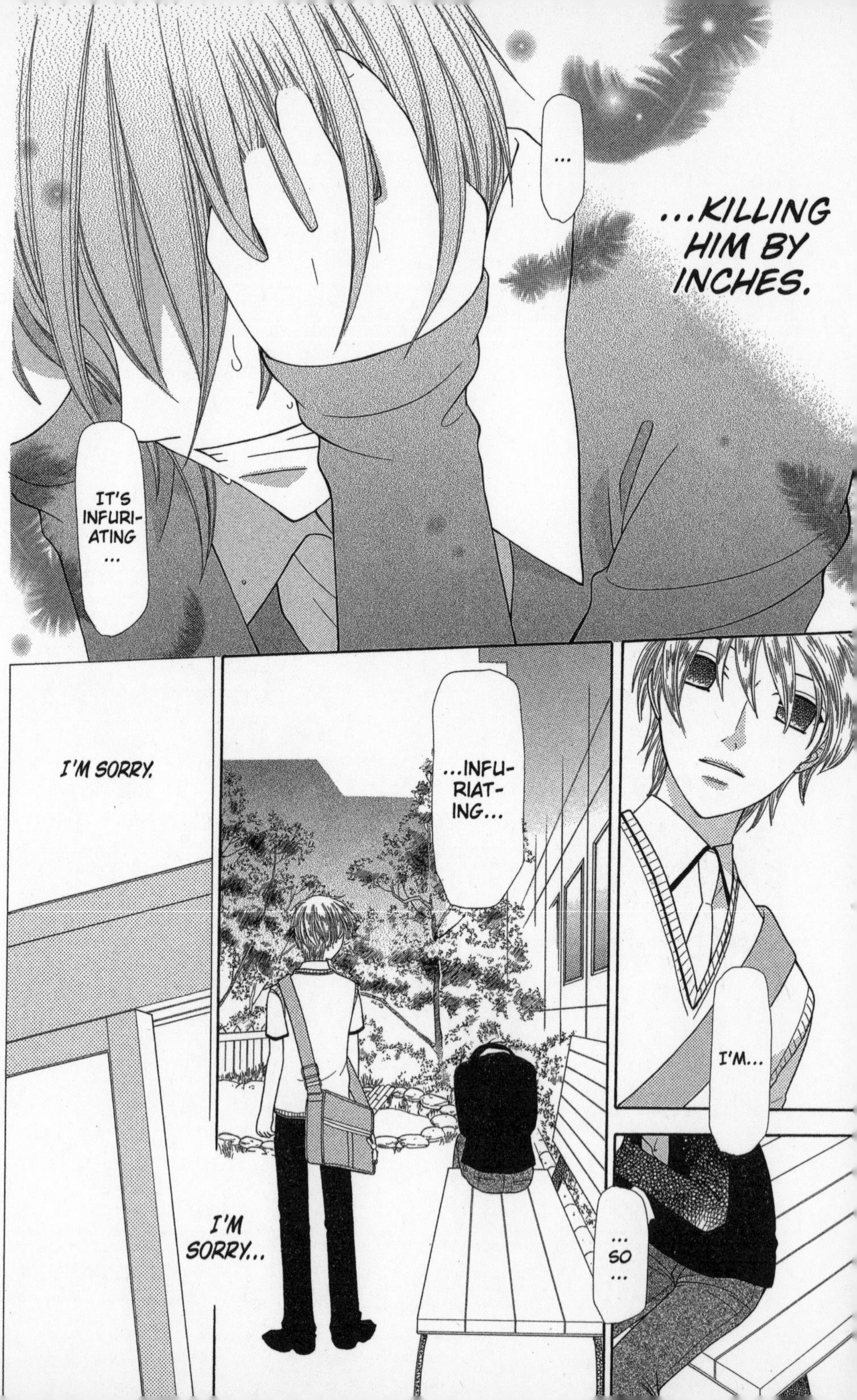
...
...KILLING HIM BY INCHES.
IT'S INFURI-ATING...
I'M...
...SO...
...INFU-RIAT-ING...
I'M SORRY...
I'M SORRY.

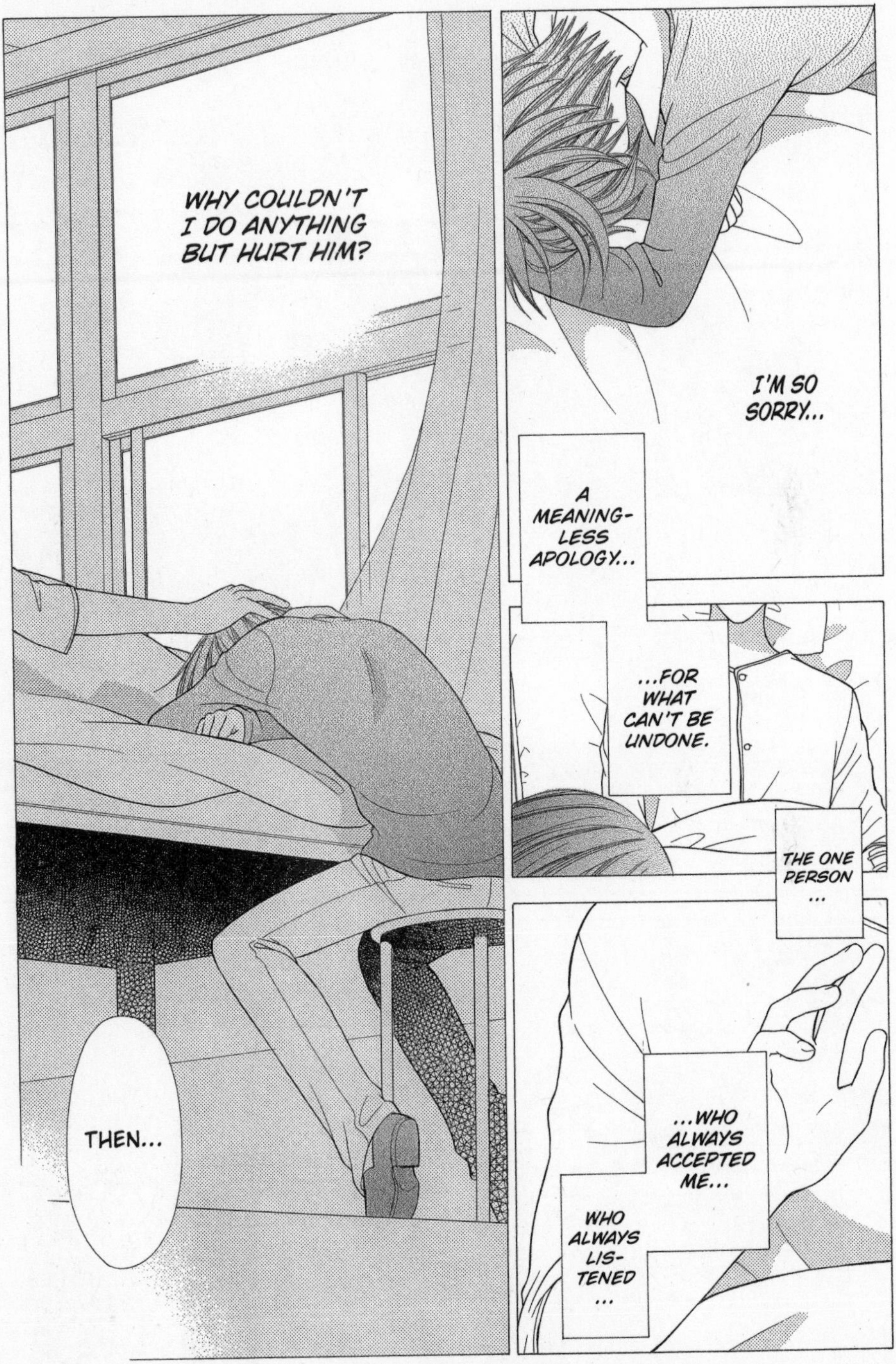

I'M SO SORRY...
A MEANING-LESS APOLOGY...
...FOR WHAT CAN'T BE UNDONE.
THE ONE PERSON...
...WHO ALWAYS ACCEPTED ME...
WHO ALWAYS LIS-TENED...
WHY COULDN'T I DO ANYTHING BUT HURT HIM?
THEN...

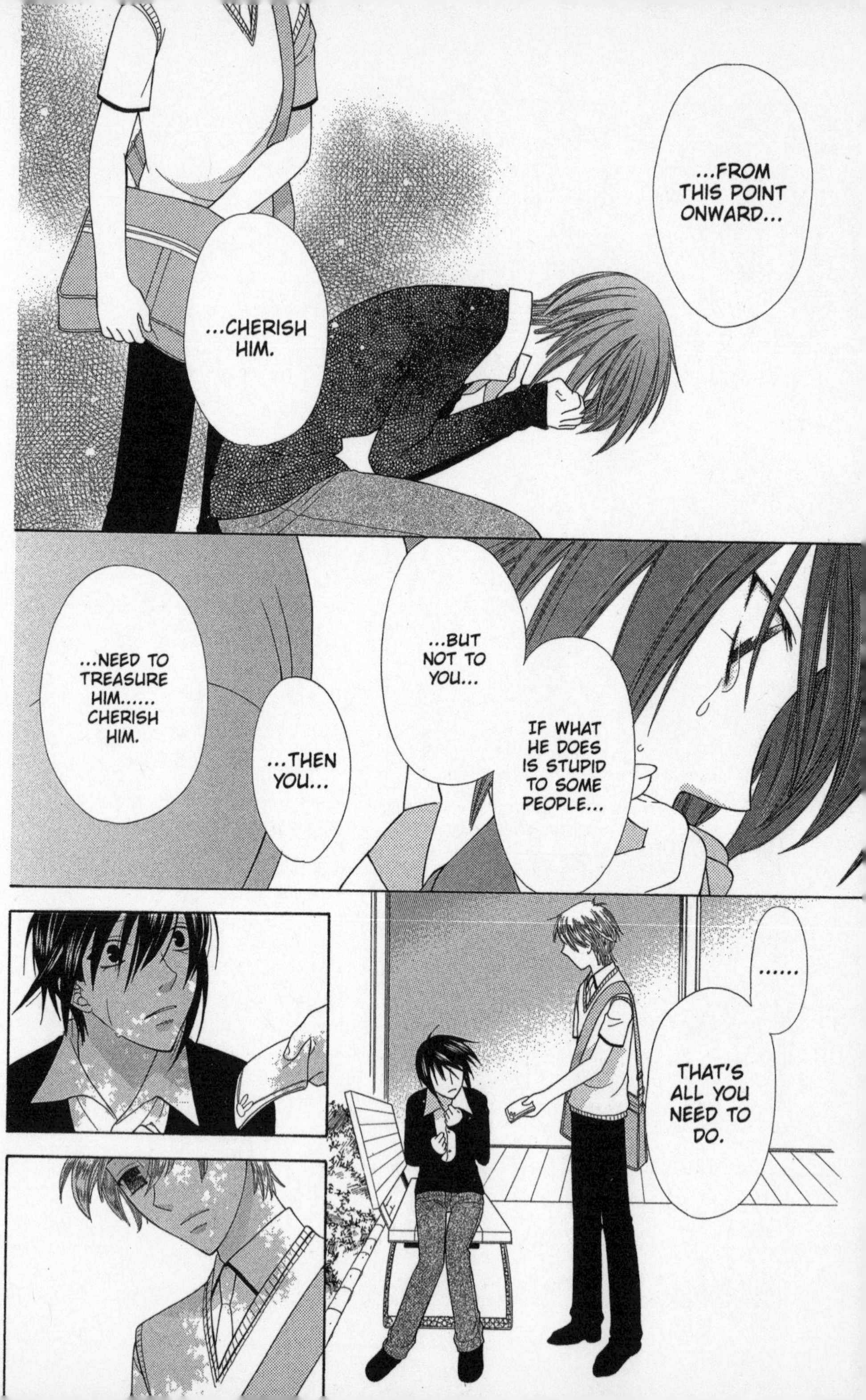
...FROM THIS POINT ONWARD...
...CHERISH HIM.
IF WHAT HE DOES IS STUPID TO SOME PEOPLE...
...BUT NOT TO YOU...
...THEN YOU...
...NEED TO TREASURE HIM...... CHERISH HIM.
......
THAT'S ALL YOU NEED TO DO.

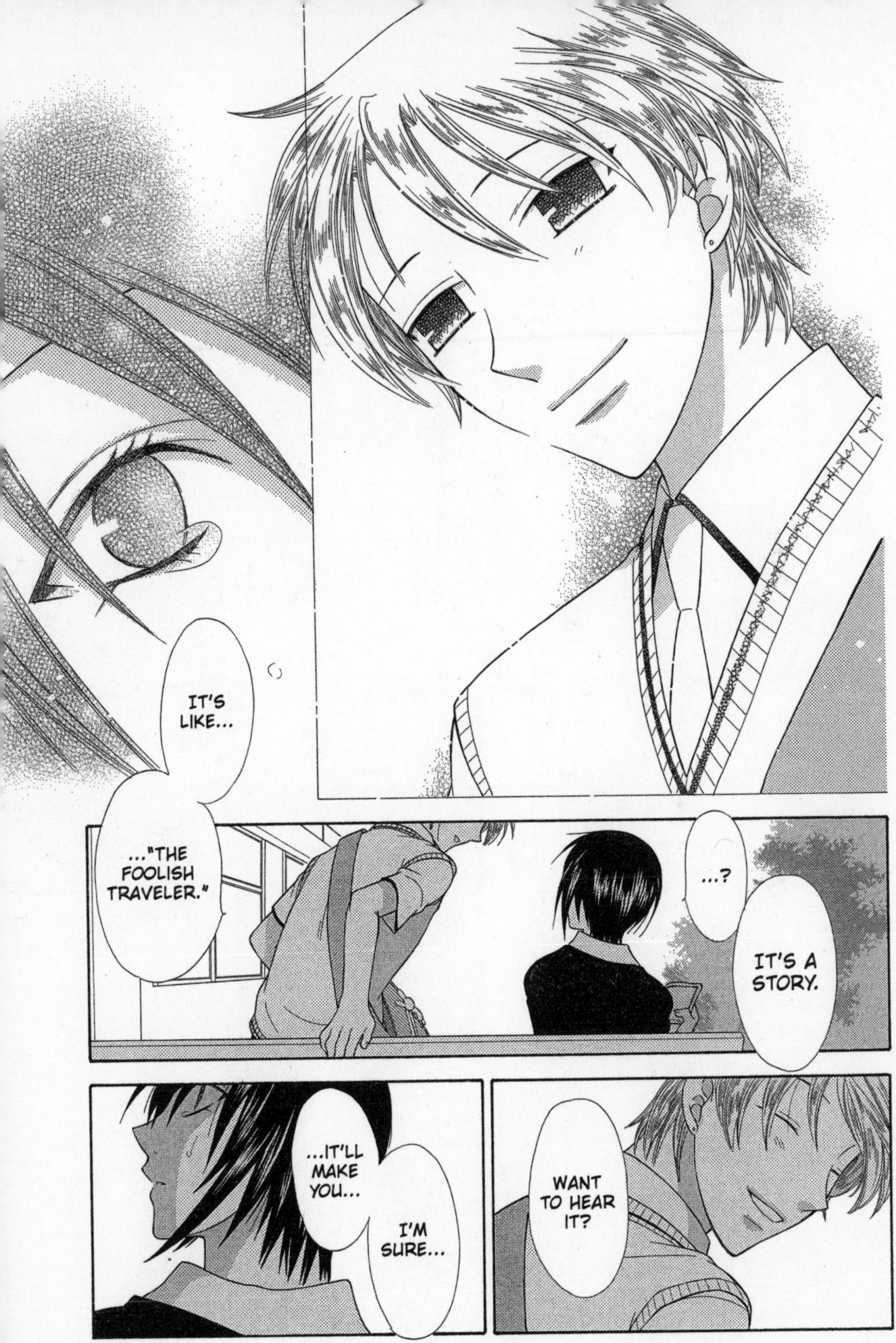
IT'S LIKE...
..."THE FOOLISH TRAVELER."
...?
IT'S A STORY.
WANT TO HEAR IT?
...IT'LL MAKE YOU...
I'M SURE...

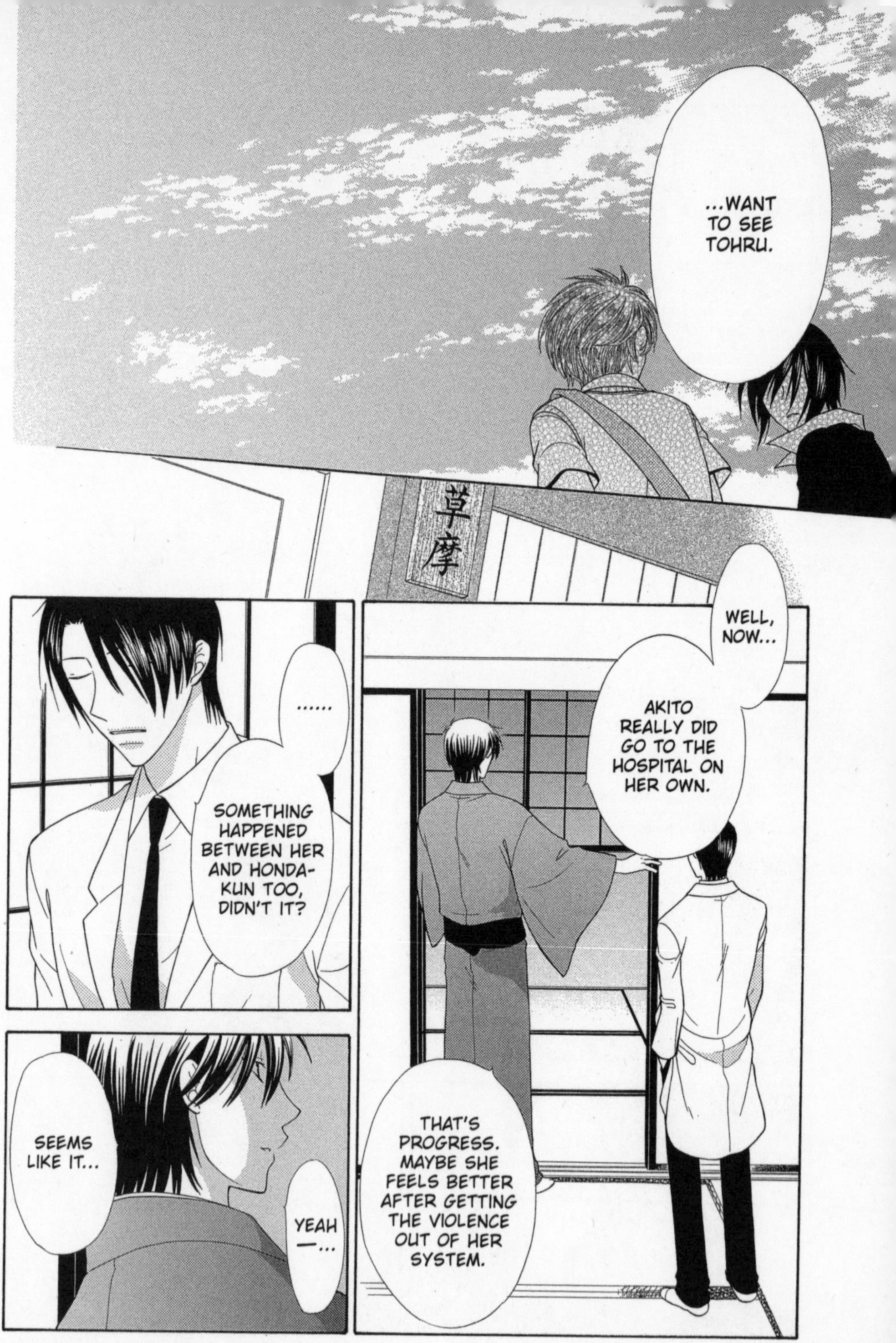
...WANT TO SEE TOHRU.
草摩
WELL, NOW...
AKITO REALLY DID GO TO THE HOSPITAL ON HER OWN.
THAT'S PROGRESS. MAYBE SHE FEELS BETTER AFTER GETTING THE VIOLENCE OUT OF HER SYSTEM.
......
SOMETHING HAPPENED BETWEEN HER AND HONDA-KUN TOO, DIDN'T IT?
SEEMS LIKE IT...
YEAH—...

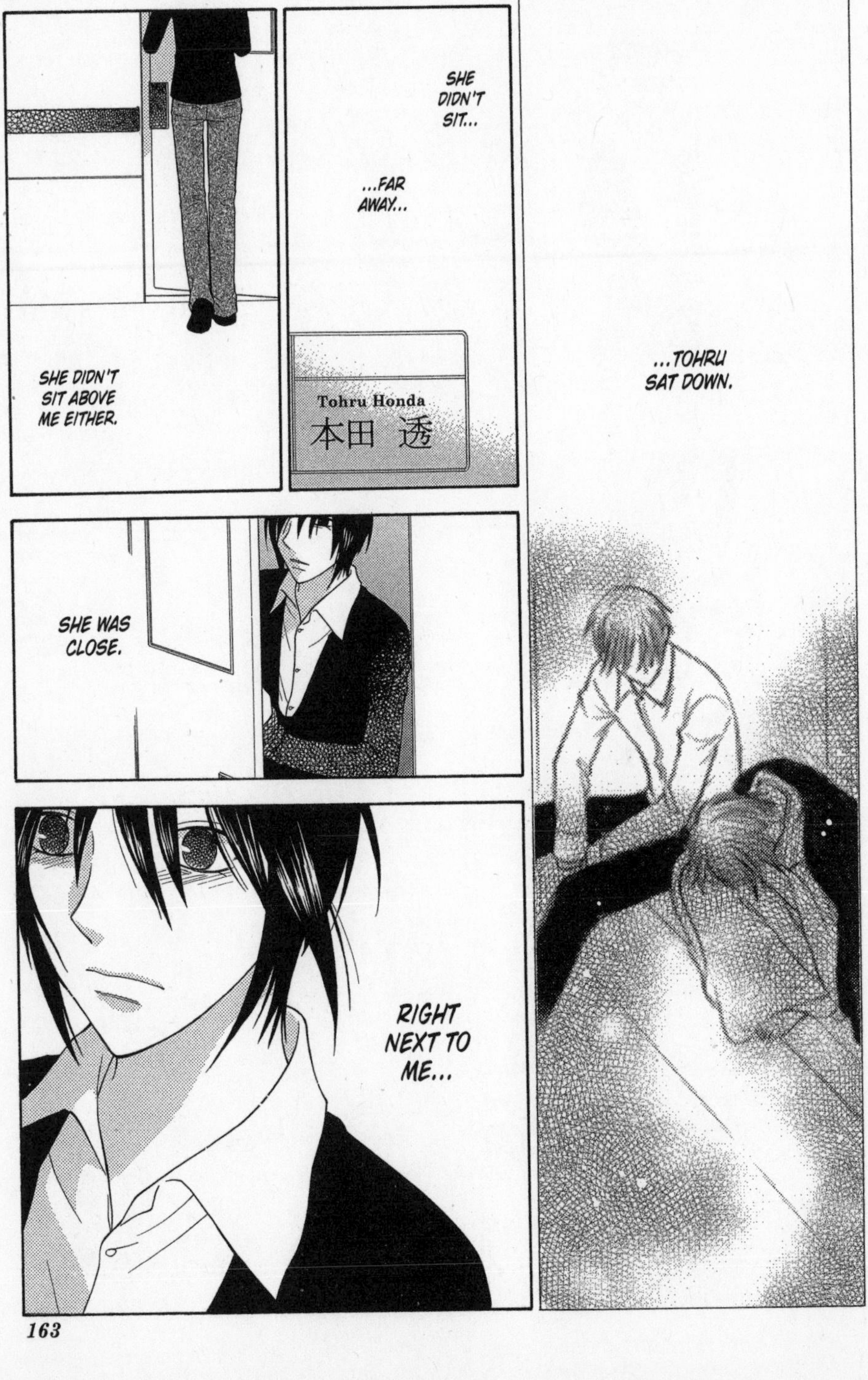
SHE DIDN'T SIT...
...FAR AWAY...
Tohru Honda
本田 透
SHE DIDN'T SIT ABOVE ME EITHER.
SHE WAS CLOSE.
RIGHT NEXT TO ME...
...TOHRU SAT DOWN.

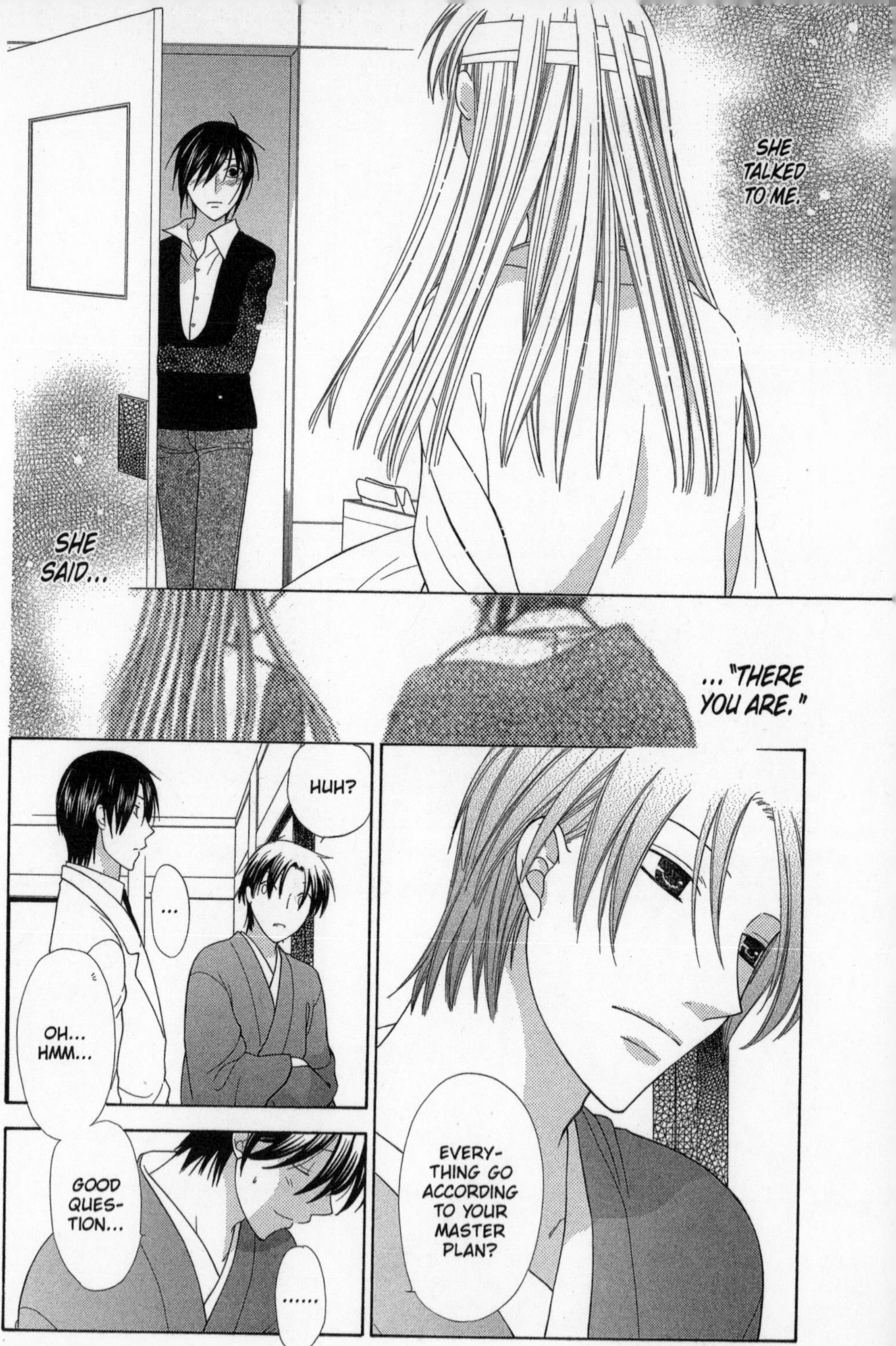
SHE TALKED TO ME.
SHE SAID...
... "THERE YOU ARE."
EVERY-THING GO ACCORDING TO YOUR MASTER PLAN?
HUH?
...
OH... HMM...
GOOD QUES-TION...
......

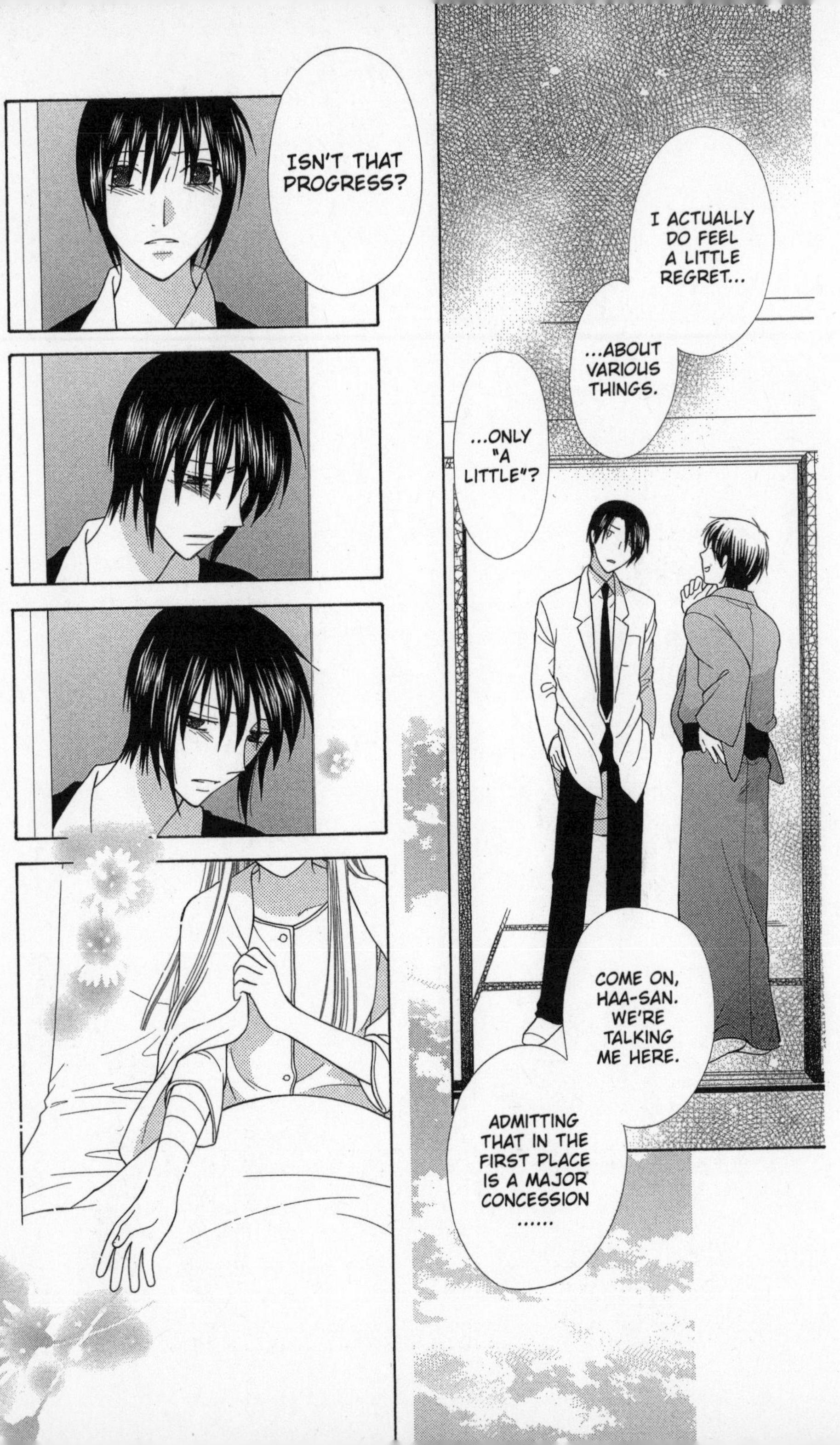
I ACTUALLY DO FEEL A LITTLE REGRET...
...ABOUT VARIOUS THINGS.
...ONLY "A LITTLE"?
COME ON, HAA-SAN. WE'RE TALKING ME HERE.
ADMITTING THAT IN THE FIRST PLACE IS A MAJOR CONCESSION ......
ISN'T THAT PROGRESS?

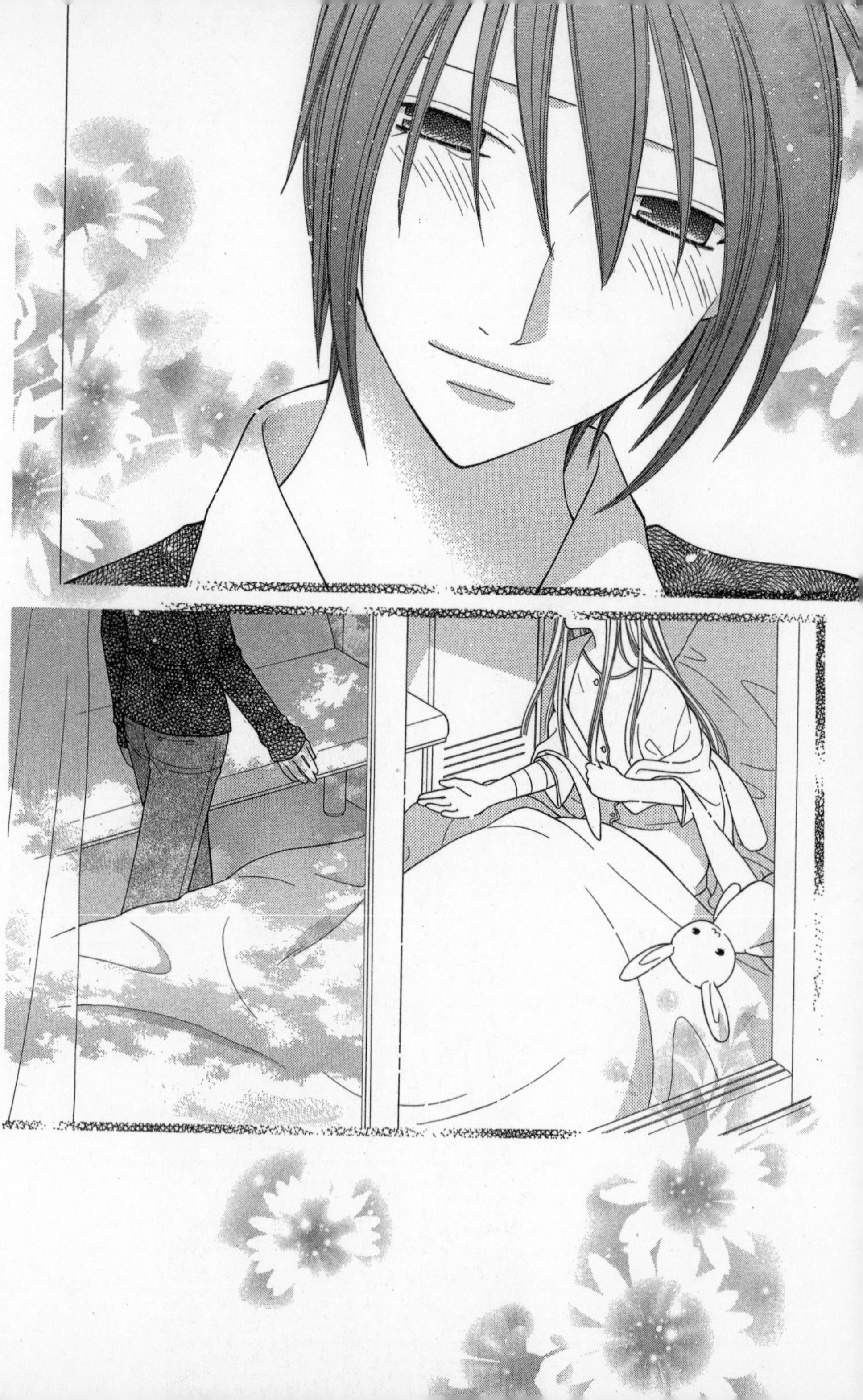

Chapter 125

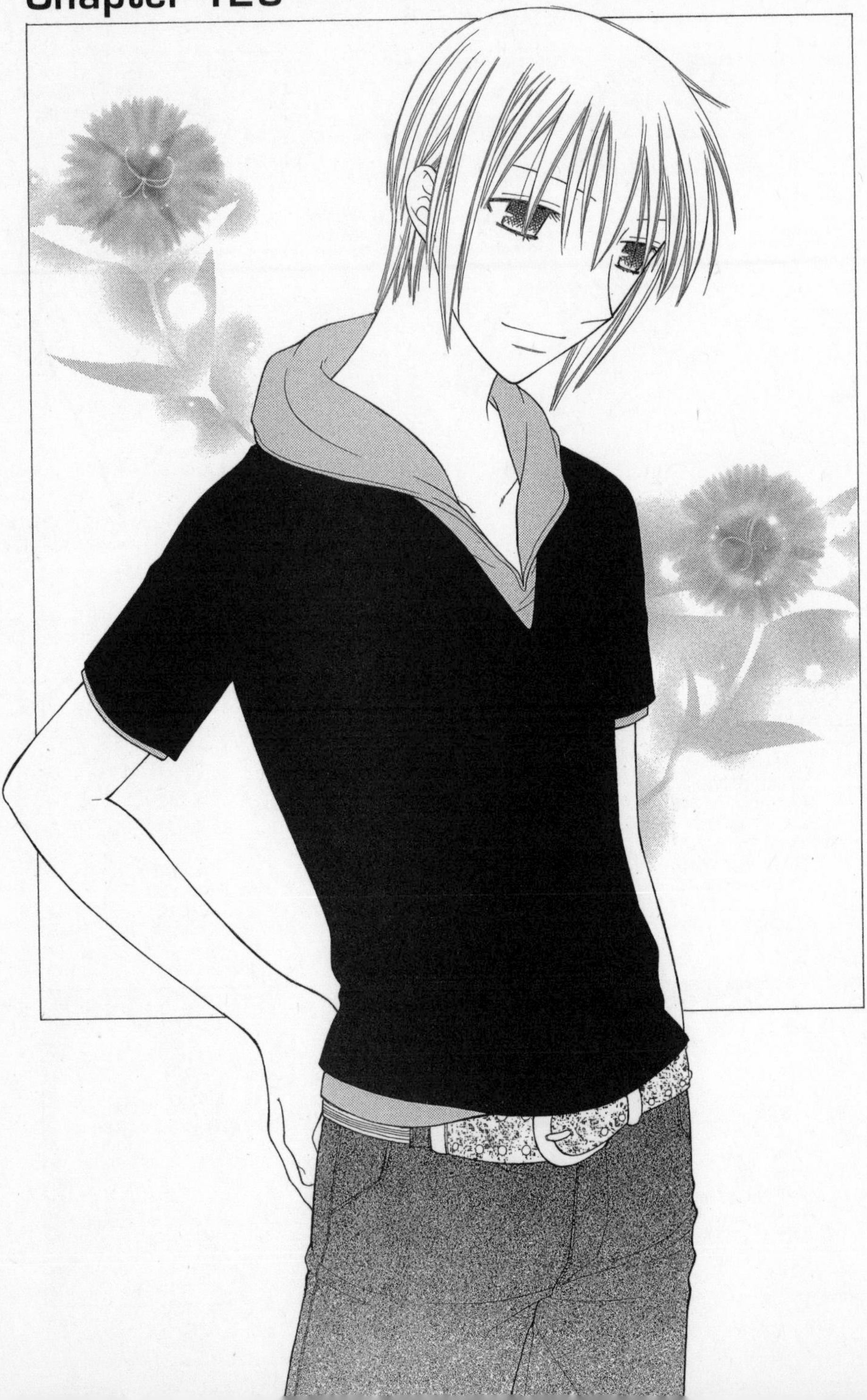

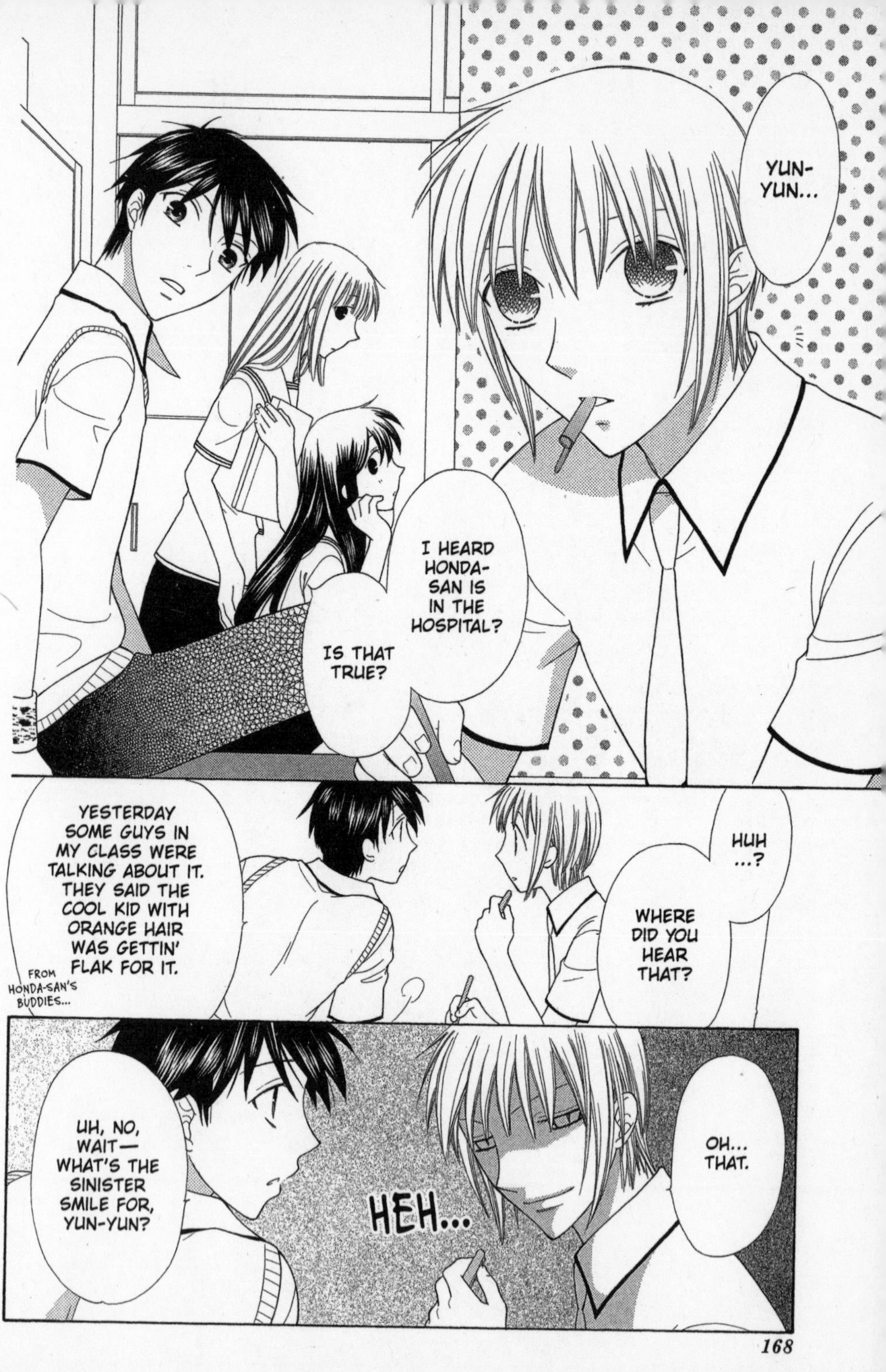
YUN-YUN...
I HEARD HONDA-SAN IS IN THE HOSPITAL?
IS THAT TRUE?
HUH ...?
WHERE DID YOU HEAR THAT?
YESTERDAY SOME GUYS IN MY CLASS WERE TALKING ABOUT IT. THEY SAID THE COOL KID WITH ORANGE HAIR WAS GETTIN' FLAK FOR IT.
FROM HONDA-SAN'S BUDDIES...
OH... THAT.
HEH...
UH, NO, WAIT— WHAT'S THE SINISTER SMILE FOR, YUN-YUN?

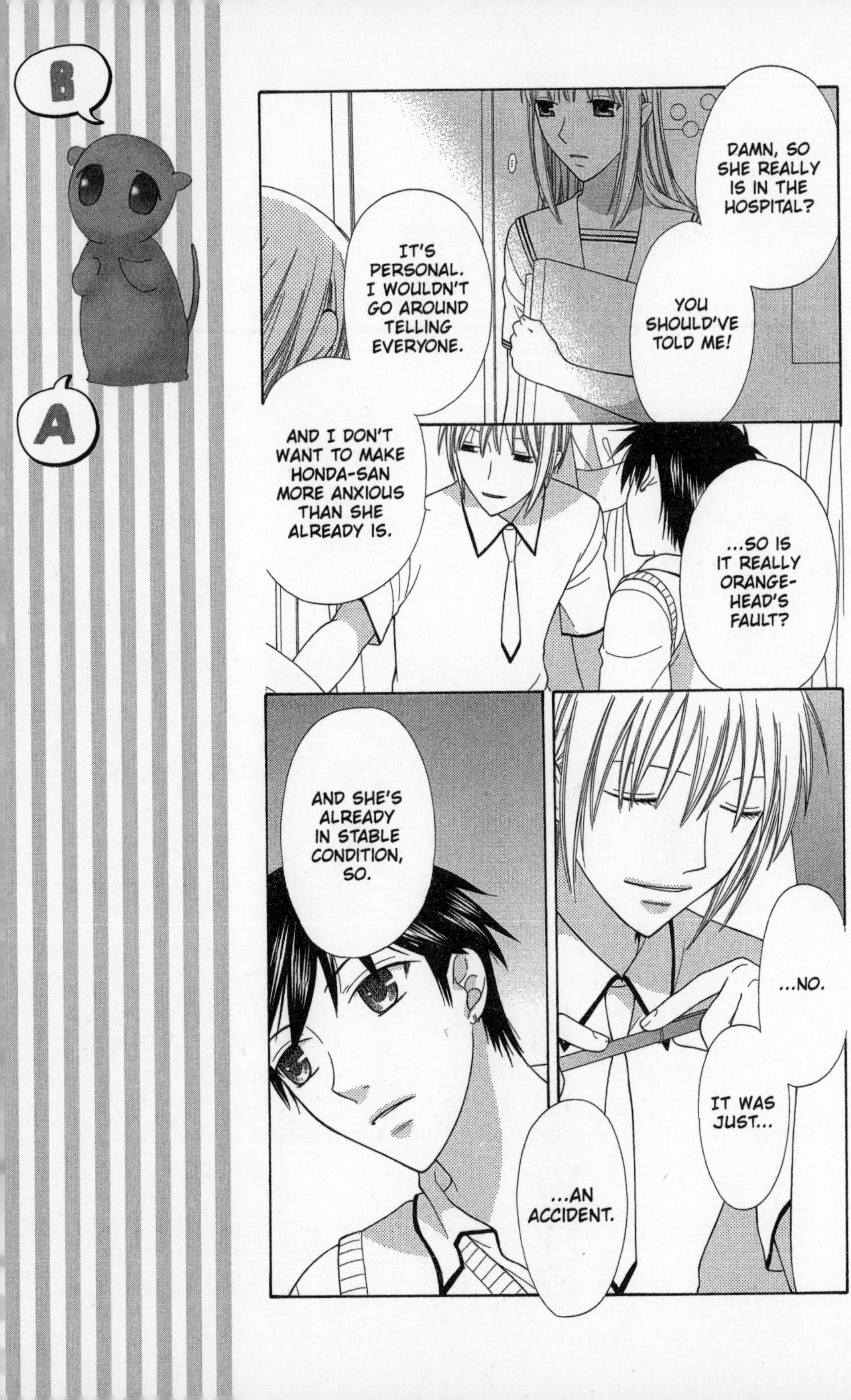
DAMN, SO SHE REALLY IS IN THE HOSPITAL?
YOU SHOULD'VE TOLD ME!
IT'S PERSONAL. I WOULDN'T GO AROUND TELLING EVERYONE.
AND I DON'T WANT TO MAKE HONDA-SAN MORE ANXIOUS THAN SHE ALREADY IS.
...SO IS IT REALLY ORANGE-HEAD'S FAULT?
...NO.
IT WAS JUST...
...AN ACCIDENT.
AND SHE'S ALREADY IN STABLE CONDITION, SO.

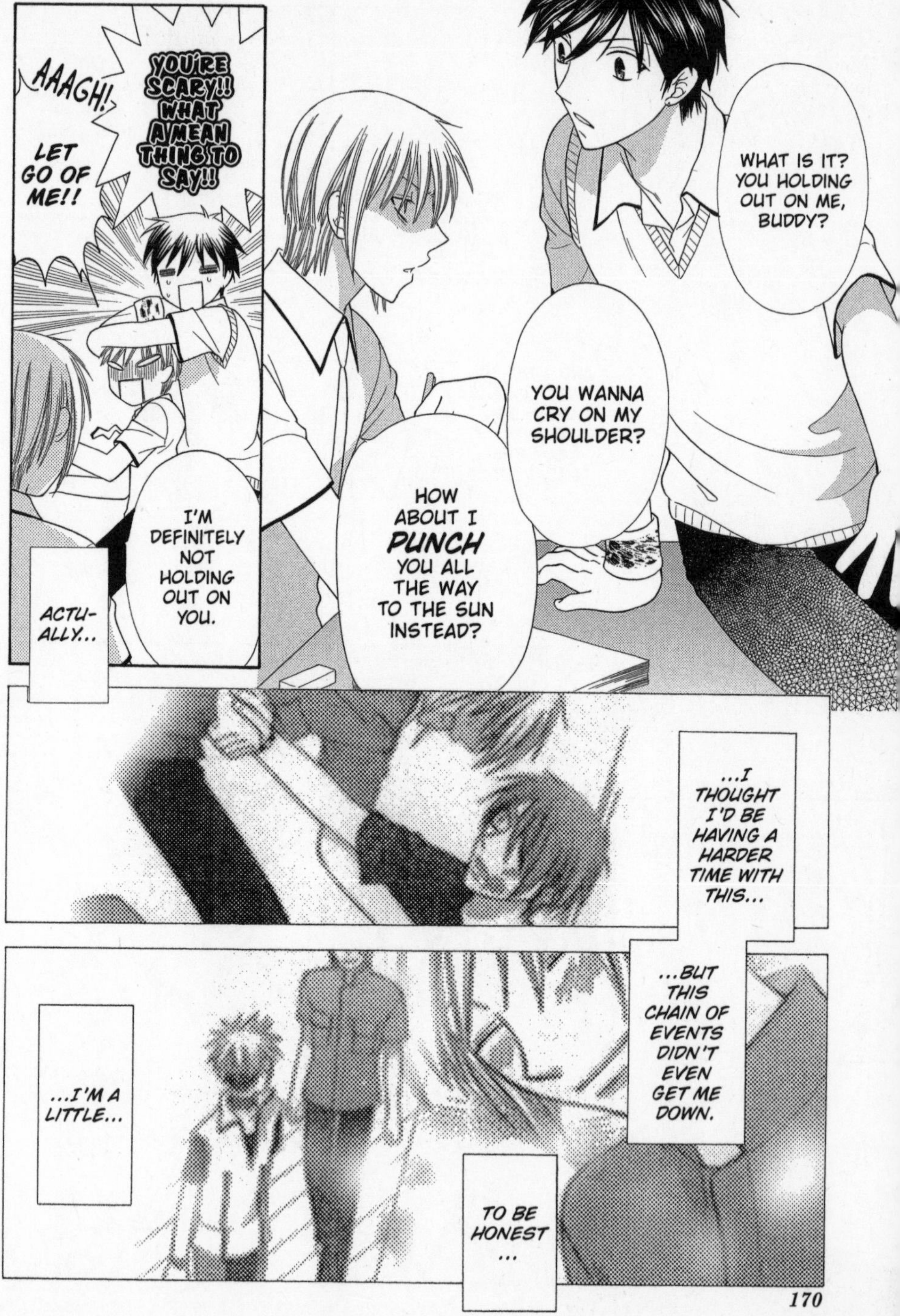
WHAT IS IT? YOU HOLDING OUT ON ME, BUDDY?
YOU WANNA CRY ON MY SHOULDER?
HOW ABOUT I PUNCH YOU ALL THE WAY TO THE SUN INSTEAD?
YOU'RE SCARY!! WHAT A MEAN THING TO SAY!!
AAAGH!
LET GO OF ME!!
I'M DEFINITELY NOT HOLDING OUT ON YOU.
ACTU-ALLY...
...I THOUGHT I'D BE HAVING A HARDER TIME WITH THIS...
...BUT THIS CHAIN OF EVENTS DIDN'T EVEN GET ME DOWN.
TO BE HONEST...
...I'M A LITTLE...

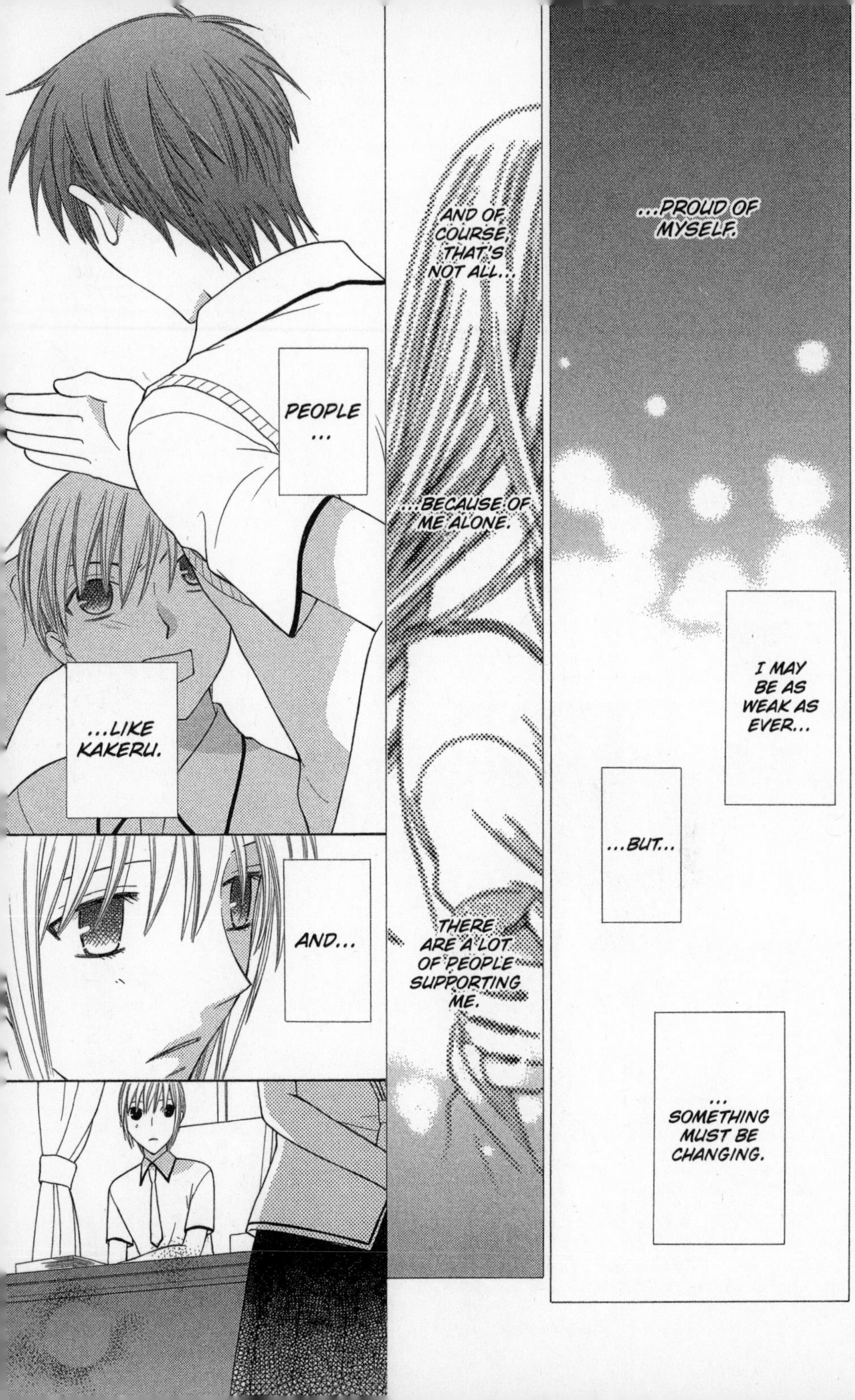

...PROUD OF MYSELF.
I MAY BE AS WEAK AS EVER...
...BUT...
...SOMETHING MUST BE CHANGING.
AND OF COURSE, THAT'S NOT ALL...
...BECAUSE OF ME ALONE.
THERE ARE A LOT OF PEOPLE SUPPORTING ME.
PEOPLE...
...LIKE KAKERU.
AND...

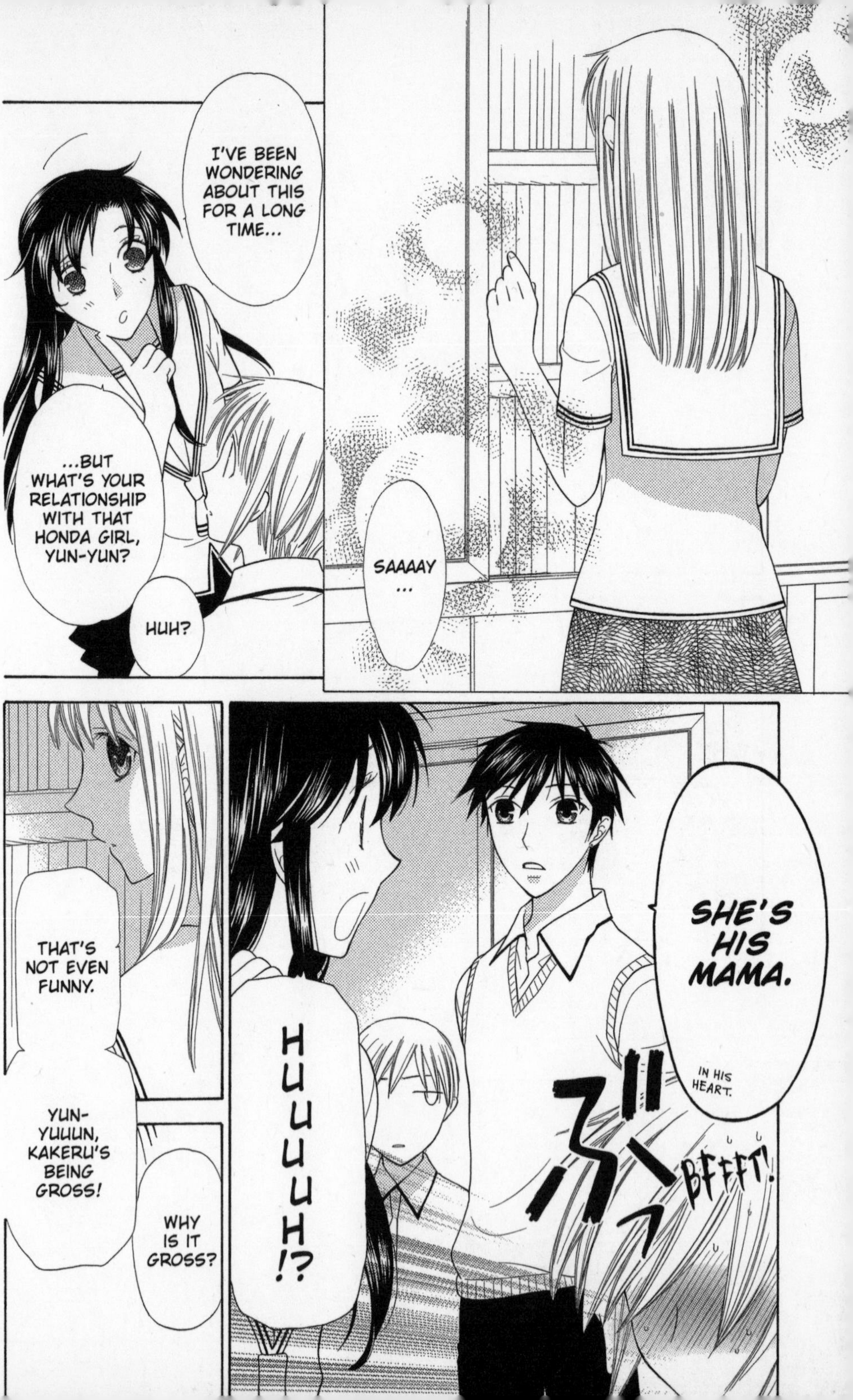
SAAAAY...
I'VE BEEN WONDERING ABOUT THIS FOR A LONG TIME...
...BUT WHAT'S YOUR RELATIONSHIP WITH THAT HONDA GIRL, YUN-YUN?
HUH?
SHE'S HIS MAMA.
IN HIS HEART.
BFFFT!
HUUUUH!?
THAT'S NOT EVEN FUNNY.
YUN-YUUUN, KAKERU'S BEING GROSS!
WHY IS IT GROSS?

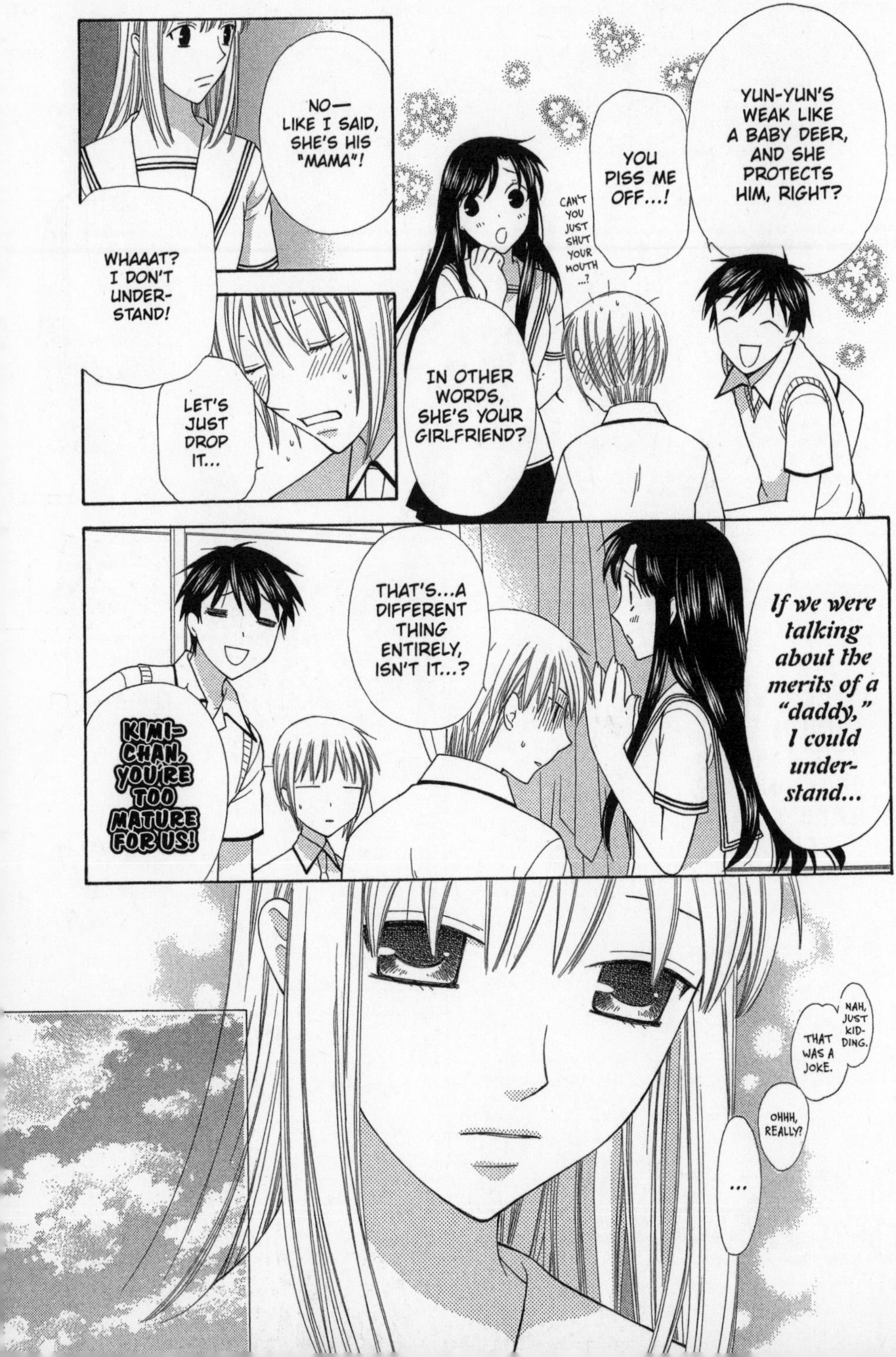
YUN-YUN'S WEAK LIKE A BABY DEER, AND SHE PROTECTS HIM, RIGHT?
YOU PISS ME OFF...!
CAN'T YOU JUST SHUT YOUR MOUTH ...?
IN OTHER WORDS, SHE'S YOUR GIRLFRIEND?
NO— LIKE I SAID, SHE'S HIS "MAMA"!
WHAAAT? I DON'T UNDER-STAND!
LET'S JUST DROP IT...
If we were talking about the merits of a "daddy," I could under-stand...
THAT'S...A DIFFERENT THING ENTIRELY, ISN'T IT...?
KIMI-CHAN, YOU'RE TOO MATURE FOR US!
NAH, JUST KID-DING.
THAT WAS A JOKE.
OHHH, REALLY?
...

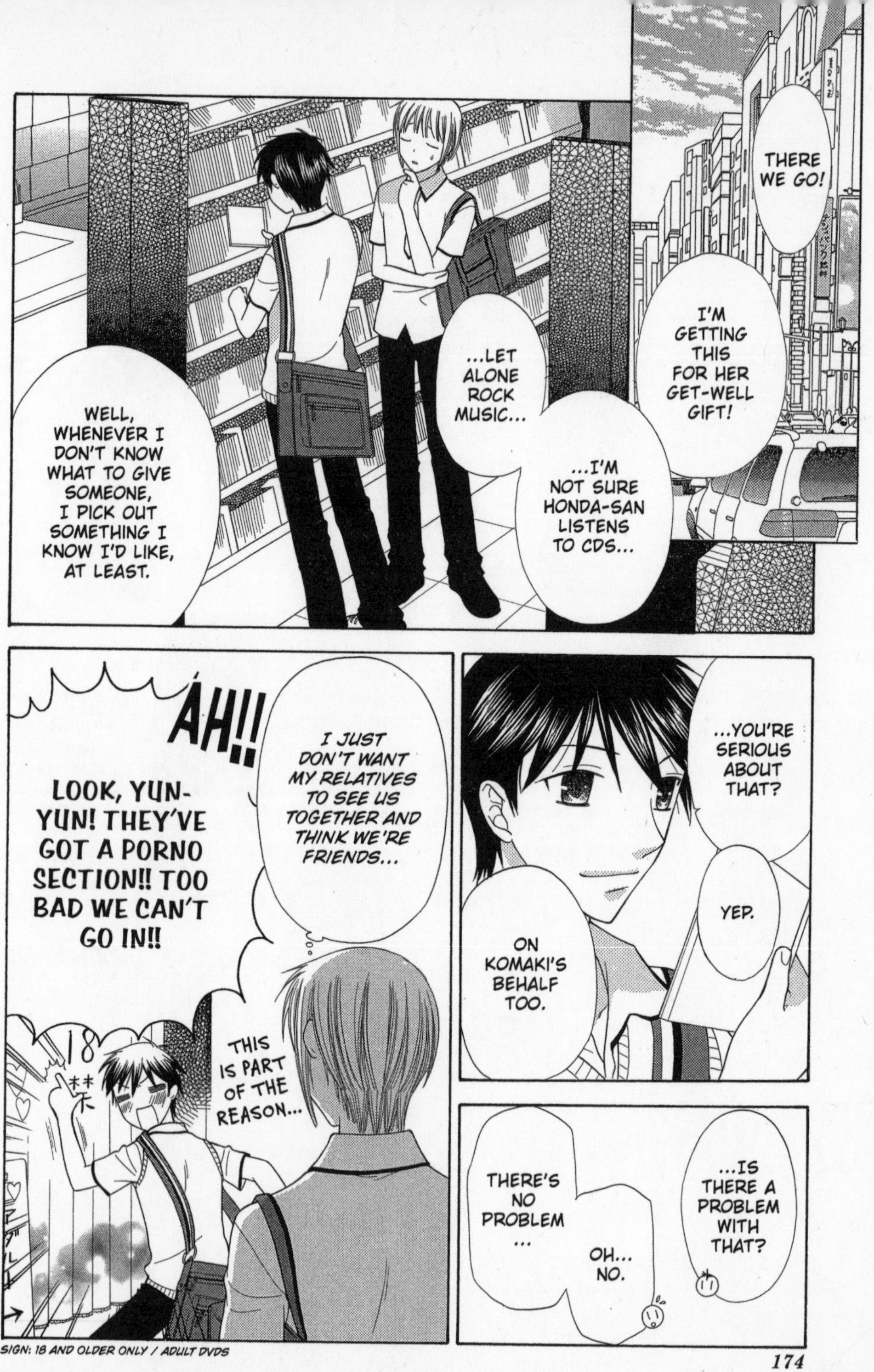
THERE WE GO!
I'M GETTING THIS FOR HER GET-WELL GIFT!
...I'M NOT SURE HONDA-SAN LISTENS TO CDS...
...LET ALONE ROCK MUSIC...
WELL, WHENEVER I DON'T KNOW WHAT TO GIVE SOMEONE, I PICK OUT SOMETHING I KNOW I'D LIKE, AT LEAST.
...YOU'RE SERIOUS ABOUT THAT?
YEP.
ON KOMAKI'S BEHALF TOO.
...IS THERE A PROBLEM WITH THAT?
THERE'S NO PROBLEM ...
OH... NO.
I JUST DON'T WANT MY RELATIVES TO SEE US TOGETHER AND THINK WE'RE FRIENDS...
AH!!
LOOK, YUN-YUN! THEY'VE GOT A PORNO SECTION!! TOO BAD WE CAN'T GO IN!!
THIS IS PART OF THE REASON...

SIGN: 18 AND OLDER ONLY / ADULT DVDS

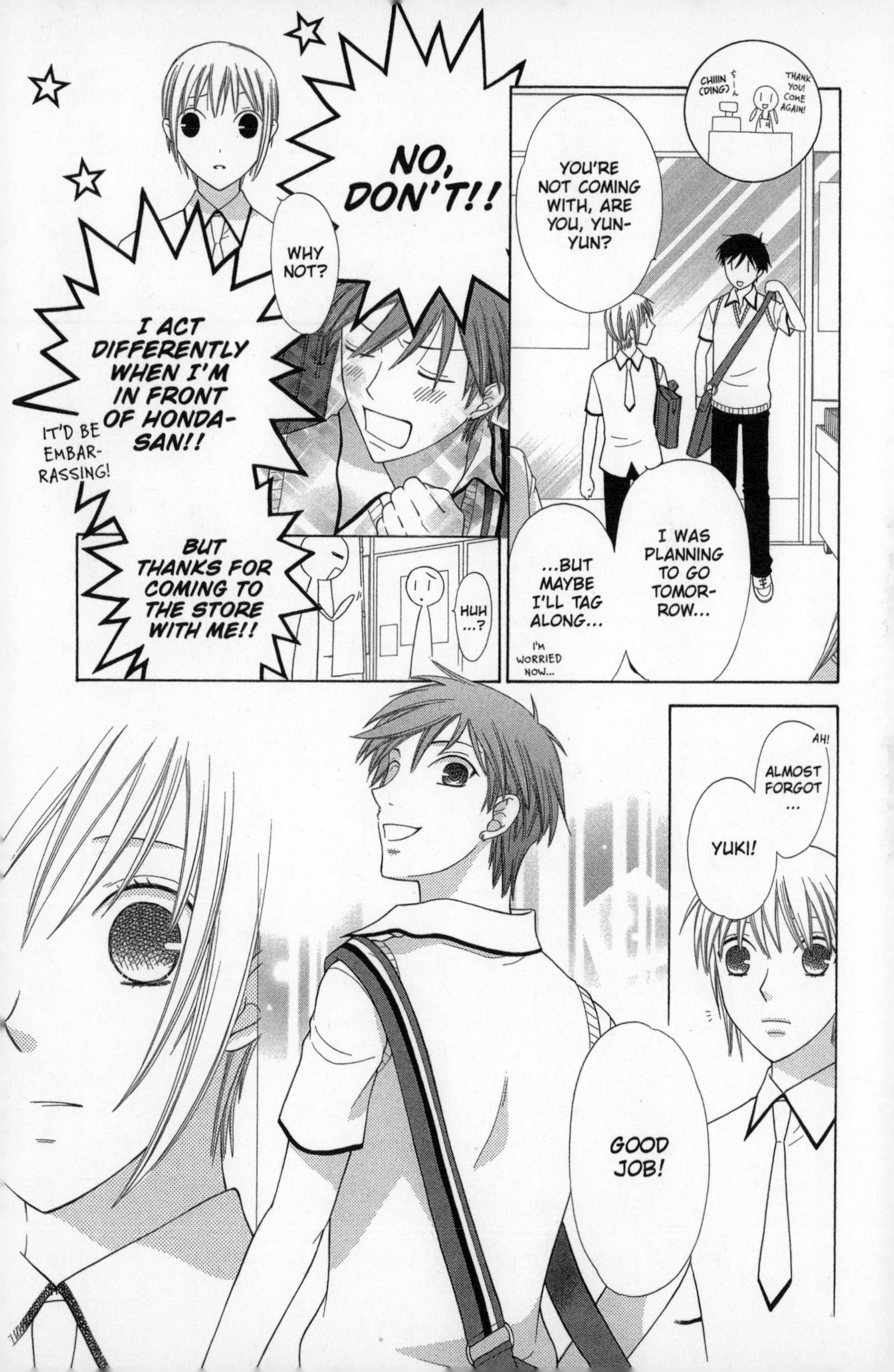
CHIIIN (DING)
THANK YOU! COME AGAIN!
YOU'RE NOT COMING WITH, ARE YOU, YUN-YUN?
I WAS PLANNING TO GO TOMORROW...
...BUT MAYBE I'LL TAG ALONG...
I'M WORRIED NOW...
NO, DON'T!!
WHY NOT?
I ACT DIFFERENTLY WHEN I'M IN FRONT OF HONDA-SAN!!
IT'D BE EMBARRASSING!
HUH ...?
BUT THANKS FOR COMING TO THE STORE WITH ME!!
AH!
ALMOST FORGOT ...
YUKI!
GOOD JOB!

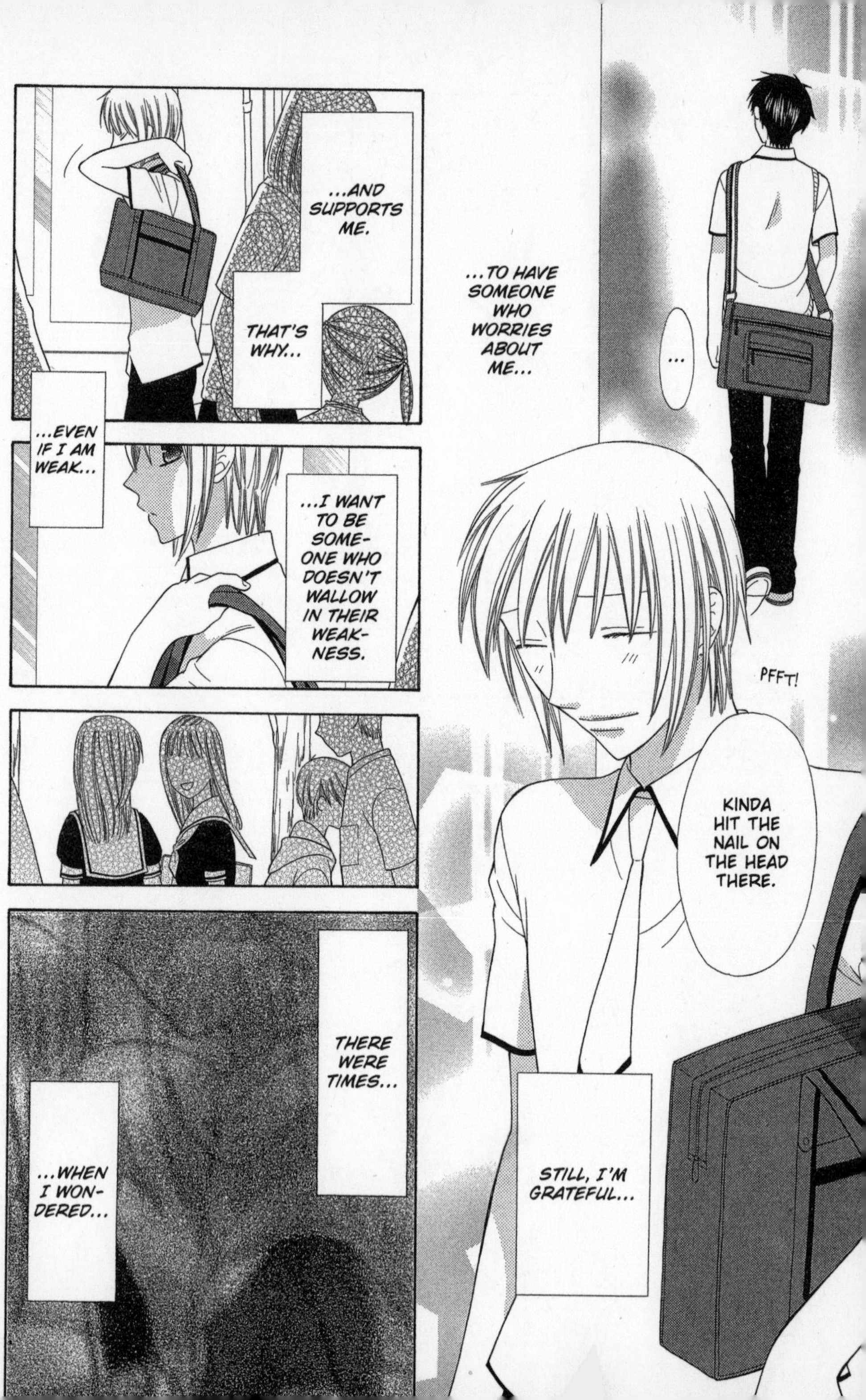
...
PFFT!
KINDA HIT THE NAIL ON THE HEAD THERE.
STILL, I'M GRATEFUL...
...TO HAVE SOMEONE WHO WORRIES ABOUT ME...
...AND SUPPORTS ME.
THAT'S WHY...
...EVEN IF I AM WEAK...
...I WANT TO BE SOME-ONE WHO DOESN'T WALLOW IN THEIR WEAK-NESS.
THERE WERE TIMES...
...WHEN I WON-DERED...

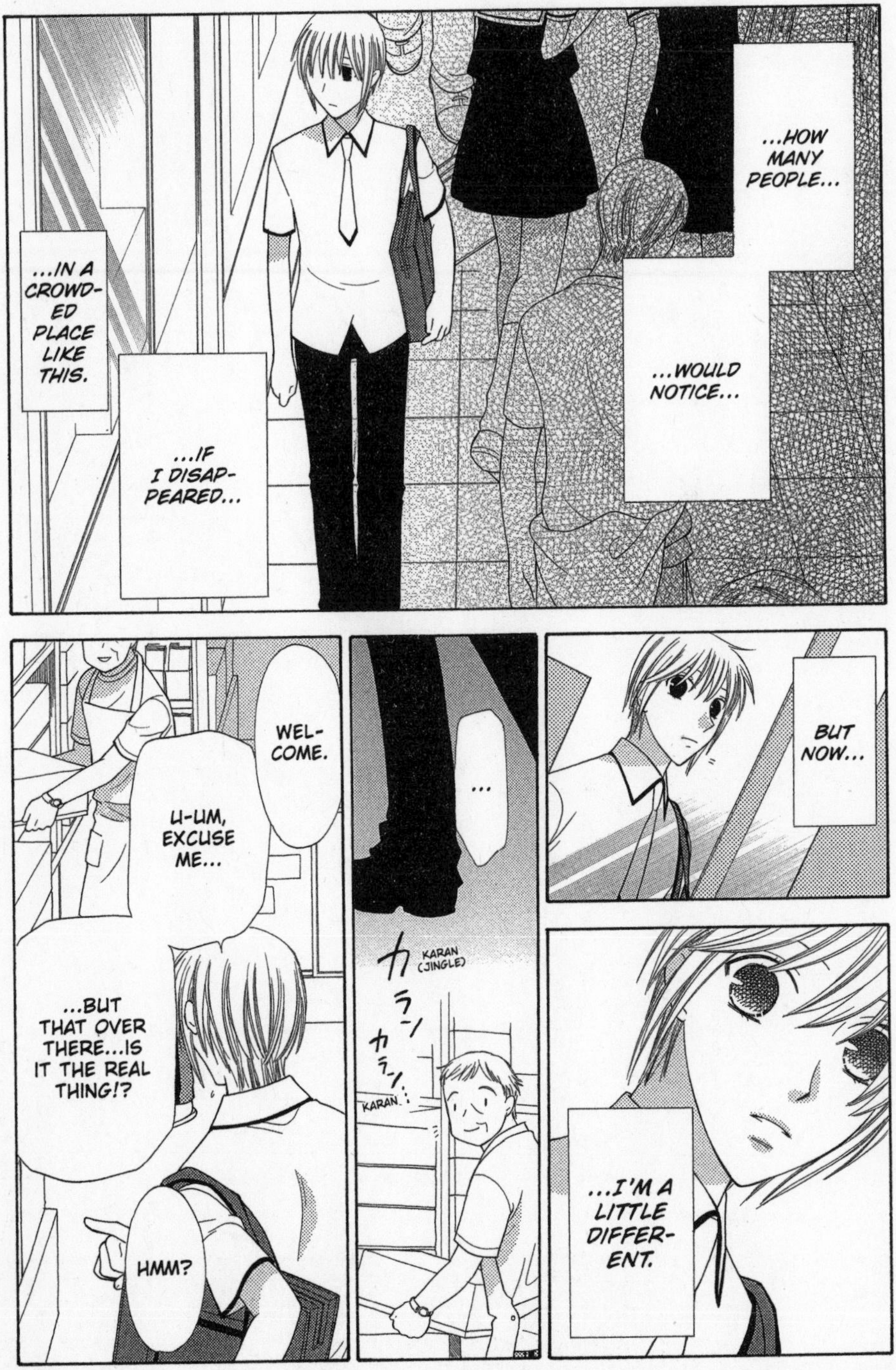
...HOW MANY PEOPLE...
...WOULD NOTICE...
...IF I DISAPPEARED...
...IN A CROWDED PLACE LIKE THIS.
BUT NOW...
...I'M A LITTLE DIFFERENT.
...
カラン KARAN (JINGLE)
カラン KARAN
WELCOME.
U-UM, EXCUSE ME...
...BUT THAT OVER THERE...IS IT THE REAL THING!?
HMM?

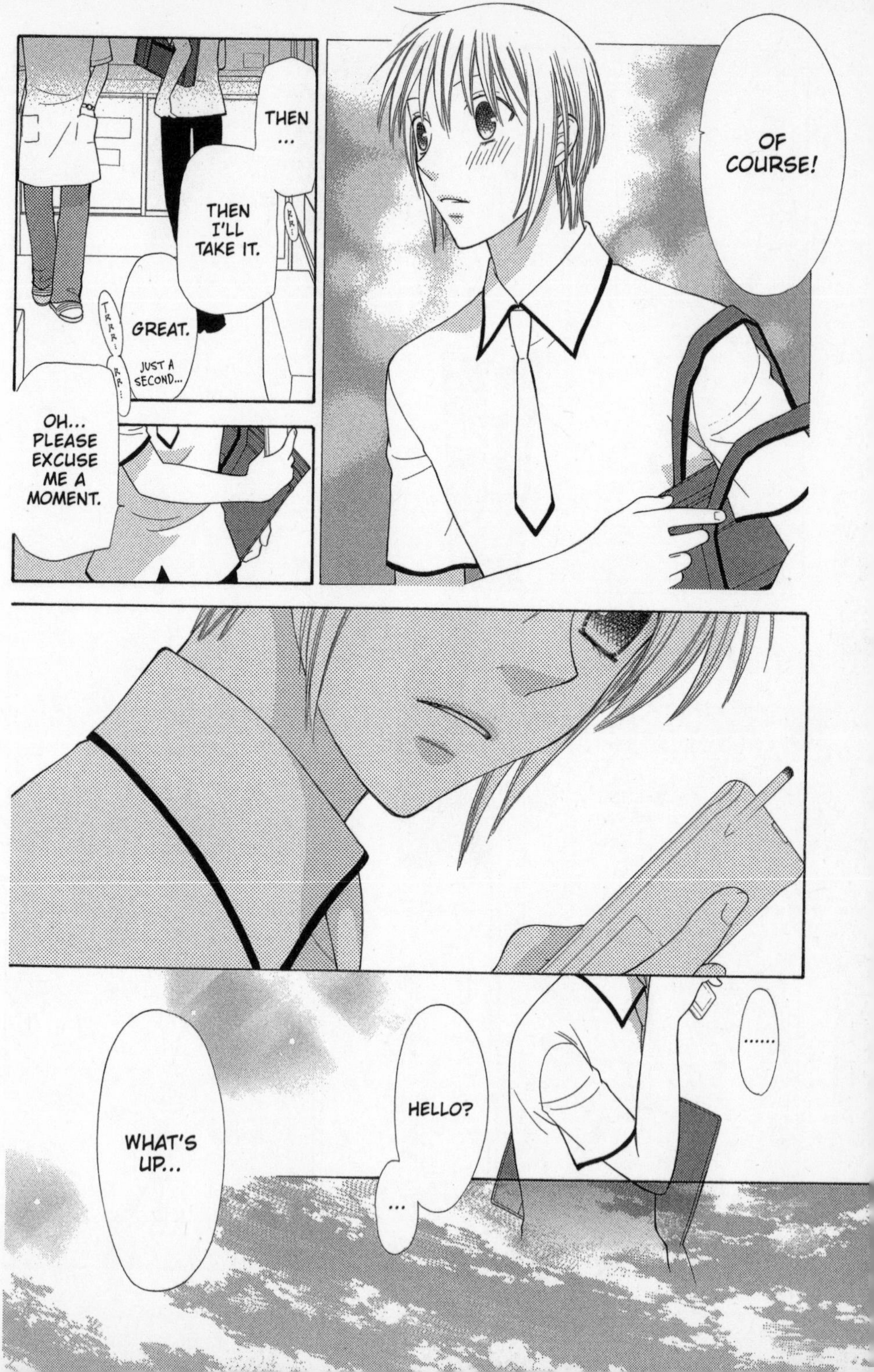

OF COURSE!
THEN ...
THEN I'LL TAKE IT.
GREAT.
JUST A SECOND...
OH... PLEASE EXCUSE ME A MOMENT.
......
HELLO?
...
WHAT'S UP...

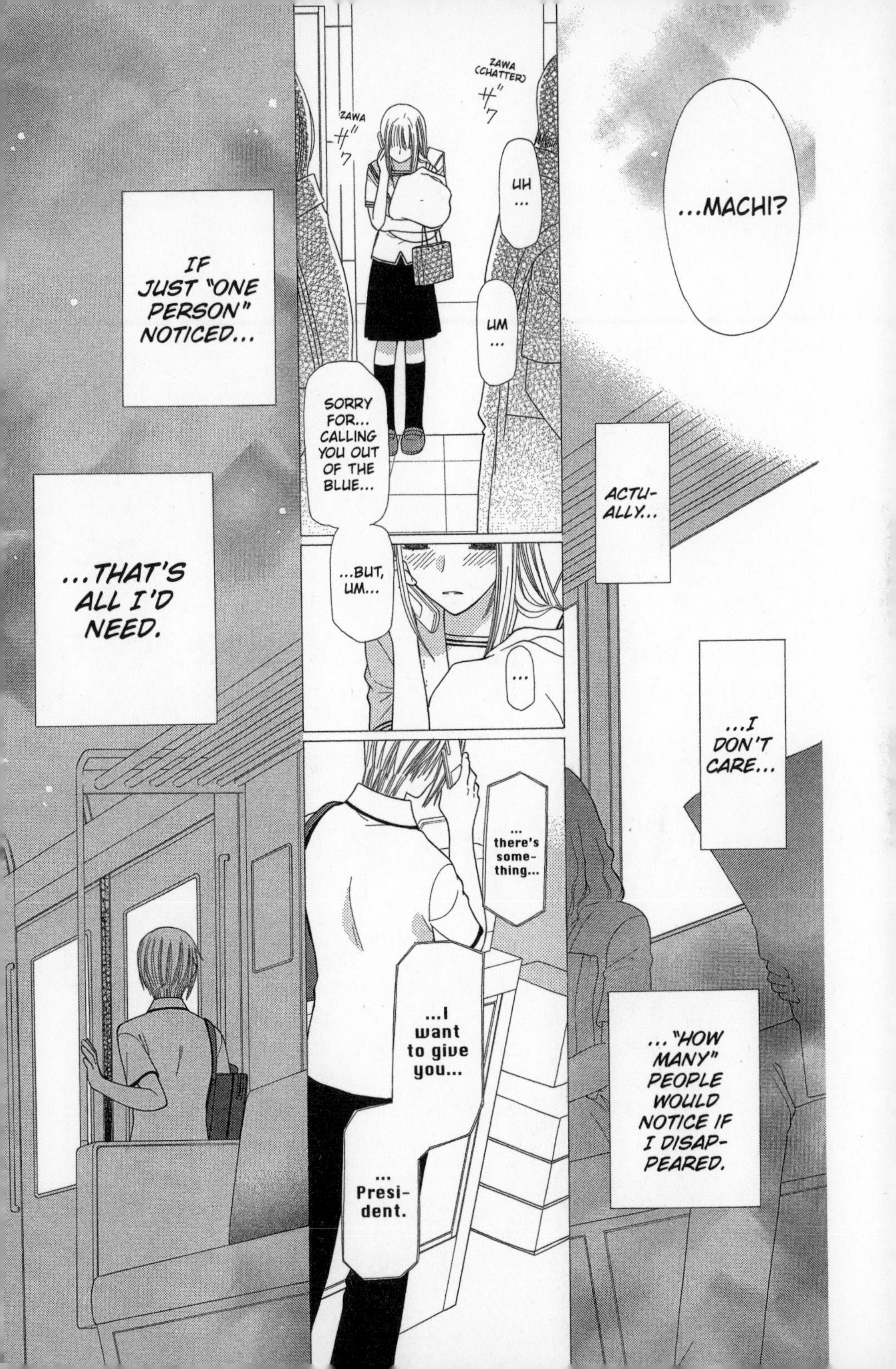
...MACHI?
ACTU-ALLY...
...I DON'T CARE...
..."HOW MANY" PEOPLE WOULD NOTICE IF I DISAPPEARED.
ZAWA (CHATTER)
ザワ
ZAWA
ザワ
UH...
UM...
SORRY FOR... CALLING YOU OUT OF THE BLUE...
...BUT, UM...
...
...there's something...
...I want to give you...
...President.
IF JUST "ONE PERSON" NOTICED...
...THAT'S ALL I'D NEED.

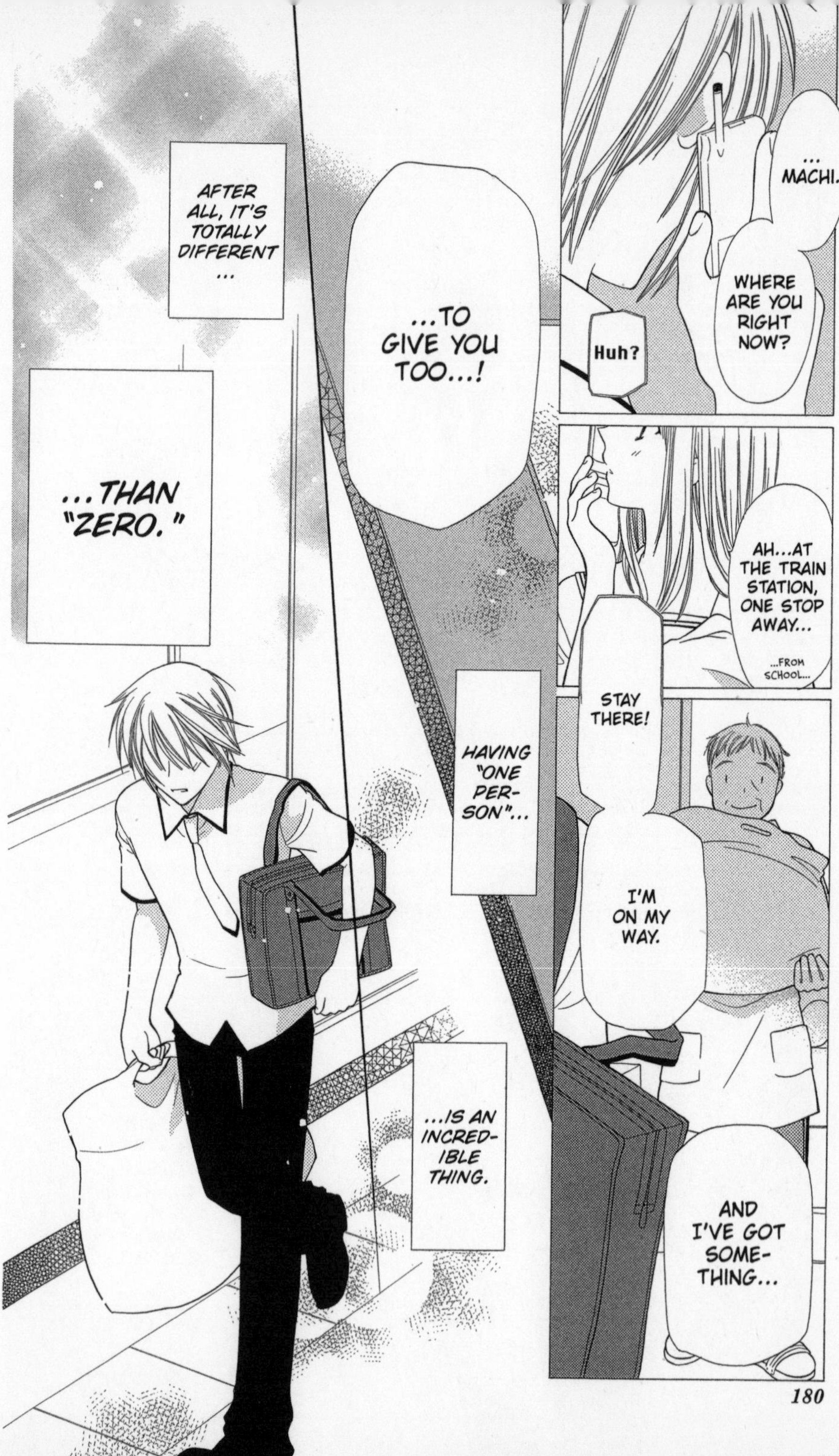
...MACHI.
WHERE ARE YOU RIGHT NOW?
Huh?
AH...AT THE TRAIN STATION, ONE STOP AWAY...
...FROM SCHOOL...
STAY THERE!
I'M ON MY WAY.
AND I'VE GOT SOMETHING...
...TO GIVE YOU TOO...!
HAVING "ONE PERSON"...
...IS AN INCREDIBLE THING.
AFTER ALL, IT'S TOTALLY DIFFERENT...
...THAN "ZERO."

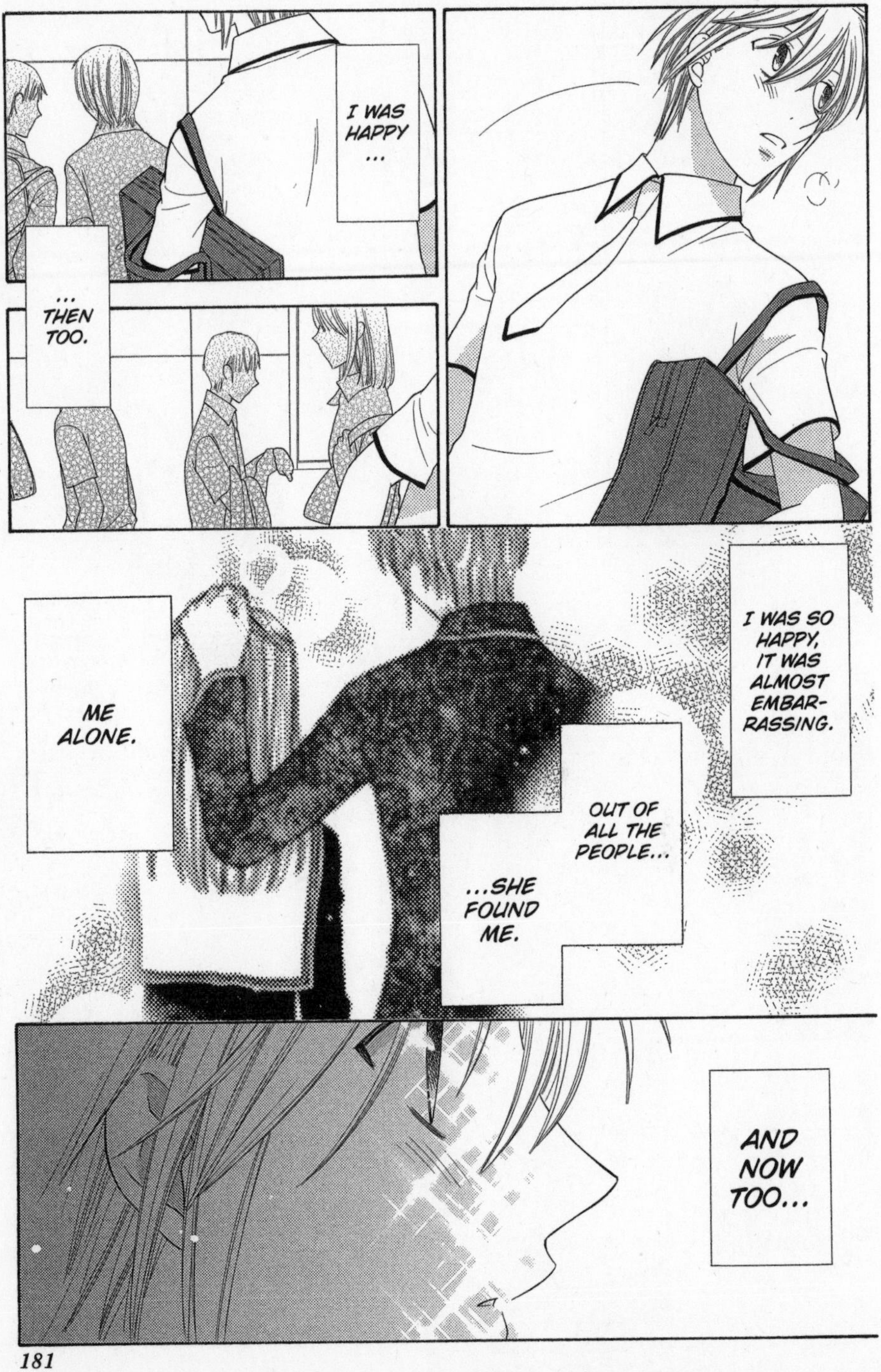
I WAS HAPPY ...
... THEN TOO.
I WAS SO HAPPY, IT WAS ALMOST EMBARRASSING.
OUT OF ALL THE PEOPLE...
...SHE FOUND ME.
ME ALONE.
AND NOW TOO...

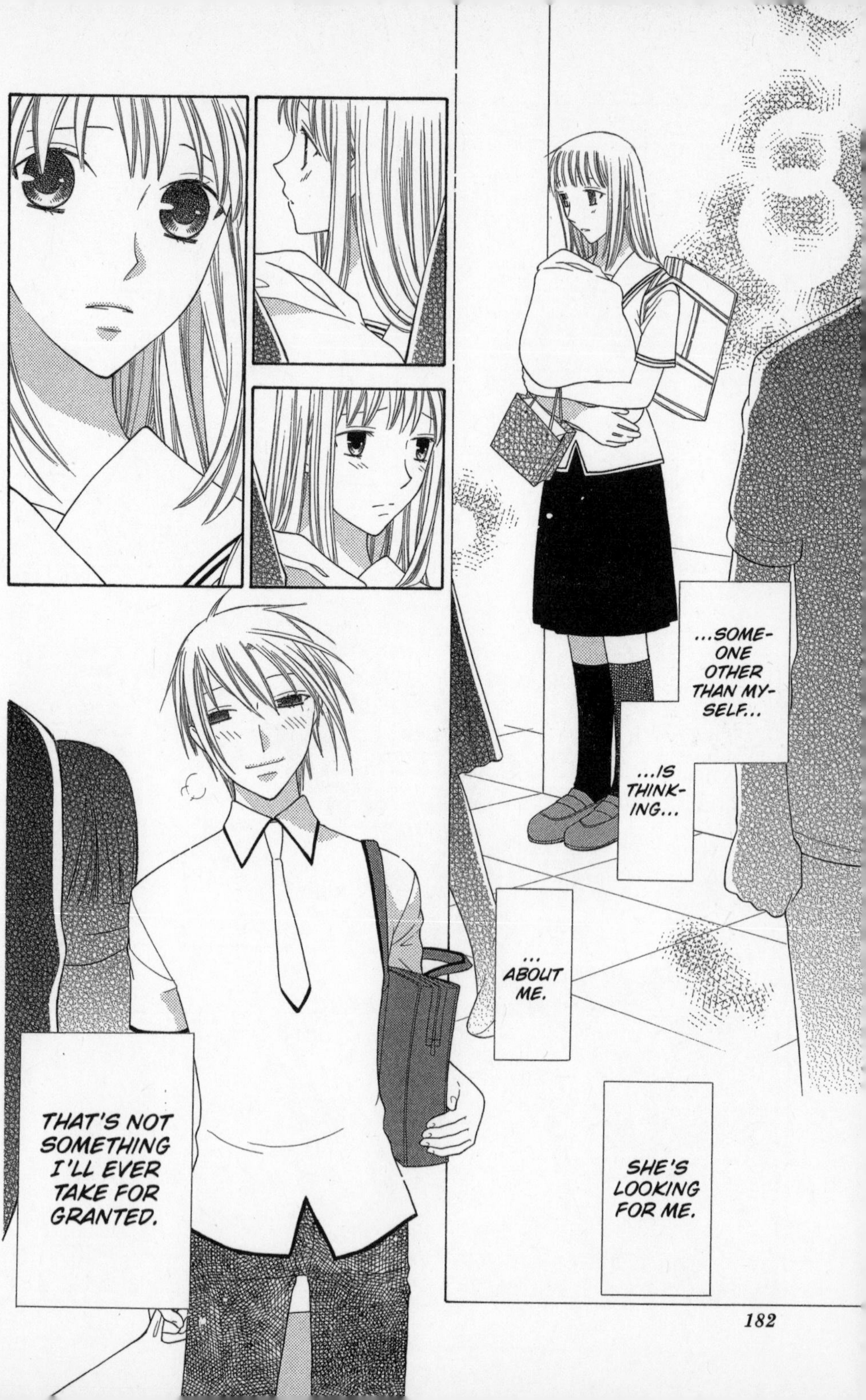
...SOME-ONE OTHER THAN MY-SELF...
...IS THINKING...
...ABOUT ME.
SHE'S LOOKING FOR ME.
THAT'S NOT SOMETHING I'LL EVER TAKE FOR GRANTED.

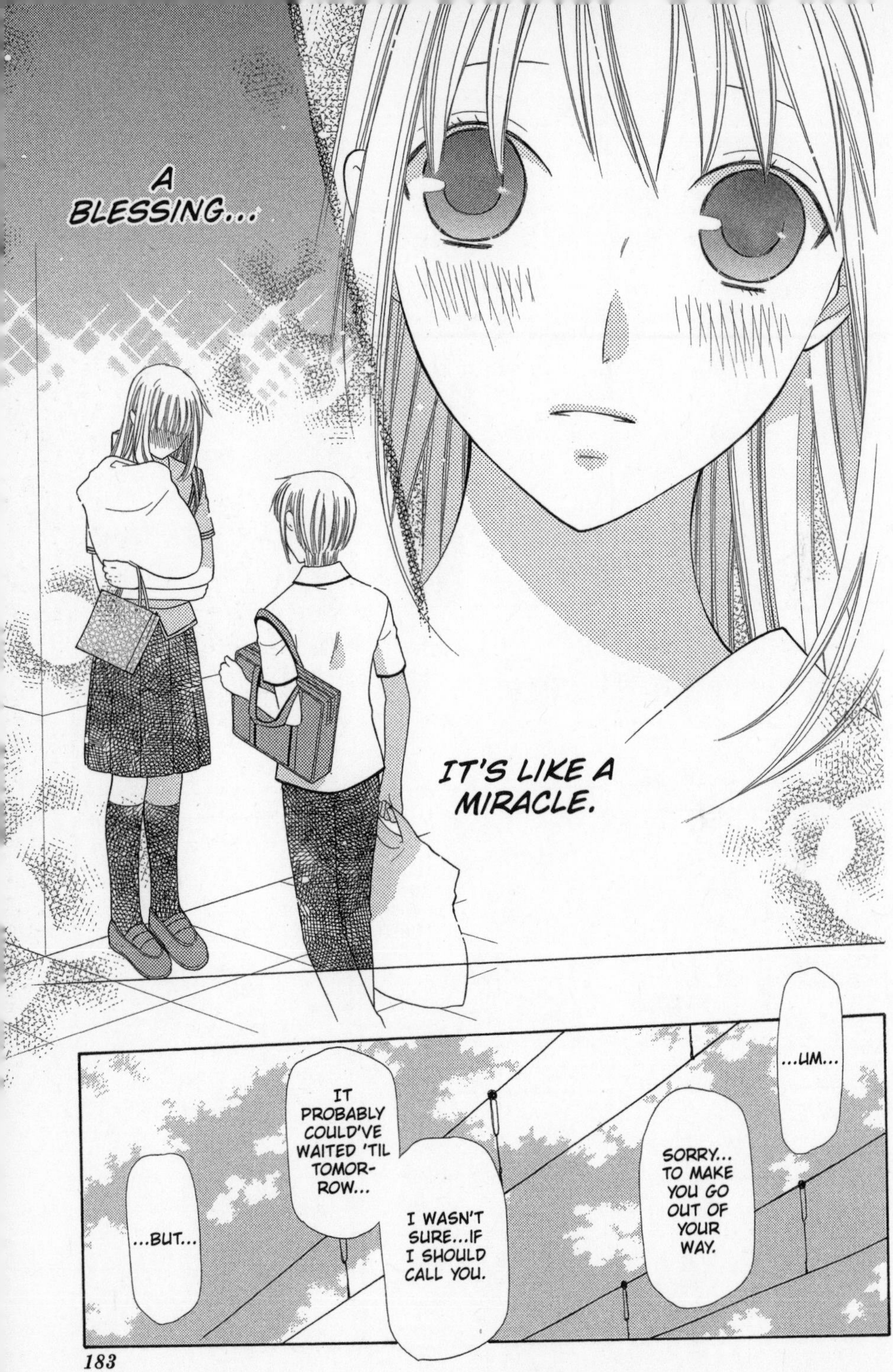
A BLESSING...
IT'S LIKE A MIRACLE.
...UM...
SORRY... TO MAKE YOU GO OUT OF YOUR WAY.
IT PROBABLY COULD'VE WAITED 'TIL TOMOR-ROW...
I WASN'T SURE...IF I SHOULD CALL YOU.
...BUT...

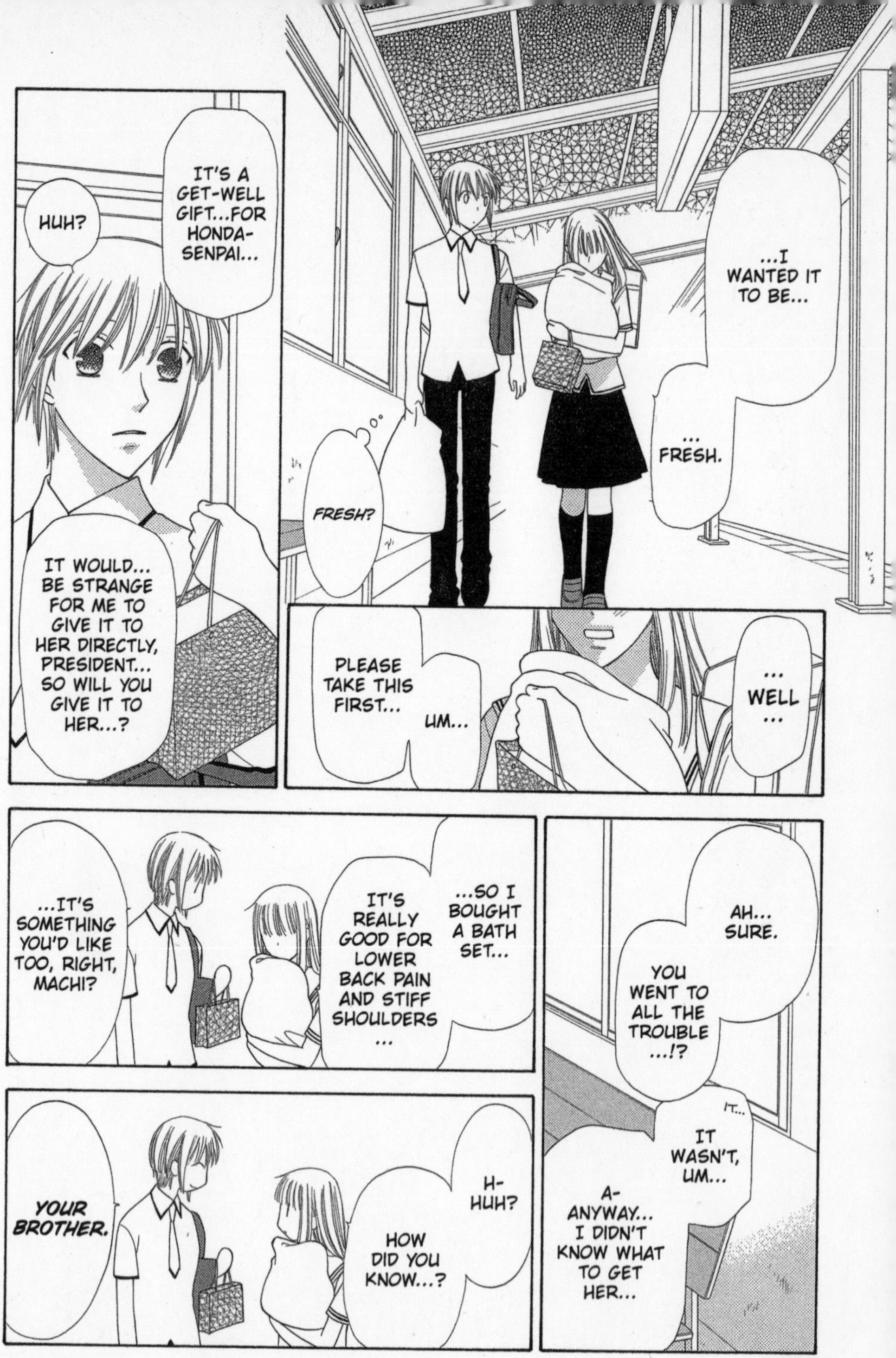
...I WANTED IT TO BE...
...FRESH.
FRESH?
...WELL...
UM...
PLEASE TAKE THIS FIRST...
IT'S A GET-WELL GIFT...FOR HONDA-SENPAI...
HUH?
IT WOULD... BE STRANGE FOR ME TO GIVE IT TO HER DIRECTLY, PRESIDENT... SO WILL YOU GIVE IT TO HER...?
AH... SURE.
YOU WENT TO ALL THE TROUBLE...!?
IT...
IT WASN'T, UM...
A-ANYWAY... I DIDN'T KNOW WHAT TO GET HER...
...SO I BOUGHT A BATH SET...
IT'S REALLY GOOD FOR LOWER BACK PAIN AND STIFF SHOULDERS...
...IT'S SOMETHING YOU'D LIKE TOO, RIGHT, MACHI?
H-HUH?
HOW DID YOU KNOW...?
YOUR BROTHER.

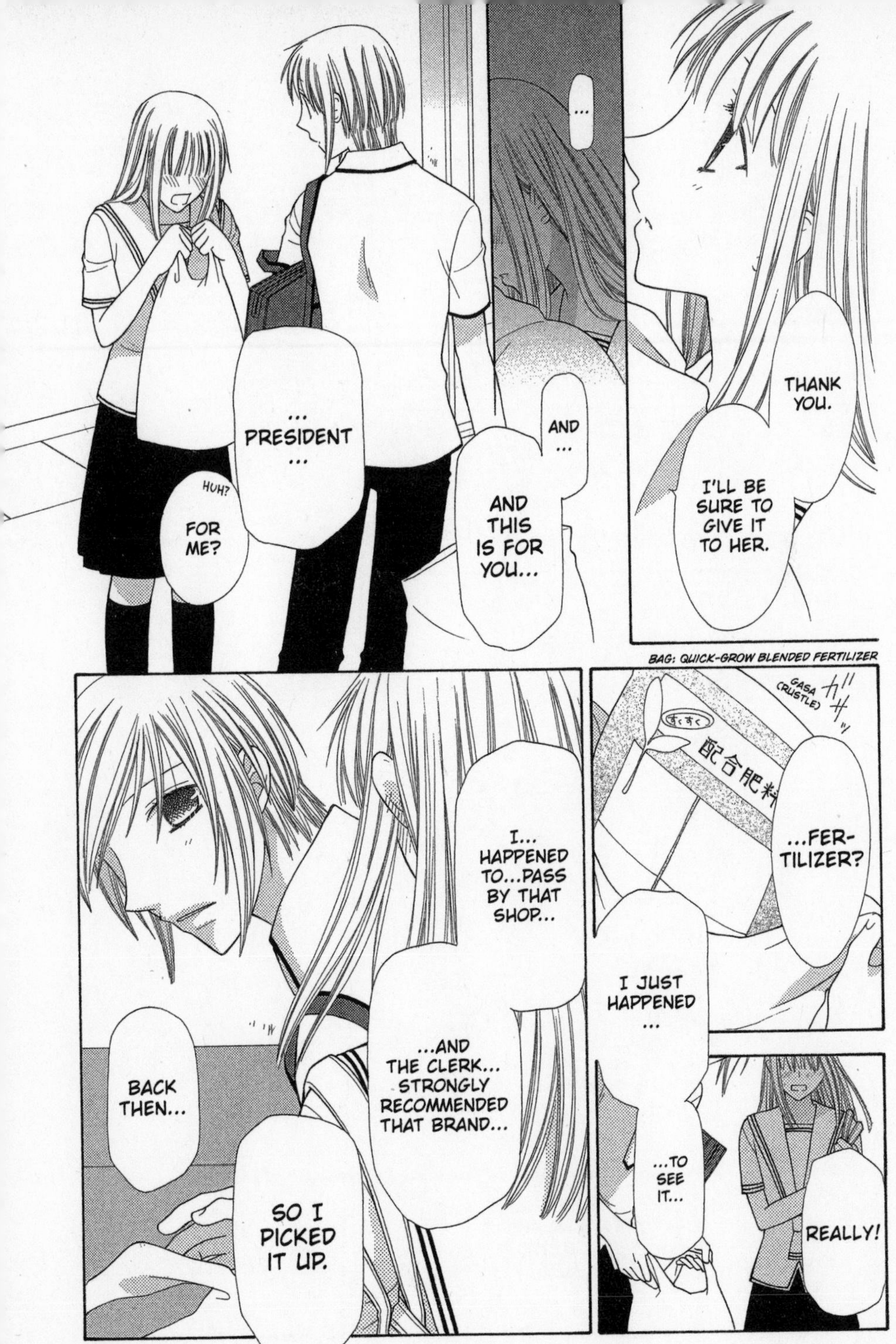
THANK YOU.
I'LL BE SURE TO GIVE IT TO HER.
...
AND ...
AND THIS IS FOR YOU...
... PRESIDENT ...
HUH?
FOR ME?
BAG: QUICK-GROW BLENDED FERTILIZER
GASA (RUSTLE)
ガサ
すくすく
配合肥料
...FER-TILIZER?
I JUST HAPPENED ...
REALLY!
...TO SEE IT...
I... HAPPENED TO...PASS BY THAT SHOP...
...AND THE CLERK... STRONGLY RECOMMENDED THAT BRAND...
BACK THEN...
SO I PICKED IT UP.

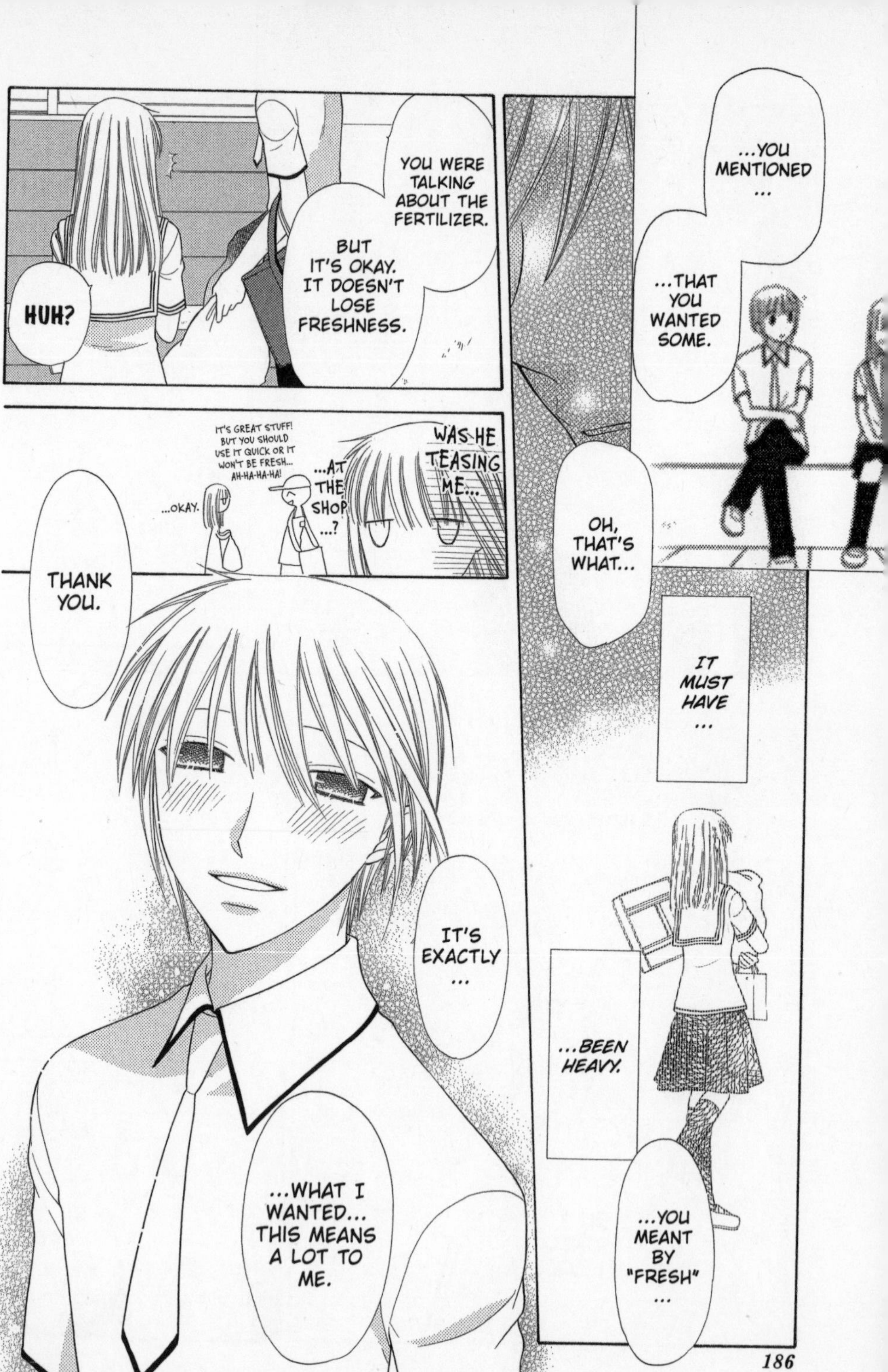
...YOU MENTIONED ...
...THAT YOU WANTED SOME.
OH, THAT'S WHAT...
...YOU MEANT BY "FRESH" ...
IT MUST HAVE ...
...BEEN HEAVY.
YOU WERE TALKING ABOUT THE FERTILIZER.
BUT IT'S OKAY. IT DOESN'T LOSE FRESHNESS.
HUH?
WAS HE TEASING ME...
...AT THE SHOP ...?
IT'S GREAT STUFF! BUT YOU SHOULD USE IT QUICK OR IT WON'T BE FRESH... AH-HA-HA-HA!
...OKAY.
THANK YOU.
IT'S EXACTLY ...
...WHAT I WANTED... THIS MEANS A LOT TO ME.

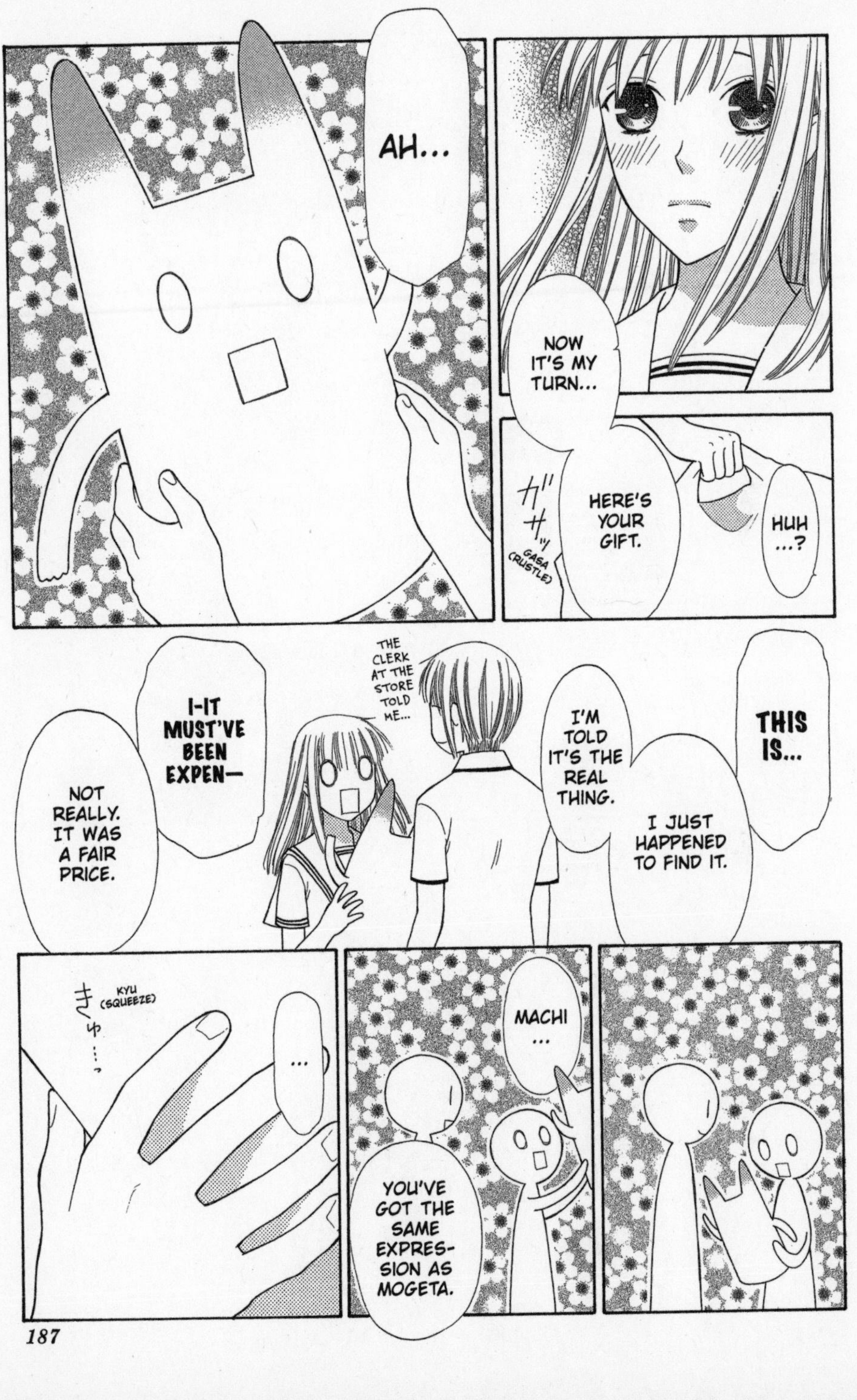
NOW IT'S MY TURN...
HERE'S YOUR GIFT.
HUH ...?
ガサッ
GASA (RUSTLE)
AH...
THIS IS...
I'M TOLD IT'S THE REAL THING.
I JUST HAPPENED TO FIND IT.
THE CLERK AT THE STORE TOLD ME...
I-IT MUST'VE BEEN EXPEN—
NOT REALLY. IT WAS A FAIR PRICE.
MACHI ...
YOU'VE GOT THE SAME EXPRES-SION AS MOGETA.
...
きゅ…
KYU (SQUEEZE)

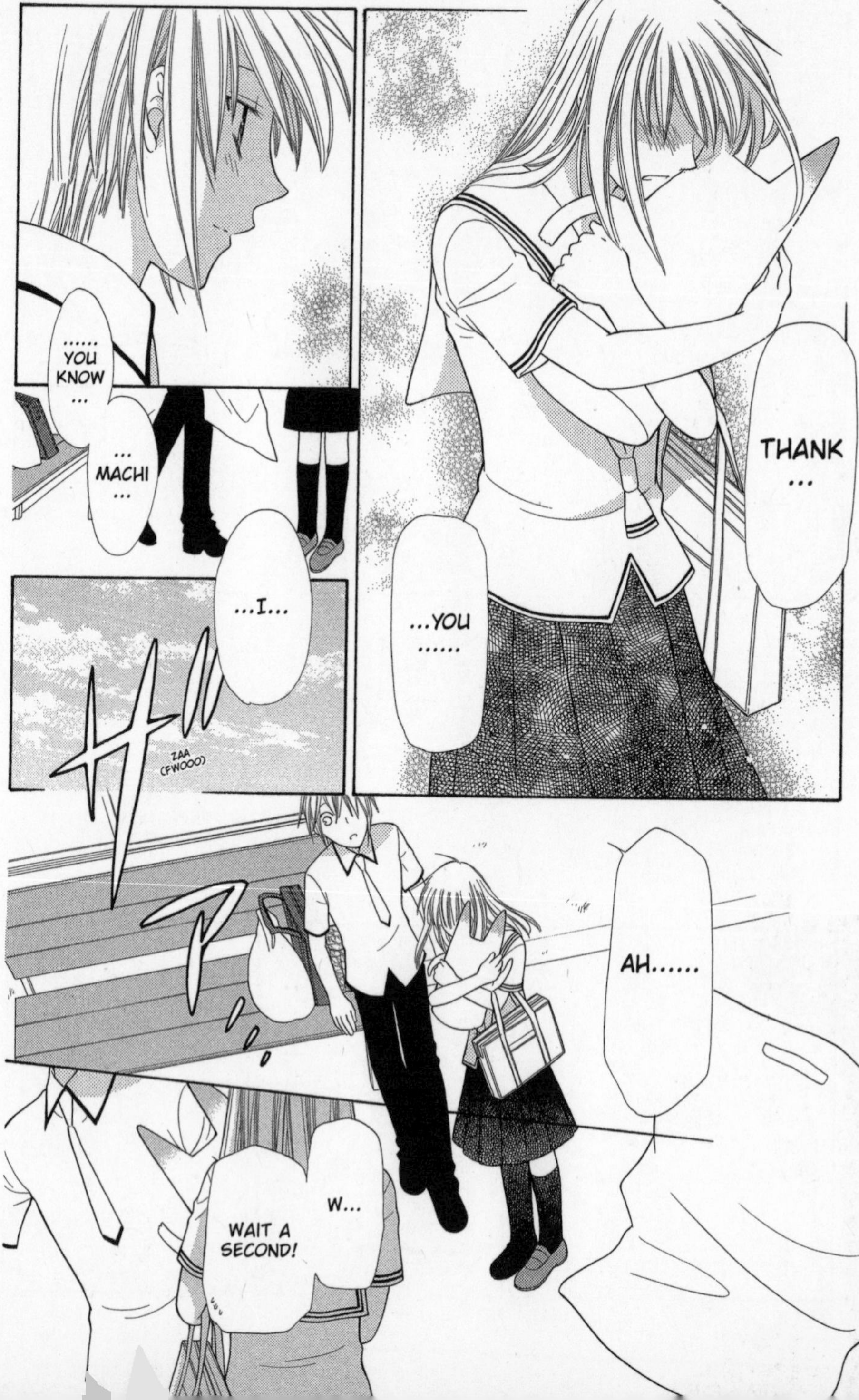
THANK ...
...YOU ......
...... YOU KNOW ...
... MACHI ...
...I...
ZAA (FWOOO)
AH......
W...
WAIT A SECOND!

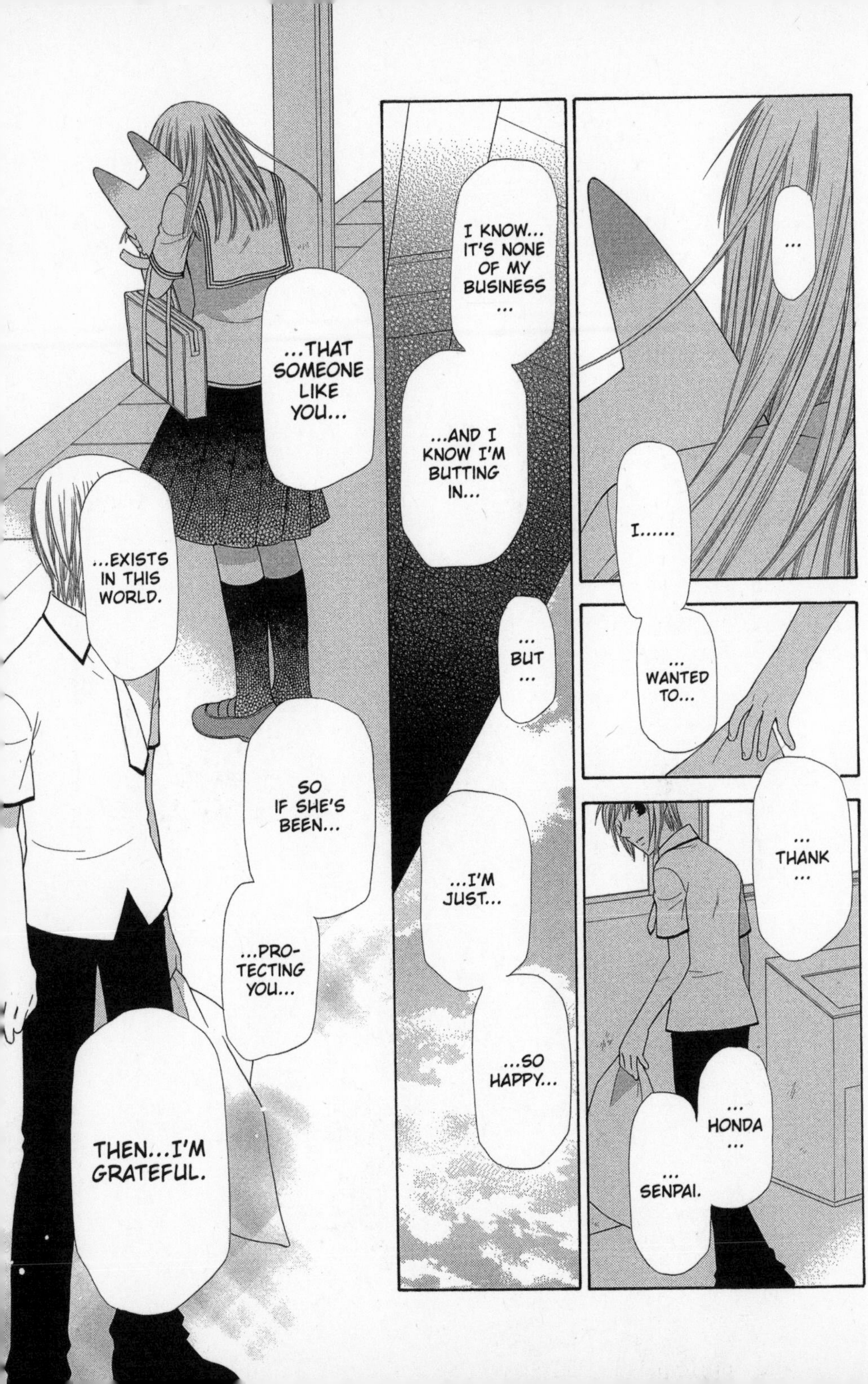
...
I......
... WANTED TO...
... THANK ...
... HONDA ...
... SENPAI.
I KNOW... IT'S NONE OF MY BUSINESS ...
...AND I KNOW I'M BUTTING IN...
... BUT ...
...I'M JUST...
...SO HAPPY...
...THAT SOMEONE LIKE YOU...
...EXISTS IN THIS WORLD.
SO IF SHE'S BEEN...
...PRO-TECTING YOU...
THEN...I'M GRATEFUL.

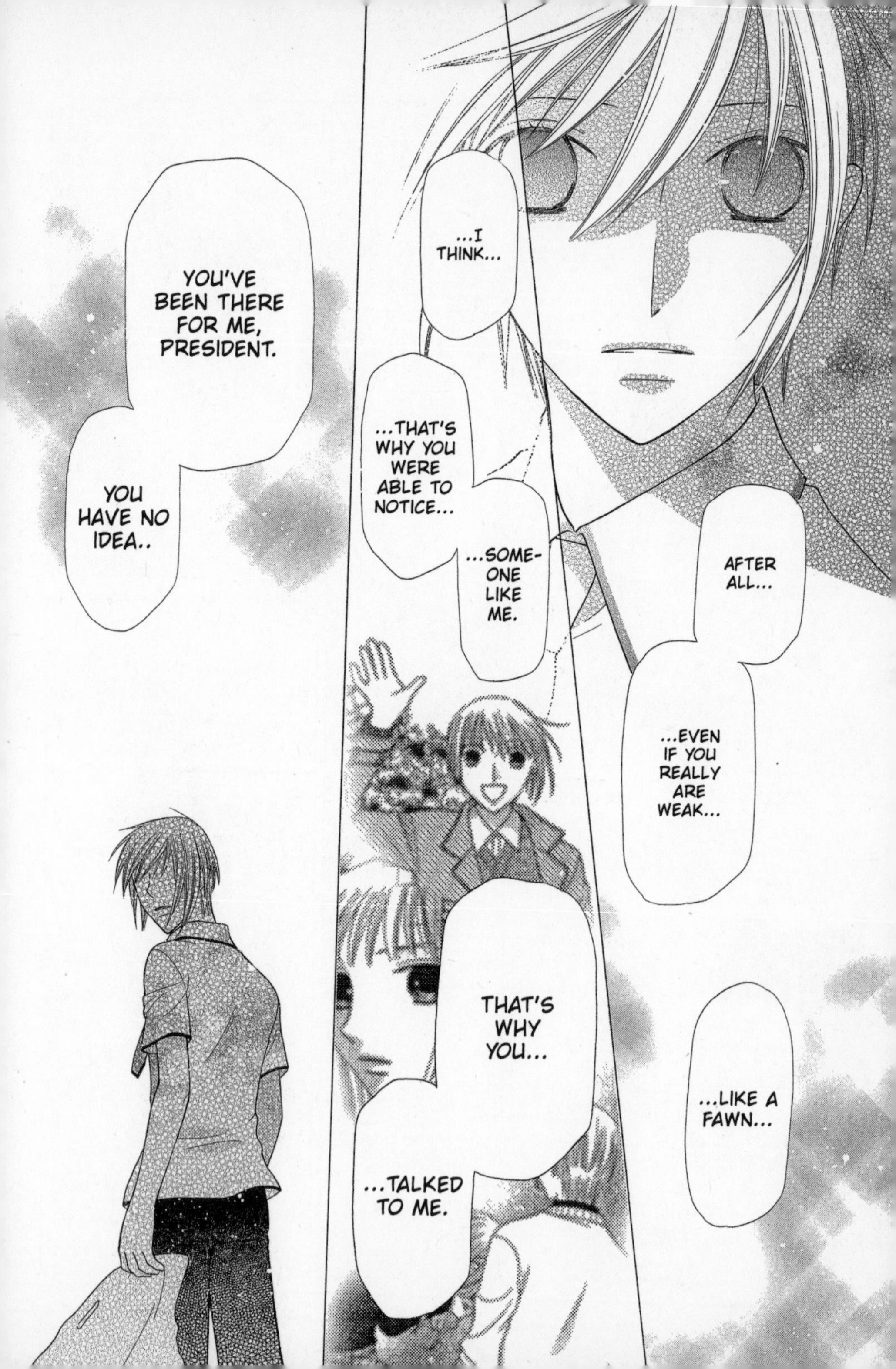
...I THINK...
...THAT'S WHY YOU WERE ABLE TO NOTICE...
...SOME-ONE LIKE ME.
AFTER ALL...
...EVEN IF YOU REALLY ARE WEAK...
...LIKE A FAWN...
THAT'S WHY YOU...
...TALKED TO ME.
YOU'VE BEEN THERE FOR ME, PRESIDENT.
YOU HAVE NO IDEA..

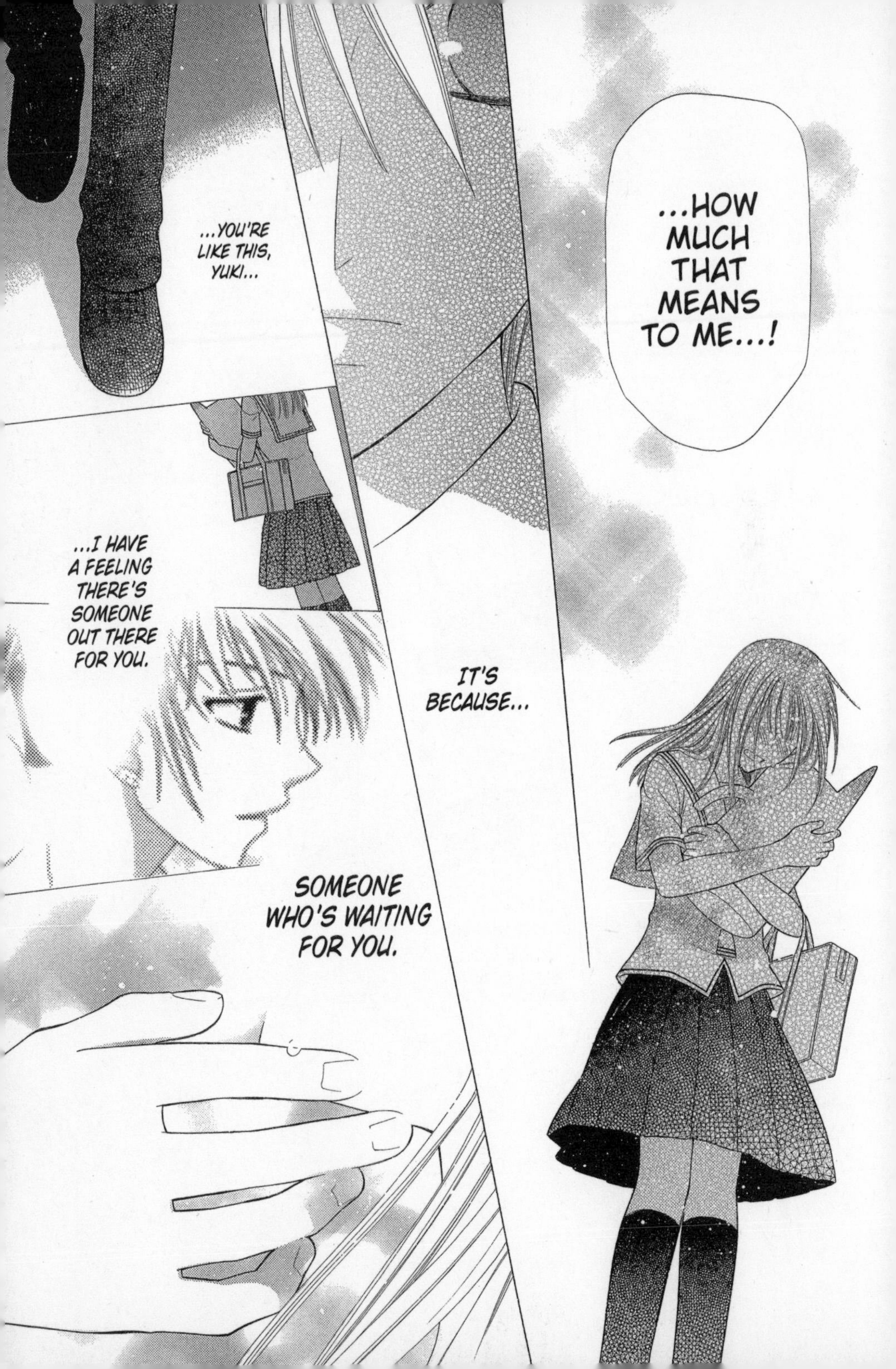
...HOW MUCH THAT MEANS TO ME...!
IT'S BECAUSE...
...YOU'RE LIKE THIS, YUKI...
...I HAVE A FEELING THERE'S SOMEONE OUT THERE FOR YOU.
SOMEONE WHO'S WAITING FOR YOU.

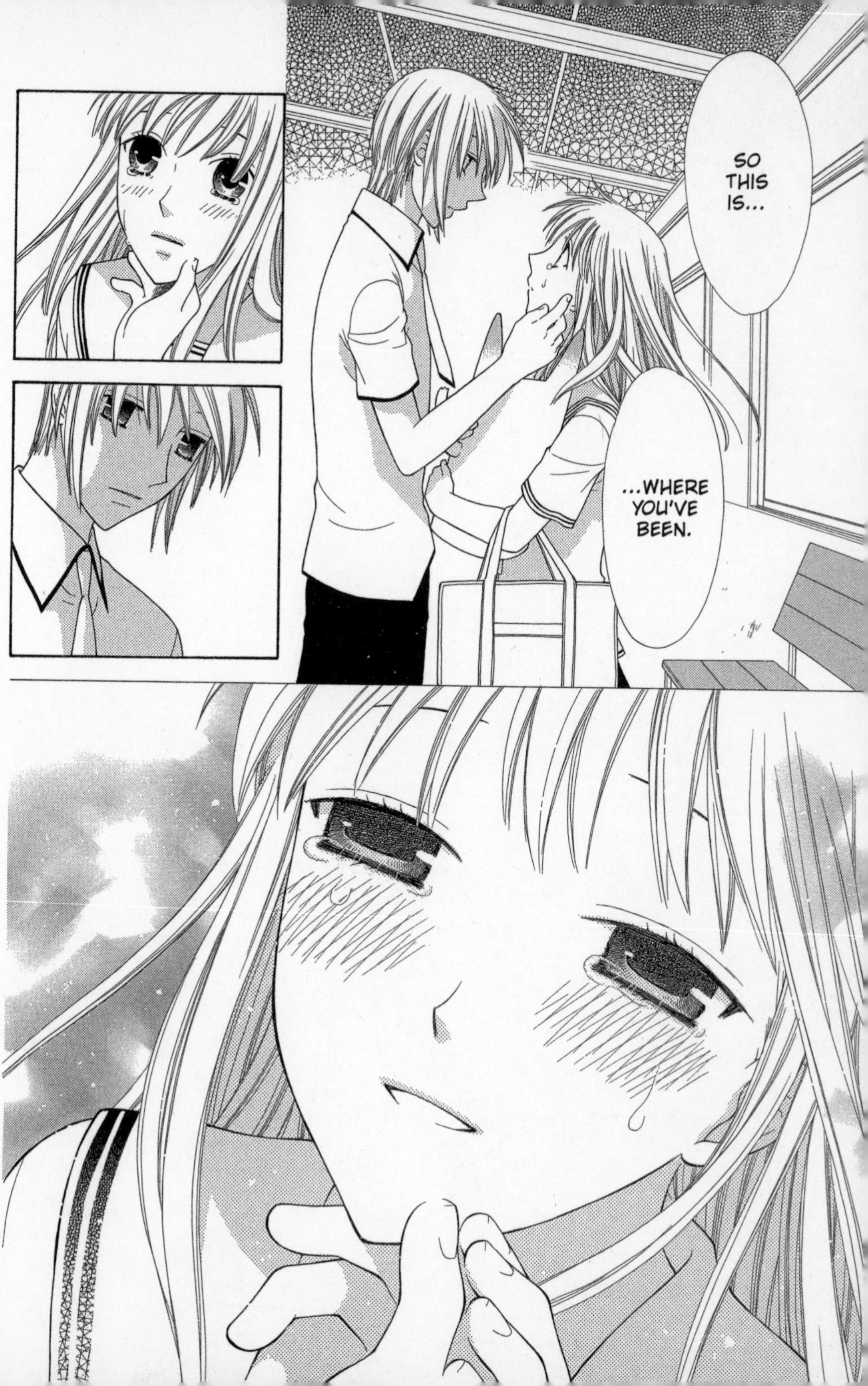
SO THIS IS...
...WHERE YOU'VE BEEN.

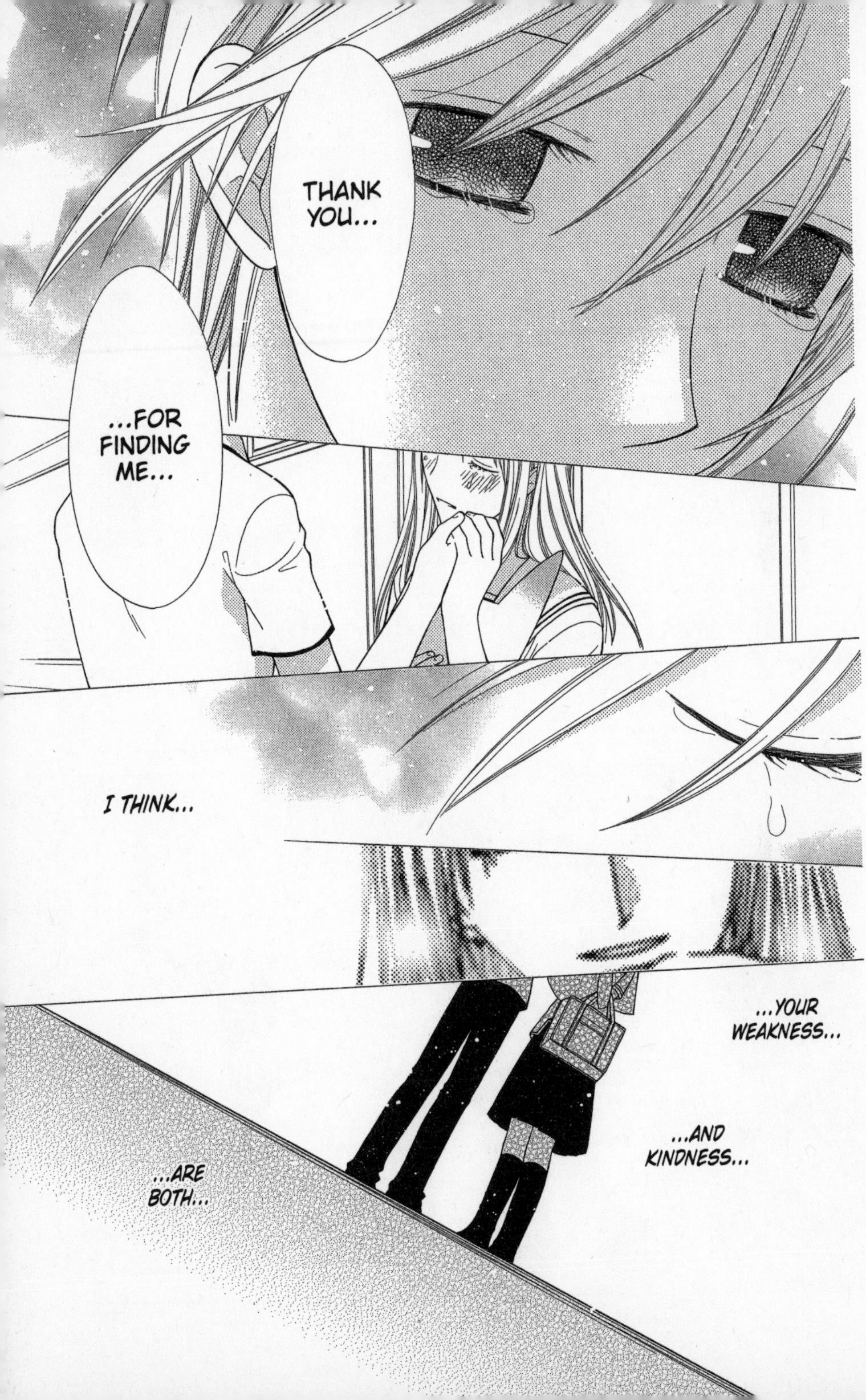
THANK YOU...
...FOR FINDING ME...
I THINK...
...YOUR WEAKNESS...
...AND KINDNESS...
...ARE BOTH...

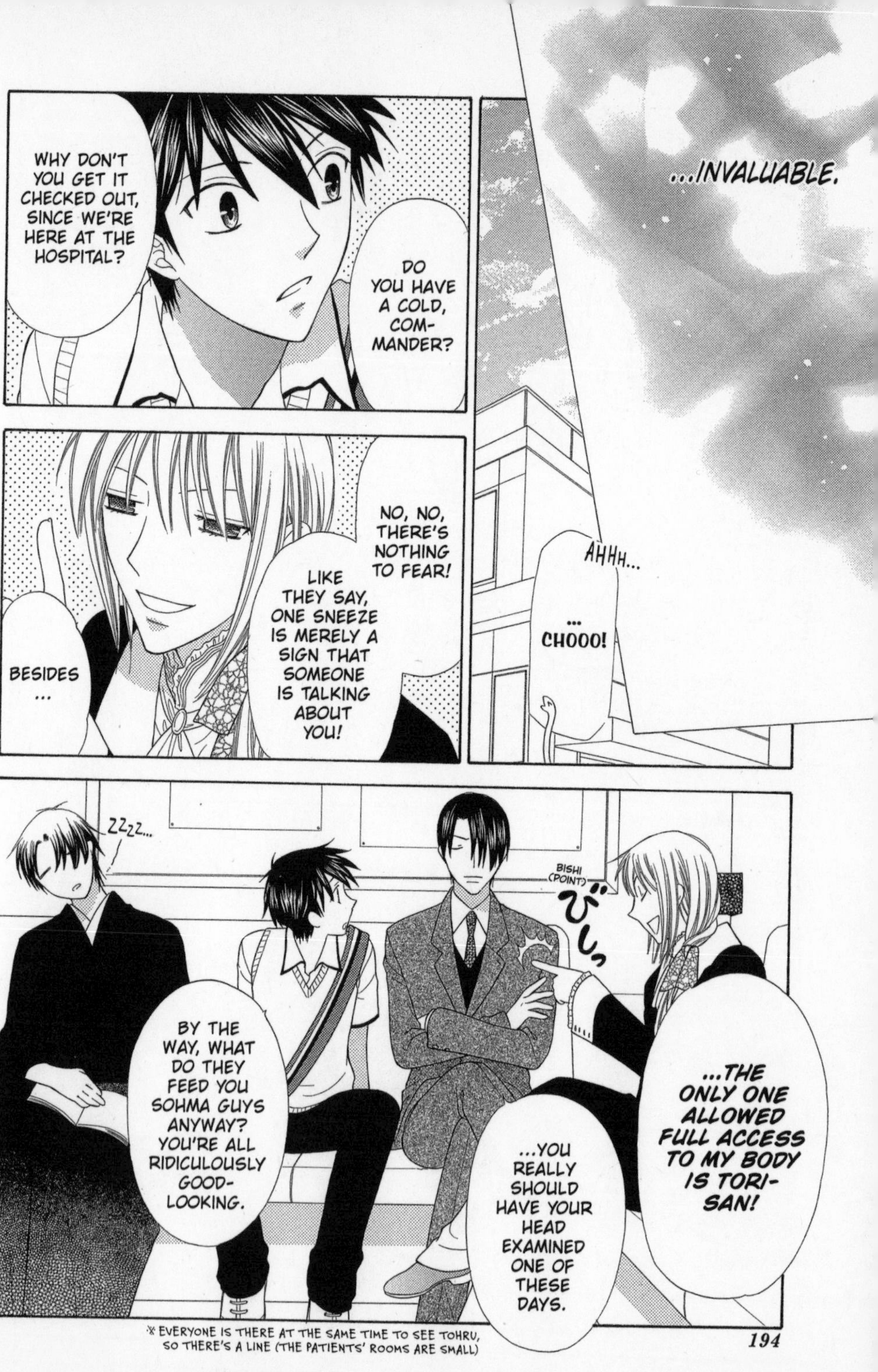
...INVALUABLE.
AHHH...
...CHOOO!
DO YOU HAVE A COLD, COM-MANDER?
WHY DON'T YOU GET IT CHECKED OUT, SINCE WE'RE HERE AT THE HOSPITAL?
NO, NO, THERE'S NOTHING TO FEAR!
LIKE THEY SAY, ONE SNEEZE IS MERELY A SIGN THAT SOMEONE IS TALKING ABOUT YOU!
BESIDES...
BISHI (POINT)
...THE ONLY ONE ALLOWED FULL ACCESS TO MY BODY IS TORI-SAN!
...YOU REALLY SHOULD HAVE YOUR HEAD EXAMINED ONE OF THESE DAYS.
ZZZZ...
BY THE WAY, WHAT DO THEY FEED YOU SOHMA GUYS ANYWAY? YOU'RE ALL RIDICULOUSLY GOOD-LOOKING.

※ EVERYONE IS THERE AT THE SAME TIME TO SEE TOHRU, SO THERE'S A LINE (THE PATIENTS' ROOMS ARE SMALL)

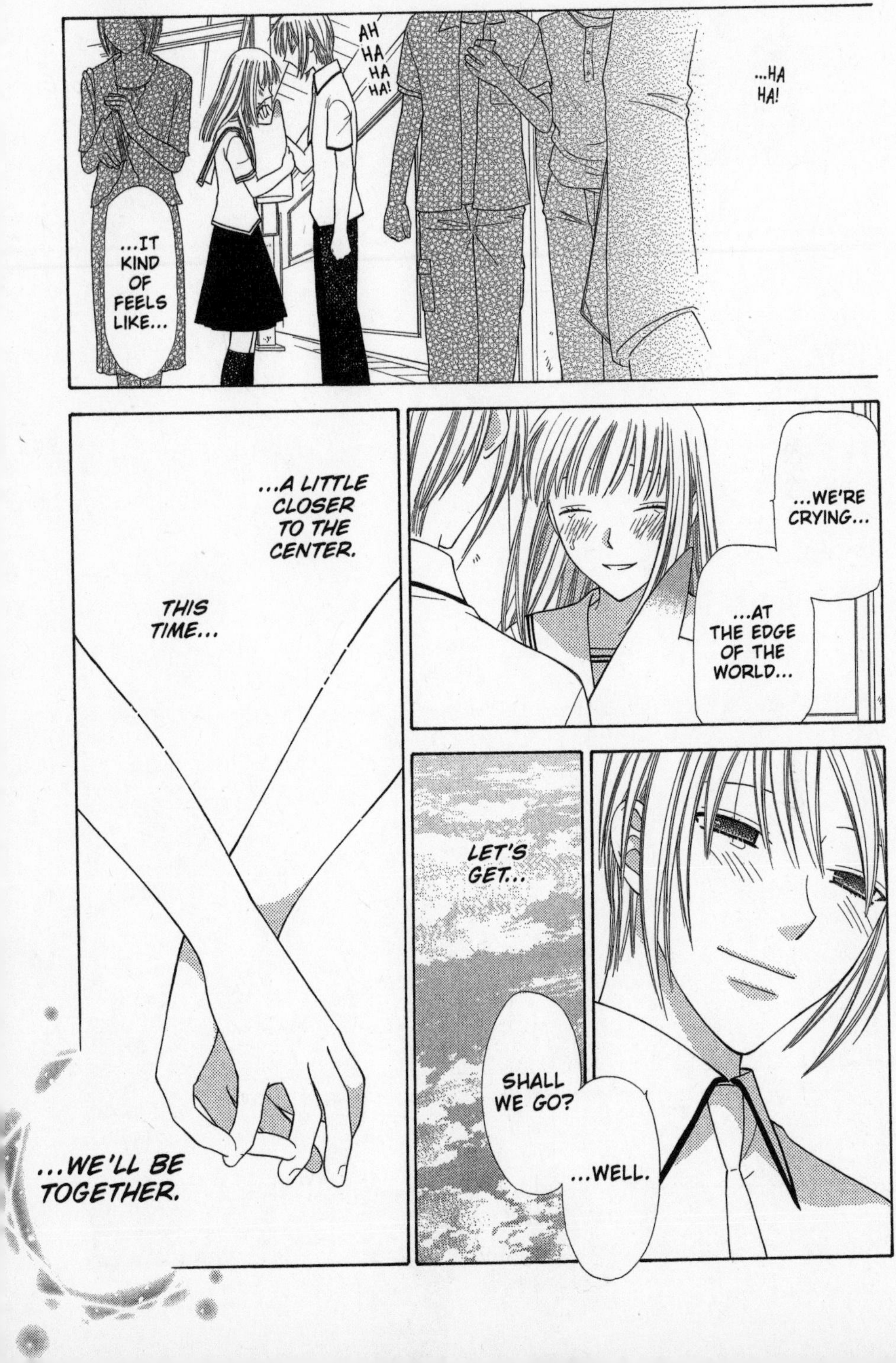
...HA HA!
AH HA HA HA!
...IT KIND OF FEELS LIKE...
...WE'RE CRYING...
...AT THE EDGE OF THE WORLD...
SHALL WE GO?
...WELL.
LET'S GET...
...A LITTLE CLOSER TO THE CENTER.
THIS TIME...
...WE'LL BE TOGETHER.

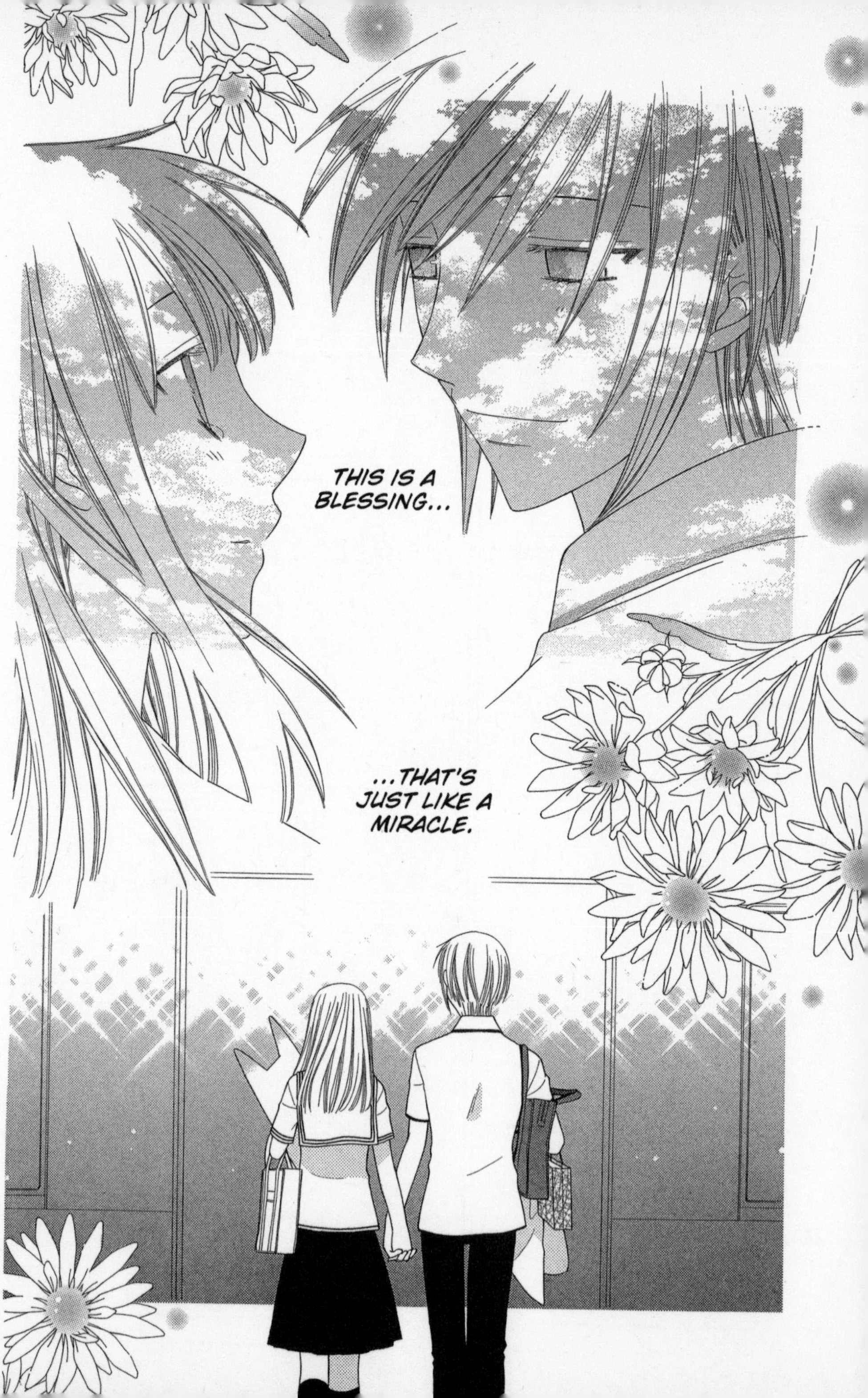
THIS IS A BLESSING...
...THAT'S JUST LIKE A MIRACLE.

COLLECTOR'S EDITION

Fruits Basket

COLLECTOR'S EDITION

Fruits
Basket

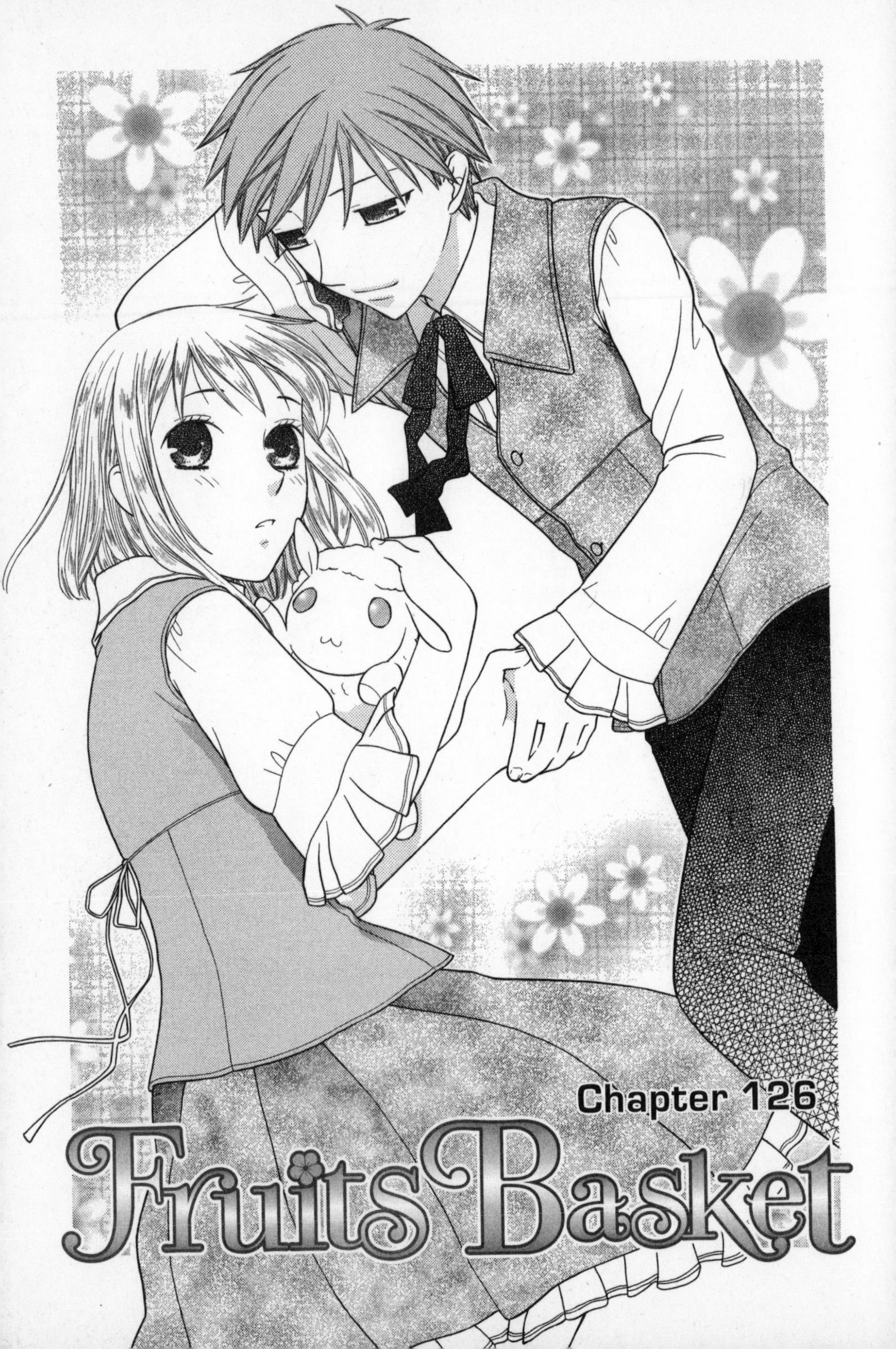
Chapter 126
Fruits Basket

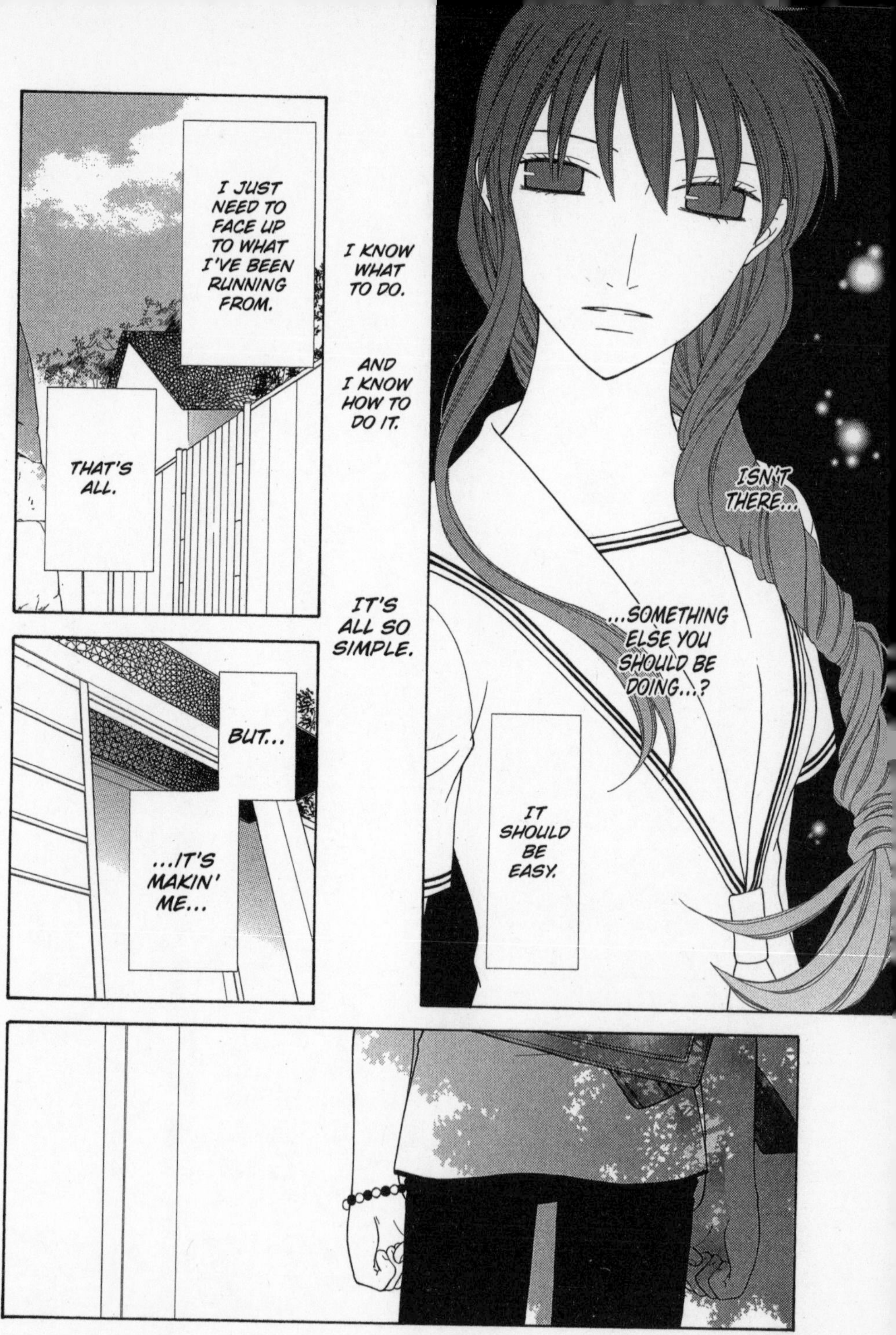
ISN'T THERE...
...SOMETHING ELSE YOU SHOULD BE DOING...?
IT SHOULD BE EASY.
I KNOW WHAT TO DO.
AND I KNOW HOW TO DO IT.
I JUST NEED TO FACE UP TO WHAT I'VE BEEN RUNNING FROM.
THAT'S ALL.
IT'S ALL SO SIMPLE.
BUT...
...IT'S MAKIN' ME...

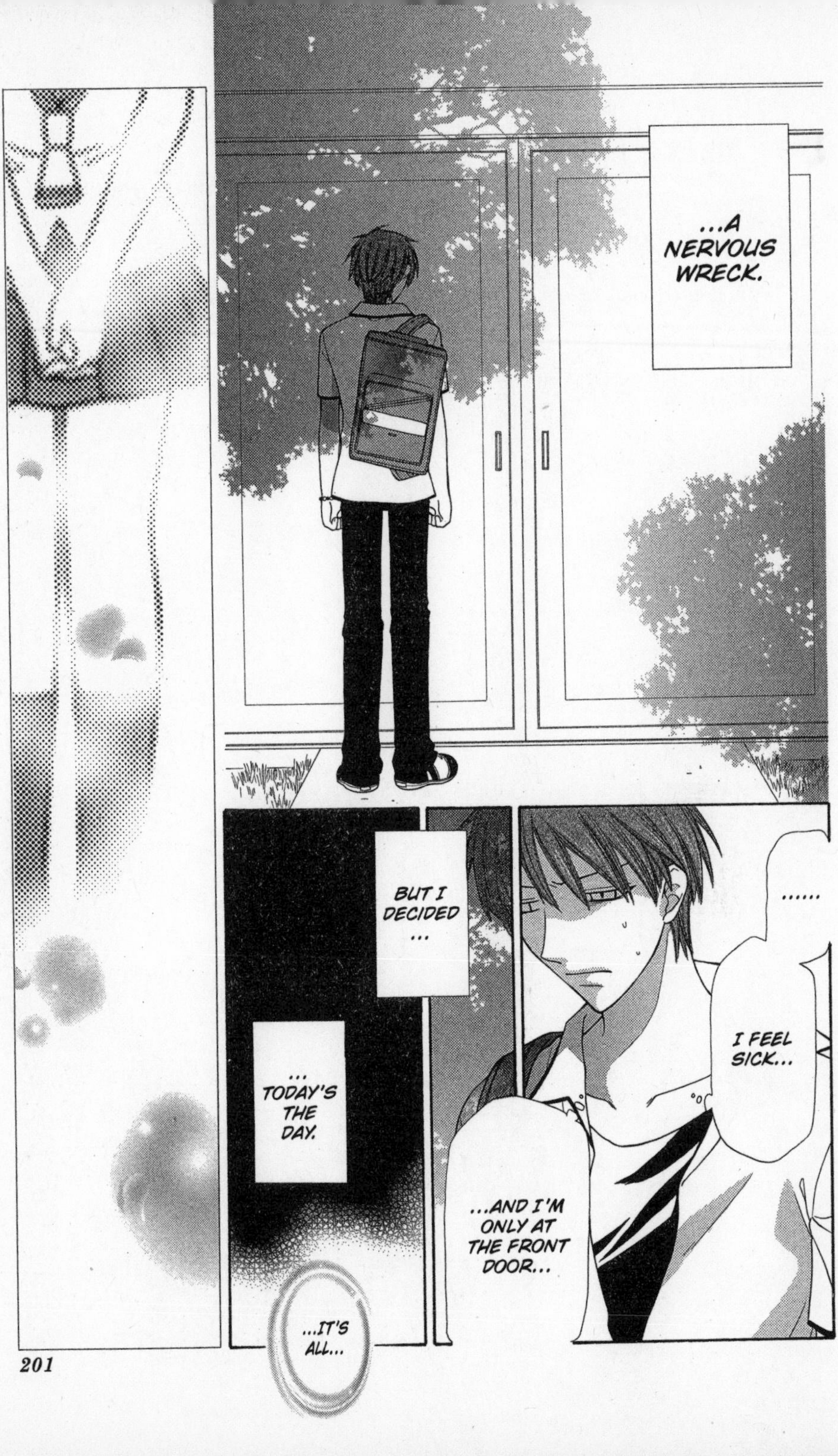
...A NERVOUS WRECK.
......
I FEEL SICK...
...AND I'M ONLY AT THE FRONT DOOR...
BUT I DECIDED ...
... TODAY'S THE DAY.
...IT'S ALL...

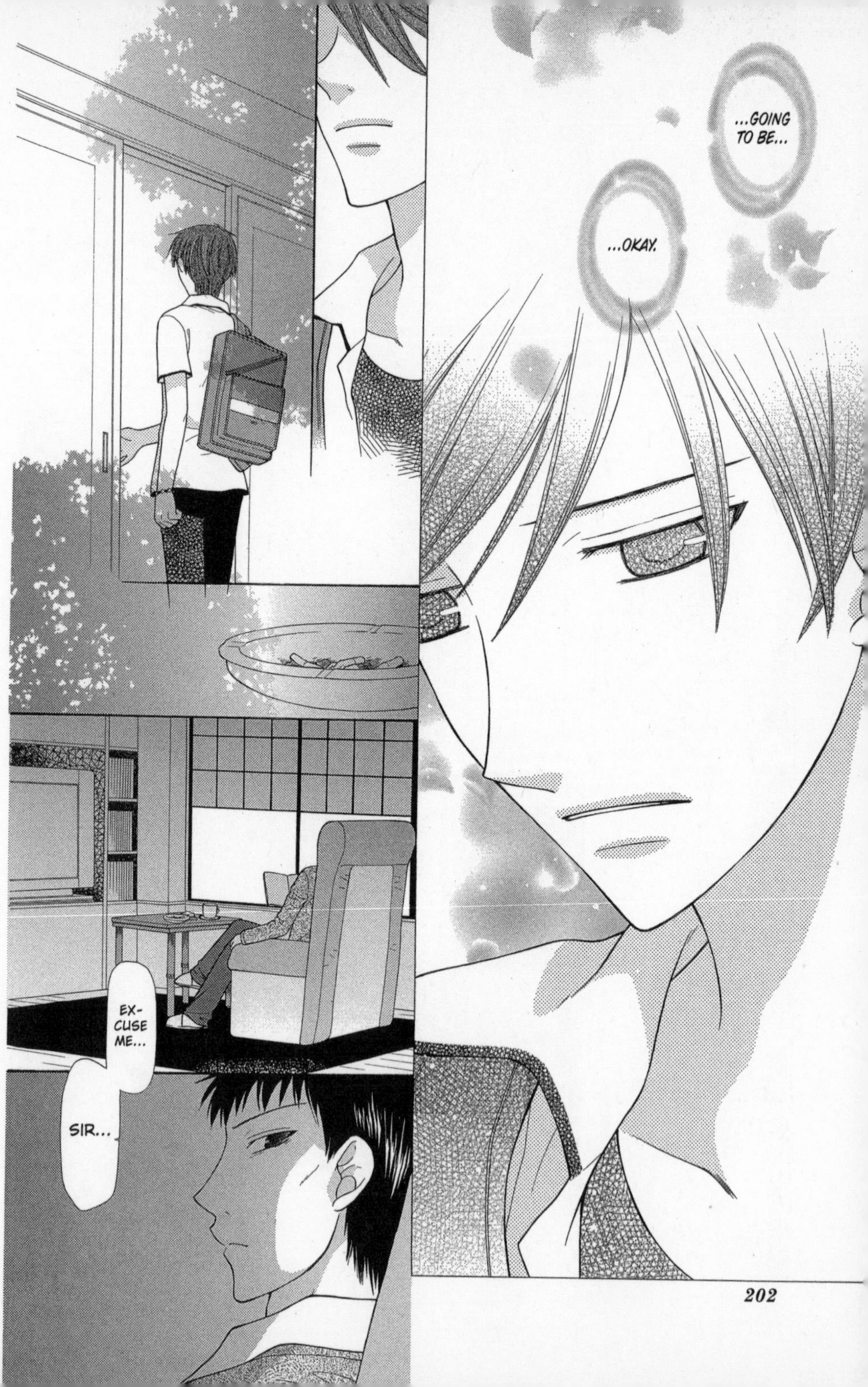
...GOING TO BE...
...OKAY.
EX-CUSE ME...
SIR...

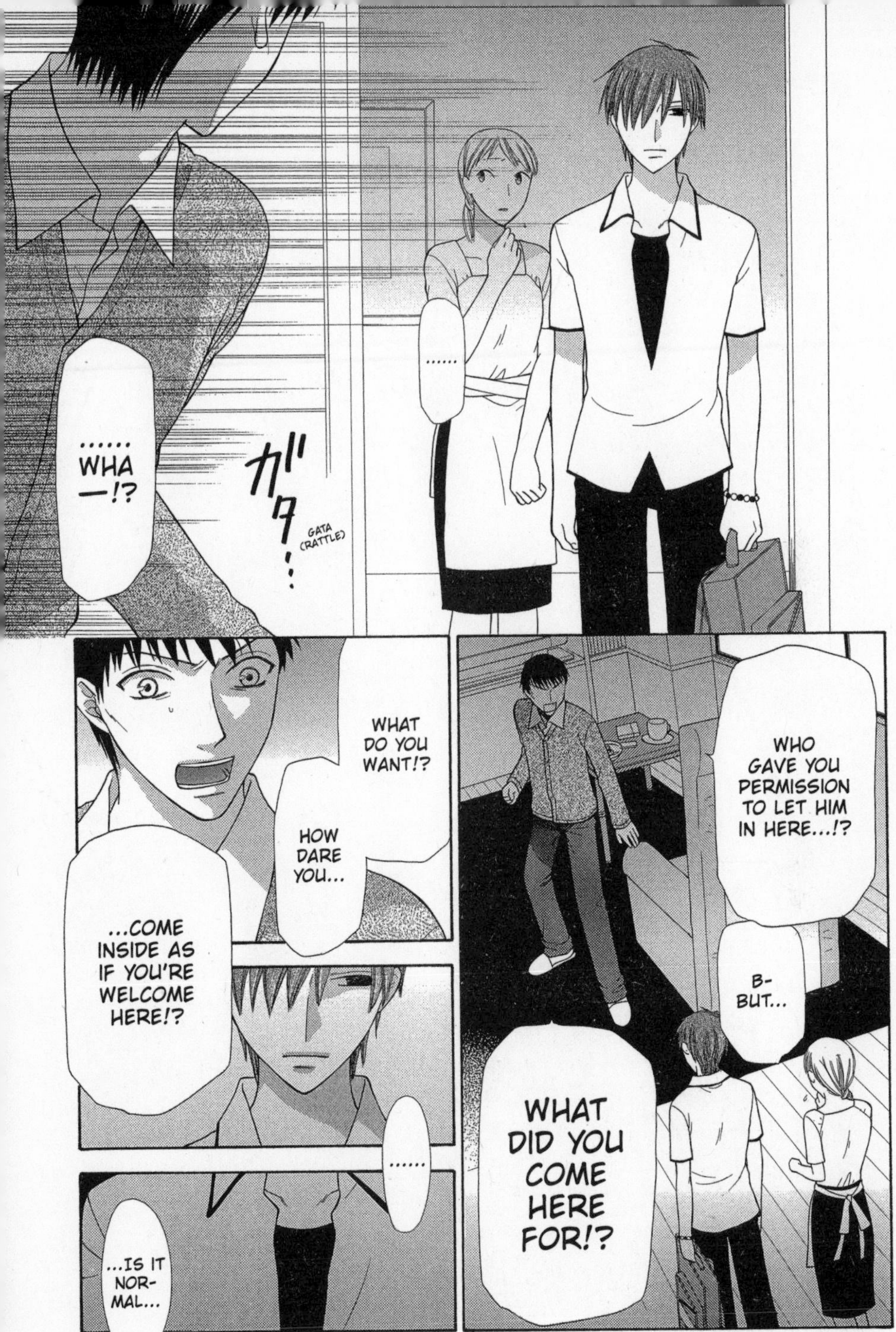
……
ガタッ
GATA (RATTLE)
……WHA—!?
WHO GAVE YOU PERMISSION TO LET HIM IN HERE...!?
B-BUT...
WHAT DID YOU COME HERE FOR!?
WHAT DO YOU WANT!?
HOW DARE YOU...
...COME INSIDE AS IF YOU'RE WELCOME HERE!?
……
...IS IT NOR-MAL...

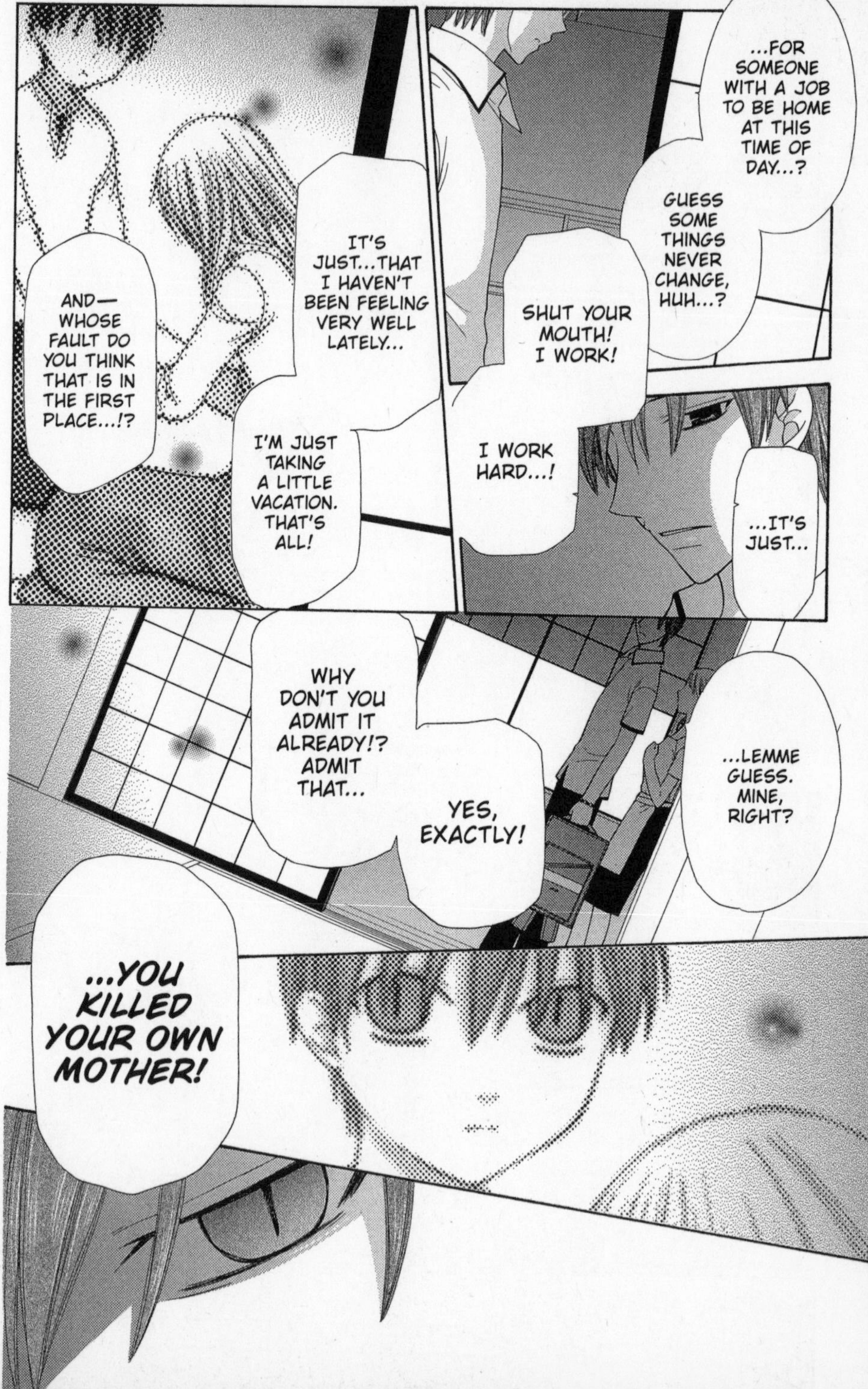
...FOR SOMEONE WITH A JOB TO BE HOME AT THIS TIME OF DAY...?
GUESS SOME THINGS NEVER CHANGE, HUH...?
SHUT YOUR MOUTH! I WORK!
I WORK HARD...!
...IT'S JUST...
IT'S JUST...THAT I HAVEN'T BEEN FEELING VERY WELL LATELY...
I'M JUST TAKING A LITTLE VACATION. THAT'S ALL!
AND—WHOSE FAULT DO YOU THINK THAT IS IN THE FIRST PLACE...!?
...LEMME GUESS. MINE, RIGHT?
YES, EXACTLY!
WHY DON'T YOU ADMIT IT ALREADY!? ADMIT THAT...
...YOU KILLED YOUR OWN MOTHER!

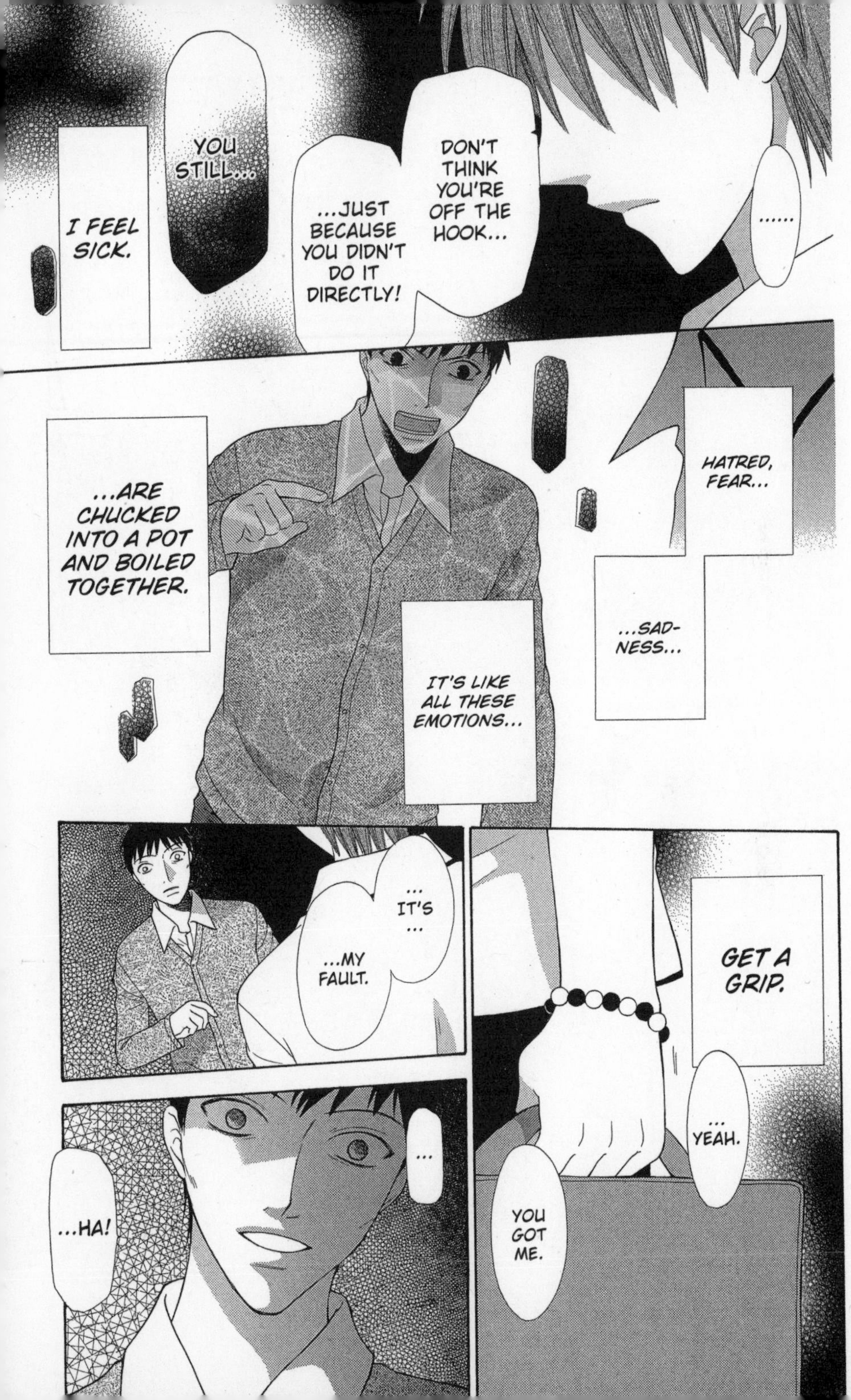
......
DON'T THINK YOU'RE OFF THE HOOK...
...JUST BECAUSE YOU DIDN'T DO IT DIRECTLY!
YOU STILL...
I FEEL SICK.
HATRED, FEAR...
...SADNESS...
IT'S LIKE ALL THESE EMOTIONS...
...ARE CHUCKED INTO A POT AND BOILED TOGETHER.
GET A GRIP.
...YEAH.
YOU GOT ME.
...IT'S...
...MY FAULT.
...
...HA!

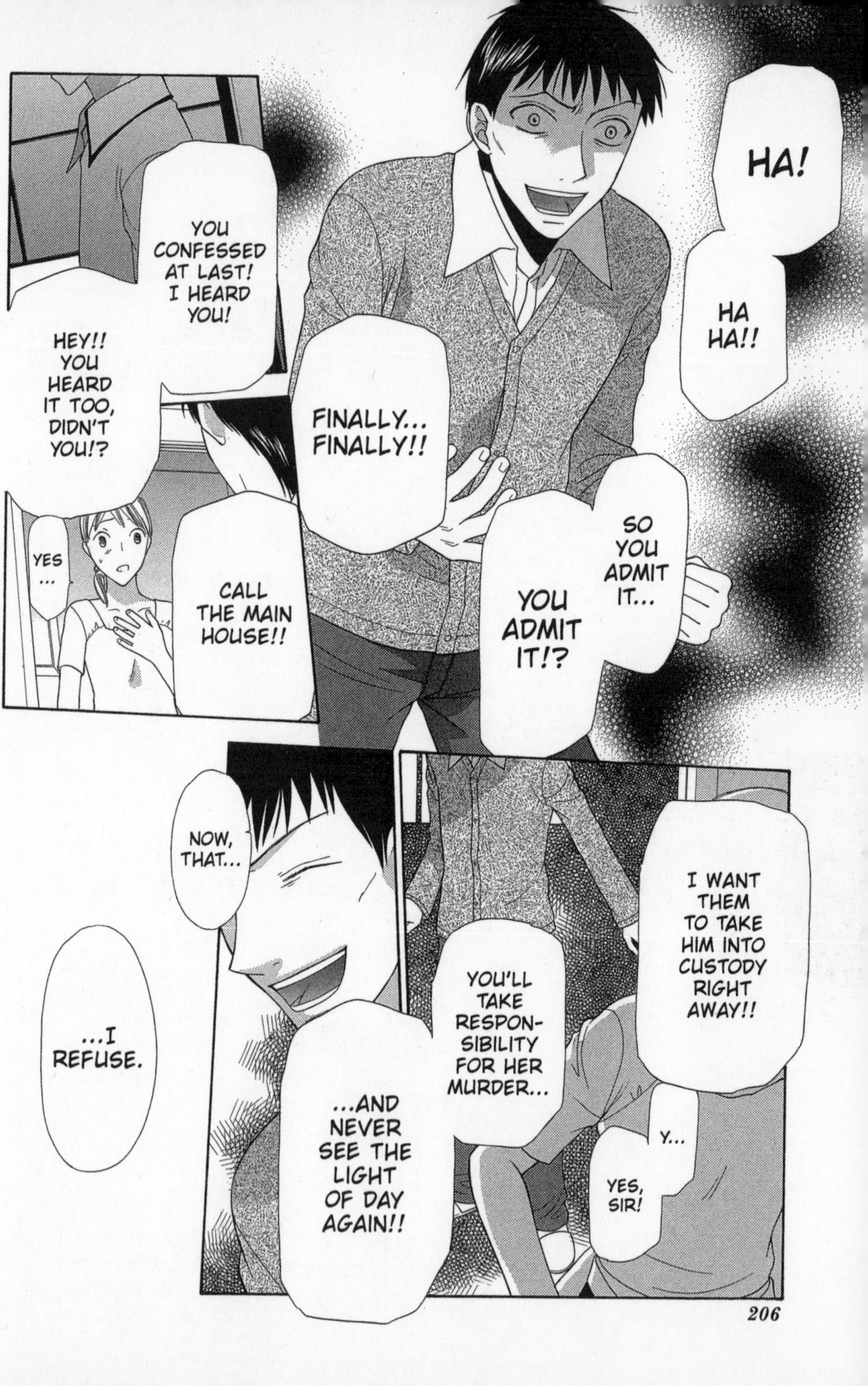
HA!
HA HA!!
SO YOU ADMIT IT...
YOU ADMIT IT!?
FINALLY... FINALLY!!
YOU CONFESSED AT LAST! I HEARD YOU!
HEY!! YOU HEARD IT TOO, DIDN'T YOU!?
CALL THE MAIN HOUSE!!
YES...
I WANT THEM TO TAKE HIM INTO CUSTODY RIGHT AWAY!!
YOU'LL TAKE RESPON-SIBILITY FOR HER MURDER...
...AND NEVER SEE THE LIGHT OF DAY AGAIN!!
Y...
YES, SIR!
NOW, THAT...
...I REFUSE.

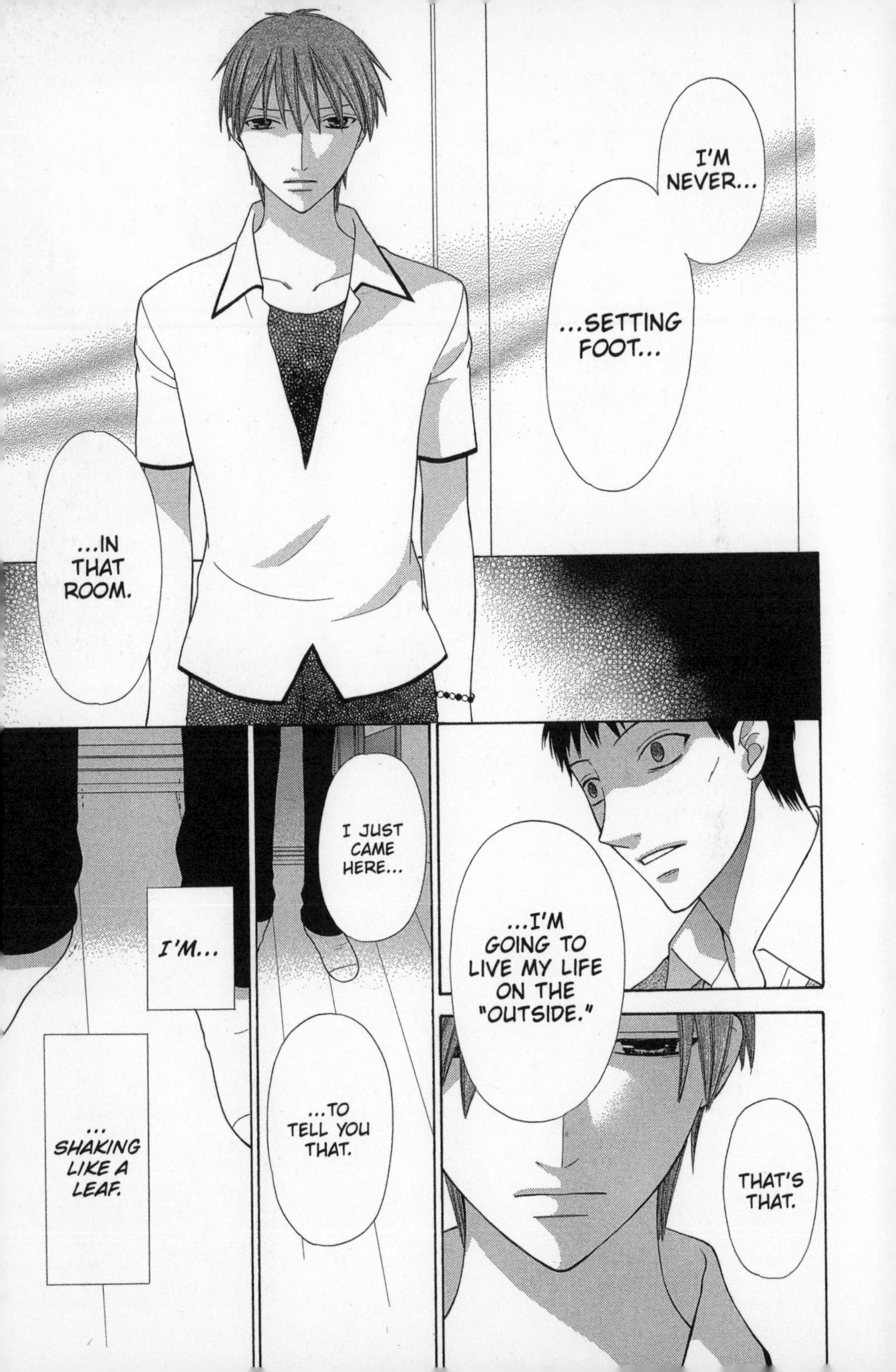

I'M NEVER...
...SETTING FOOT...
...IN THAT ROOM.
...I'M GOING TO LIVE MY LIFE ON THE "OUTSIDE."
THAT'S THAT.
I JUST CAME HERE...
...TO TELL YOU THAT.
I'M...
...SHAKING LIKE A LEAF.

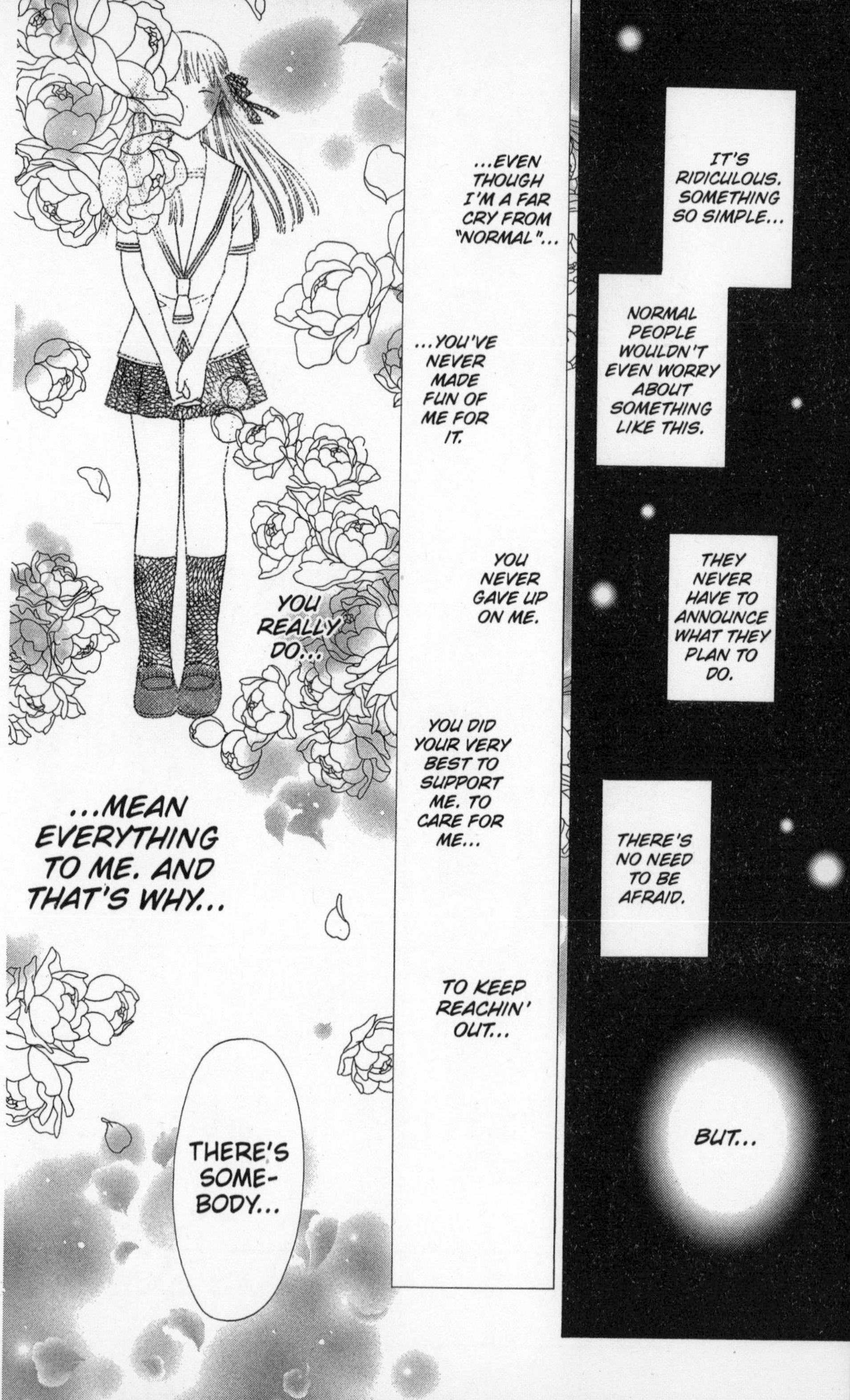
IT'S RIDICULOUS. SOMETHING SO SIMPLE...
NORMAL PEOPLE WOULDN'T EVEN WORRY ABOUT SOMETHING LIKE THIS.
THEY NEVER HAVE TO ANNOUNCE WHAT THEY PLAN TO DO.
THERE'S NO NEED TO BE AFRAID.
BUT...
...EVEN THOUGH I'M A FAR CRY FROM "NORMAL"...
...YOU'VE NEVER MADE FUN OF ME FOR IT.
YOU NEVER GAVE UP ON ME.
YOU DID YOUR VERY BEST TO SUPPORT ME. TO CARE FOR ME...
TO KEEP REACHIN' OUT...
YOU REALLY DO...
...MEAN EVERYTHING TO ME. AND THAT'S WHY...
THERE'S SOME-BODY...

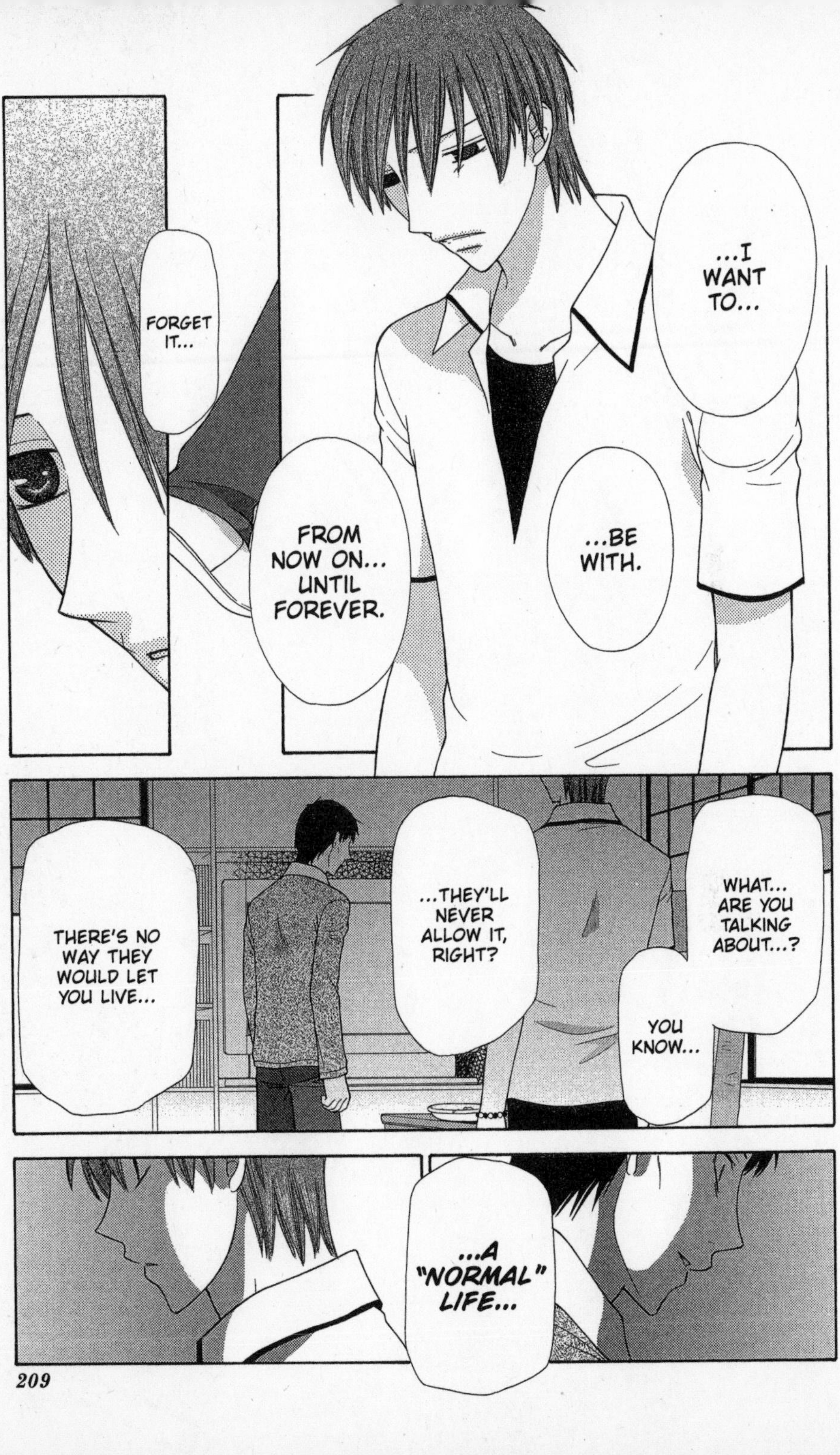
...I WANT TO...
...BE WITH.
FROM NOW ON... UNTIL FOREVER.
FORGET IT...
WHAT... ARE YOU TALKING ABOUT...?
YOU KNOW...
...THEY'LL NEVER ALLOW IT, RIGHT?
THERE'S NO WAY THEY WOULD LET YOU LIVE...
...A "NORMAL" LIFE...

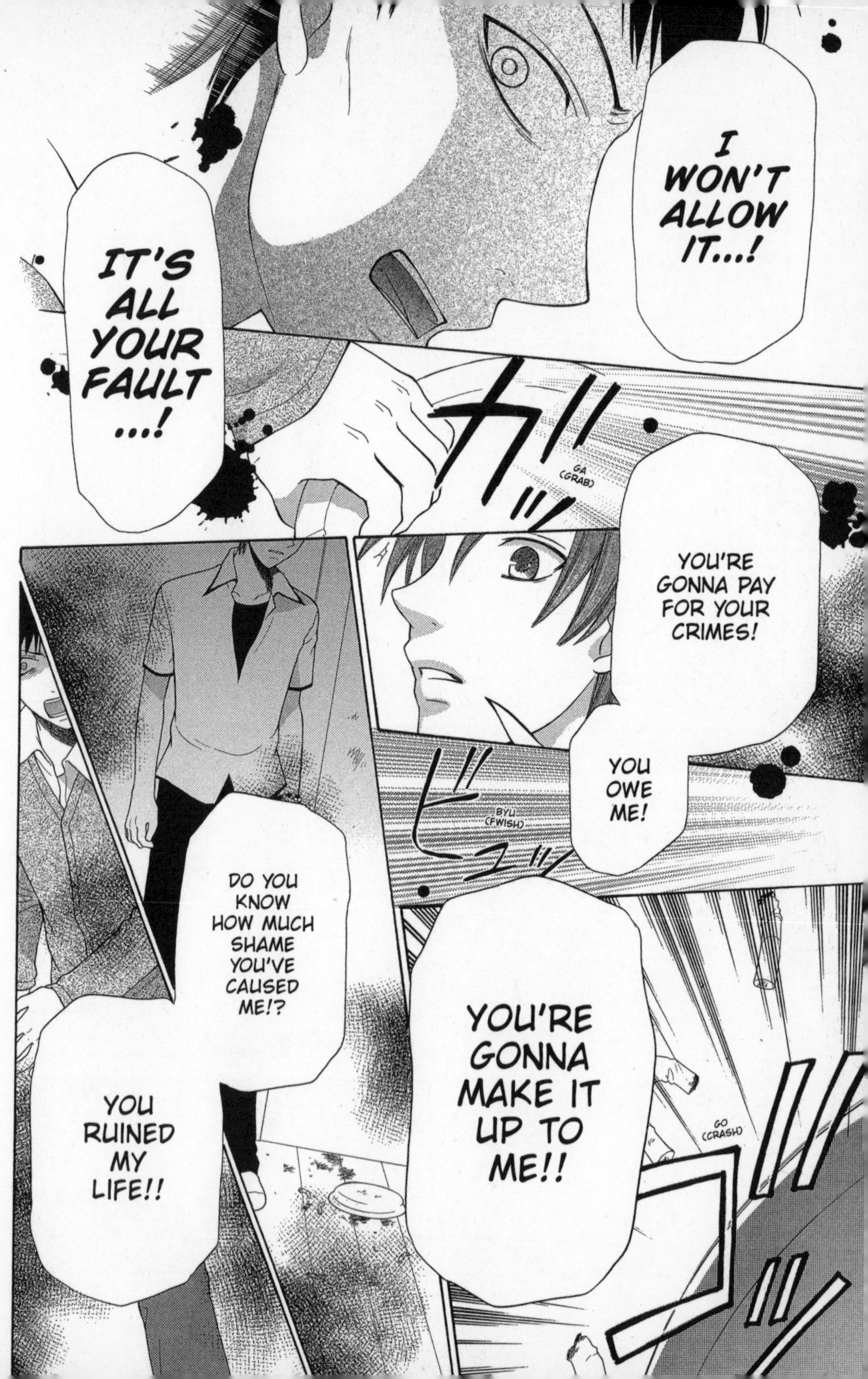
I WON'T ALLOW IT...!
IT'S ALL YOUR FAULT...!
GA (GRAB)
YOU'RE GONNA PAY FOR YOUR CRIMES!
YOU OWE ME!
BYU (FWISH)
YOU'RE GONNA MAKE IT UP TO ME!!
GO (CRASH)
DO YOU KNOW HOW MUCH SHAME YOU'VE CAUSED ME!?
YOU RUINED MY LIFE!!

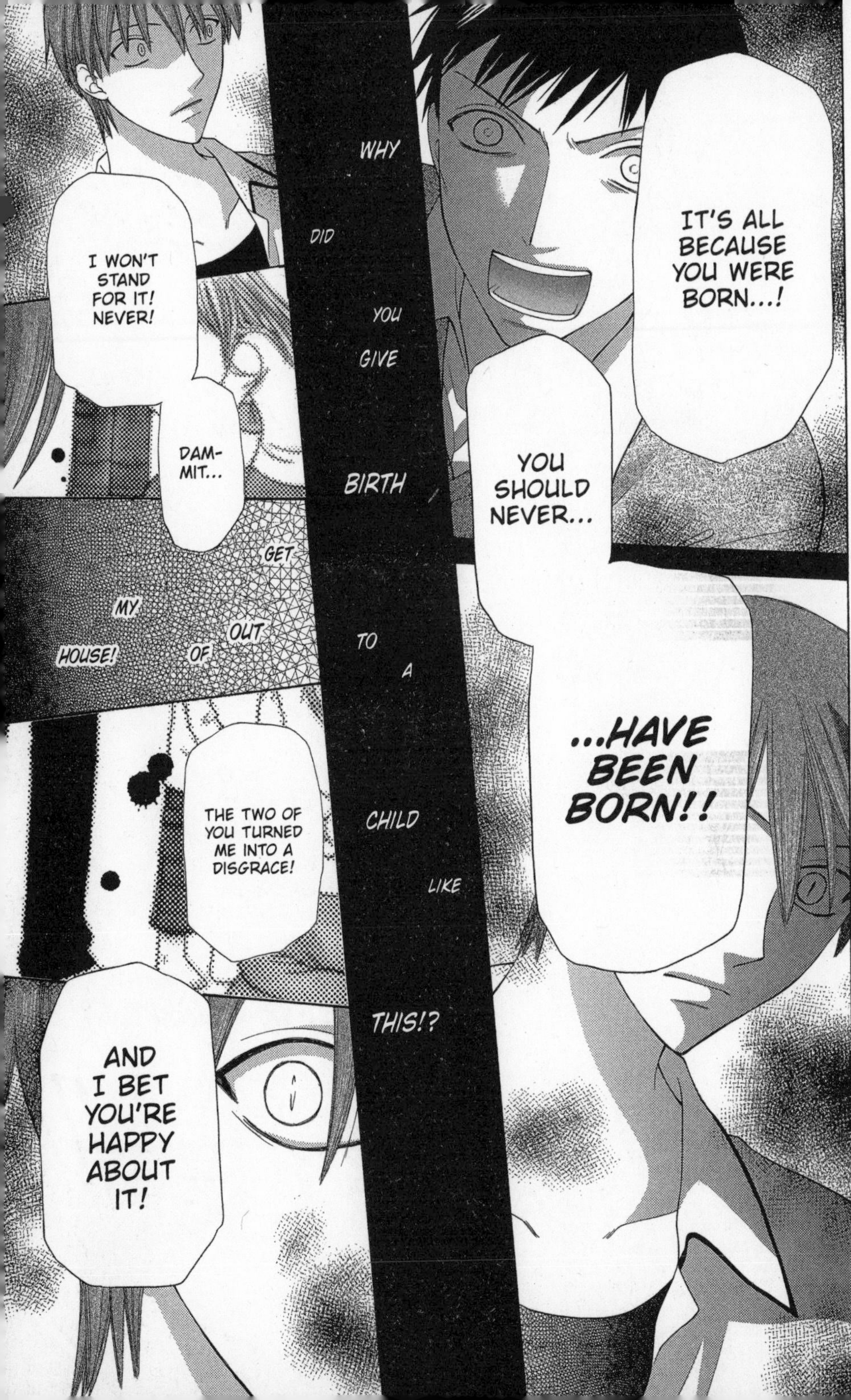
IT'S ALL BECAUSE YOU WERE BORN...!
YOU SHOULD NEVER...
...HAVE BEEN BORN!!
WHY DID YOU GIVE BIRTH TO A CHILD LIKE THIS!?
I WON'T STAND FOR IT! NEVER!
DAM-MIT...
GET OUT OF MY HOUSE!
THE TWO OF YOU TURNED ME INTO A DISGRACE!
AND I BET YOU'RE HAPPY ABOUT IT!

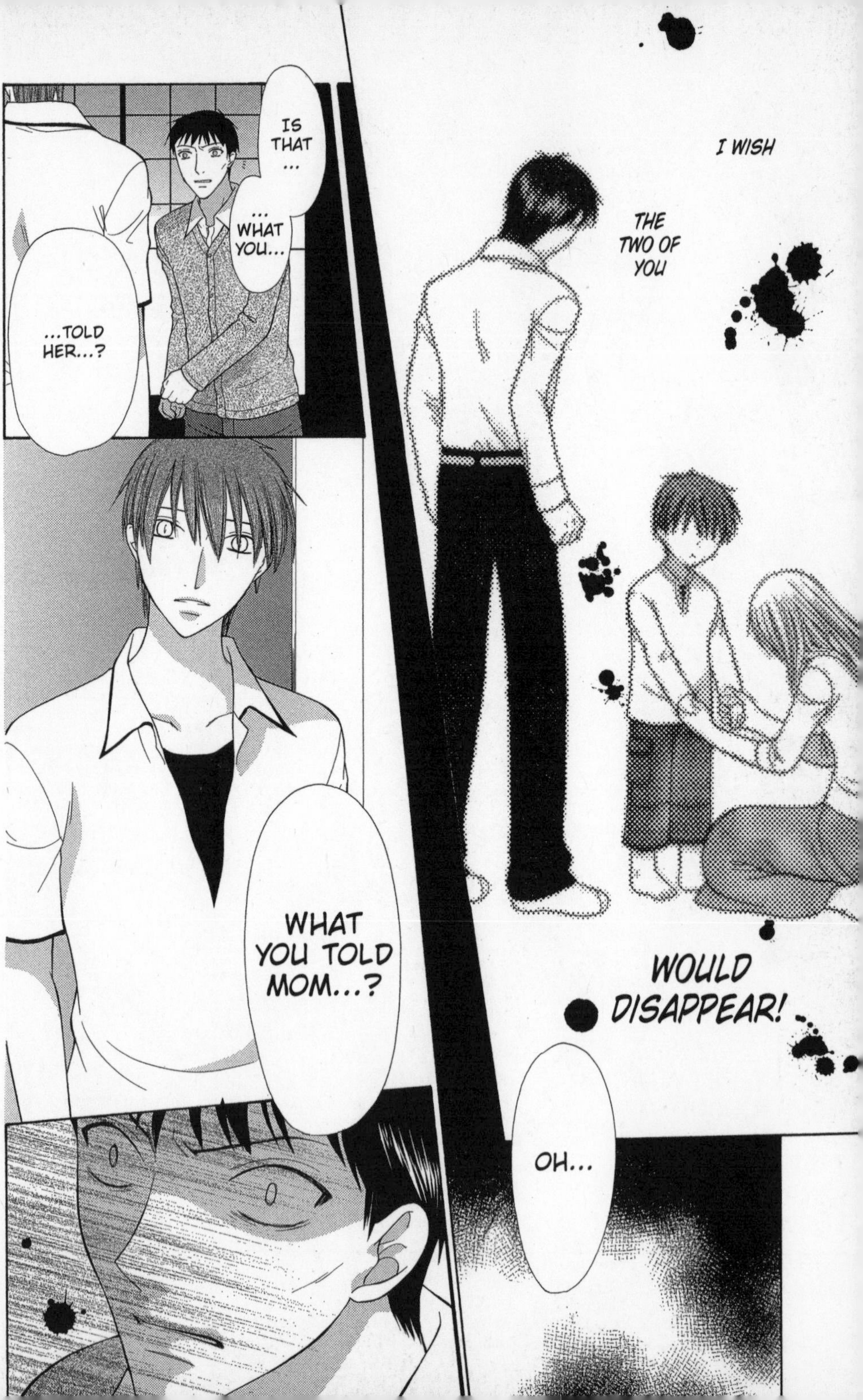
IS THAT ...
... WHAT YOU...
...TOLD HER...?
WHAT YOU TOLD MOM...?
I WISH
THE TWO OF YOU
WOULD DISAPPEAR!
OH...

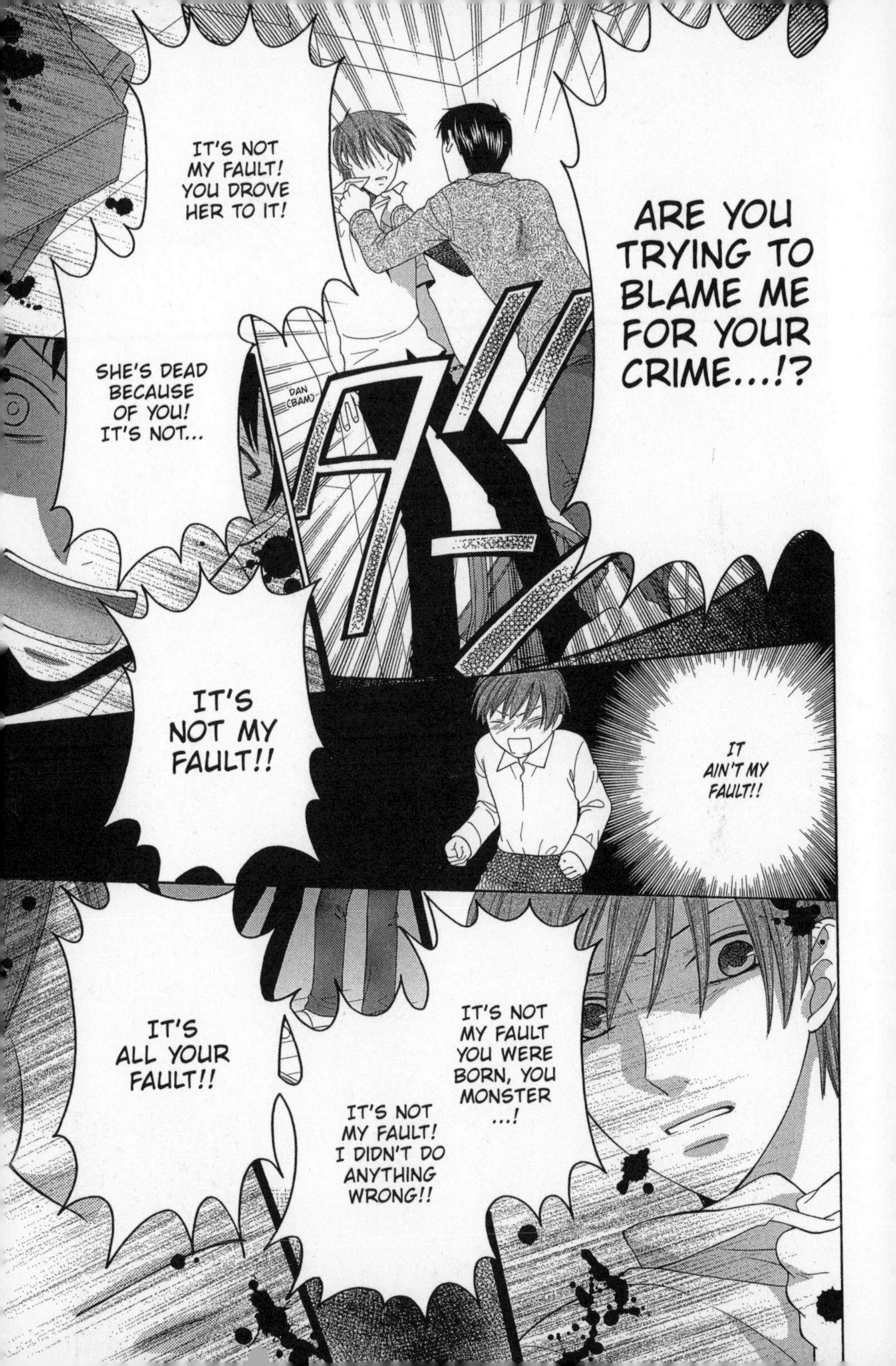
ARE YOU TRYING TO BLAME ME FOR YOUR CRIME...!?
IT'S NOT MY FAULT! YOU DROVE HER TO IT!
DAN (BAM)
SHE'S DEAD BECAUSE OF YOU! IT'S NOT...
IT AIN'T MY FAULT!!
IT'S NOT MY FAULT!!
IT'S NOT MY FAULT YOU WERE BORN, YOU MONSTER ...!
IT'S NOT MY FAULT! I DIDN'T DO ANYTHING WRONG!!
IT'S ALL YOUR FAULT!!

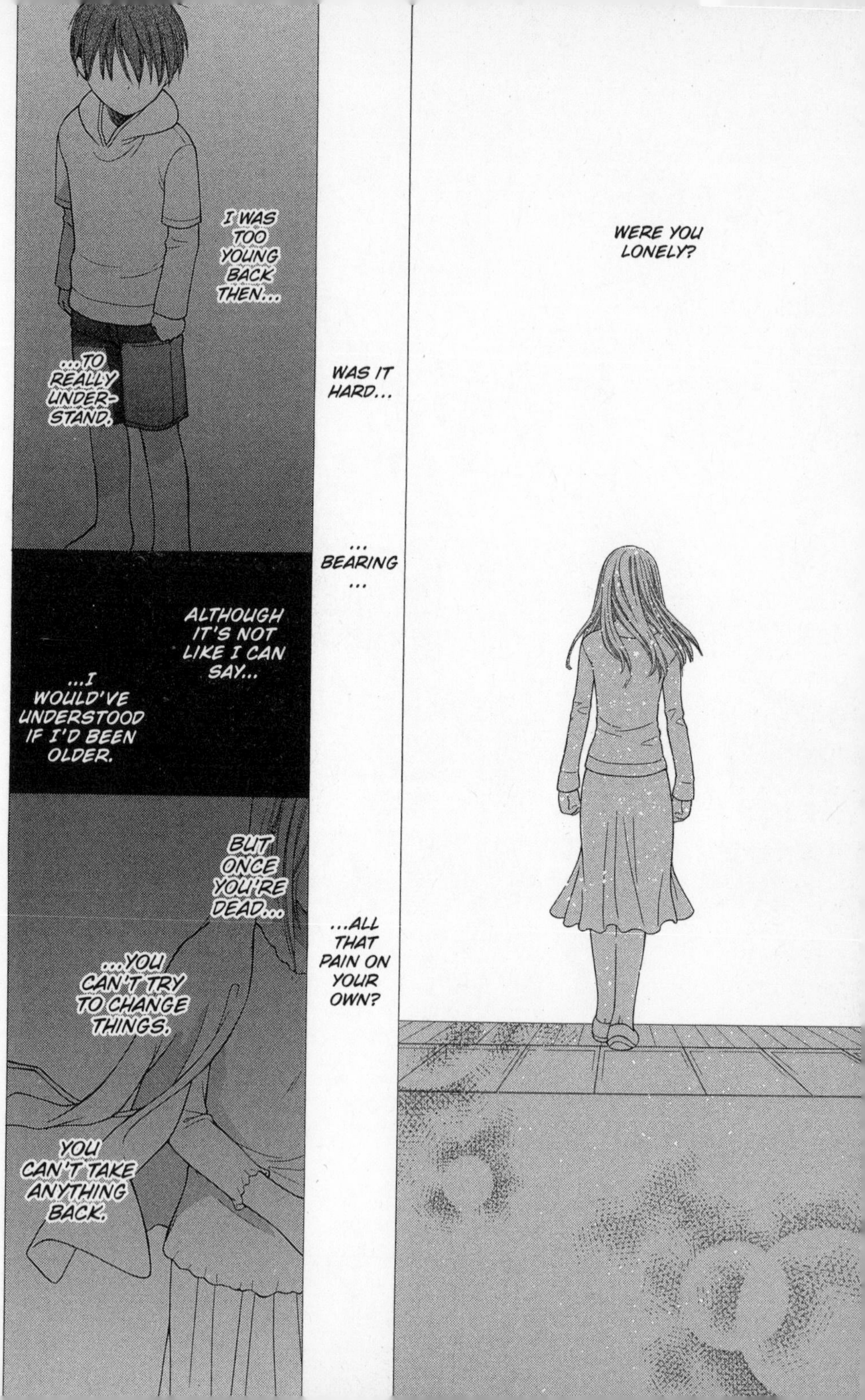
WERE YOU LONELY?
WAS IT HARD...
...BEARING...
...ALL THAT PAIN ON YOUR OWN?
I WAS TOO YOUNG BACK THEN...
...TO REALLY UNDERSTAND.
ALTHOUGH IT'S NOT LIKE I CAN SAY...
...I WOULD'VE UNDERSTOOD IF I'D BEEN OLDER.
BUT ONCE YOU'RE DEAD...
...YOU CAN'T TRY TO CHANGE THINGS.
YOU CAN'T TAKE ANYTHING BACK.

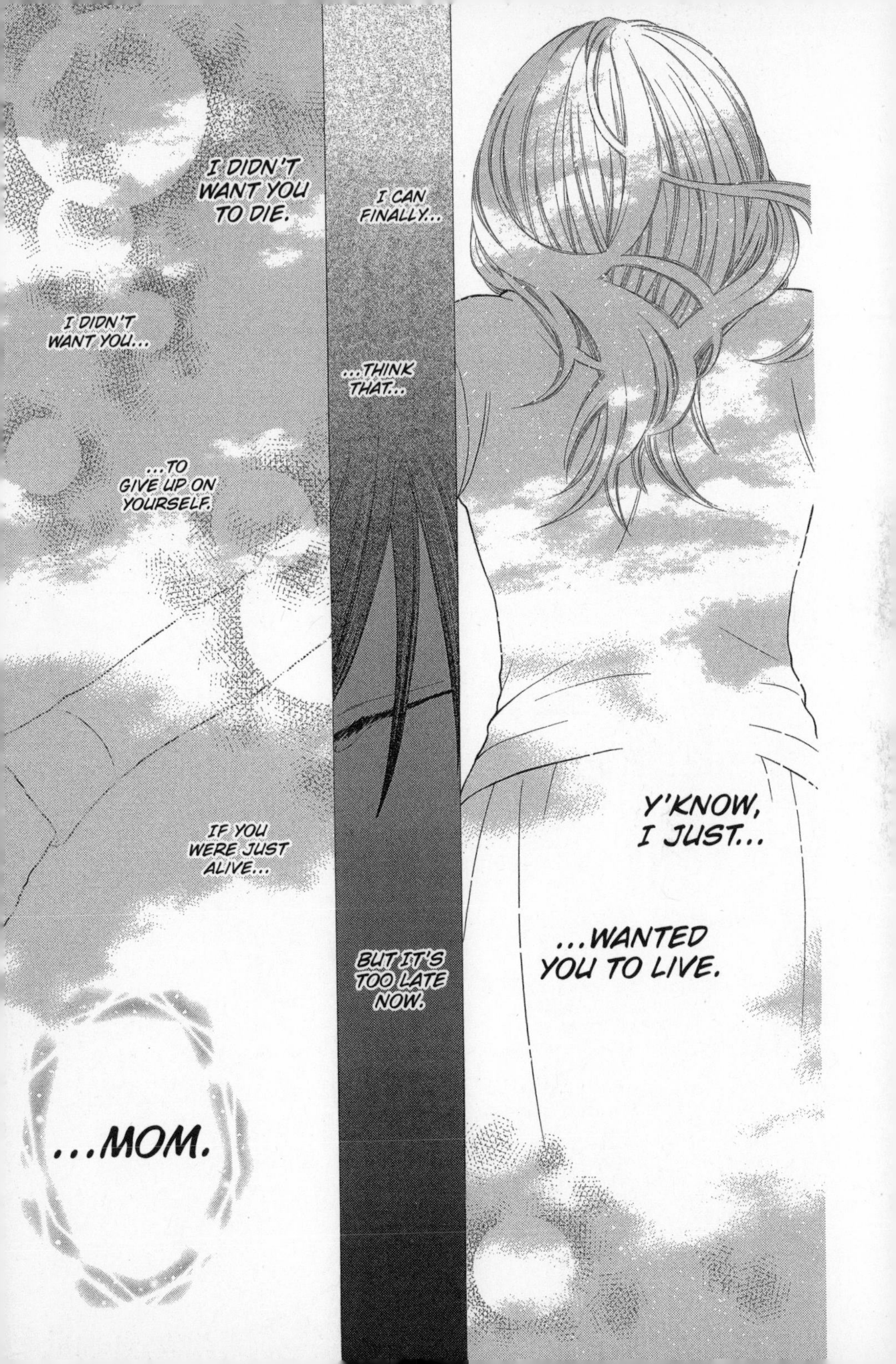
Y'KNOW, I JUST...
...WANTED YOU TO LIVE.
I CAN FINALLY...
...THINK THAT...
BUT IT'S TOO LATE NOW.
I DIDN'T WANT YOU TO DIE.
I DIDN'T WANT YOU...
...TO GIVE UP ON YOURSELF.
IF YOU WERE JUST ALIVE...
...MOM.

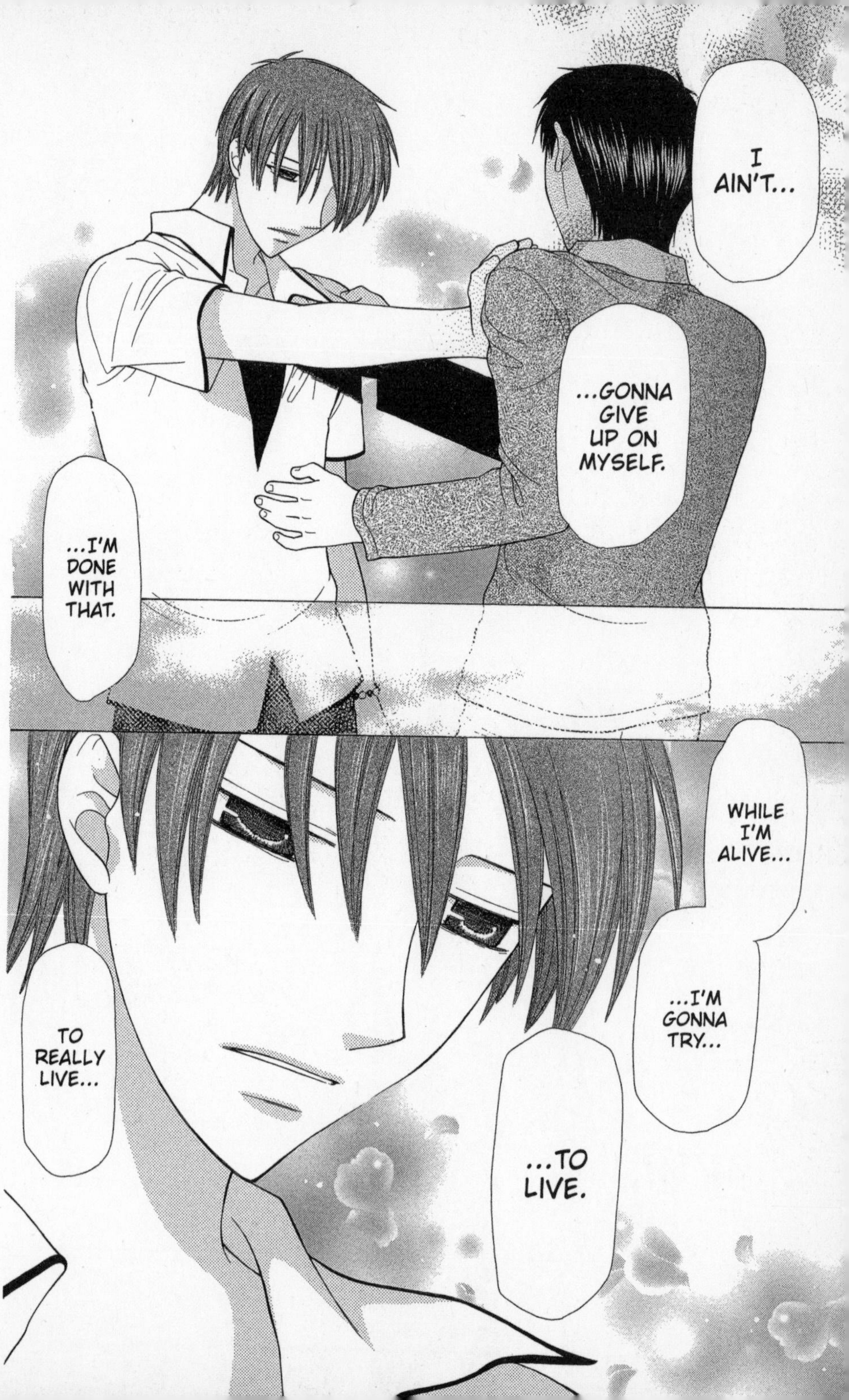
I AIN'T...
...GONNA GIVE UP ON MYSELF.
...I'M DONE WITH THAT.
WHILE I'M ALIVE...
...I'M GONNA TRY...
...TO LIVE.
TO REALLY LIVE...

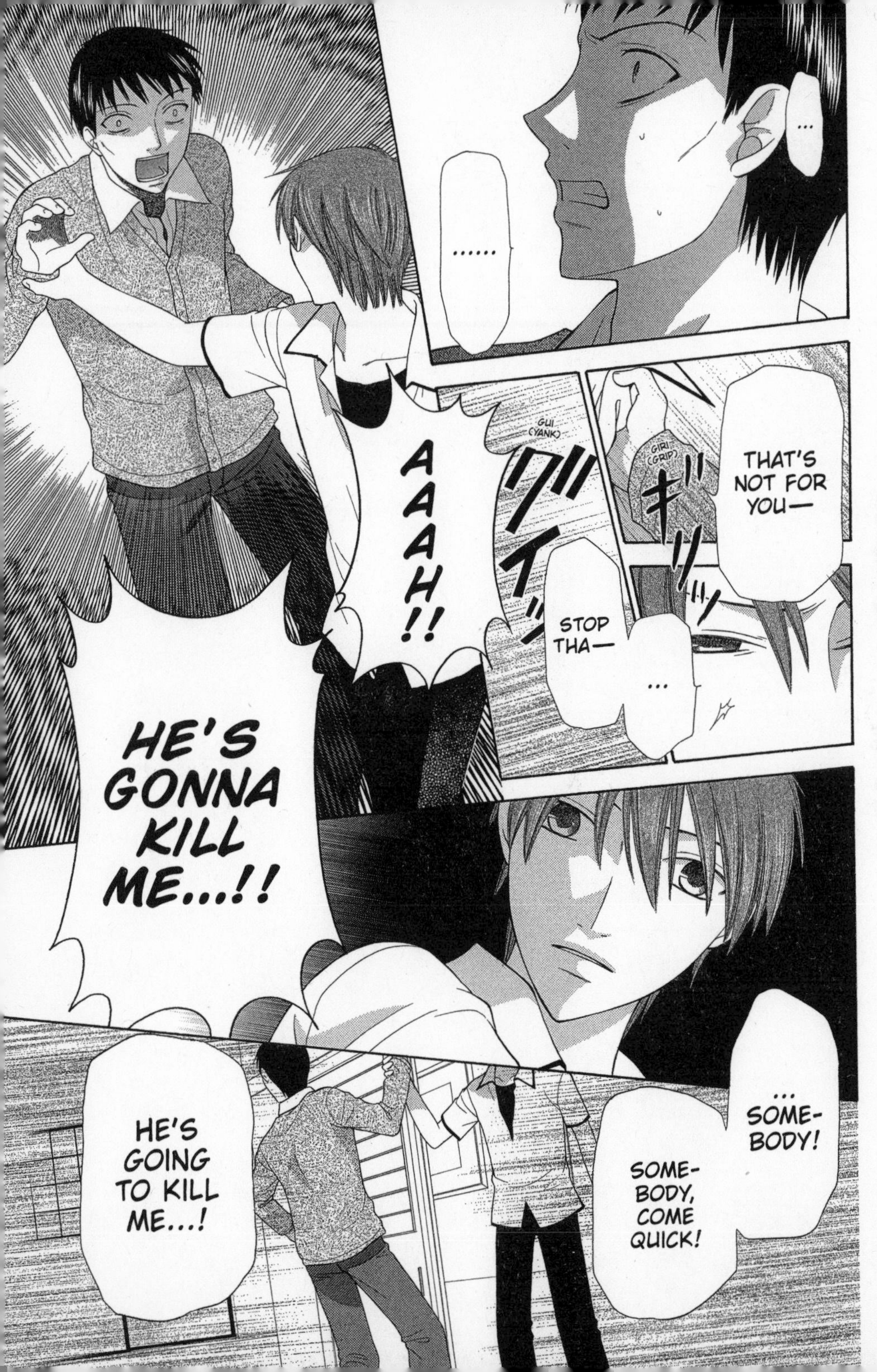
...
......
THAT'S NOT FOR YOU—
GIRI (GRIP)
STOP THA—
...
GUI (YANK)
AAAAH!!
HE'S GONNA KILL ME...!!
... SOMEBODY!
SOMEBODY, COME QUICK!
HE'S GOING TO KILL ME...!

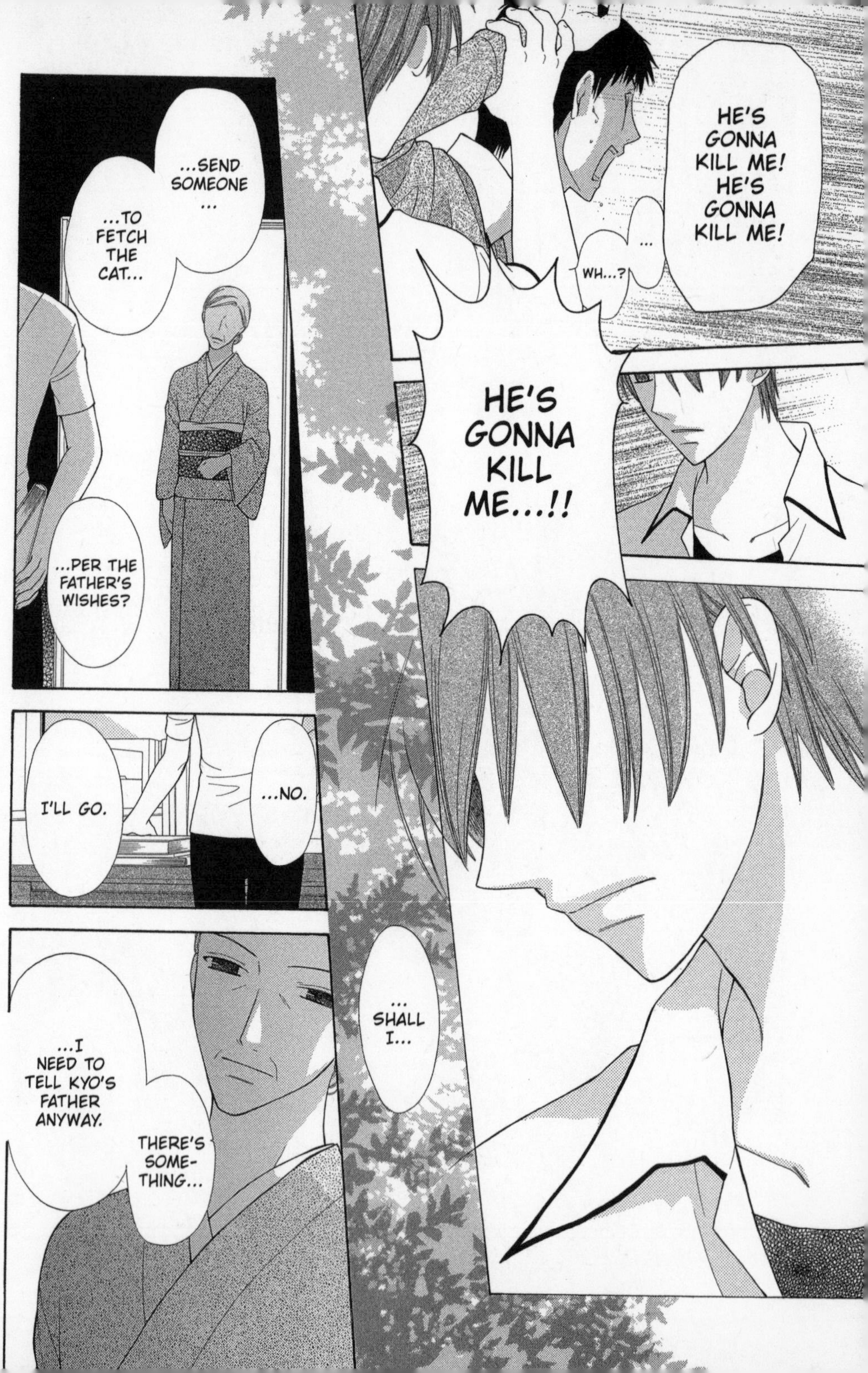
HE'S GONNA KILL ME! HE'S GONNA KILL ME!
...
WH...?
HE'S GONNA KILL ME...!!
...SHALL I...
...SEND SOMEONE ...
...TO FETCH THE CAT...
...PER THE FATHER'S WISHES?
...NO.
I'LL GO.
THERE'S SOME-THING...
...I NEED TO TELL KYO'S FATHER ANYWAY.

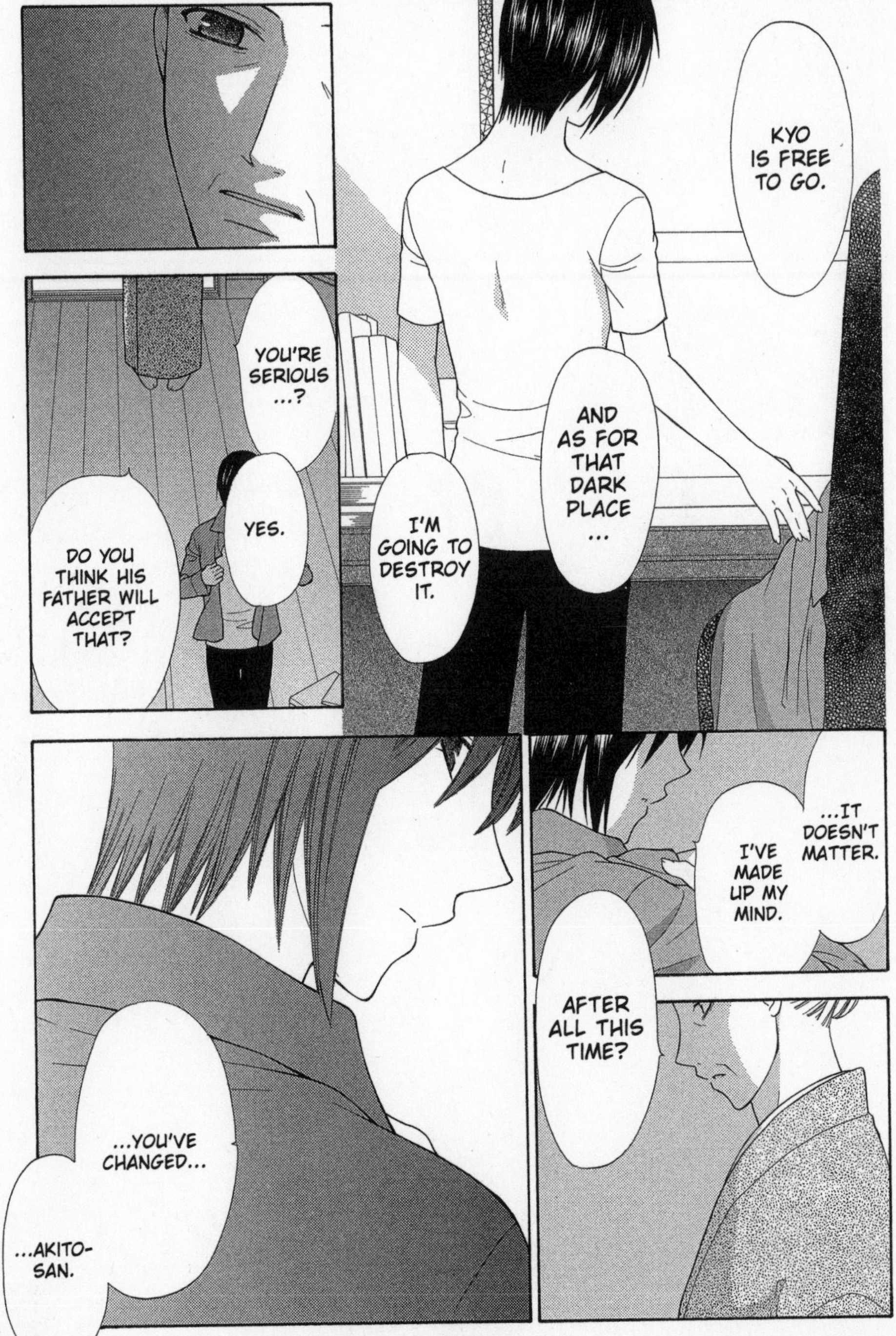
KYO IS FREE TO GO.
AND AS FOR THAT DARK PLACE...
I'M GOING TO DESTROY IT.
YOU'RE SERIOUS...?
YES.
DO YOU THINK HIS FATHER WILL ACCEPT THAT?
...IT DOESN'T MATTER.
I'VE MADE UP MY MIND.
AFTER ALL THIS TIME?
...YOU'VE CHANGED...
...AKITO-SAN.

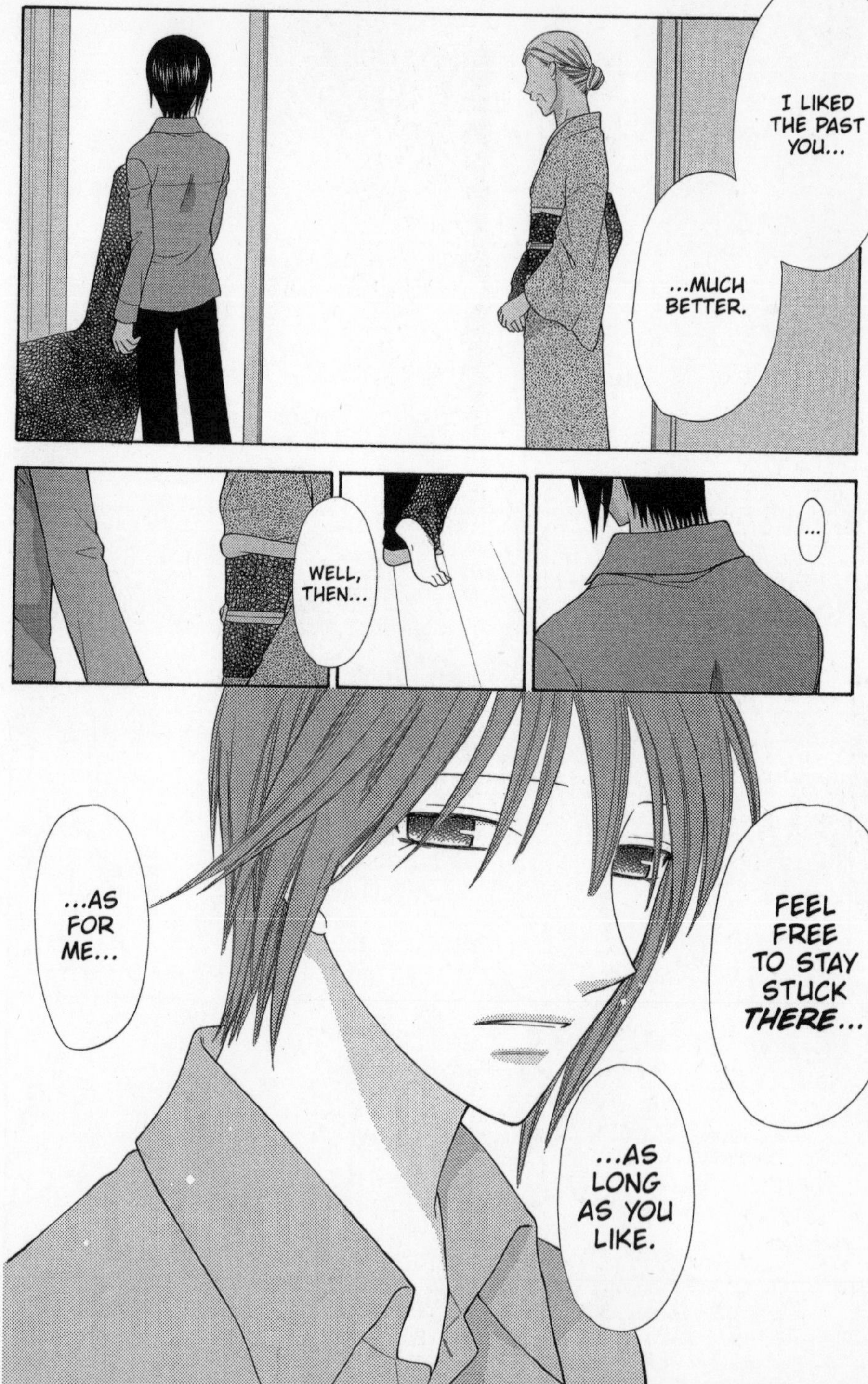
I LIKED THE PAST YOU...
...MUCH BETTER.
...
WELL, THEN...
FEEL FREE TO STAY STUCK *THERE*...
...AS FOR ME...
...AS LONG AS YOU LIKE.

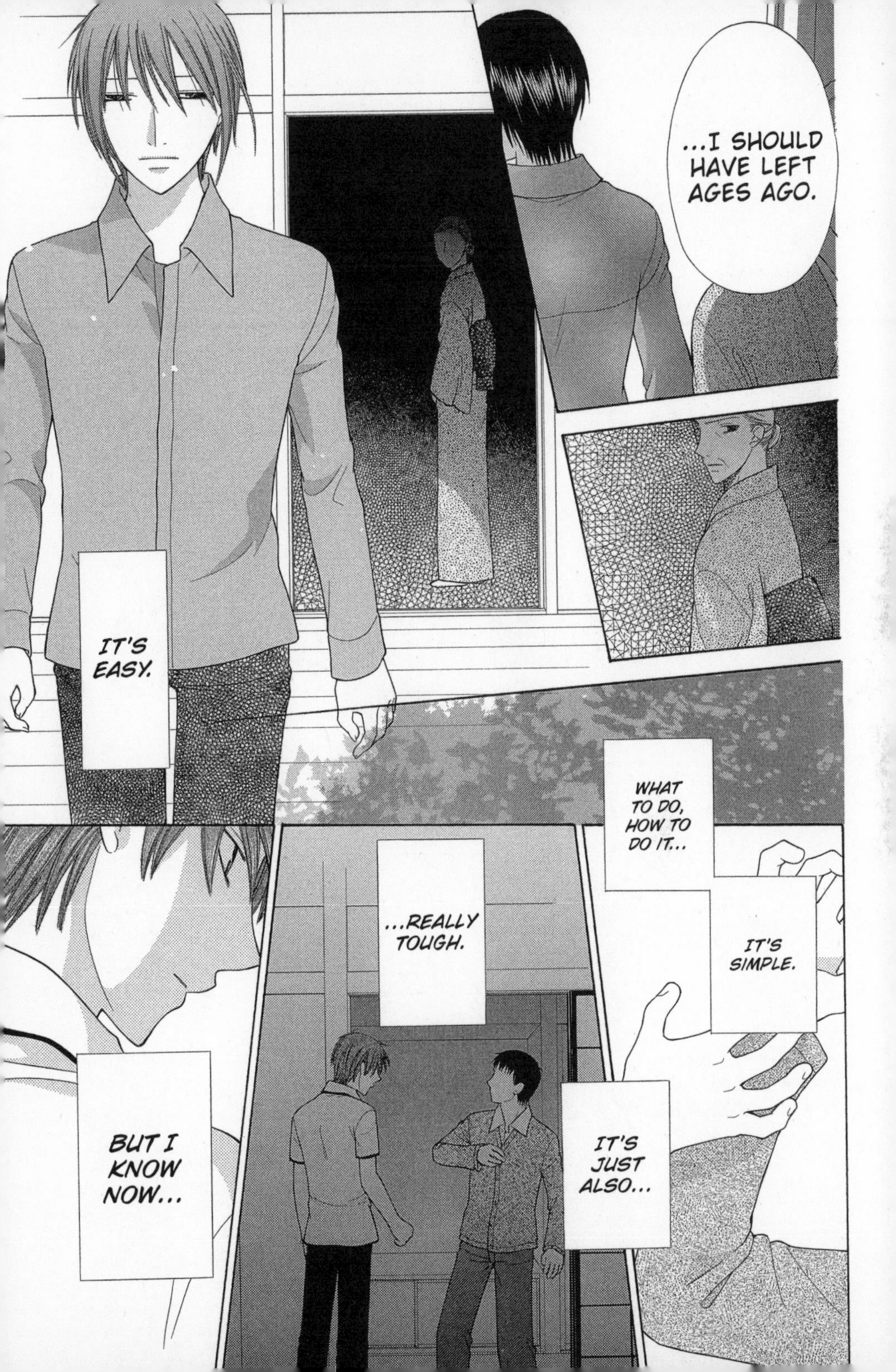
...I SHOULD HAVE LEFT AGES AGO.
IT'S EASY.
WHAT TO DO, HOW TO DO IT...
IT'S SIMPLE.
IT'S JUST ALSO...
...REALLY TOUGH.
BUT I KNOW NOW...

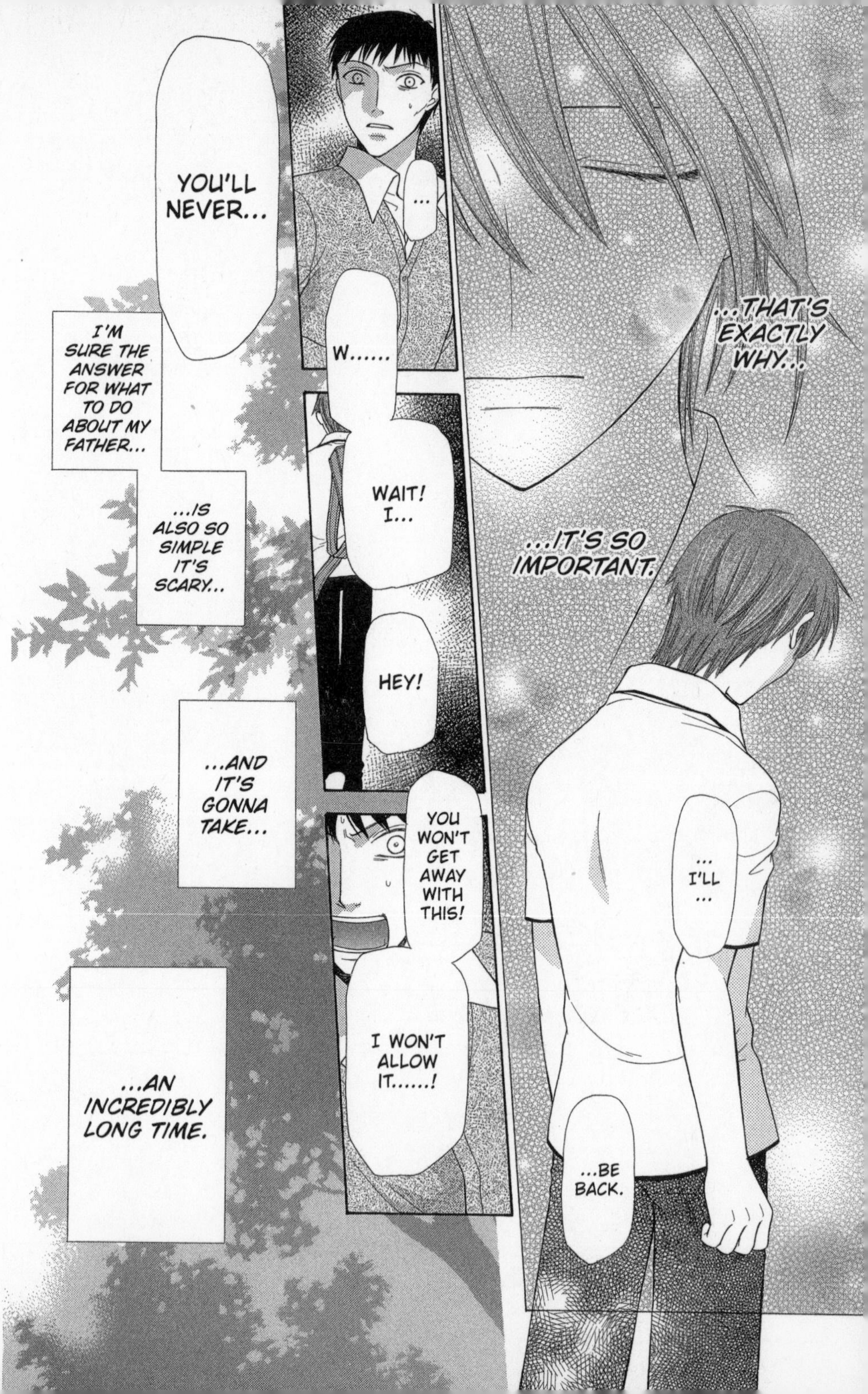
...THAT'S EXACTLY WHY...
...IT'S SO IMPORTANT.
...I'LL...
...BE BACK.
...
W......
WAIT! I...
HEY!
YOU WON'T GET AWAY WITH THIS!
I WON'T ALLOW IT......!
YOU'LL NEVER...
I'M SURE THE ANSWER FOR WHAT TO DO ABOUT MY FATHER...
...IS ALSO SO SIMPLE IT'S SCARY...
...AND IT'S GONNA TAKE...
...AN INCREDIBLY LONG TIME.

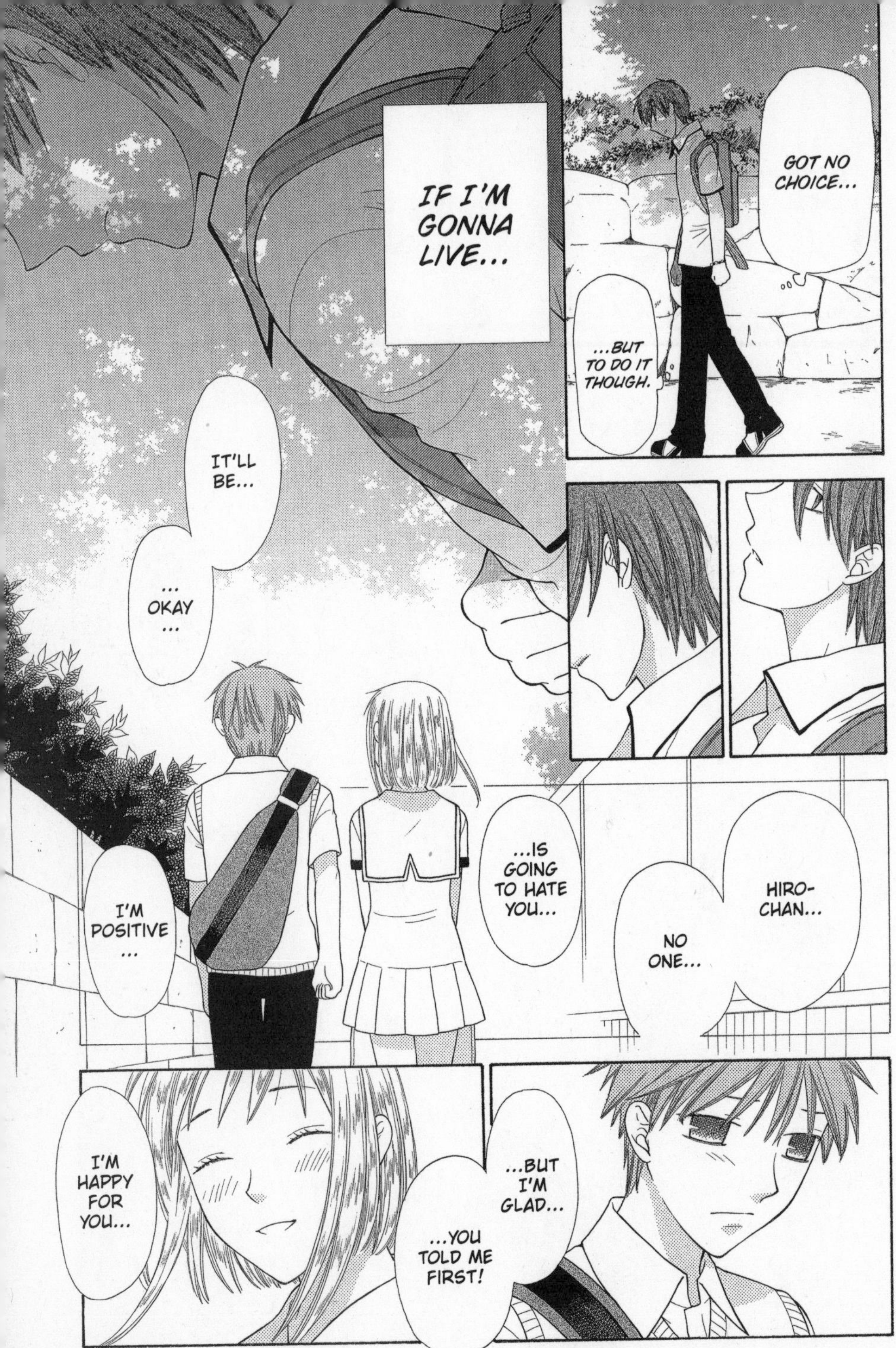
GOT NO CHOICE...
...BUT TO DO IT THOUGH.
IF I'M GONNA LIVE...
IT'LL BE...
...OKAY...
HIRO-CHAN...
NO ONE...
...IS GOING TO HATE YOU...
I'M POSITIVE...
I'M HAPPY FOR YOU...
...BUT I'M GLAD...
...YOU TOLD ME FIRST!

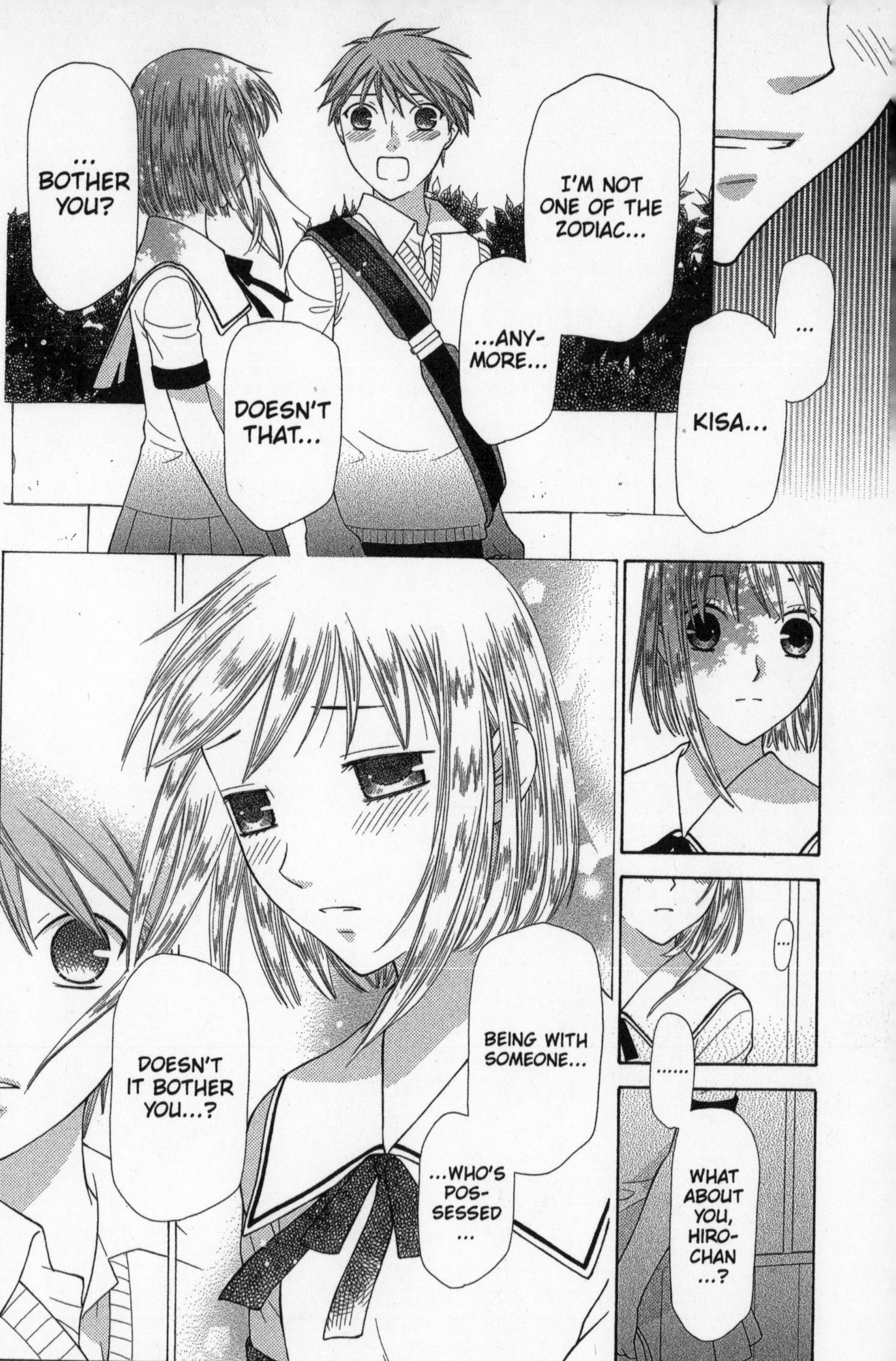
...
KISA...
I'M NOT ONE OF THE ZODIAC...
...ANY-MORE...
DOESN'T THAT...
...BOTHER YOU?
...
......
WHAT ABOUT YOU, HIRO-CHAN ...?
BEING WITH SOMEONE...
...WHO'S POS-SESSED ...
DOESN'T IT BOTHER YOU...?

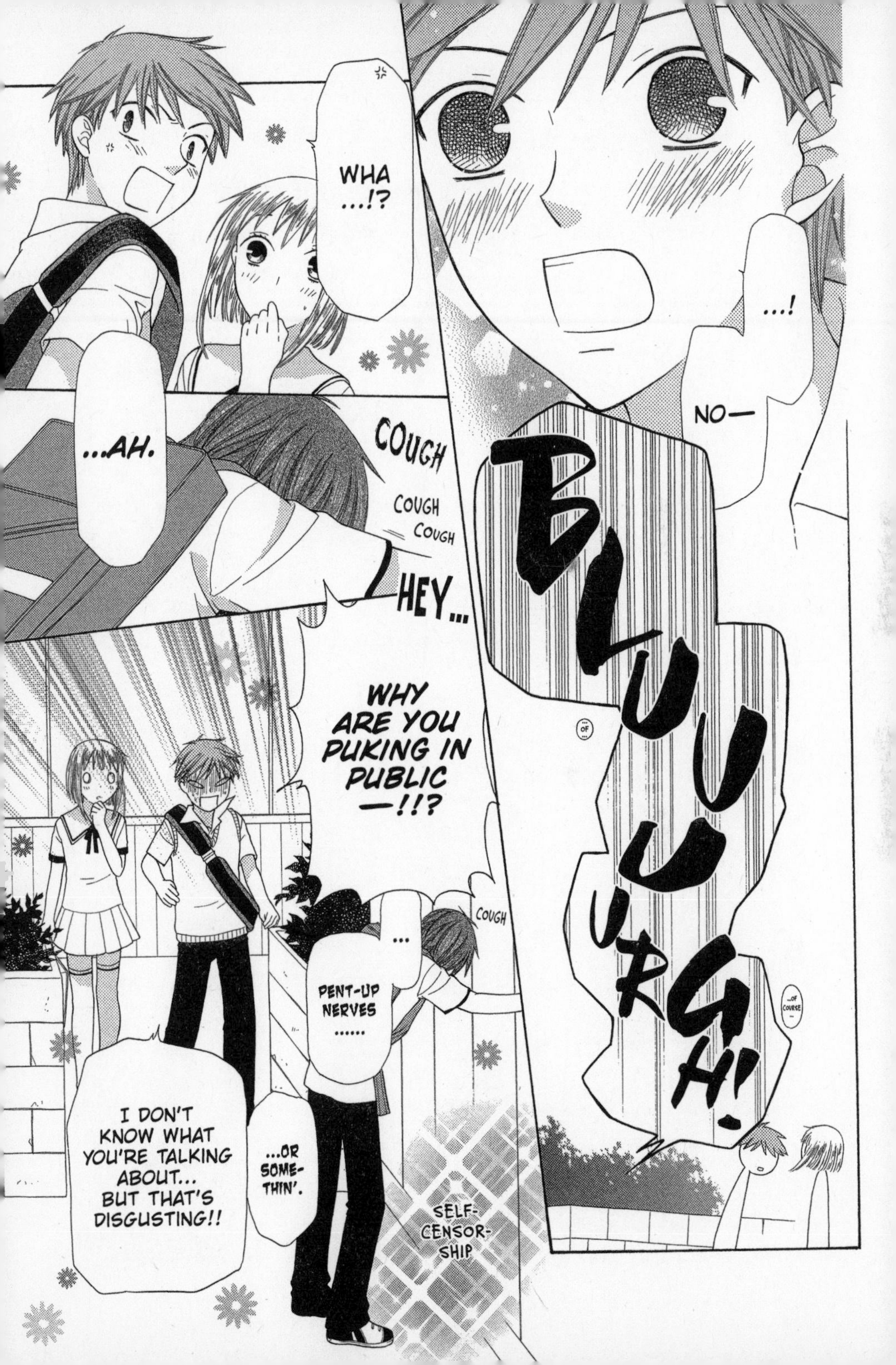
...!
NO—
BLUUUURGH!
...OF
...OF COURSE...
WHA ...!?
COUGH
...AH.
COUGH COUGH
HEY...
WHY ARE YOU PUKING IN PUBLIC —!!?
COUGH
...
PENT-UP NERVES ......
...OR SOME-THIN'.
I DON'T KNOW WHAT YOU'RE TALKING ABOUT... BUT THAT'S DISGUSTING!!
SELF-CENSOR-SHIP

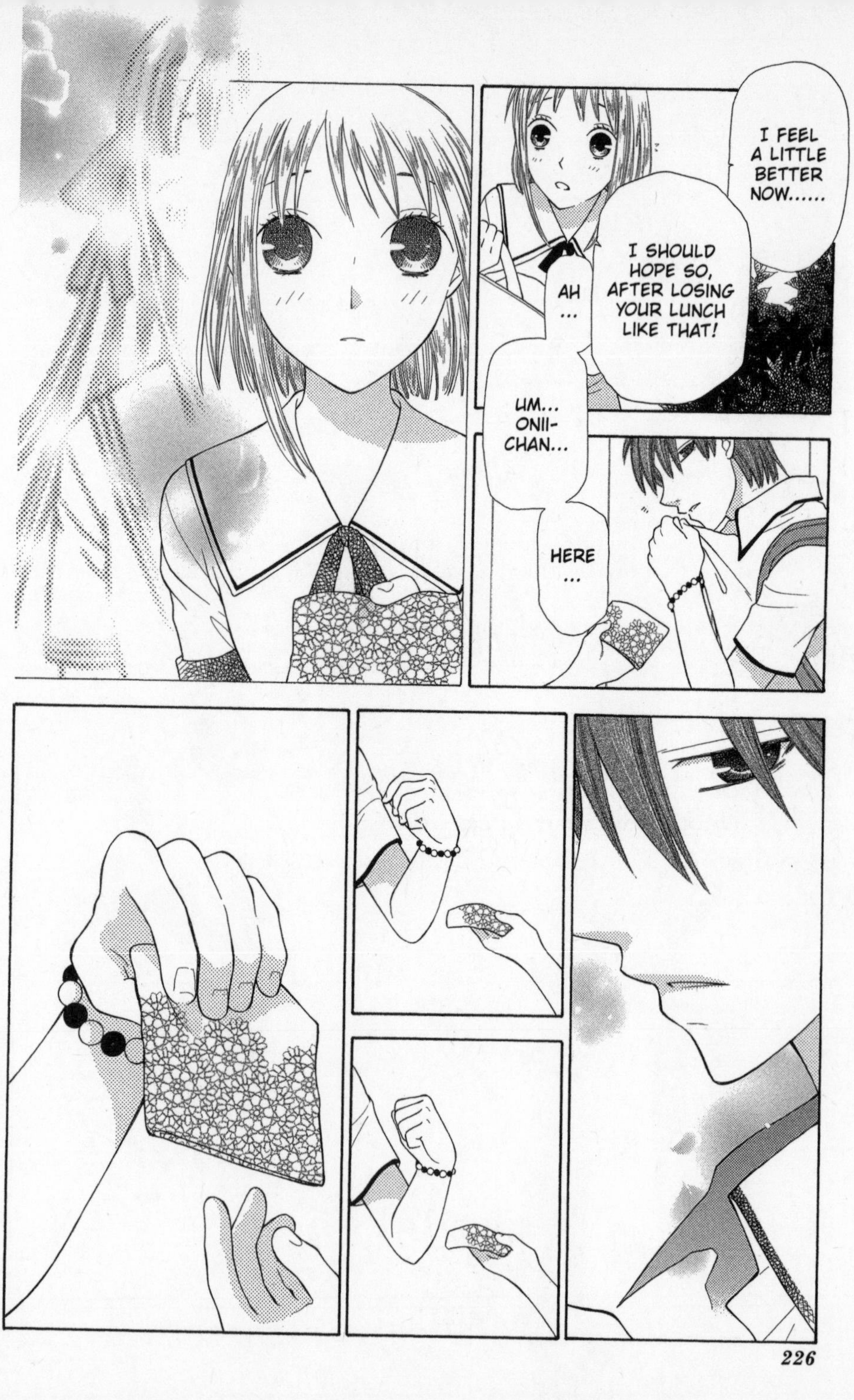
I FEEL A LITTLE BETTER NOW......
I SHOULD HOPE SO, AFTER LOSING YOUR LUNCH LIKE THAT!
AH ...
UM... ONII-CHAN...
HERE ...

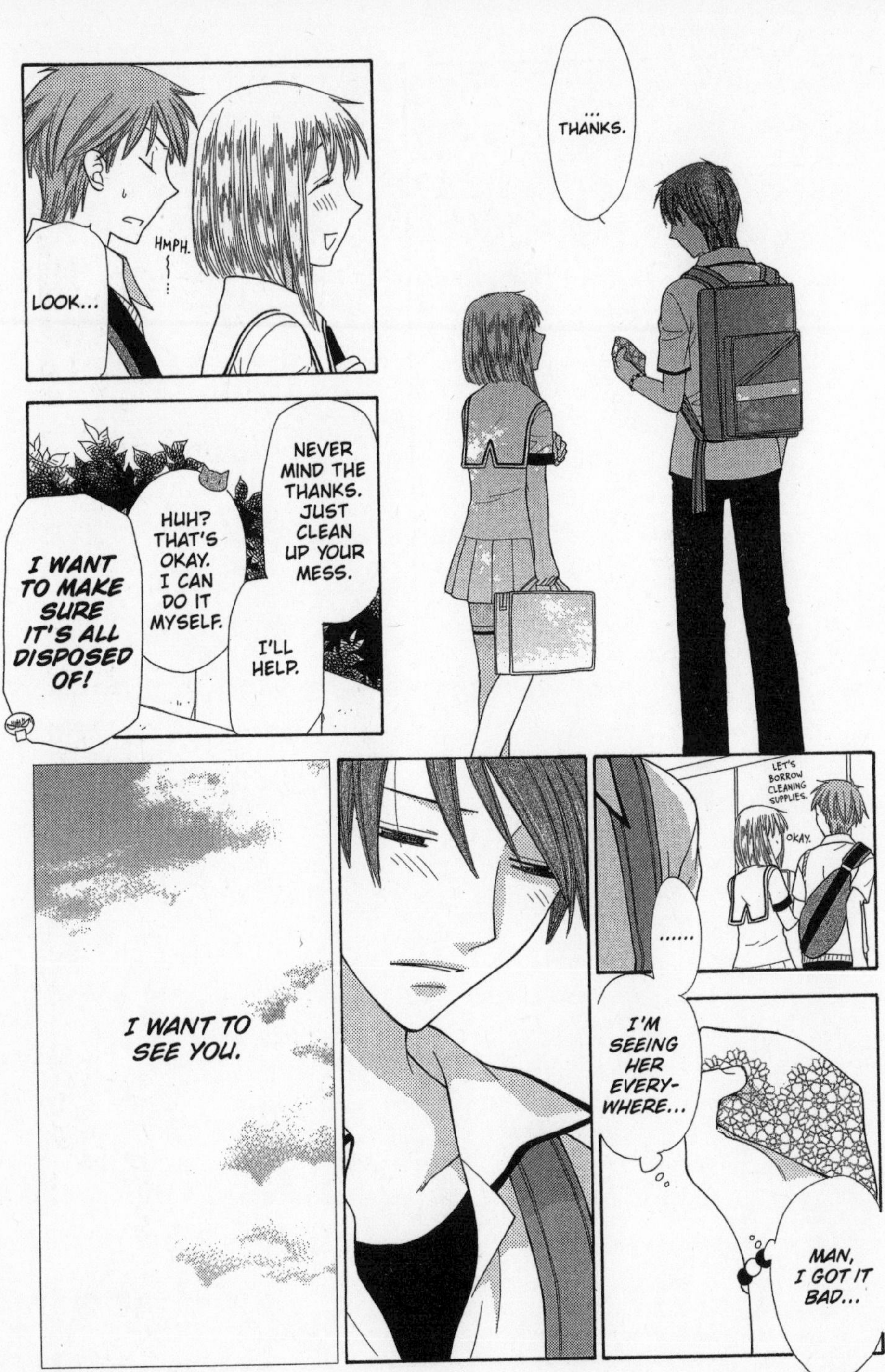
... THANKS.
HMPH.
LOOK...
NEVER MIND THE THANKS. JUST CLEAN UP YOUR MESS.
HUH? THAT'S OKAY. I CAN DO IT MYSELF.
I'LL HELP.
I WANT TO MAKE SURE IT'S ALL DISPOSED OF!
LET'S BORROW CLEANING SUPPLIES.
OKAY.
......
I'M SEEING HER EVERYWHERE...
MAN, I GOT IT BAD...
I WANT TO SEE YOU.

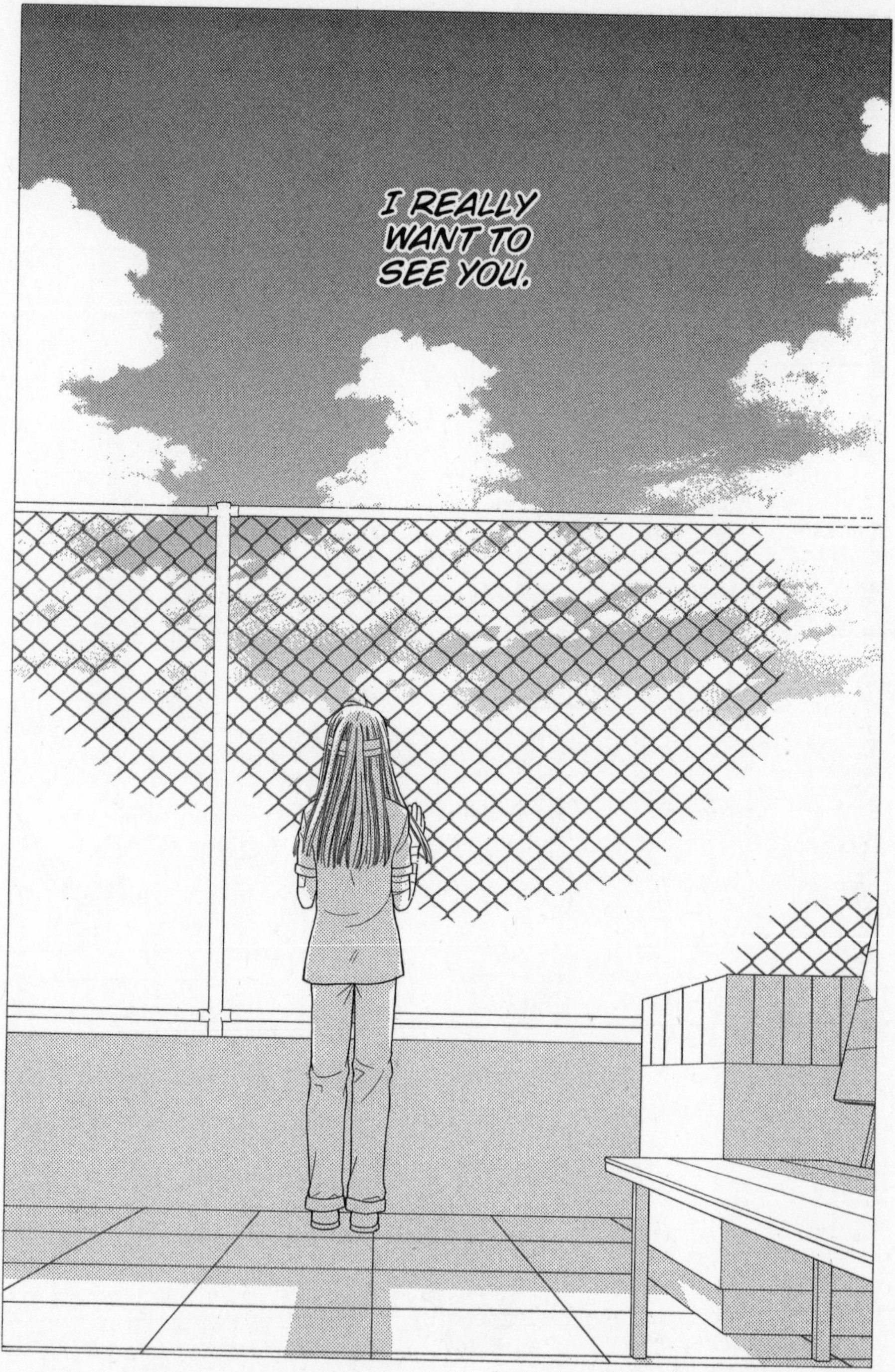
I REALLY WANT TO SEE YOU.

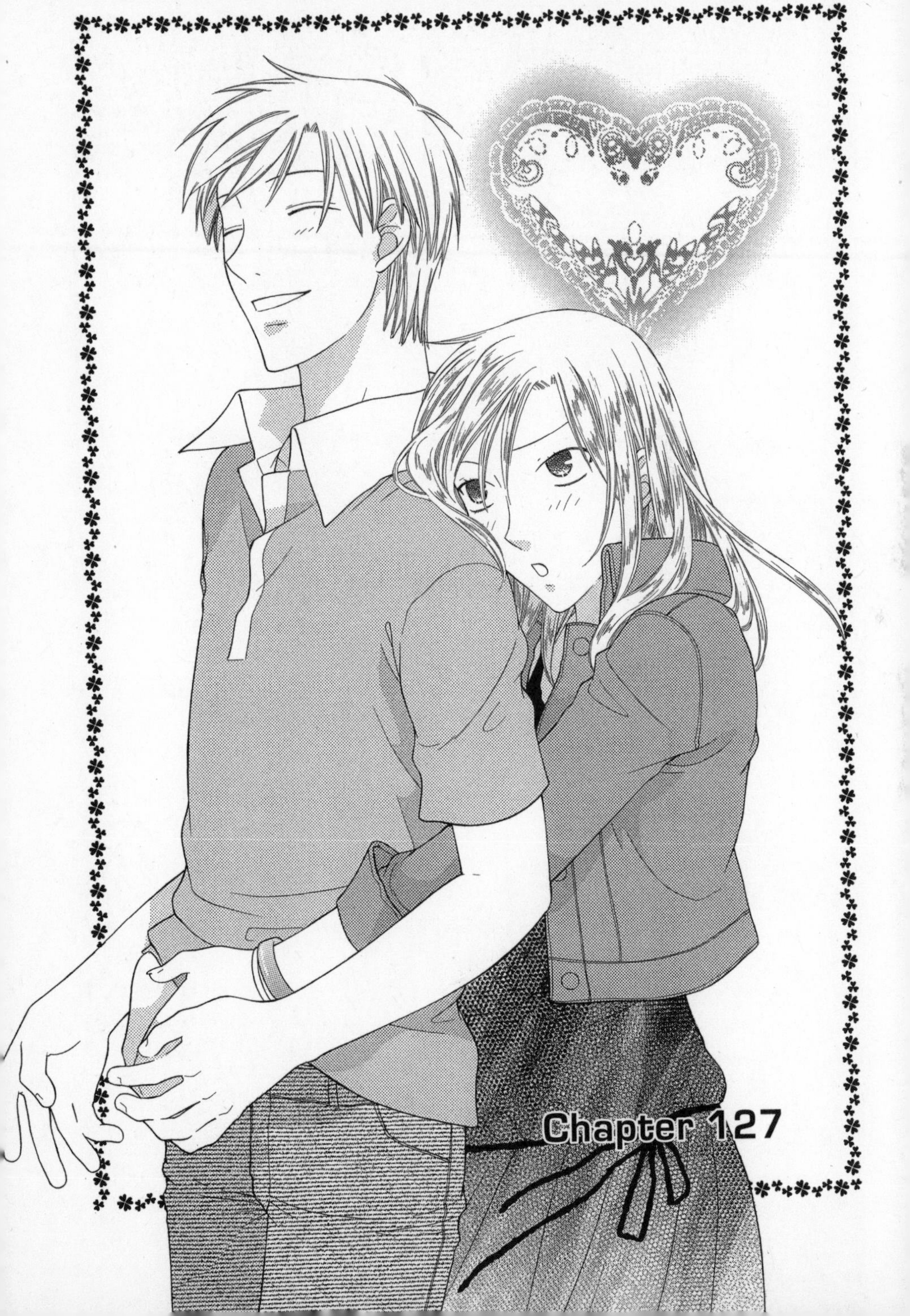
Chapter 127

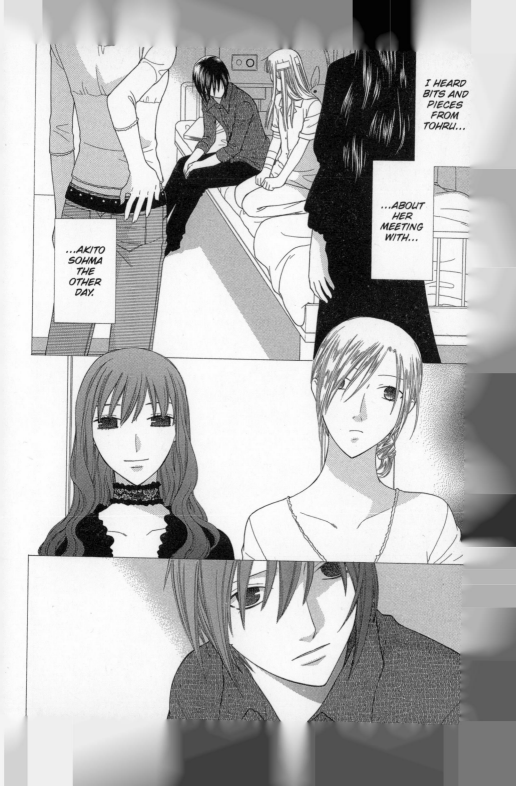

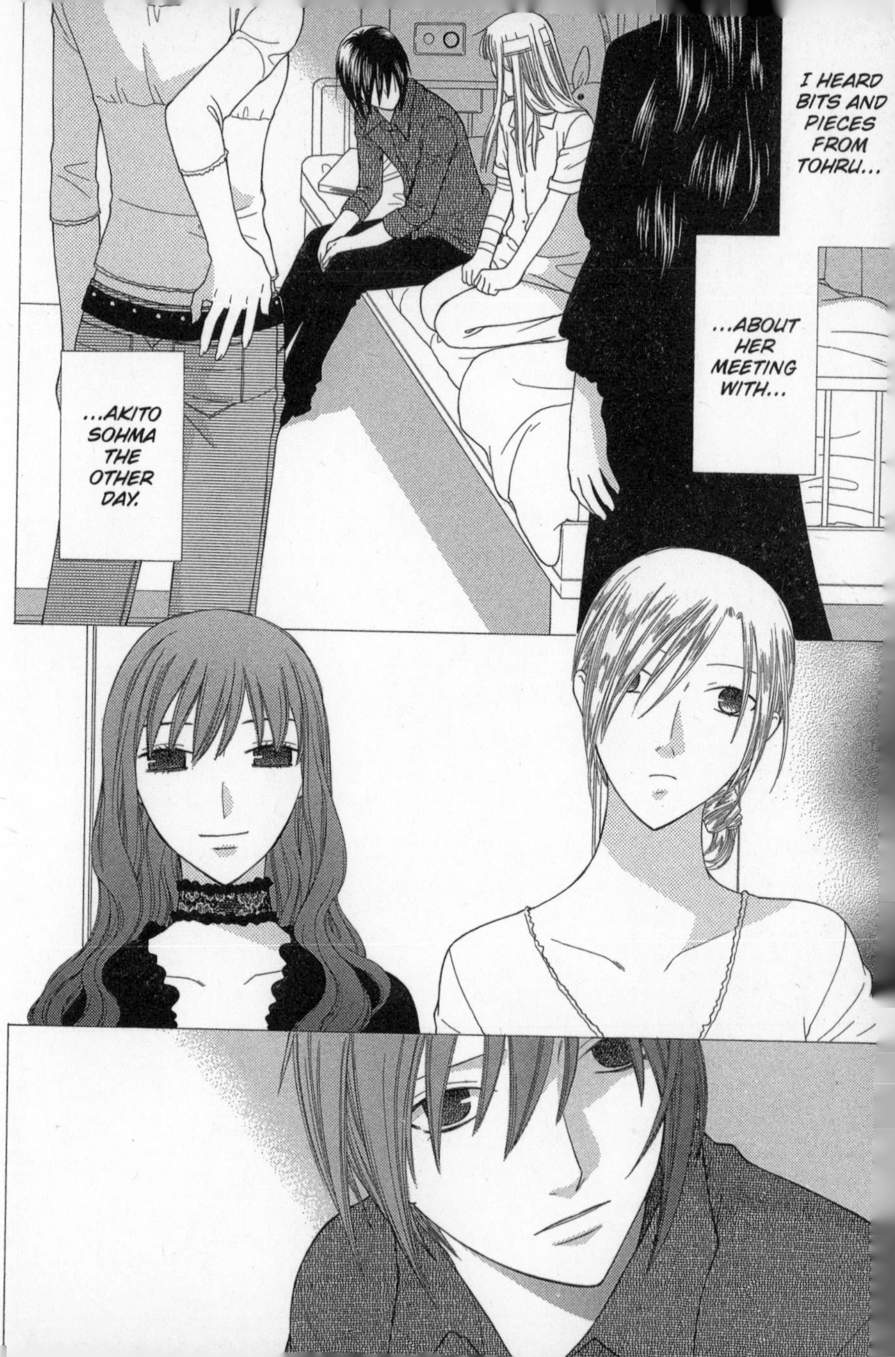
I HEARD BITS AND PIECES FROM TOHRU...
...ABOUT HER MEETING WITH...
...AKITO SOHMA THE OTHER DAY.

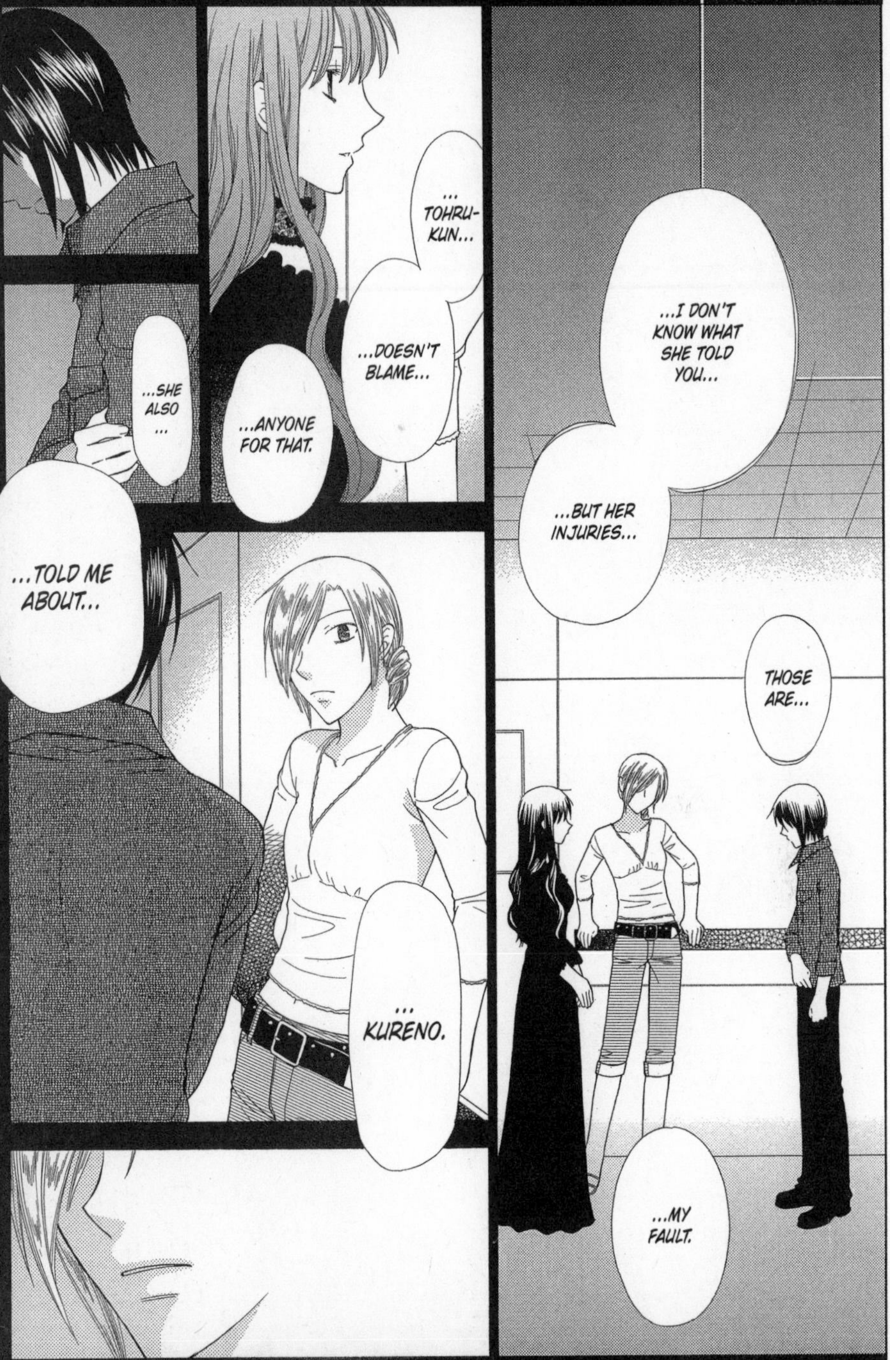
...I DON'T KNOW WHAT SHE TOLD YOU...
...BUT HER INJURIES...
THOSE ARE...
...MY FAULT.
... TOHRU-KUN...
...DOESN'T BLAME...
...ANYONE FOR THAT.
...SHE ALSO ...
...TOLD ME ABOUT...
... KURENO.

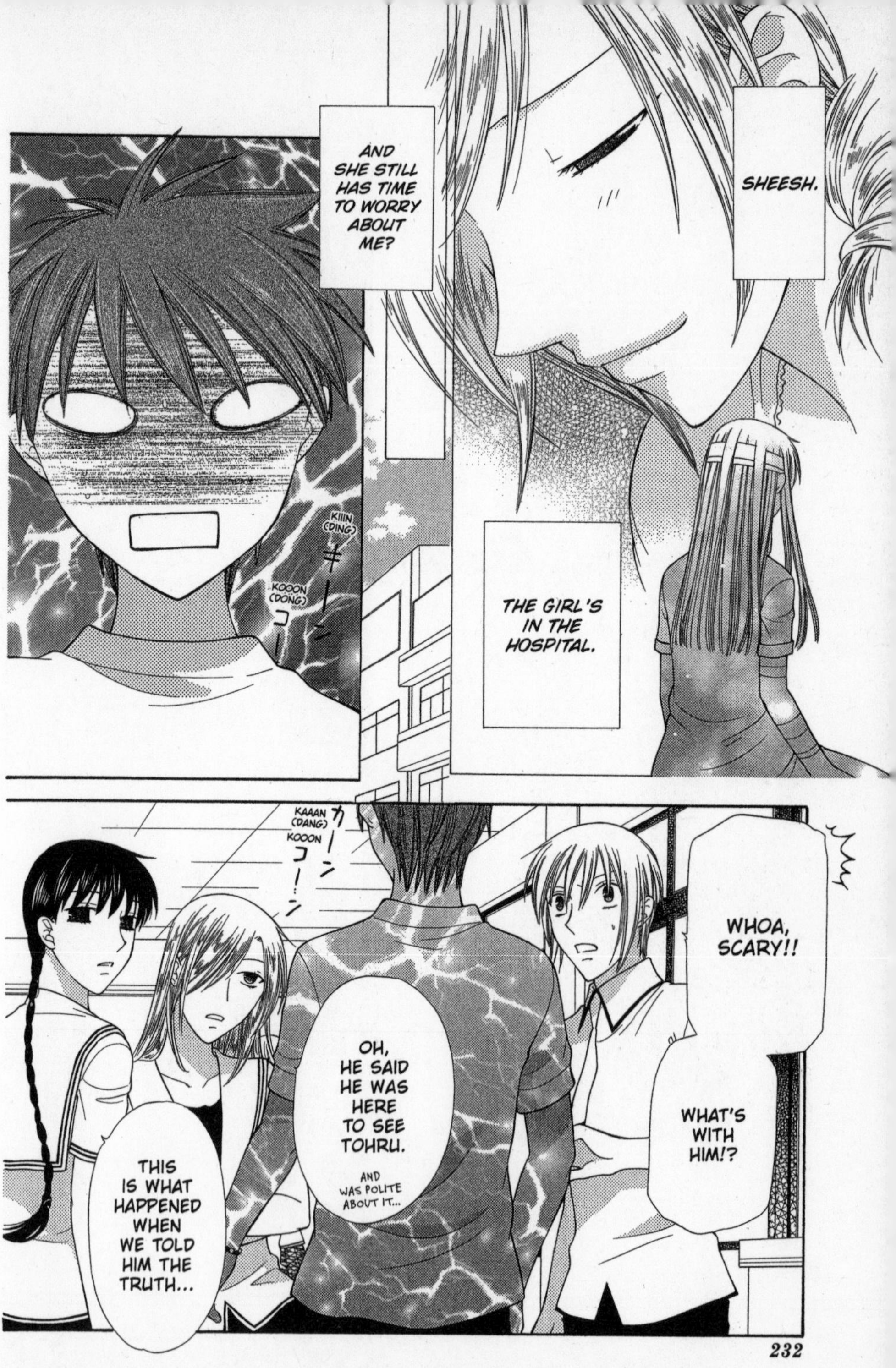
SHEESH.
AND SHE STILL HAS TIME TO WORRY ABOUT ME?
THE GIRL'S IN THE HOSPITAL.
KIIN (DING)
KOOON (DONG)
WHOA, SCARY!!
WHAT'S WITH HIM!?
KAAAN (DANG)
KOOON
OH, HE SAID HE WAS HERE TO SEE TOHRU.
AND WAS POLITE ABOUT IT...
THIS IS WHAT HAPPENED WHEN WE TOLD HIM THE TRUTH...

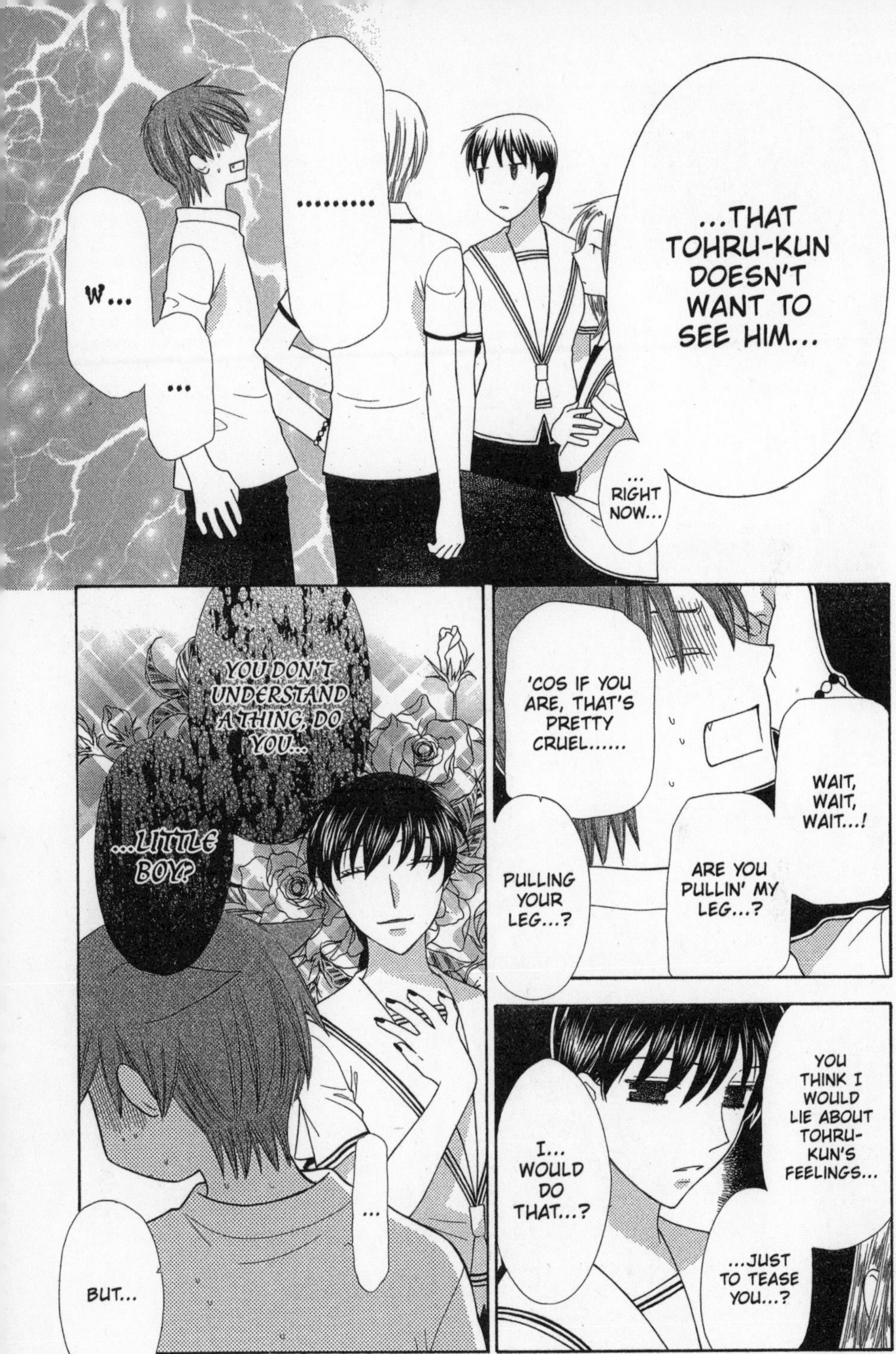
...THAT TOHRU-KUN DOESN'T WANT TO SEE HIM...
...RIGHT NOW...
....
W...
...
WAIT, WAIT, WAIT...!
ARE YOU PULLIN' MY LEG...?
'COS IF YOU ARE, THAT'S PRETTY CRUEL......
PULLING YOUR LEG...?
YOU THINK I WOULD LIE ABOUT TOHRU-KUN'S FEELINGS...
...JUST TO TEASE YOU...?
I... WOULD DO THAT...?
YOU DON'T UNDERSTAND A THING, DO YOU...
...LITTLE BOY?
...
BUT...

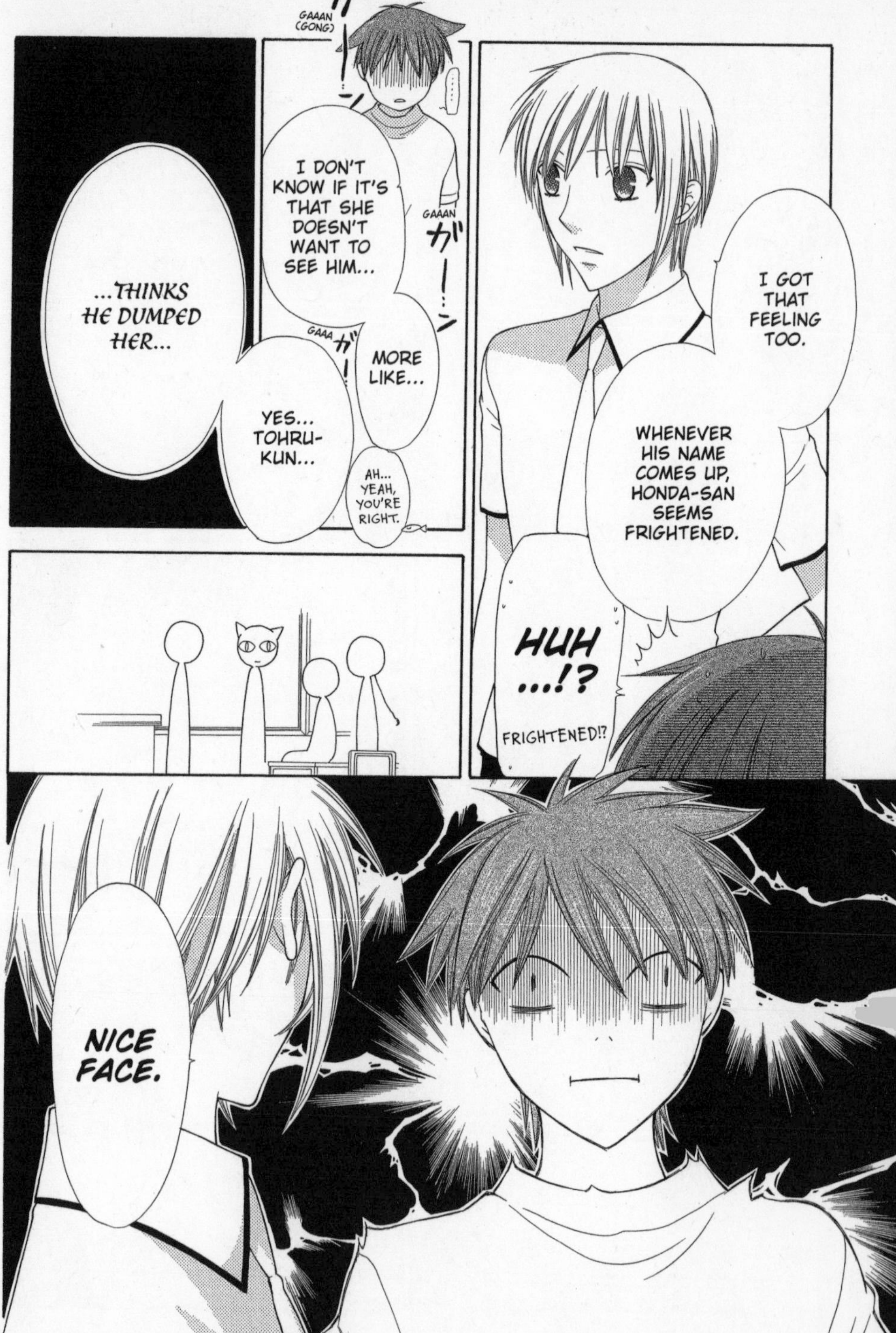
I GOT THAT FEELING TOO.
WHENEVER HIS NAME COMES UP, HONDA-SAN SEEMS FRIGHTENED.
HUH ...!?
FRIGHTENED!?
GAAAN (GONG)
ガーン
I DON'T KNOW IF IT'S THAT SHE DOESN'T WANT TO SEE HIM...
GAAAN
ガーン
MORE LIKE...
GAAA
ガ
YES... TOHRU-KUN...
...THINKS HE DUMPED HER...
AH... YEAH, YOU'RE RIGHT.
NICE FACE.

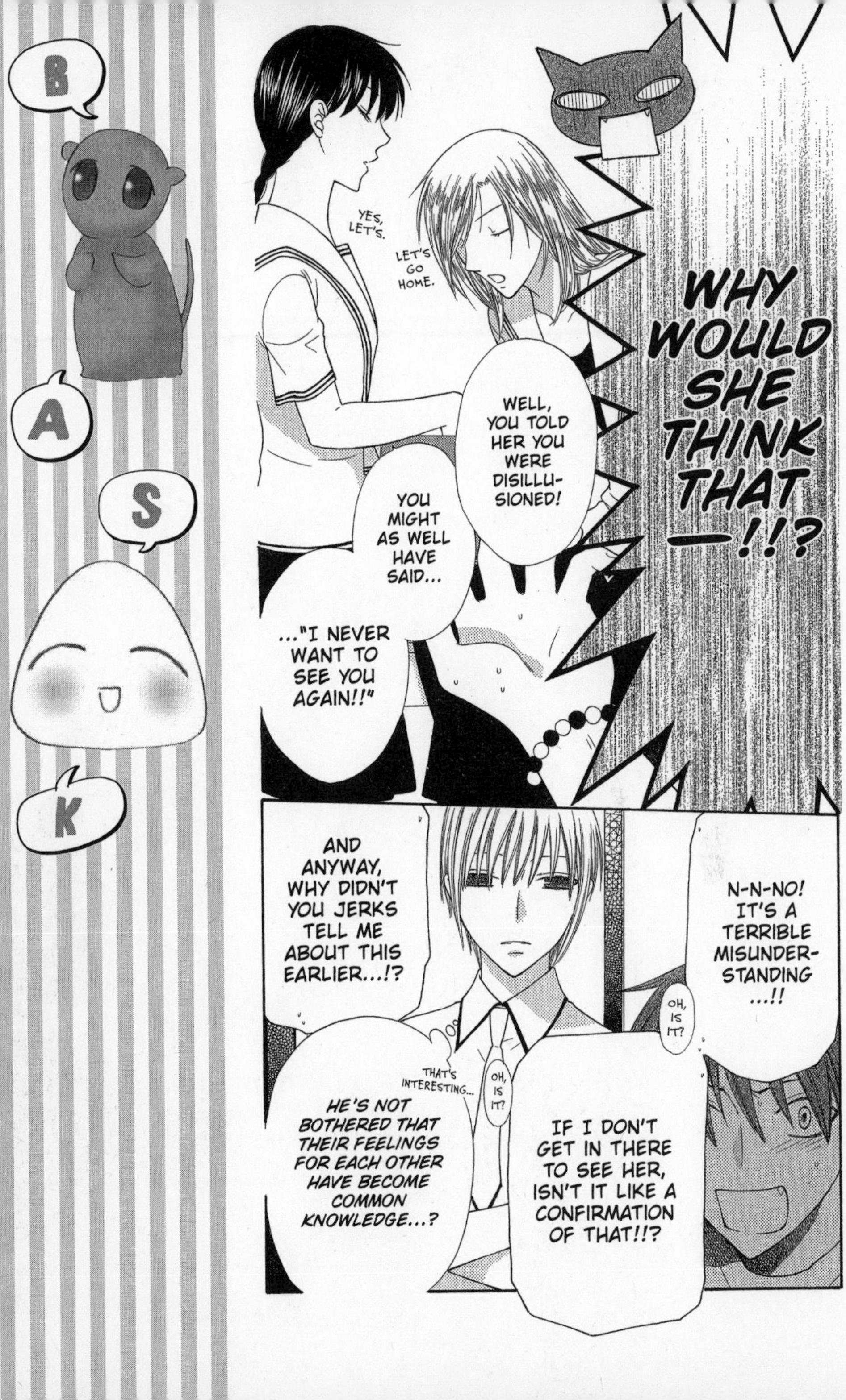
B
A
S
K
WHY WOULD SHE THINK THAT—!!?
LET'S GO HOME.
YES, LET'S.
WELL, YOU TOLD HER YOU WERE DISILLU-SIONED!
YOU MIGHT AS WELL HAVE SAID...
..."I NEVER WANT TO SEE YOU AGAIN!!"
N-N-NO! IT'S A TERRIBLE MISUNDER-STANDING ...!!
AND ANYWAY, WHY DIDN'T YOU JERKS TELL ME ABOUT THIS EARLIER...!?
OH, IS IT?
IF I DON'T GET IN THERE TO SEE HER, ISN'T IT LIKE A CONFIRMATION OF THAT!!?
OH, IS IT?
THAT'S INTERESTING...
HE'S NOT BOTHERED THAT THEIR FEELINGS FOR EACH OTHER HAVE BECOME COMMON KNOWLEDGE...?

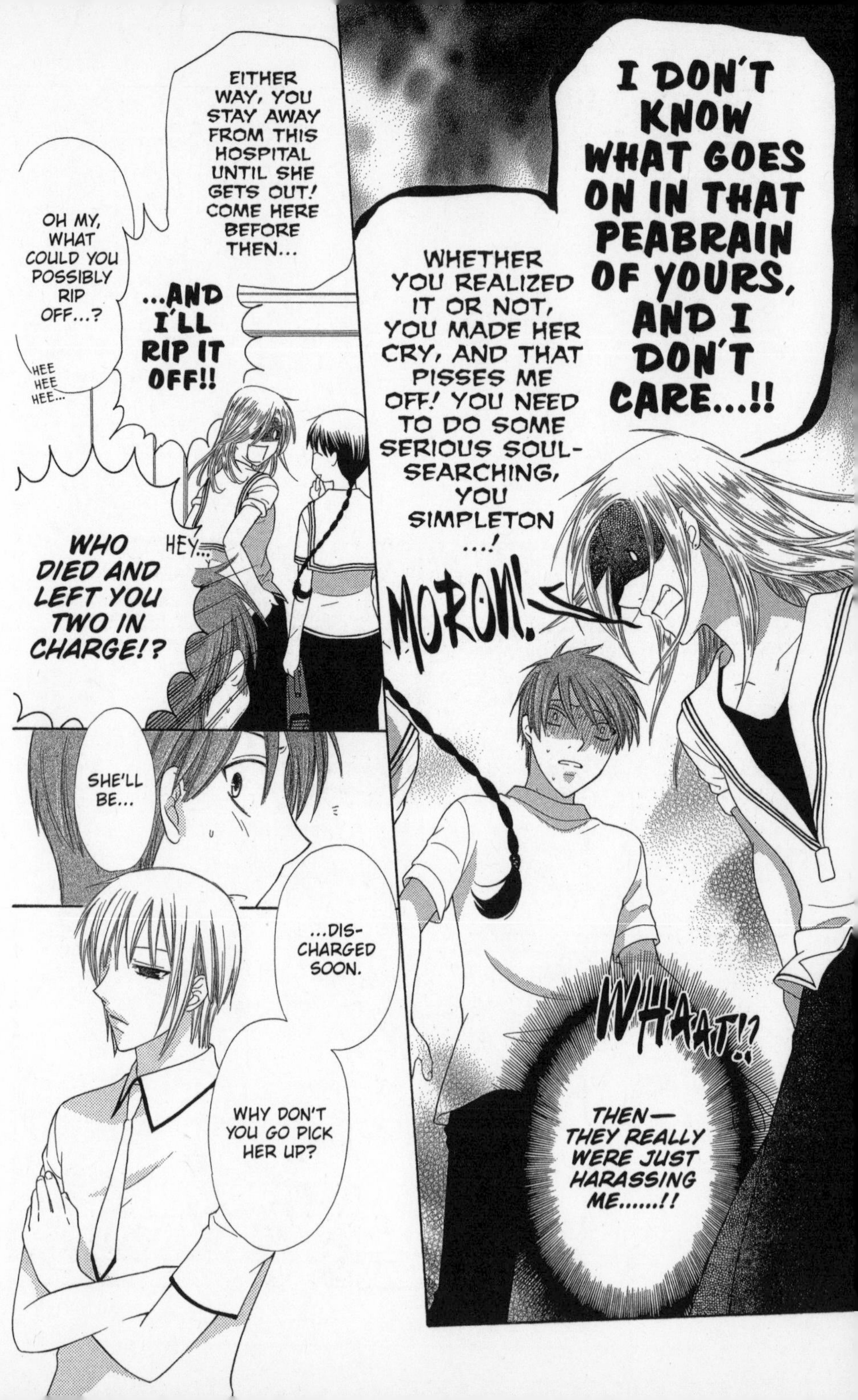

I DON'T KNOW WHAT GOES ON IN THAT PEABRAIN OF YOURS, AND I DON'T CARE...!!
WHETHER YOU REALIZED IT OR NOT, YOU MADE HER CRY, AND THAT PISSES ME OFF! YOU NEED TO DO SOME SERIOUS SOUL-SEARCHING, YOU SIMPLETON ...!
MORON!
WHAAT!?
THEN—THEY REALLY WERE JUST HARASSING ME......!!
EITHER WAY, YOU STAY AWAY FROM THIS HOSPITAL UNTIL SHE GETS OUT! COME HERE BEFORE THEN...
...AND I'LL RIP IT OFF!!
OH MY, WHAT COULD YOU POSSIBLY RIP OFF...?
HEE HEE HEE...
HEY...
WHO DIED AND LEFT YOU TWO IN CHARGE!?
SHE'LL BE...
...DIS-CHARGED SOON.
WHY DON'T YOU GO PICK HER UP?

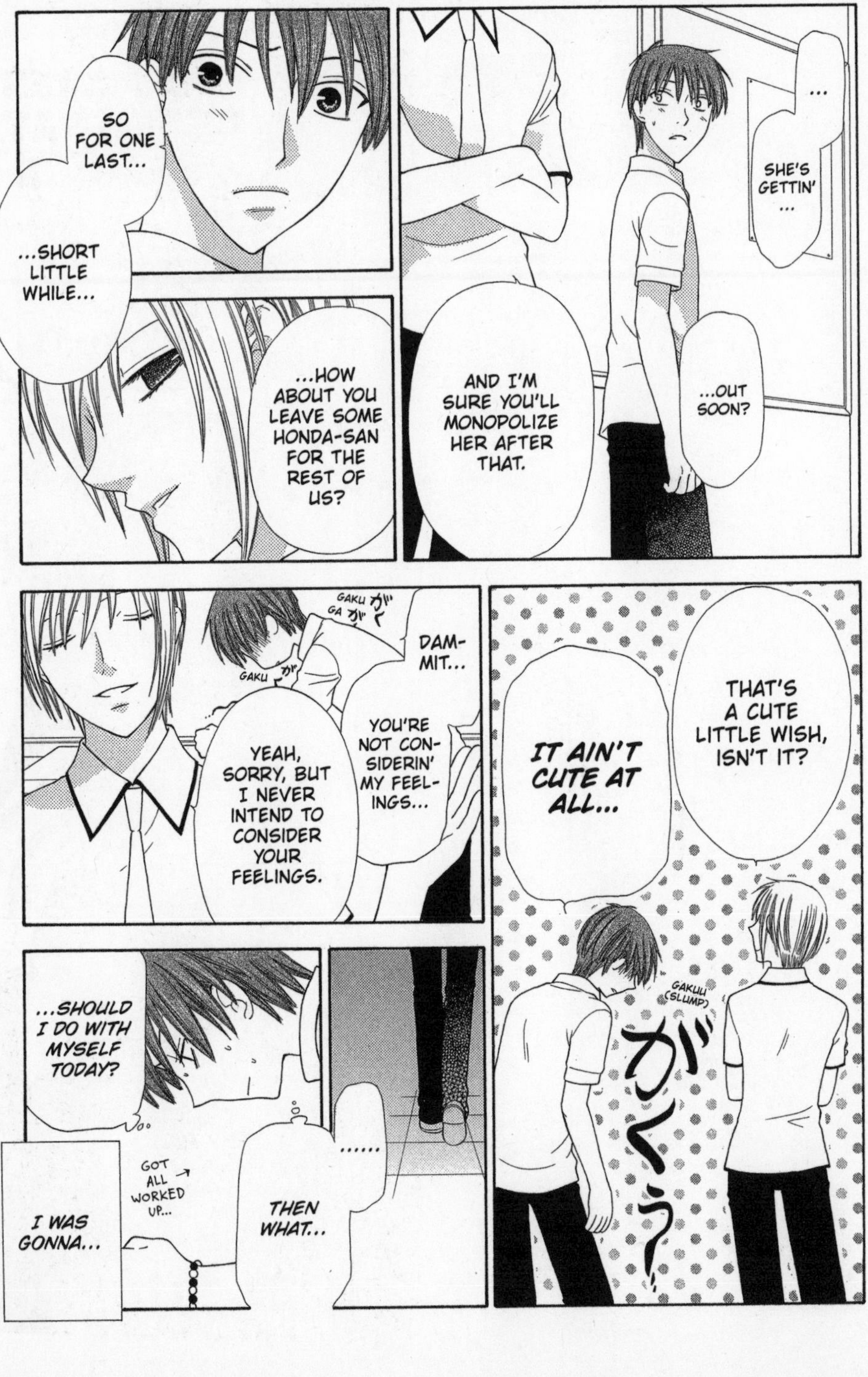
...
SHE'S GETTIN' ...
...OUT SOON?
AND I'M SURE YOU'LL MONOPOLIZE HER AFTER THAT.
SO FOR ONE LAST...
...SHORT LITTLE WHILE...
...HOW ABOUT YOU LEAVE SOME HONDA-SAN FOR THE REST OF US?
THAT'S A CUTE LITTLE WISH, ISN'T IT?
IT AIN'T CUTE AT ALL...
GAKUU (SLUMP)
がくぅ
DAM-MIT...
GAKU GA がくがく
GAKU が
YOU'RE NOT CON-SIDERIN' MY FEEL-INGS...
YEAH, SORRY, BUT I NEVER INTEND TO CONSIDER YOUR FEELINGS.
......
THEN WHAT...
...SHOULD I DO WITH MYSELF TODAY?
GOT ALL WORKED UP...
I WAS GONNA...

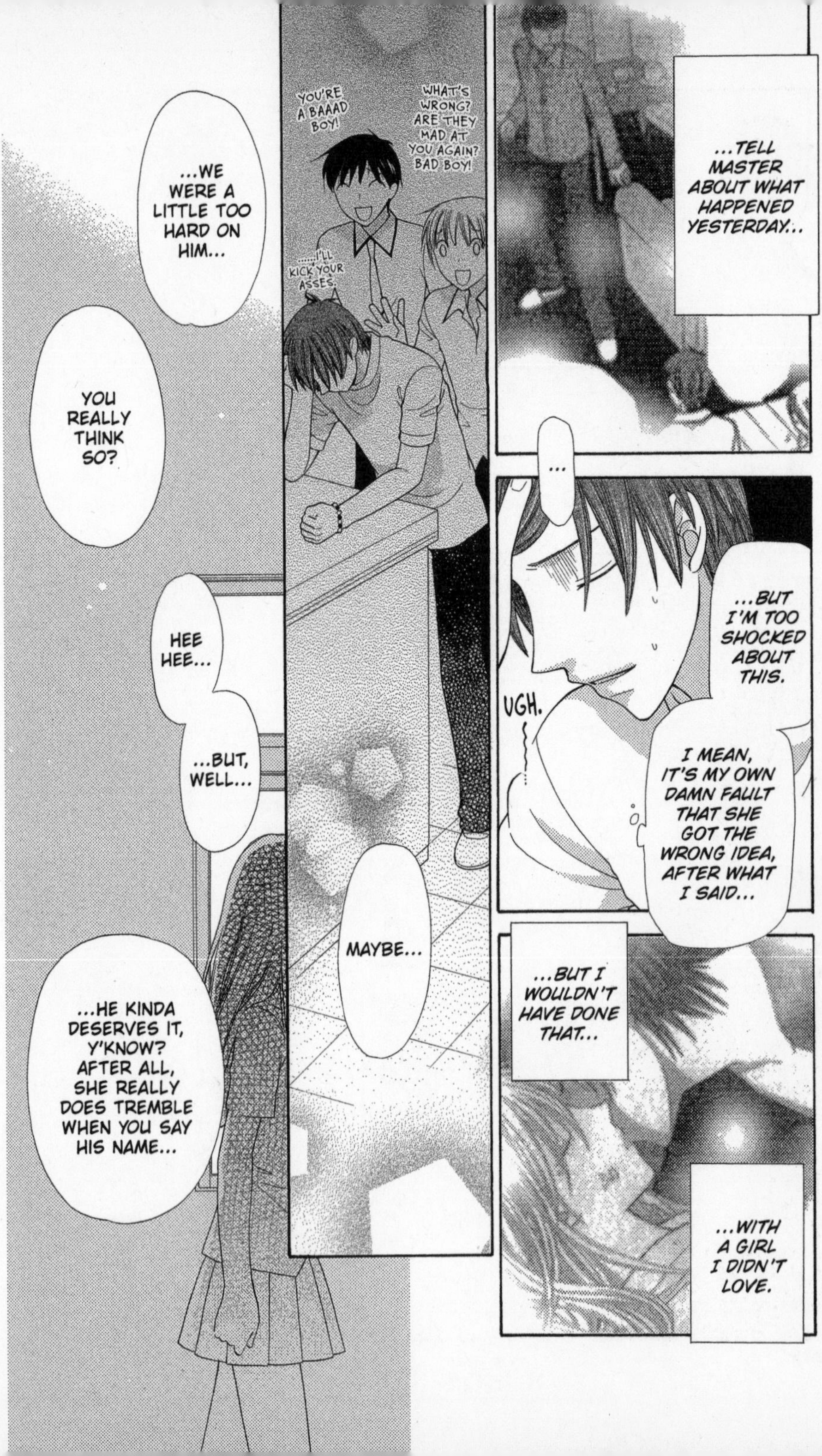
...TELL MASTER ABOUT WHAT HAPPENED YESTERDAY...
...
...BUT I'M TOO SHOCKED ABOUT THIS.
UGH.
I MEAN, IT'S MY OWN DAMN FAULT THAT SHE GOT THE WRONG IDEA, AFTER WHAT I SAID...
...BUT I WOULDN'T HAVE DONE THAT...
...WITH A GIRL I DIDN'T LOVE.
WHAT'S WRONG? ARE THEY MAD AT YOU AGAIN? BAD BOY!
YOU'RE A BAAAD BOY!
......I'LL KICK YOUR ASSES.
MAYBE...
...WE WERE A LITTLE TOO HARD ON HIM...
YOU REALLY THINK SO?
HEE HEE...
...BUT, WELL...
...HE KINDA DESERVES IT, Y'KNOW? AFTER ALL, SHE REALLY DOES TREMBLE WHEN YOU SAY HIS NAME...

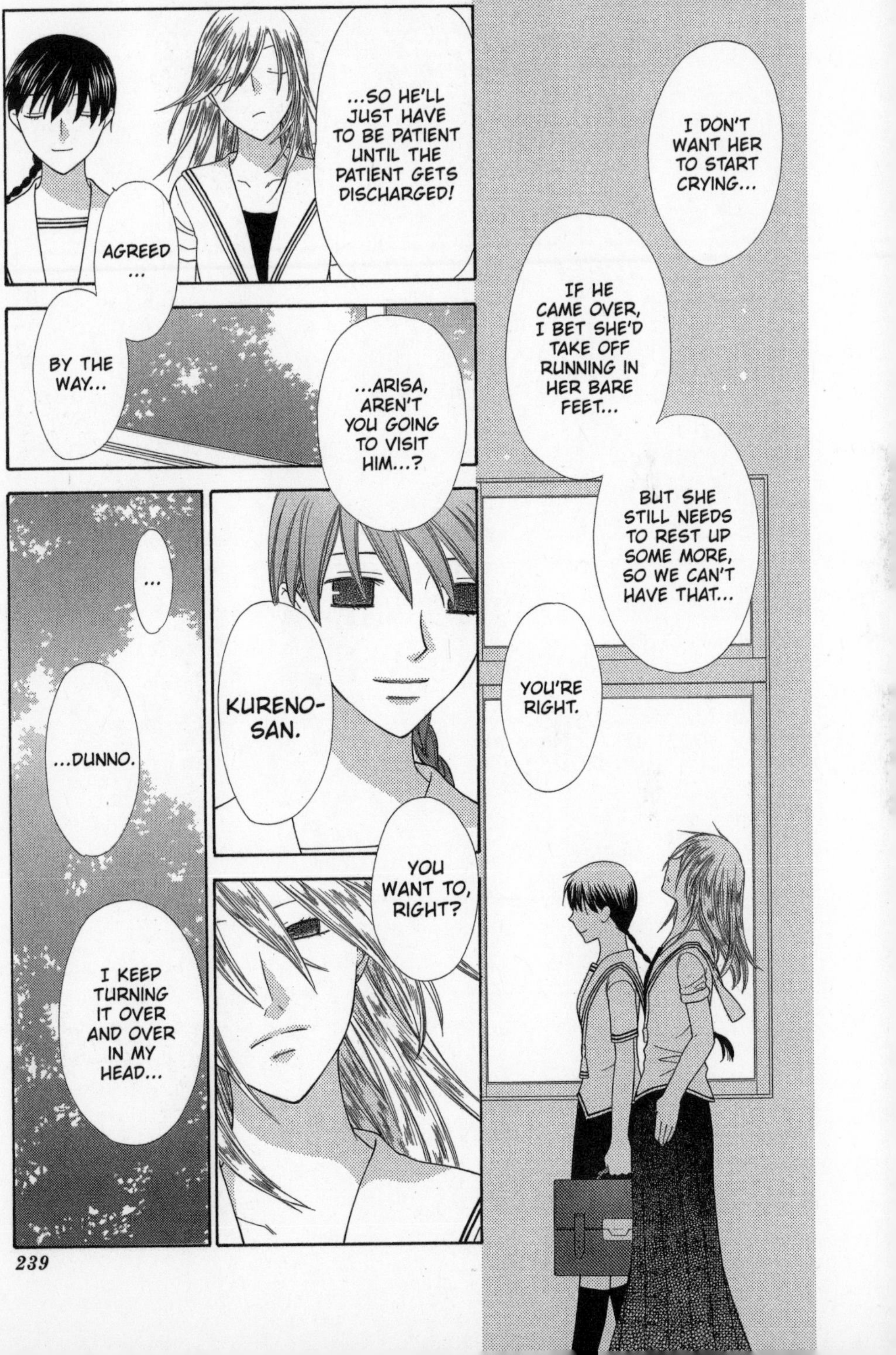

I DON'T WANT HER TO START CRYING...
IF HE CAME OVER, I BET SHE'D TAKE OFF RUNNING IN HER BARE FEET...
BUT SHE STILL NEEDS TO REST UP SOME MORE, SO WE CAN'T HAVE THAT...
YOU'RE RIGHT.
...SO HE'LL JUST HAVE TO BE PATIENT UNTIL THE PATIENT GETS DISCHARGED!
AGREED ...
BY THE WAY...
...ARISA, AREN'T YOU GOING TO VISIT HIM...?
KURENO-SAN.
YOU WANT TO, RIGHT?
...
...DUNNO.
I KEEP TURNING IT OVER AND OVER IN MY HEAD...

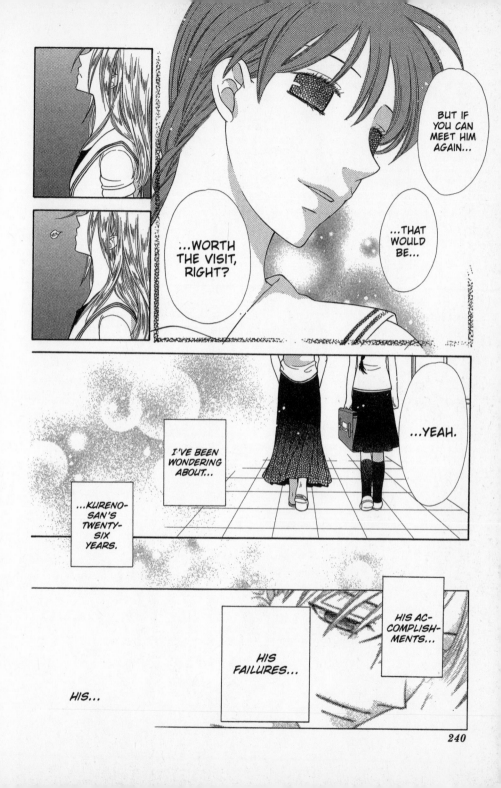

BUT IF YOU CAN MEET HIM AGAIN...

...THAT WOULD BE...

...WORTH THE VISIT, RIGHT?

...YEAH.

I'VE BEEN WONDERING ABOUT...

...KURENO-SAN'S TWENTY-SIX YEARS.

HIS AC-COMPLISH-MENTS...

HIS FAILURES...

HIS...

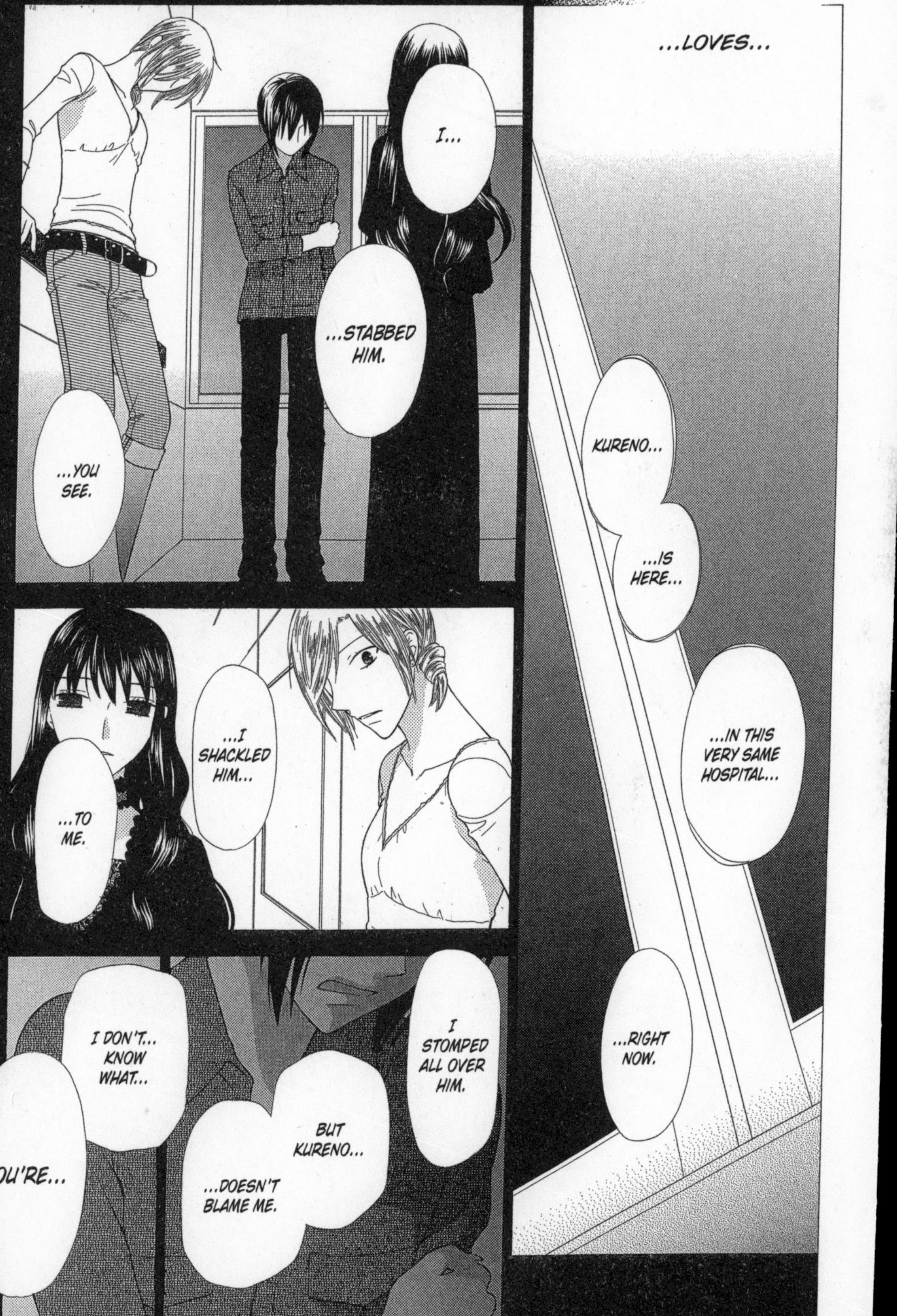
...LOVES...
KURENO...
...IS HERE...
...IN THIS VERY SAME HOSPITAL...
...RIGHT NOW.
I...
...STABBED HIM.
...YOU SEE.
...I SHACKLED HIM...
...TO ME.
I STOMPED ALL OVER HIM.
BUT KURENO...
...DOESN'T BLAME ME.
I DON'T... KNOW WHAT...
YOU'RE...

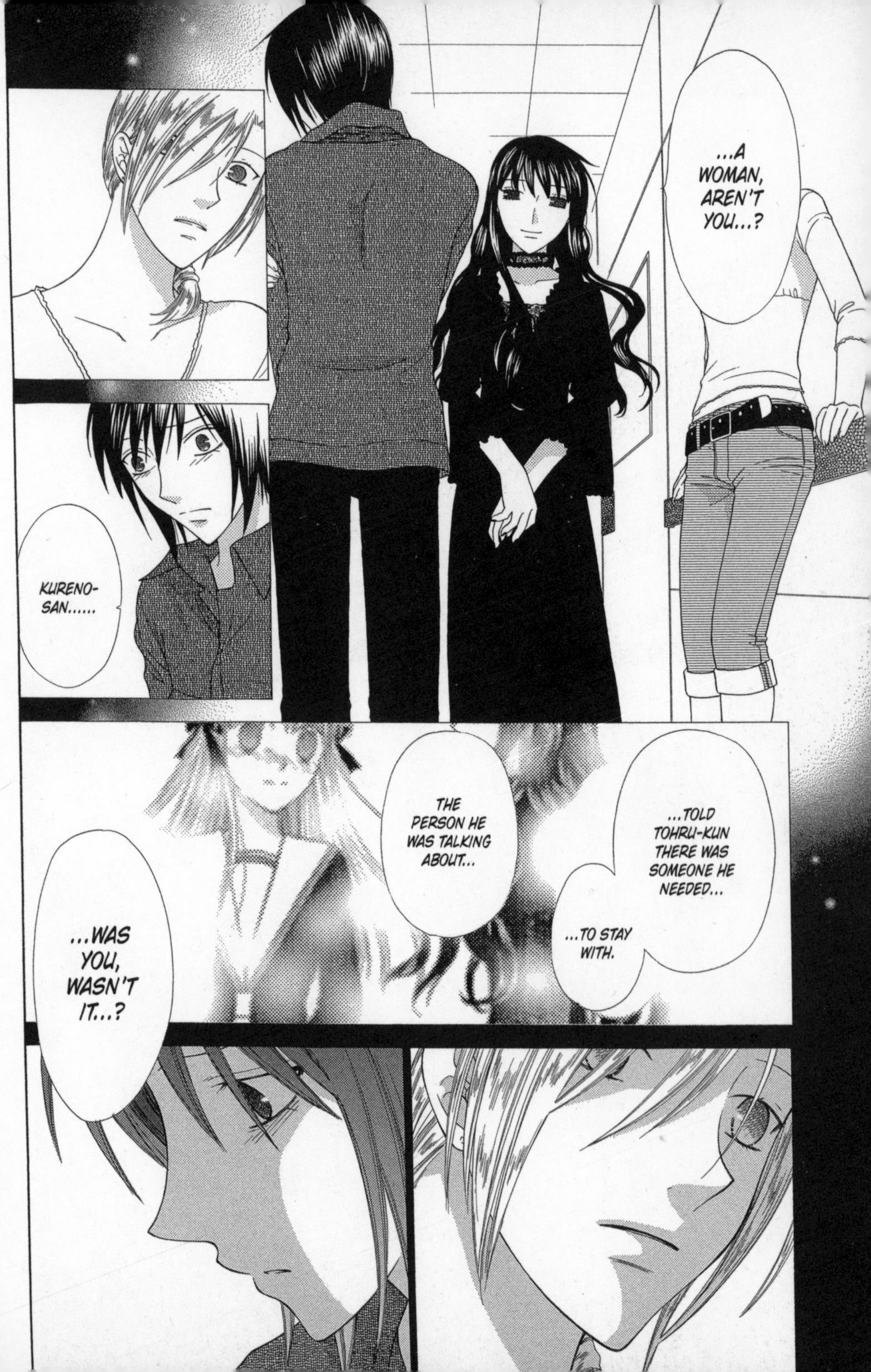
...A WOMAN, AREN'T YOU...?
KURENO-SAN......
...TOLD TOHRU-KUN THERE WAS SOMEONE HE NEEDED...
...TO STAY WITH.
THE PERSON HE WAS TALKING ABOUT...
...WAS YOU, WASN'T IT...?

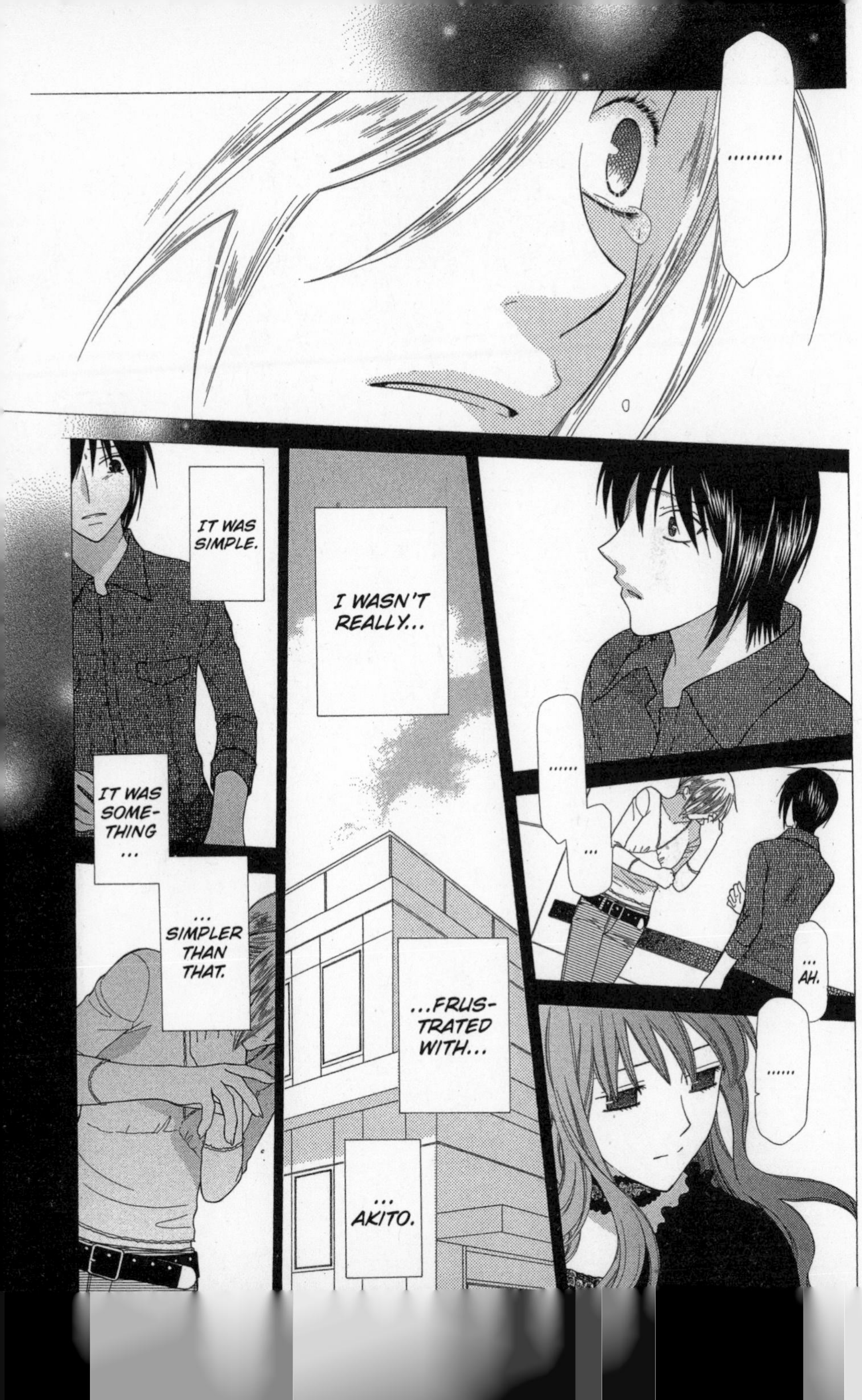

....
......
...
... AH.
......
I WASN'T REALLY...
...FRUS-TRATED WITH...
... AKITO.
IT WAS SIMPLE.
IT WAS SOME-THING ...
... SIMPLER THAN THAT.

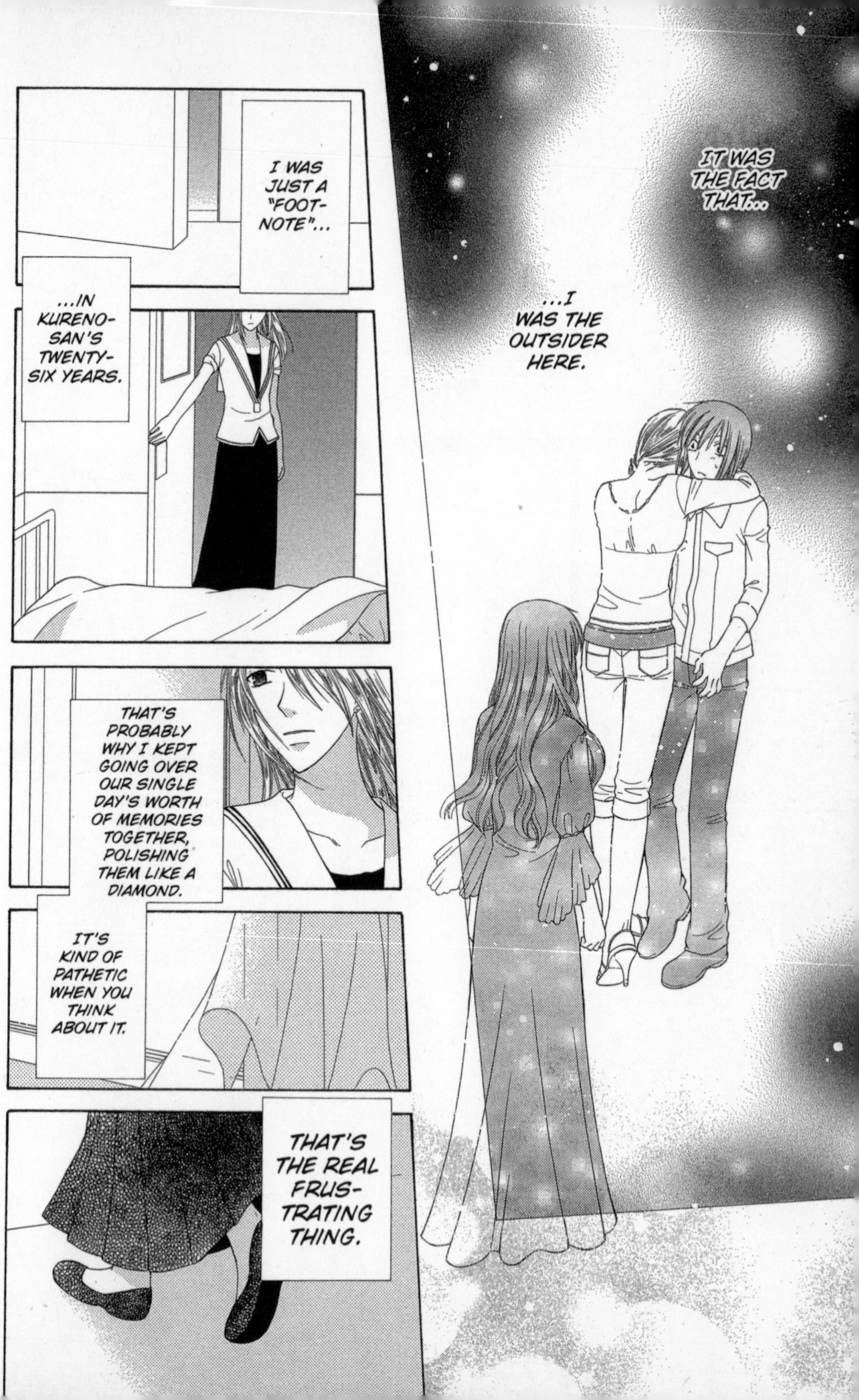
IT WAS THE FACT THAT...
...I WAS THE OUTSIDER HERE.
I WAS JUST A "FOOT-NOTE"...
...IN KURENO-SAN'S TWENTY-SIX YEARS.
THAT'S PROBABLY WHY I KEPT GOING OVER OUR SINGLE DAY'S WORTH OF MEMORIES TOGETHER, POLISHING THEM LIKE A DIAMOND.
IT'S KIND OF PATHETIC WHEN YOU THINK ABOUT IT.
THAT'S THE REAL FRUS-TRATING THING.

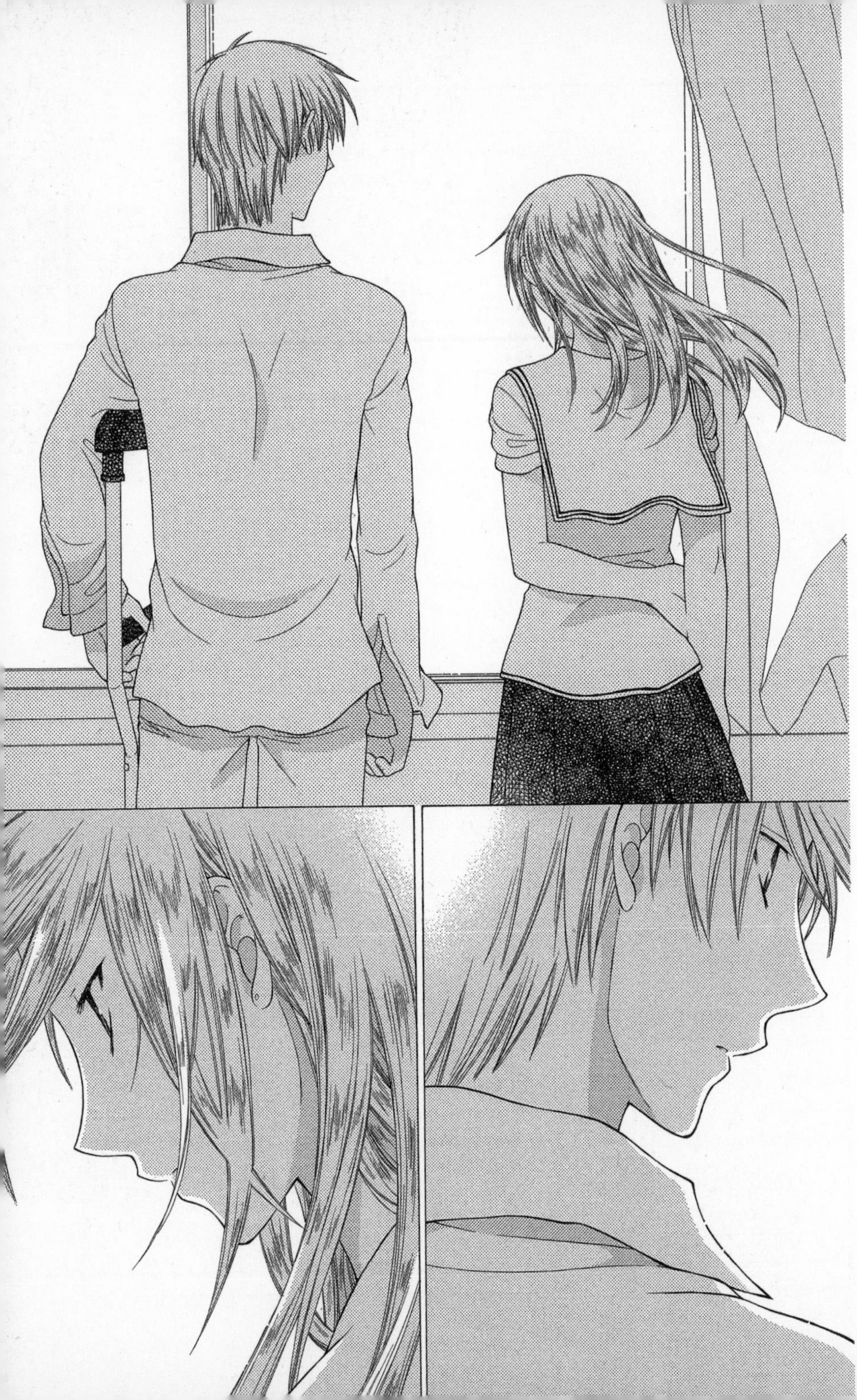

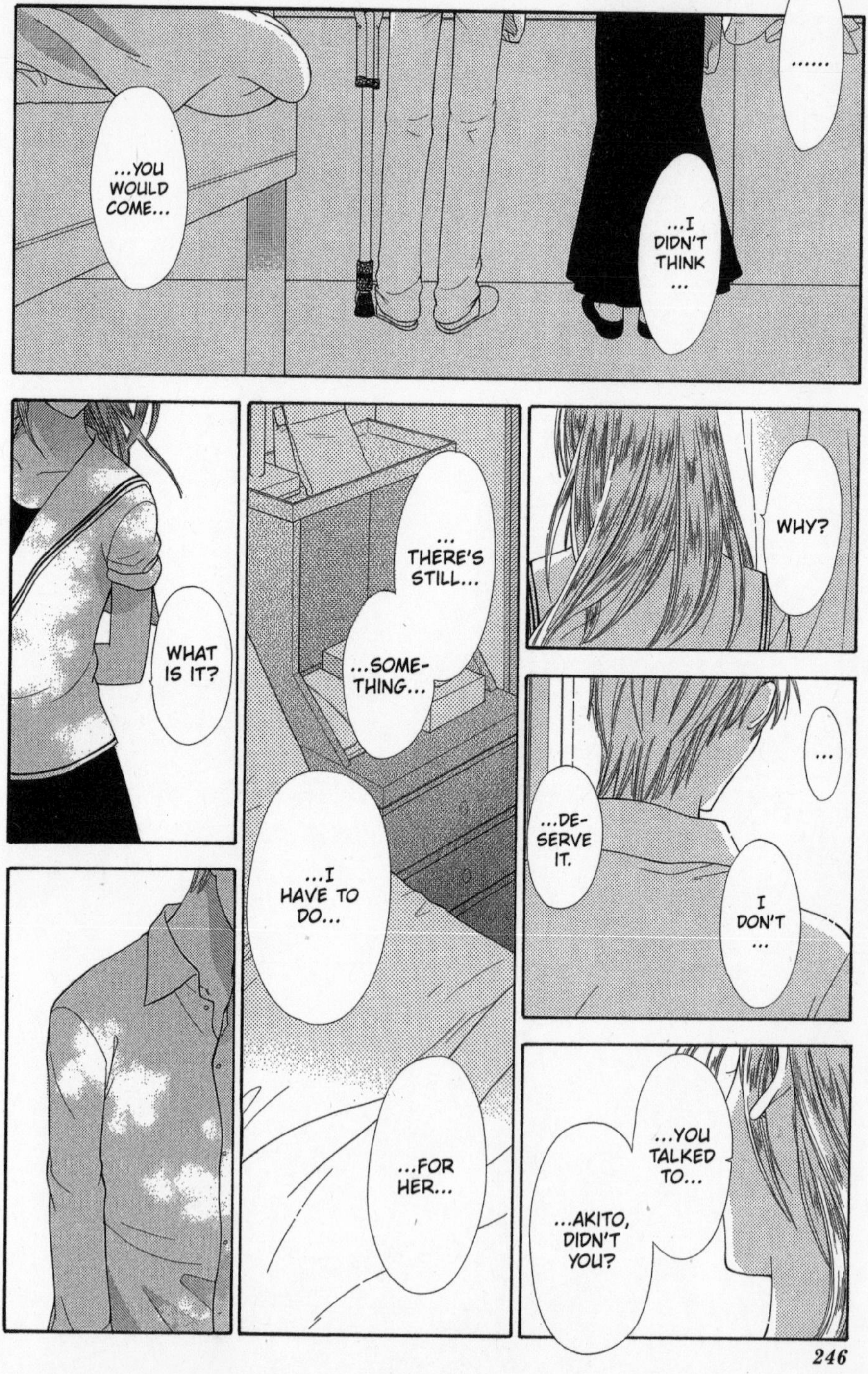
......
...I DIDN'T THINK ...
...YOU WOULD COME...
WHY?
...
I DON'T ...
...DE-SERVE IT.
...YOU TALKED TO...
...AKITO, DIDN'T YOU?
... THERE'S STILL...
...SOME-THING...
...I HAVE TO DO...
...FOR HER...
WHAT IS IT?

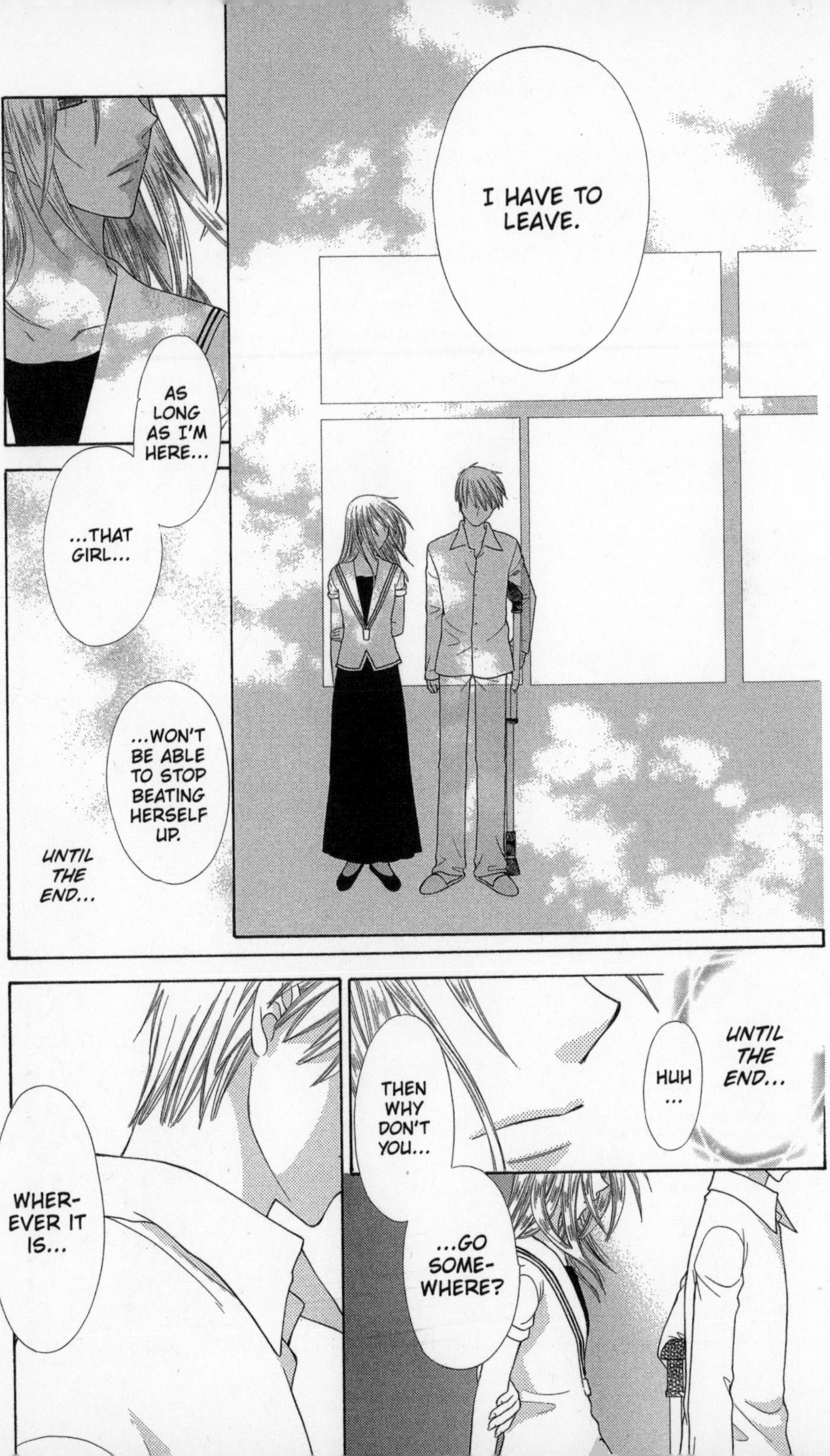
I HAVE TO LEAVE.
AS LONG AS I'M HERE...
...THAT GIRL...
...WON'T BE ABLE TO STOP BEATING HERSELF UP.
UNTIL THE END...
UNTIL THE END...
HUH...
THEN WHY DON'T YOU...
...GO SOMEWHERE?
WHER-EVER IT IS...

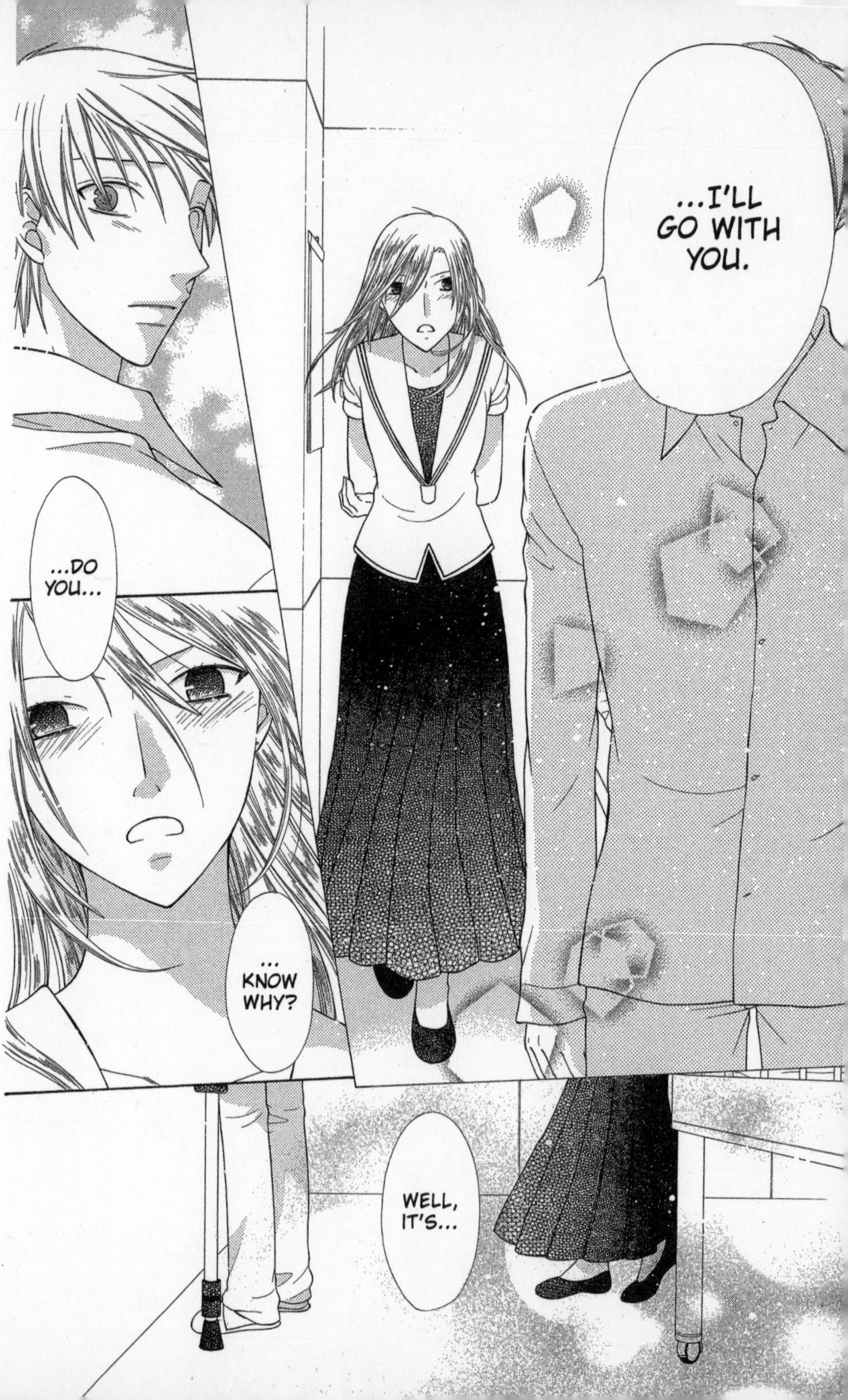
...I'LL GO WITH YOU.
...DO YOU...
... KNOW WHY?
WELL, IT'S...

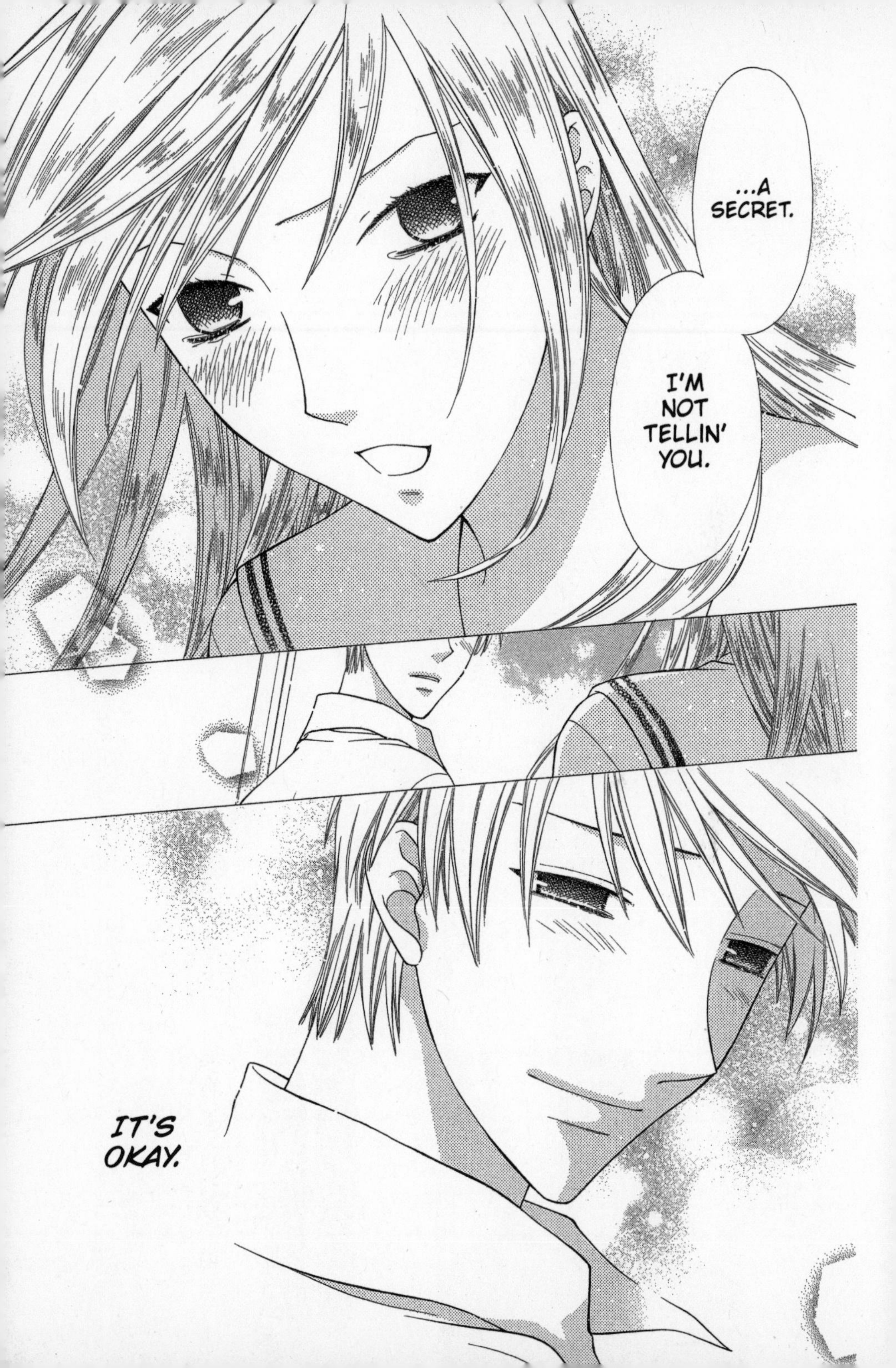
...A SECRET.
I'M NOT TELLIN' YOU.
IT'S OKAY.

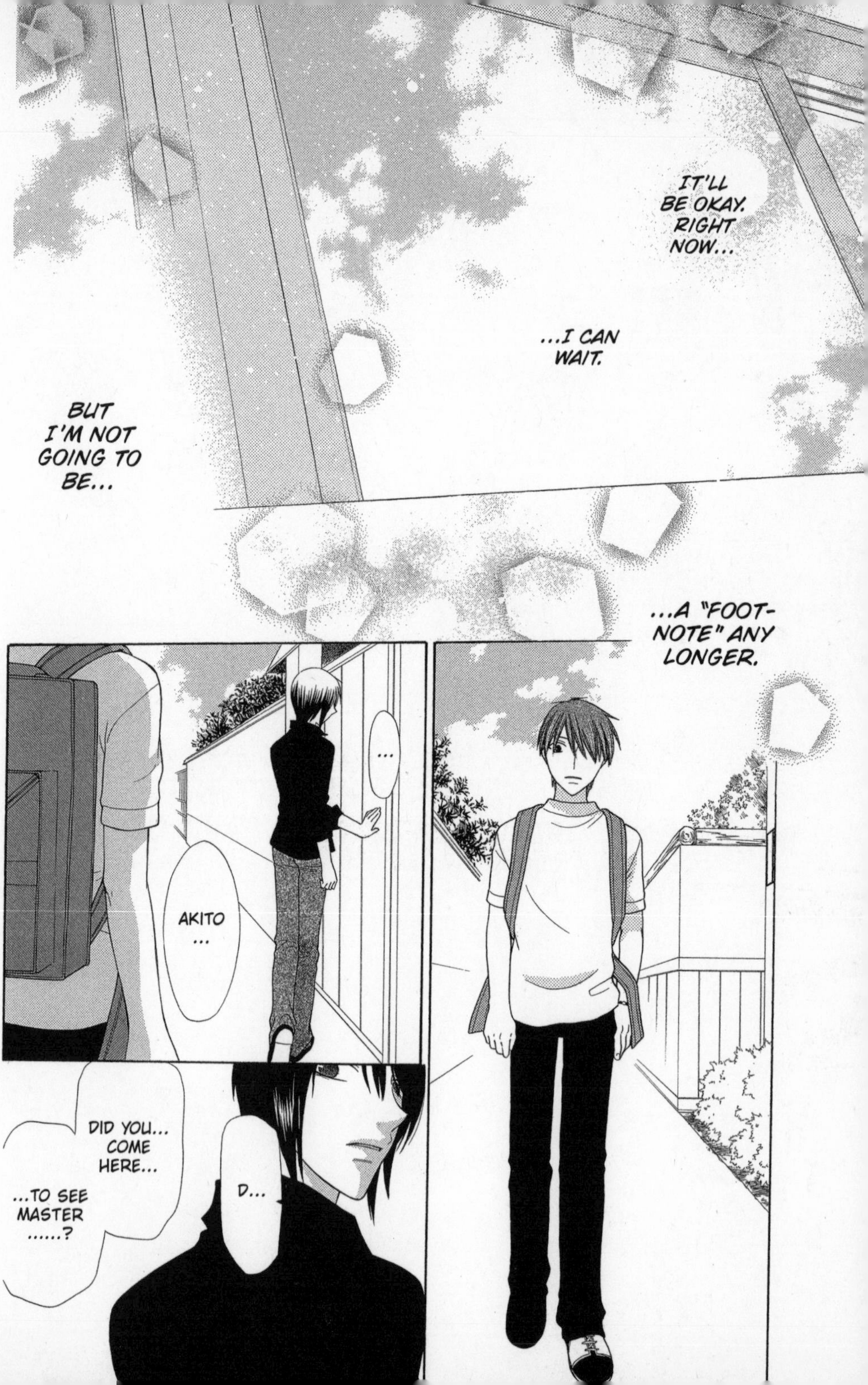
IT'LL BE OKAY. RIGHT NOW...
...I CAN WAIT.
BUT I'M NOT GOING TO BE...
...A "FOOT-NOTE" ANY LONGER.
...
AKITO ...
D...
DID YOU... COME HERE...
...TO SEE MASTER ......?

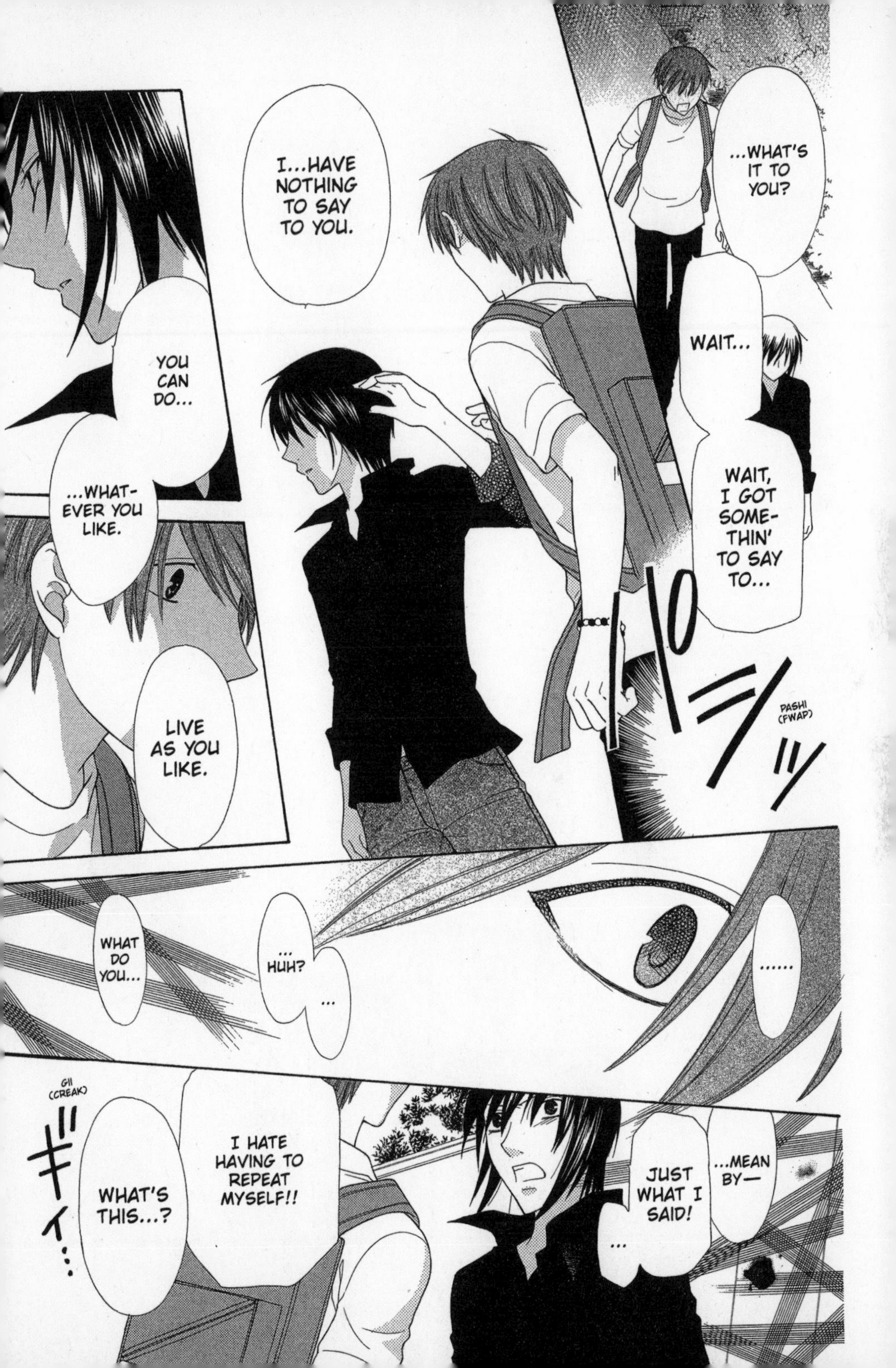
...WHAT'S IT TO YOU?
WAIT...
WAIT, I GOT SOMETHIN' TO SAY TO...
PASHI (FWAP)
I...HAVE NOTHING TO SAY TO YOU.
YOU CAN DO...
...WHATEVER YOU LIKE.
LIVE AS YOU LIKE.
......
... HUH? ...
WHAT DO YOU...
...MEAN BY—
JUST WHAT I SAID! ...
I HATE HAVING TO REPEAT MYSELF!!
WHAT'S THIS...?
GII (CREAK)
ギイ…

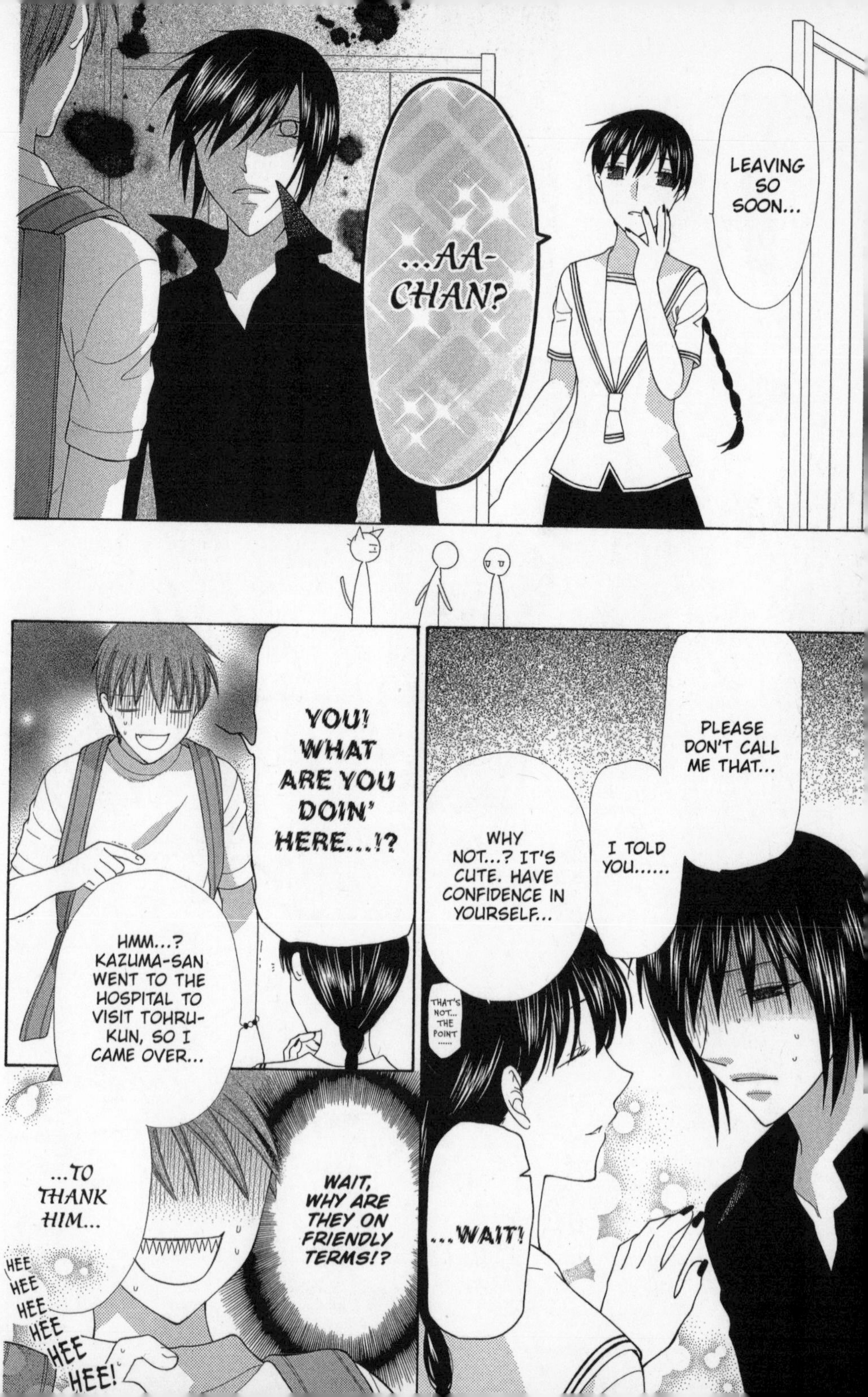
LEAVING SO SOON...
...AA-CHAN?
PLEASE DON'T CALL ME THAT...
I TOLD YOU......
WHY NOT...? IT'S CUTE. HAVE CONFIDENCE IN YOURSELF...
THAT'S NOT... THE POINT ......
YOU! WHAT ARE YOU DOIN' HERE...!?
HMM...? KAZUMA-SAN WENT TO THE HOSPITAL TO VISIT TOHRU-KUN, SO I CAME OVER...
...WAIT!
WAIT, WHY ARE THEY ON FRIENDLY TERMS!?
...TO THANK HIM...
HEE HEE HEE HEE HEE HEE!

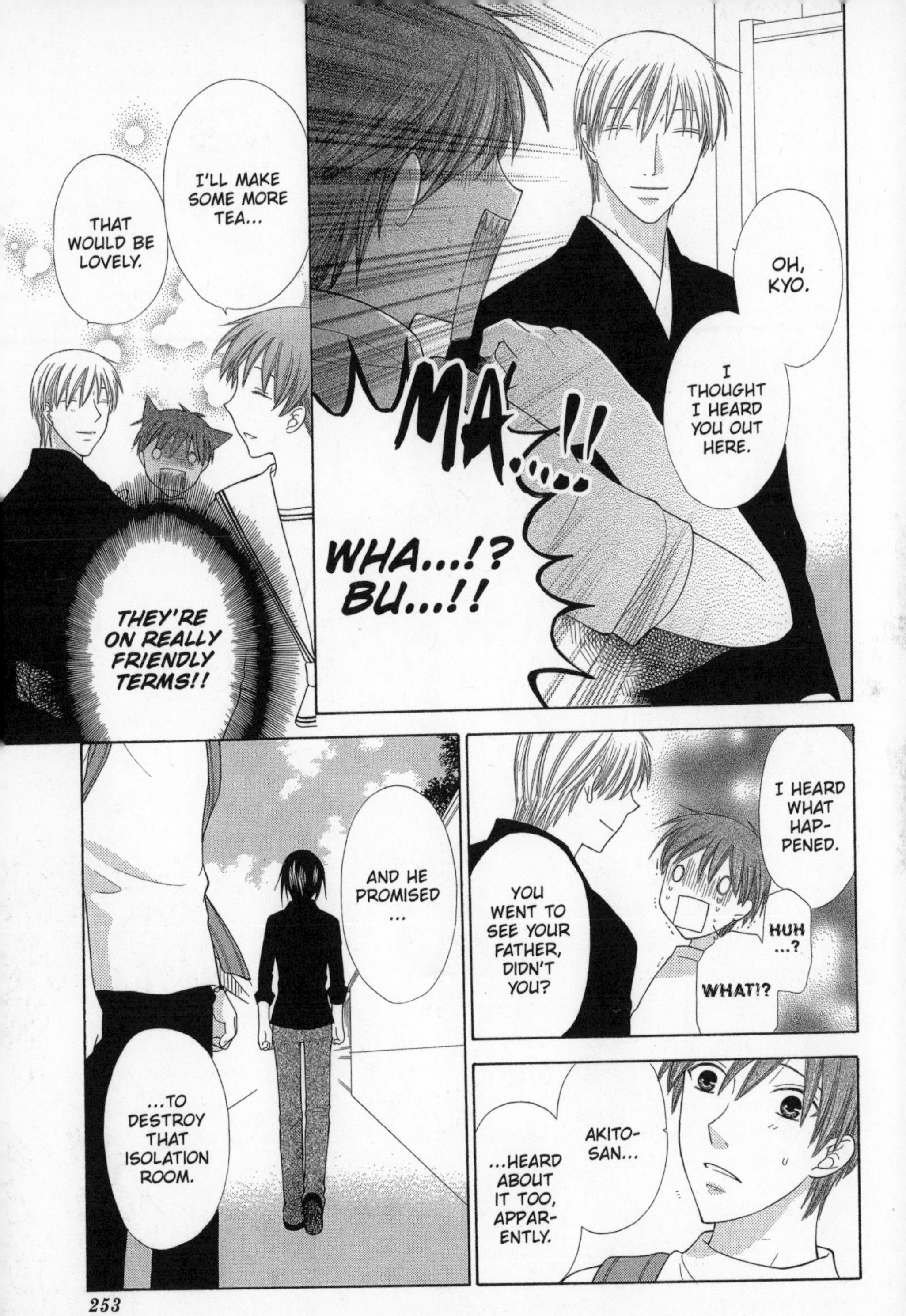
OH, KYO.
I THOUGHT I HEARD YOU OUT HERE.
MA...!!
WHA...!? BU...!!
I'LL MAKE SOME MORE TEA...
THAT WOULD BE LOVELY.
THEY'RE ON REALLY FRIENDLY TERMS!!
I HEARD WHAT HAPPENED.
HUH...?
WHAT!?
YOU WENT TO SEE YOUR FATHER, DIDN'T YOU?
AKITO-SAN...
...HEARD ABOUT IT TOO, APPARENTLY.
AND HE PROMISED...
...TO DESTROY THAT ISOLATION ROOM.

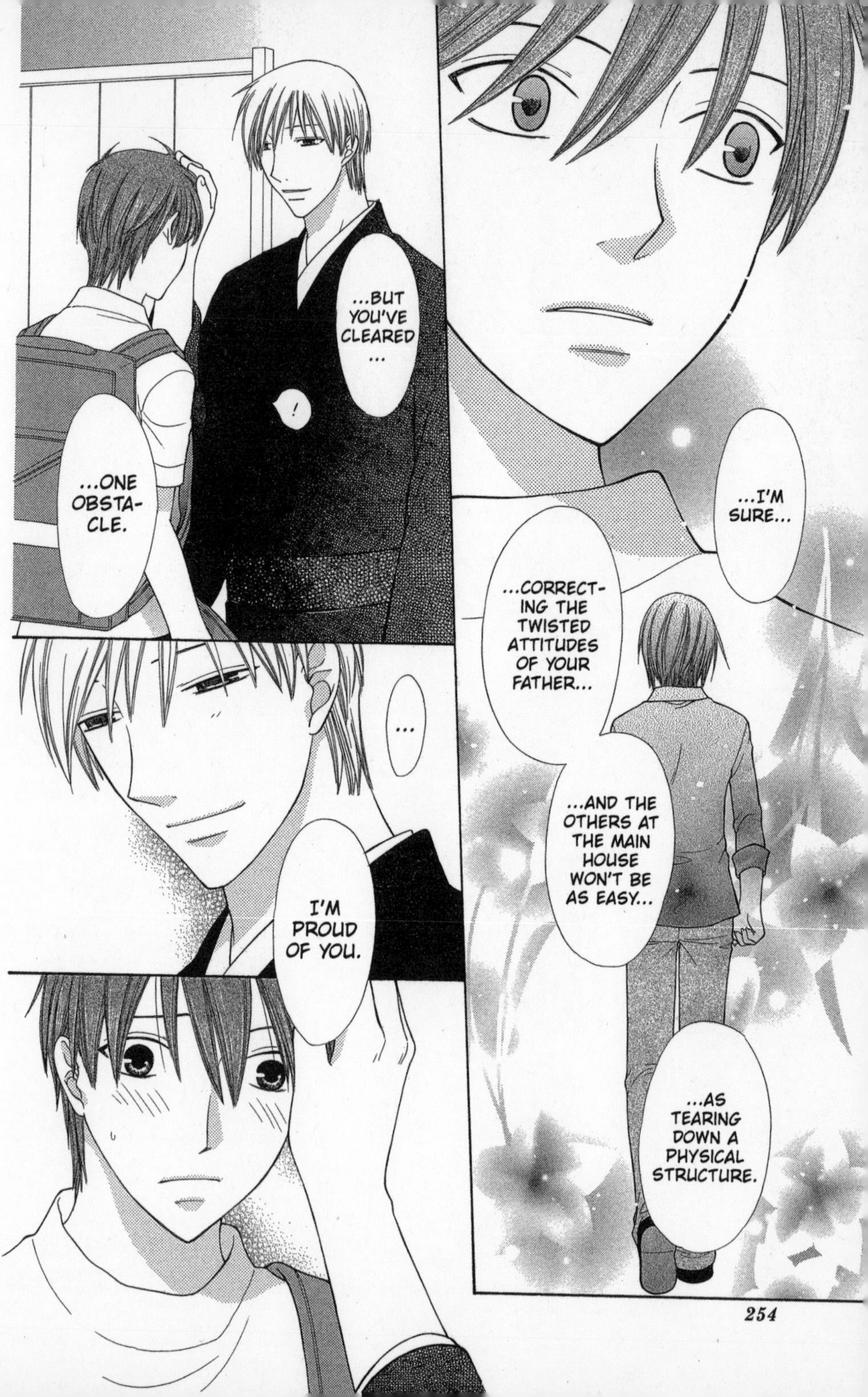
...I'M SURE...
...CORRECTING THE TWISTED ATTITUDES OF YOUR FATHER...
...AND THE OTHERS AT THE MAIN HOUSE WON'T BE AS EASY...
...AS TEARING DOWN A PHYSICAL STRUCTURE.
...BUT YOU'VE CLEARED...
!
...ONE OBSTACLE.
...
I'M PROUD OF YOU.

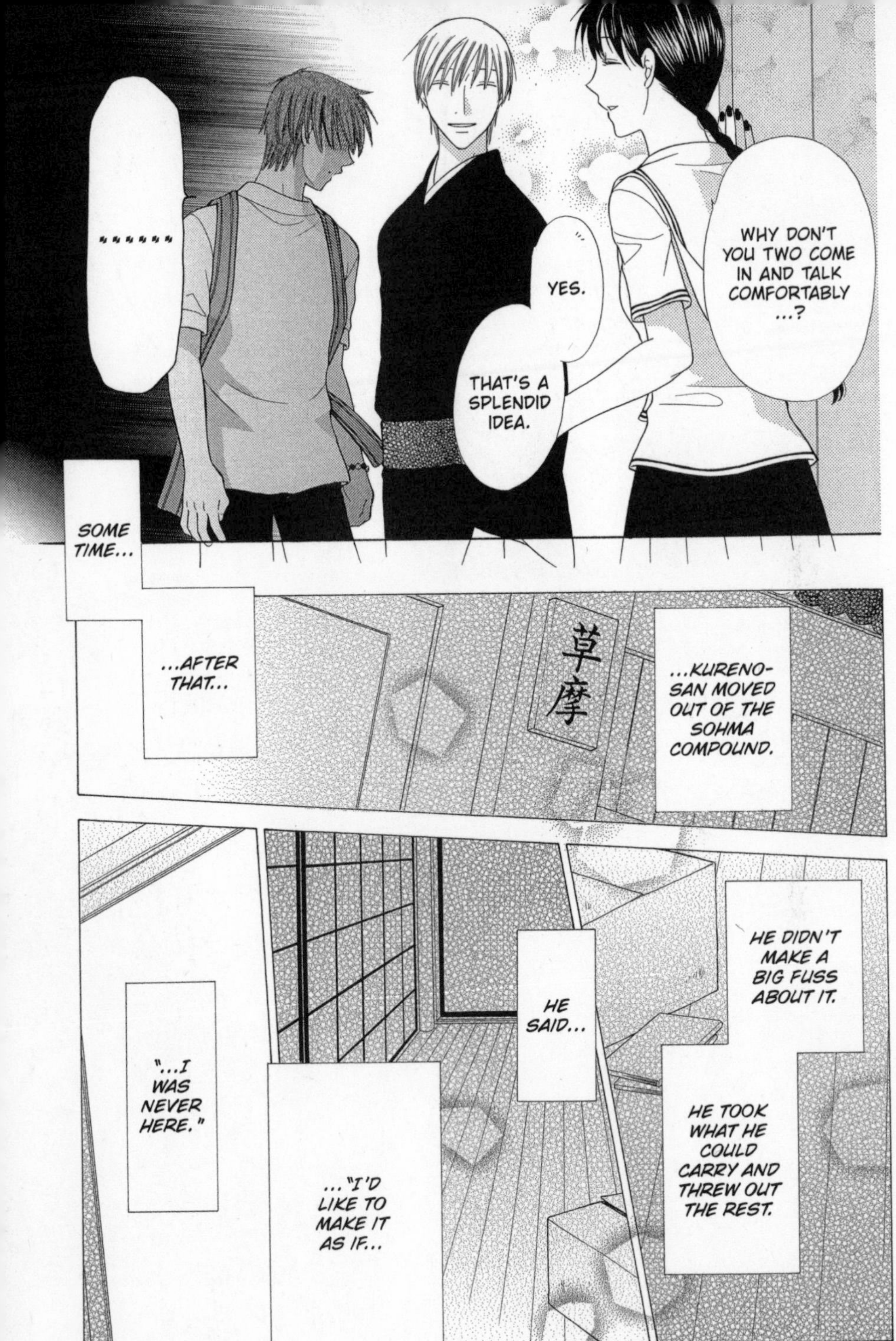
WHY DON'T YOU TWO COME IN AND TALK COMFORTABLY ...?
YES.
THAT'S A SPLENDID IDEA.
......
SOME TIME...
...AFTER THAT...
草摩
...KURENO-SAN MOVED OUT OF THE SOHMA COMPOUND.
HE DIDN'T MAKE A BIG FUSS ABOUT IT.
HE TOOK WHAT HE COULD CARRY AND THREW OUT THE REST.
HE SAID...
..."I'D LIKE TO MAKE IT AS IF...
"...I WAS NEVER HERE."

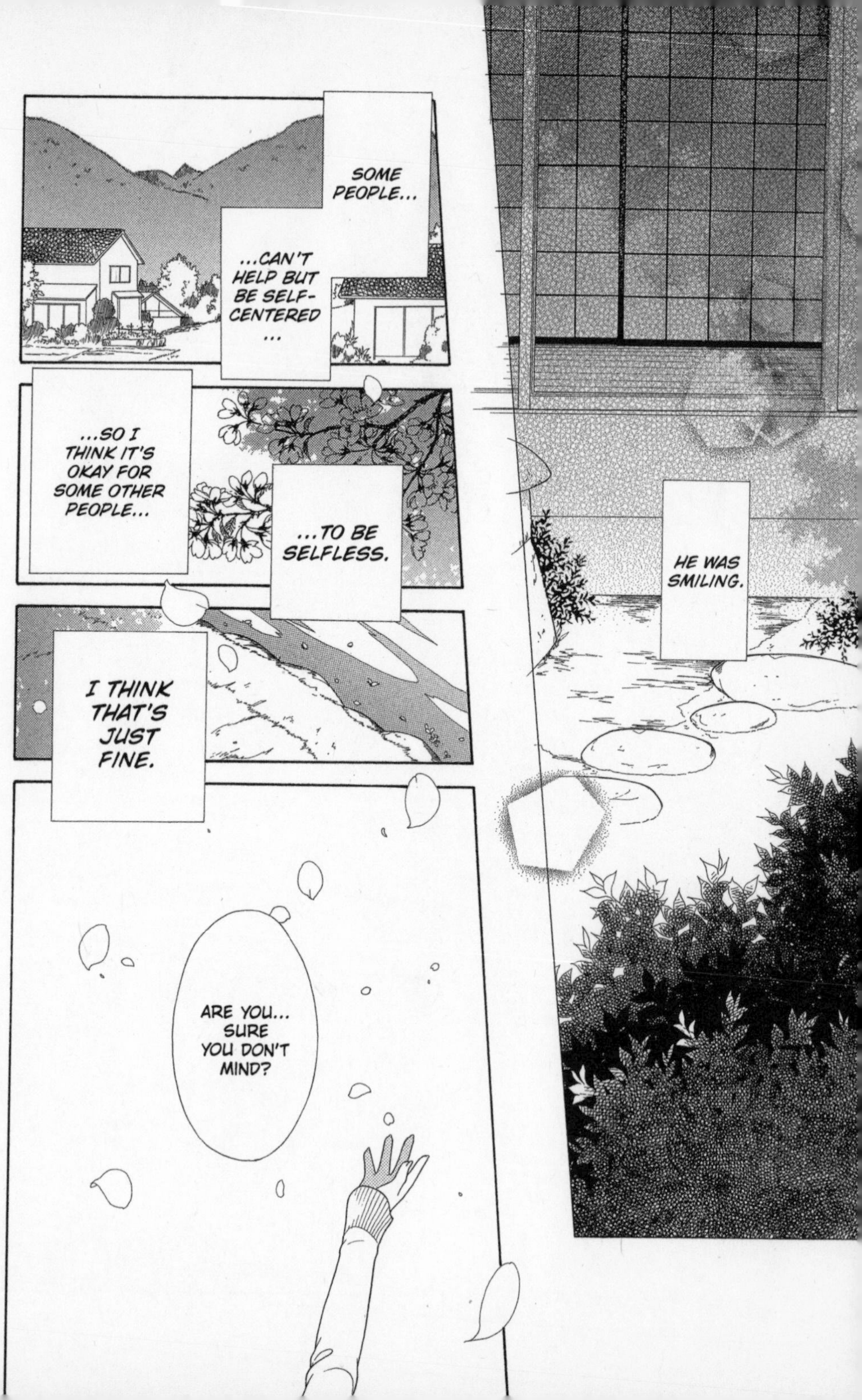
HE WAS SMILING.
SOME PEOPLE...
...CAN'T HELP BUT BE SELF-CENTERED...
...SO I THINK IT'S OKAY FOR SOME OTHER PEOPLE...
...TO BE SELFLESS.
I THINK THAT'S JUST FINE.
ARE YOU... SURE YOU DON'T MIND?

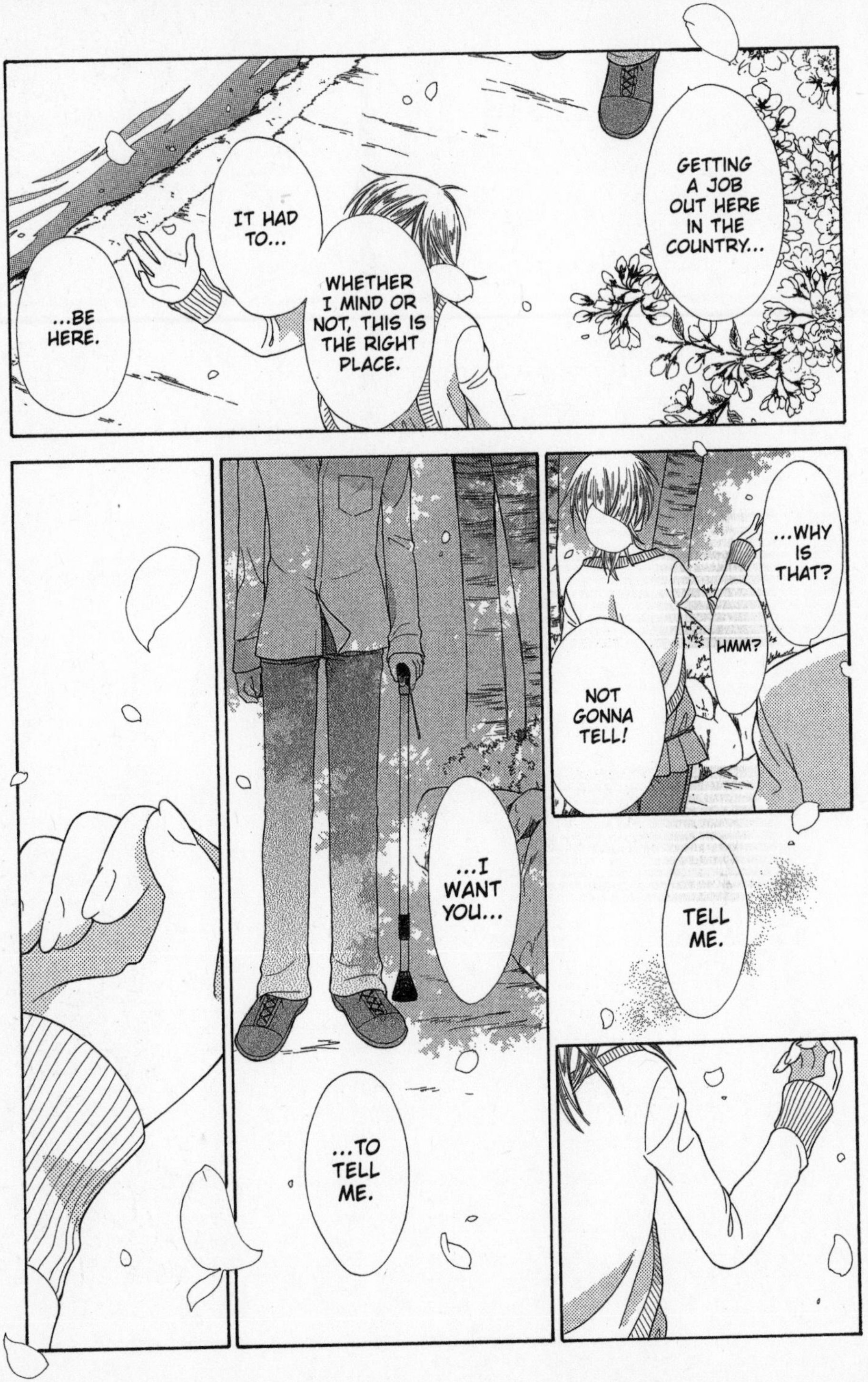
GETTING A JOB OUT HERE IN THE COUNTRY...
WHETHER I MIND OR NOT, THIS IS THE RIGHT PLACE.
IT HAD TO...
...BE HERE.
...WHY IS THAT?
HMM?
NOT GONNA TELL!
TELL ME.
...I WANT YOU...
...TO TELL ME.

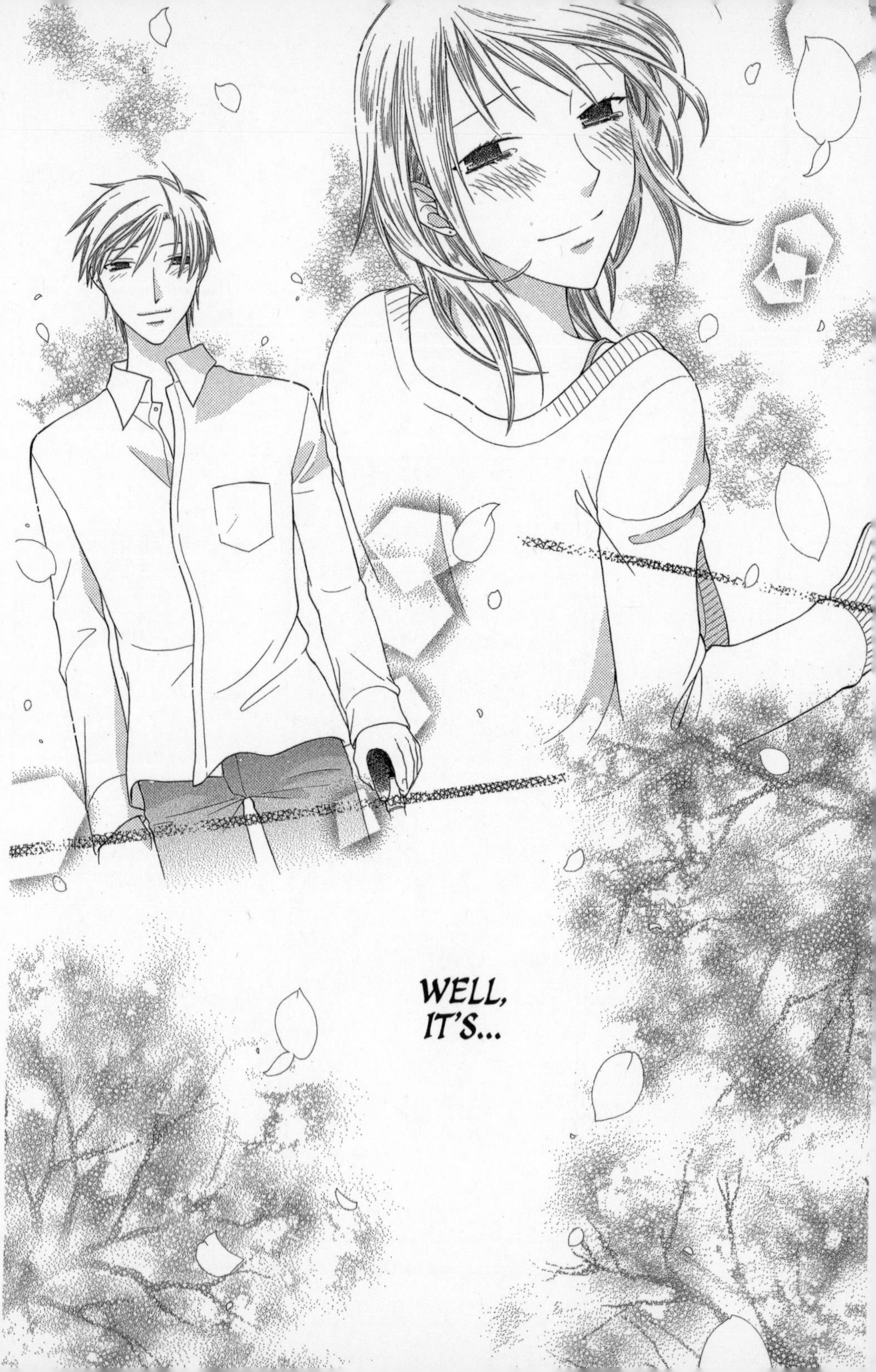
WELL, IT'S...

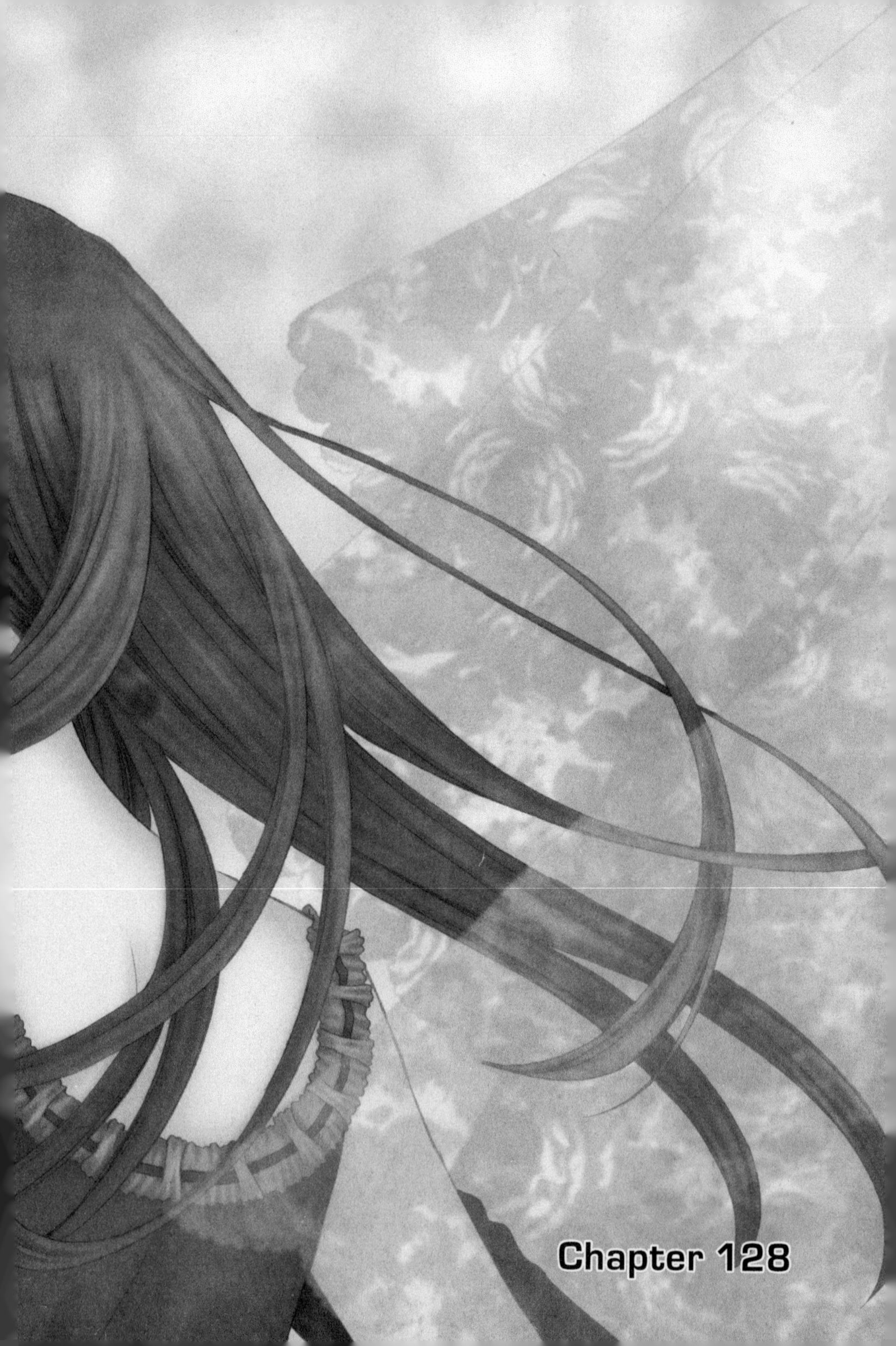
Chapter 128

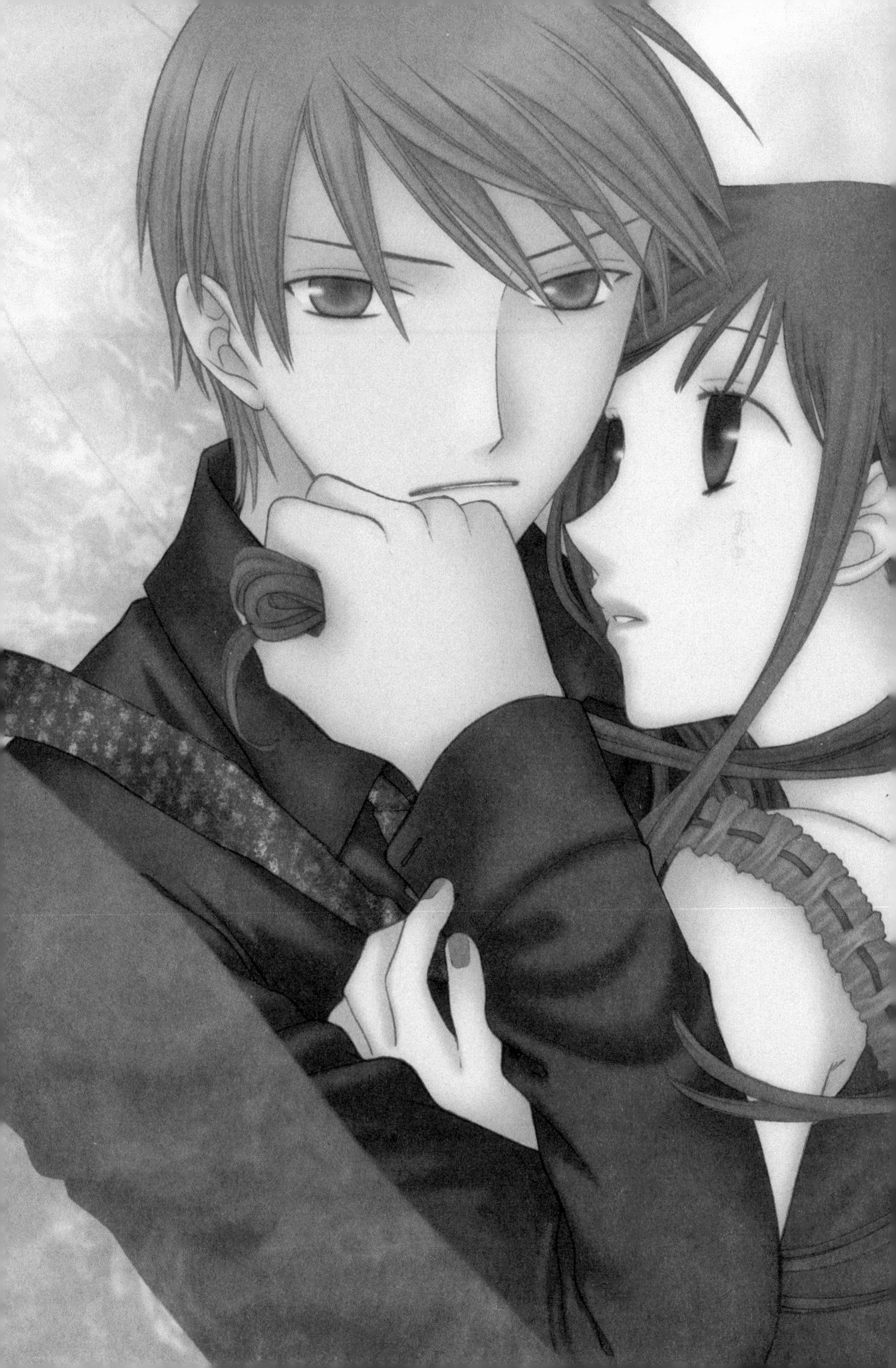

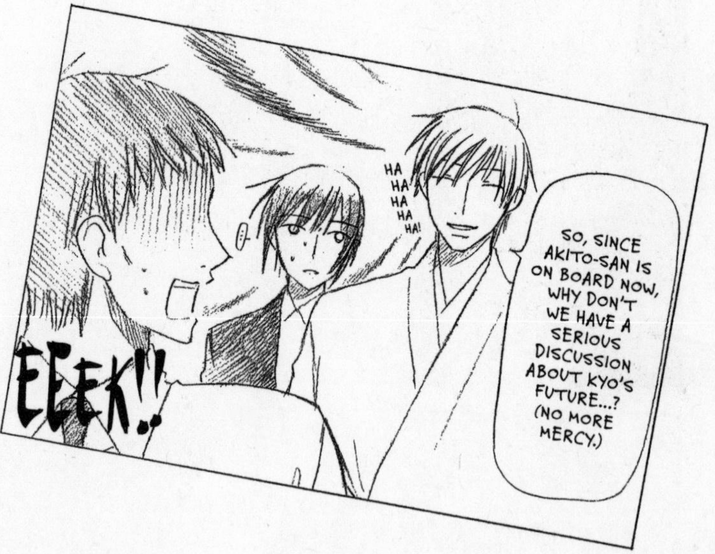
SO, SINCE AKITO-SAN IS ON BOARD NOW, WHY DON'T WE HAVE A SERIOUS DISCUSSION ABOUT KYO'S FUTURE...? (NO MORE MERCY.)
HA HA HA HA HA!
EEEK!!

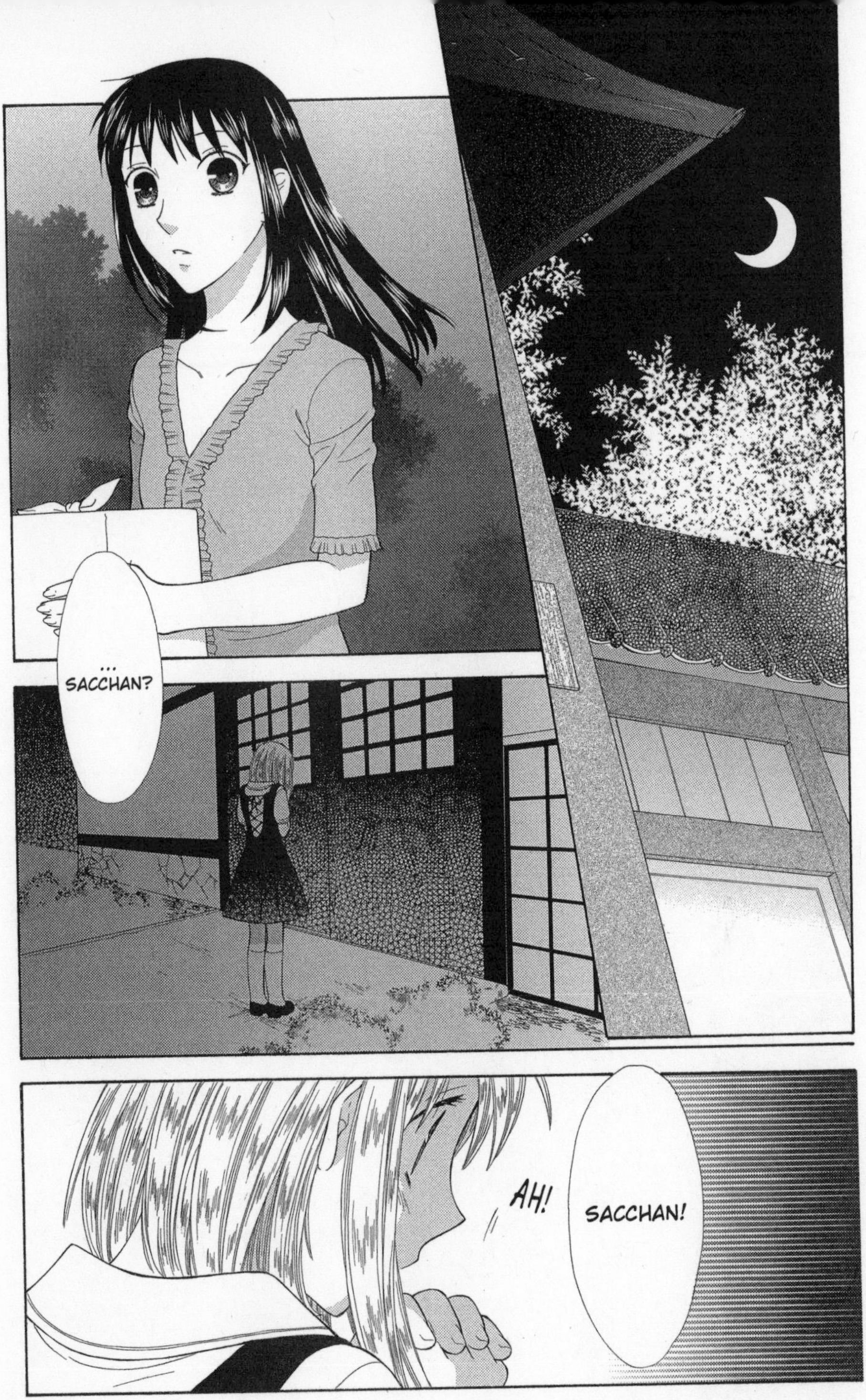
... SACCHAN?
SACCHAN!
AH!

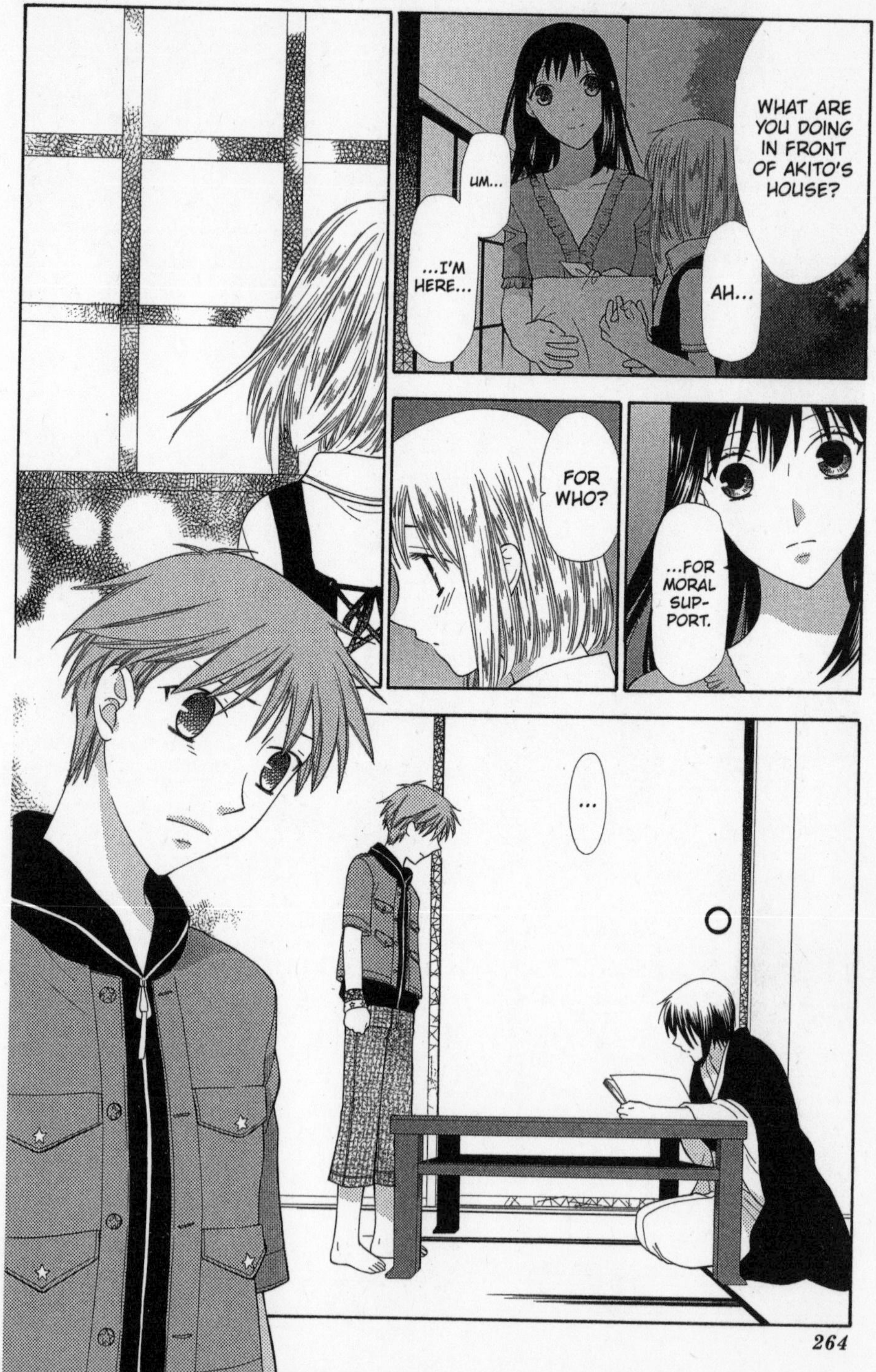
WHAT ARE YOU DOING IN FRONT OF AKITO'S HOUSE?
AH...
UM...
...I'M HERE...
...FOR MORAL SUP-PORT.
FOR WHO?
...

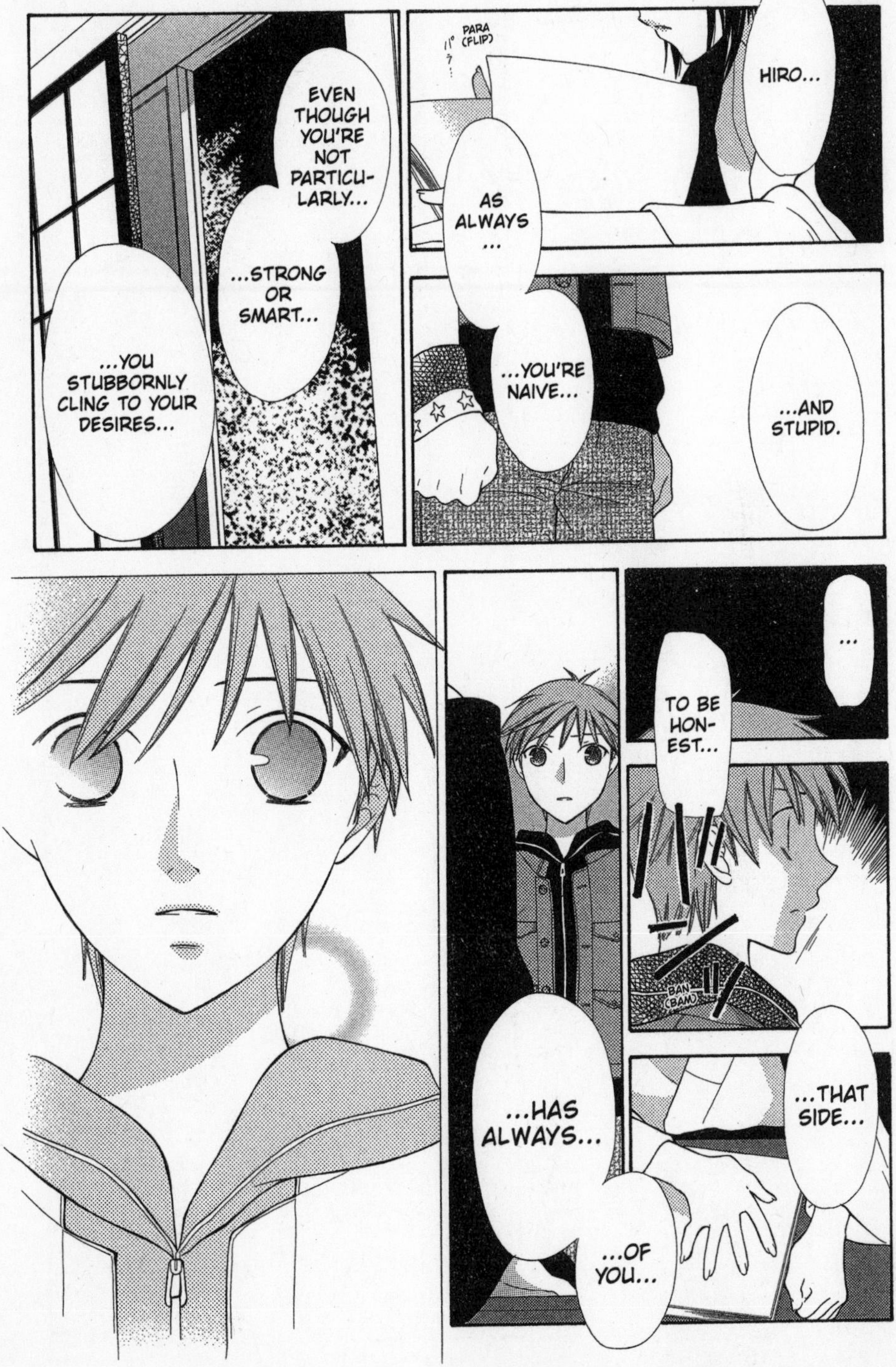
HIRO...
PARA (FLIP)
AS ALWAYS ...
...YOU'RE NAIVE...
...AND STUPID.
EVEN THOUGH YOU'RE NOT PARTICU-LARLY...
...STRONG OR SMART...
...YOU STUBBORNLY CLING TO YOUR DESIRES...
...
TO BE HON-EST...
BAN (BAM)
...THAT SIDE...
...HAS ALWAYS...
...OF YOU...

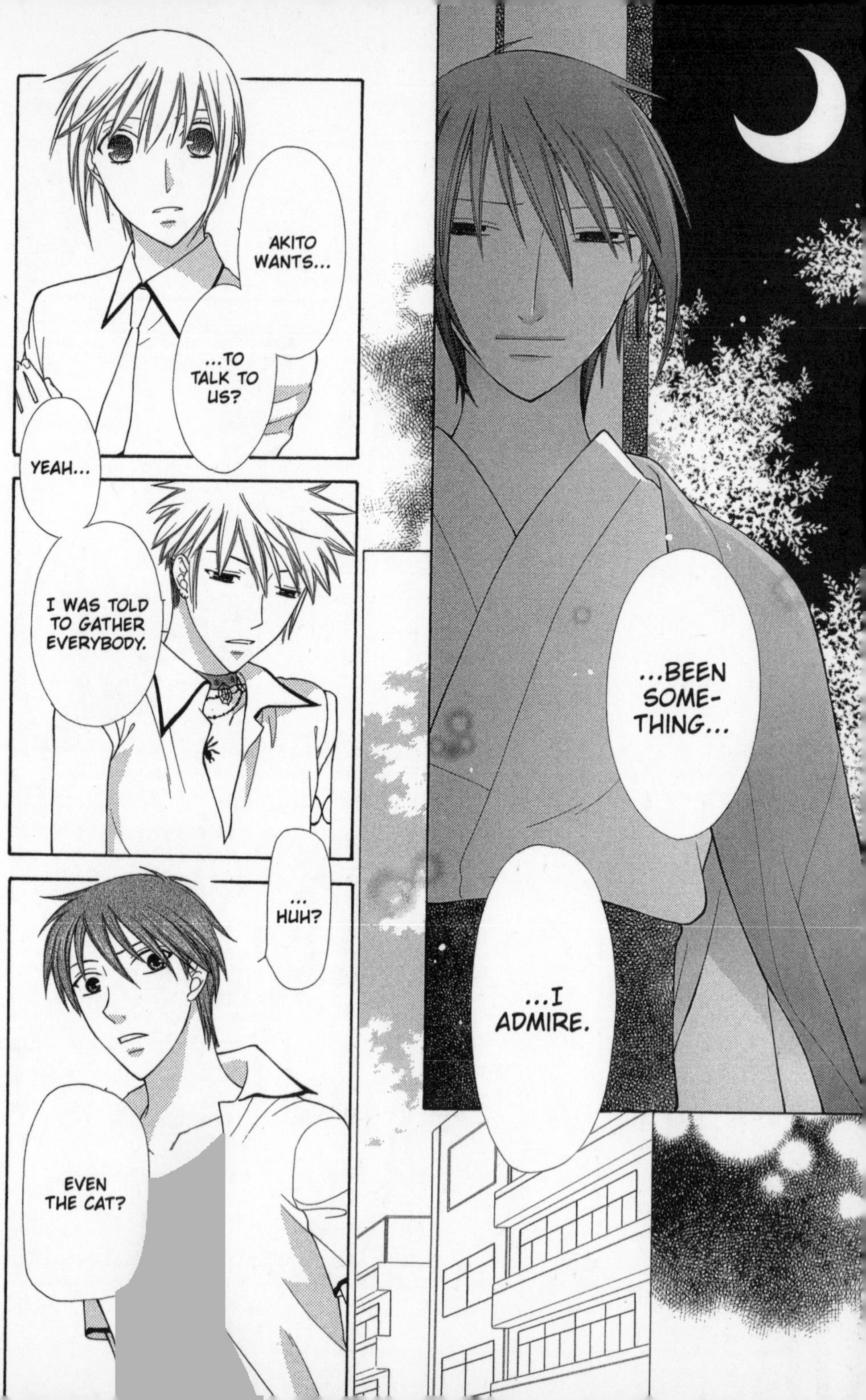
...BEEN SOME-THING...
...I ADMIRE.
AKITO WANTS...
...TO TALK TO US?
YEAH...
I WAS TOLD TO GATHER EVERYBODY.
...HUH?
EVEN THE CAT?

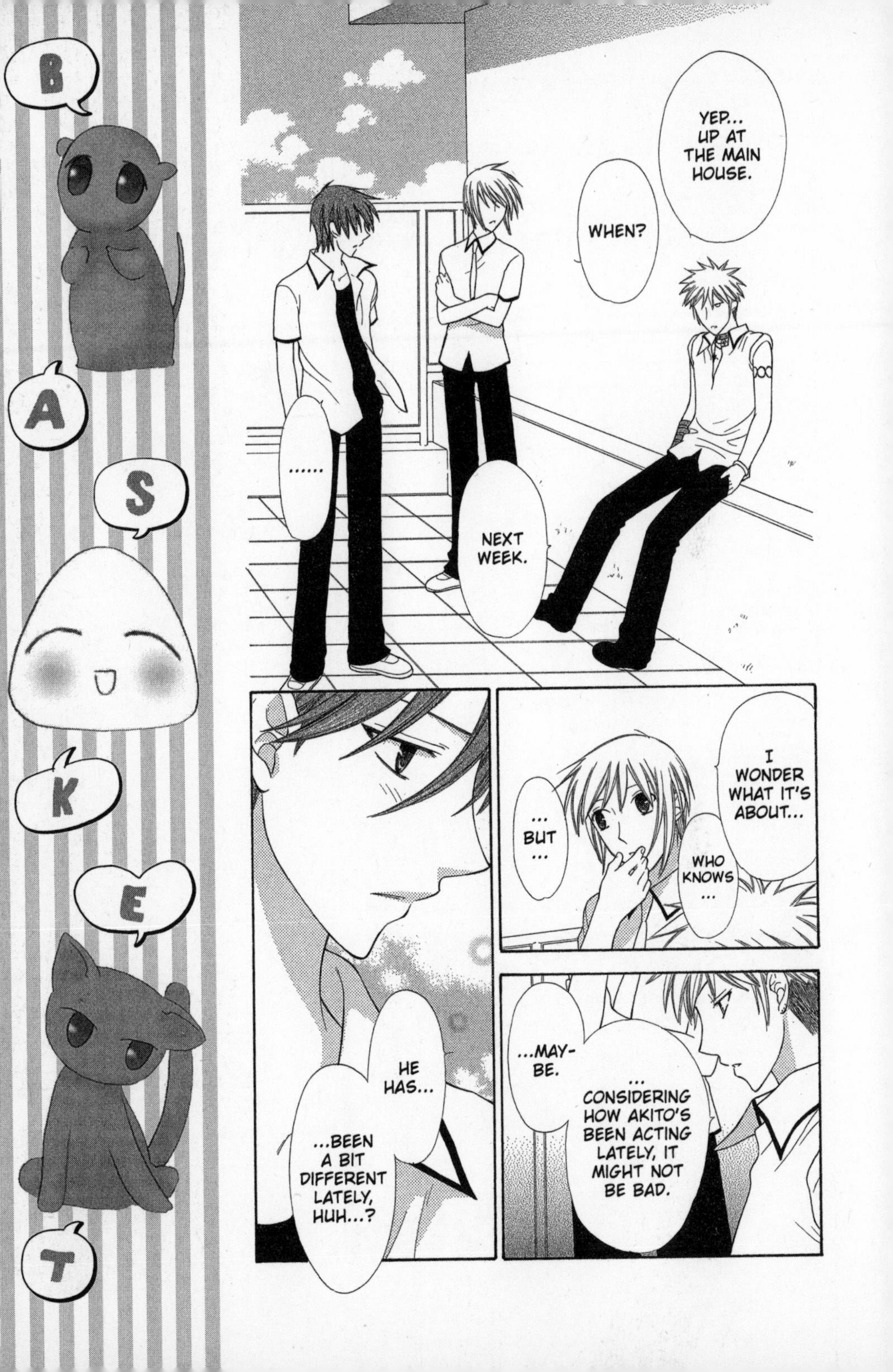
B
A
S
K
E
T
YEP... UP AT THE MAIN HOUSE.
WHEN?
NEXT WEEK.
......
I WONDER WHAT IT'S ABOUT...
WHO KNOWS...
... BUT ...
... CONSIDERING HOW AKITO'S BEEN ACTING LATELY, IT MIGHT NOT BE BAD.
...MAY-BE.
HE HAS...
...BEEN A BIT DIFFERENT LATELY, HUH...?

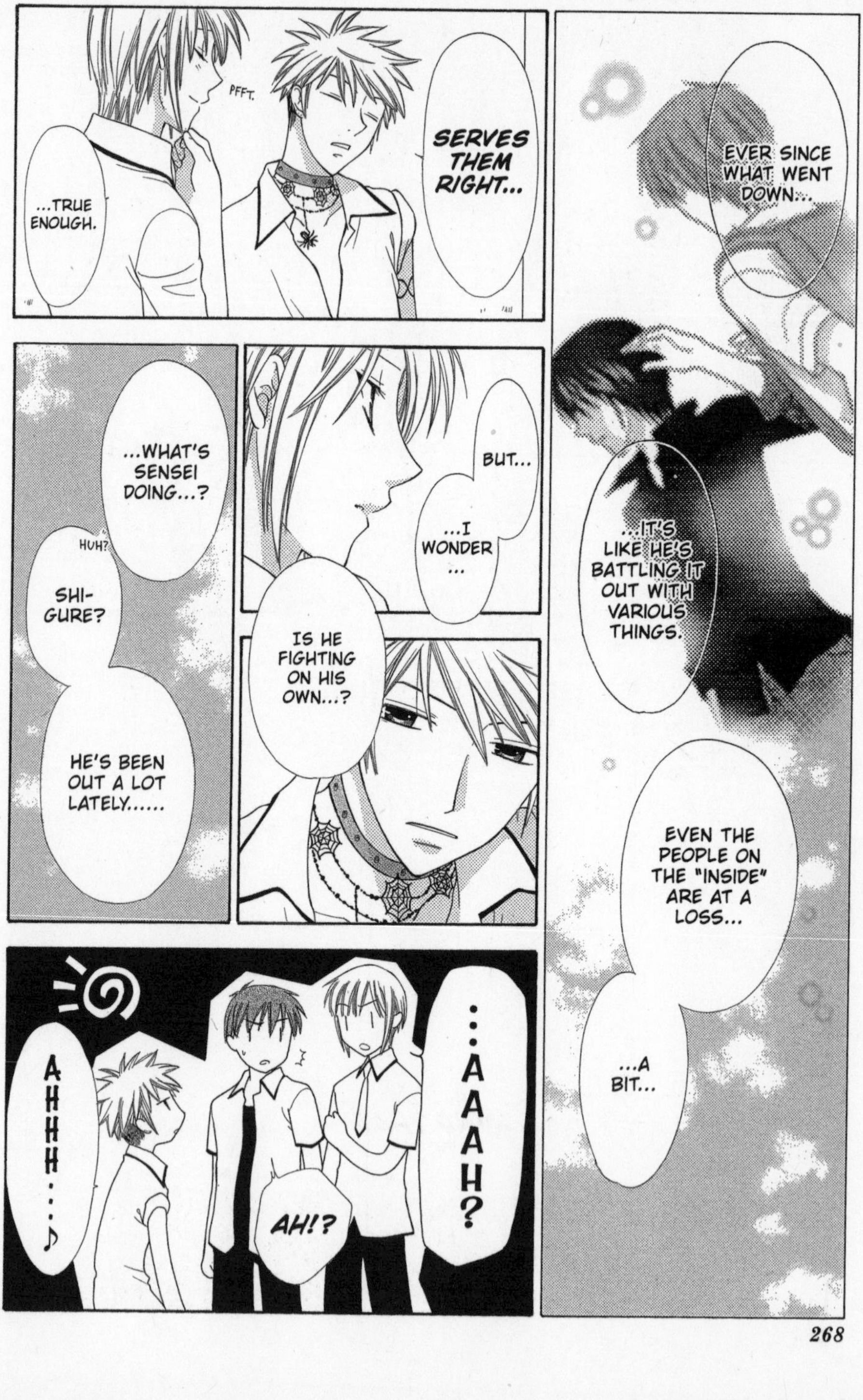
EVER SINCE WHAT WENT DOWN...
...IT'S LIKE HE'S BATTLING IT OUT WITH VARIOUS THINGS.
EVEN THE PEOPLE ON THE "INSIDE" ARE AT A LOSS...
...A BIT...
SERVES THEM RIGHT...
PFFT.
...TRUE ENOUGH.
BUT...
...I WONDER...
IS HE FIGHTING ON HIS OWN...?
...WHAT'S SENSEI DOING...?
HUH?
SHI-GURE?
HE'S BEEN OUT A LOT LATELY......
...AAAAH?
AH!?
AHHH...♪

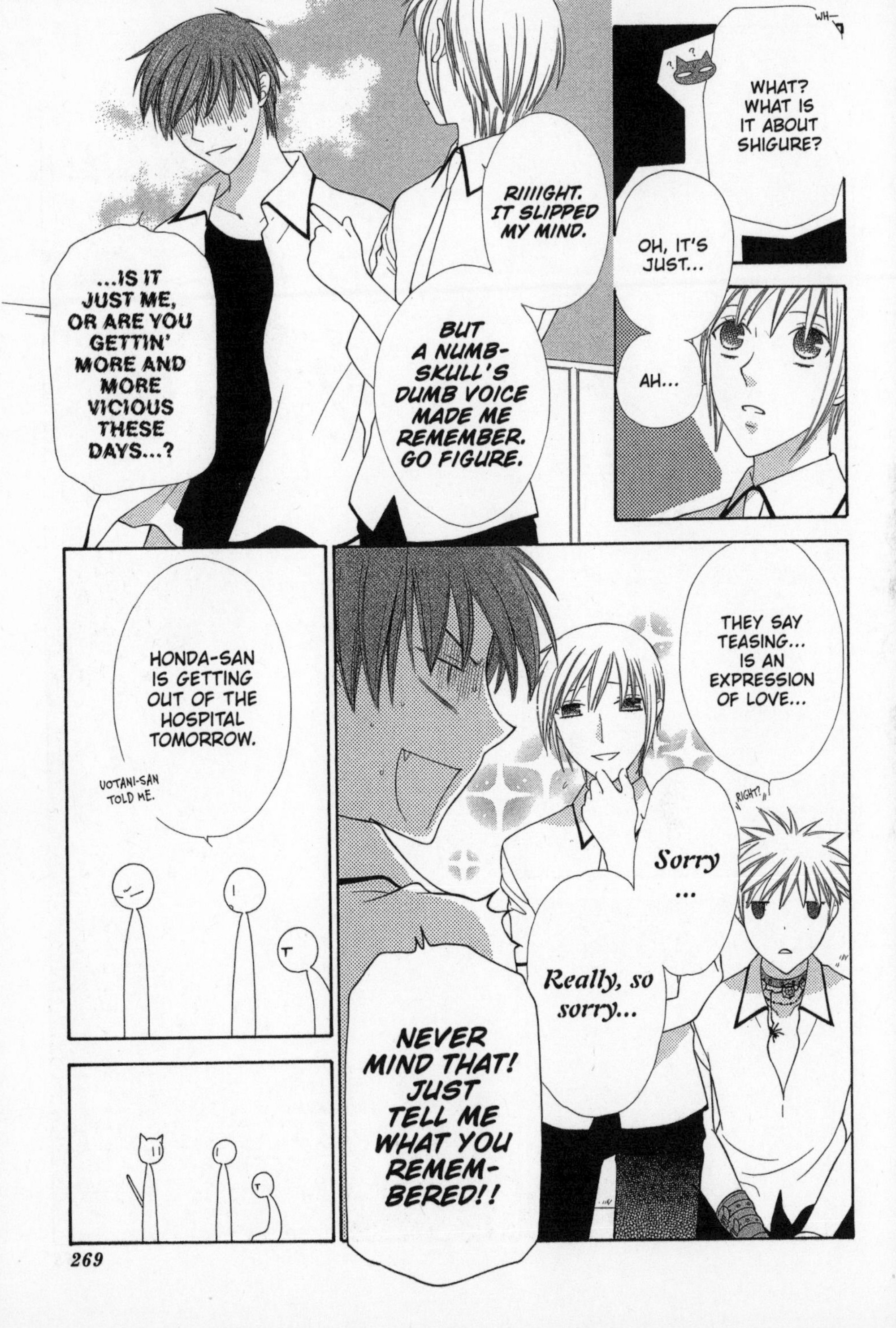
WH—
WHAT? WHAT IS IT ABOUT SHIGURE?
OH, IT'S JUST...
AH...
RIIIIGHT. IT SLIPPED MY MIND.
BUT A NUMB-SKULL'S DUMB VOICE MADE ME REMEMBER. GO FIGURE.
...IS IT JUST ME, OR ARE YOU GETTIN' MORE AND MORE VICIOUS THESE DAYS...?
THEY SAY TEASING... IS AN EXPRESSION OF LOVE...
RIGHT?
Sorry ...
Really, so sorry...
NEVER MIND THAT! JUST TELL ME WHAT YOU REMEM-BERED!!
HONDA-SAN IS GETTING OUT OF THE HOSPITAL TOMORROW.
UOTANI-SAN TOLD ME.

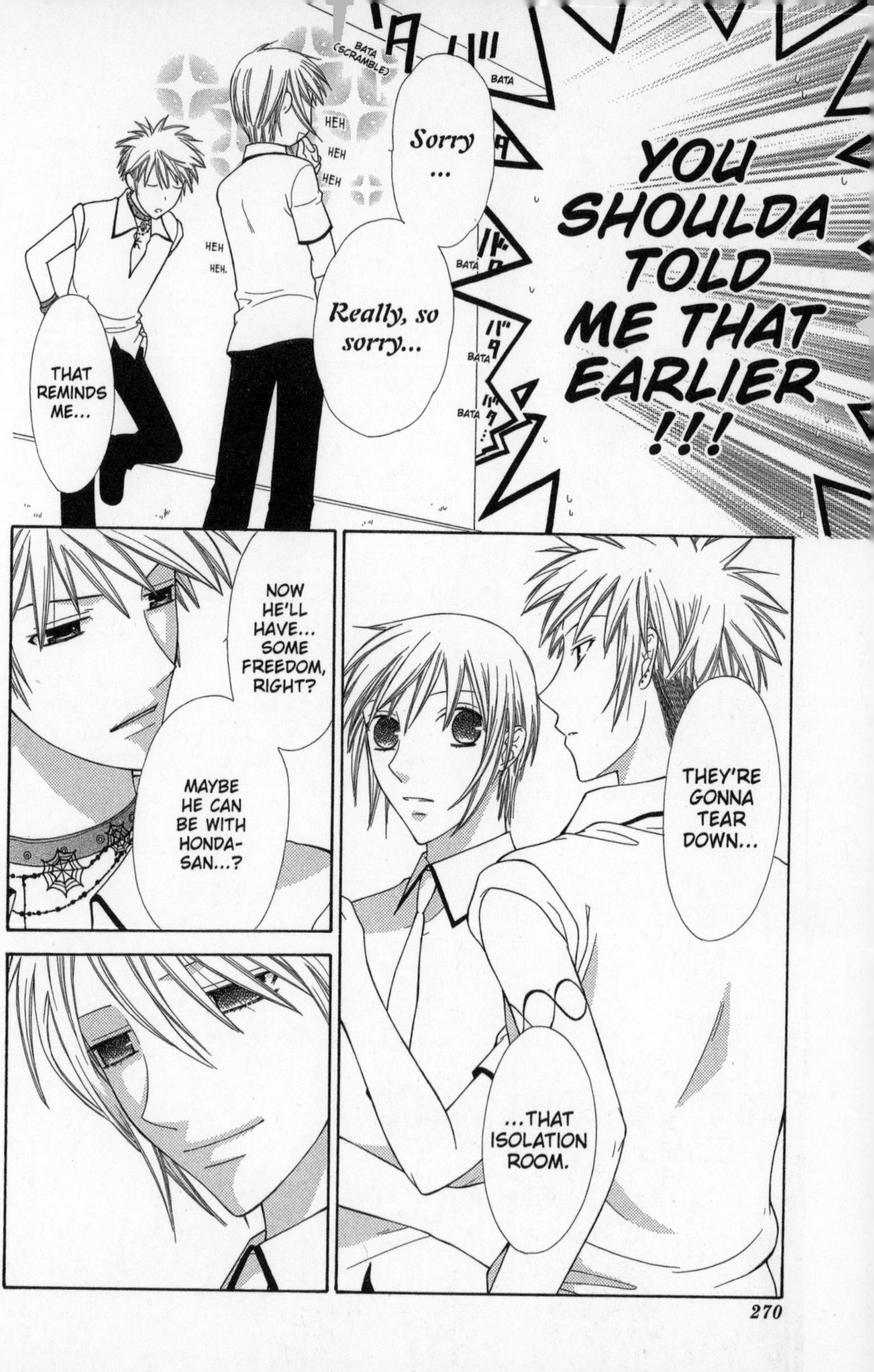
YOU SHOULDA TOLD ME THAT EARLIER!!!
BATA (SCRAMBLE)
BATA
BATA
BATA
BATA
Sorry...
Really, so sorry...
HEH HEH HEH
HEH HEH.
THAT REMINDS ME...
THEY'RE GONNA TEAR DOWN...
...THAT ISOLATION ROOM.
NOW HE'LL HAVE... SOME FREEDOM, RIGHT?
MAYBE HE CAN BE WITH HONDA-SAN...?

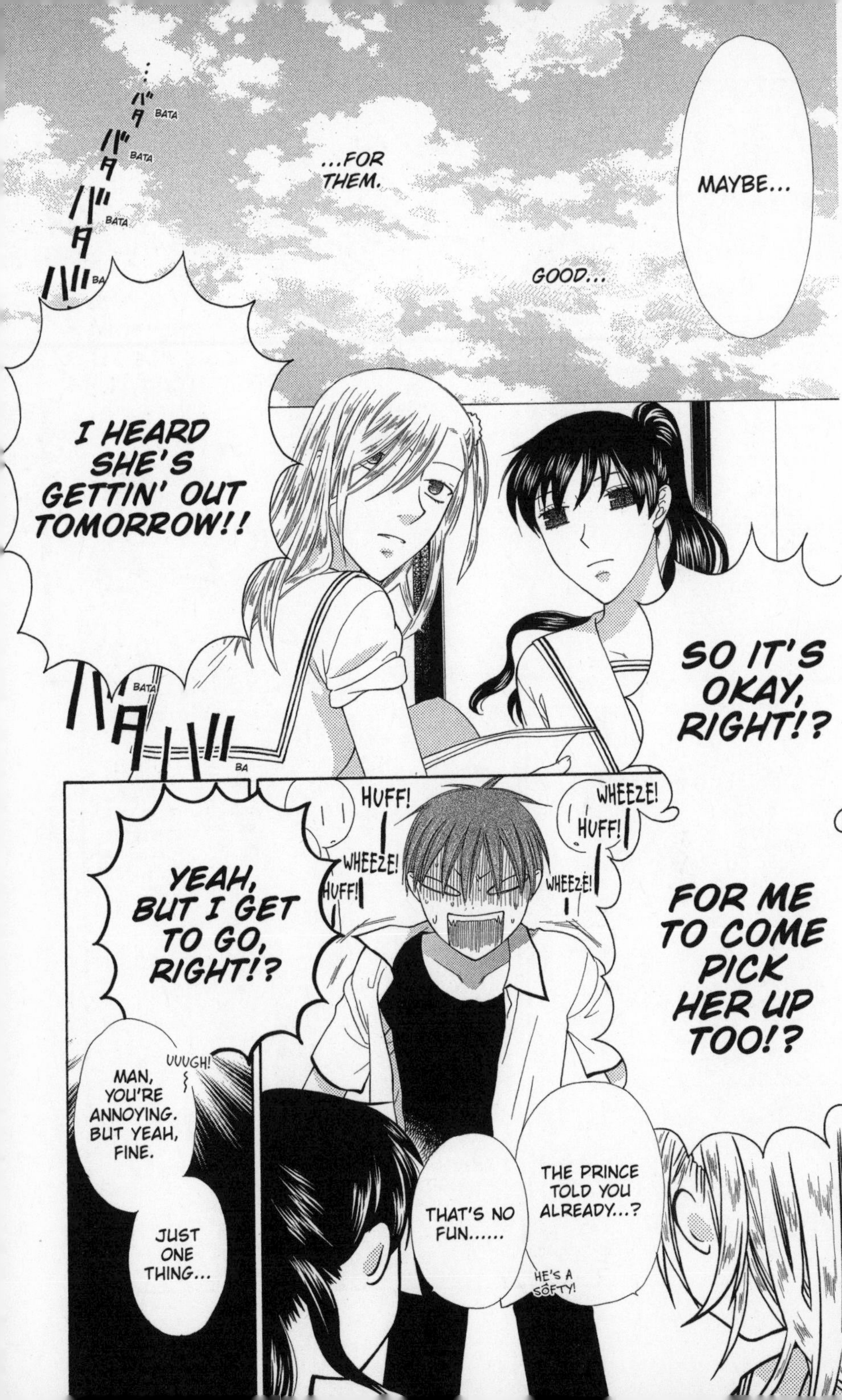
MAYBE...
GOOD...
...FOR THEM.
...バタ BATA
バタ BATA
バタ BATA
バ BA
I HEARD SHE'S GETTIN' OUT TOMORROW!!
バタバ BATA BA
SO IT'S OKAY, RIGHT!?
FOR ME TO COME PICK HER UP TOO!?
WHEEZE! HUFF!
HUFF!
WHEEZE!
WHEEZE! HUFF!
YEAH, BUT I GET TO GO, RIGHT!?
THE PRINCE TOLD YOU ALREADY...?
HE'S A SOFTY!
THAT'S NO FUN......
UUUGH!
MAN, YOU'RE ANNOYING. BUT YEAH, FINE.
JUST ONE THING...

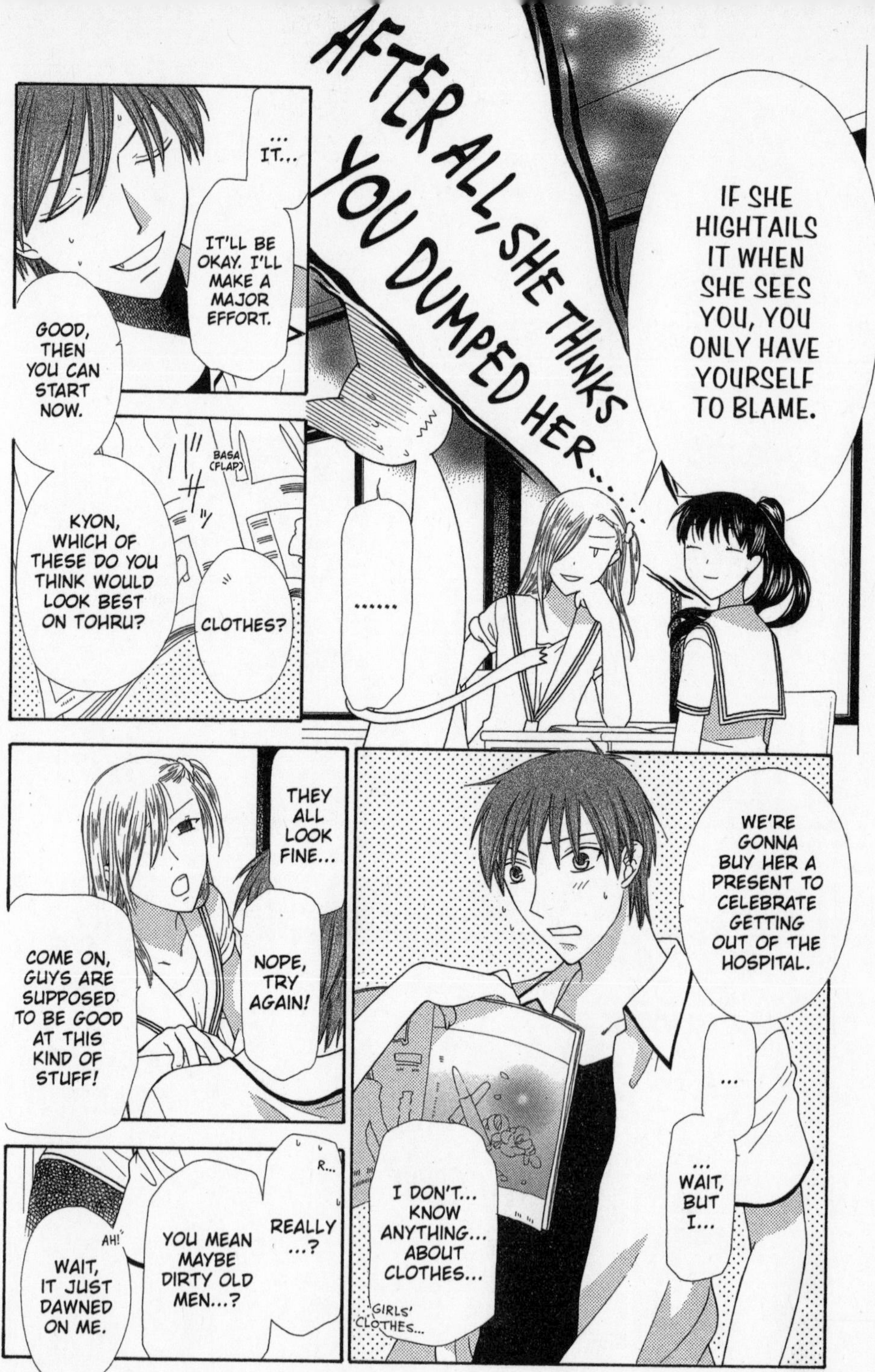
IF SHE HIGHTAILS IT WHEN SHE SEES YOU, YOU ONLY HAVE YOURSELF TO BLAME.
AFTER ALL, SHE THINKS YOU DUMPED HER......
......
... IT...
IT'LL BE OKAY. I'LL MAKE A MAJOR EFFORT.
GOOD, THEN YOU CAN START NOW.
BASA (FLAP)
KYON, WHICH OF THESE DO YOU THINK WOULD LOOK BEST ON TOHRU?
CLOTHES?
WE'RE GONNA BUY HER A PRESENT TO CELEBRATE GETTING OUT OF THE HOSPITAL.
...
... WAIT, BUT I...
I DON'T... KNOW ANYTHING... ABOUT CLOTHES...
GIRLS' CLOTHES...
THEY ALL LOOK FINE...
NOPE, TRY AGAIN!
COME ON, GUYS ARE SUPPOSED TO BE GOOD AT THIS KIND OF STUFF!
R...
REALLY ...?
YOU MEAN MAYBE DIRTY OLD MEN...?
AH!
WAIT, IT JUST DAWNED ON ME.

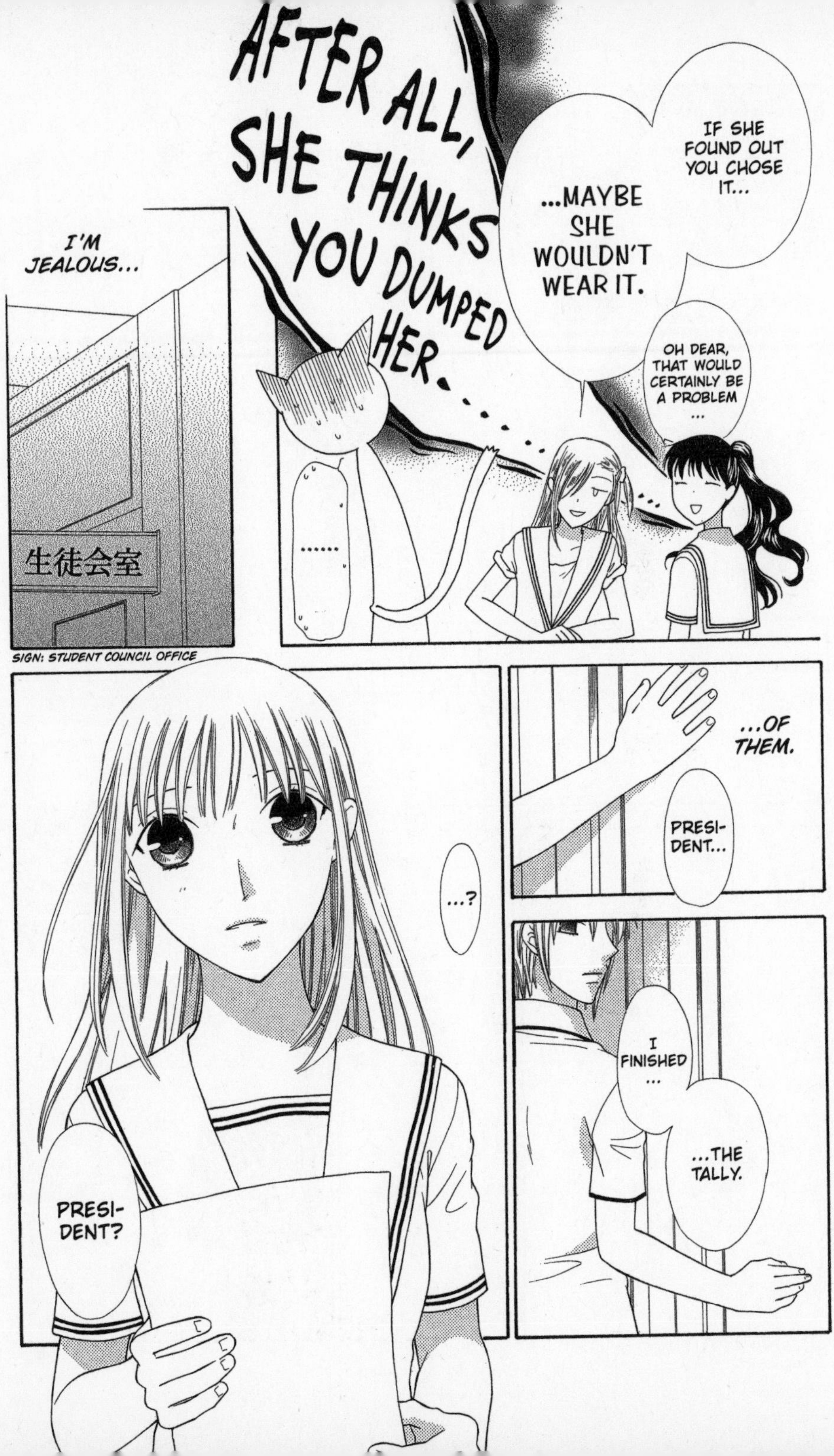
IF SHE FOUND OUT YOU CHOSE IT...
...MAYBE SHE WOULDN'T WEAR IT.
OH DEAR, THAT WOULD CERTAINLY BE A PROBLEM...
AFTER ALL, SHE THINKS YOU DUMPED HER...
......
I'M JEALOUS...
生徒会室
SIGN: STUDENT COUNCIL OFFICE
...OF THEM.
PRESI-DENT...
I FINISHED...
...THE TALLY.
...?
PRESI-DENT?

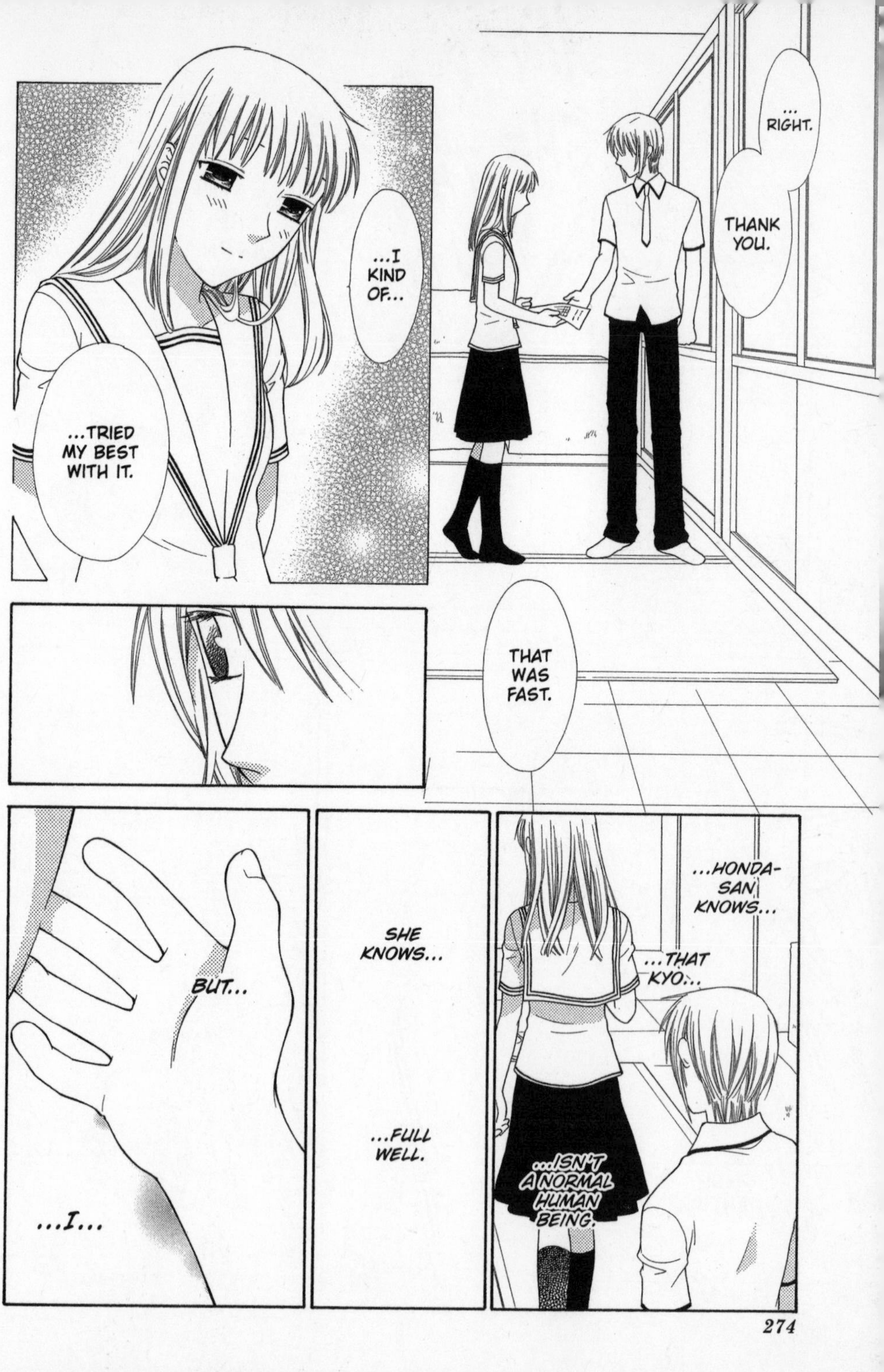

...RIGHT.
THANK YOU.
THAT WAS FAST.
...I KIND OF...
...TRIED MY BEST WITH IT.
...HONDA-SAN KNOWS...
...THAT KYO...
...ISN'T A NORMAL HUMAN BEING.
SHE KNOWS...
...FULL WELL.
BUT...
...I...

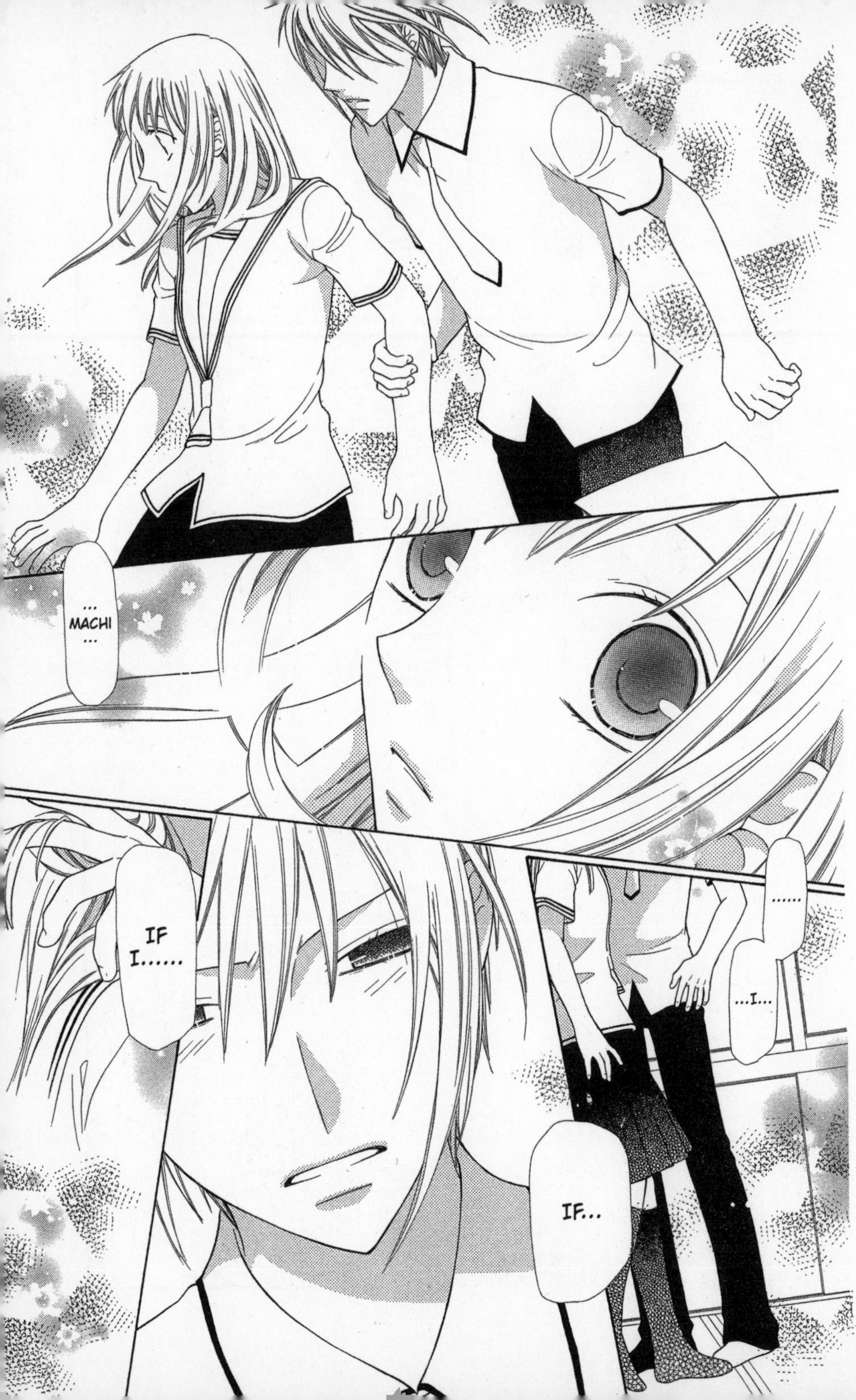

...MACHI...
......
...I...
IF...
IF I......

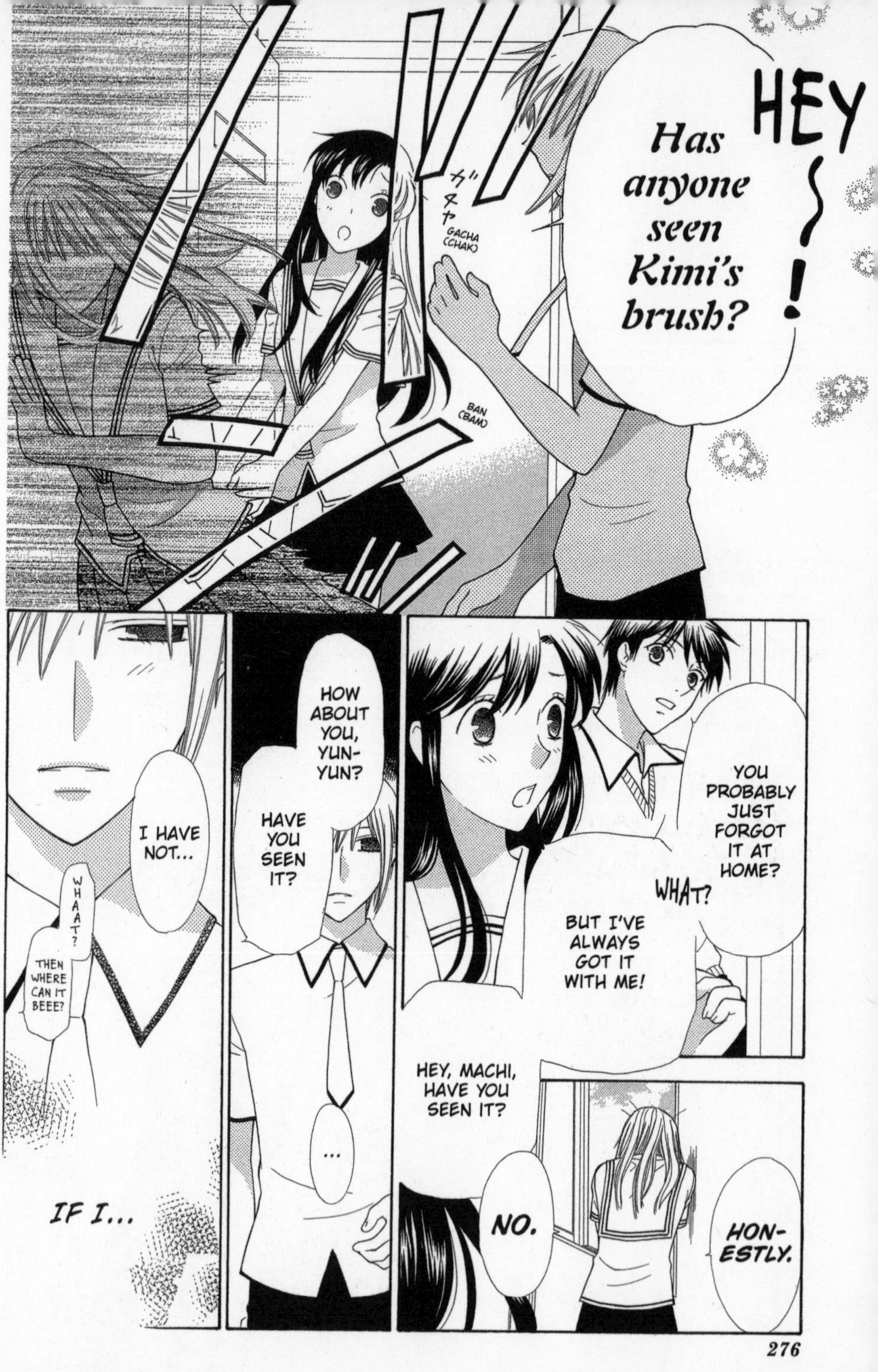

HEY~!
Has anyone seen Kimi's brush?
ガタッ
GACHA (CHAK)
BAN (BAM)
YOU PROBABLY JUST FORGOT IT AT HOME?
WHAT?
BUT I'VE ALWAYS GOT IT WITH ME!
HEY, MACHI, HAVE YOU SEEN IT?
HON-ESTLY.
NO.
HOW ABOUT YOU, YUN-YUN?
HAVE YOU SEEN IT?
...
I HAVE NOT...
WHAAT?
THEN WHERE CAN IT BEEE?
IF I...

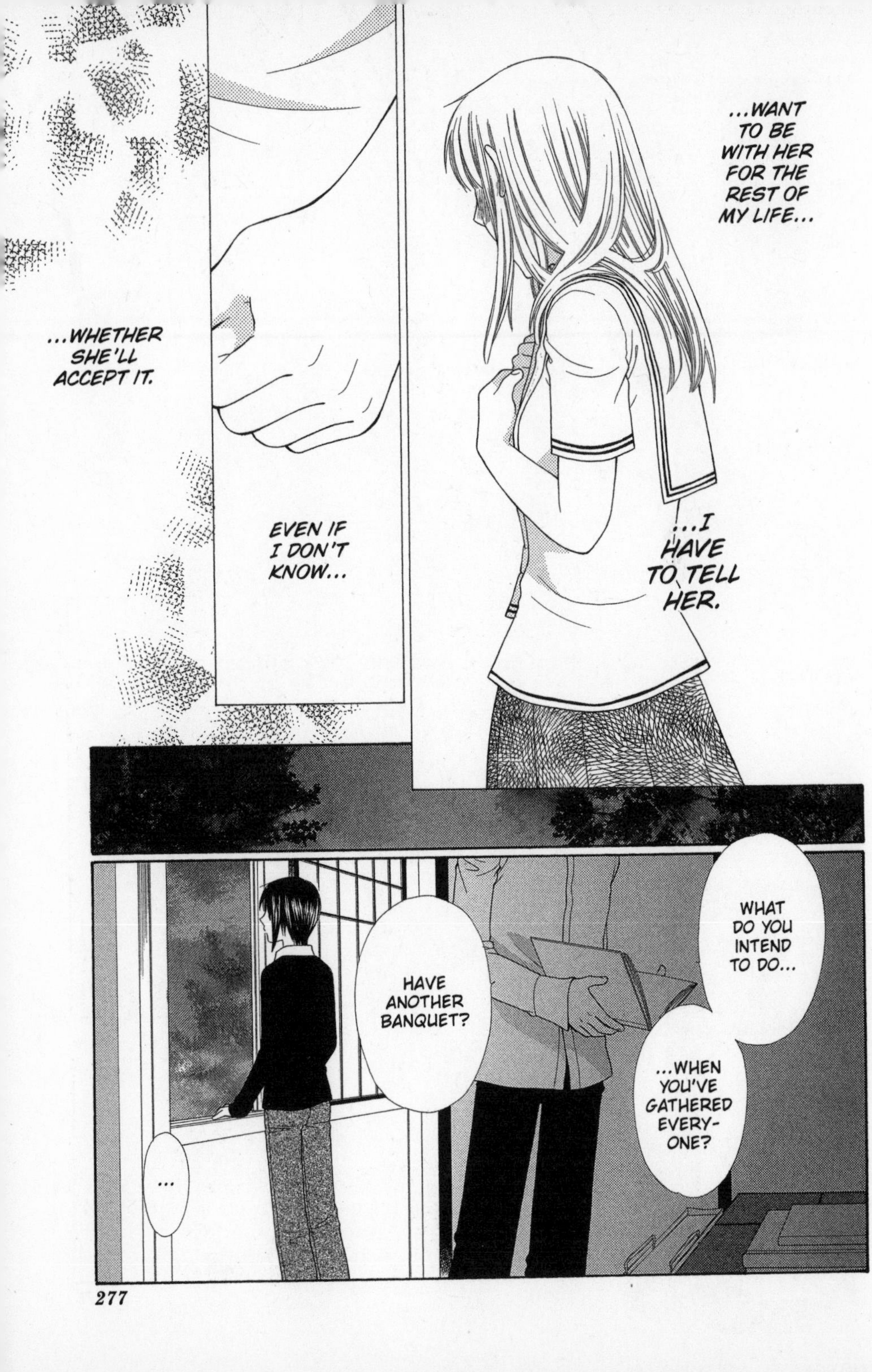
...WANT TO BE WITH HER FOR THE REST OF MY LIFE...
...WHETHER SHE'LL ACCEPT IT.
EVEN IF I DON'T KNOW...
...I HAVE TO TELL HER.
WHAT DO YOU INTEND TO DO...
...WHEN YOU'VE GATHERED EVERY-ONE?
HAVE ANOTHER BANQUET?
...

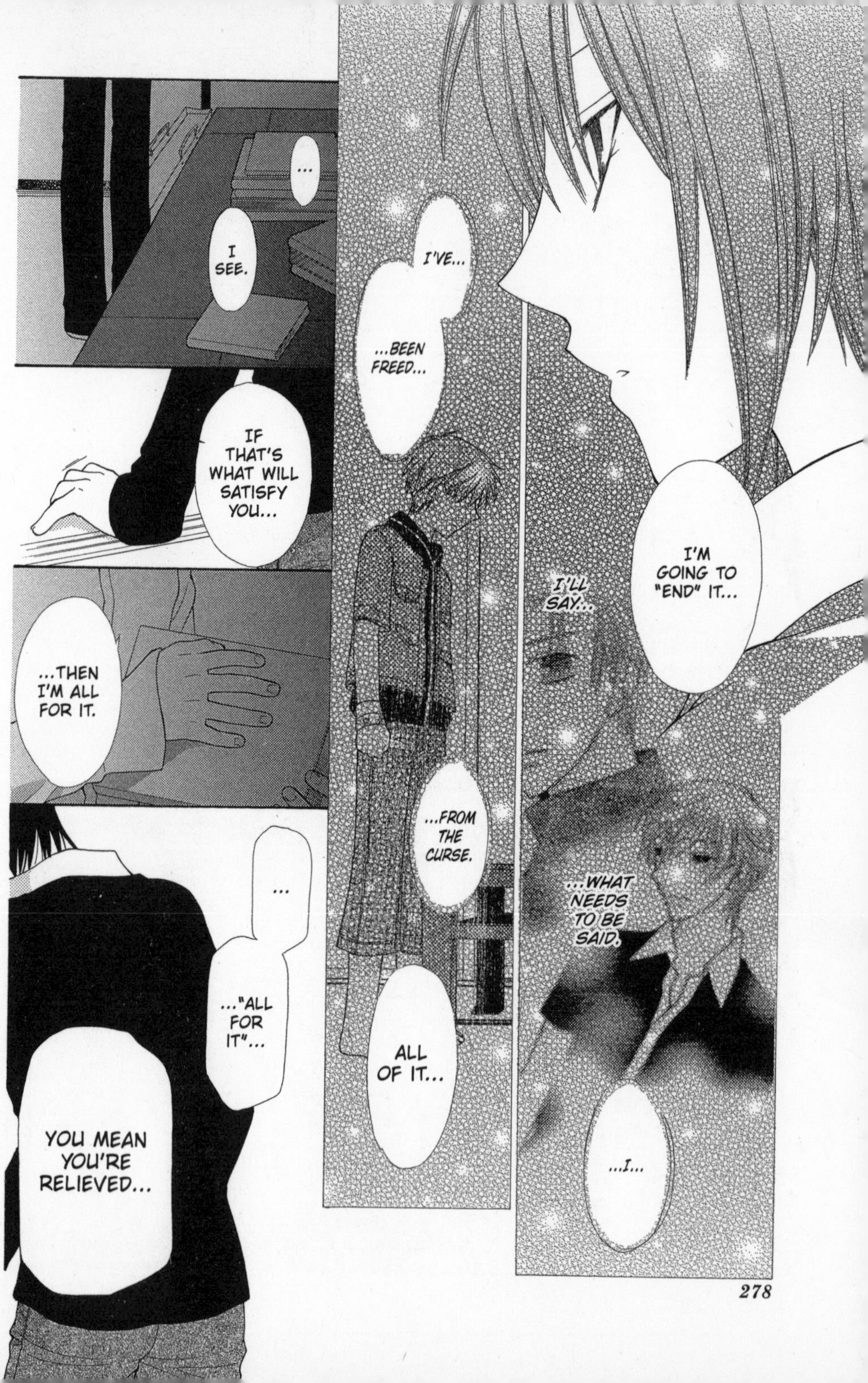
I'M GOING TO "END" IT...
I'LL SAY...
...WHAT NEEDS TO BE SAID.
...I...
I'VE...
...BEEN FREED...
...FROM THE CURSE.
ALL OF IT...
...
I SEE.
IF THAT'S WHAT WILL SATISFY YOU...
...THEN I'M ALL FOR IT.
...
..."ALL FOR IT"...
YOU MEAN YOU'RE RELIEVED...

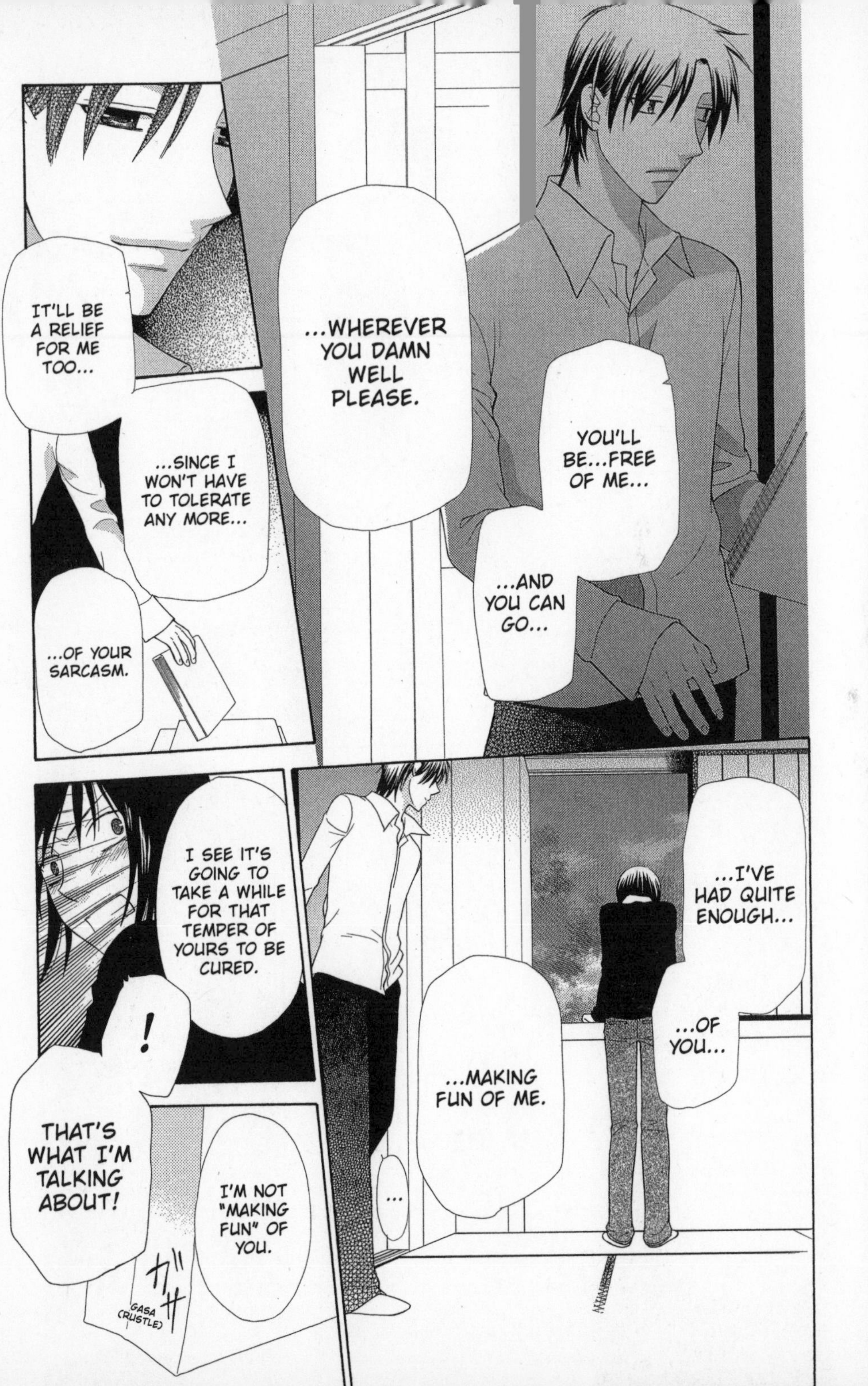
YOU'LL BE...FREE OF ME...
...AND YOU CAN GO...
...WHEREVER YOU DAMN WELL PLEASE.
IT'LL BE A RELIEF FOR ME TOO...
...SINCE I WON'T HAVE TO TOLERATE ANY MORE...
...OF YOUR SARCASM.
...I'VE HAD QUITE ENOUGH...
...OF YOU...
...MAKING FUN OF ME.
...
I SEE IT'S GOING TO TAKE A WHILE FOR THAT TEMPER OF YOURS TO BE CURED.
!
I'M NOT "MAKING FUN" OF YOU.
THAT'S WHAT I'M TALKING ABOUT!
GASA (RUSTLE)

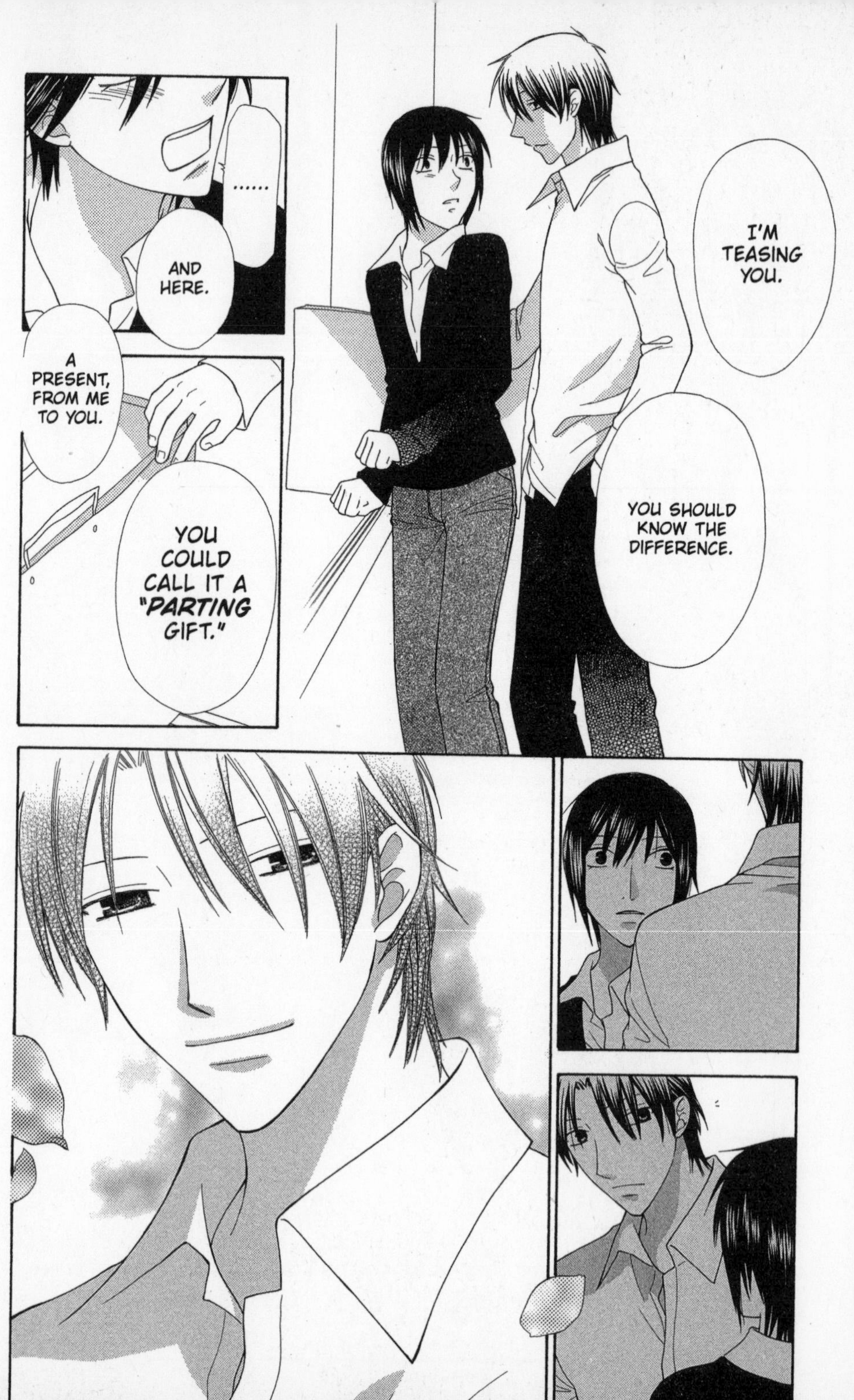

I'M TEASING YOU.
YOU SHOULD KNOW THE DIFFERENCE.
......
AND HERE.
A PRESENT, FROM ME TO YOU.
YOU COULD CALL IT A "PARTING GIFT."

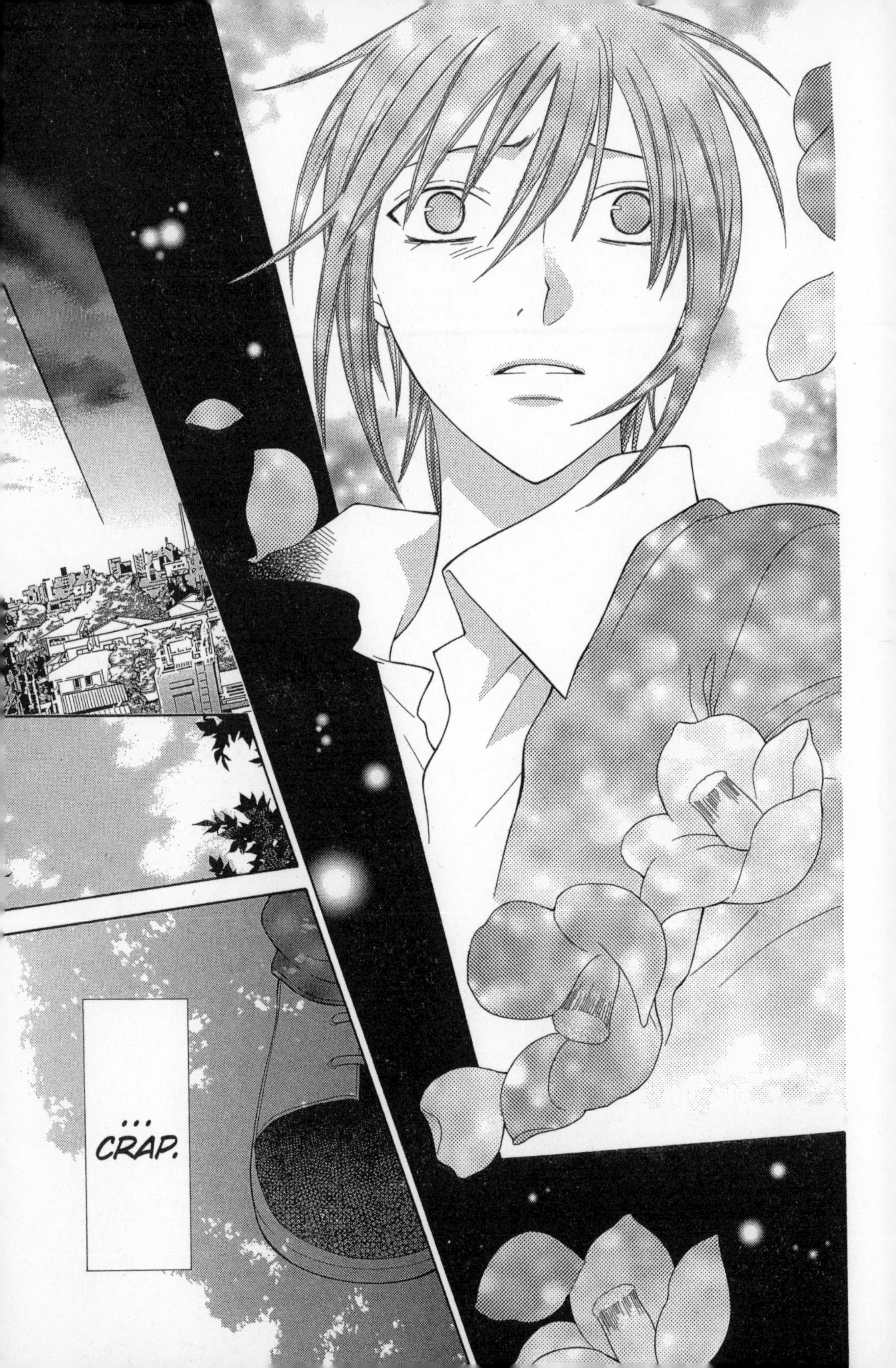
...CRAP.

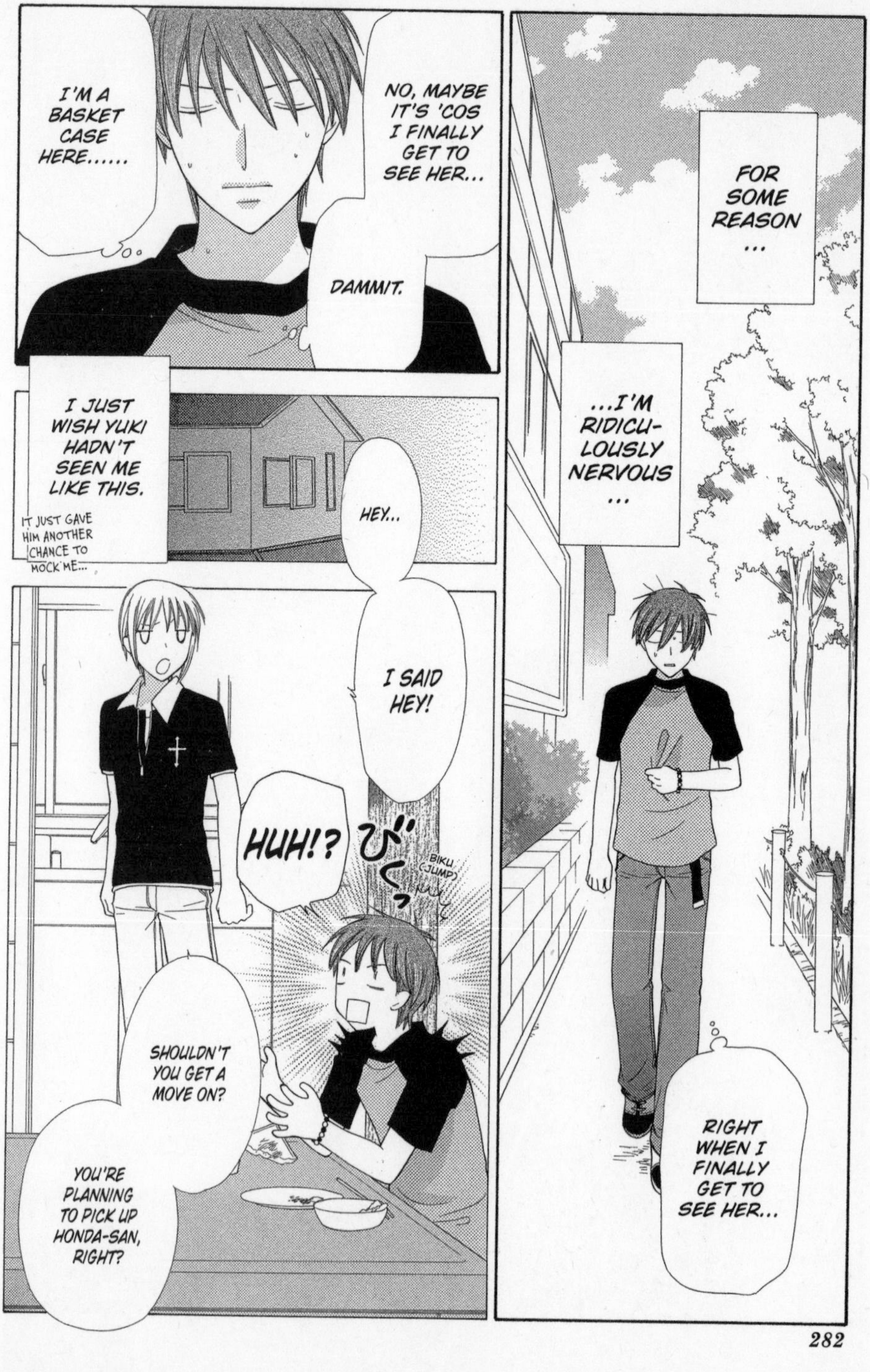
FOR SOME REASON ...
...I'M RIDICULOUSLY NERVOUS ...
RIGHT WHEN I FINALLY GET TO SEE HER...
NO, MAYBE IT'S 'COS I FINALLY GET TO SEE HER...
I'M A BASKET CASE HERE......
DAMMIT.
I JUST WISH YUKI HADN'T SEEN ME LIKE THIS.
IT JUST GAVE HIM ANOTHER CHANCE TO MOCK ME...
HEY...
I SAID HEY!
HUH!?
びくっ
BIKU (JUMP)
SHOULDN'T YOU GET A MOVE ON?
YOU'RE PLANNING TO PICK UP HONDA-SAN, RIGHT?

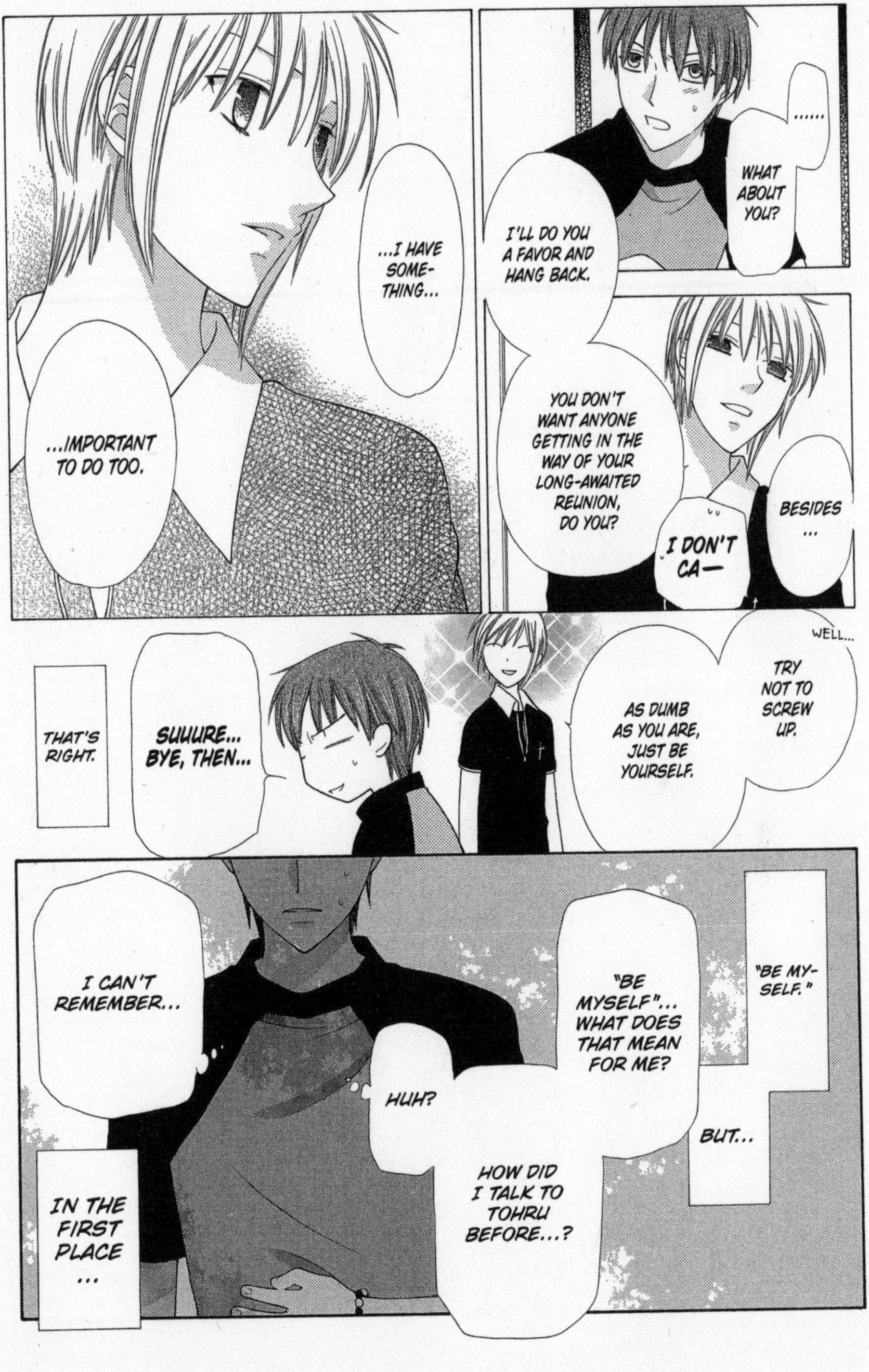
......
WHAT ABOUT YOU?
I'LL DO YOU A FAVOR AND HANG BACK.
YOU DON'T WANT ANYONE GETTING IN THE WAY OF YOUR LONG-AWAITED REUNION, DO YOU?
I DON'T CA—
BESIDES ...
...I HAVE SOME-THING...
...IMPORTANT TO DO TOO.
WELL...
TRY NOT TO SCREW UP.
AS DUMB AS YOU ARE, JUST BE YOURSELF.
SUUURE... BYE, THEN...
THAT'S RIGHT.
"BE MY-SELF."
BUT...
"BE MYSELF"... WHAT DOES THAT MEAN FOR ME?
HOW DID I TALK TO TOHRU BEFORE...?
HUH?
I CAN'T REMEMBER...
IN THE FIRST PLACE ...

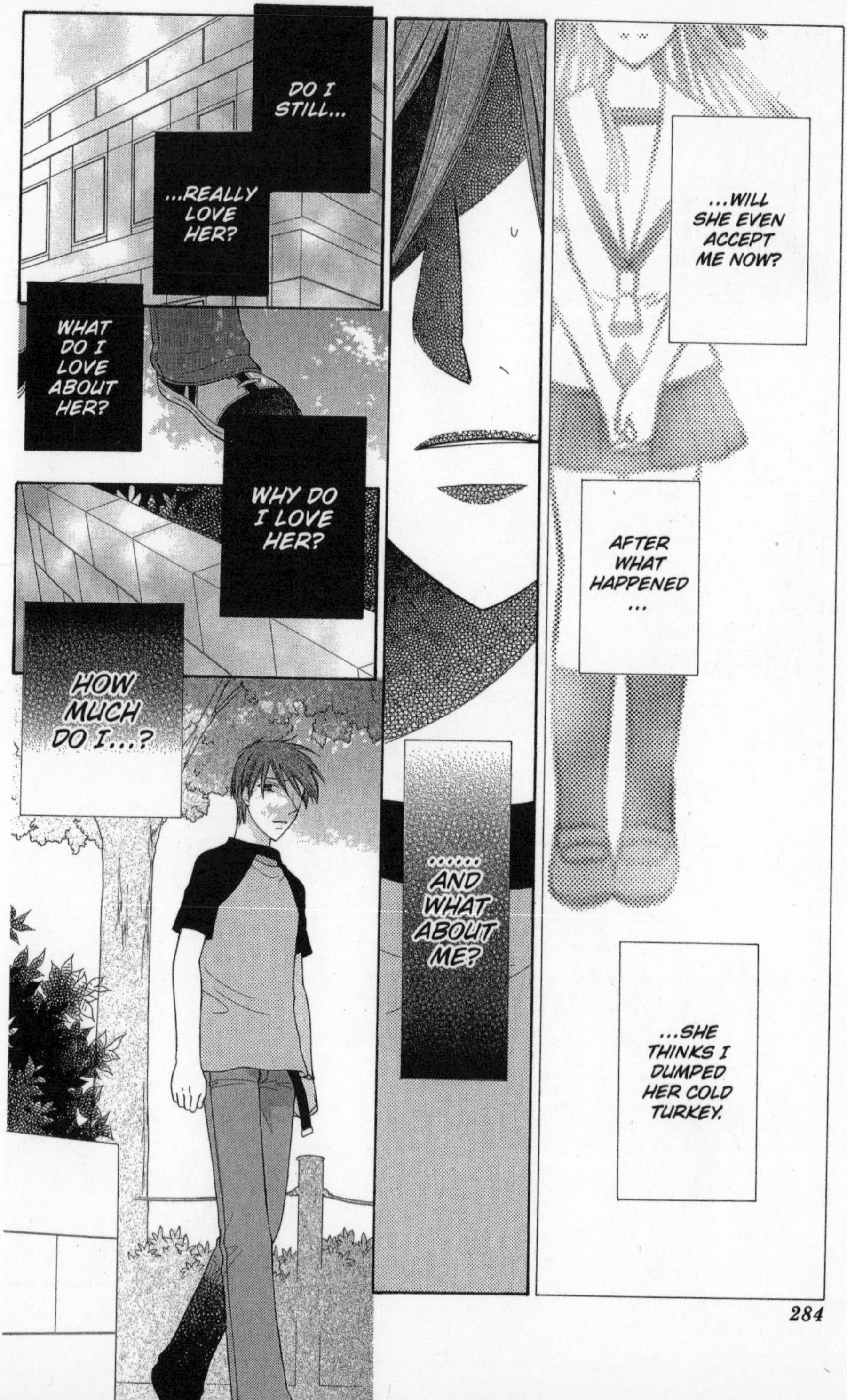
...WILL SHE EVEN ACCEPT ME NOW?
AFTER WHAT HAPPENED...
...SHE THINKS I DUMPED HER COLD TURKEY.
......AND WHAT ABOUT ME?
DO I STILL...
...REALLY LOVE HER?
WHAT DO I LOVE ABOUT HER?
WHY DO I LOVE HER?
HOW MUCH DO I...?

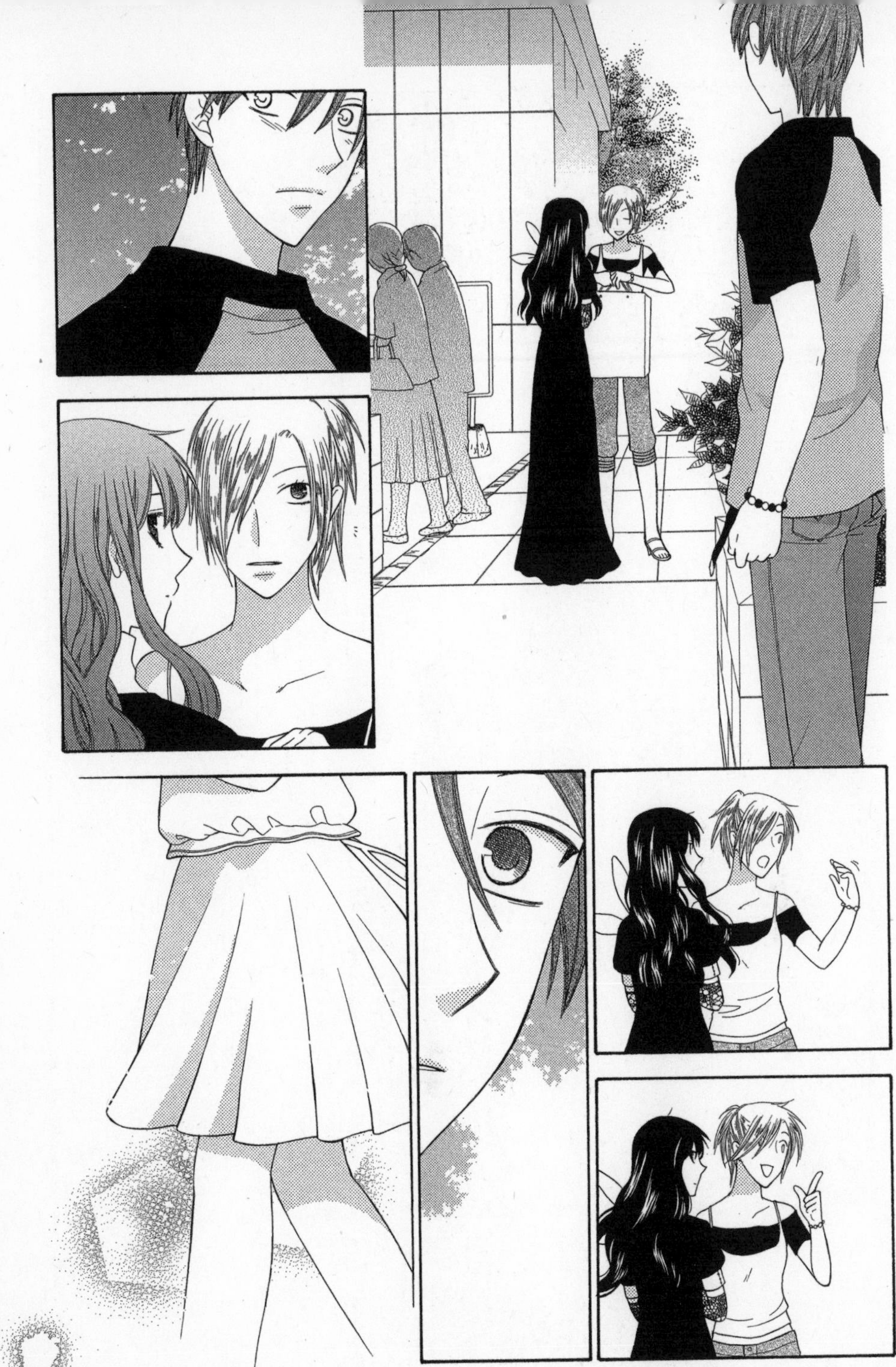

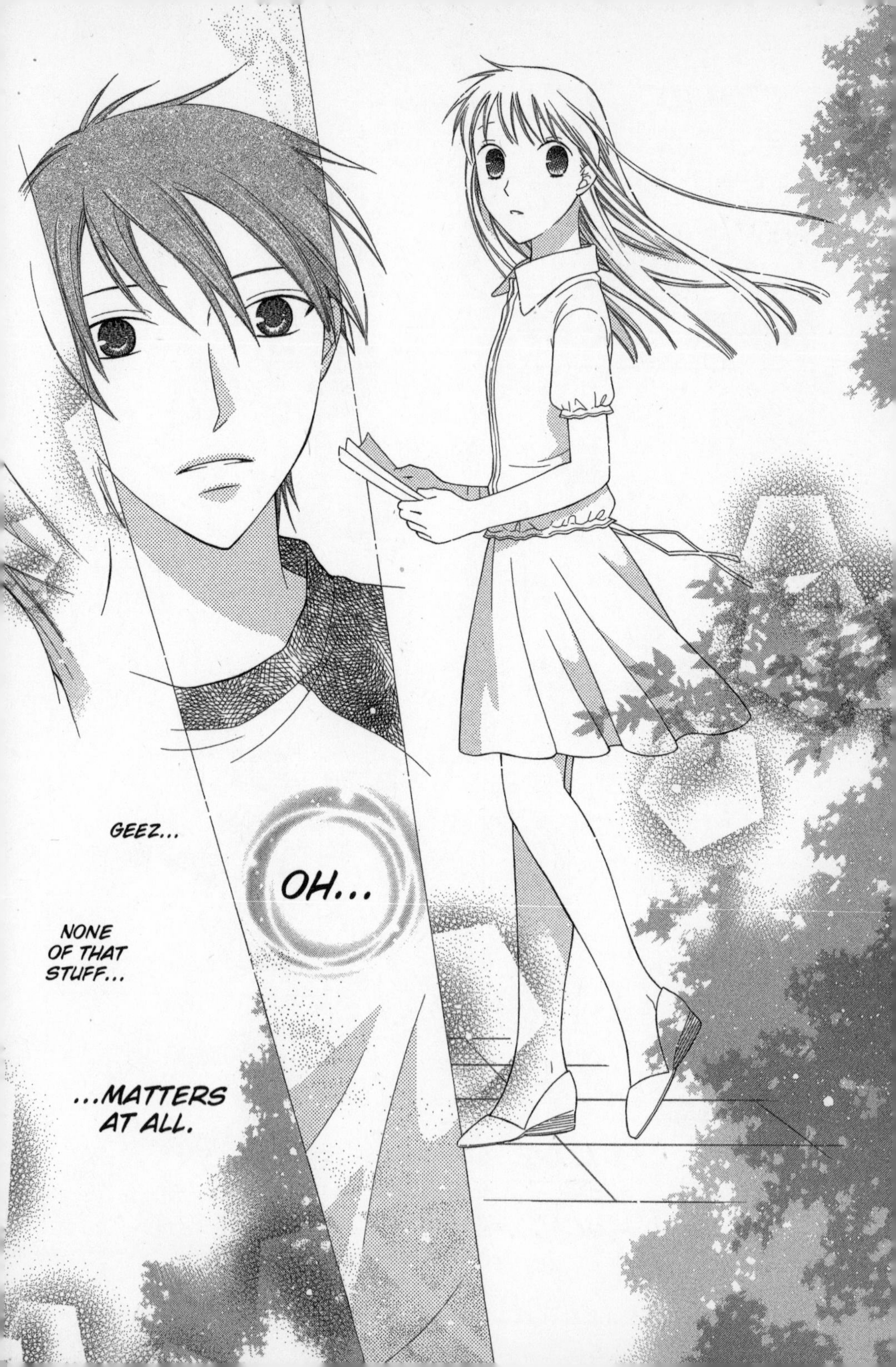
GEEZ...
OH...
NONE OF THAT STUFF...
...MATTERS AT ALL.

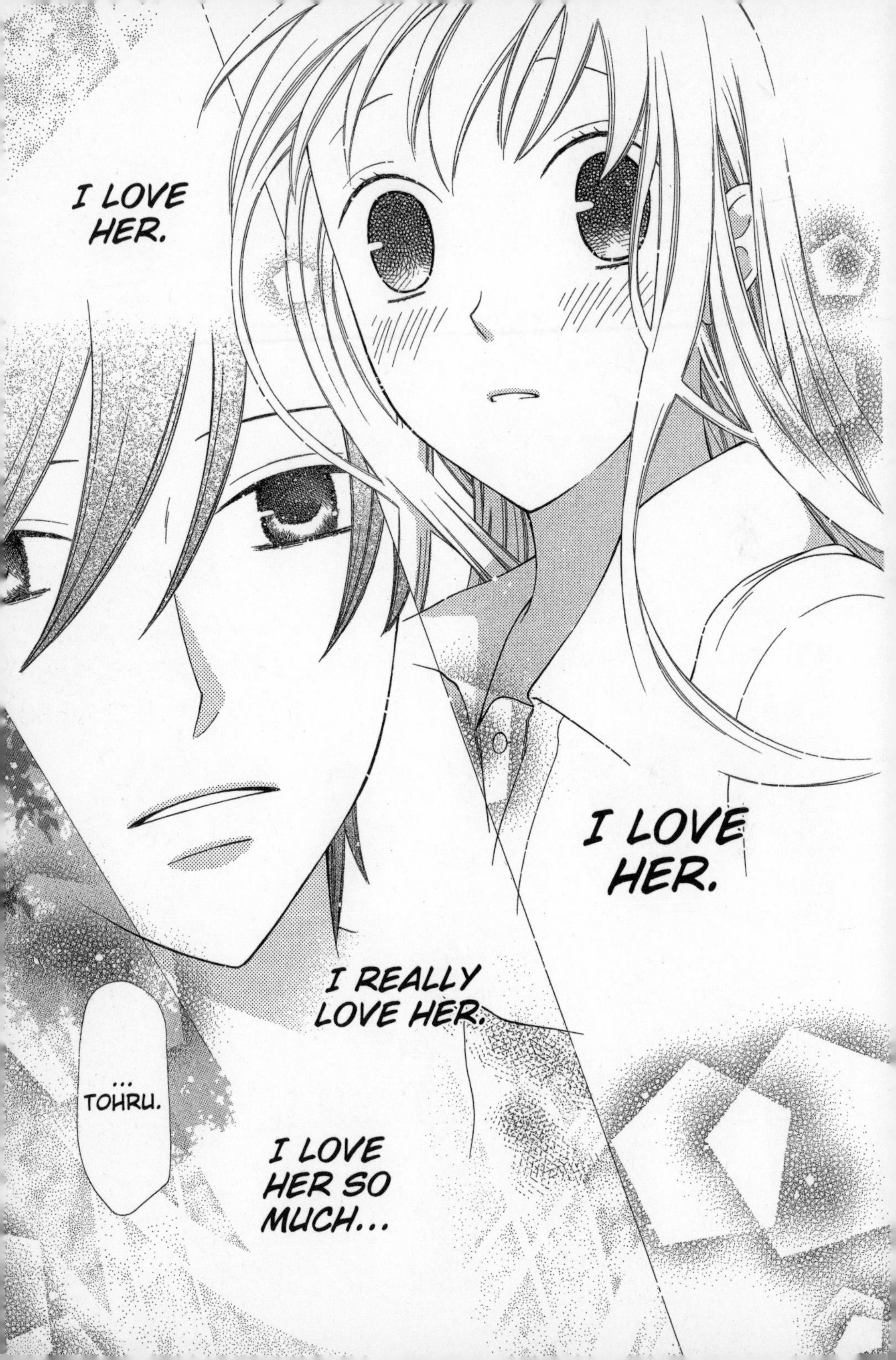
I LOVE HER.
I LOVE HER.
I REALLY LOVE HER.
...TOHRU.
I LOVE HER SO MUCH...

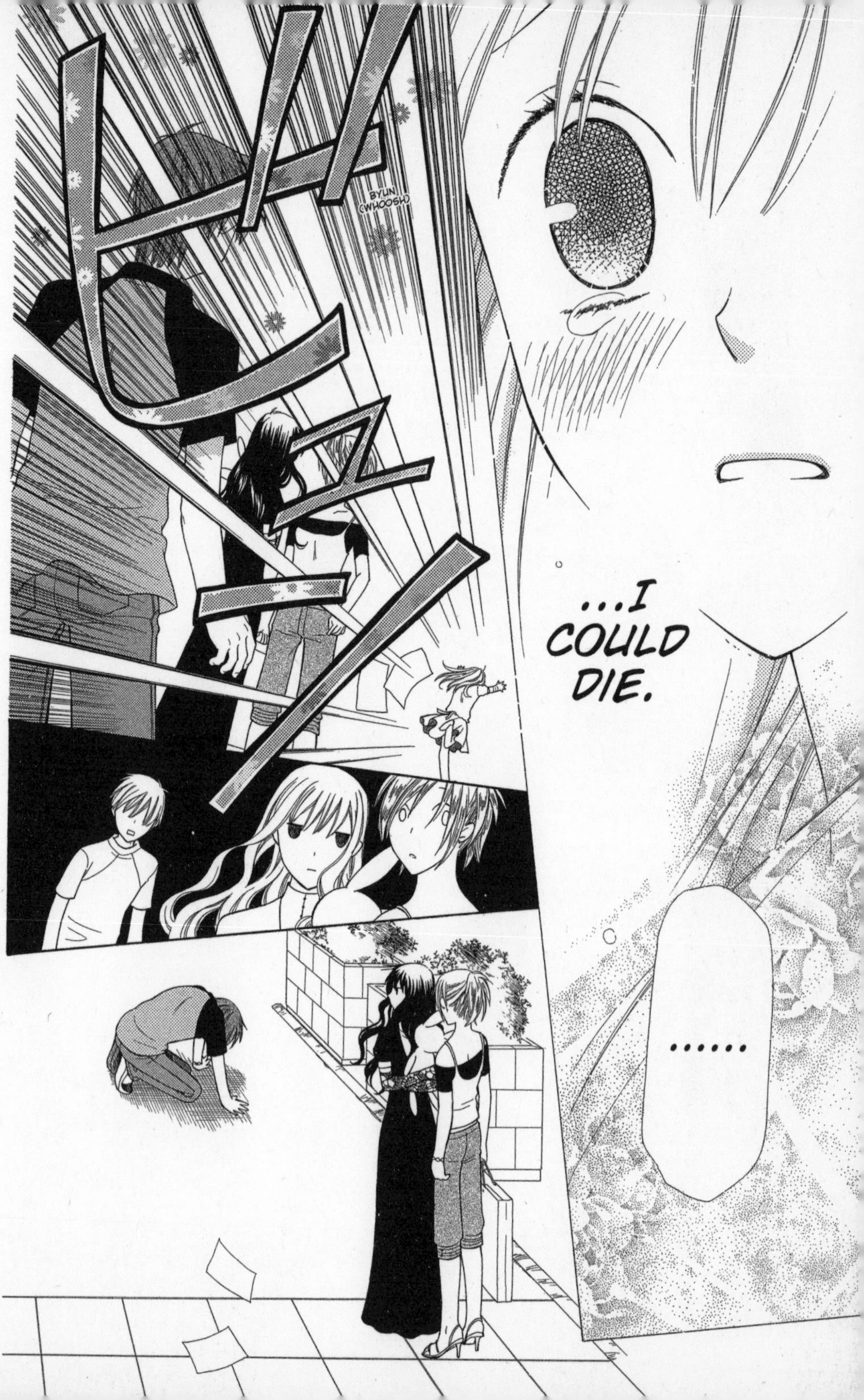
...I COULD DIE.
......
BYUN (WHOOSH)

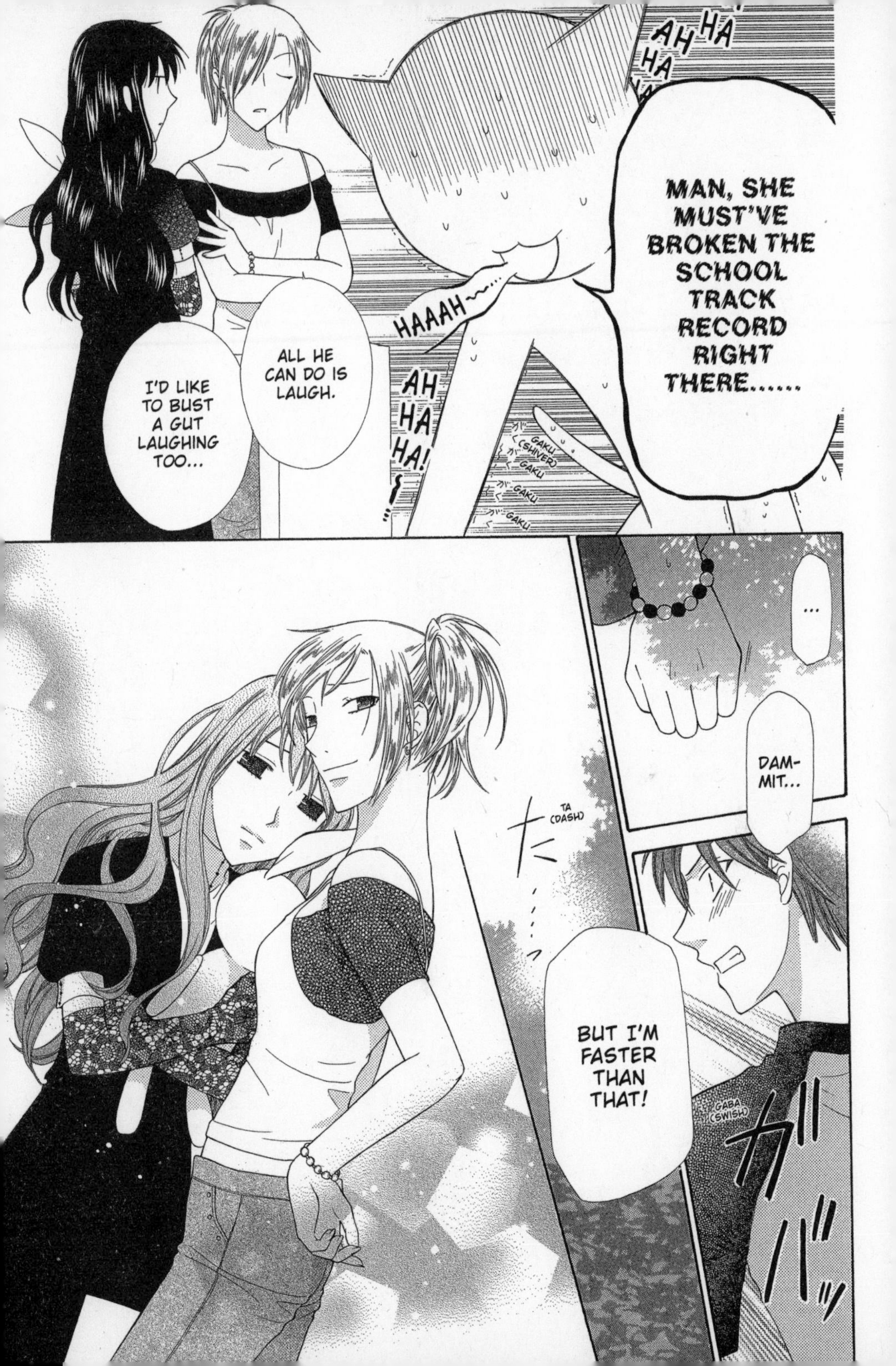
MAN, SHE MUST'VE BROKEN THE SCHOOL TRACK RECORD RIGHT THERE......
AH HA HA HA
HAAAH~
AH HA HA!
GAKU (SHIVER) GAKU
GAKU
GAKU
ALL HE CAN DO IS LAUGH.
I'D LIKE TO BUST A GUT LAUGHING TOO...
...
DAM-MIT...
GABA (SWISH)
TA (DASH)
BUT I'M FASTER THAN THAT!

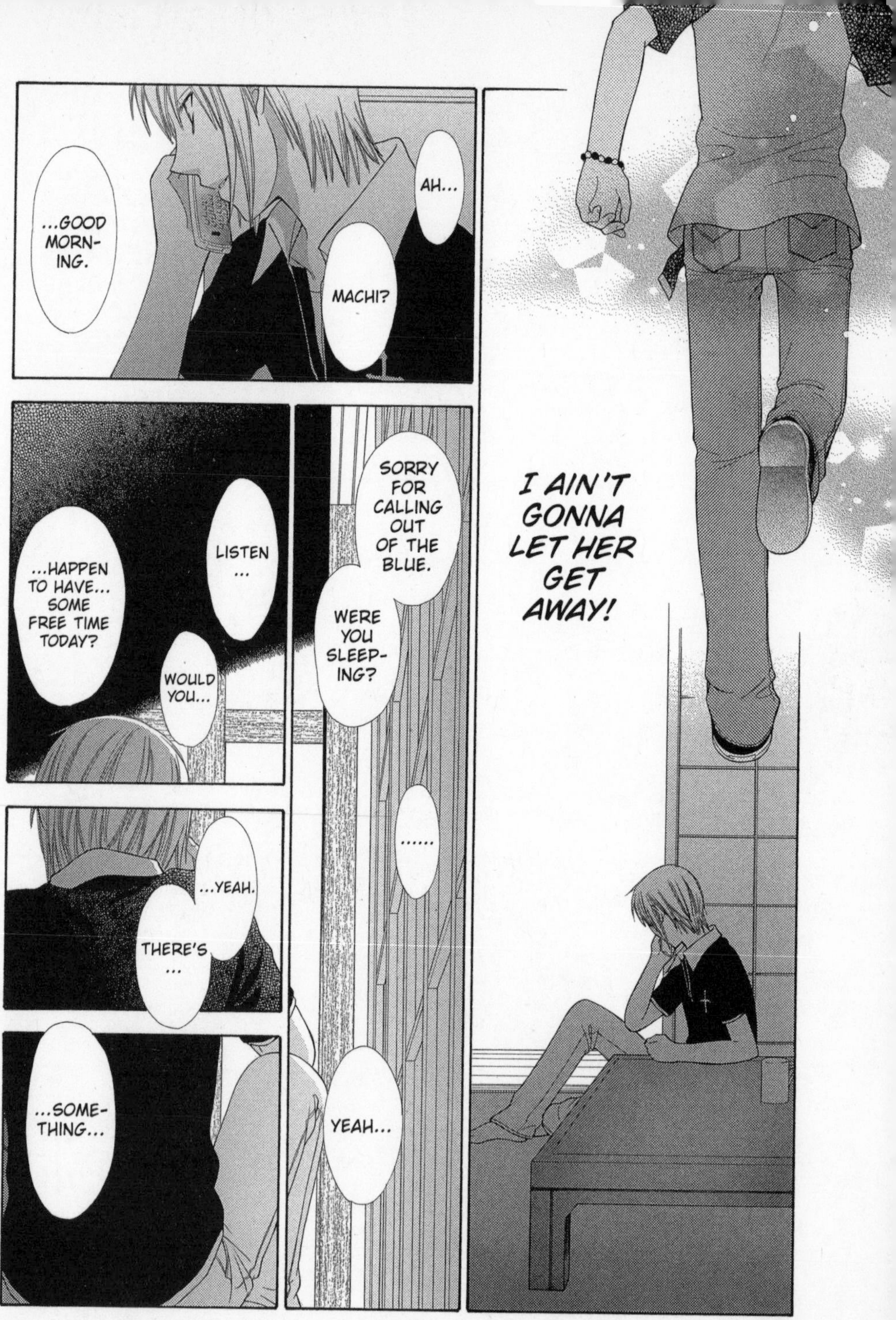
I AIN'T GONNA LET HER GET AWAY!
AH...
MACHI?
...GOOD MORNING.
SORRY FOR CALLING OUT OF THE BLUE.
WERE YOU SLEEPING?
......
YEAH...
LISTEN...
WOULD YOU...
...HAPPEN TO HAVE... SOME FREE TIME TODAY?
...YEAH.
THERE'S...
...SOMETHING...

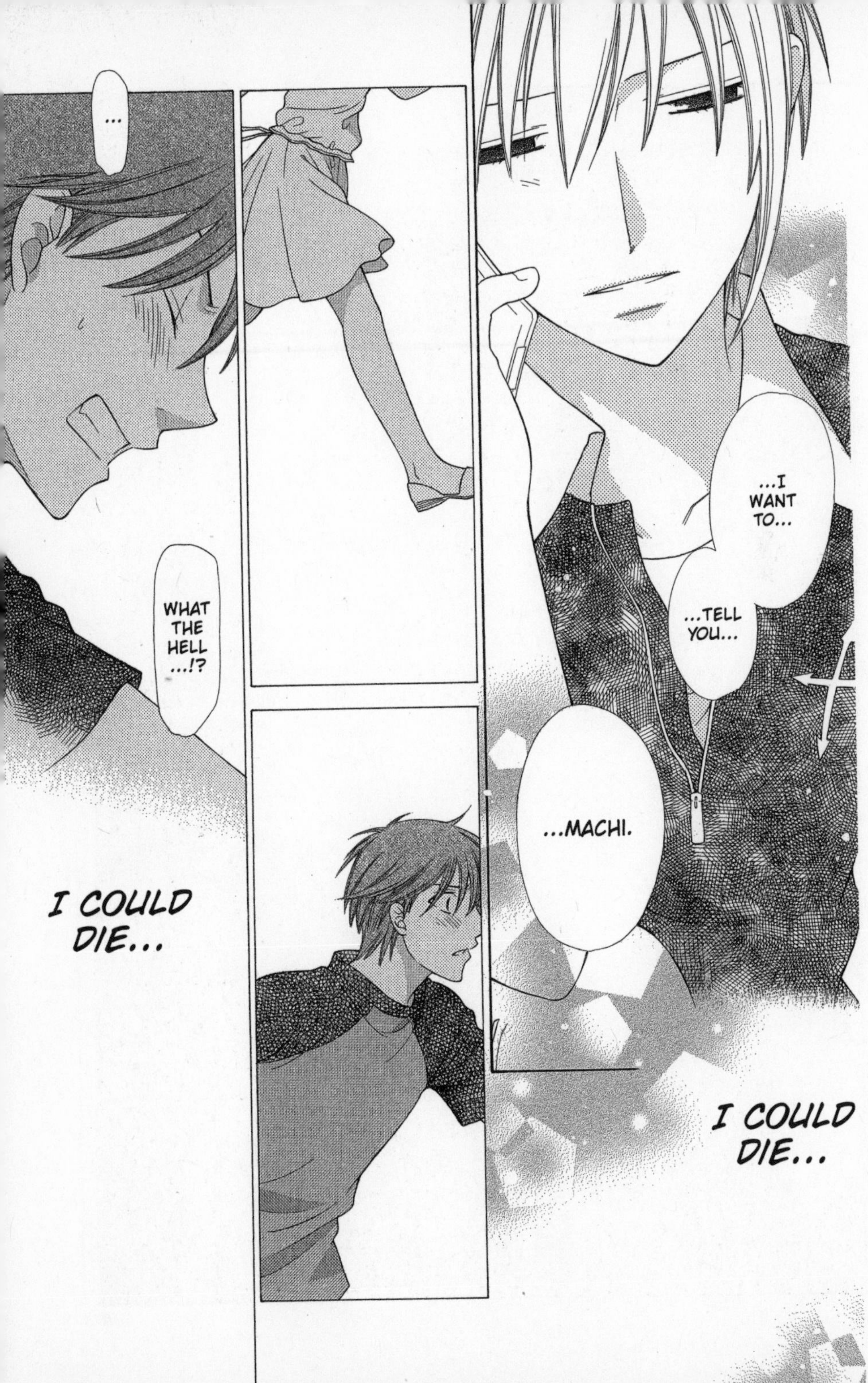
...I WANT TO...
...TELL YOU...
...MACHI.
I COULD DIE...
...
WHAT THE HELL ...!?
I COULD DIE...

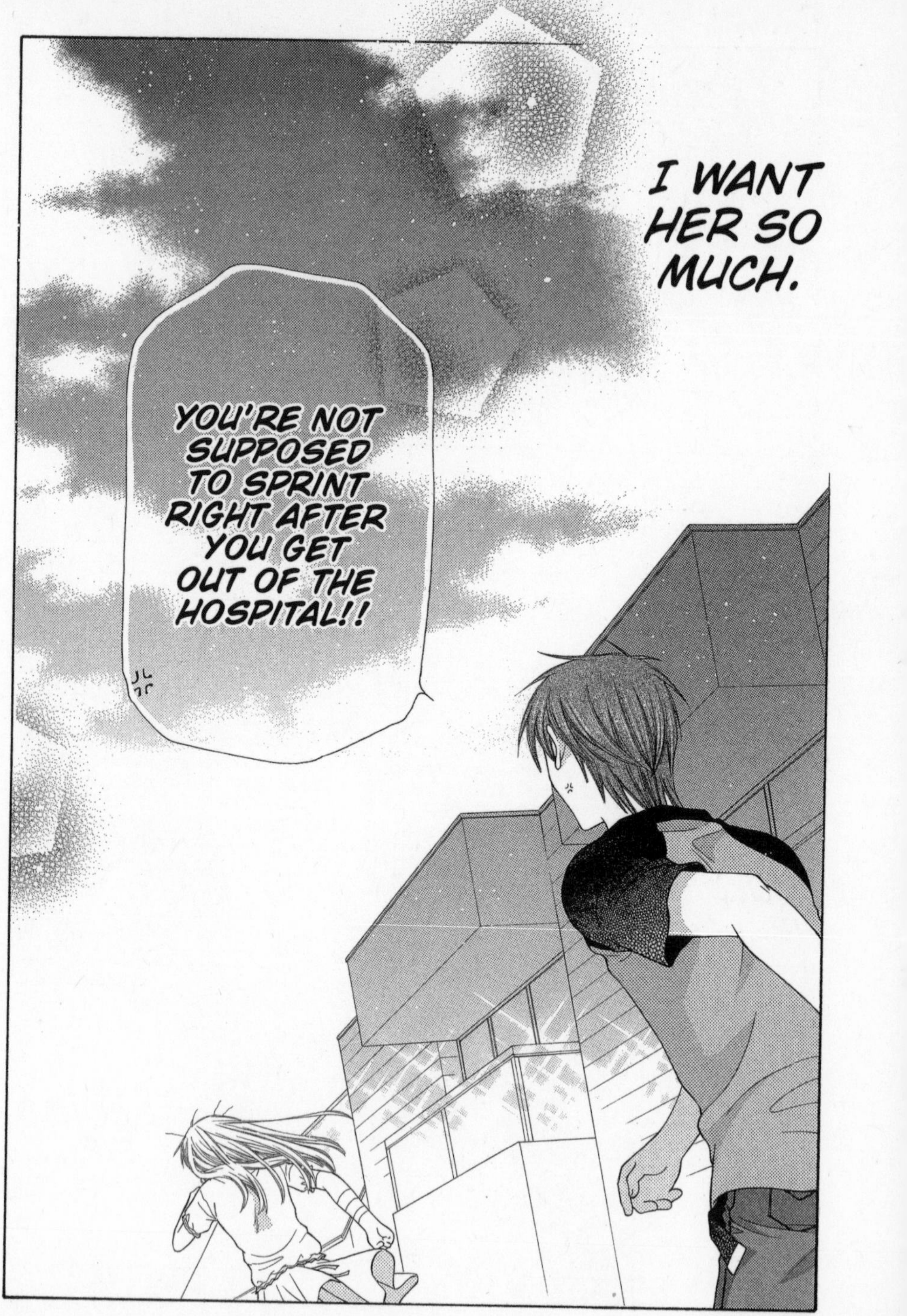
I WANT HER SO MUCH.
YOU'RE NOT SUPPOSED TO SPRINT RIGHT AFTER YOU GET OUT OF THE HOSPITAL!!

Chapter 129

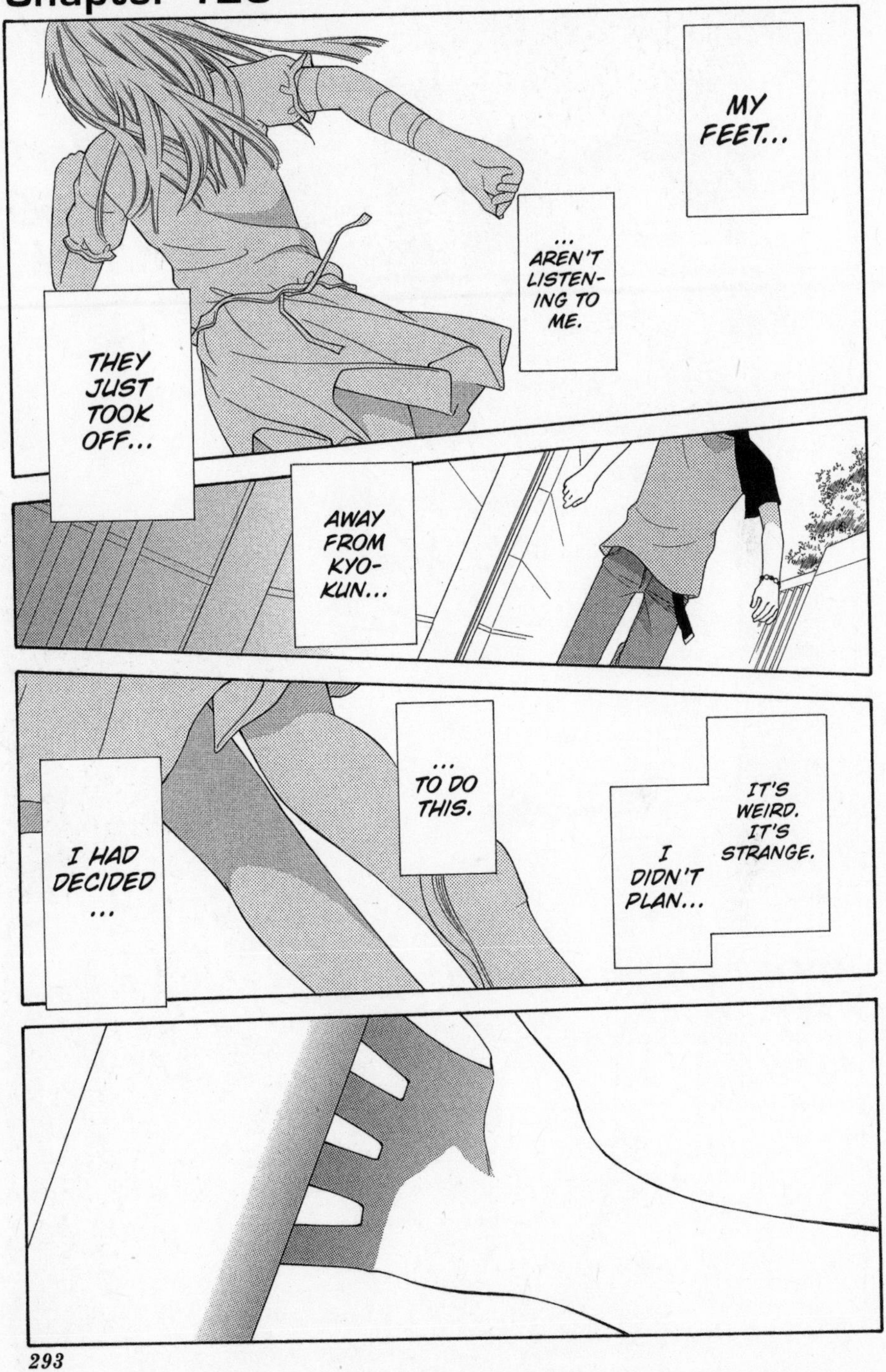
MY FEET...
... AREN'T LISTENING TO ME.
THEY JUST TOOK OFF...
AWAY FROM KYO-KUN...
IT'S WEIRD. IT'S STRANGE.
I DIDN'T PLAN...
... TO DO THIS.
I HAD DECIDED ...

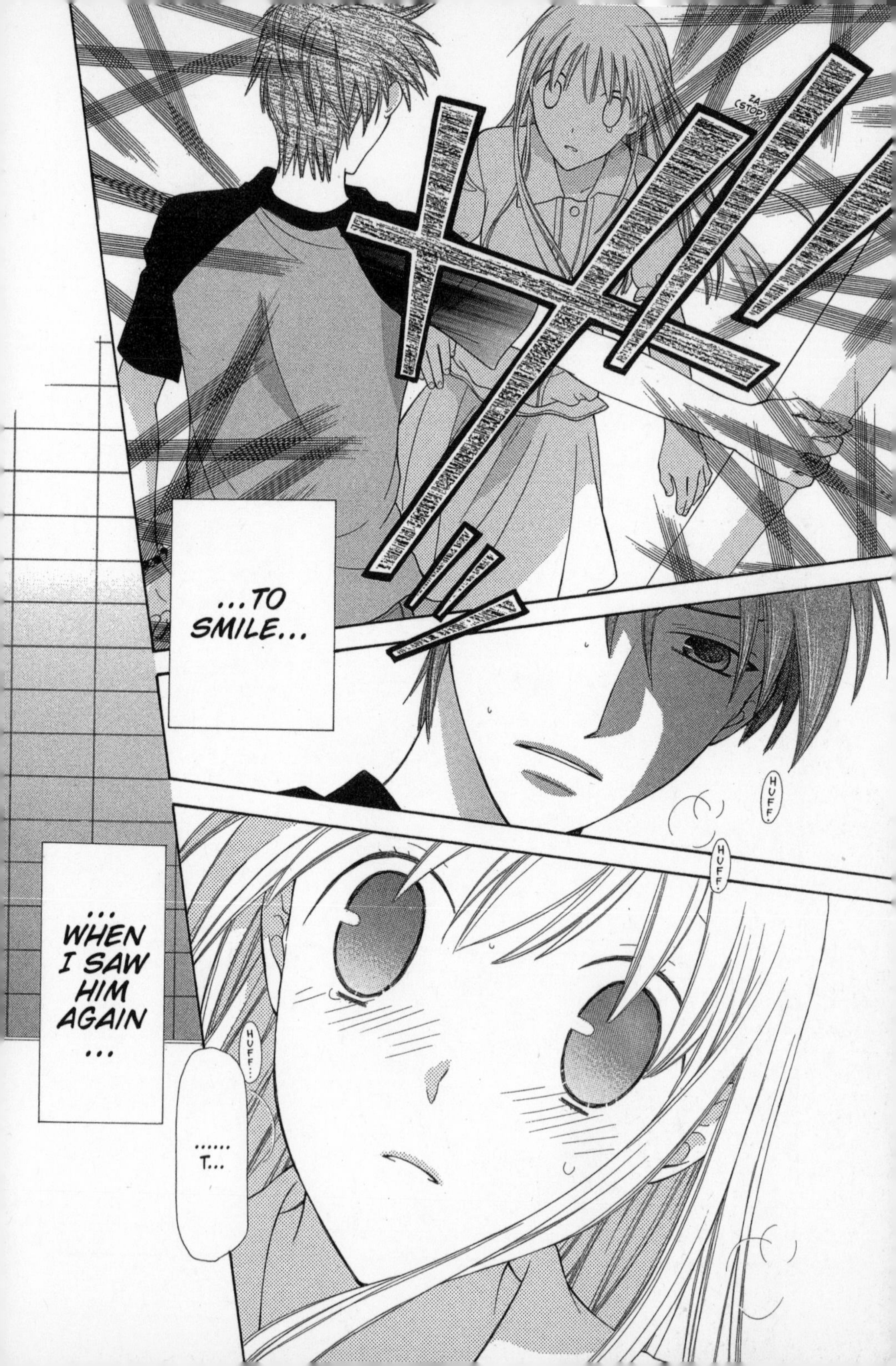
ZA (STOP)
...TO SMILE...
HUFF.
HUFF.
HUFF...
......T...
...WHEN I SAW HIM AGAIN...

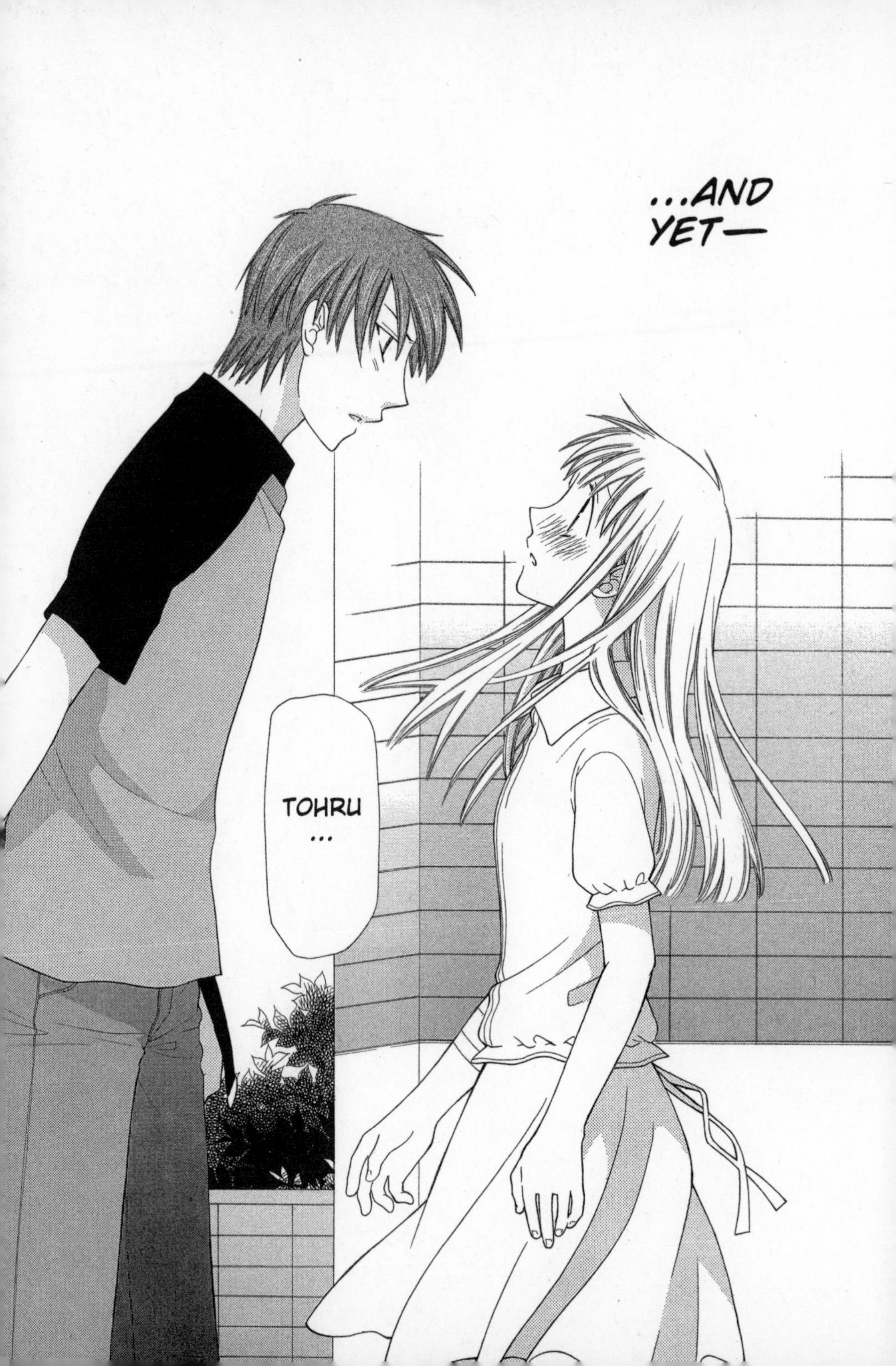
...AND YET—
TOHRU ...

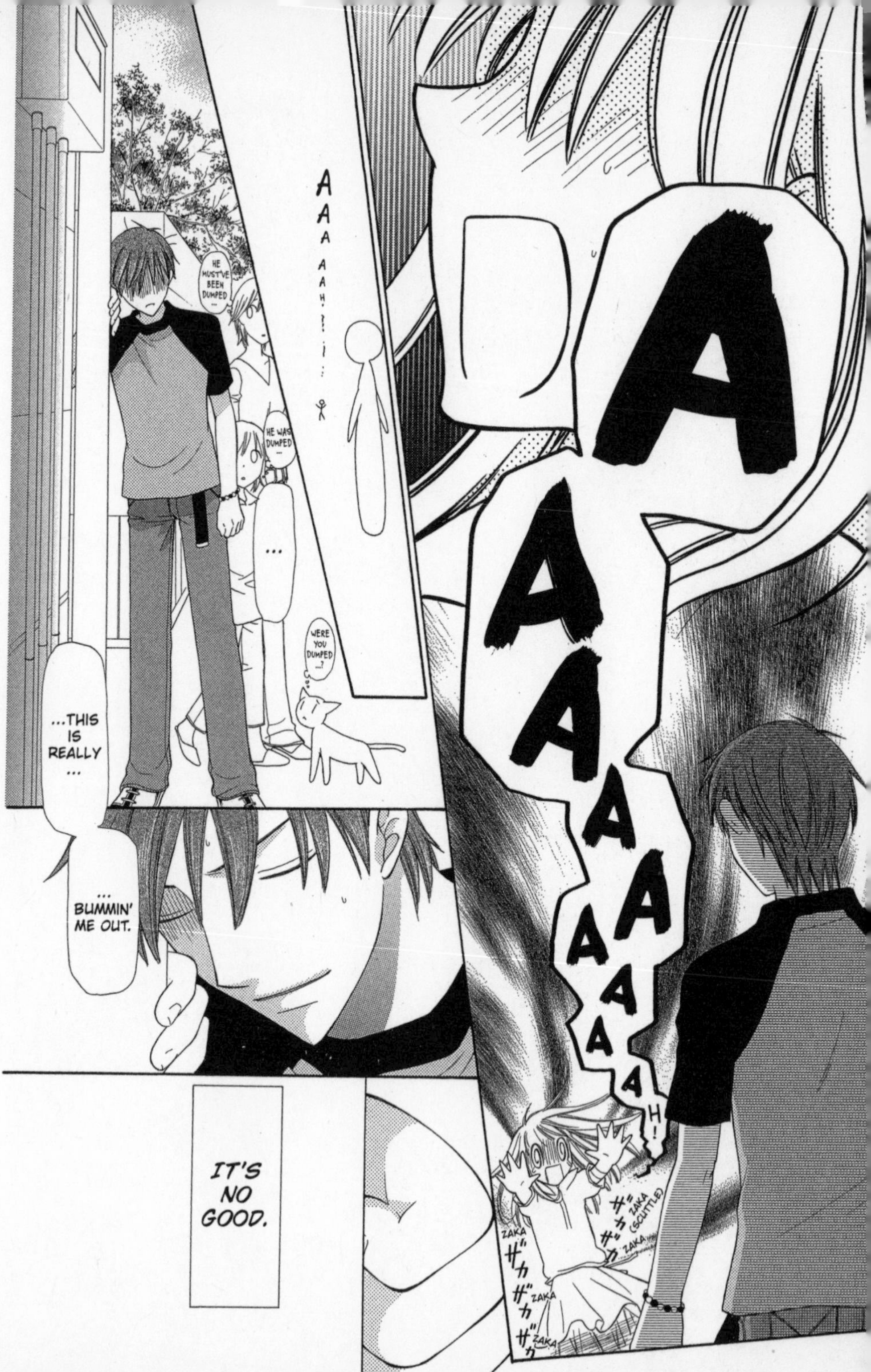

AAAAAAAAAAAAH!
ZAKA (SCUTTLE)
ZAKA
ZAKA
ZAKA
ZAKA
AAAAAH?!...
HE MUST'VE BEEN DUMPED...
HE WAS DUMPED...
...
WERE YOU DUMPED...?
...THIS IS REALLY...
...BUMMIN' ME OUT.
IT'S NO GOOD.

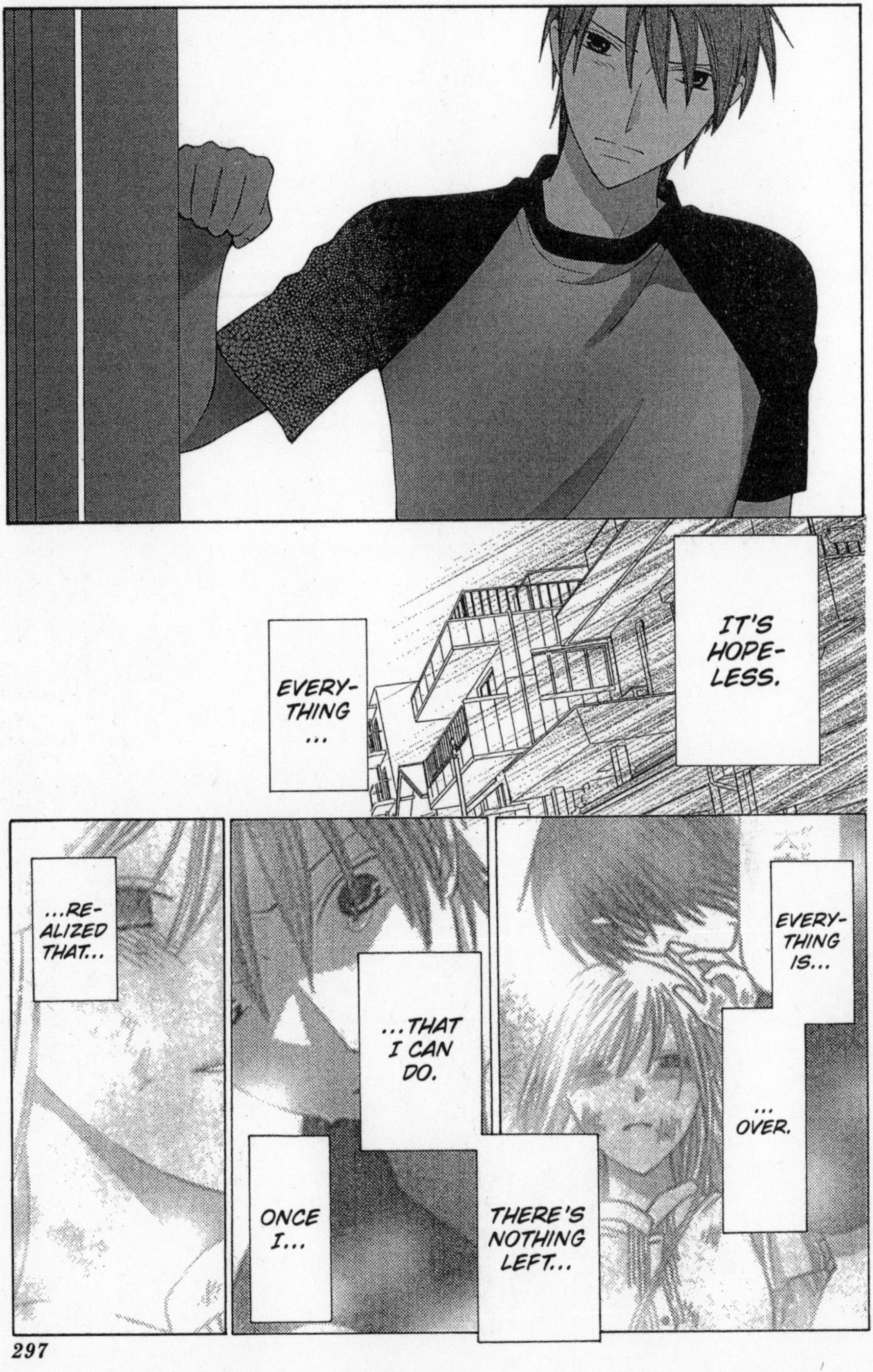
IT'S HOPE-LESS.
EVERY-THING ...
EVERY-THING IS...
... OVER.
THERE'S NOTHING LEFT...
...THAT I CAN DO.
ONCE I...
...RE-ALIZED THAT...

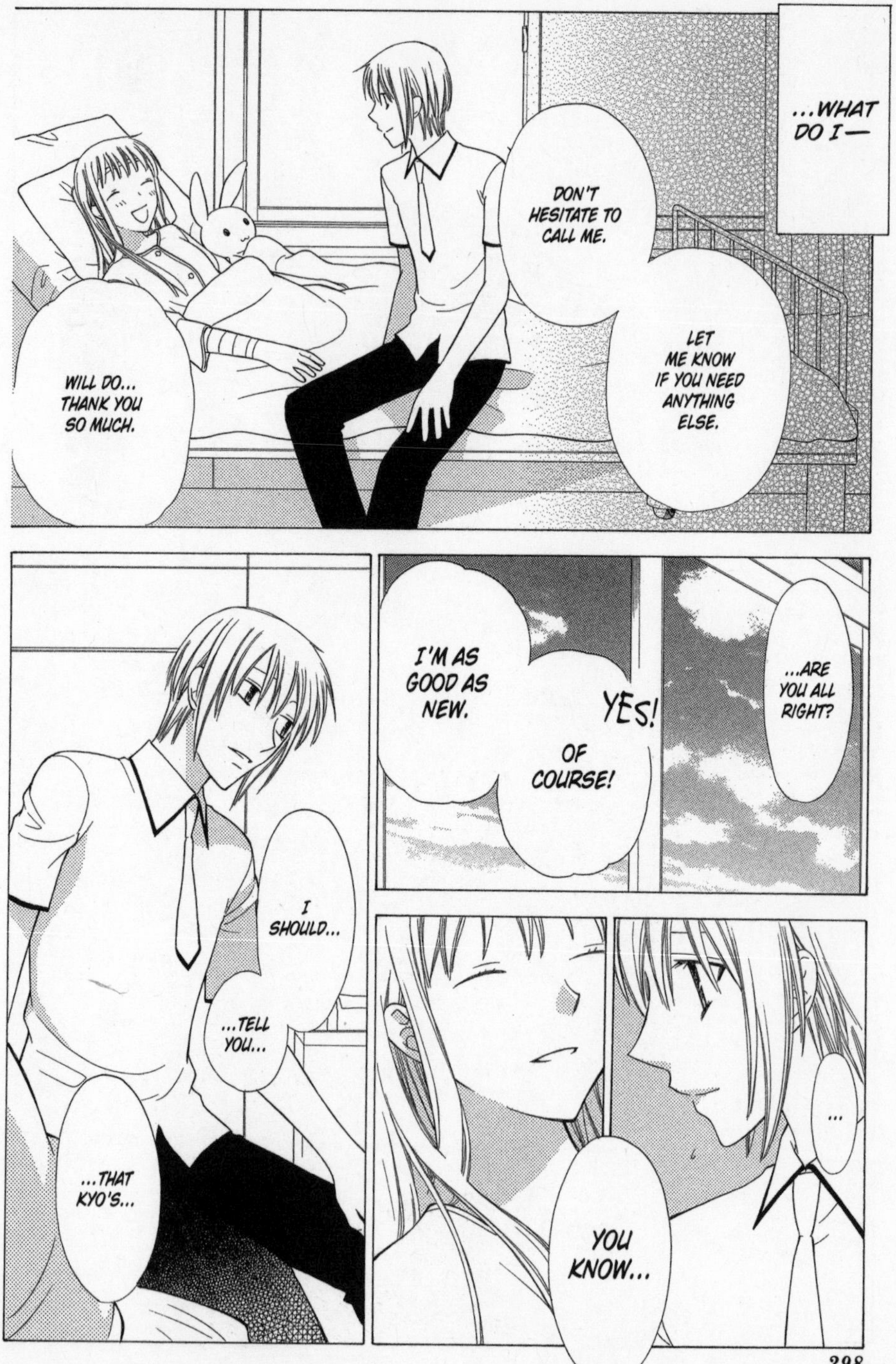
...WHAT DO I—
DON'T HESITATE TO CALL ME.
LET ME KNOW IF YOU NEED ANYTHING ELSE.
WILL DO... THANK YOU SO MUCH.
...ARE YOU ALL RIGHT?
YES! OF COURSE! I'M AS GOOD AS NEW.
...
YOU KNOW...
I SHOULD...
...TELL YOU...
...THAT KYO'S...

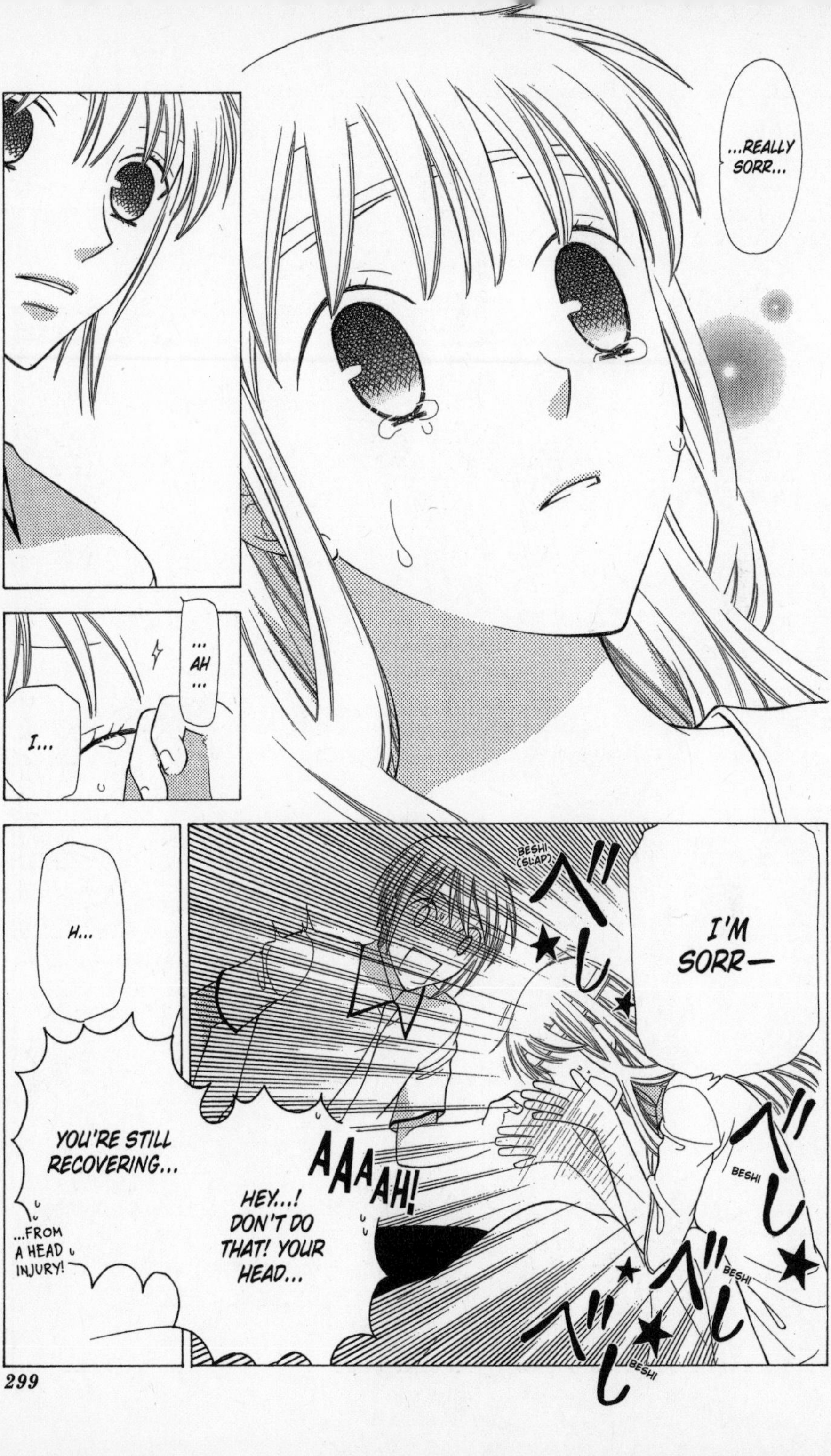
...REALLY SORR...
...AH...
I...
I'M SORR—
BESHI (SLAP)
BESHI
BESHI
BESHI
AAAAH!
HEY...! DON'T DO THAT! YOUR HEAD...
H...
YOU'RE STILL RECOVERING...
...FROM A HEAD INJURY!

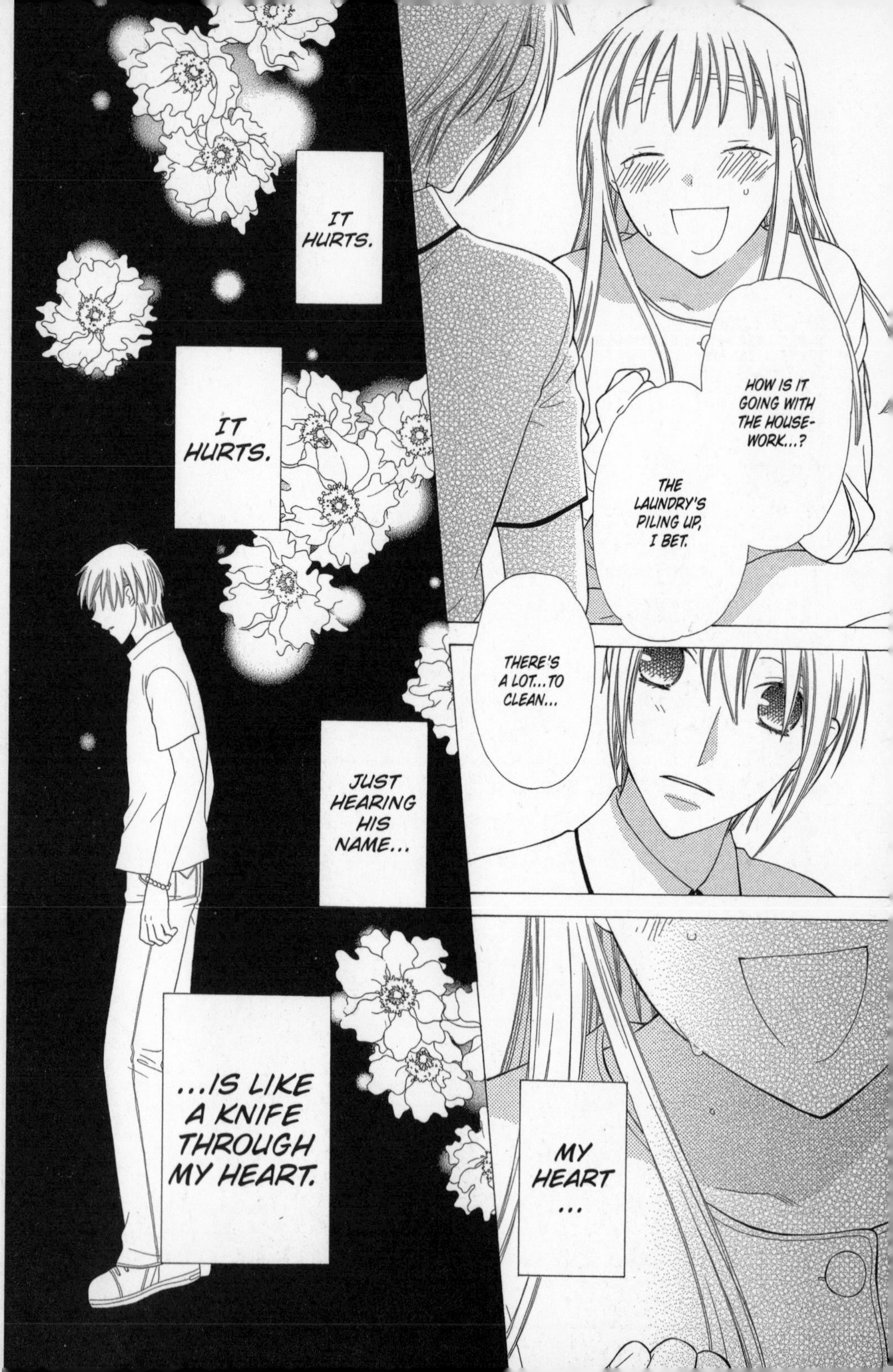
HOW IS IT GOING WITH THE HOUSE-WORK...?
THE LAUNDRY'S PILING UP, I BET.
THERE'S A LOT...TO CLEAN...
MY HEART ...
IT HURTS.
IT HURTS.
JUST HEARING HIS NAME...
...IS LIKE A KNIFE THROUGH MY HEART.

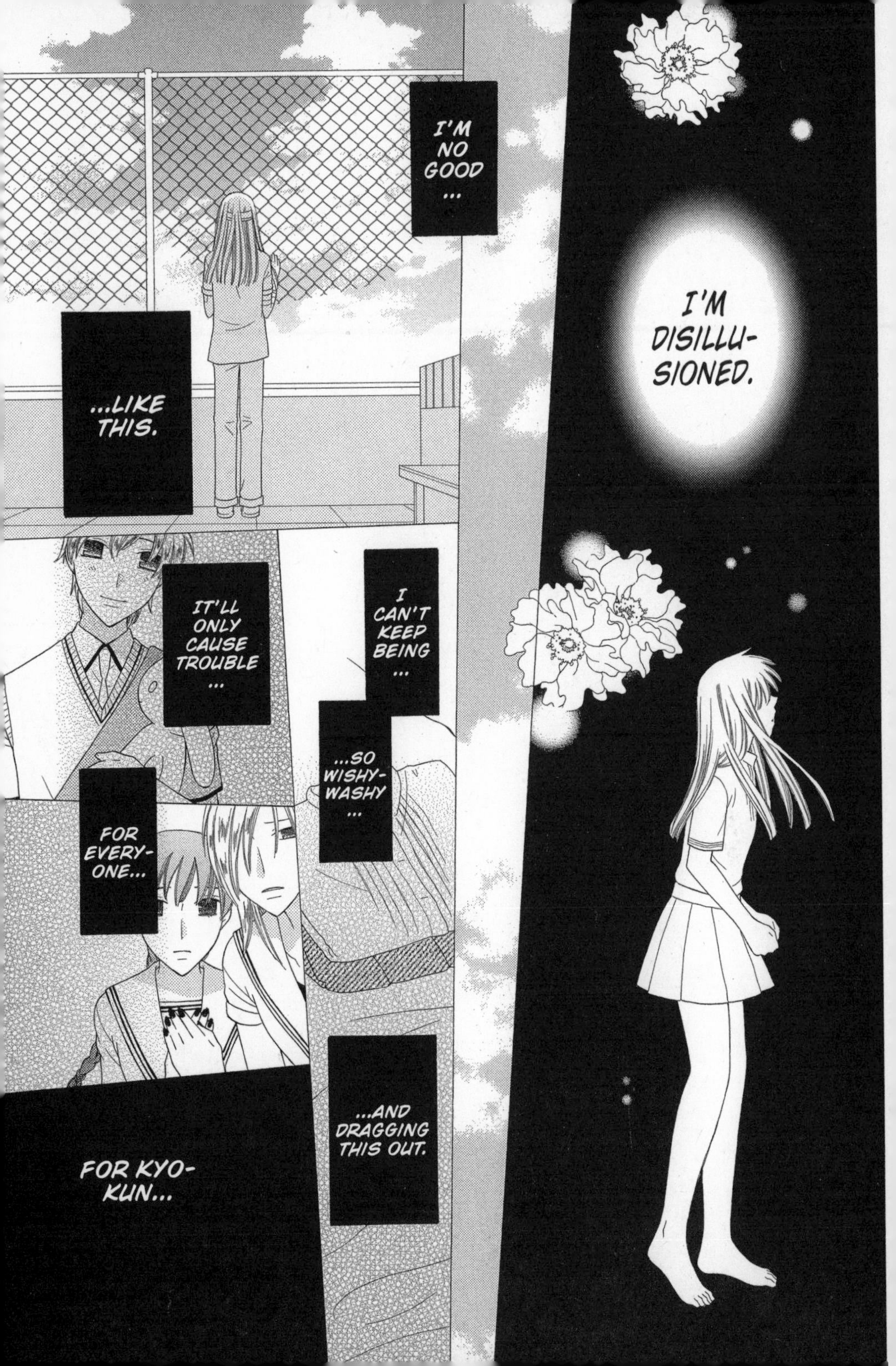
I'M DISILLUSIONED.
I'M NO GOOD...
...LIKE THIS.
I CAN'T KEEP BEING...
...SO WISHY-WASHY...
...AND DRAGGING THIS OUT.
IT'LL ONLY CAUSE TROUBLE...
FOR EVERYONE...
FOR KYO-KUN...

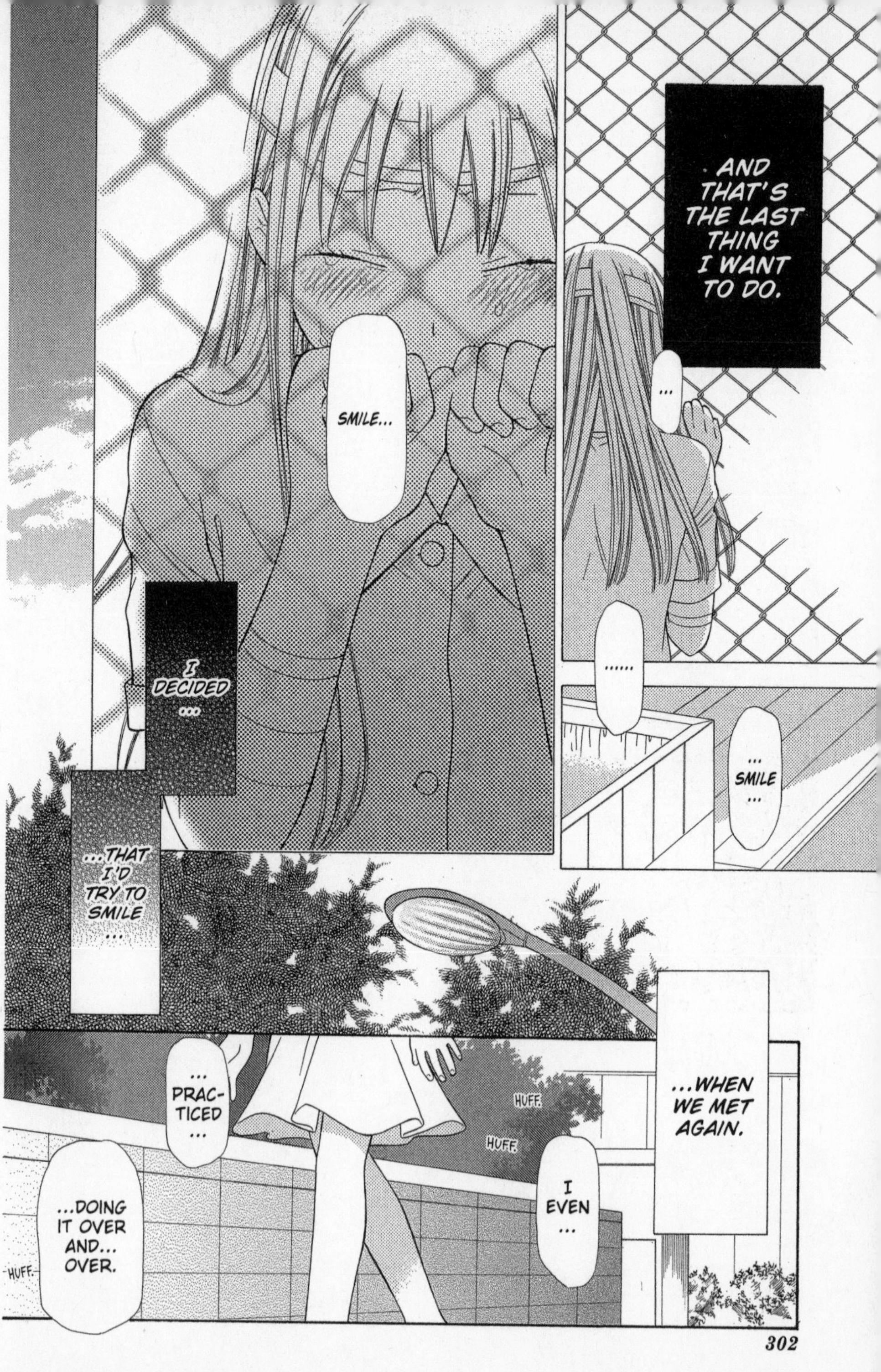
AND THAT'S THE LAST THING I WANT TO DO.
...
......
...SMILE...
SMILE...
I DECIDED...
...THAT I'D TRY TO SMILE...
...WHEN WE MET AGAIN.
I EVEN...
HUFF.
HUFF.
...PRACTICED...
...DOING IT OVER AND... OVER.
HUFF.

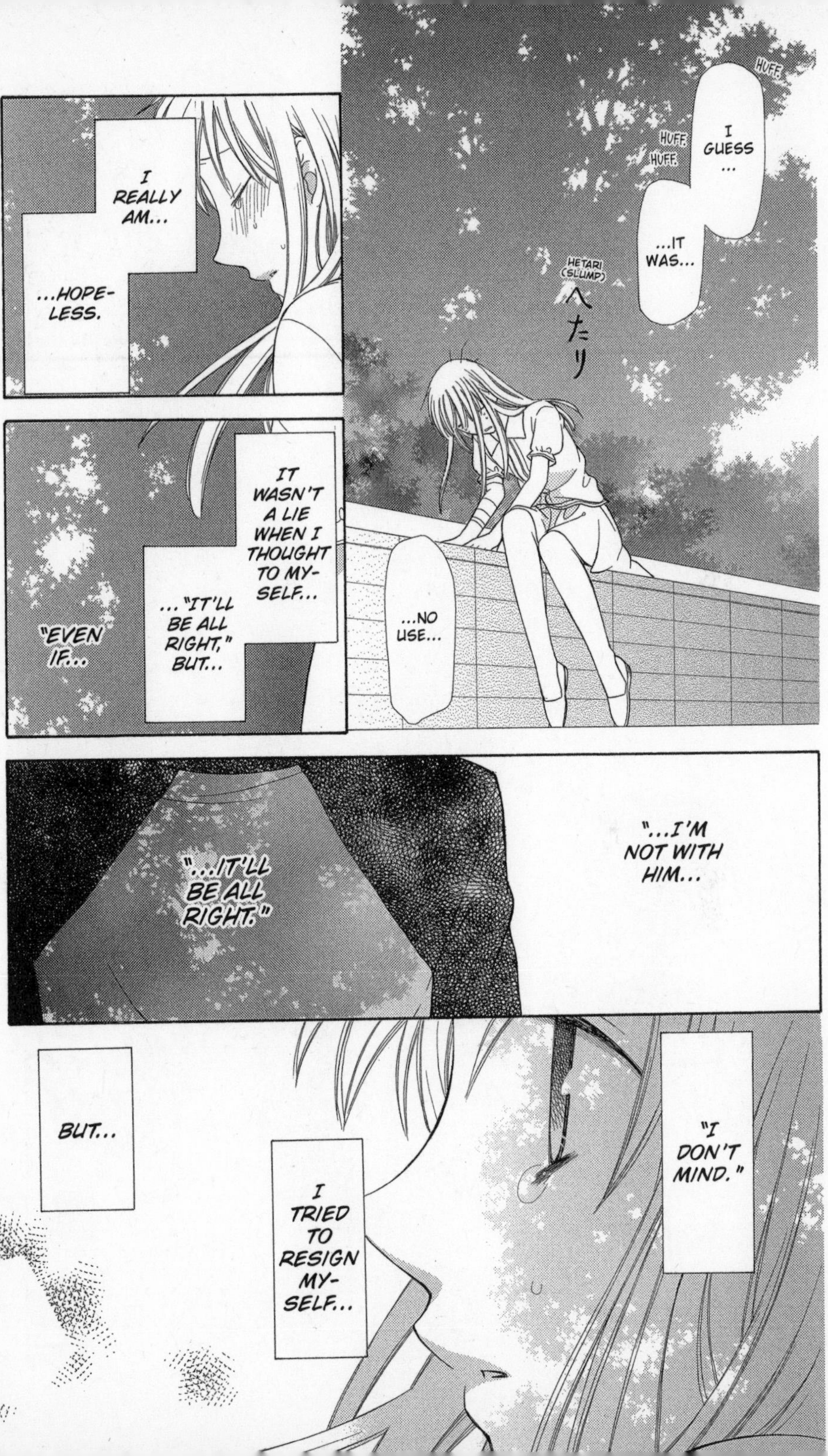
HUFF
I GUESS...
HUFF
HUFF
...IT WAS...
HETARI (SLUMP)
へたり
...NO USE...
I REALLY AM...
...HOPE-LESS.
IT WASN'T A LIE WHEN I THOUGHT TO MY-SELF...
..."IT'LL BE ALL RIGHT," BUT...
"EVEN IF...
"...I'M NOT WITH HIM...
"...IT'LL BE ALL RIGHT."
"I DON'T MIND."
I TRIED TO RESIGN MY-SELF...
BUT...

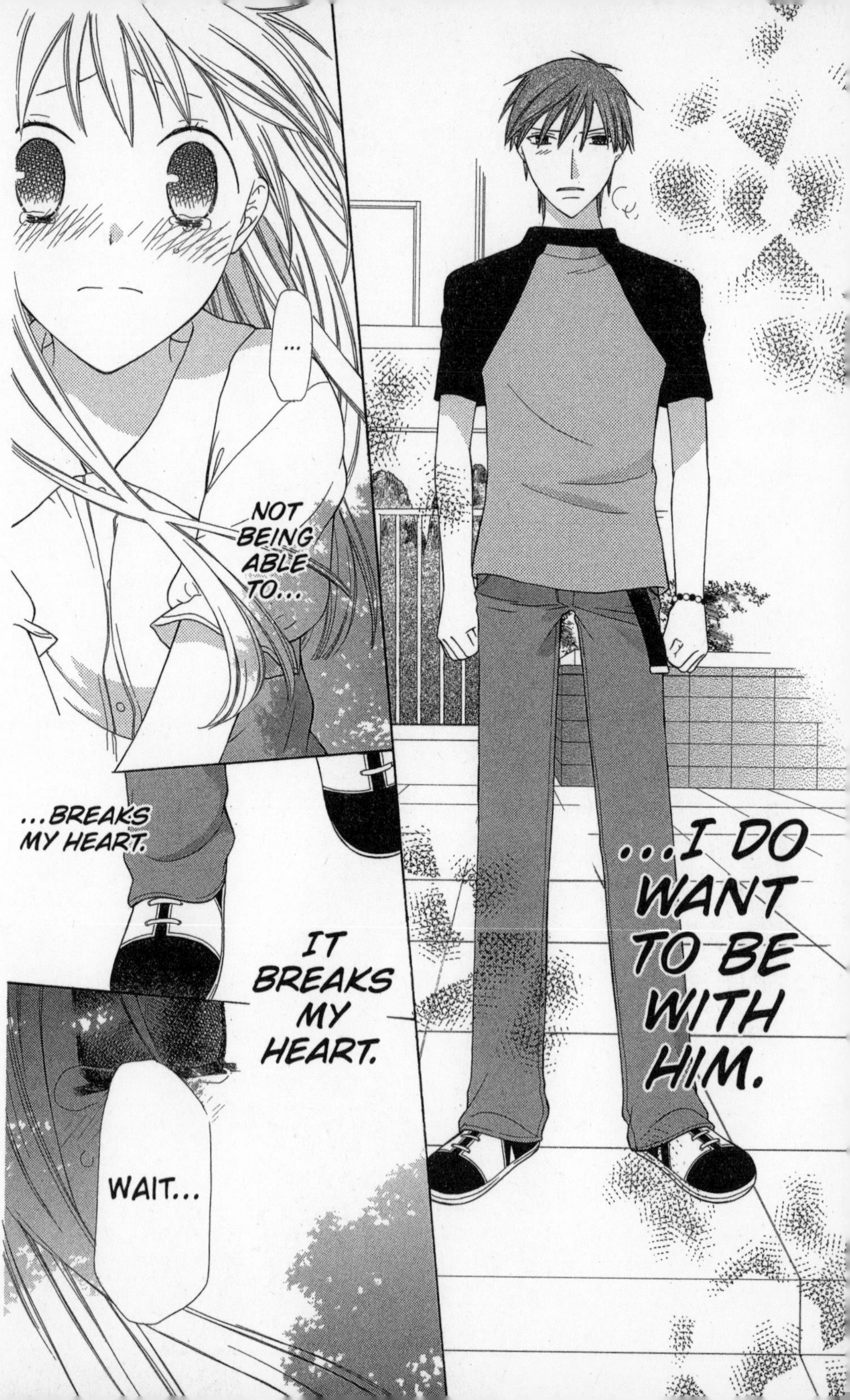
...I DO WANT TO BE WITH HIM.
...
NOT BEING ABLE TO...
...BREAKS MY HEART.
IT BREAKS MY HEART.
WAIT...

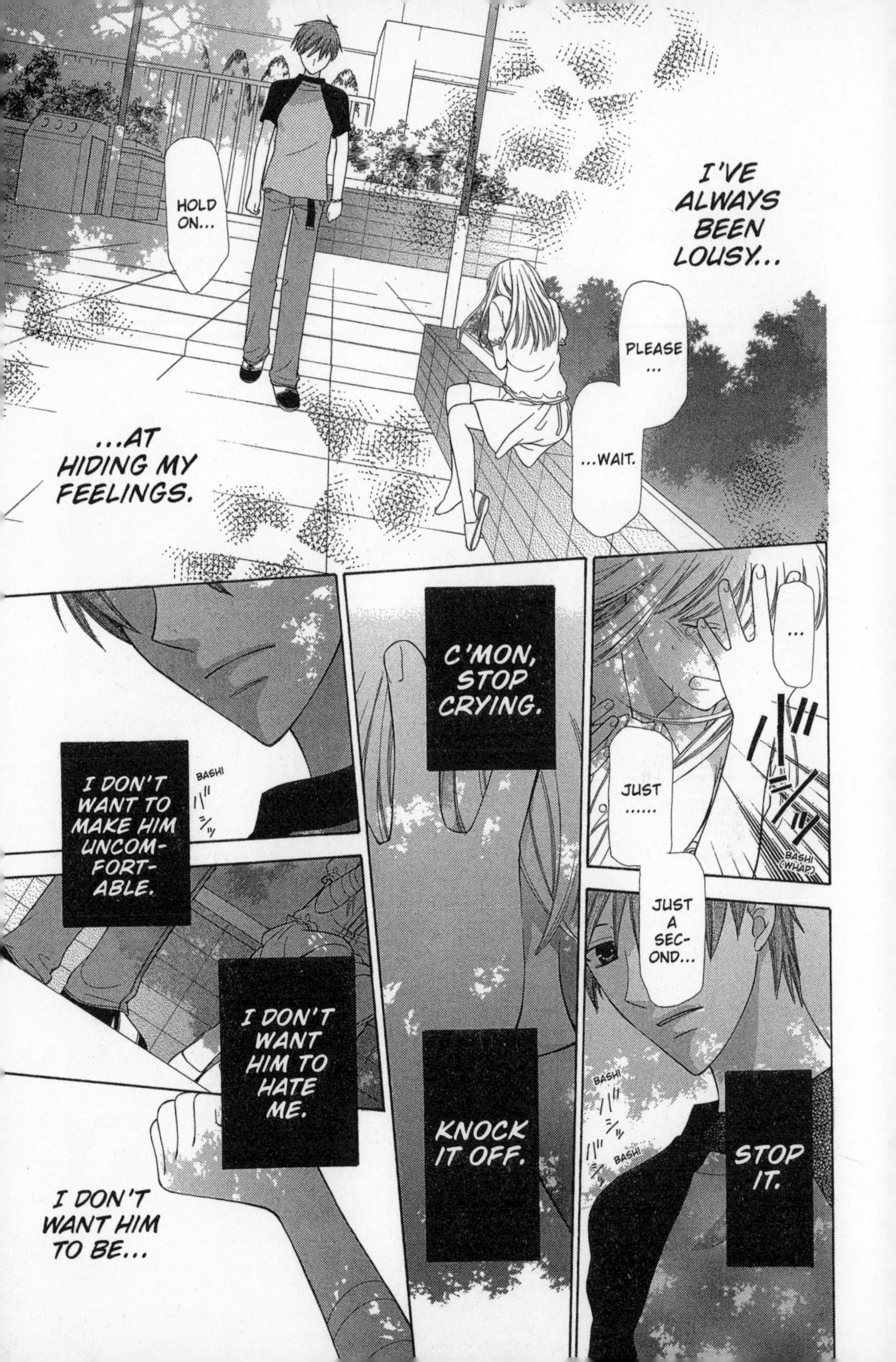
I'VE ALWAYS BEEN LOUSY...
PLEASE ...
...WAIT.
HOLD ON...
...AT HIDING MY FEELINGS.
...
JUST ......
BASHI (WHAP)
JUST A SEC- OND...
BASHI
BASHI
STOP IT.
C'MON, STOP CRYING.
KNOCK IT OFF.
I DON'T WANT TO MAKE HIM UNCOM- FORT- ABLE.
BASHI
I DON'T WANT HIM TO HATE ME.
I DON'T WANT HIM TO BE...

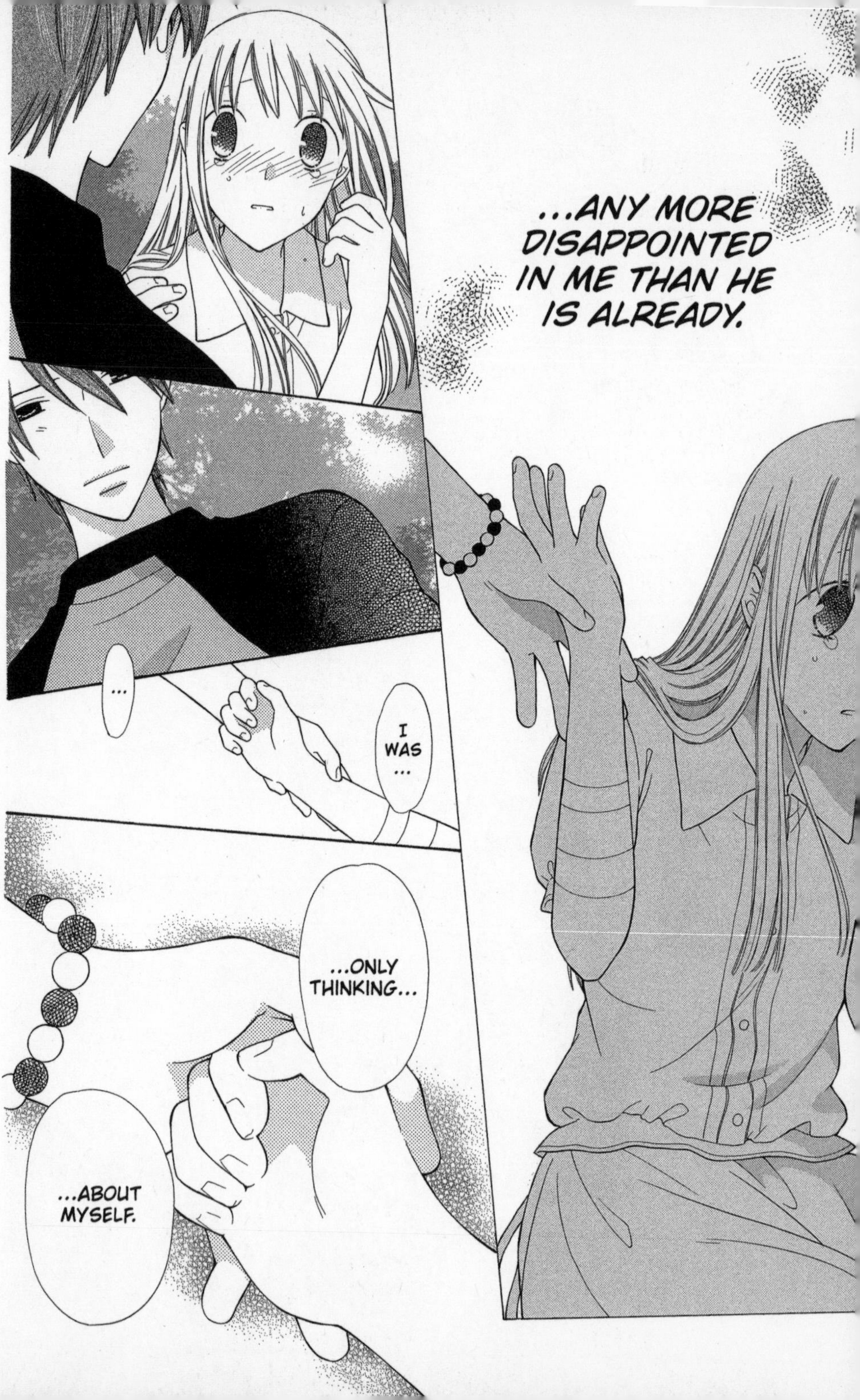
...ANY MORE DISAPPOINTED IN ME THAN HE IS ALREADY.
I WAS ...
...
...ONLY THINKING...
...ABOUT MYSELF.

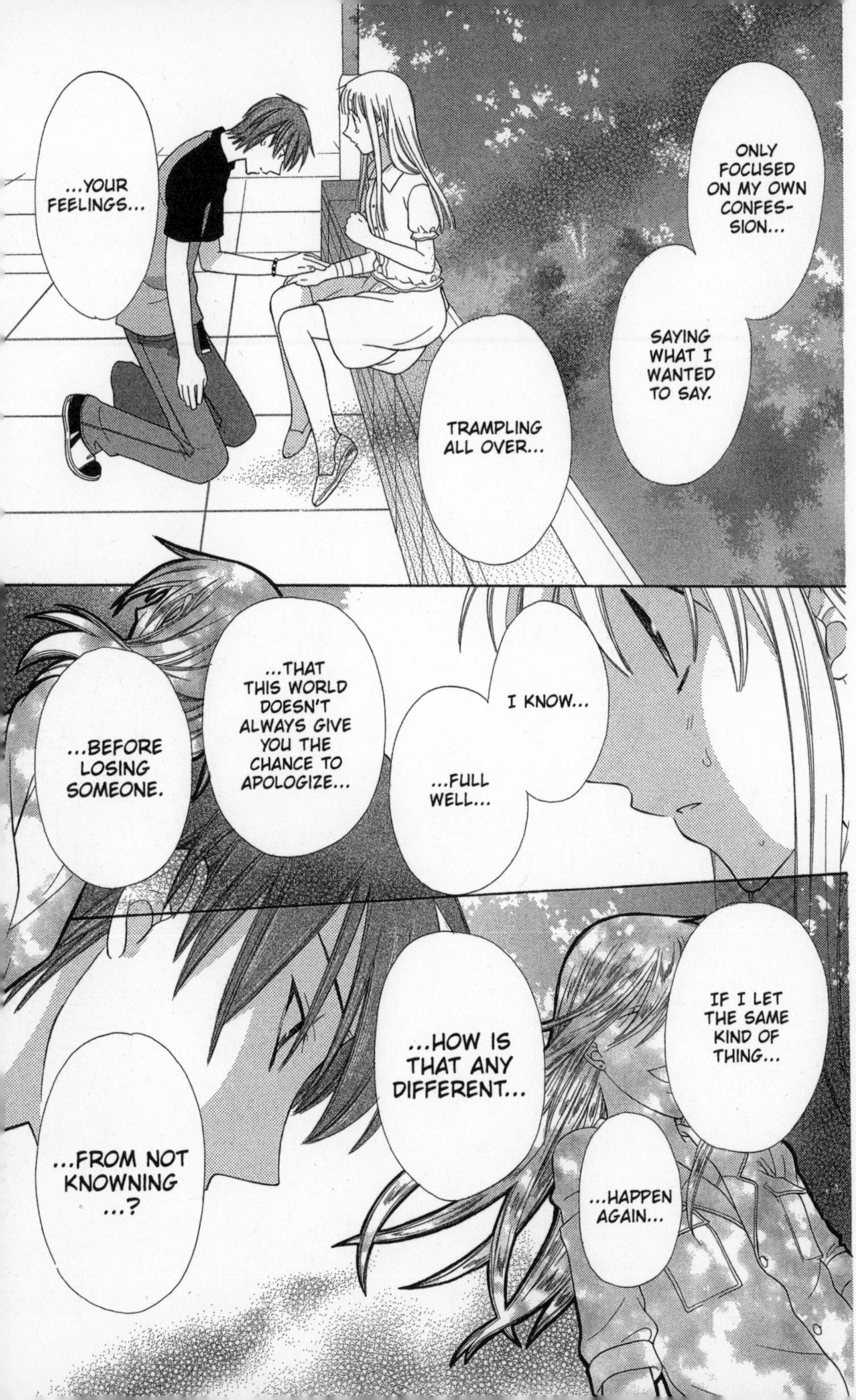
ONLY FOCUSED ON MY OWN CONFES-SION...
SAYING WHAT I WANTED TO SAY.
TRAMPLING ALL OVER...
...YOUR FEELINGS...
I KNOW...
...FULL WELL...
...THAT THIS WORLD DOESN'T ALWAYS GIVE YOU THE CHANCE TO APOLOGIZE...
...BEFORE LOSING SOMEONE.
IF I LET THE SAME KIND OF THING...
...HAPPEN AGAIN...
...HOW IS THAT ANY DIFFERENT...
...FROM NOT KNOWNING ...?

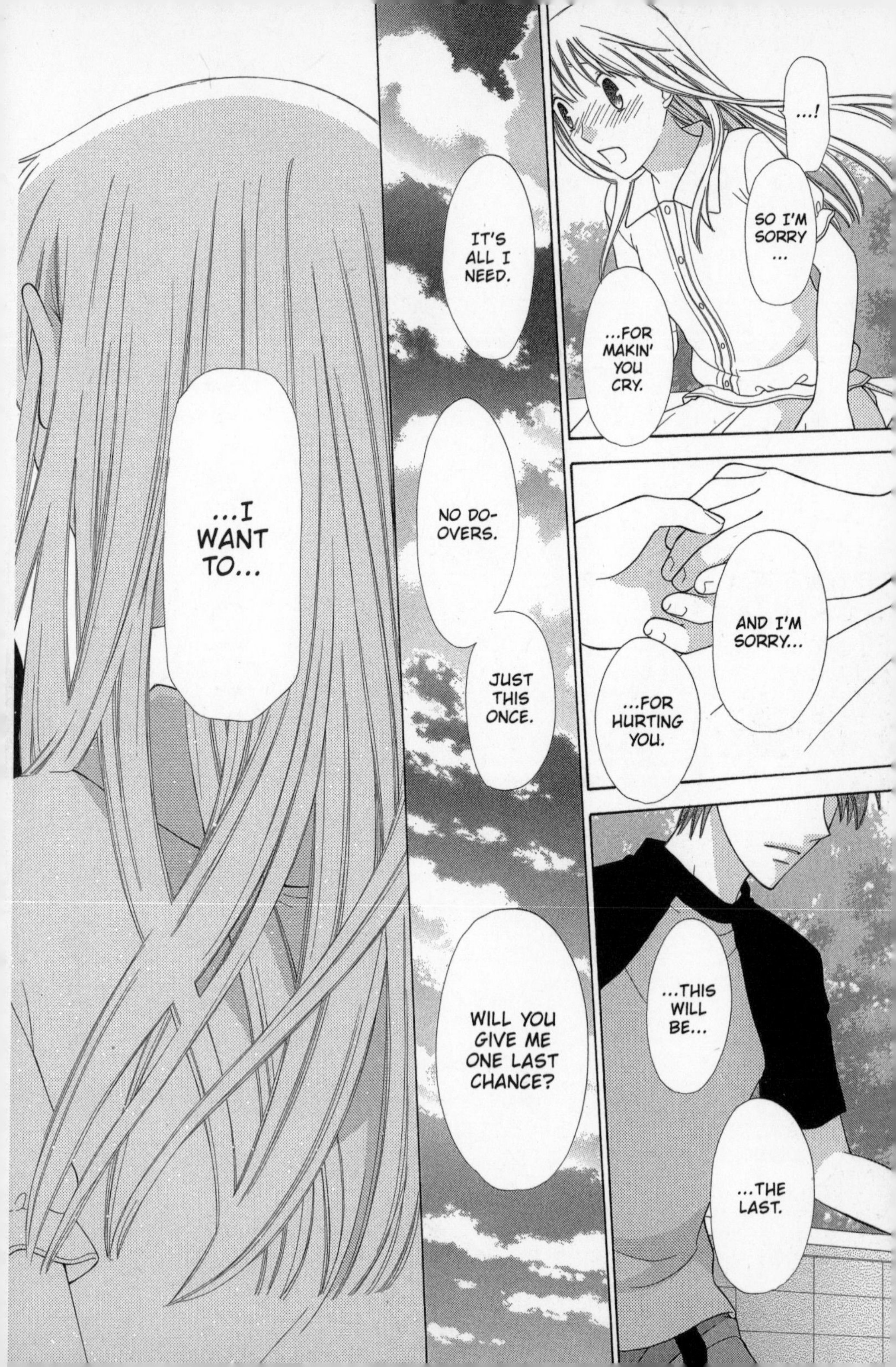
...!
SO I'M SORRY...
...FOR MAKIN' YOU CRY.
AND I'M SORRY...
...FOR HURTING YOU.
...THIS WILL BE...
...THE LAST.
IT'S ALL I NEED.
NO DO-OVERS.
JUST THIS ONCE.
WILL YOU GIVE ME ONE LAST CHANCE?
...I WANT TO...

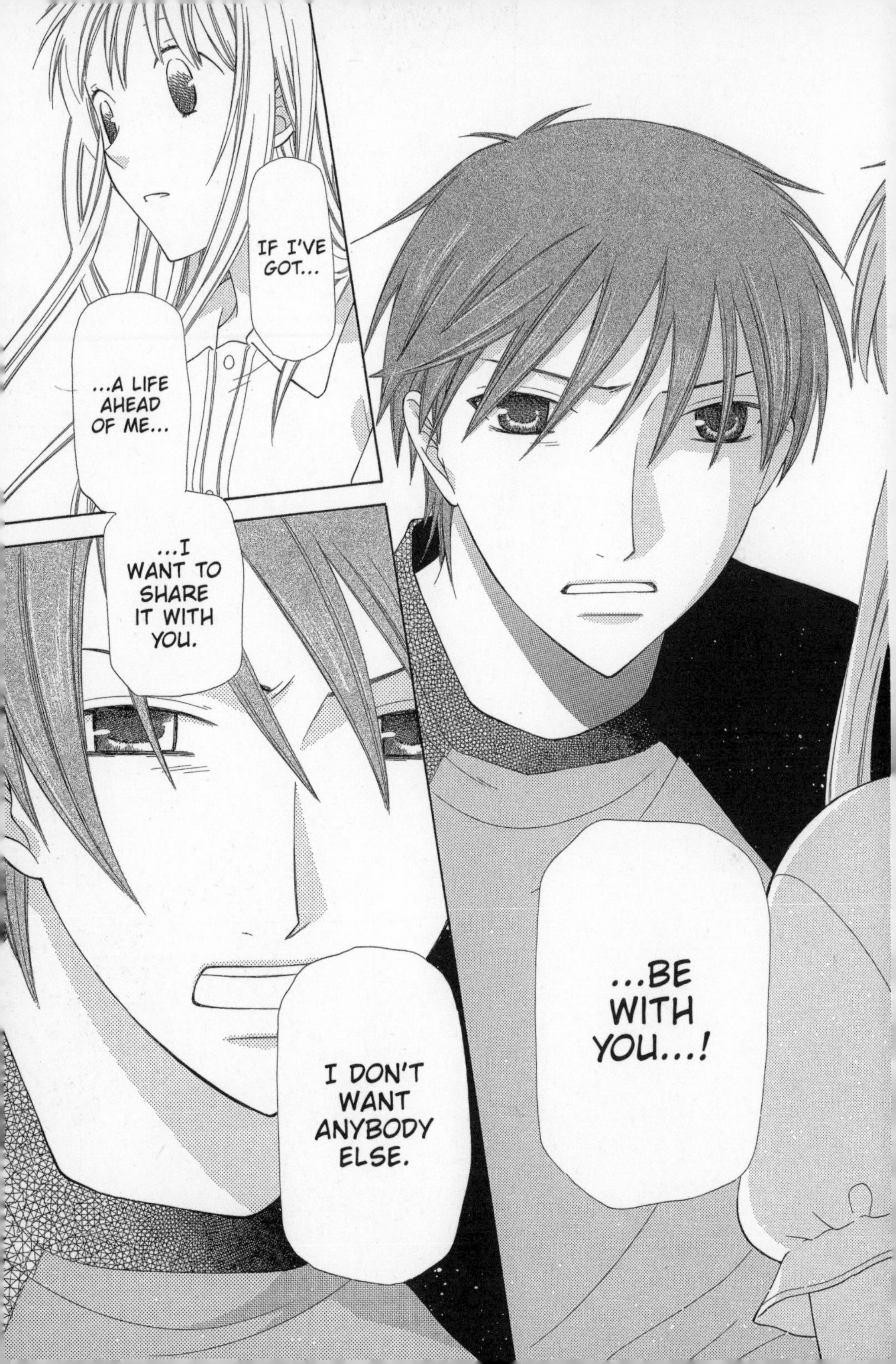
IF I'VE GOT...
...A LIFE AHEAD OF ME...
...I WANT TO SHARE IT WITH YOU.
...BE WITH YOU...!
I DON'T WANT ANYBODY ELSE.

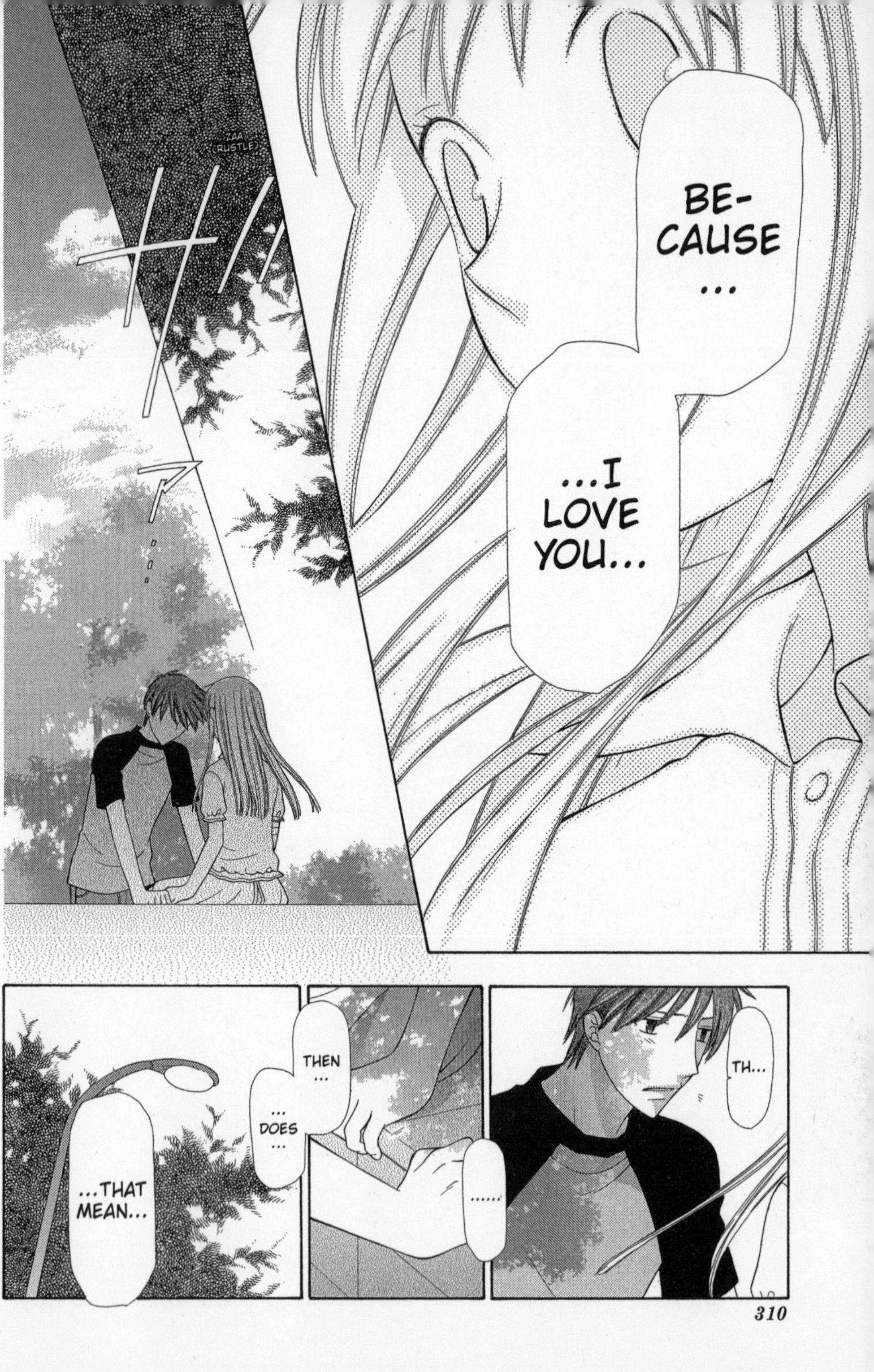
BE-CAUSE...
...I LOVE YOU...
ZAA (RUSTLE)
TH...
......
THEN...
...DOES...
...THAT MEAN...

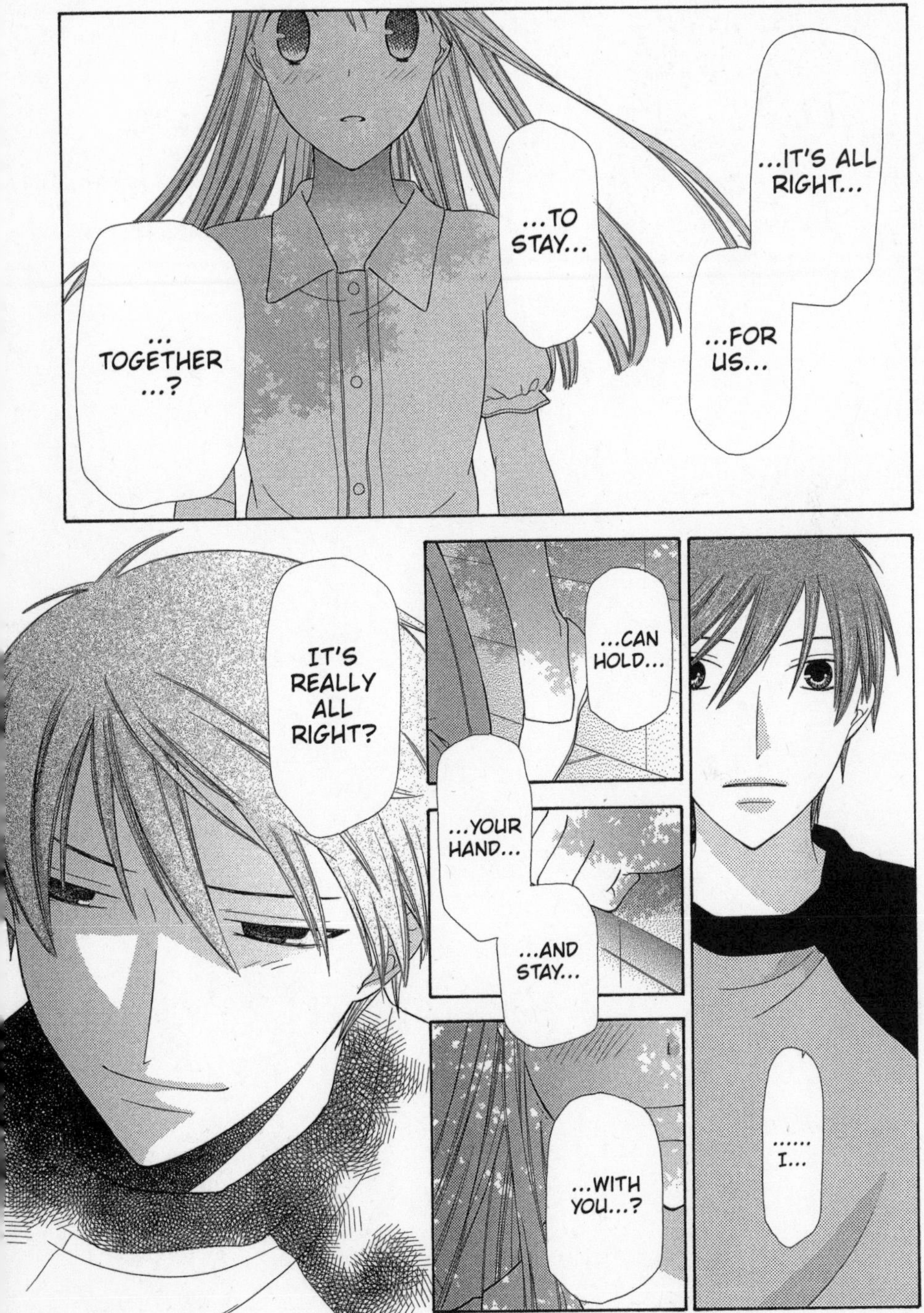
...IT'S ALL RIGHT...
...FOR US...
...TO STAY...
... TOGETHER ...?
...... I...
...CAN HOLD...
...YOUR HAND...
...AND STAY...
...WITH YOU...?
IT'S REALLY ALL RIGHT?

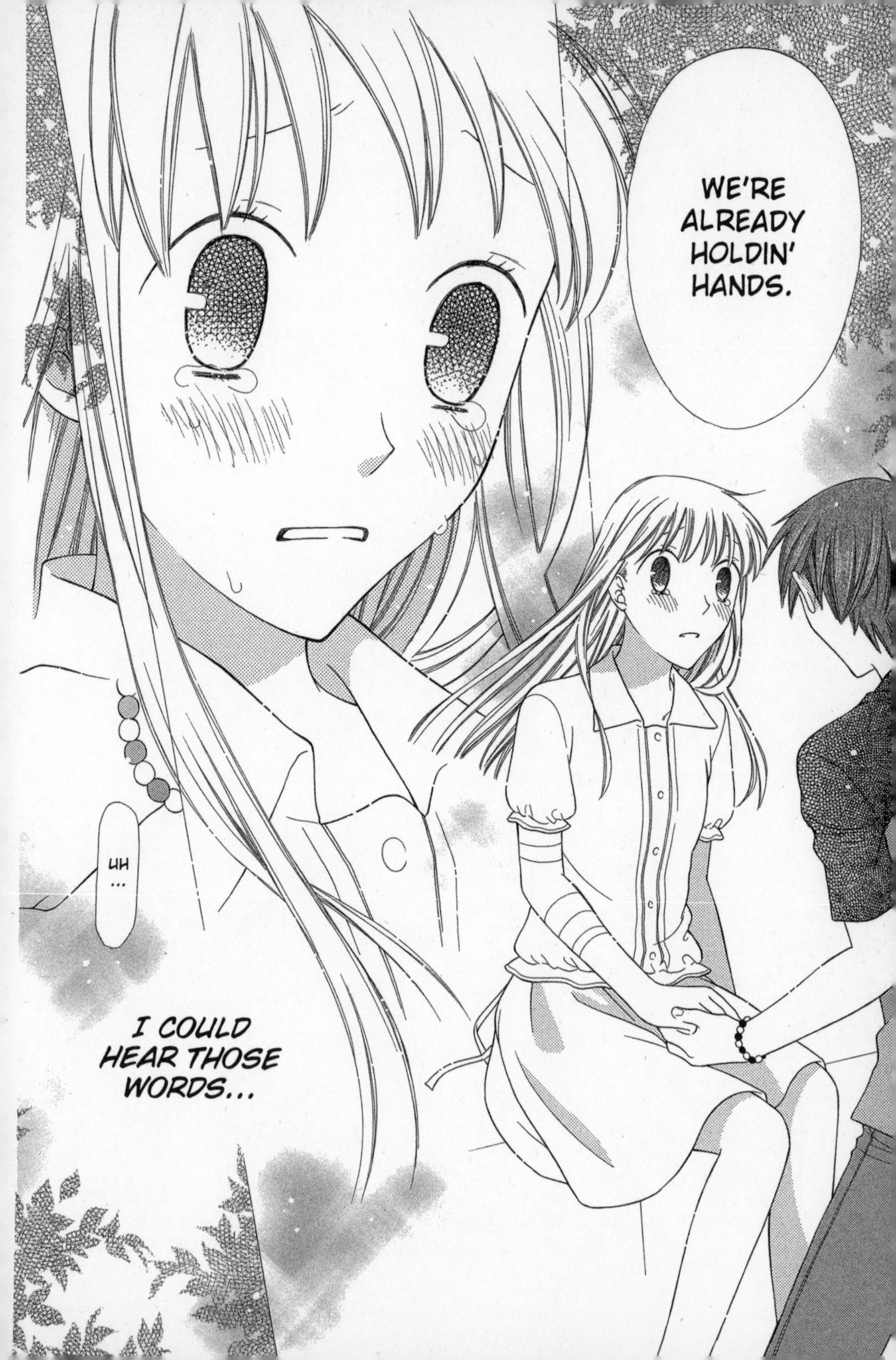
WE'RE ALREADY HOLDIN' HANDS.
UH ...
I COULD HEAR THOSE WORDS...

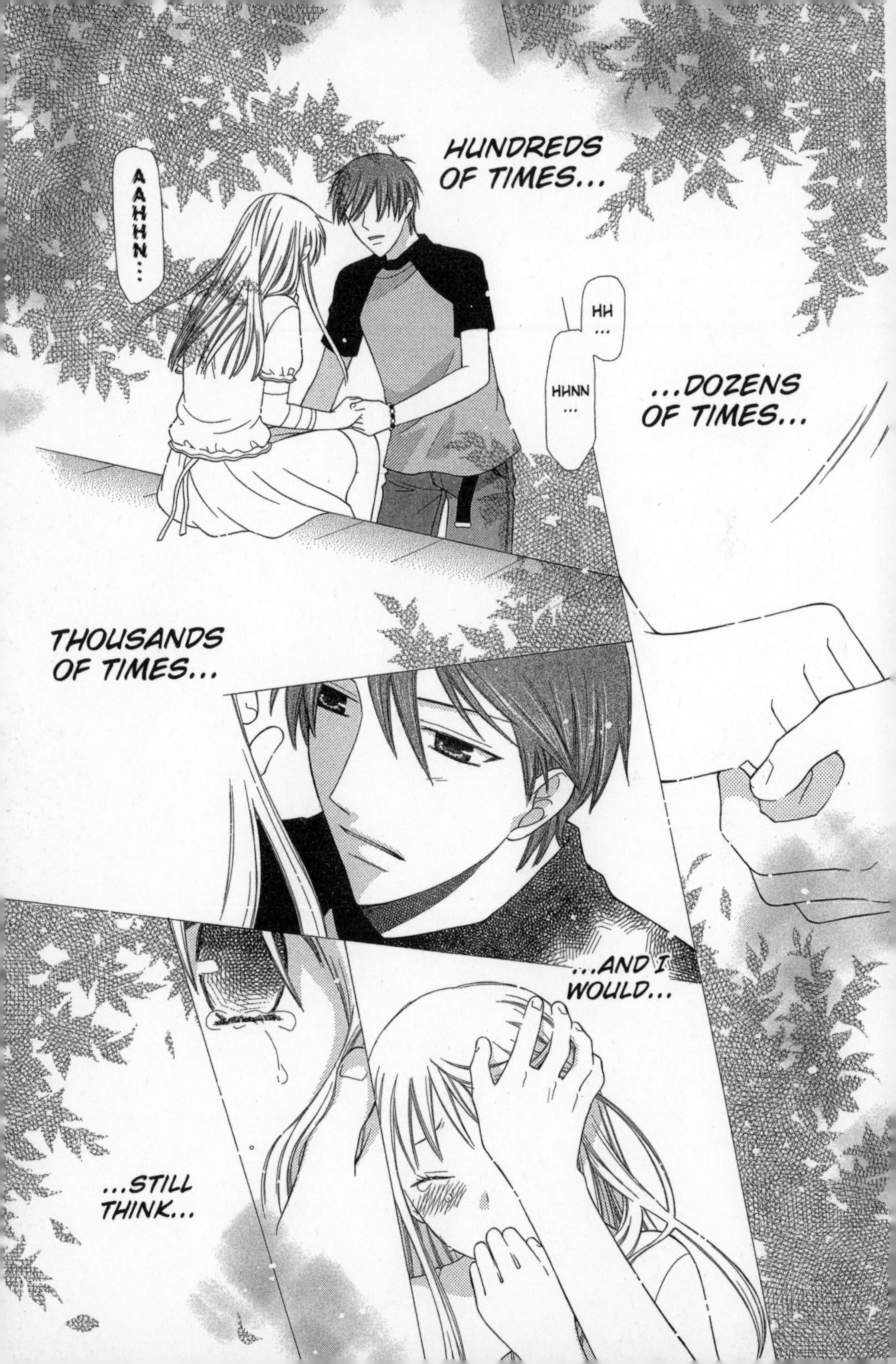
HUNDREDS OF TIMES...
HH...
HHNN...
AAHHN...
...DOZENS OF TIMES...
THOUSANDS OF TIMES...
...AND I WOULD...
...STILL THINK...

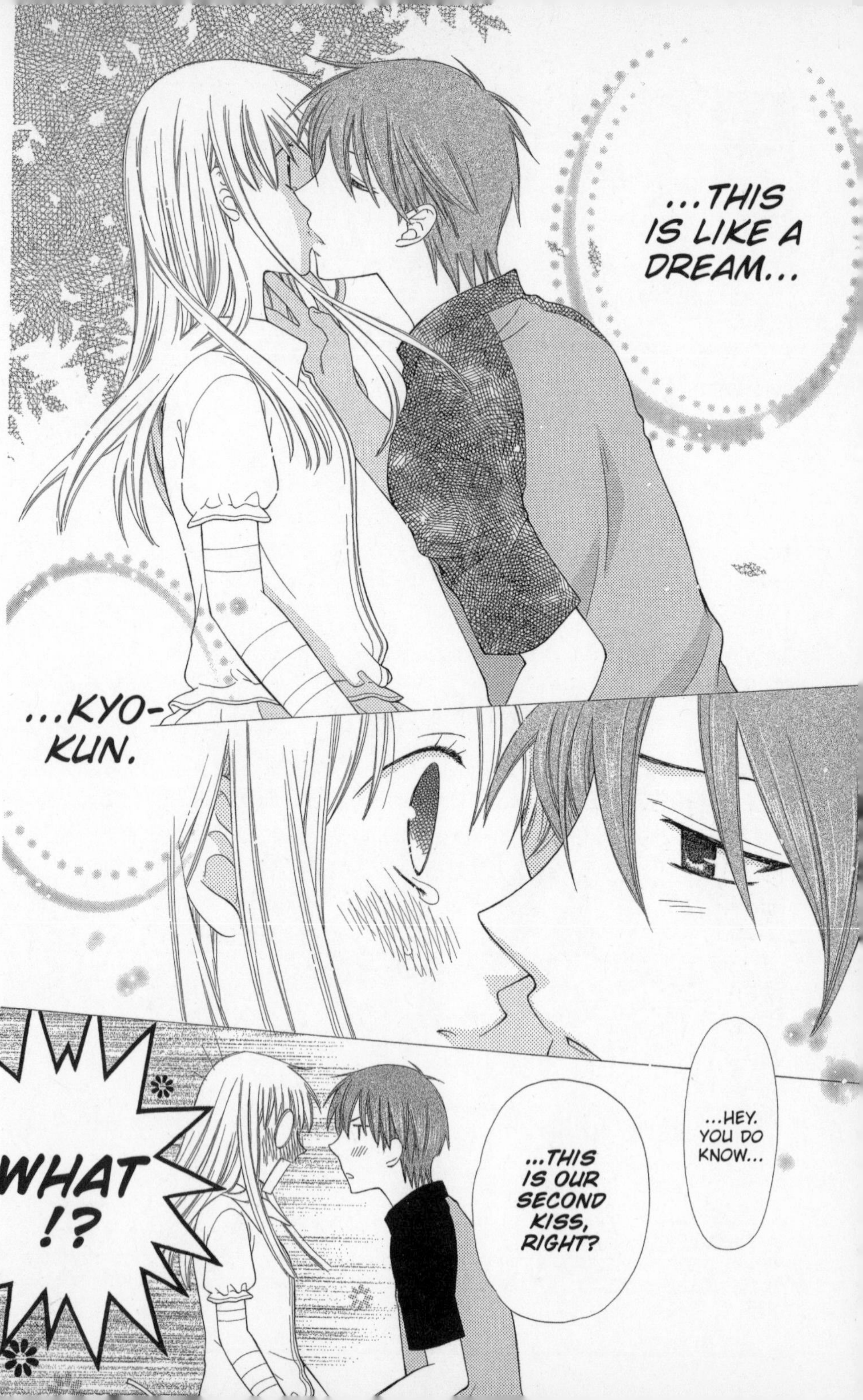
...THIS IS LIKE A DREAM...
...KYO-KUN.
...HEY. YOU DO KNOW...
...THIS IS OUR SECOND KISS, RIGHT?
WHAT!?

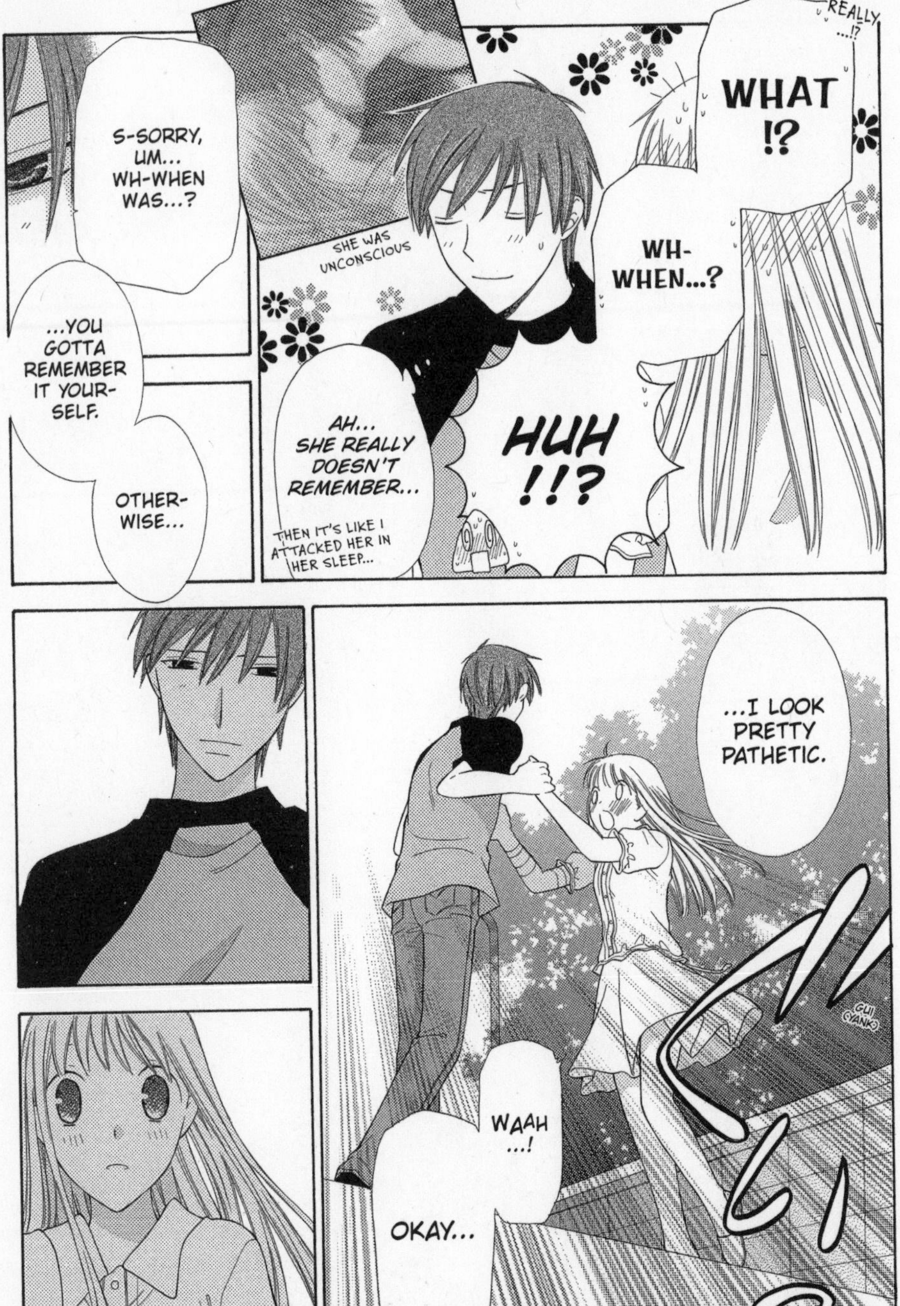

REALLY ...!?
WHAT !?
WH- WHEN...?
SHE WAS UNCONSCIOUS
HUH !!?
AH... SHE REALLY DOESN'T REMEMBER...
THEN IT'S LIKE I ATTACKED HER IN HER SLEEP...
S-SORRY, UM... WH-WHEN WAS...?
...YOU GOTTA REMEMBER IT YOURSELF.
OTHER-WISE...
...I LOOK PRETTY PATHETIC.
GUI (YANK)
WAAH ...!
OKAY...

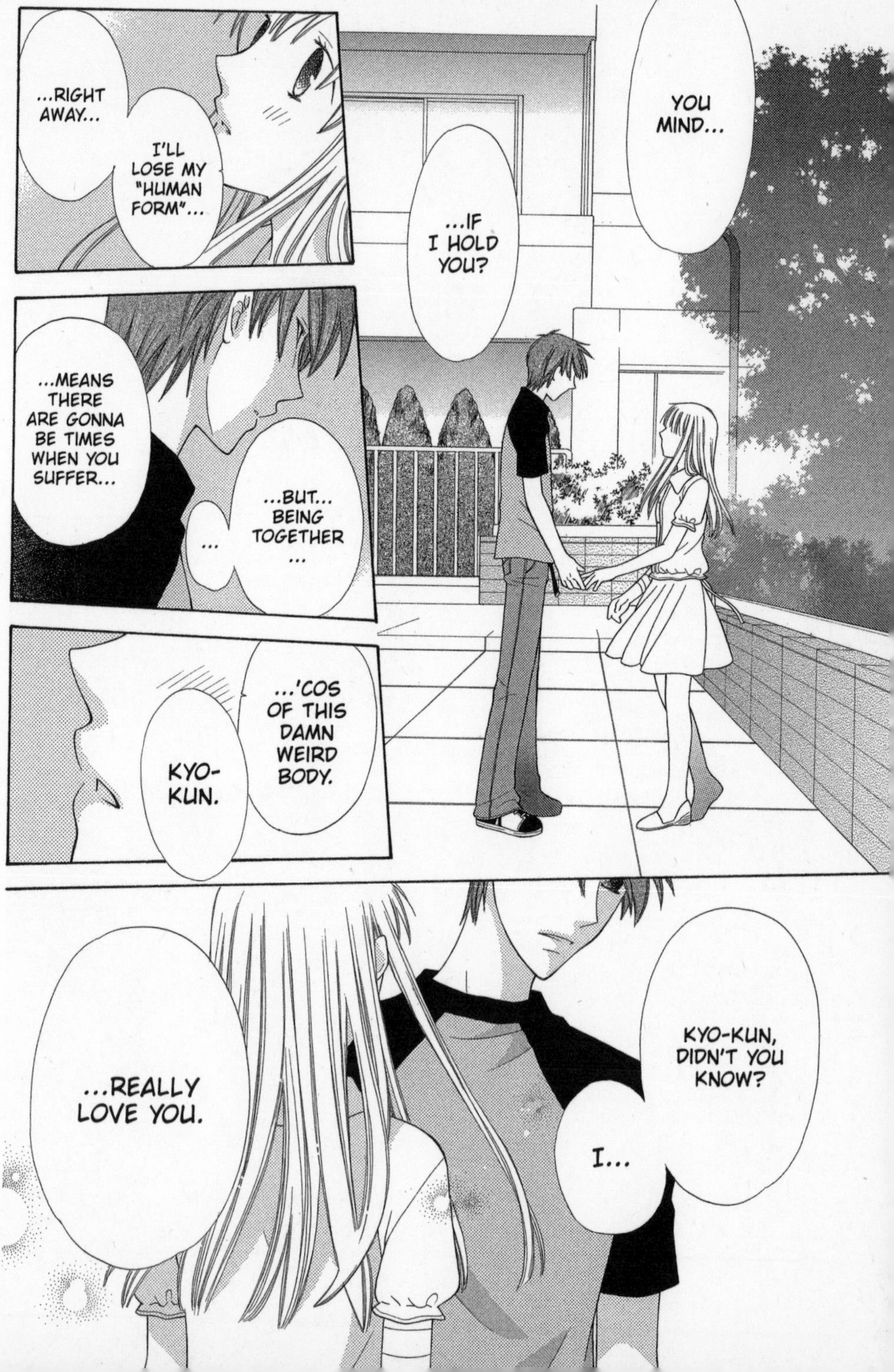
YOU MIND...
...IF I HOLD YOU?
I'LL LOSE MY "HUMAN FORM"...
...RIGHT AWAY...
...BUT... BEING TOGETHER ...
...
...MEANS THERE ARE GONNA BE TIMES WHEN YOU SUFFER...
...'COS OF THIS DAMN WEIRD BODY.
KYO-KUN.
KYO-KUN, DIDN'T YOU KNOW?
I...
...REALLY LOVE YOU.

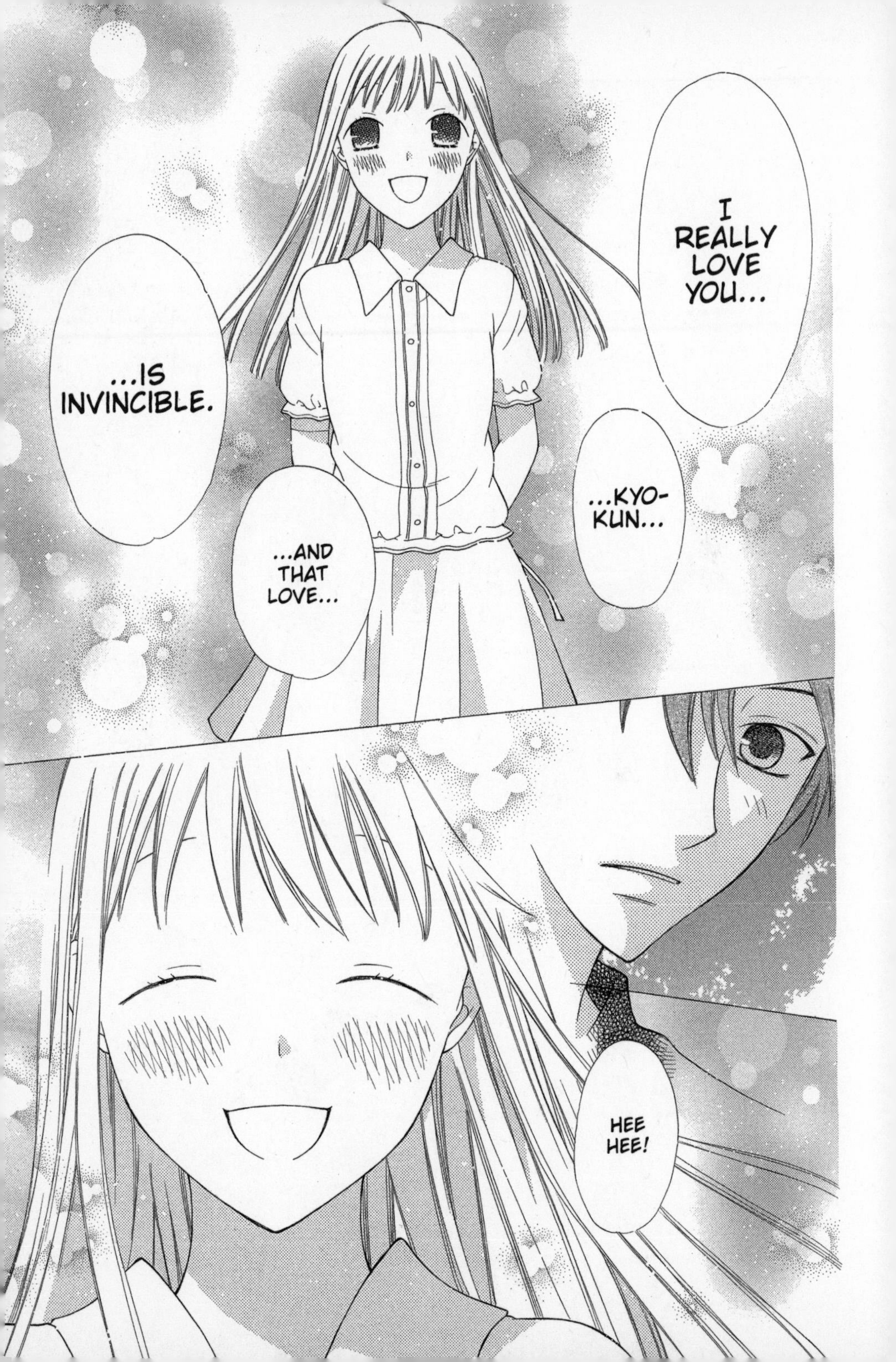
I REALLY LOVE YOU...
...KYO-KUN...
...AND THAT LOVE...
...IS INVINCIBLE.
HEE HEE!

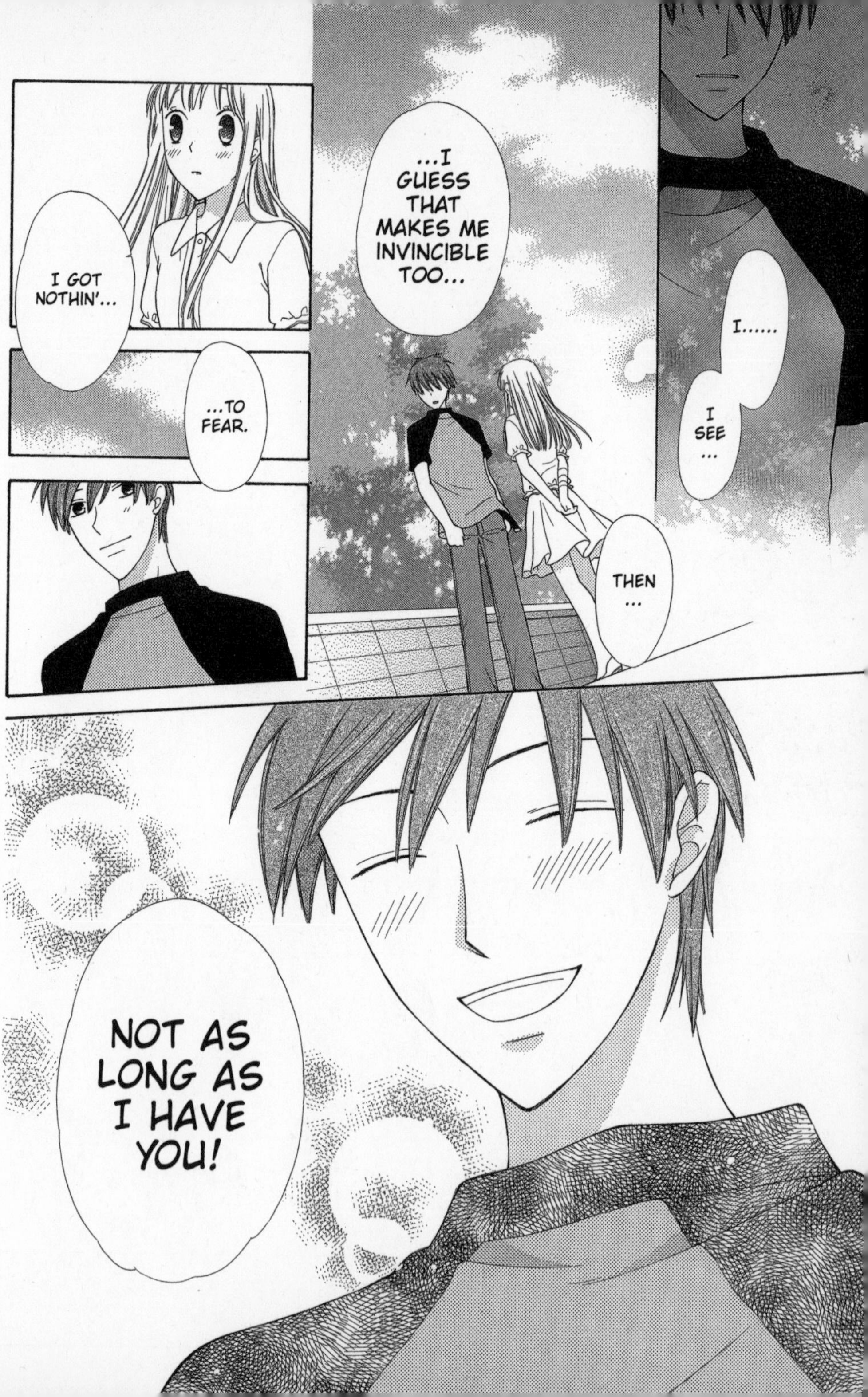
I......
I SEE ...
...I GUESS THAT MAKES ME INVINCIBLE TOO...
THEN ...
I GOT NOTHIN'...
...TO FEAR.
NOT AS LONG AS I HAVE YOU!

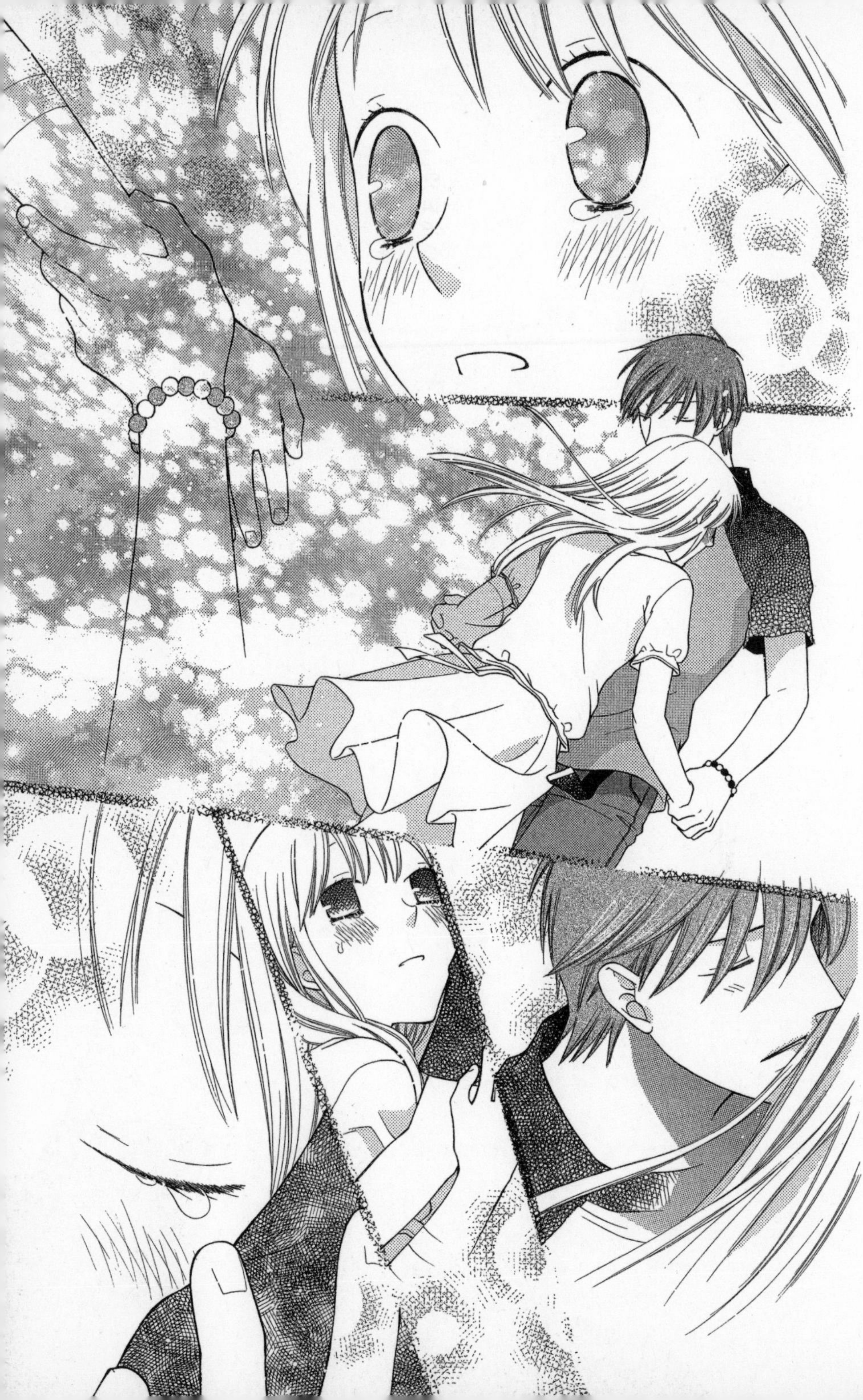

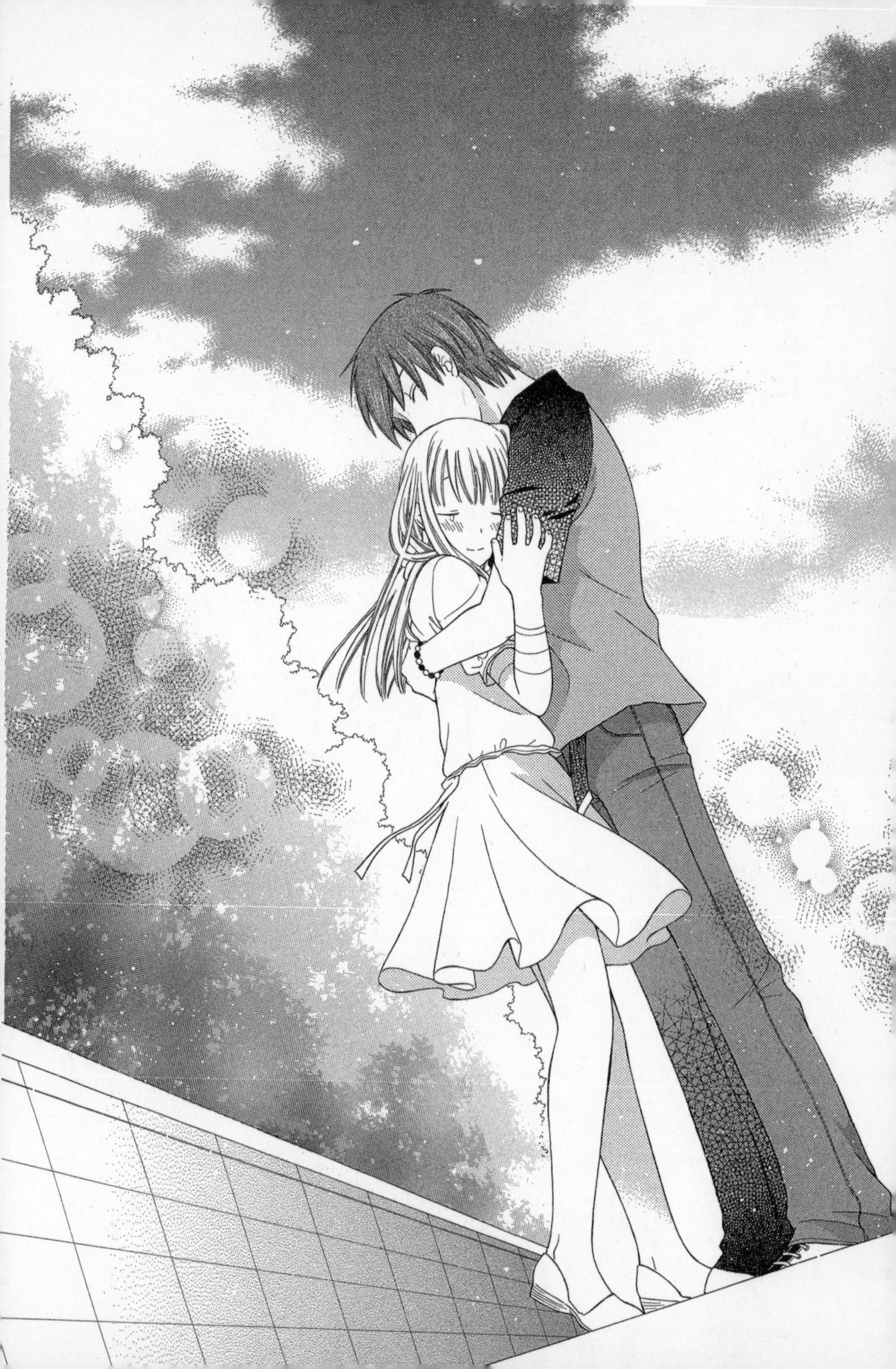

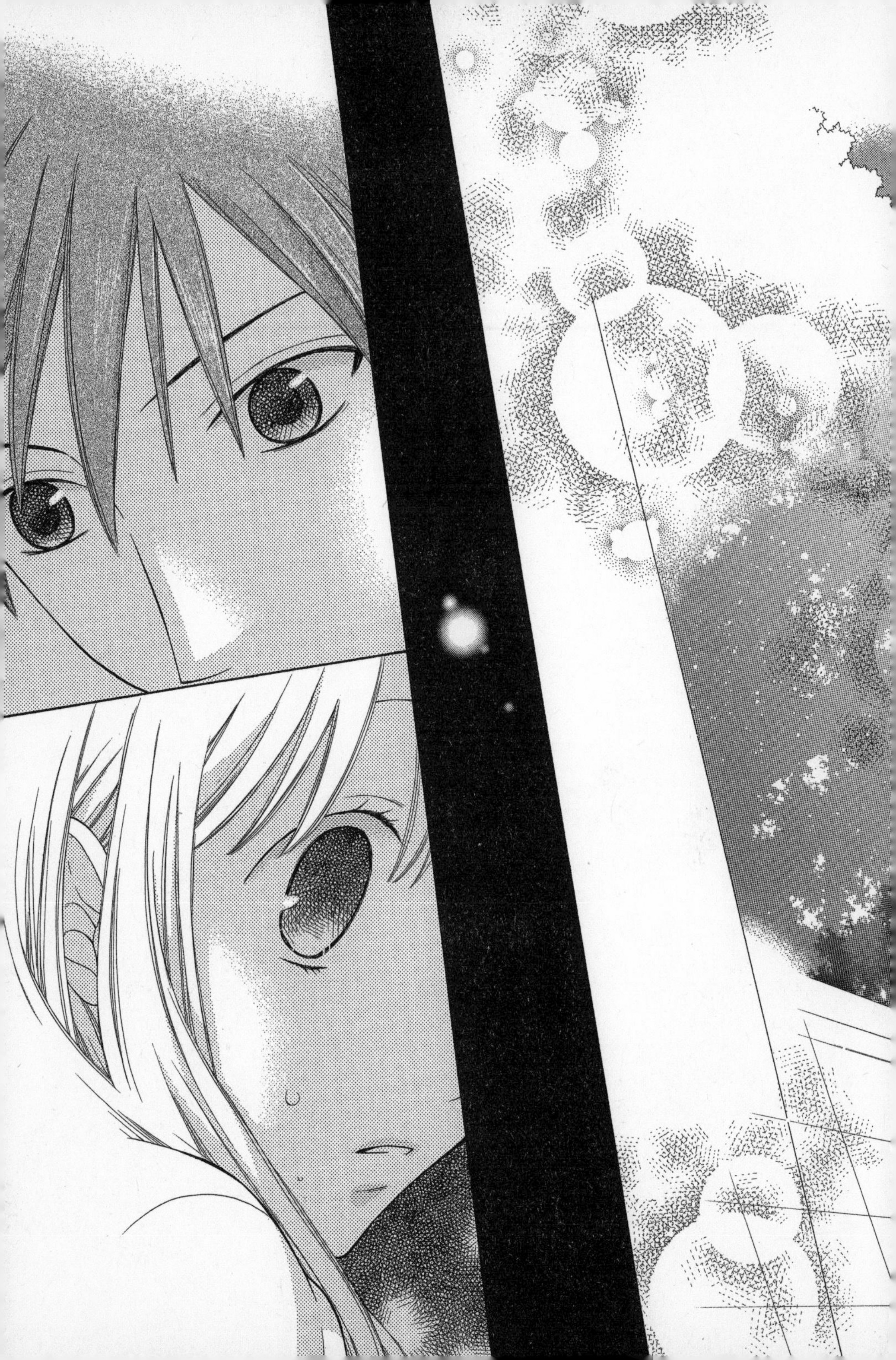

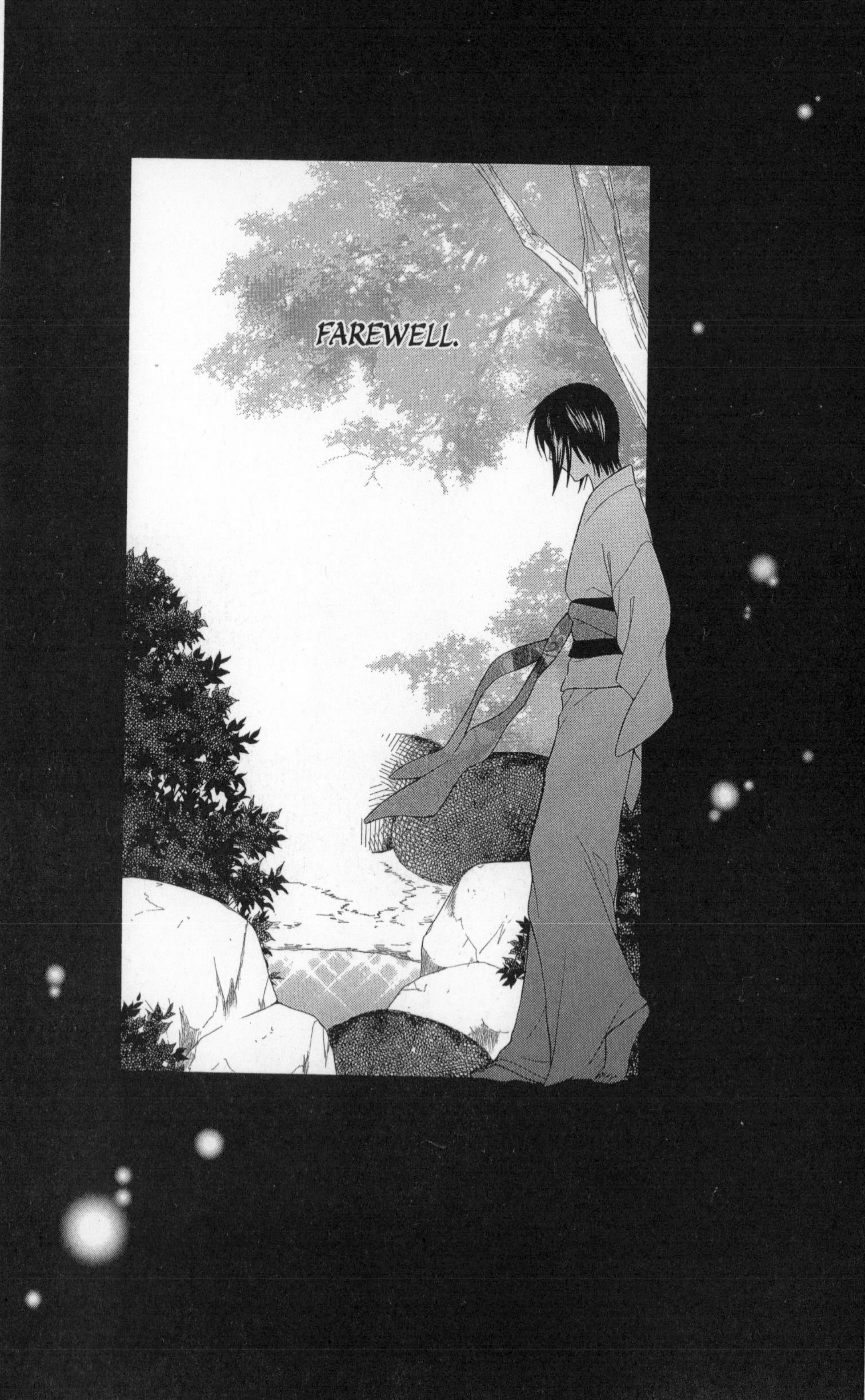
FAREWELL.

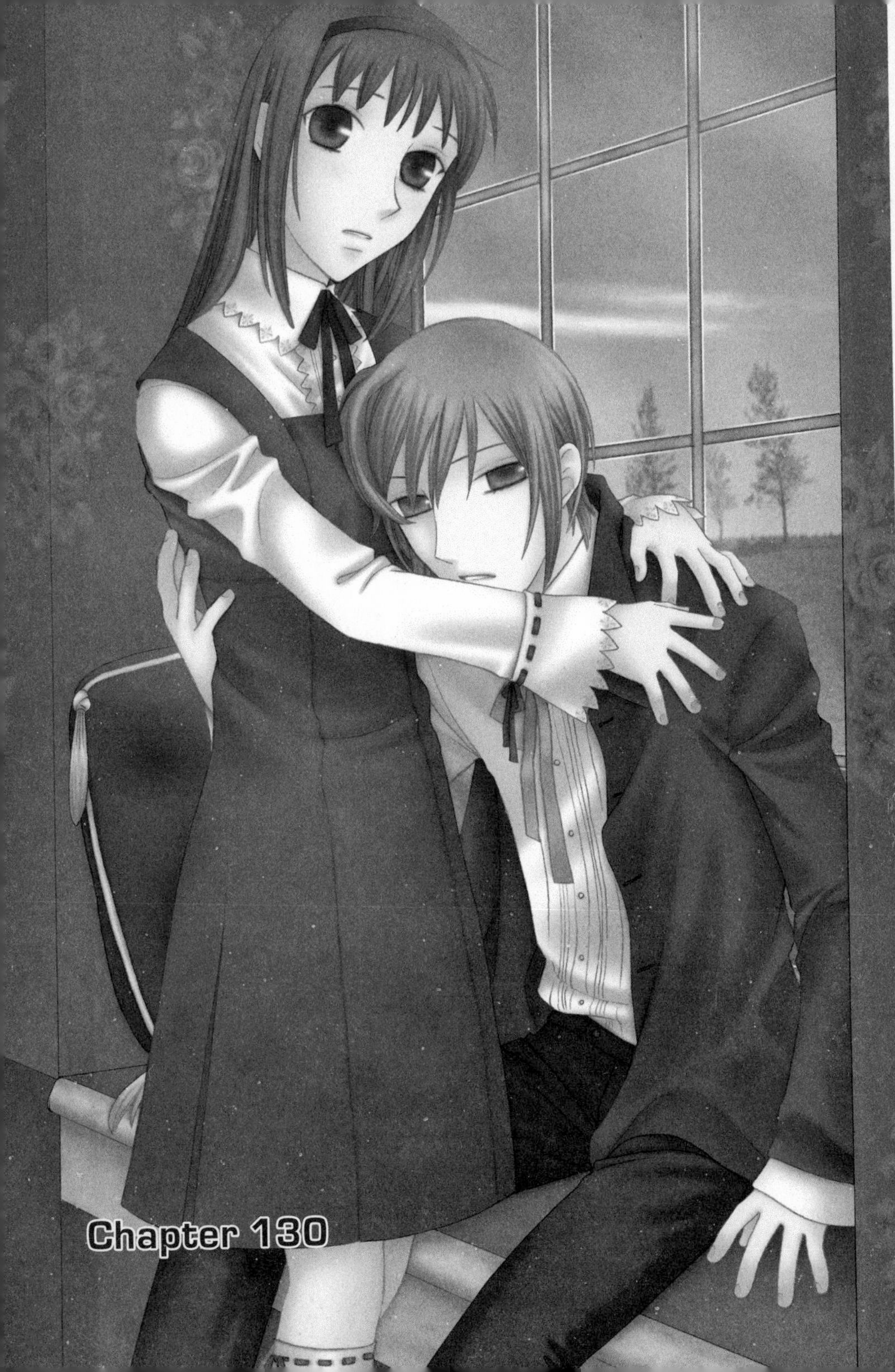
Chapter 130

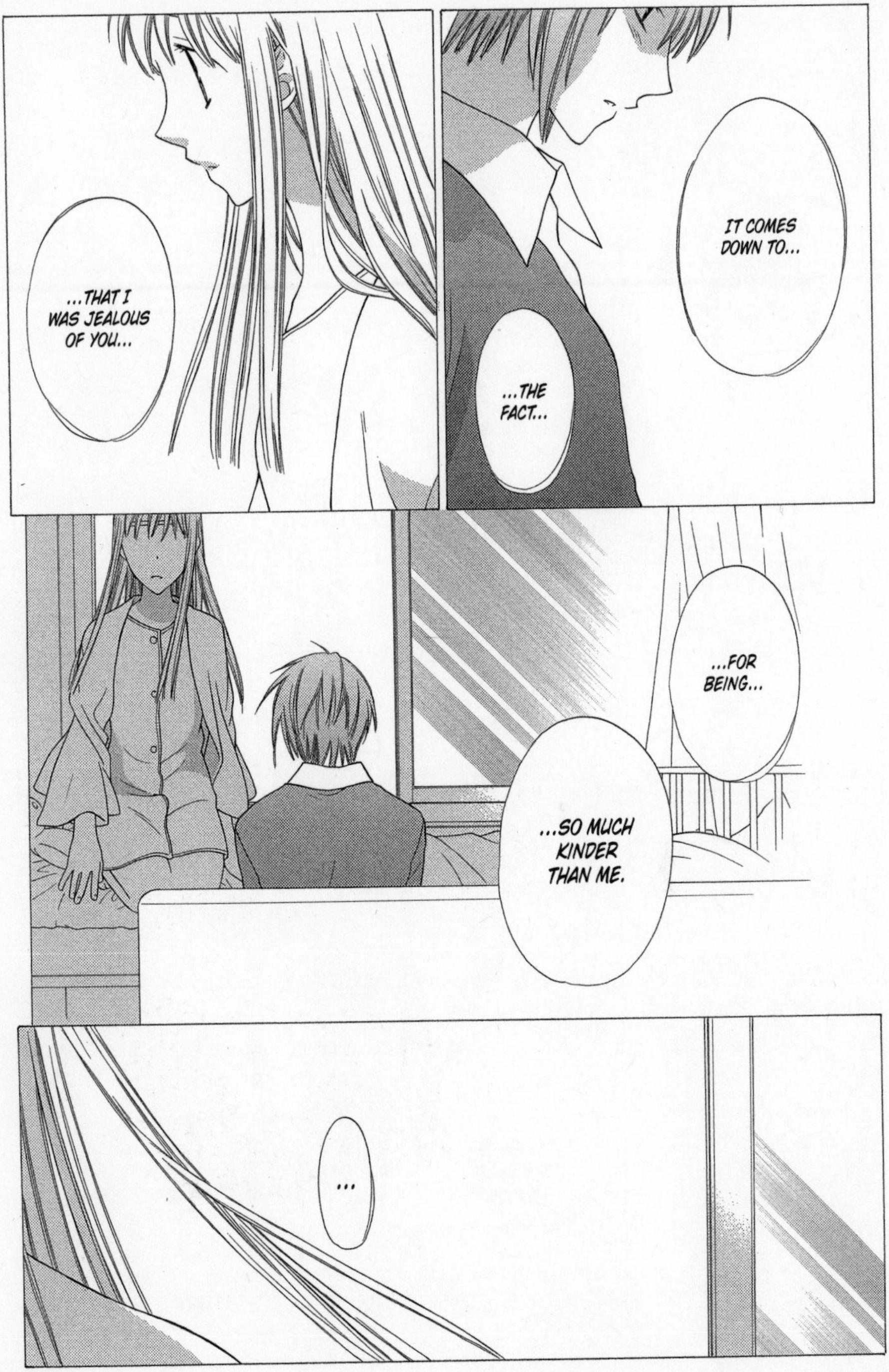
IT COMES DOWN TO...
...THE FACT...
...THAT I WAS JEALOUS OF YOU...
...FOR BEING...
...SO MUCH KINDER THAN ME.
...

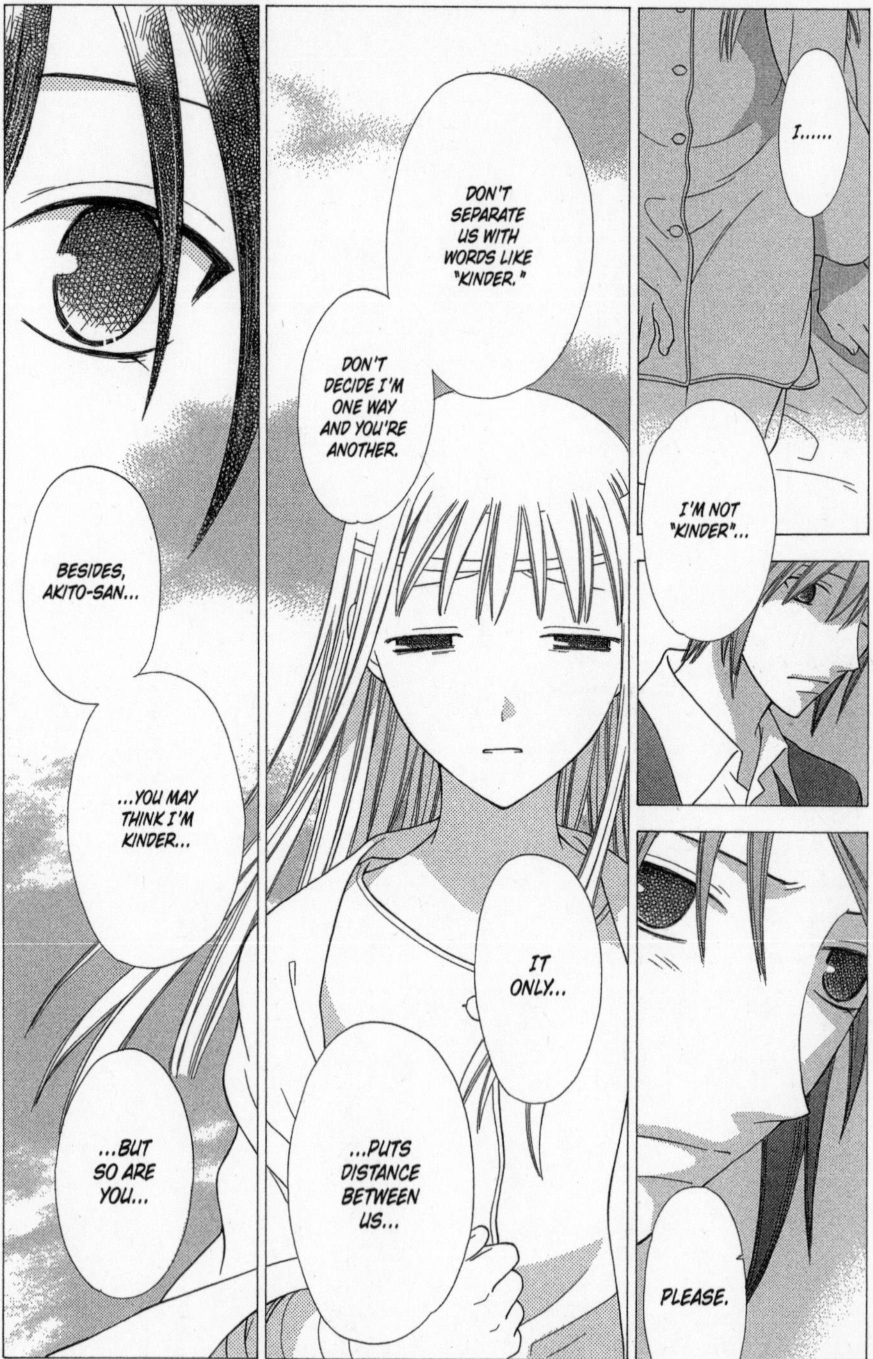
I......
I'M NOT "KINDER"...
PLEASE.
DON'T SEPARATE US WITH WORDS LIKE "KINDER."
DON'T DECIDE I'M ONE WAY AND YOU'RE ANOTHER.
IT ONLY...
...PUTS DISTANCE BETWEEN US...
BESIDES, AKITO-SAN...
...YOU MAY THINK I'M KINDER...
...BUT SO ARE YOU...

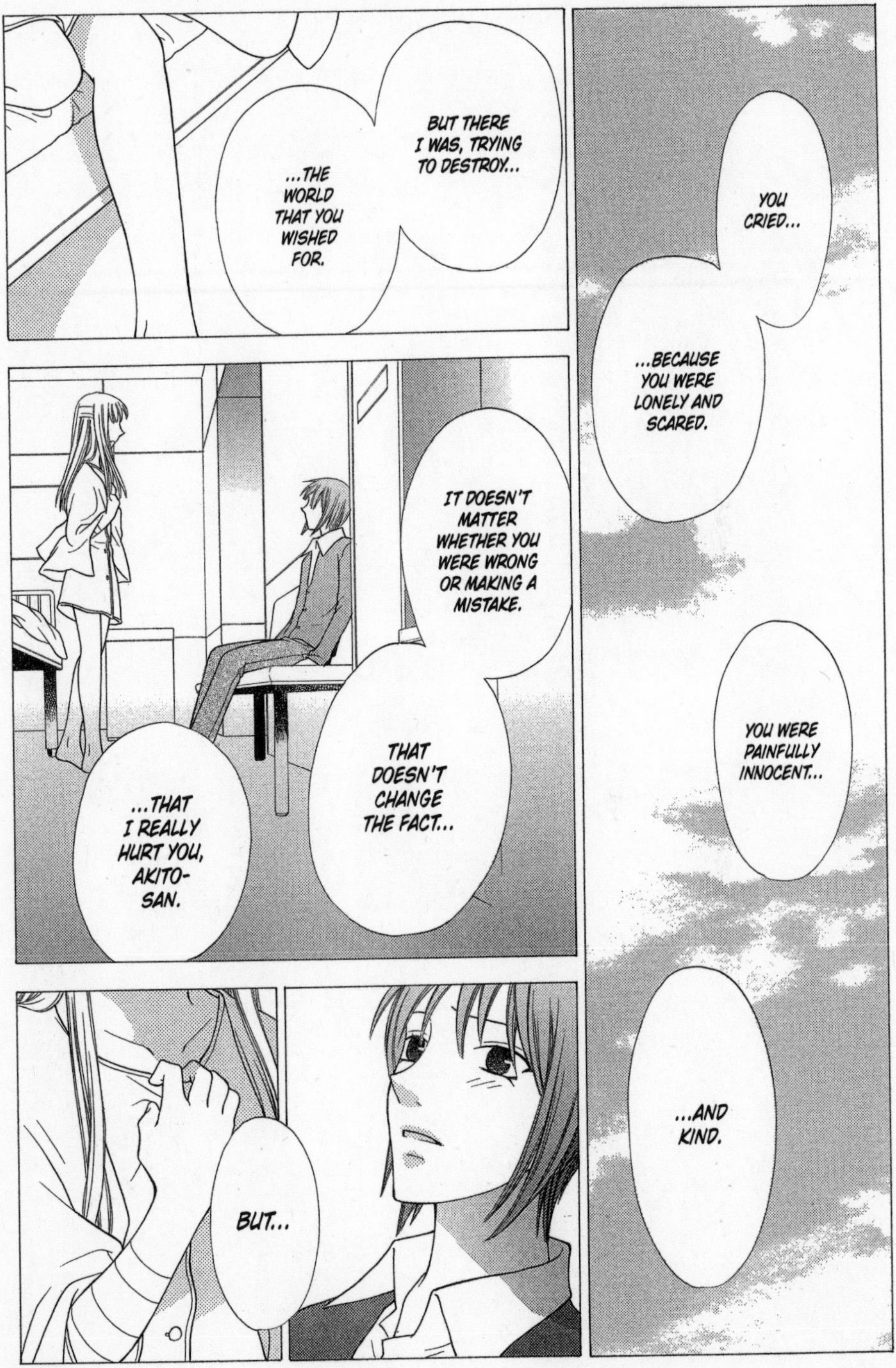
YOU CRIED...
...BECAUSE YOU WERE LONELY AND SCARED.
YOU WERE PAINFULLY INNOCENT...
...AND KIND.
BUT THERE I WAS, TRYING TO DESTROY...
...THE WORLD THAT YOU WISHED FOR.
IT DOESN'T MATTER WHETHER YOU WERE WRONG OR MAKING A MISTAKE.
THAT DOESN'T CHANGE THE FACT...
...THAT I REALLY HURT YOU, AKITO-SAN.
BUT...

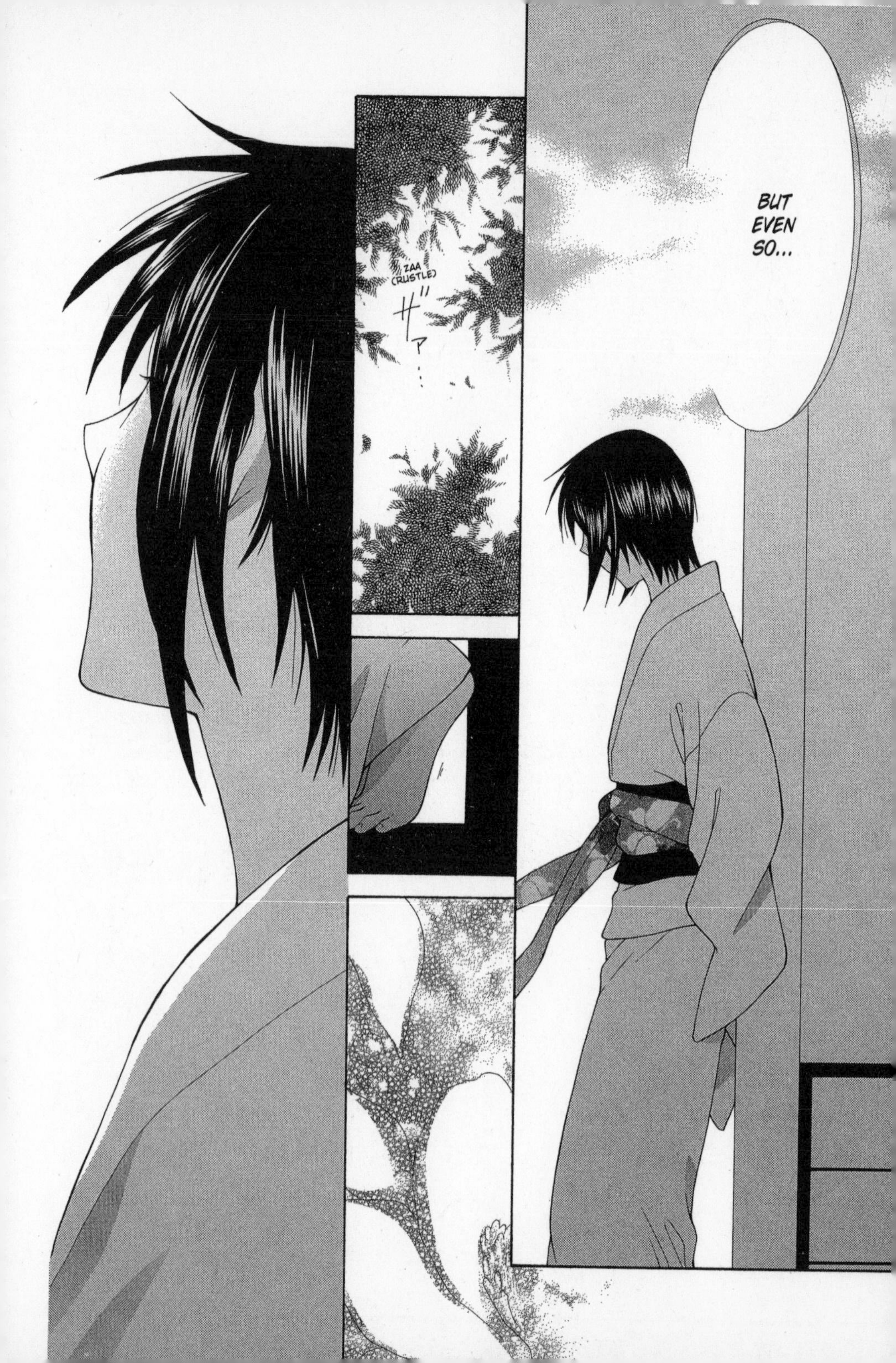
BUT EVEN SO...
ZAA (RUSTLE)
ザァ…

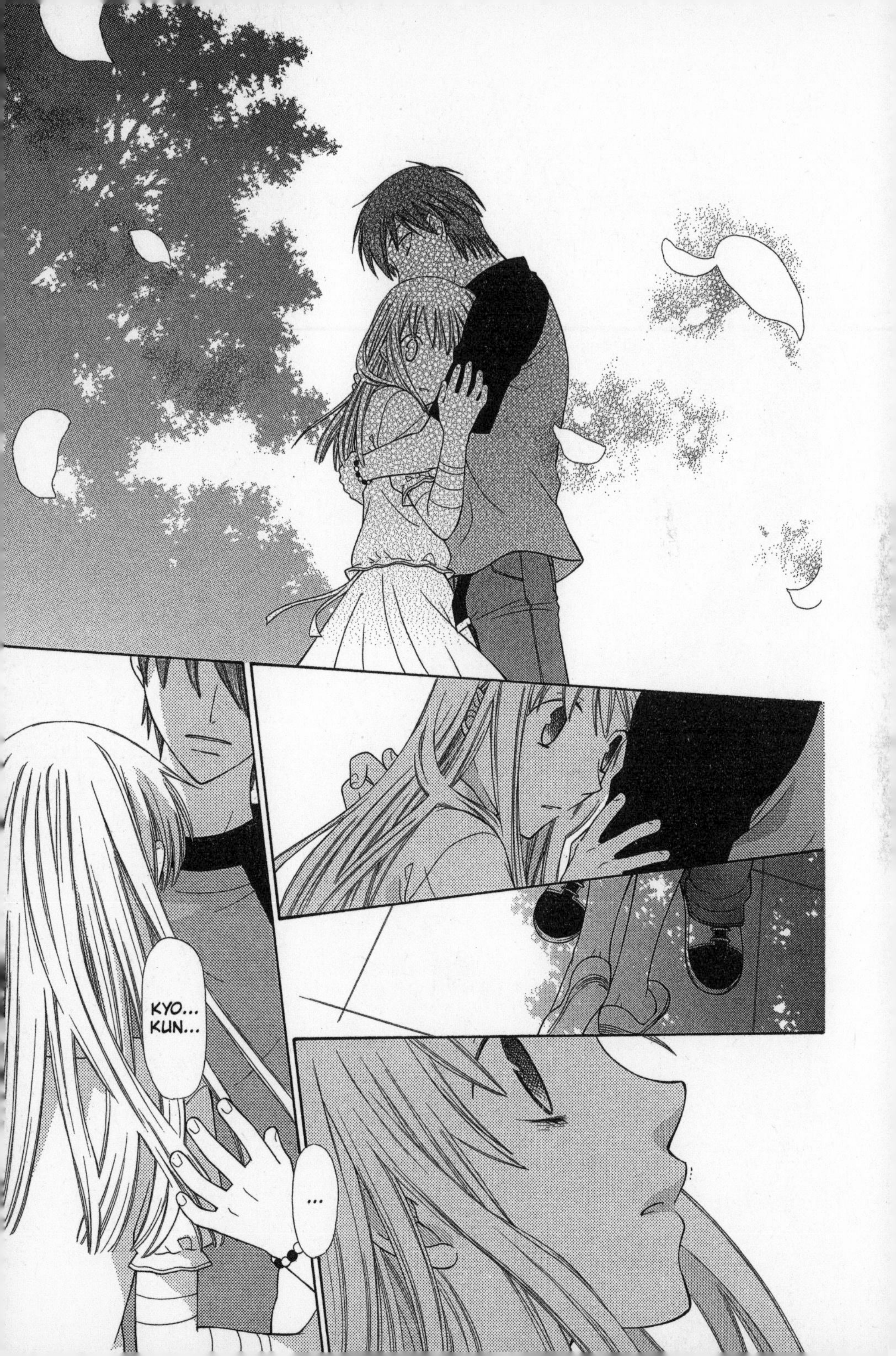
KYO... KUN...
...

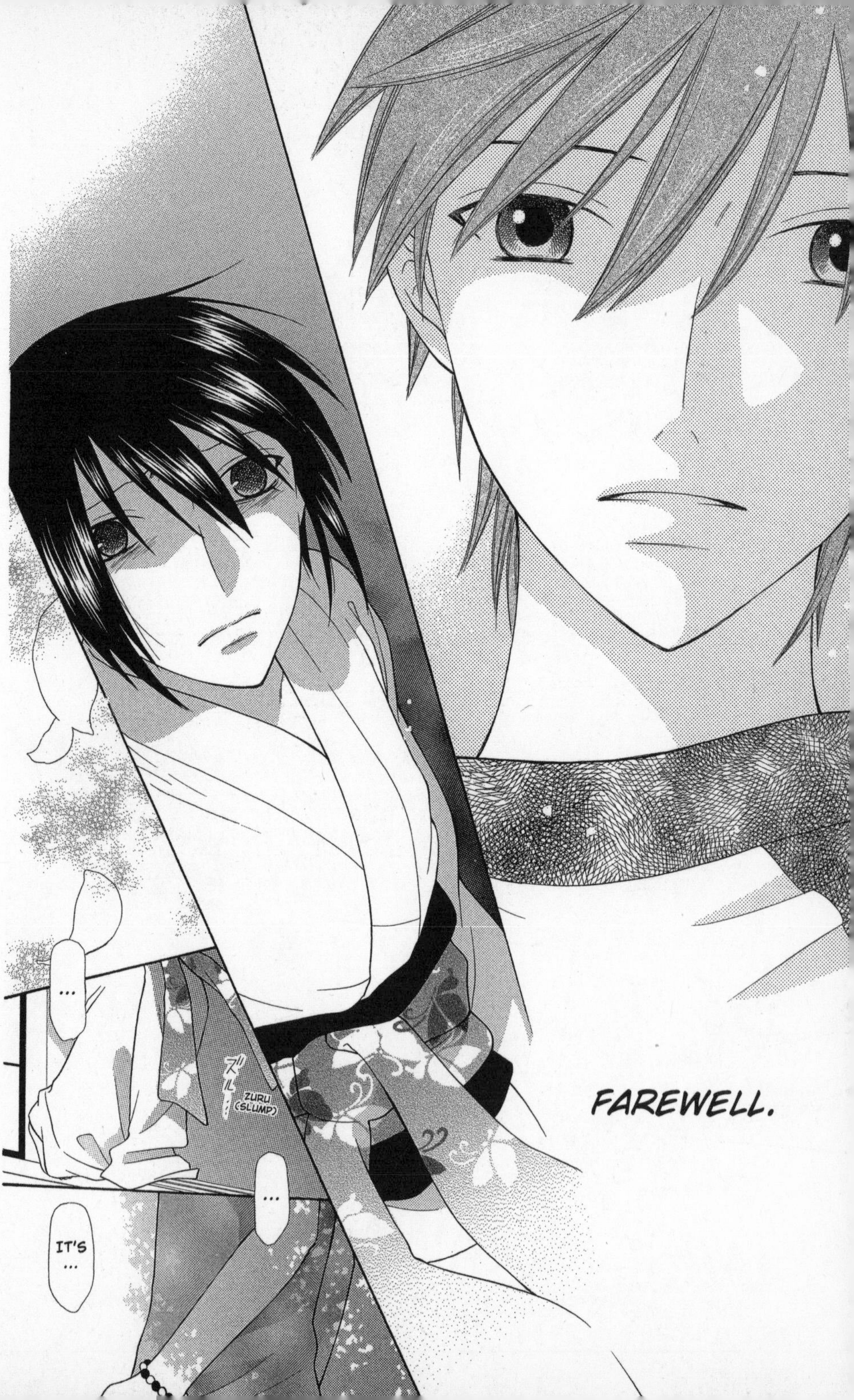
FAREWELL.
...
ズル...
ZURU (SLUMP)
...
IT'S ...

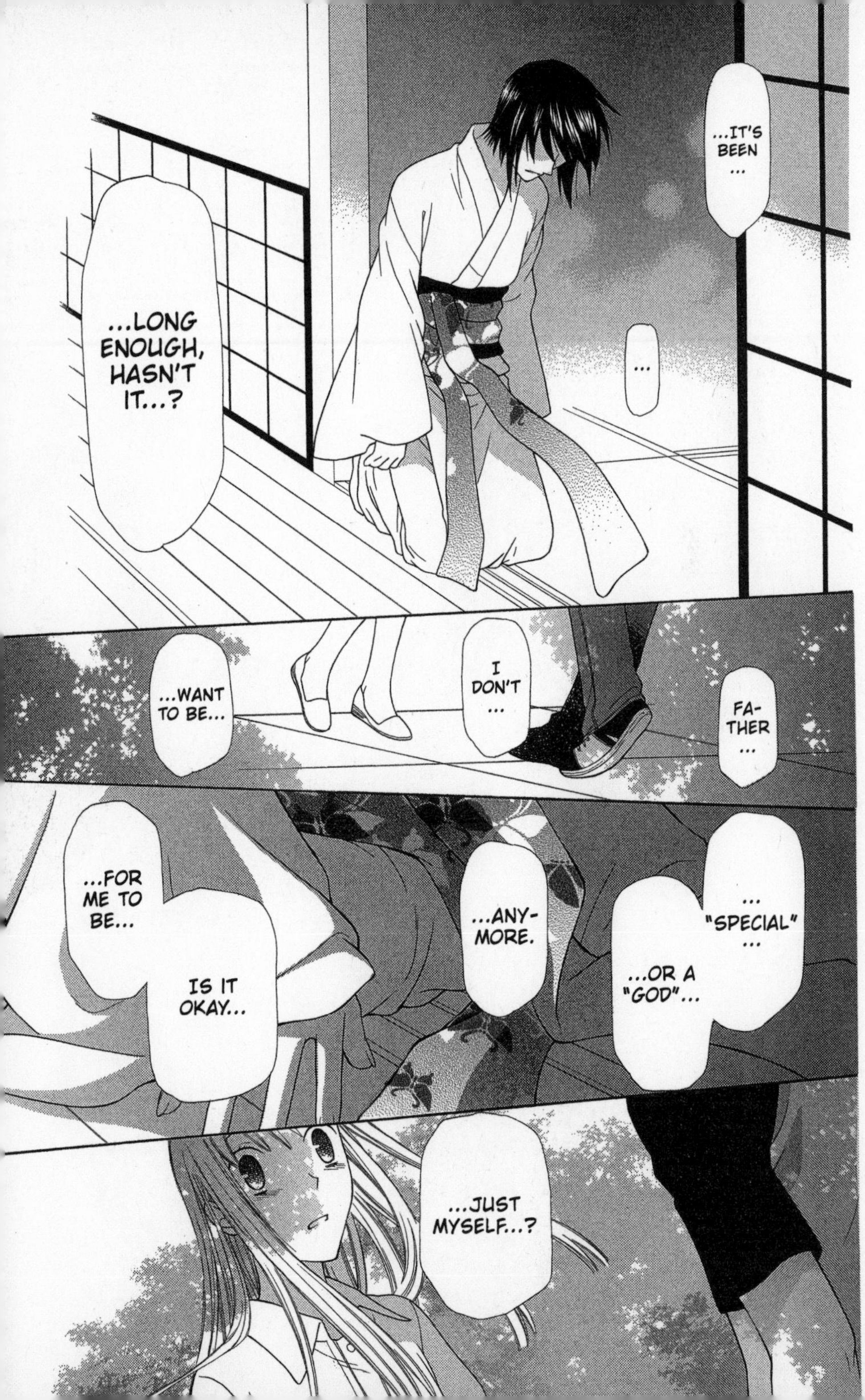
...IT'S BEEN ...
...
...LONG ENOUGH, HASN'T IT...?
FA-THER ...
I DON'T ...
...WANT TO BE...
... "SPECIAL" ...
...OR A "GOD"...
...ANY-MORE.
...FOR ME TO BE...
IS IT OKAY...
...JUST MYSELF...?

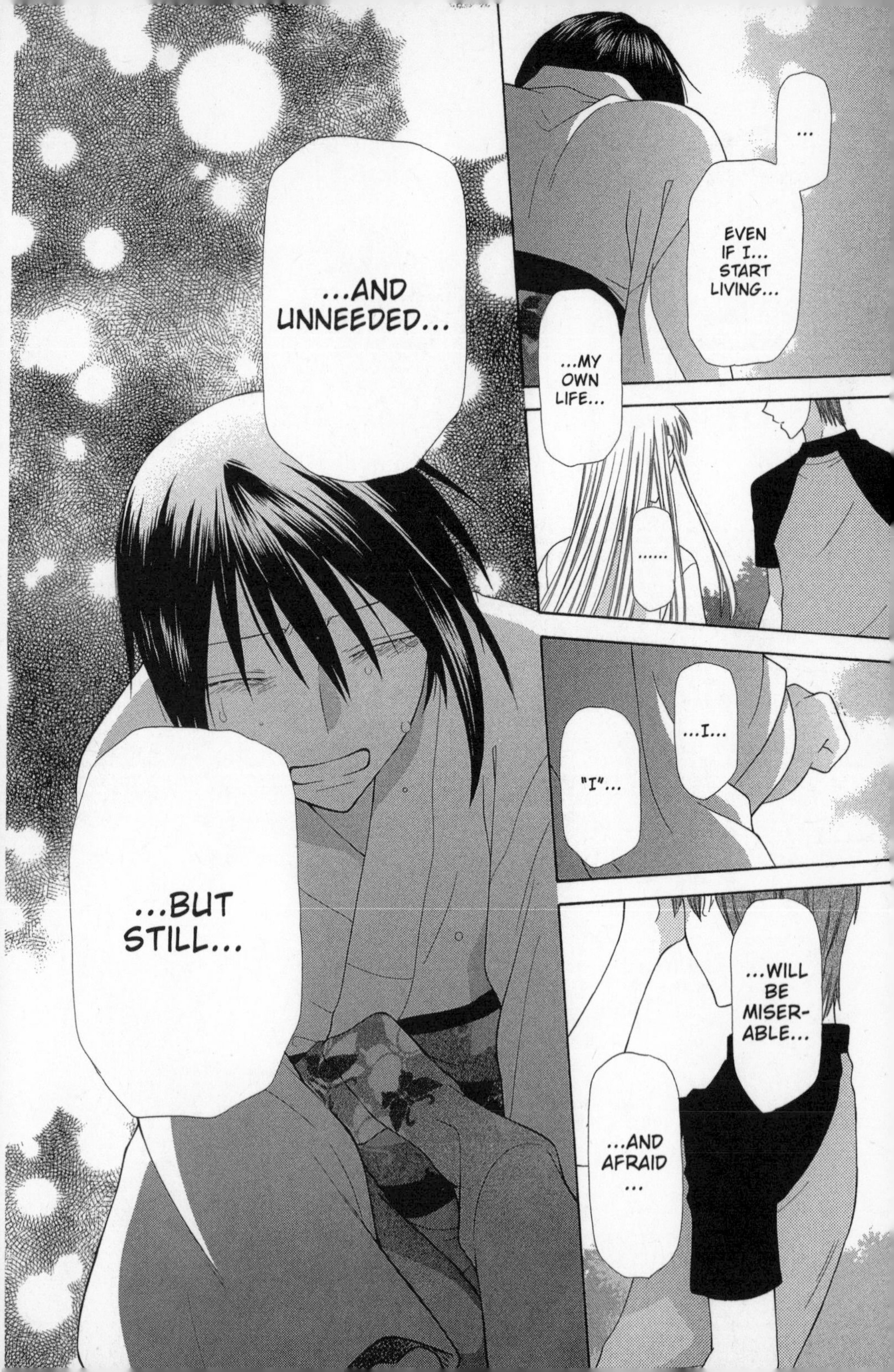
...
EVEN IF I... START LIVING...
...MY OWN LIFE...
......
...I...
"I"...
...WILL BE MISER-ABLE...
...AND AFRAID...
...AND UNNEEDED...
...BUT STILL...

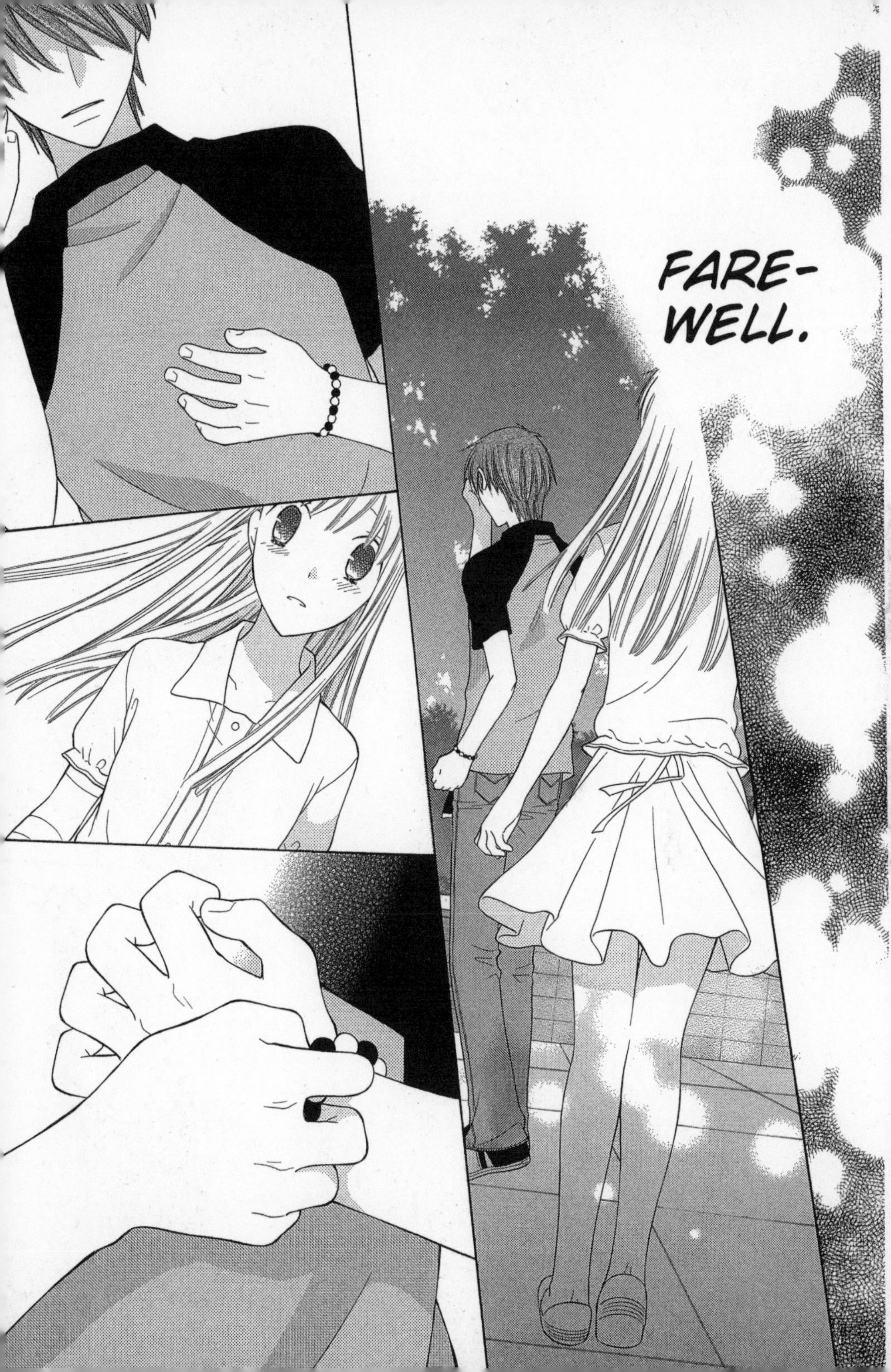
FARE-
WELL.

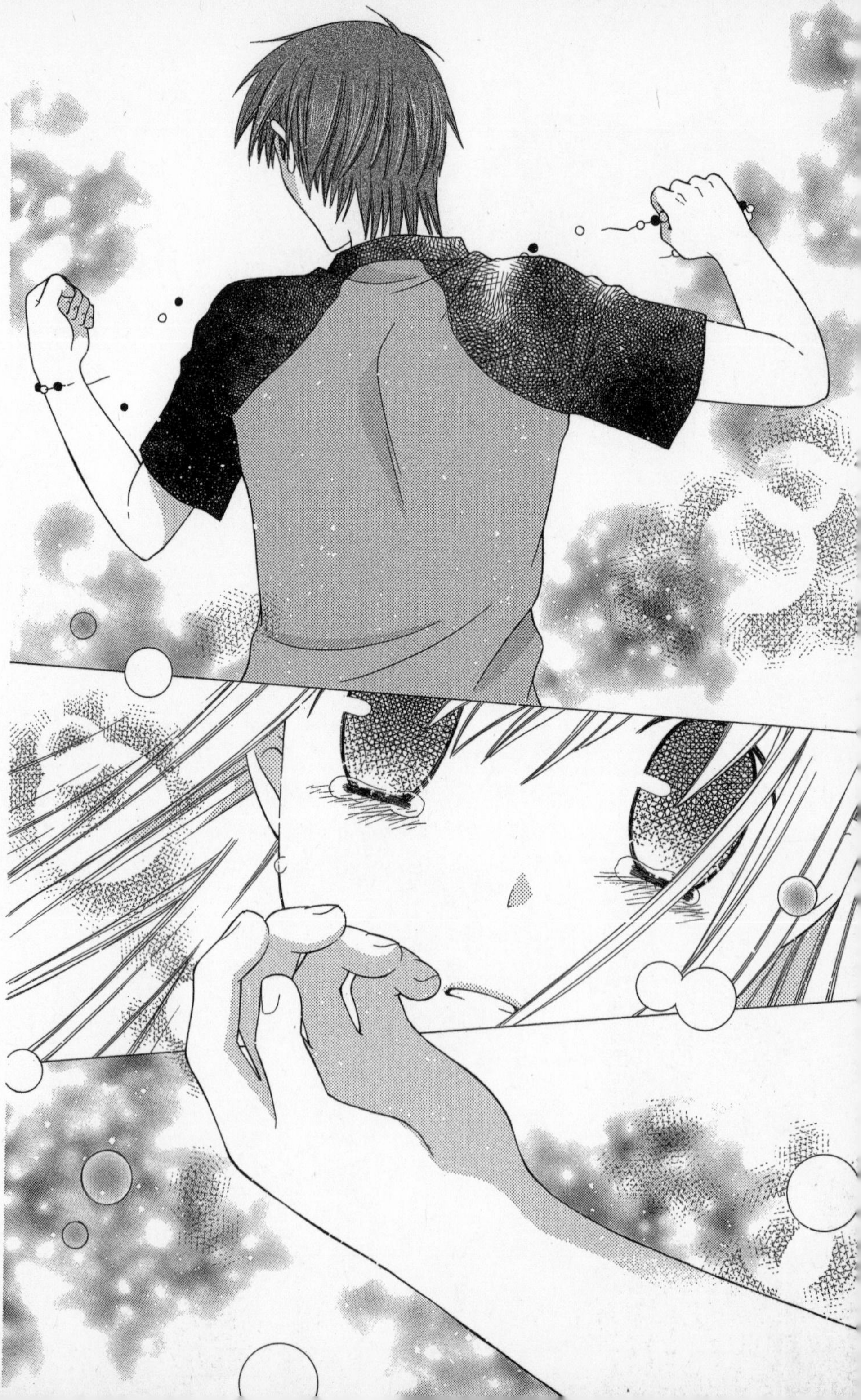

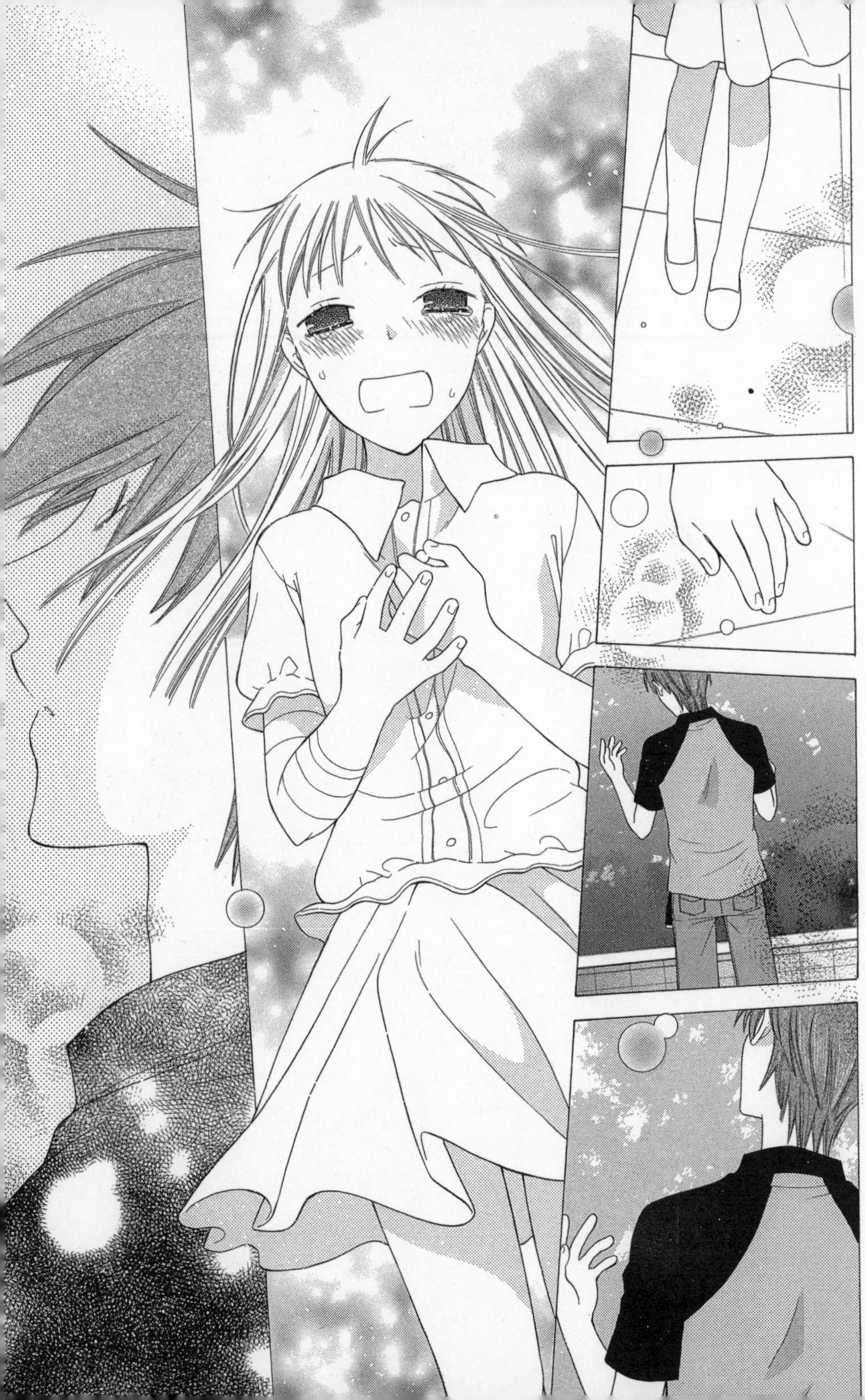

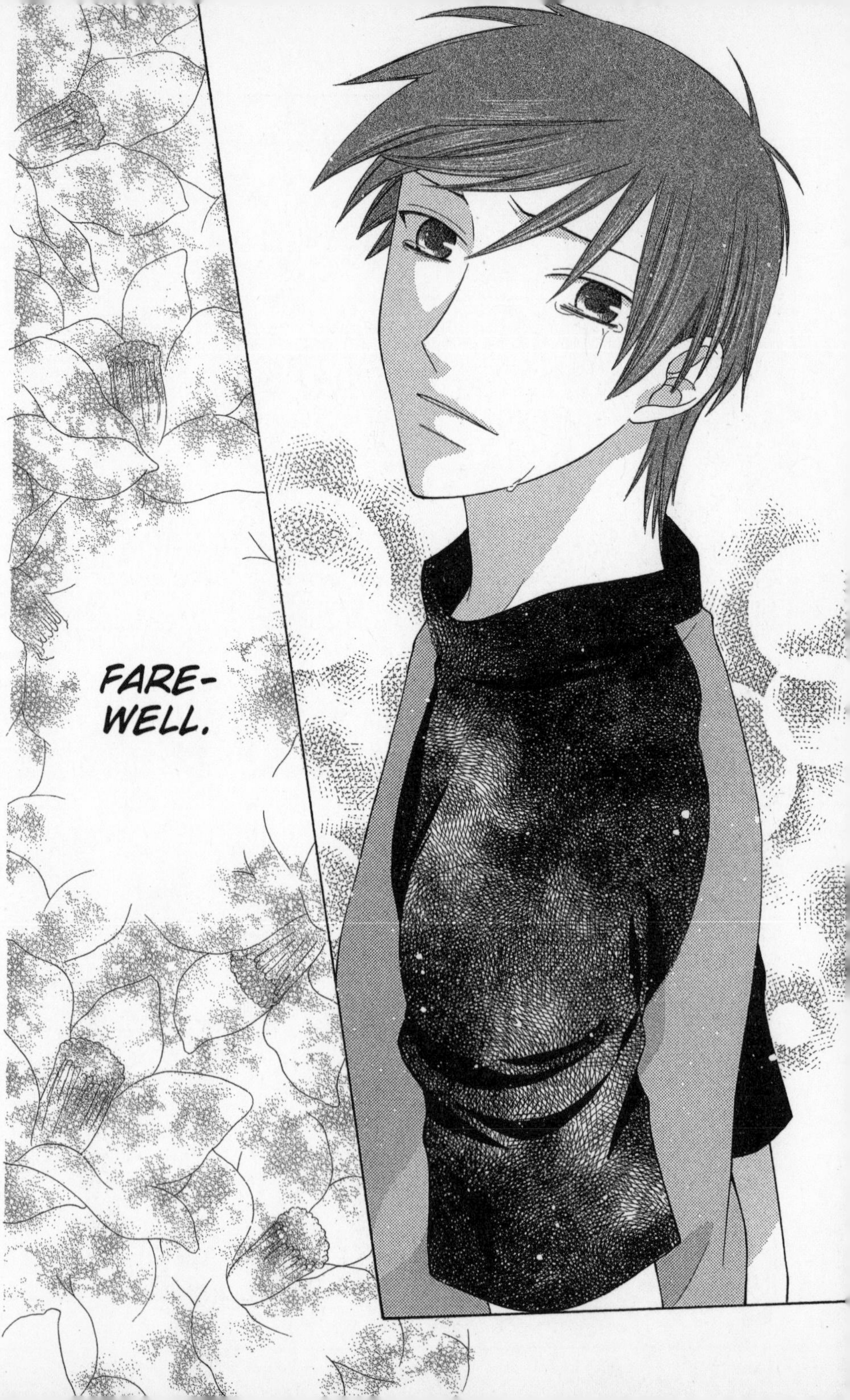
FARE-
WELL.

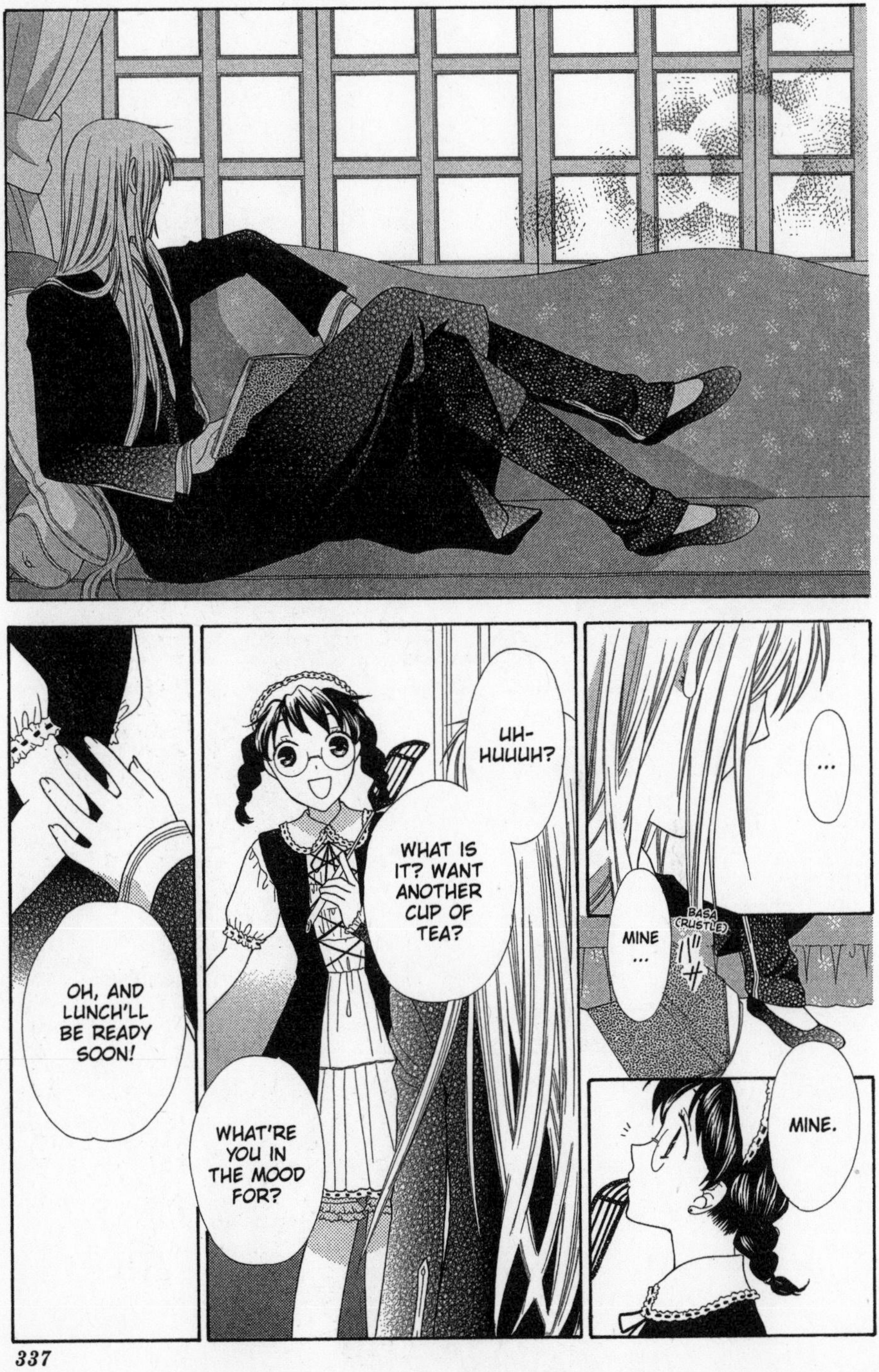
...
MINE ...
BASA (RUSTLE)
MINE.
UH-HUUUH?
WHAT IS IT? WANT ANOTHER CUP OF TEA?
WHAT'RE YOU IN THE MOOD FOR?
OH, AND LUNCH'LL BE READY SOON!

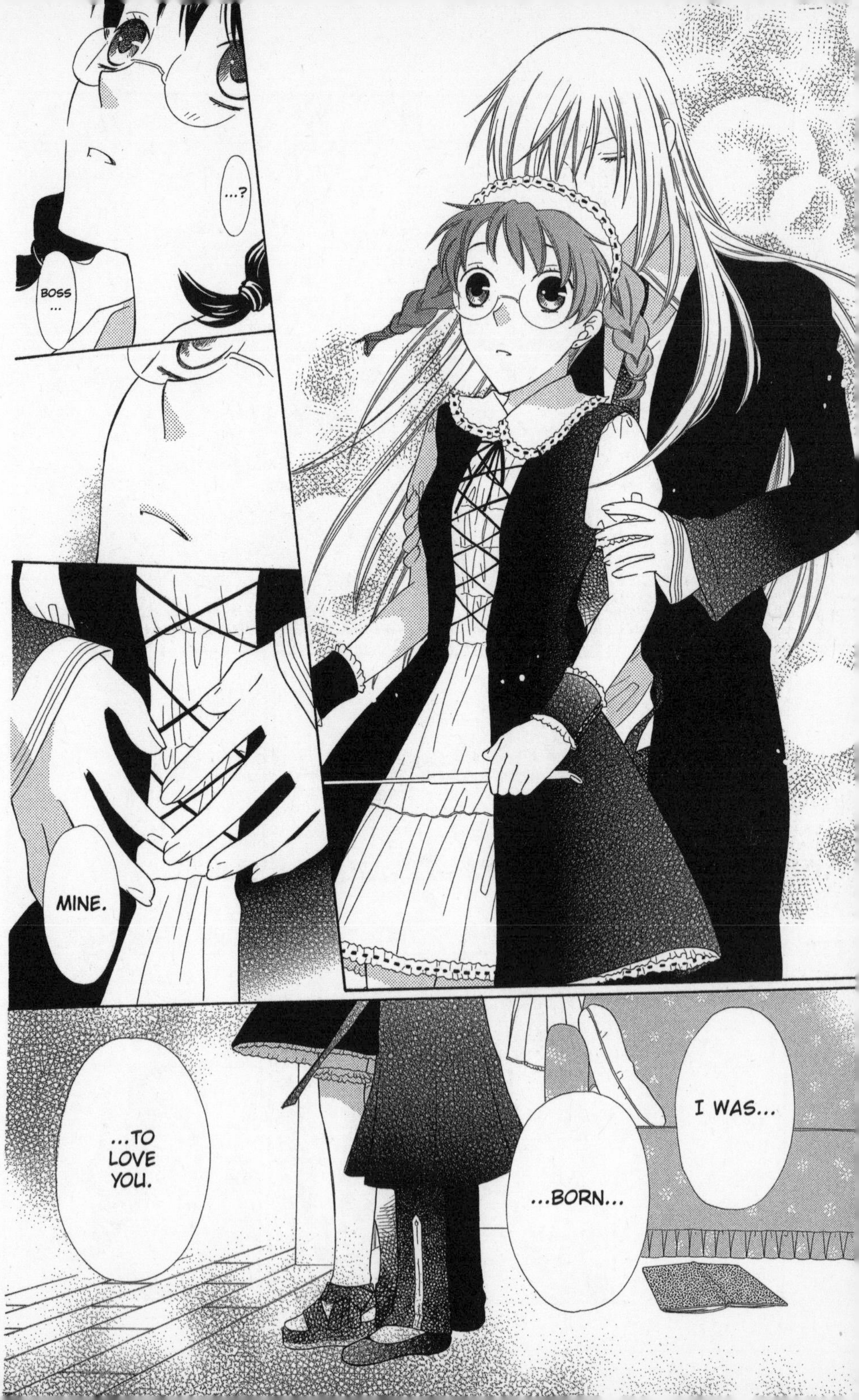
...?
BOSS...
MINE.
I WAS...
...BORN...
...TO LOVE YOU.

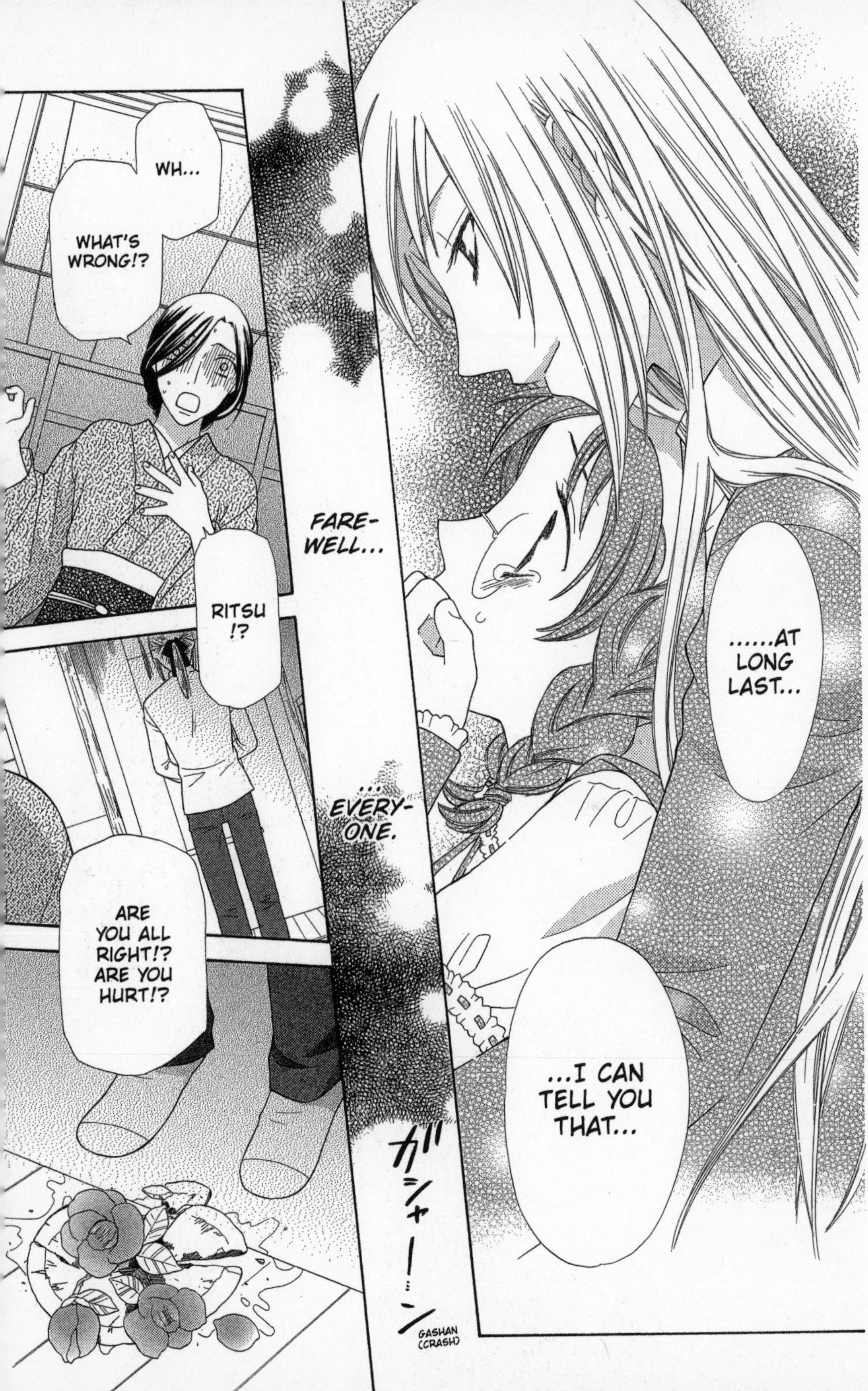
......AT LONG LAST...
...I CAN TELL YOU THAT...
FARE-WELL...
...EVERY-ONE.
ガシャーン
GASHAN (CRASH)
WH...
WHAT'S WRONG!?
RITSU!?
ARE YOU ALL RIGHT!? ARE YOU HURT!?

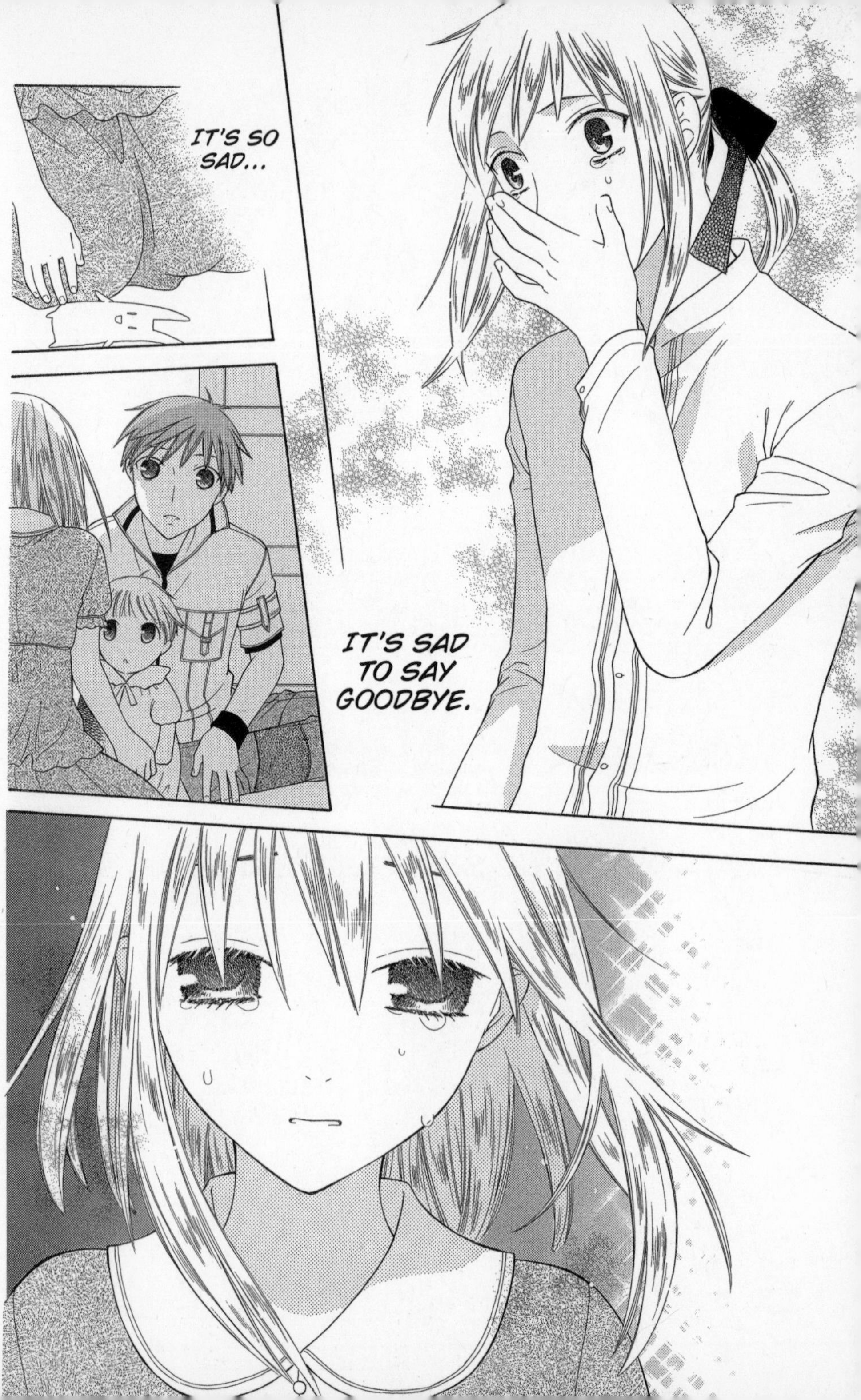
IT'S SO SAD...
IT'S SAD TO SAY GOODBYE.

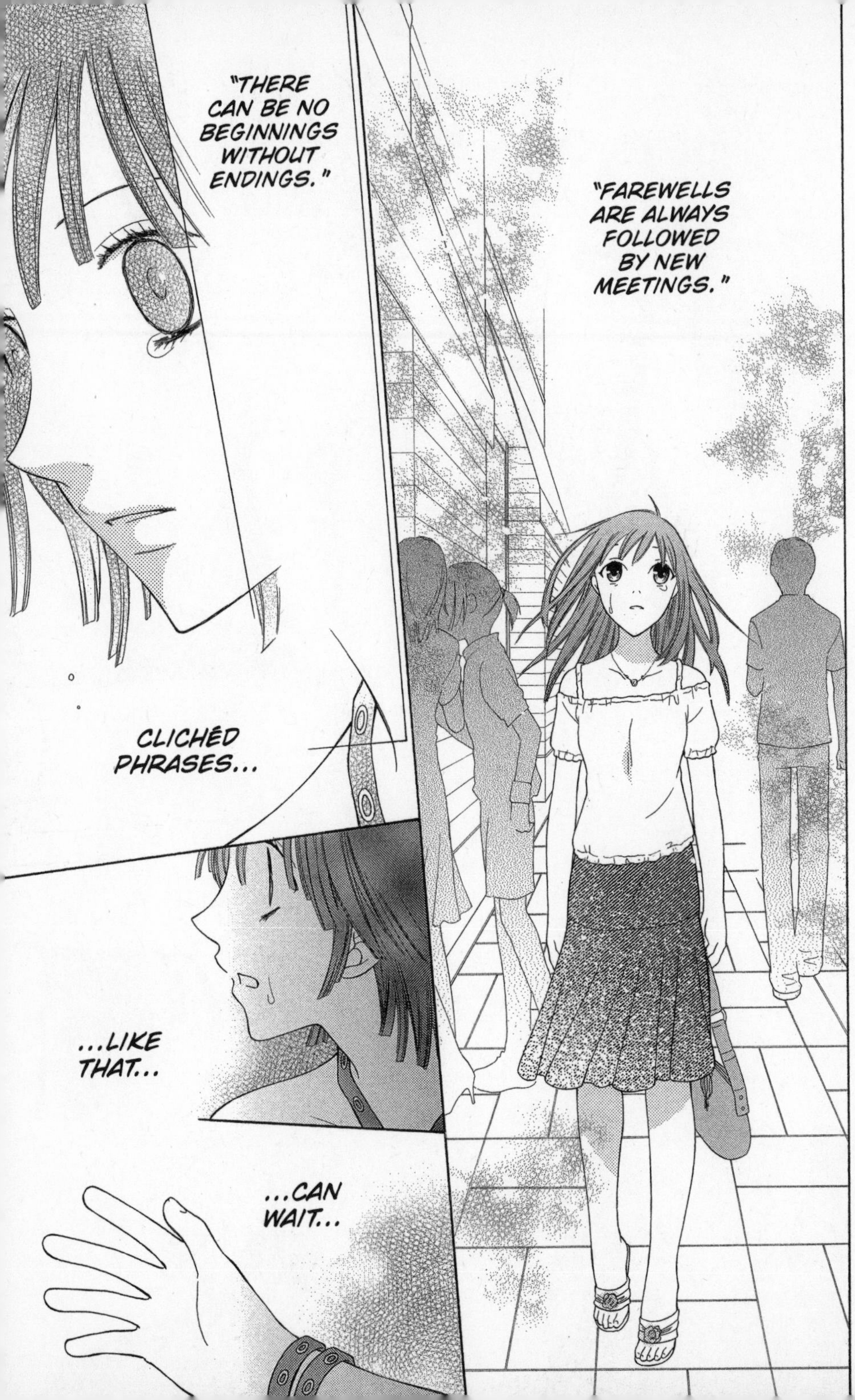
"FAREWELLS ARE ALWAYS FOLLOWED BY NEW MEETINGS."
"THERE CAN BE NO BEGINNINGS WITHOUT ENDINGS."
CLICHÉD PHRASES...
...LIKE THAT...
...CAN WAIT...

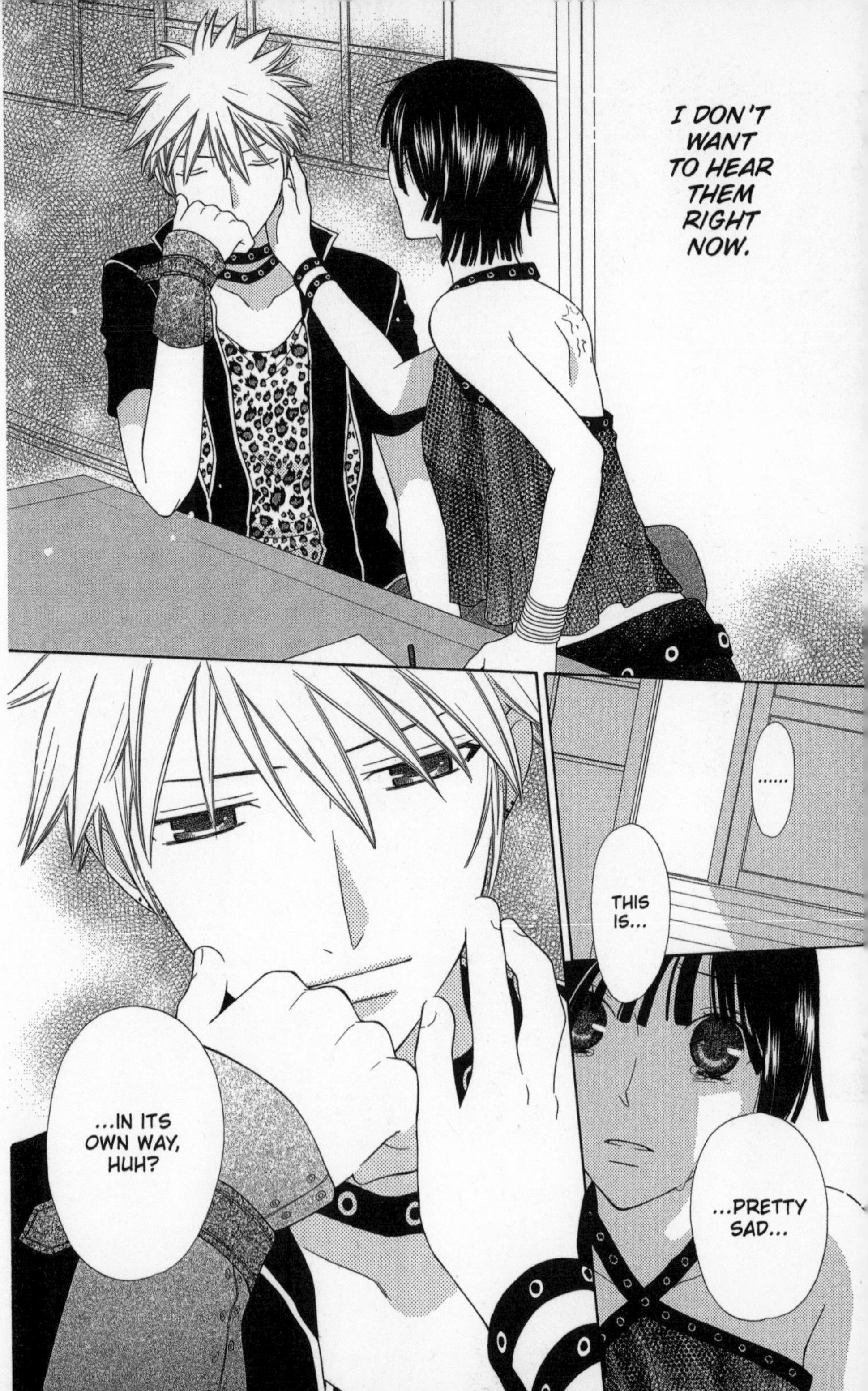
I DON'T WANT TO HEAR THEM RIGHT NOW.
......
THIS IS...
...PRETTY SAD...
...IN ITS OWN WAY, HUH?

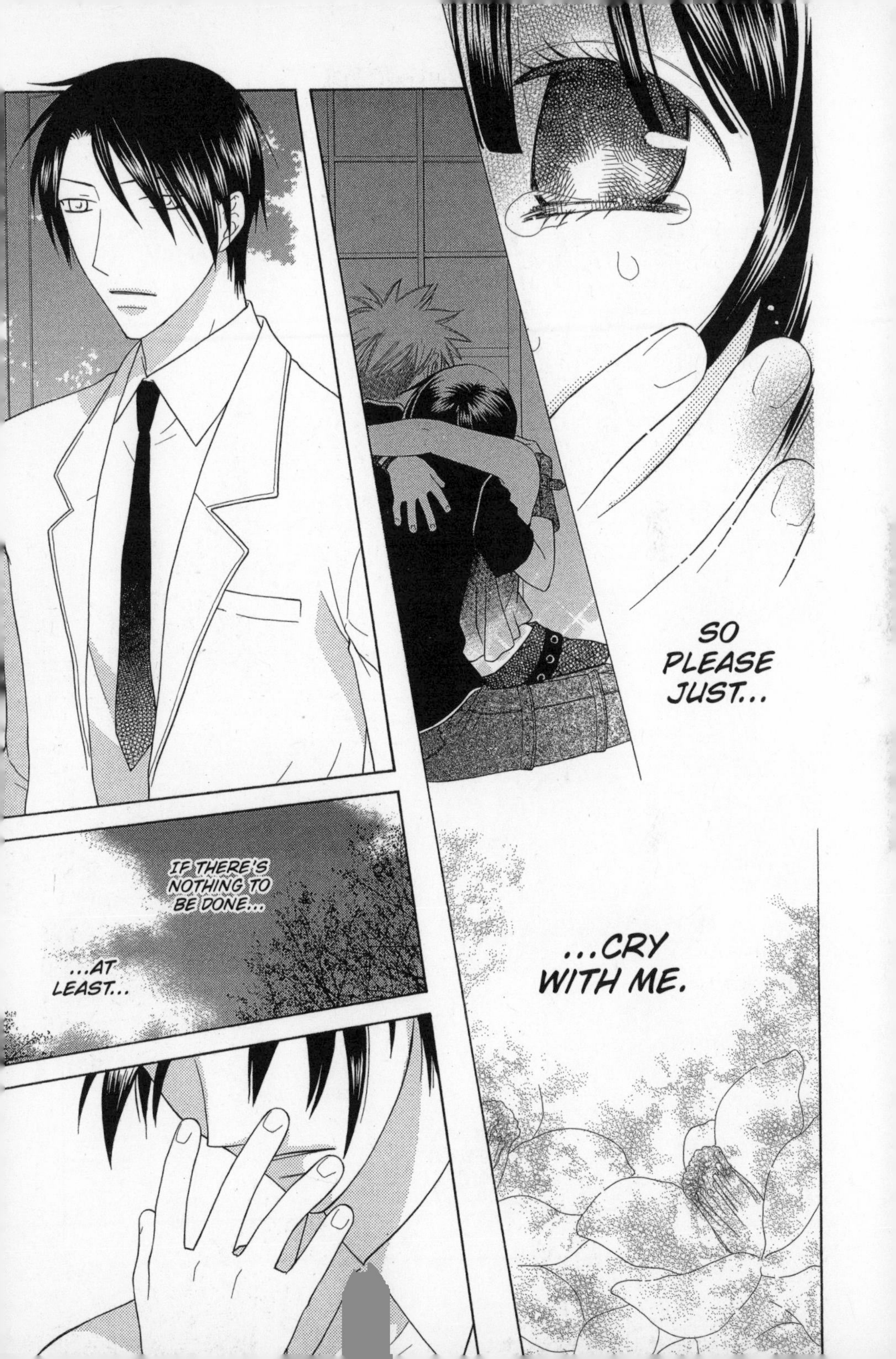
SO PLEASE JUST...
...CRY WITH ME.
IF THERE'S NOTHING TO BE DONE...
...AT LEAST...

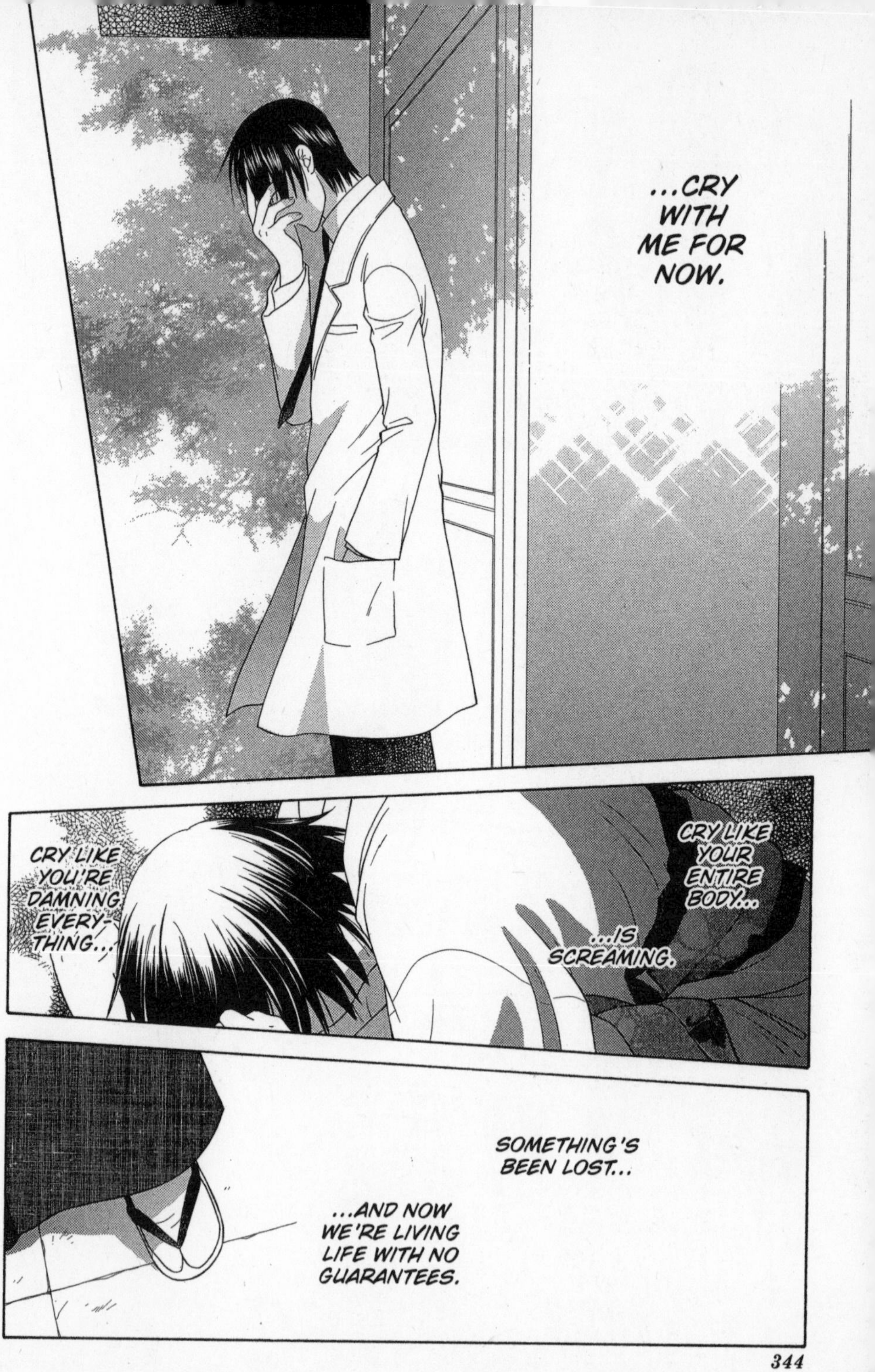
...CRY WITH ME FOR NOW.
CRY LIKE YOUR ENTIRE BODY...
...IS SCREAMING.
CRY LIKE YOU'RE DAMNING EVERY-THING...
SOMETHING'S BEEN LOST...
...AND NOW WE'RE LIVING LIFE WITH NO GUARANTEES.

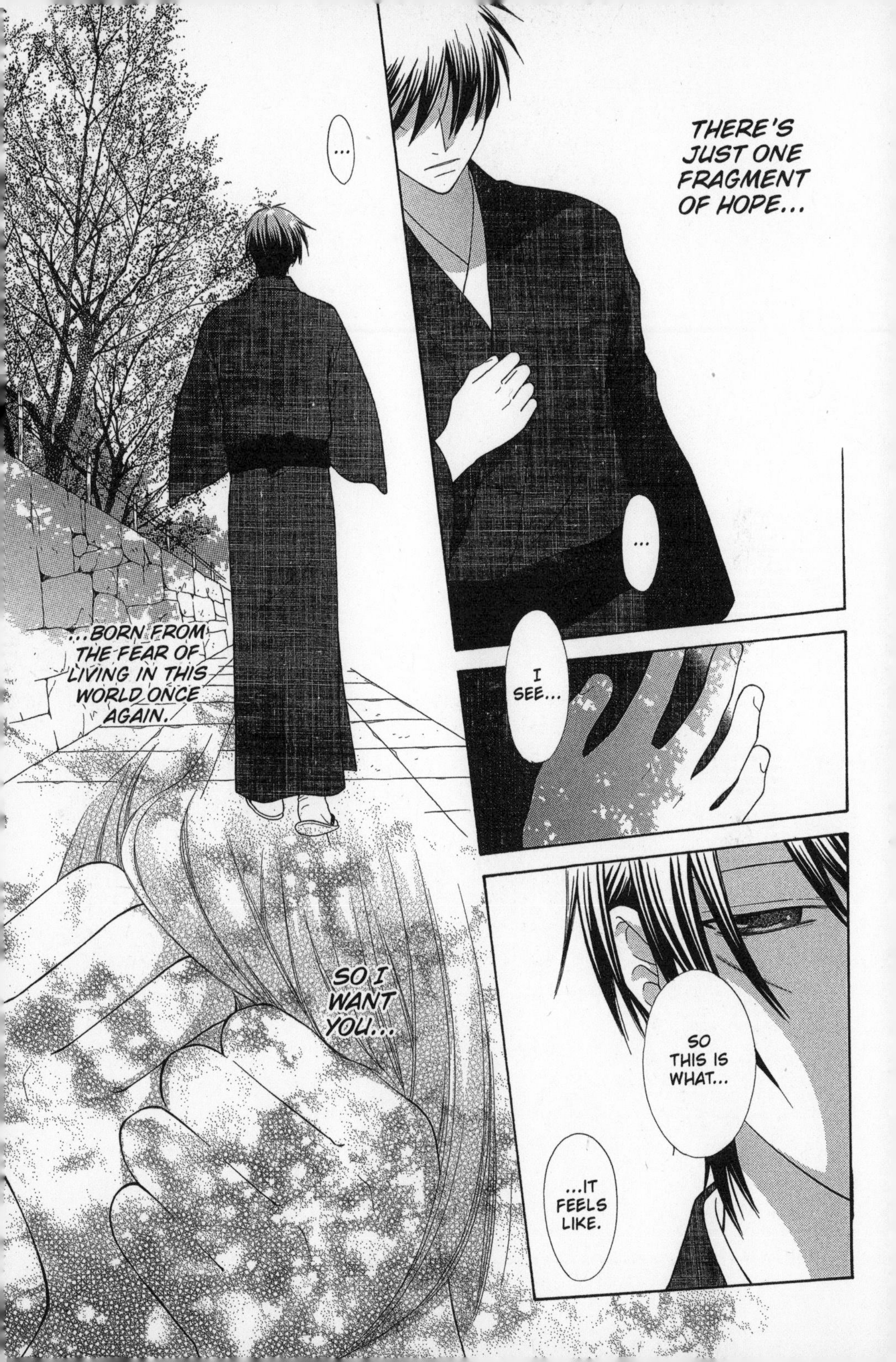
THERE'S JUST ONE FRAGMENT OF HOPE...
...
I SEE...
SO THIS IS WHAT...
...IT FEELS LIKE.
...
...BORN FROM THE FEAR OF LIVING IN THIS WORLD ONCE AGAIN.
SO I WANT YOU...

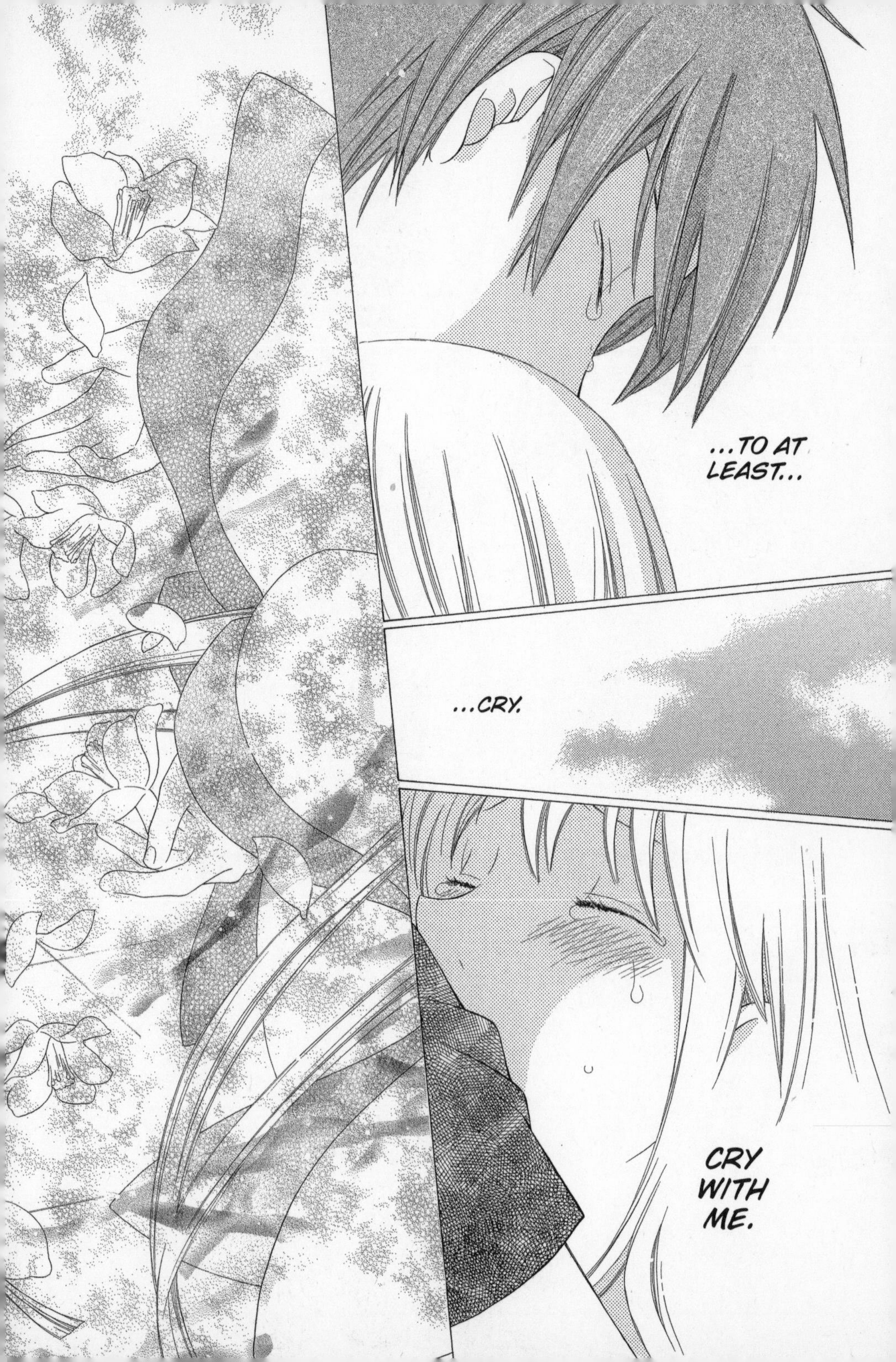
...TO AT LEAST...
...CRY.
CRY WITH ME.

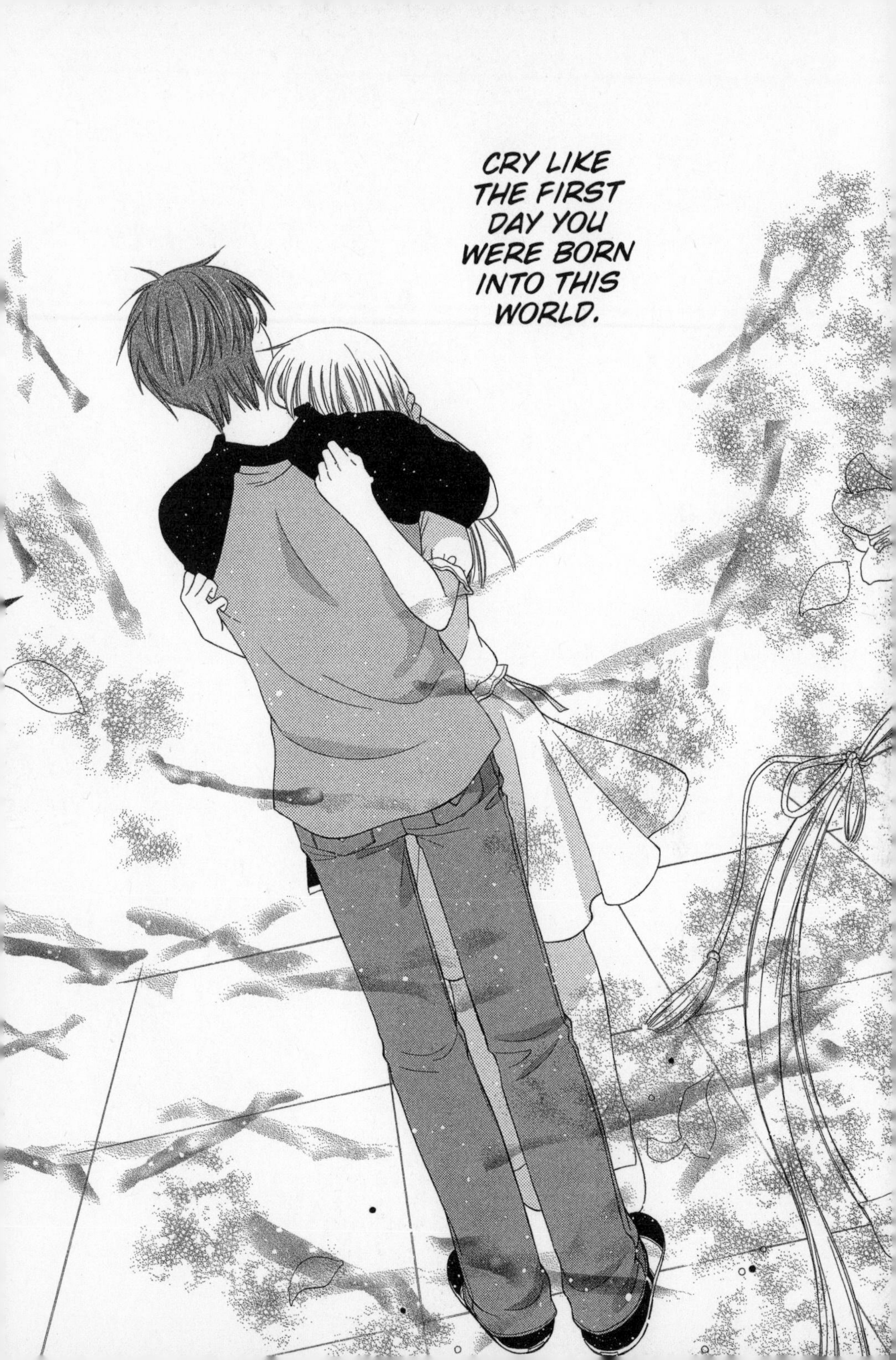
CRY LIKE THE FIRST DAY YOU WERE BORN INTO THIS WORLD.

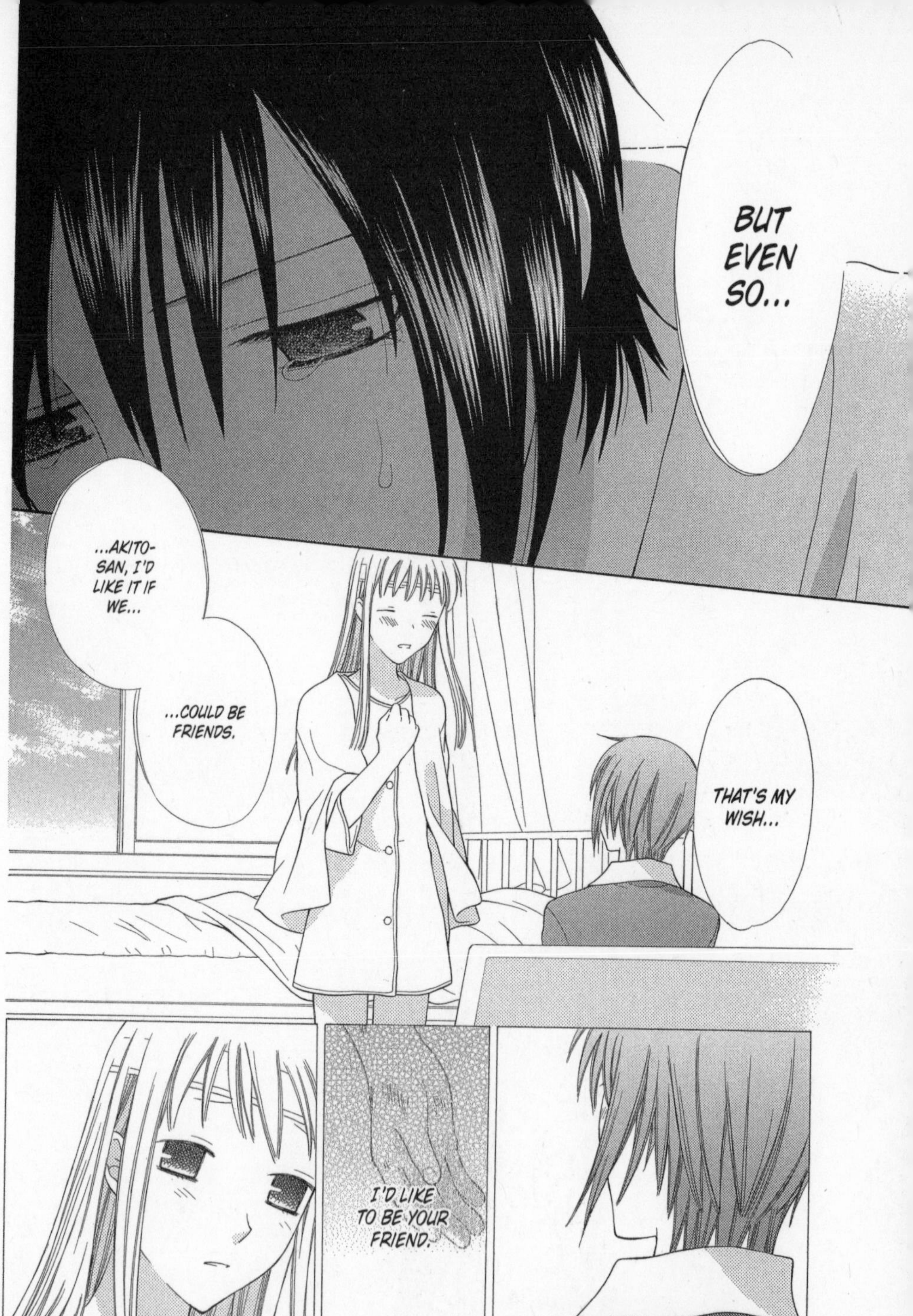
BUT EVEN SO...
...AKITO-SAN, I'D LIKE IT IF WE...
...COULD BE FRIENDS.
THAT'S MY WISH...
I'D LIKE TO BE YOUR FRIEND.

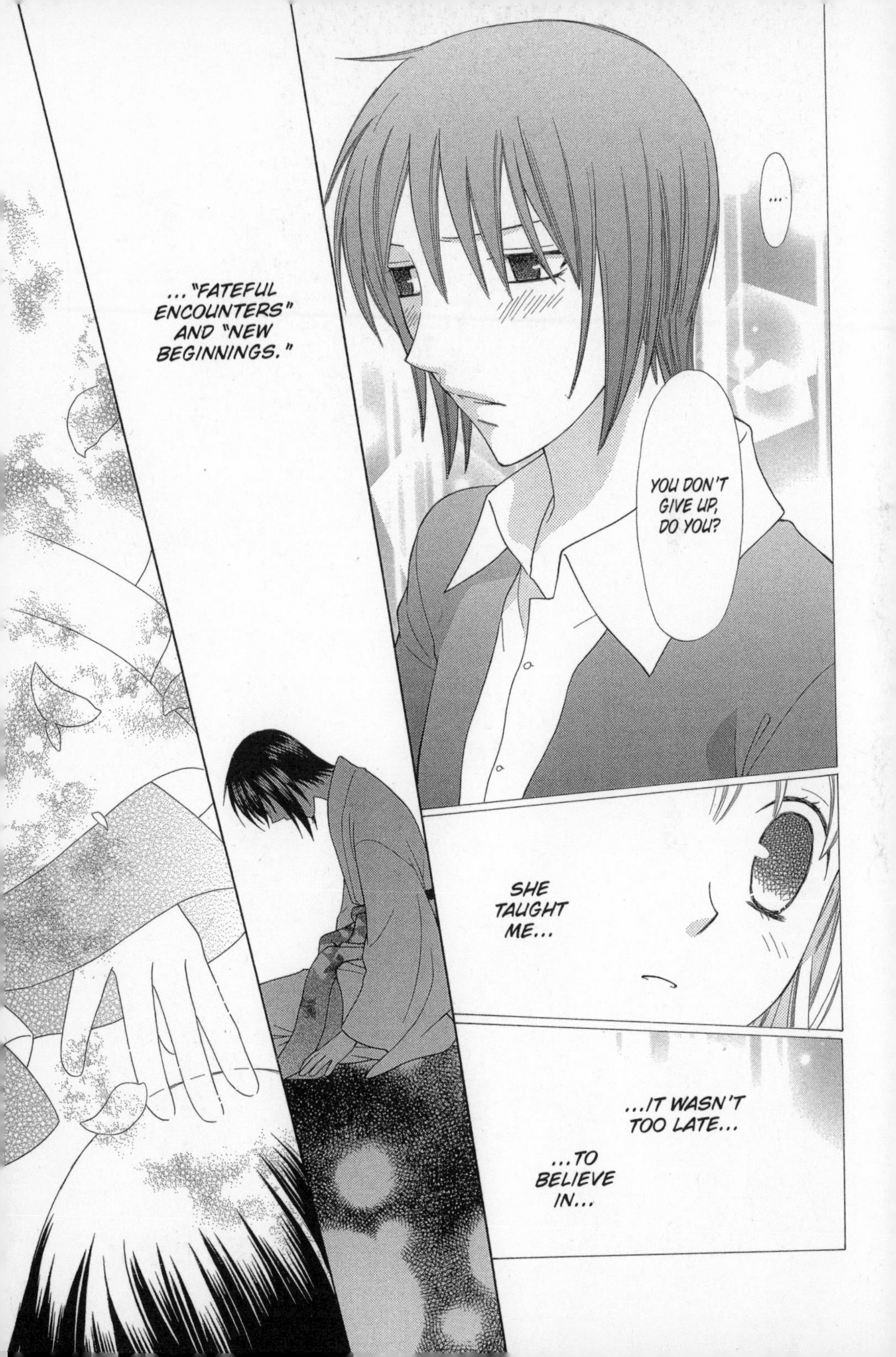

...
YOU DON'T GIVE UP, DO YOU?
SHE TAUGHT ME...
...IT WASN'T TOO LATE...
...TO BELIEVE IN...
..."FATEFUL ENCOUNTERS" AND "NEW BEGINNINGS."

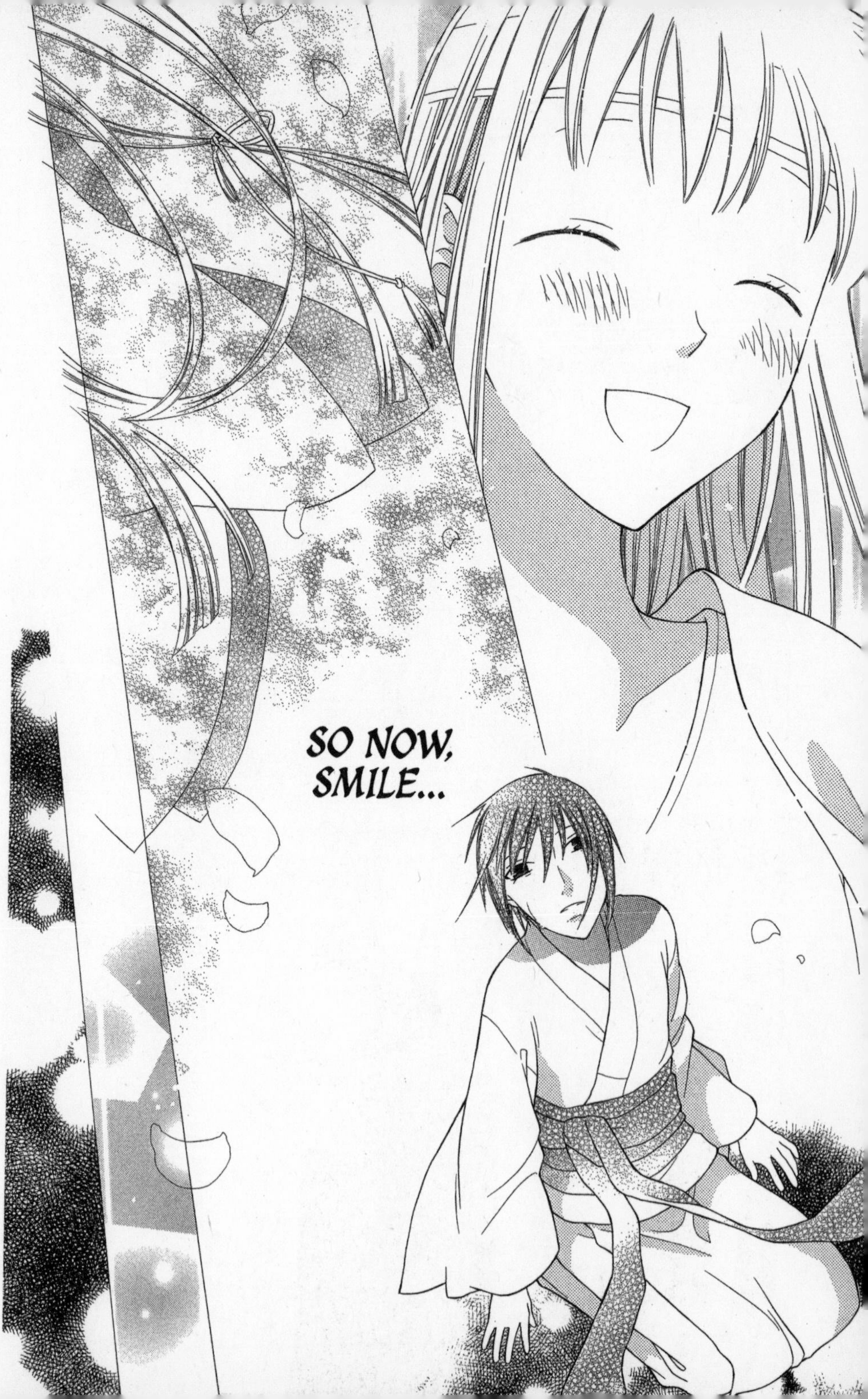
SO NOW, SMILE...

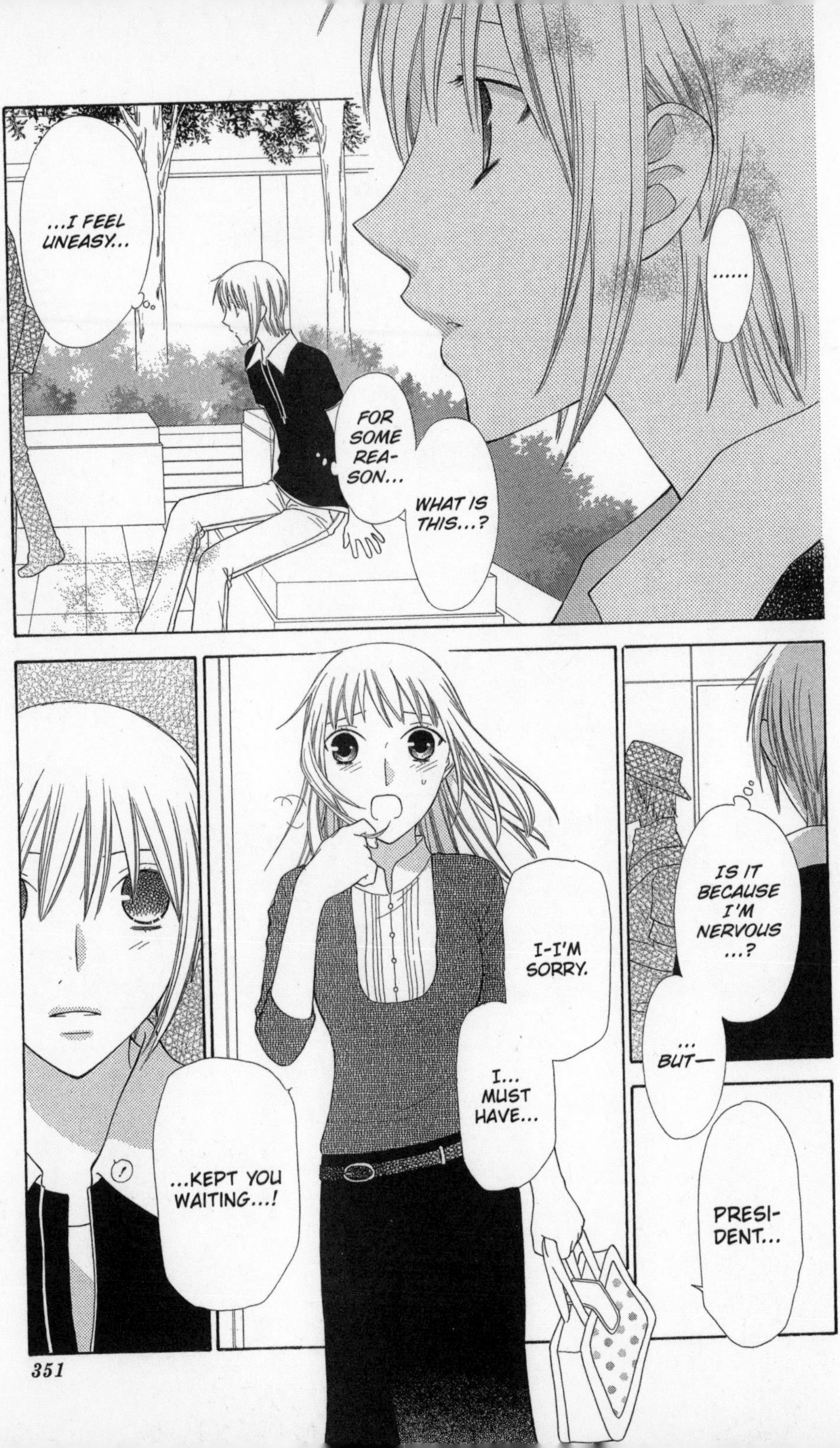
......
WHAT IS THIS...?
FOR SOME REA-SON...
...I FEEL UNEASY...
IS IT BECAUSE I'M NERVOUS ...?
... BUT—
PRESI-DENT...
I-I'M SORRY.
I... MUST HAVE...
...KEPT YOU WAITING...!
!

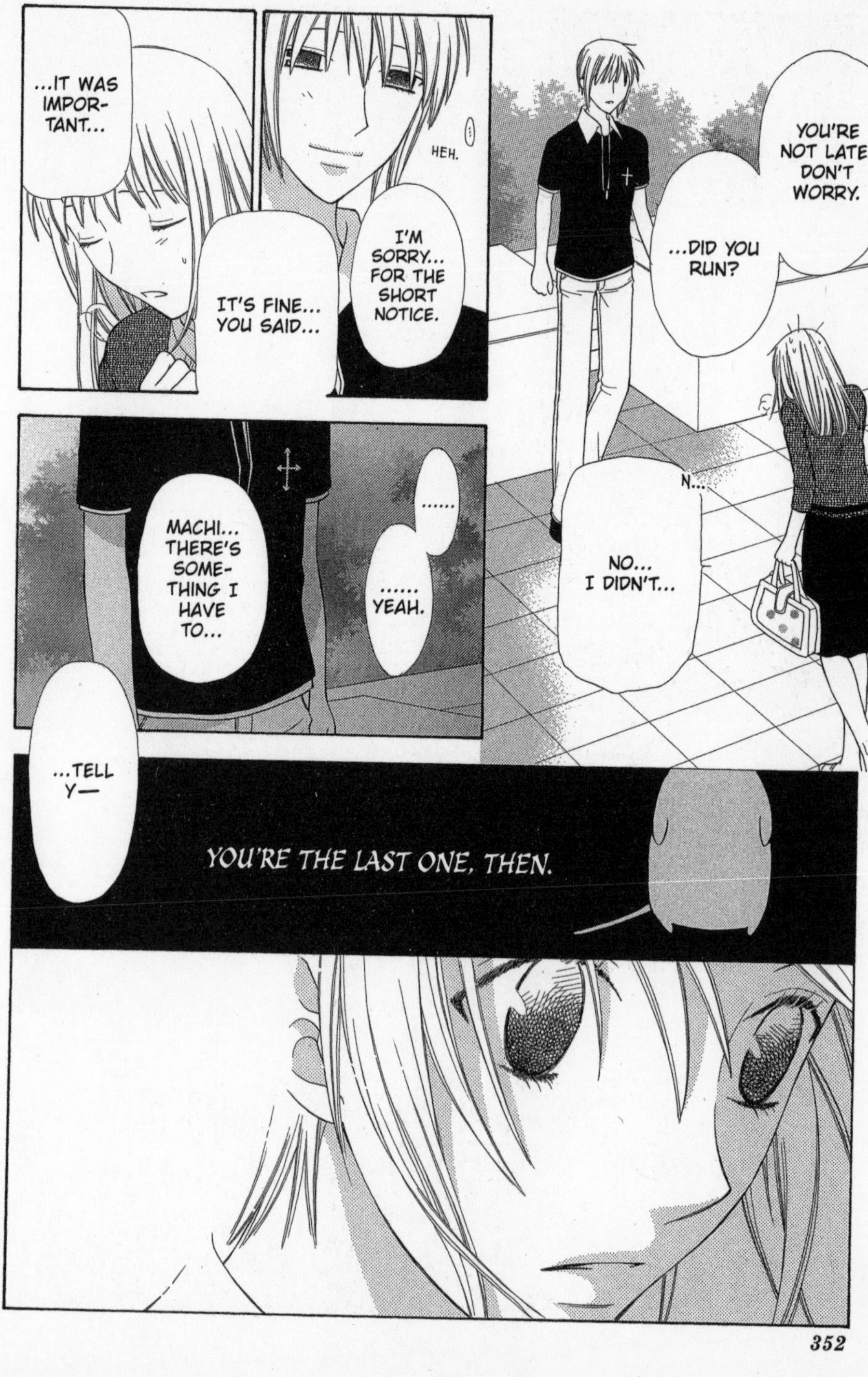
YOU'RE NOT LATE. DON'T WORRY.
...DID YOU RUN?
N...
NO... I DIDN'T...
HEH.
I'M SORRY... FOR THE SHORT NOTICE.
IT'S FINE... YOU SAID...
...IT WAS IMPORTANT...
MACHI... THERE'S SOMETHING I HAVE TO...
......
...... YEAH.
...TELL Y—
YOU'RE THE LAST ONE, THEN.

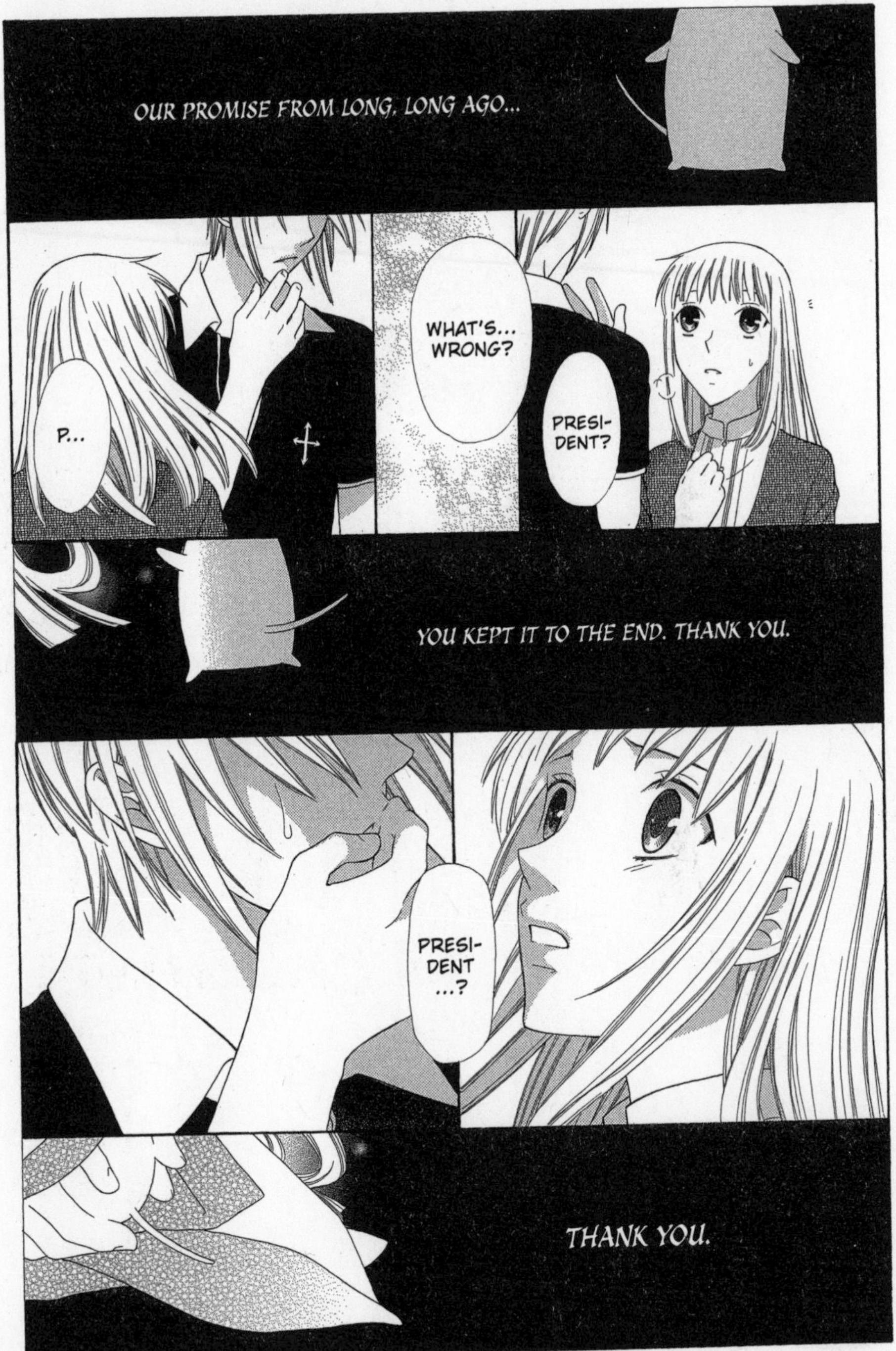
OUR PROMISE FROM LONG, LONG AGO...
PRESIDENT?
WHAT'S... WRONG?
P...
YOU KEPT IT TO THE END. THANK YOU.
PRESIDENT...?
THANK YOU.

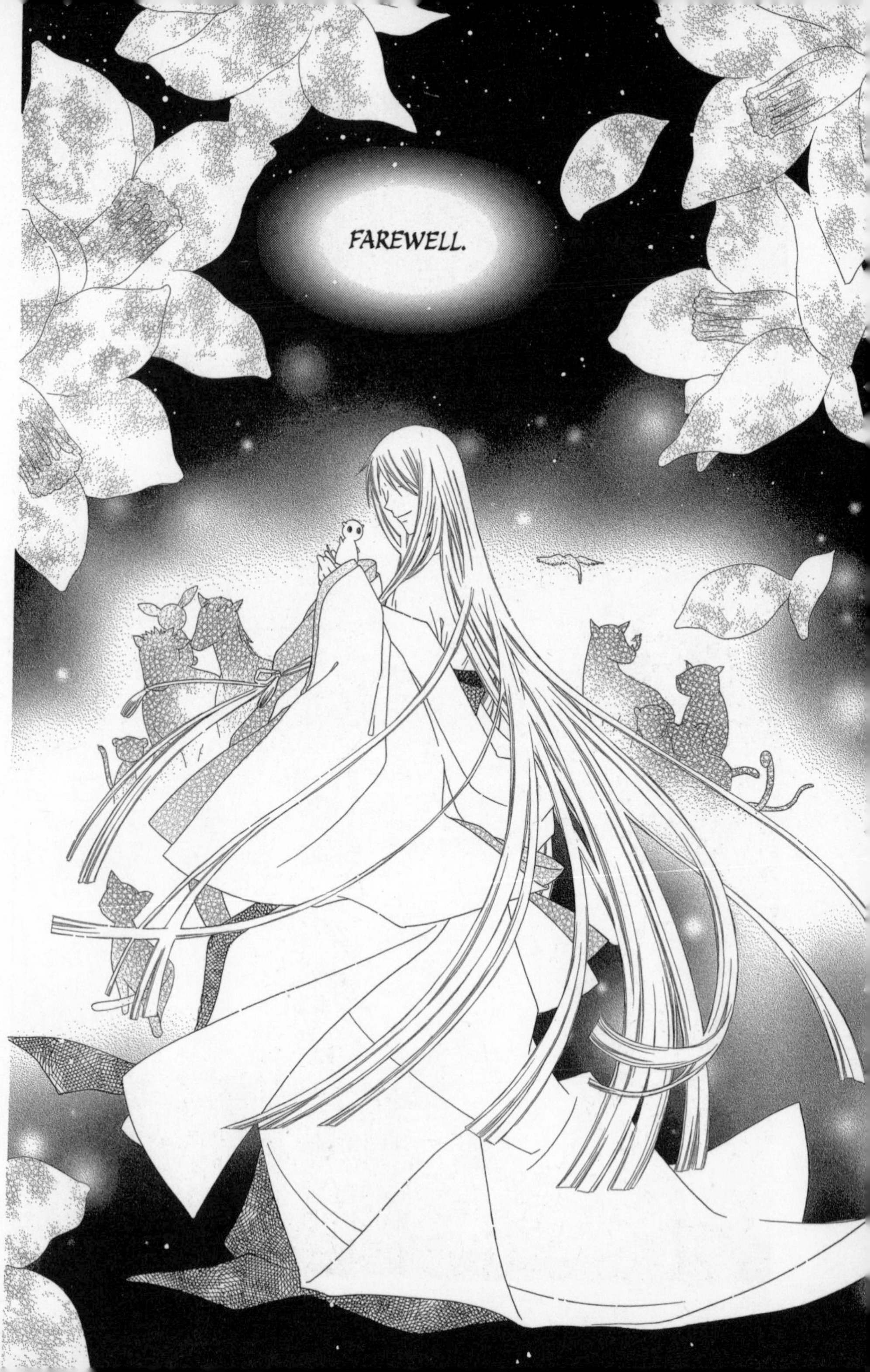
FAREWELL.

Chapter 131

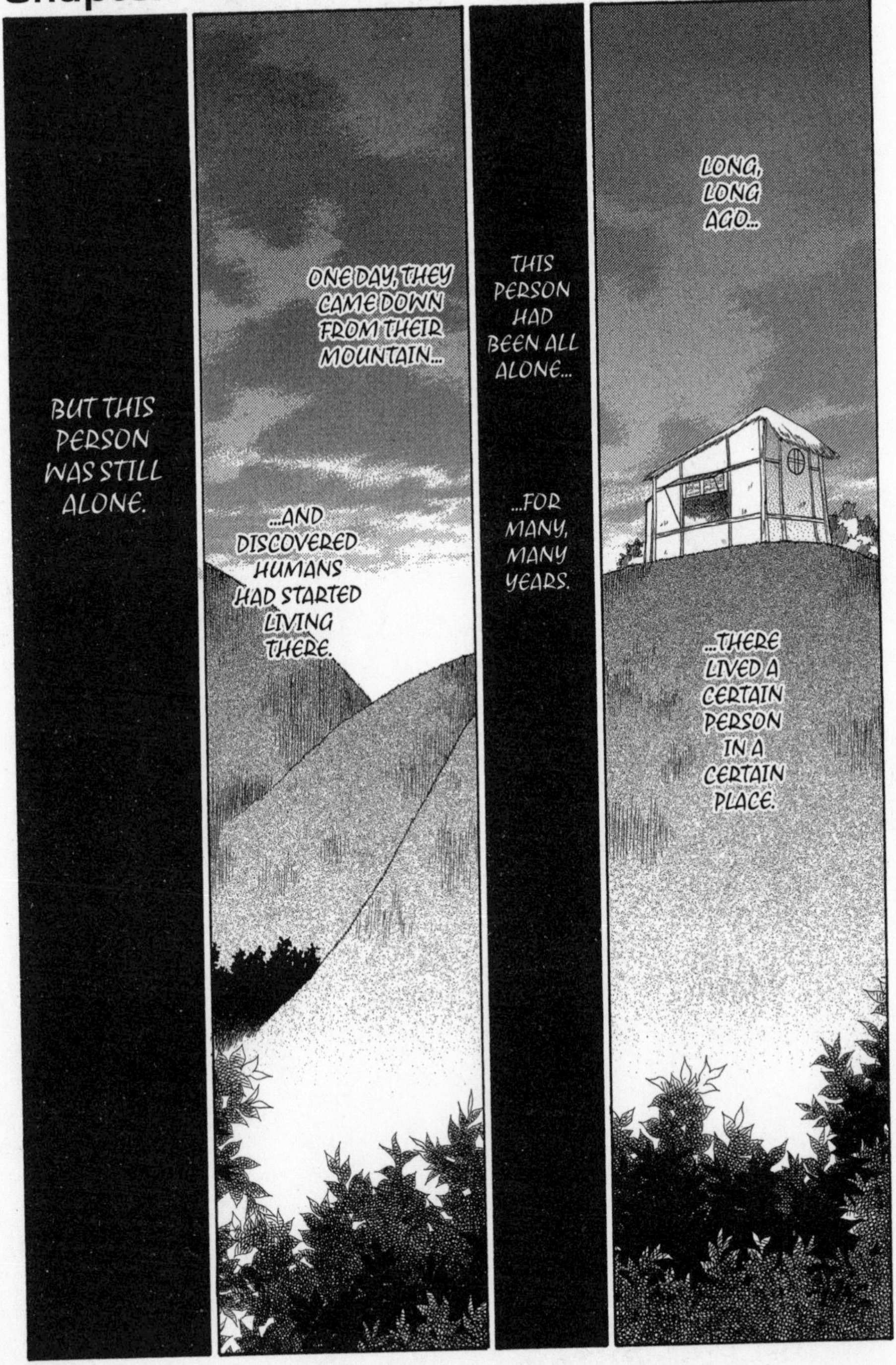
LONG, LONG AGO...
...THERE LIVED A CERTAIN PERSON IN A CERTAIN PLACE.
THIS PERSON HAD BEEN ALL ALONE...
...FOR MANY, MANY YEARS.
ONE DAY, THEY CAME DOWN FROM THEIR MOUNTAIN...
...AND DISCOVERED HUMANS HAD STARTED LIVING THERE.
BUT THIS PERSON WAS STILL ALONE.

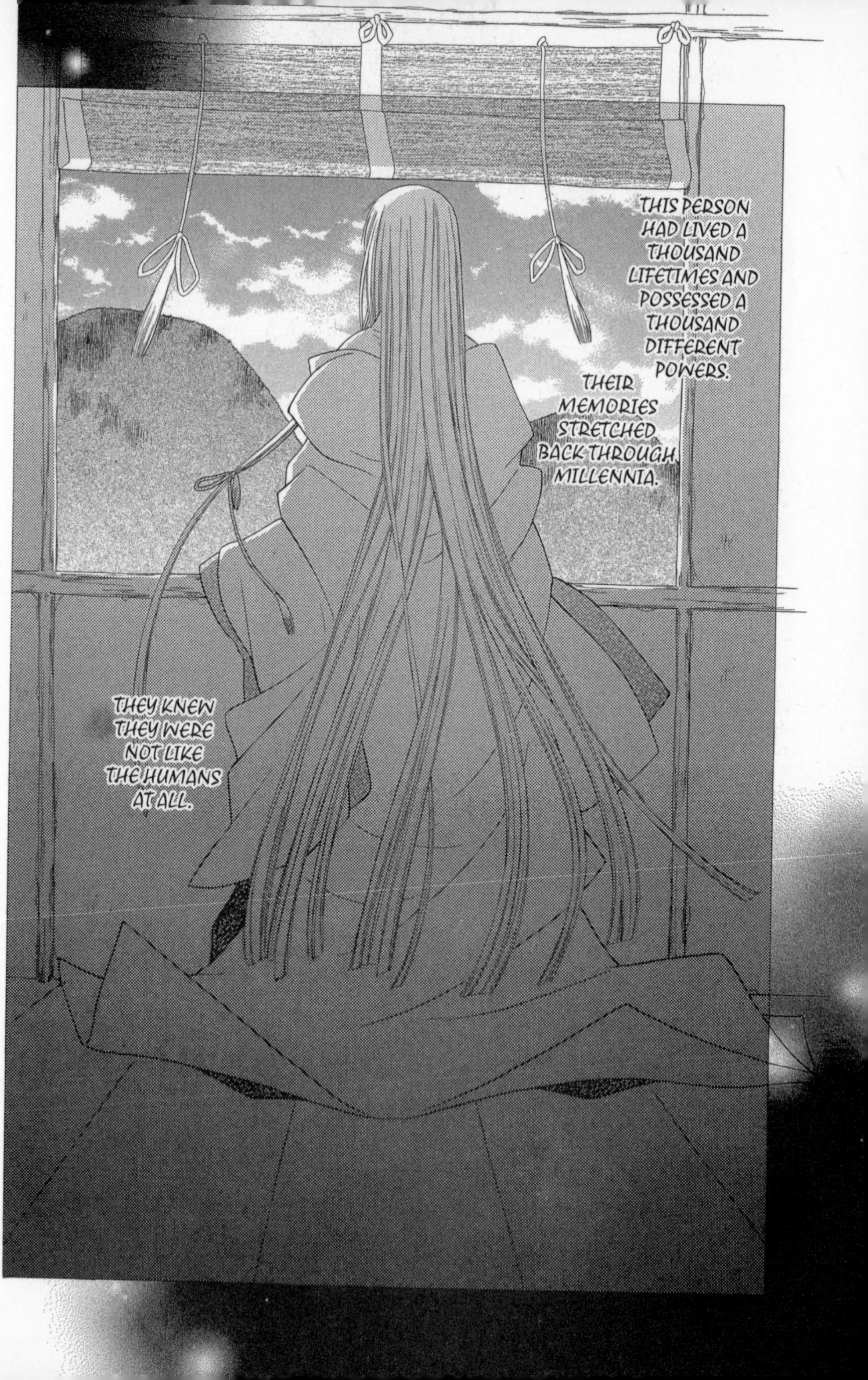
THIS PERSON HAD LIVED A THOUSAND LIFETIMES AND POSSESSED A THOUSAND DIFFERENT POWERS.
THEIR MEMORIES STRETCHED BACK THROUGH MILLENNIA.
THEY KNEW THEY WERE NOT LIKE THE HUMANS AT ALL.

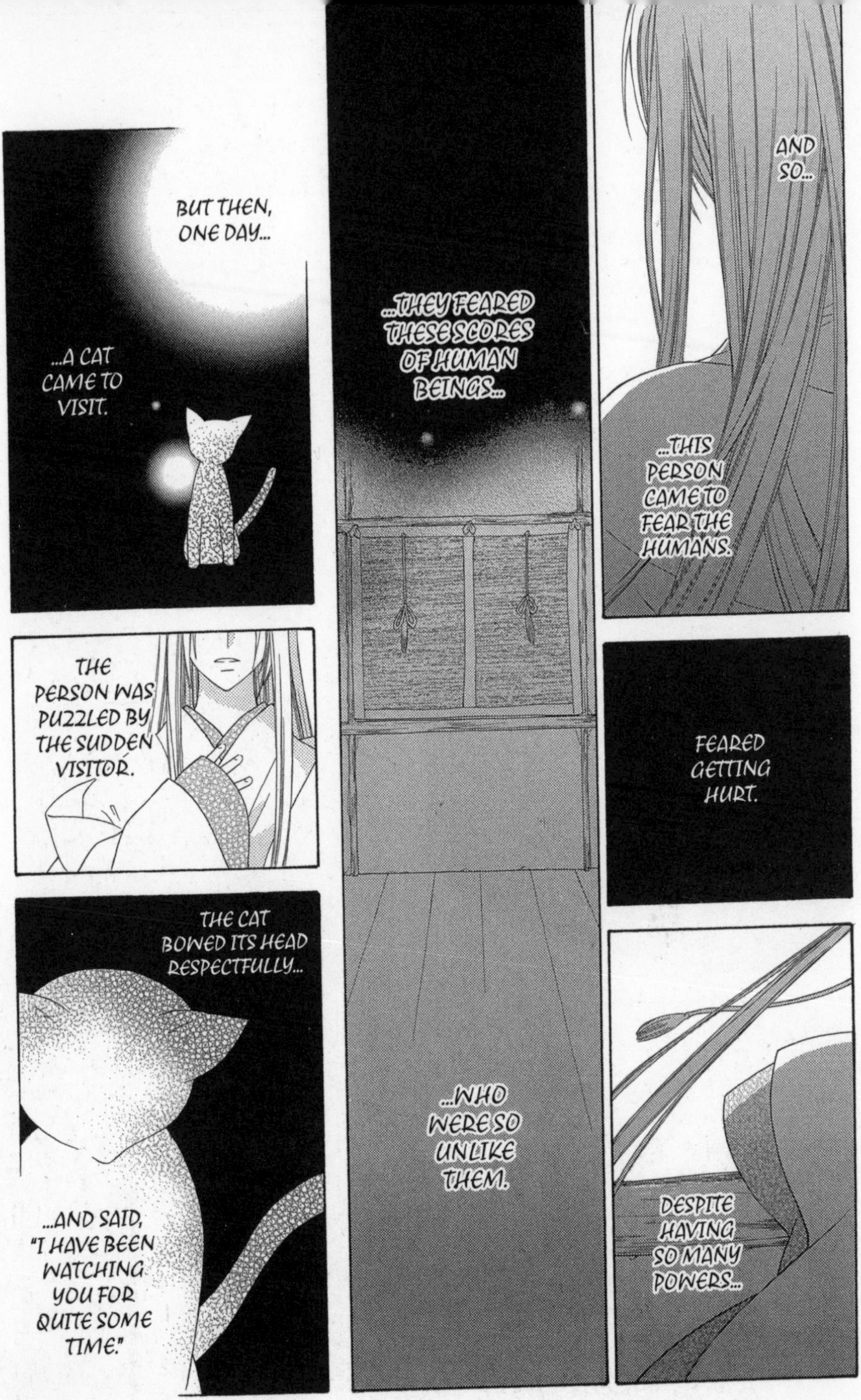
AND SO...
...THIS PERSON CAME TO FEAR THE HUMANS.
FEARED GETTING HURT.
DESPITE HAVING SO MANY POWERS...
...THEY FEARED THESE SCORES OF HUMAN BEINGS...
...WHO WERE SO UNLIKE THEM.
BUT THEN, ONE DAY...
...A CAT CAME TO VISIT.
THE PERSON WAS PUZZLED BY THE SUDDEN VISITOR.
THE CAT BOWED ITS HEAD RESPECTFULLY...
...AND SAID, "I HAVE BEEN WATCHING YOU FOR QUITE SOME TIME."

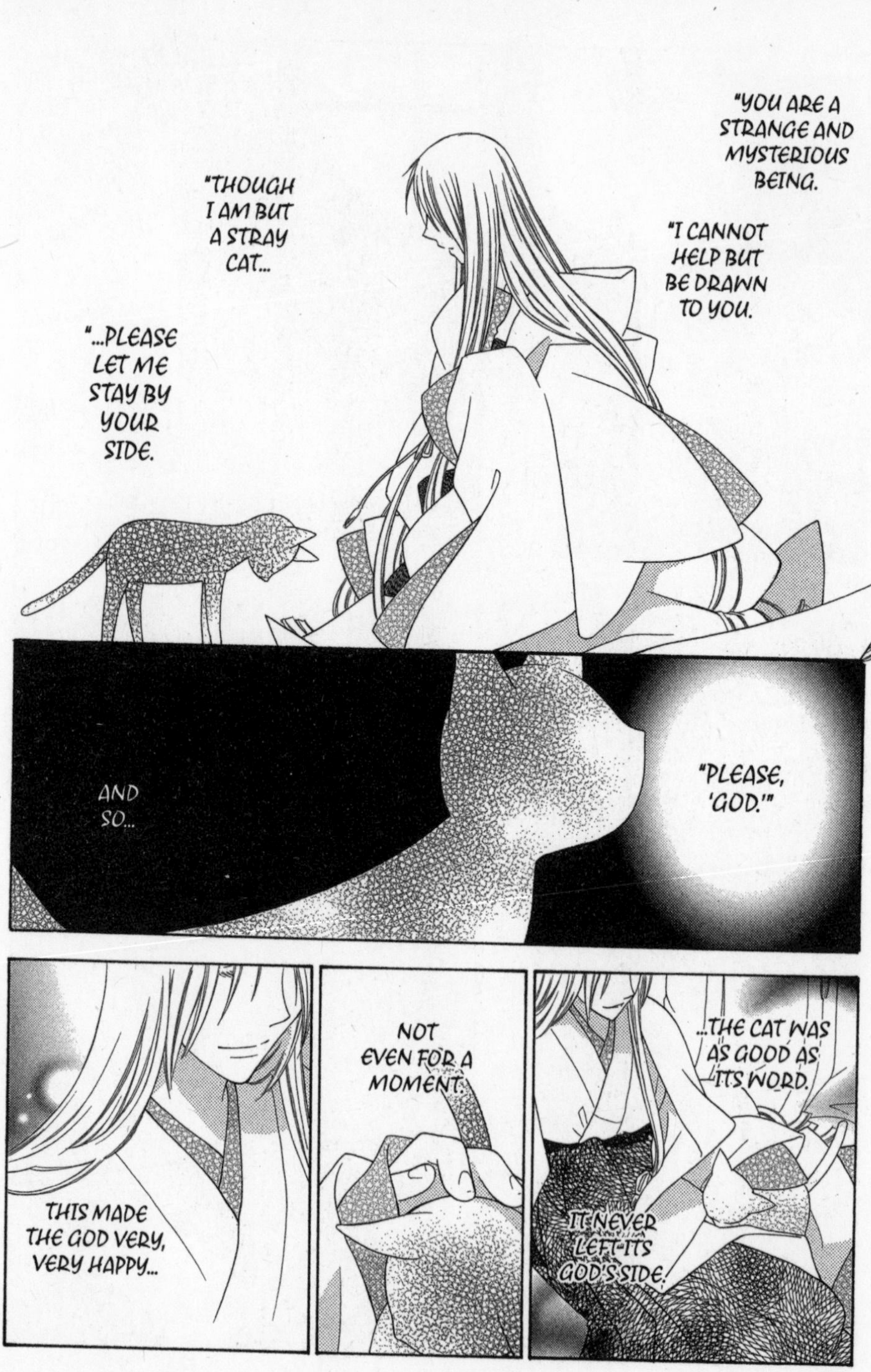
"YOU ARE A STRANGE AND MYSTERIOUS BEING.
"I CANNOT HELP BUT BE DRAWN TO YOU.
"THOUGH I AM BUT A STRAY CAT...
"...PLEASE LET ME STAY BY YOUR SIDE.
"PLEASE, 'GOD.'"
AND SO...
...THE CAT WAS AS GOOD AS ITS WORD.
IT NEVER LEFT ITS GOD'S SIDE.
NOT EVEN FOR A MOMENT.
THIS MADE THE GOD VERY, VERY HAPPY...

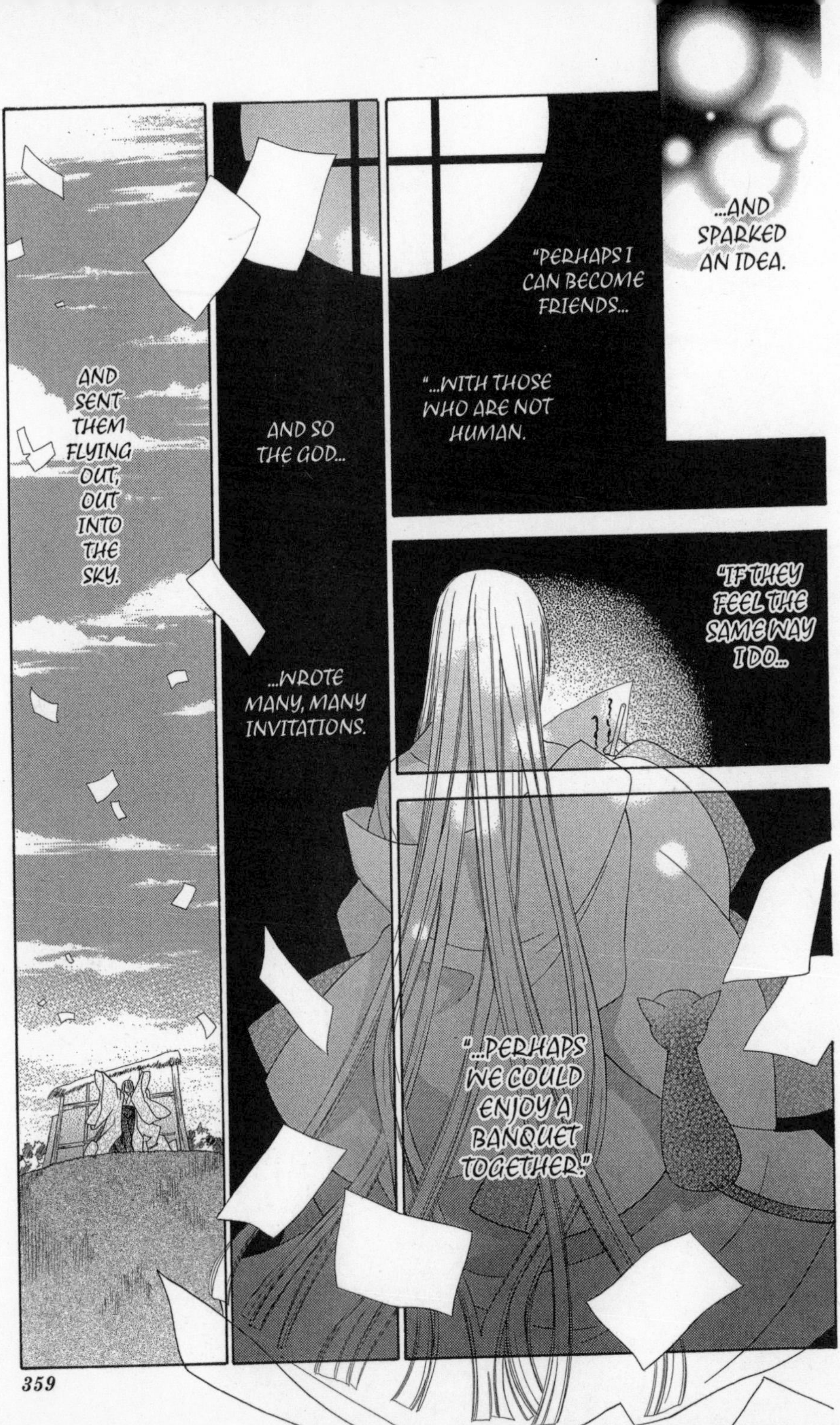
...AND SPARKED AN IDEA.
"PERHAPS I CAN BECOME FRIENDS...
"...WITH THOSE WHO ARE NOT HUMAN.
"IF THEY FEEL THE SAME WAY I DO...
"...PERHAPS WE COULD ENJOY A BANQUET TOGETHER."
AND SO THE GOD...
...WROTE MANY, MANY INVITATIONS.
AND SENT THEM FLYING OUT, OUT INTO THE SKY.

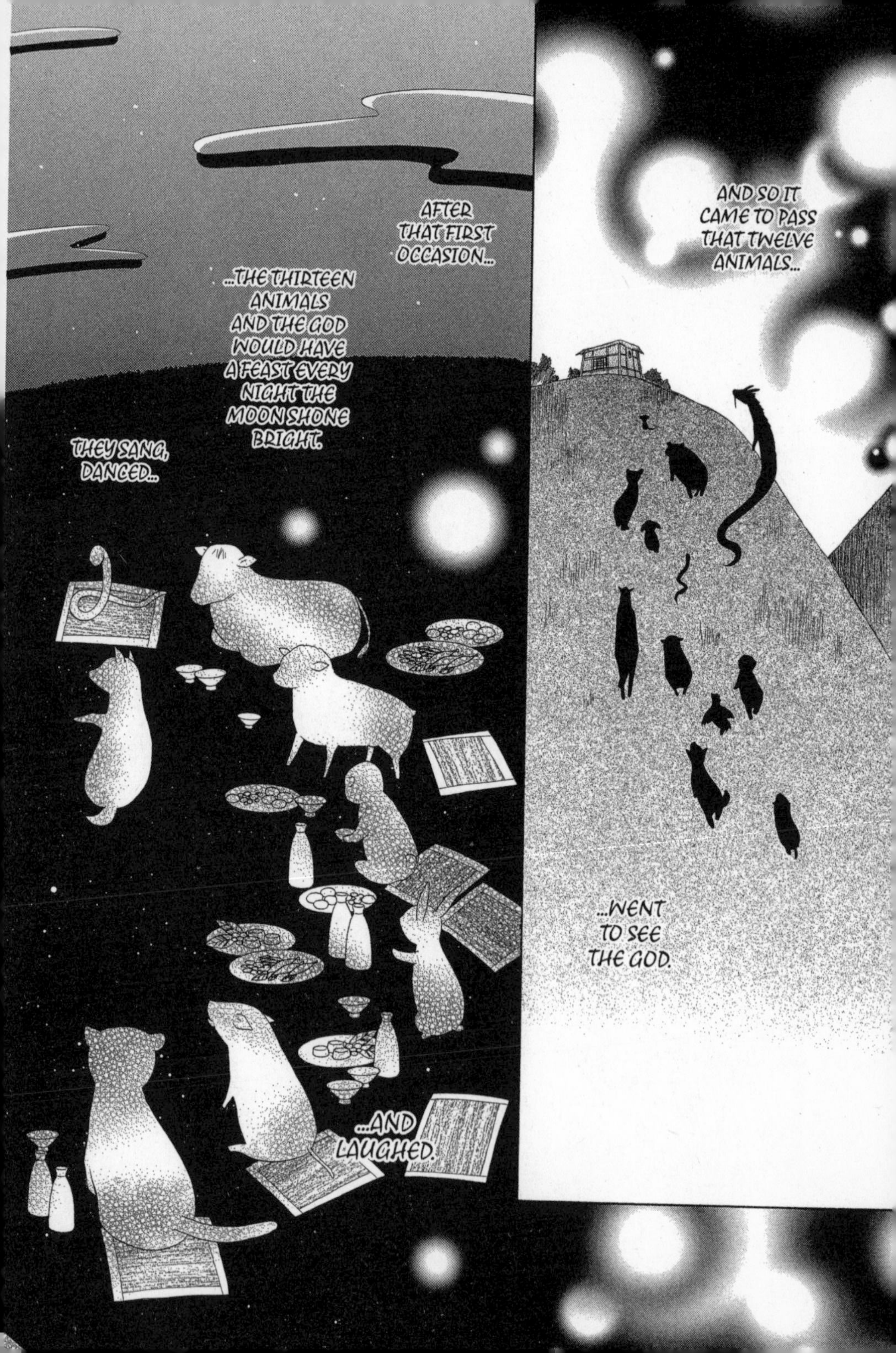
AND SO IT CAME TO PASS THAT TWELVE ANIMALS...
...WENT TO SEE THE GOD.
AFTER THAT FIRST OCCASION...
...THE THIRTEEN ANIMALS AND THE GOD WOULD HAVE A FEAST EVERY NIGHT THE MOON SHONE BRIGHT.
THEY SANG, DANCED...
...AND LAUGHED.

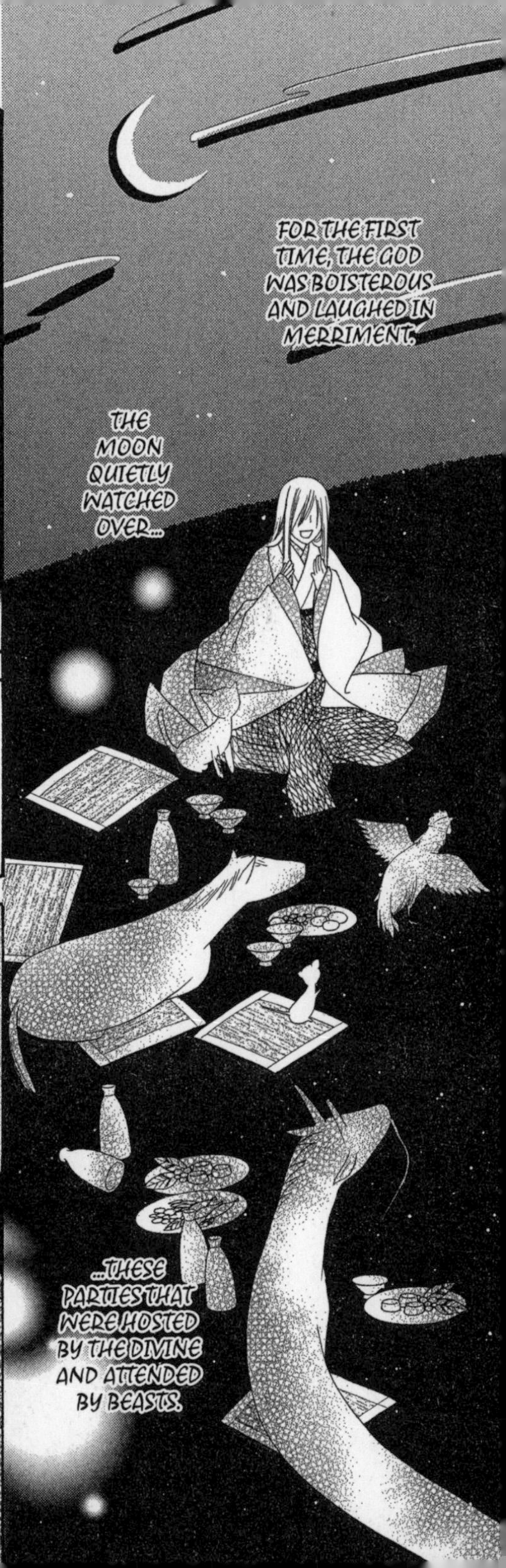
FOR THE FIRST TIME, THE GOD WAS BOISTEROUS AND LAUGHED IN MERRIMENT.
THE MOON QUIETLY WATCHED OVER...
...THESE PARTIES THAT WERE HOSTED BY THE DIVINE AND ATTENDED BY BEASTS.
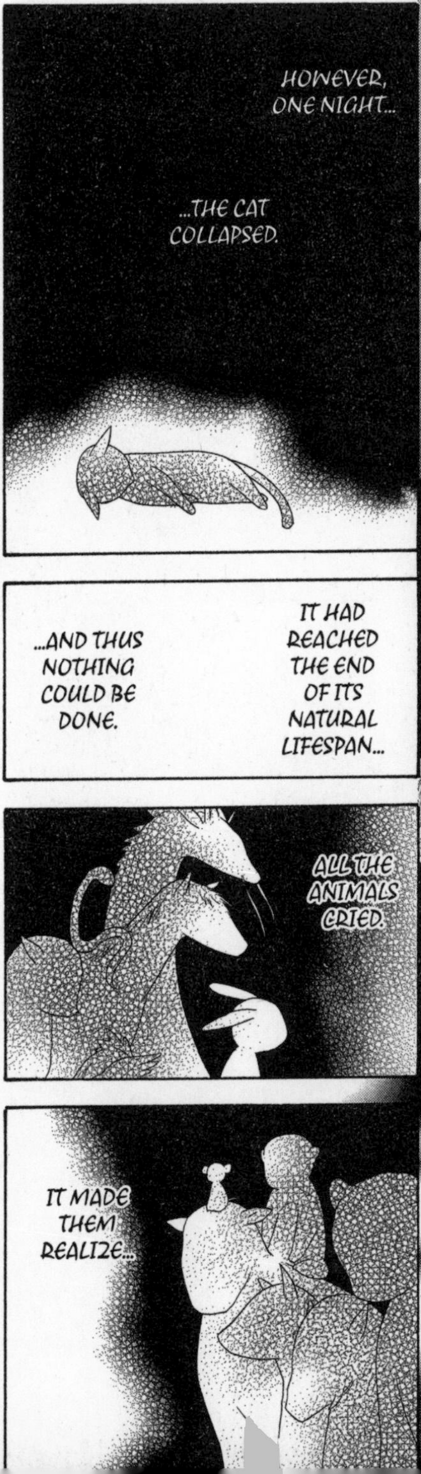
HOWEVER, ONE NIGHT...
...THE CAT COLLAPSED.
IT HAD REACHED THE END OF ITS NATURAL LIFESPAN...
...AND THUS NOTHING COULD BE DONE.
ALL THE ANIMALS CRIED.
IT MADE THEM REALIZE...

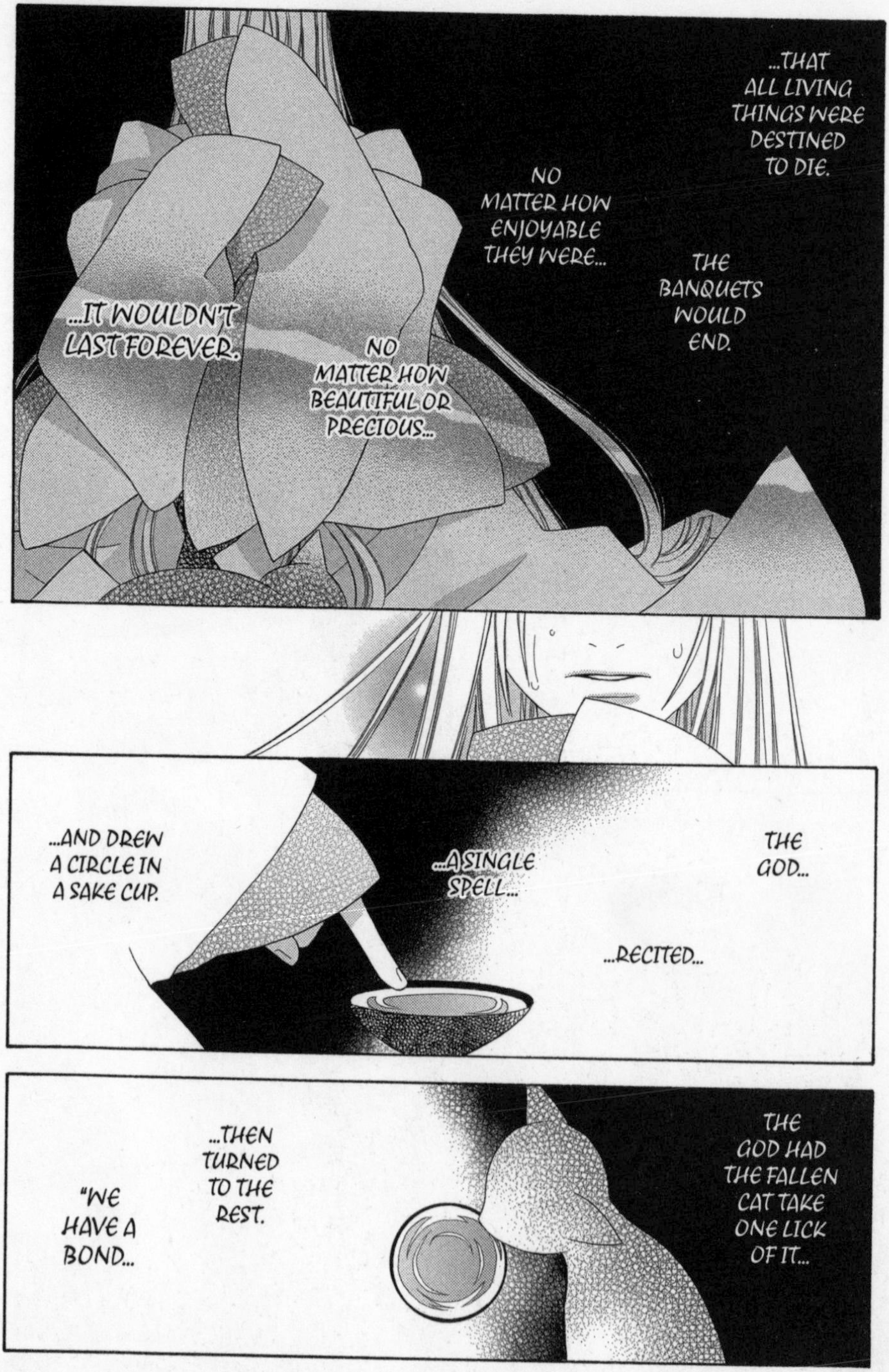
...THAT ALL LIVING THINGS WERE DESTINED TO DIE.
THE BANQUETS WOULD END.
NO MATTER HOW ENJOYABLE THEY WERE...
NO MATTER HOW BEAUTIFUL OR PRECIOUS...
...IT WOULDN'T LAST FOREVER.
THE GOD...
...RECITED...
...A SINGLE SPELL...
...AND DREW A CIRCLE IN A SAKE CUP.
THE GOD HAD THE FALLEN CAT TAKE ONE LICK OF IT...
...THEN TURNED TO THE REST.
"WE HAVE A BOND...

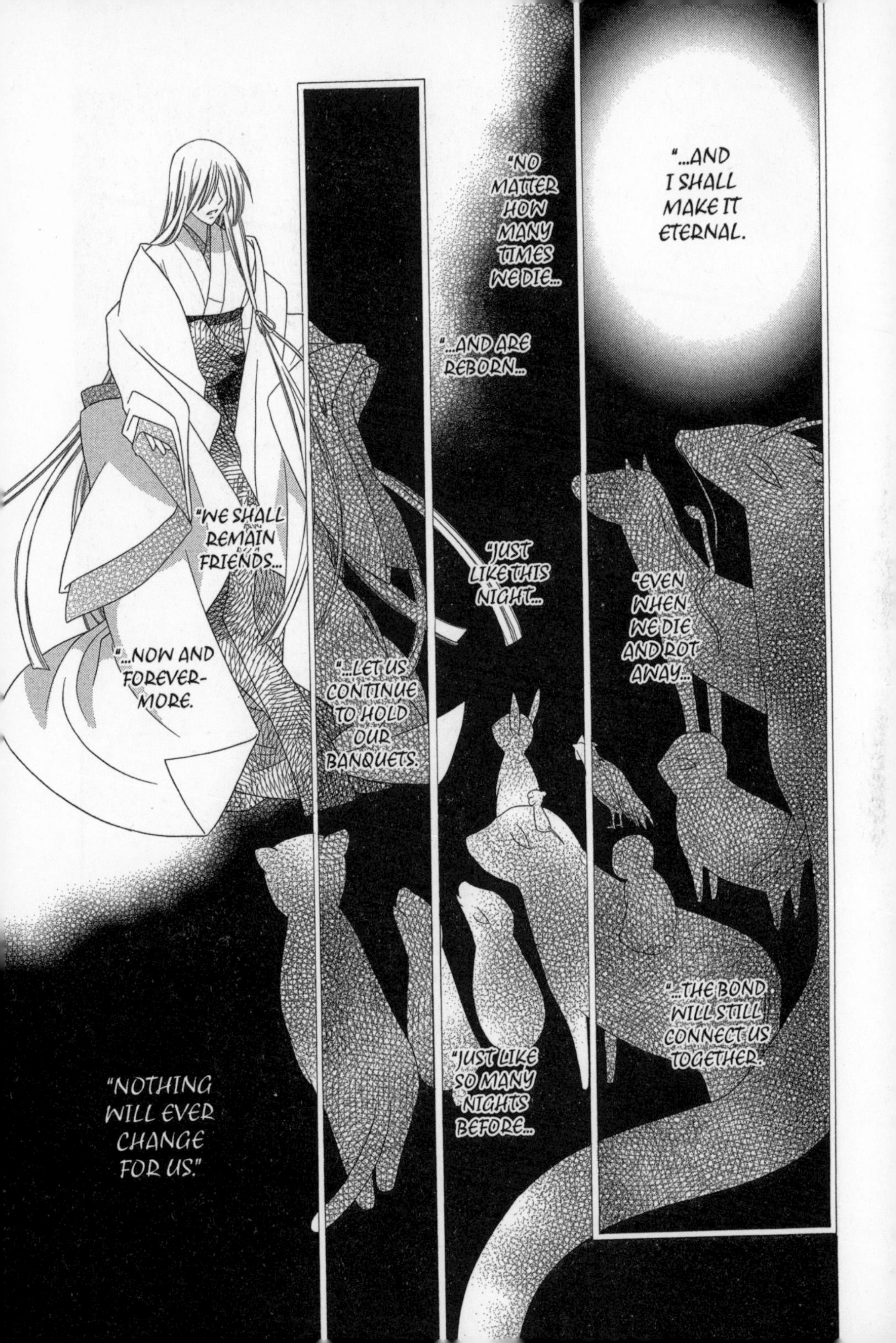
"...AND I SHALL MAKE IT ETERNAL.
"EVEN WHEN WE DIE AND ROT AWAY...
"...THE BOND WILL STILL CONNECT US TOGETHER.
"NO MATTER HOW MANY TIMES WE DIE...
"...AND ARE REBORN...
"JUST LIKE THIS NIGHT...
"JUST LIKE SO MANY NIGHTS BEFORE...
"...LET US CONTINUE TO HOLD OUR BANQUETS.
"WE SHALL REMAIN FRIENDS...
"...NOW AND FOREVER-MORE.
"NOTHING WILL EVER CHANGE FOR US."

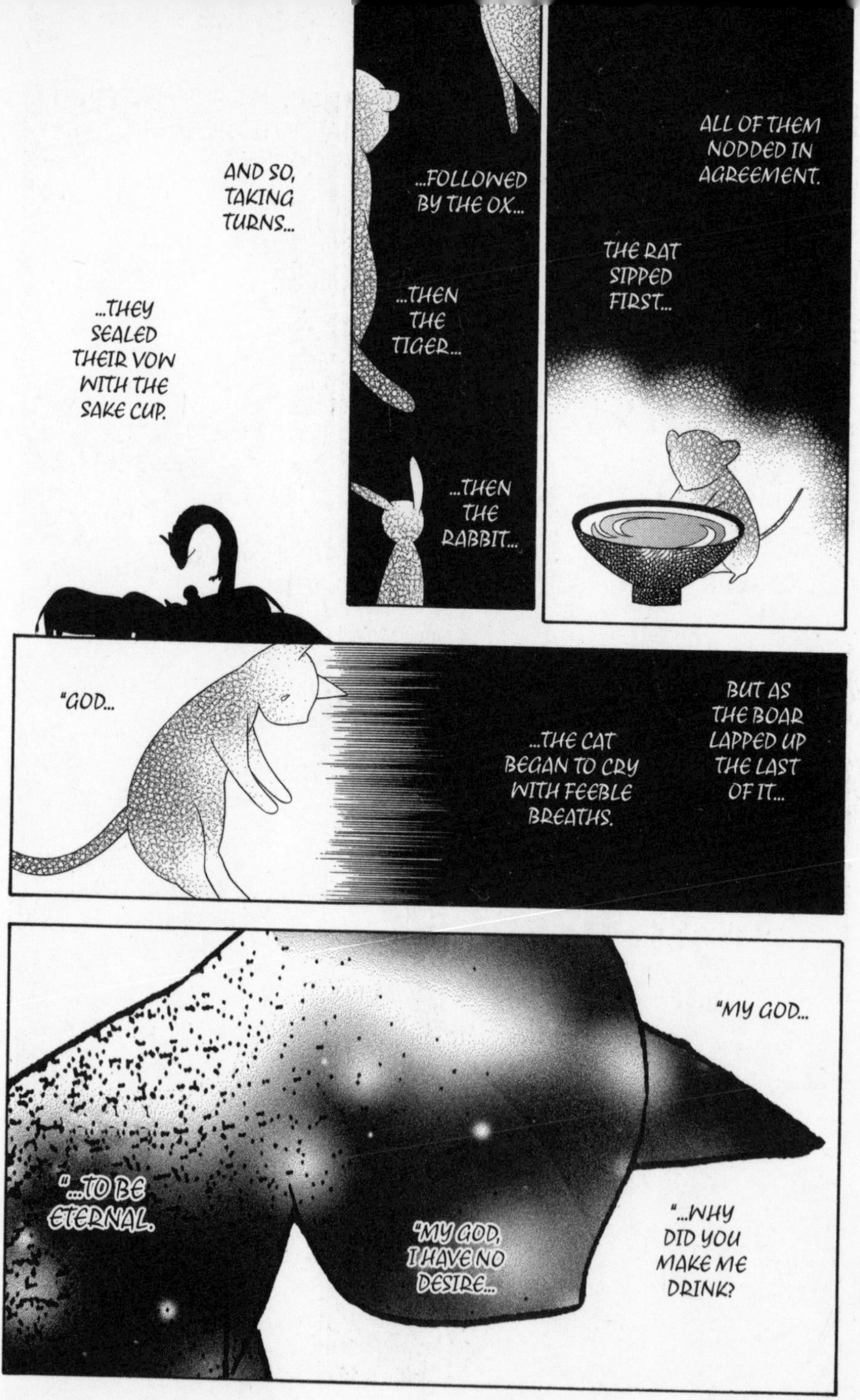
ALL OF THEM NODDED IN AGREEMENT.
THE RAT SIPPED FIRST...
...FOLLOWED BY THE OX...
...THEN THE TIGER...
...THEN THE RABBIT...
AND SO, TAKING TURNS...
...THEY SEALED THEIR VOW WITH THE SAKE CUP.
BUT AS THE BOAR LAPPED UP THE LAST OF IT...
...THE CAT BEGAN TO CRY WITH FEEBLE BREATHS.
"GOD...
"MY GOD...
"...WHY DID YOU MAKE ME DRINK?
"MY GOD, I HAVE NO DESIRE...
"...TO BE ETERNAL.

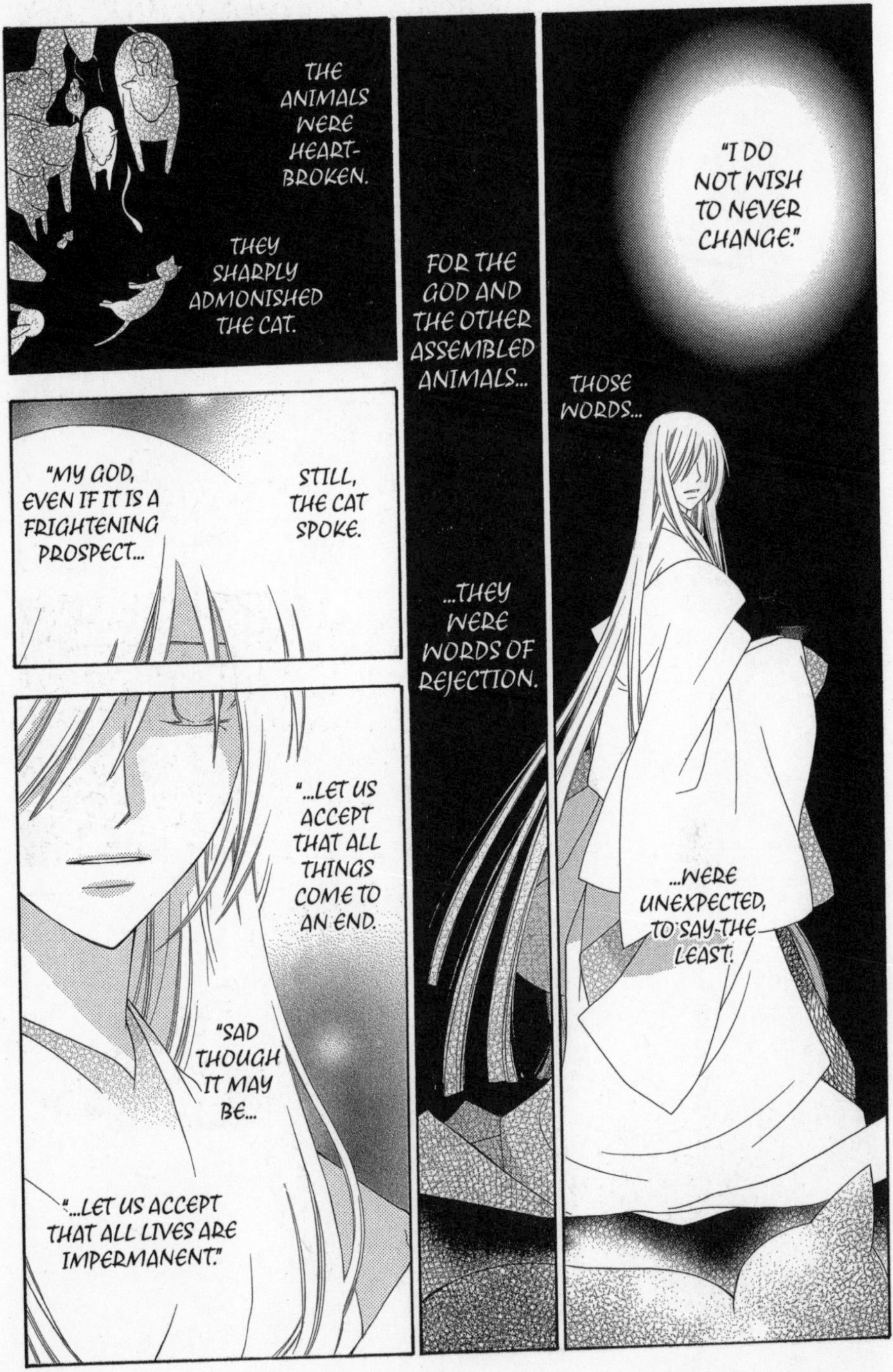
"I DO NOT WISH TO NEVER CHANGE."
THOSE WORDS...
...WERE UNEXPECTED, TO SAY THE LEAST.
FOR THE GOD AND THE OTHER ASSEMBLED ANIMALS...
...THEY WERE WORDS OF REJECTION.
THE ANIMALS WERE HEART-BROKEN.
THEY SHARPLY ADMONISHED THE CAT.
STILL, THE CAT SPOKE.
"MY GOD, EVEN IF IT IS A FRIGHTENING PROSPECT...
"...LET US ACCEPT THAT ALL THINGS COME TO AN END.
"SAD THOUGH IT MAY BE...
"...LET US ACCEPT THAT ALL LIVES ARE IMPERMANENT."

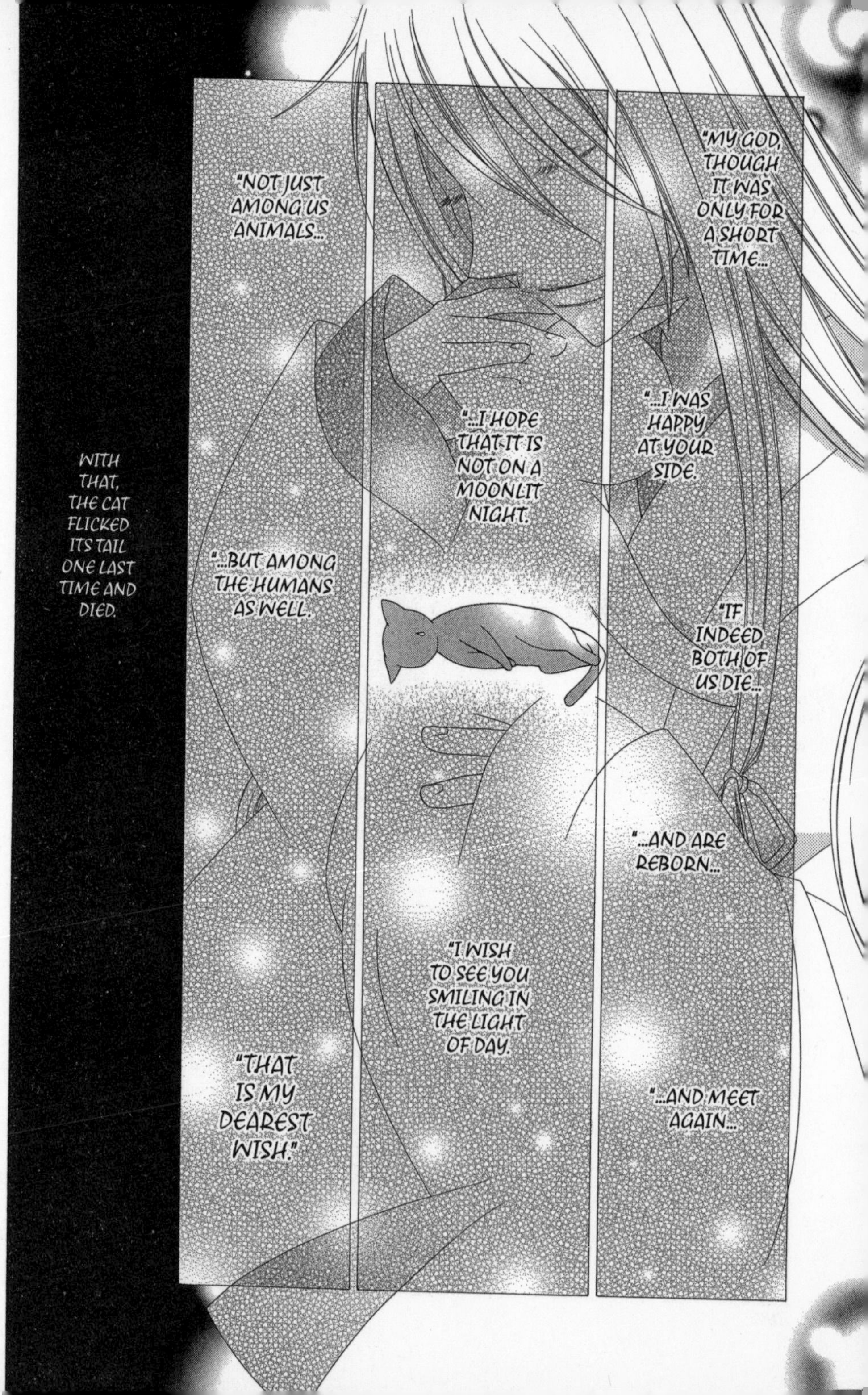
"MY GOD, THOUGH IT WAS ONLY FOR A SHORT TIME...
"...I WAS HAPPY AT YOUR SIDE.
"IF INDEED BOTH OF US DIE...
"...AND ARE REBORN...
"...AND MEET AGAIN...
"...I HOPE THAT IT IS NOT ON A MOONLIT NIGHT.
"I WISH TO SEE YOU SMILING IN THE LIGHT OF DAY.
"NOT JUST AMONG US ANIMALS...
"...BUT AMONG THE HUMANS AS WELL.
"THAT IS MY DEAREST WISH."
WITH THAT, THE CAT FLICKED ITS TAIL ONE LAST TIME AND DIED.

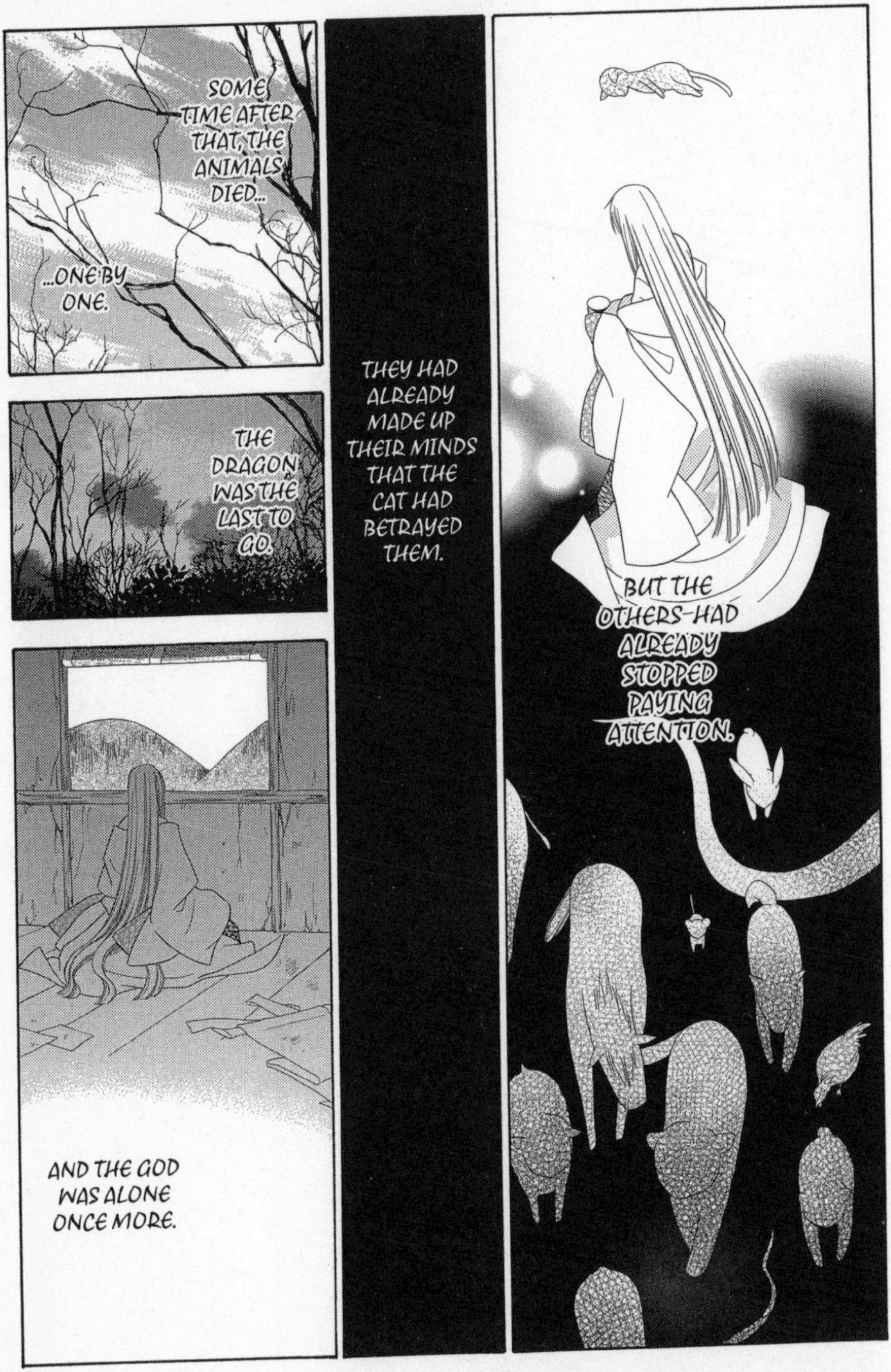
BUT THE OTHERS HAD ALREADY STOPPED PAYING ATTENTION.
THEY HAD ALREADY MADE UP THEIR MINDS THAT THE CAT HAD BETRAYED THEM.
SOME TIME AFTER THAT, THE ANIMALS DIED...
...ONE BY ONE.
THE DRAGON WAS THE LAST TO GO.
AND THE GOD WAS ALONE ONCE MORE.

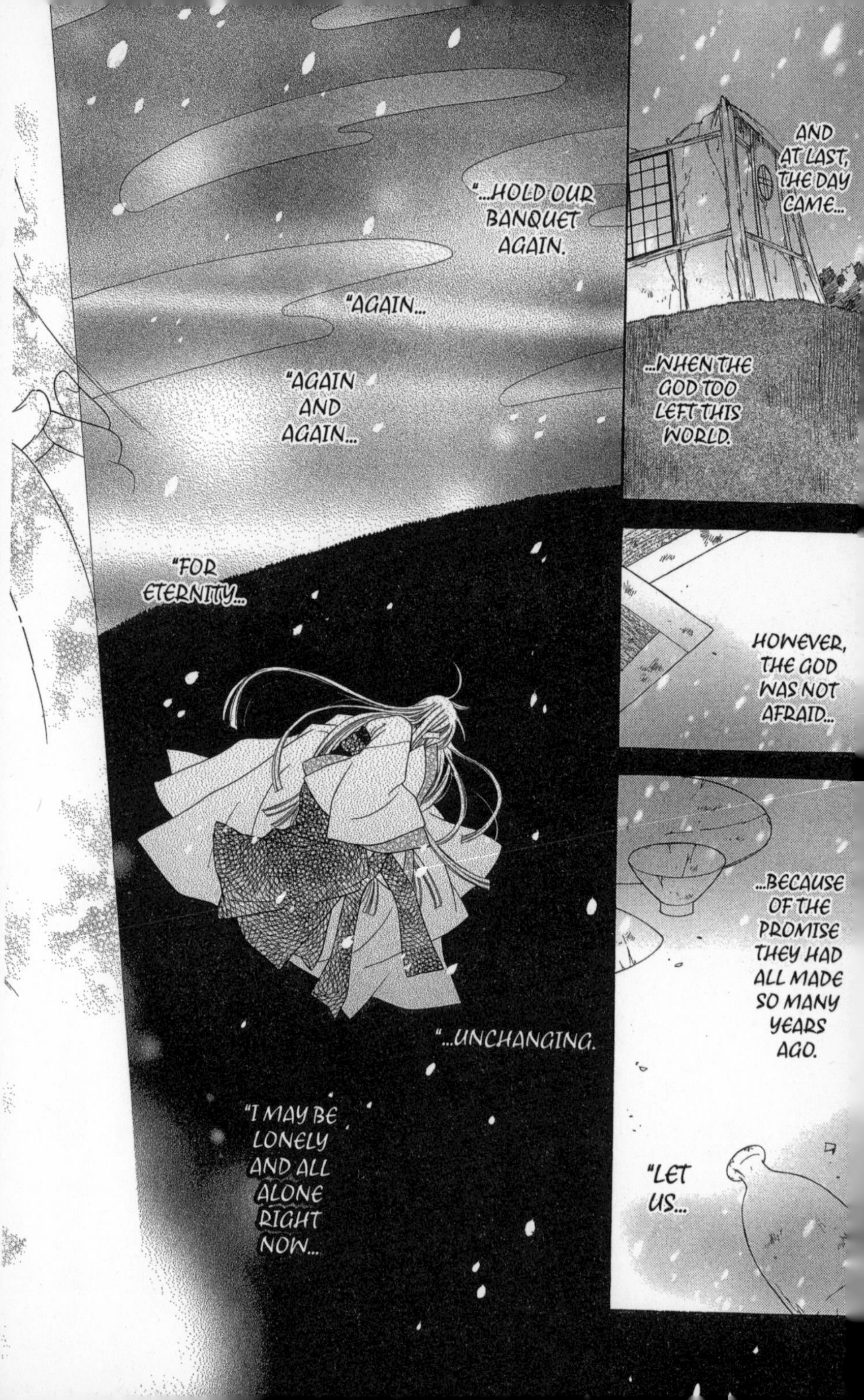
AND AT LAST, THE DAY CAME...
...WHEN THE GOD TOO LEFT THIS WORLD.
HOWEVER, THE GOD WAS NOT AFRAID...
...BECAUSE OF THE PROMISE THEY HAD ALL MADE SO MANY YEARS AGO.
"LET US...
"...HOLD OUR BANQUET AGAIN.
"AGAIN...
"AGAIN AND AGAIN...
"FOR ETERNITY...
"...UNCHANGING.
"I MAY BE LONELY AND ALL ALONE RIGHT NOW...

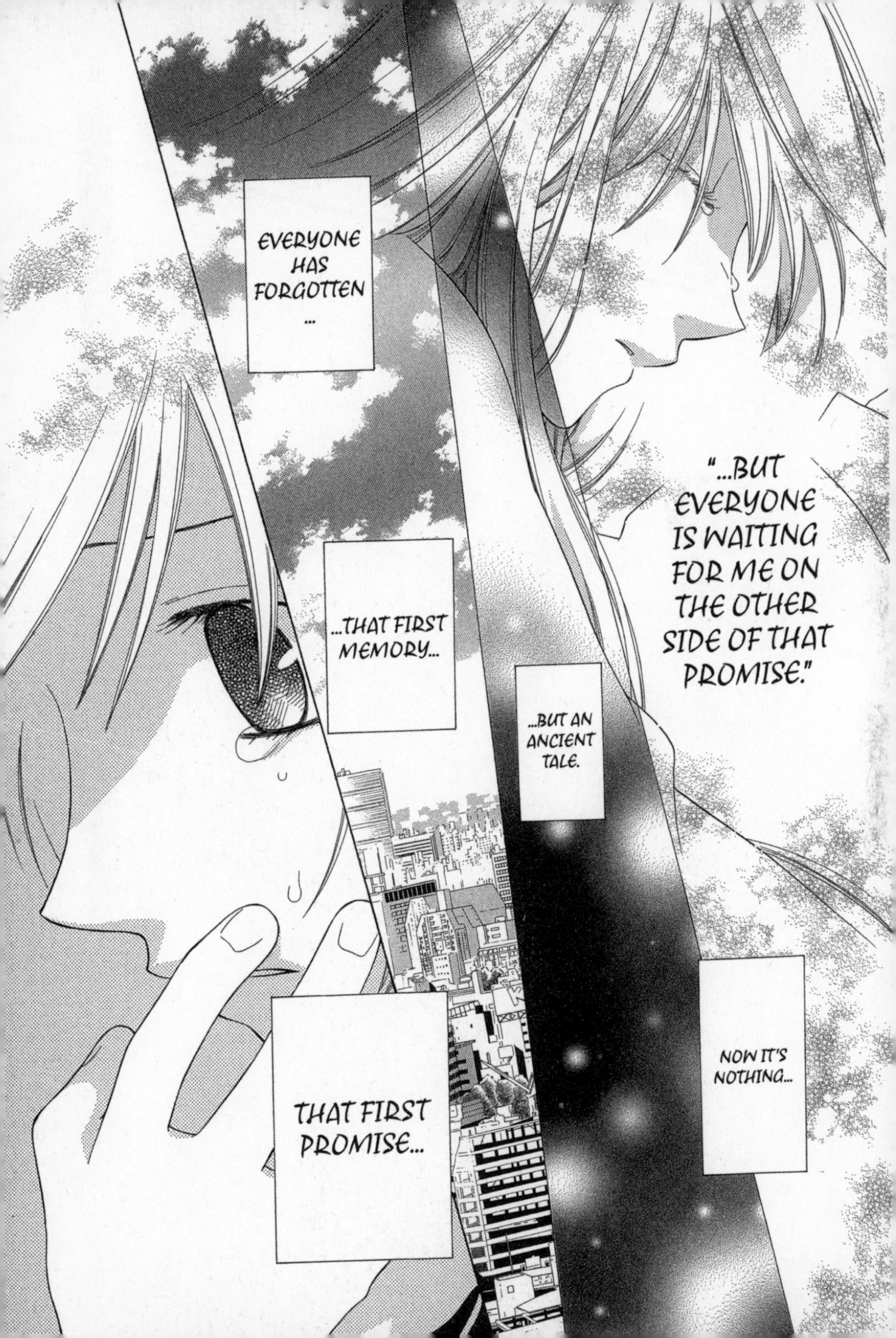
EVERYONE HAS FORGOTTEN ...
...THAT FIRST MEMORY...
"...BUT EVERYONE IS WAITING FOR ME ON THE OTHER SIDE OF THAT PROMISE."
THAT FIRST PROMISE...
NOW IT'S NOTHING...
...BUT AN ANCIENT TALE.

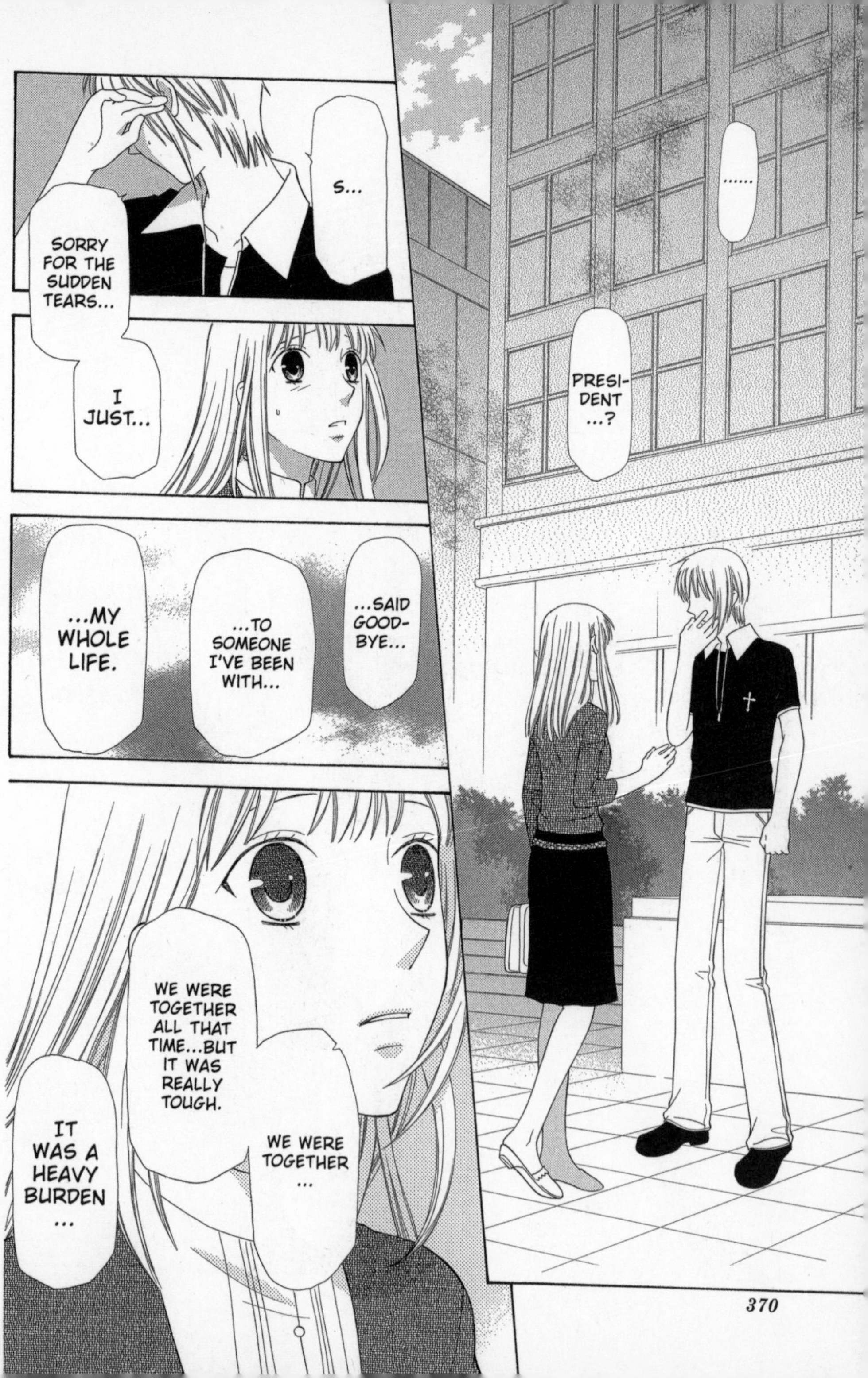
......
PRESIDENT...?
S...
SORRY FOR THE SUDDEN TEARS...
I JUST...
...SAID GOODBYE...
...TO SOMEONE I'VE BEEN WITH...
...MY WHOLE LIFE.
WE WERE TOGETHER ALL THAT TIME...BUT IT WAS REALLY TOUGH.
WE WERE TOGETHER...
IT WAS A HEAVY BURDEN...

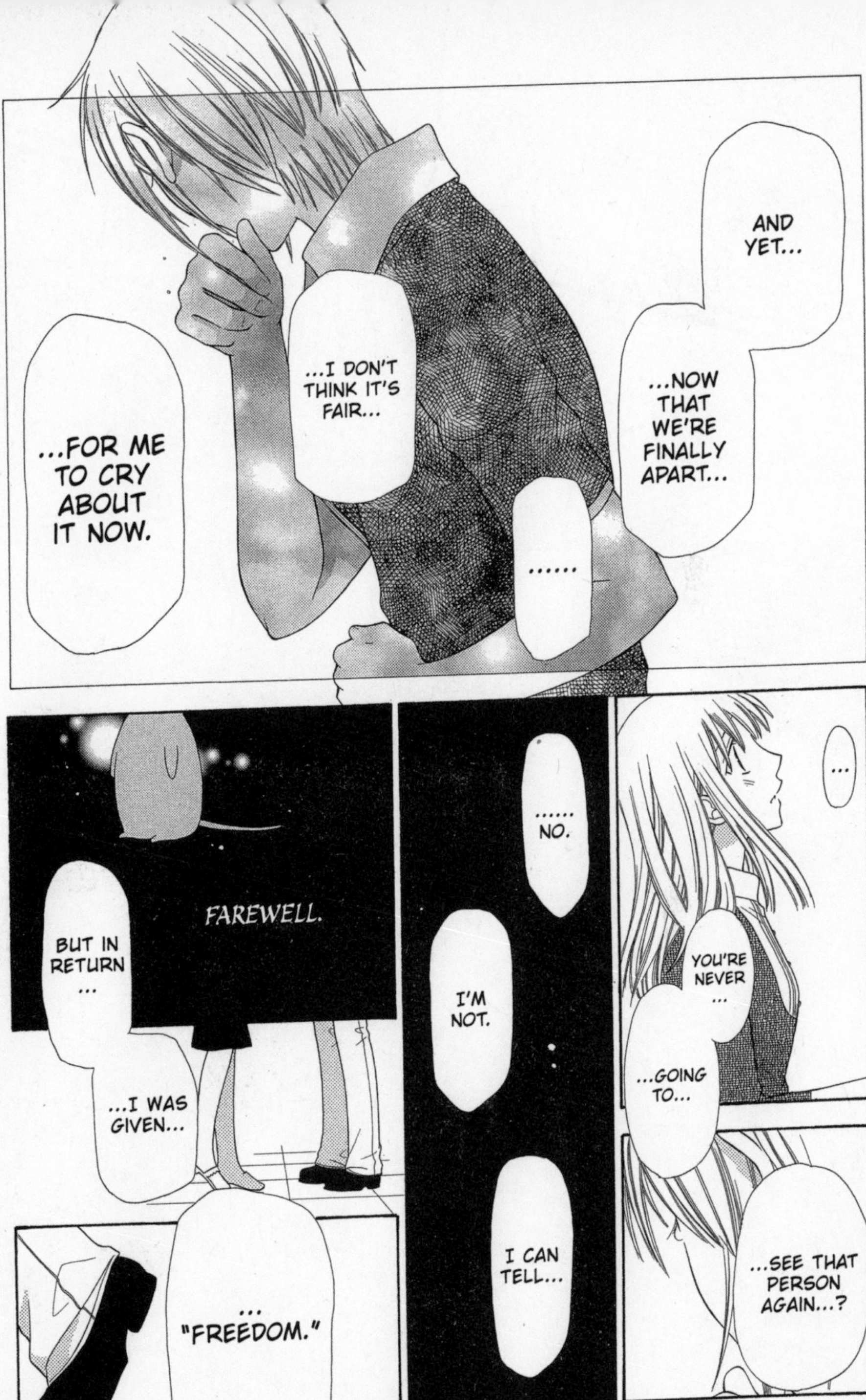
AND YET...
...NOW THAT WE'RE FINALLY APART...
......
...I DON'T THINK IT'S FAIR...
...FOR ME TO CRY ABOUT IT NOW.
...
YOU'RE NEVER ...
...GOING TO...
...SEE THAT PERSON AGAIN...?
...... NO.
I'M NOT.
I CAN TELL...
FAREWELL.
BUT IN RETURN ...
...I WAS GIVEN...
... "FREEDOM."

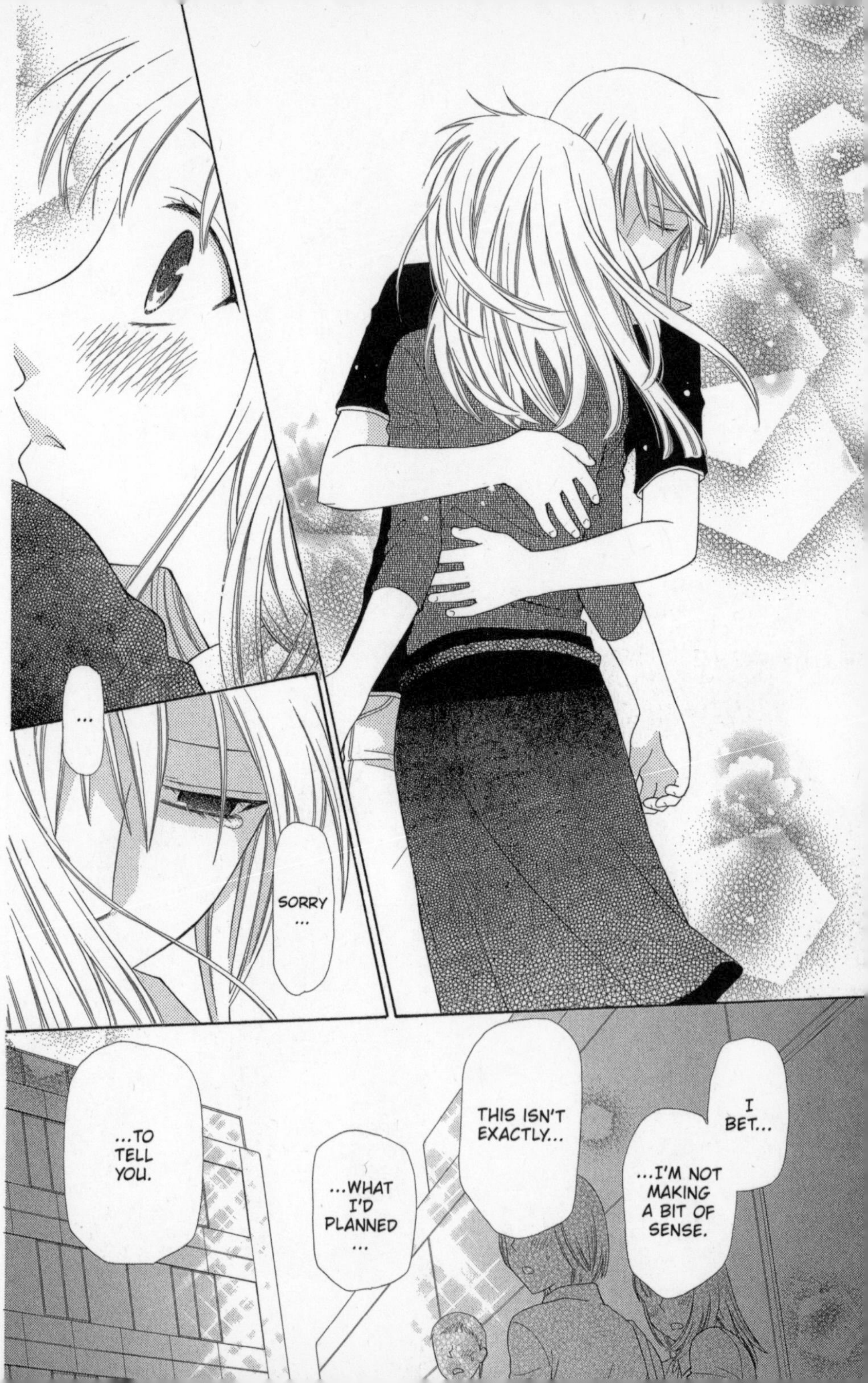
...
SORRY ...
I BET...
...I'M NOT MAKING A BIT OF SENSE.
THIS ISN'T EXACTLY...
...WHAT I'D PLANNED ...
...TO TELL YOU.

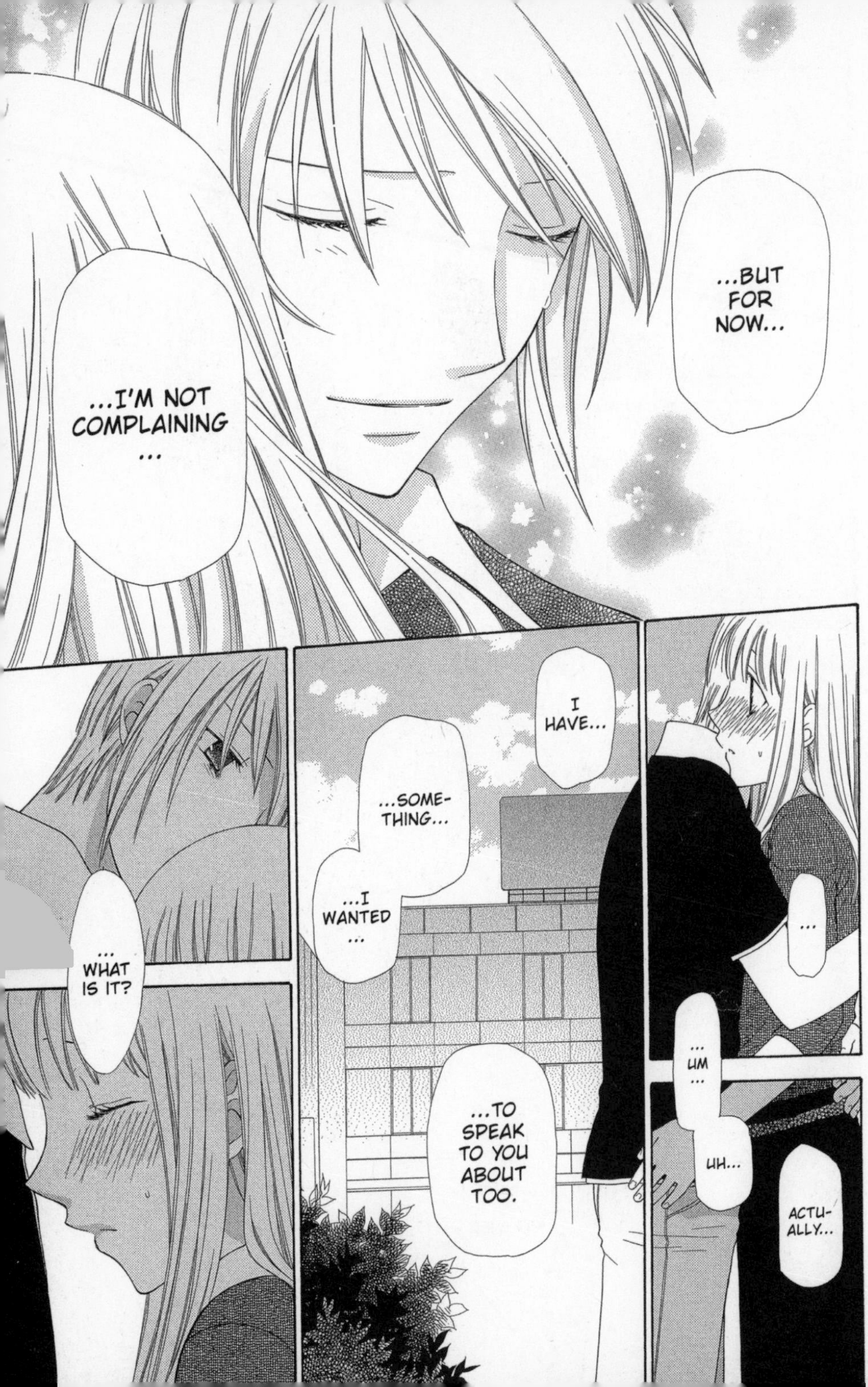

...BUT FOR NOW...
...I'M NOT COMPLAINING ...
...
... UM ...
UH...
ACTU- ALLY...
I HAVE...
...SOME- THING...
...I WANTED ...
...TO SPEAK TO YOU ABOUT TOO.
... WHAT IS IT?

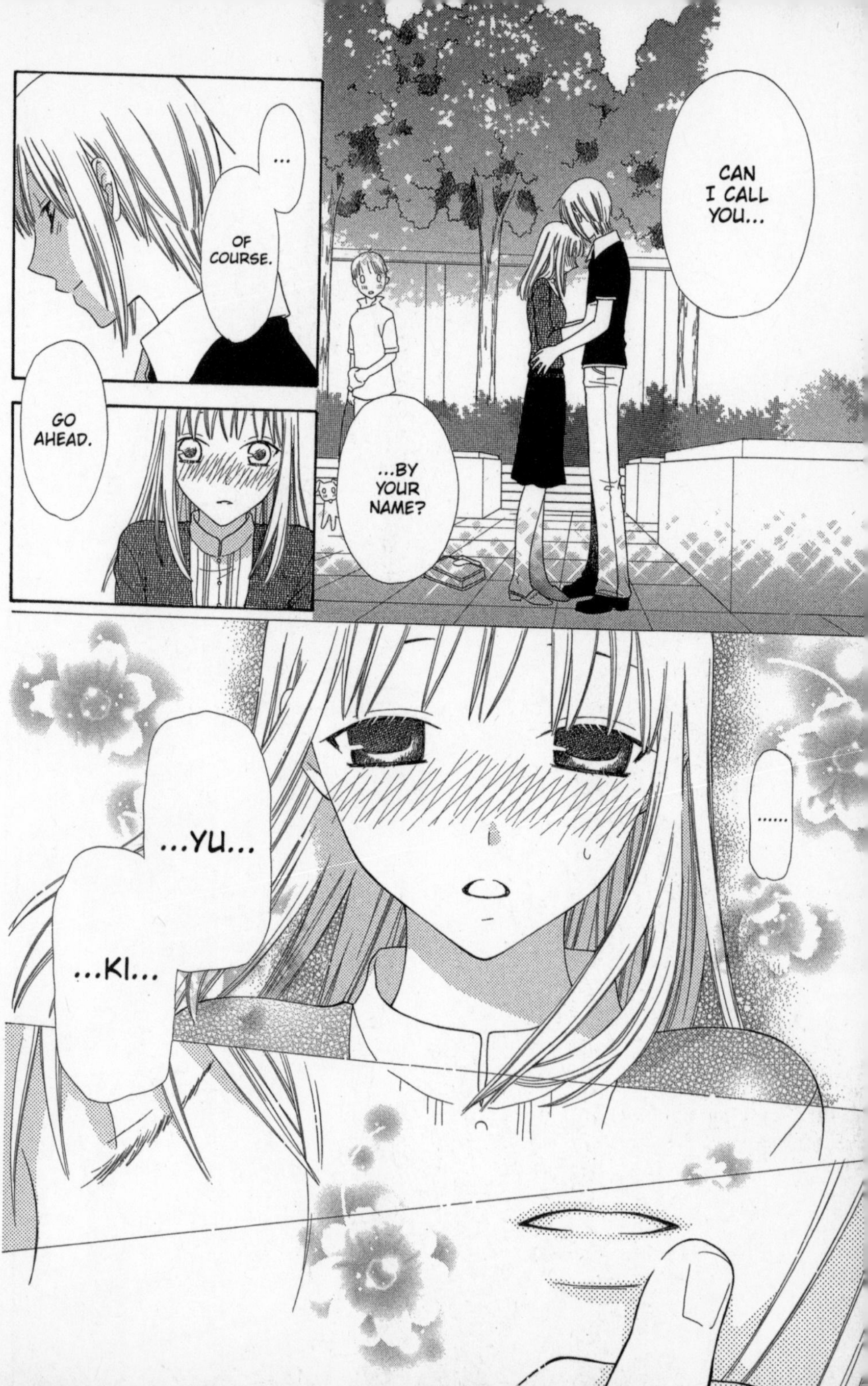
CAN I CALL YOU...
...BY YOUR NAME?
...
OF COURSE.
GO AHEAD.
......
...YU...
...KI...

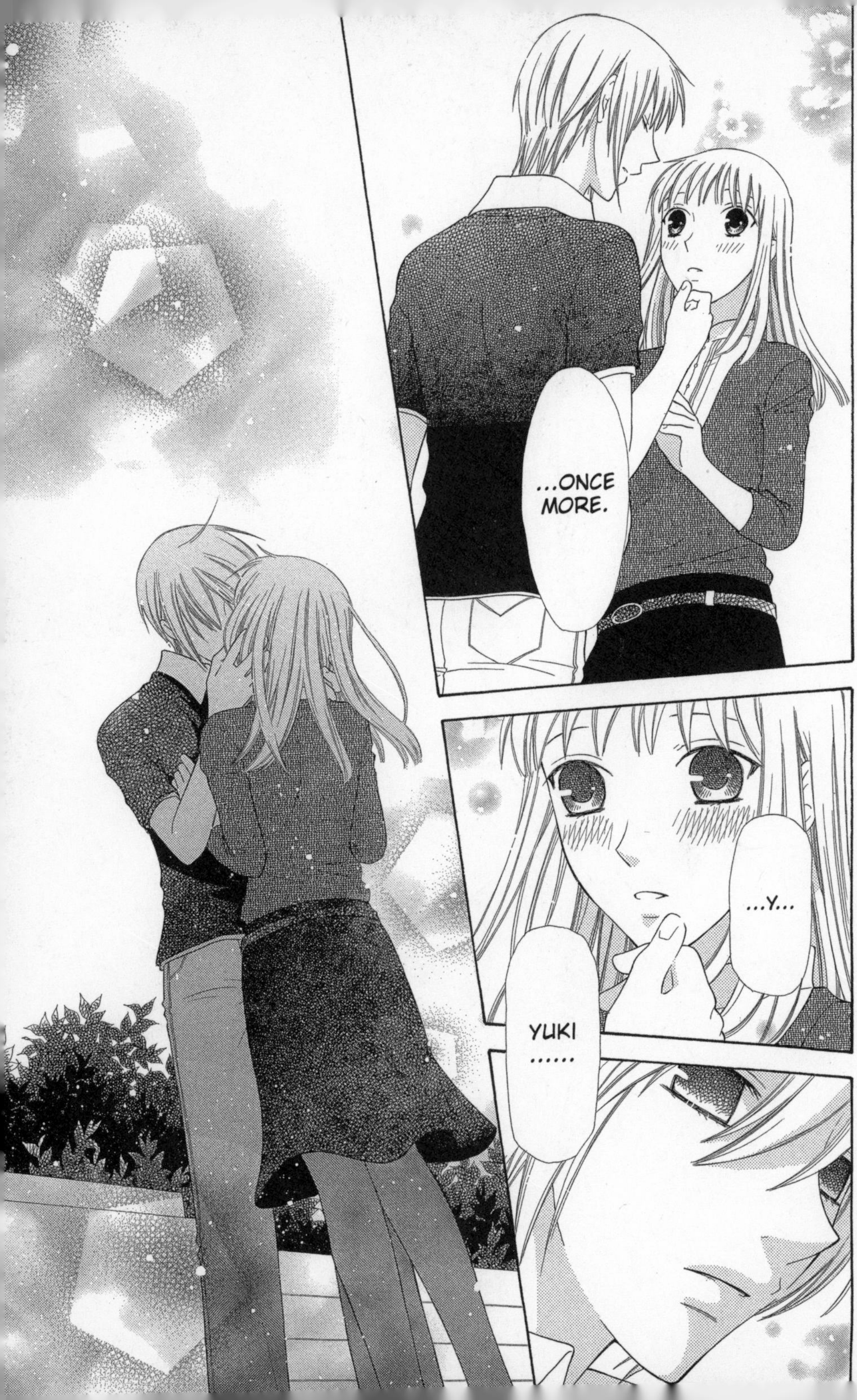
...ONCE MORE.
...Y...
YUKI ......

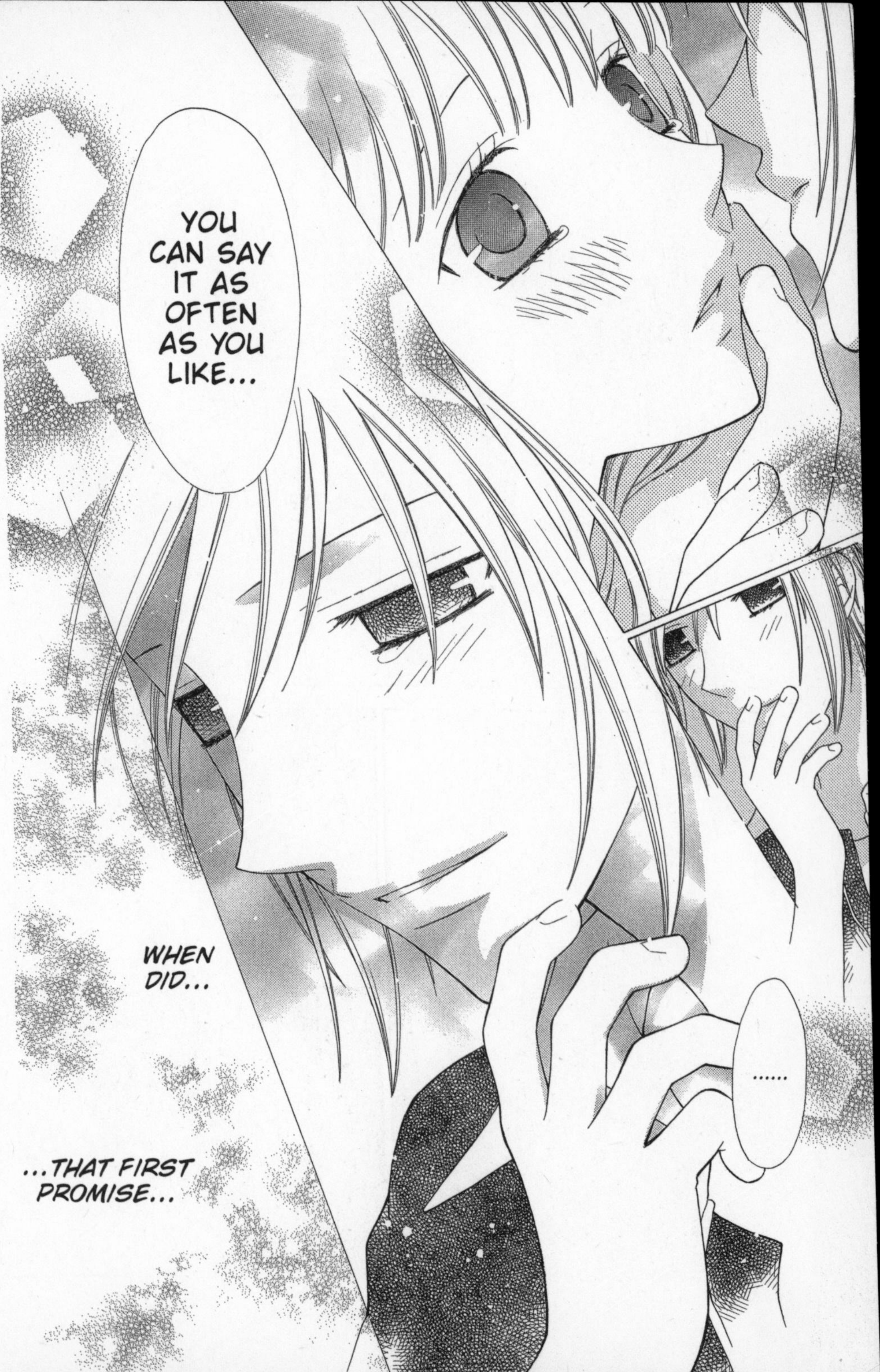
YOU CAN SAY IT AS OFTEN AS YOU LIKE...
WHEN DID...
......
...THAT FIRST PROMISE...

...TURN INTO...

...A "CURSE"?

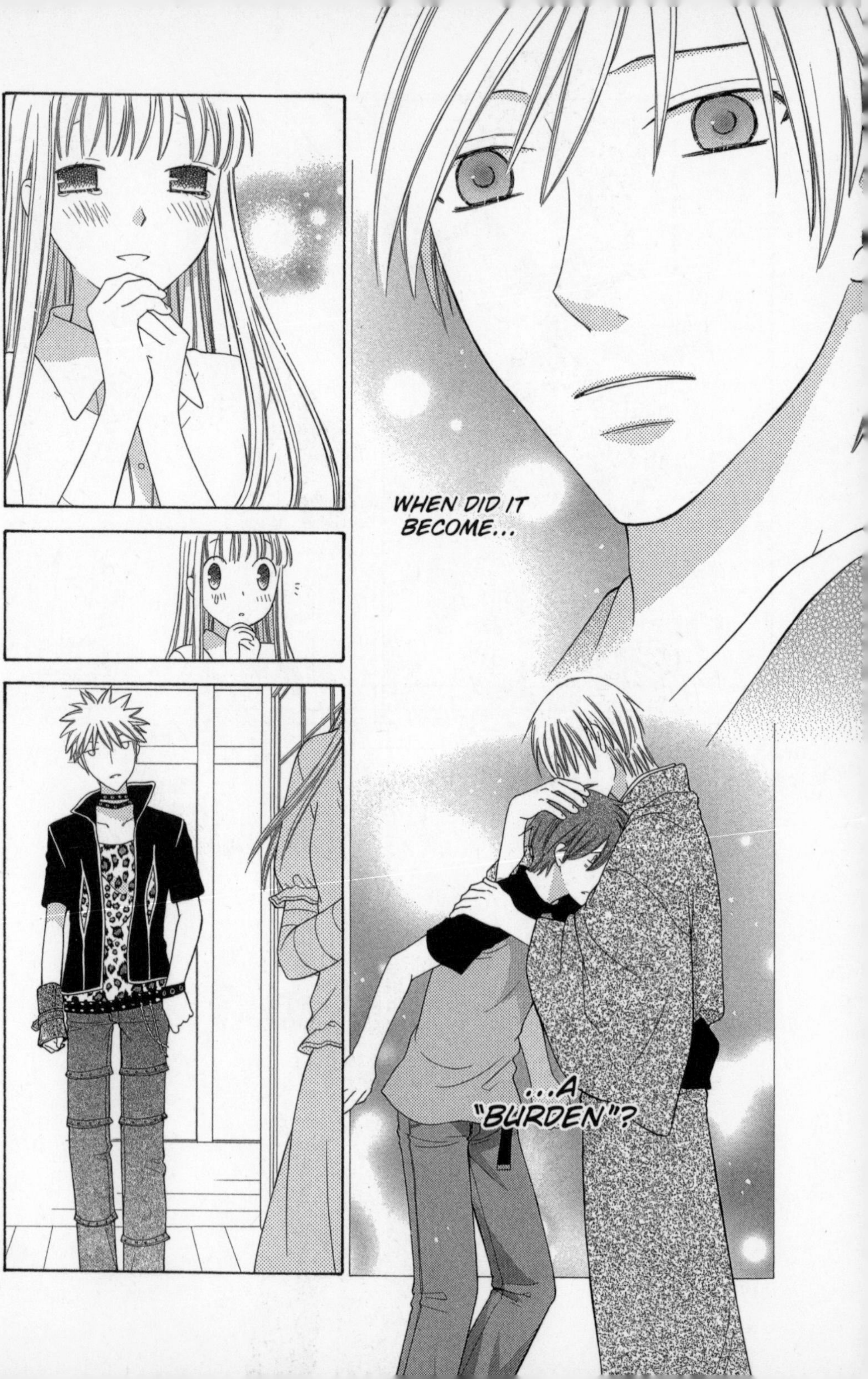
WHEN DID IT BECOME...
..."BURDEN"?

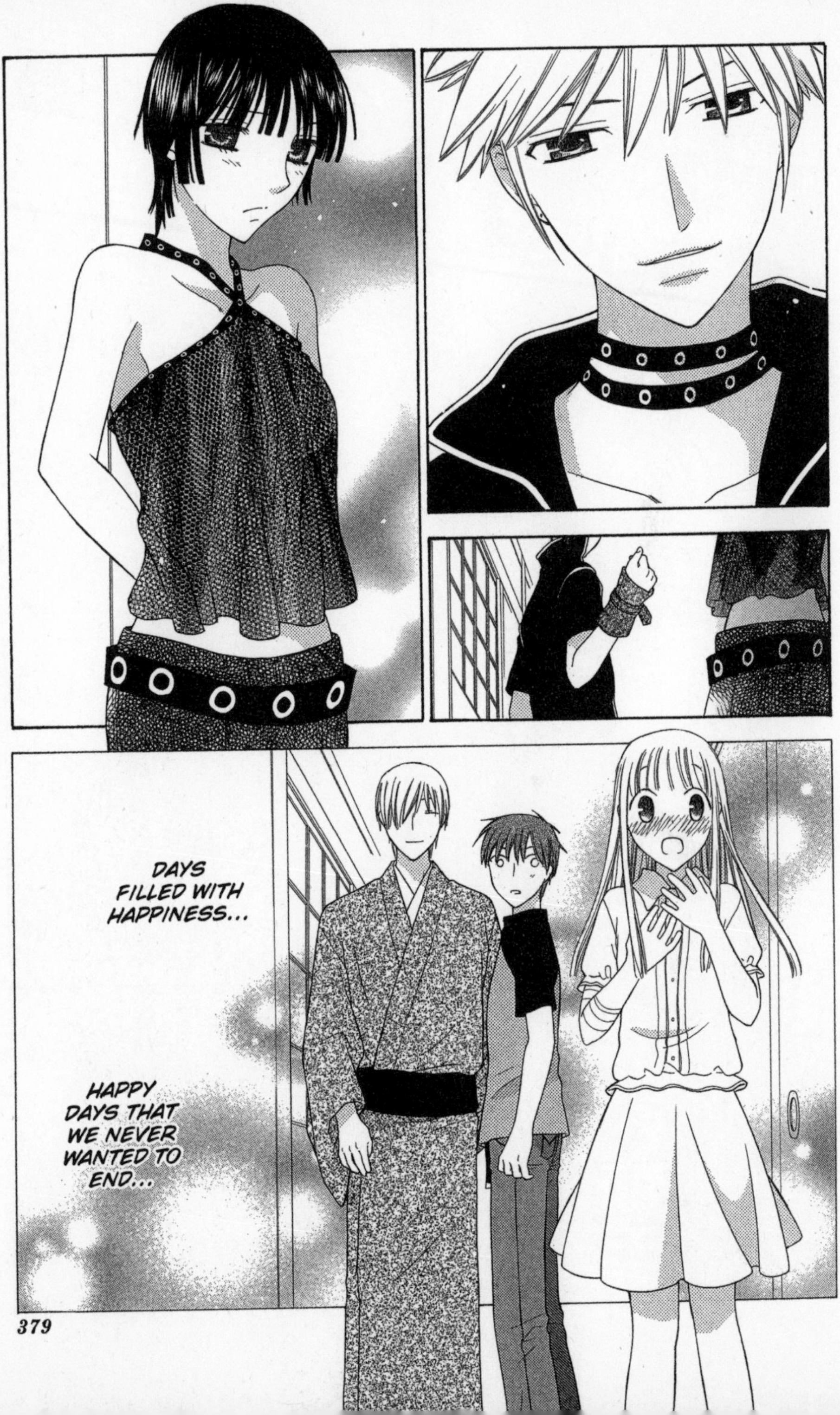
DAYS FILLED WITH HAPPINESS...
HAPPY DAYS THAT WE NEVER WANTED TO END...

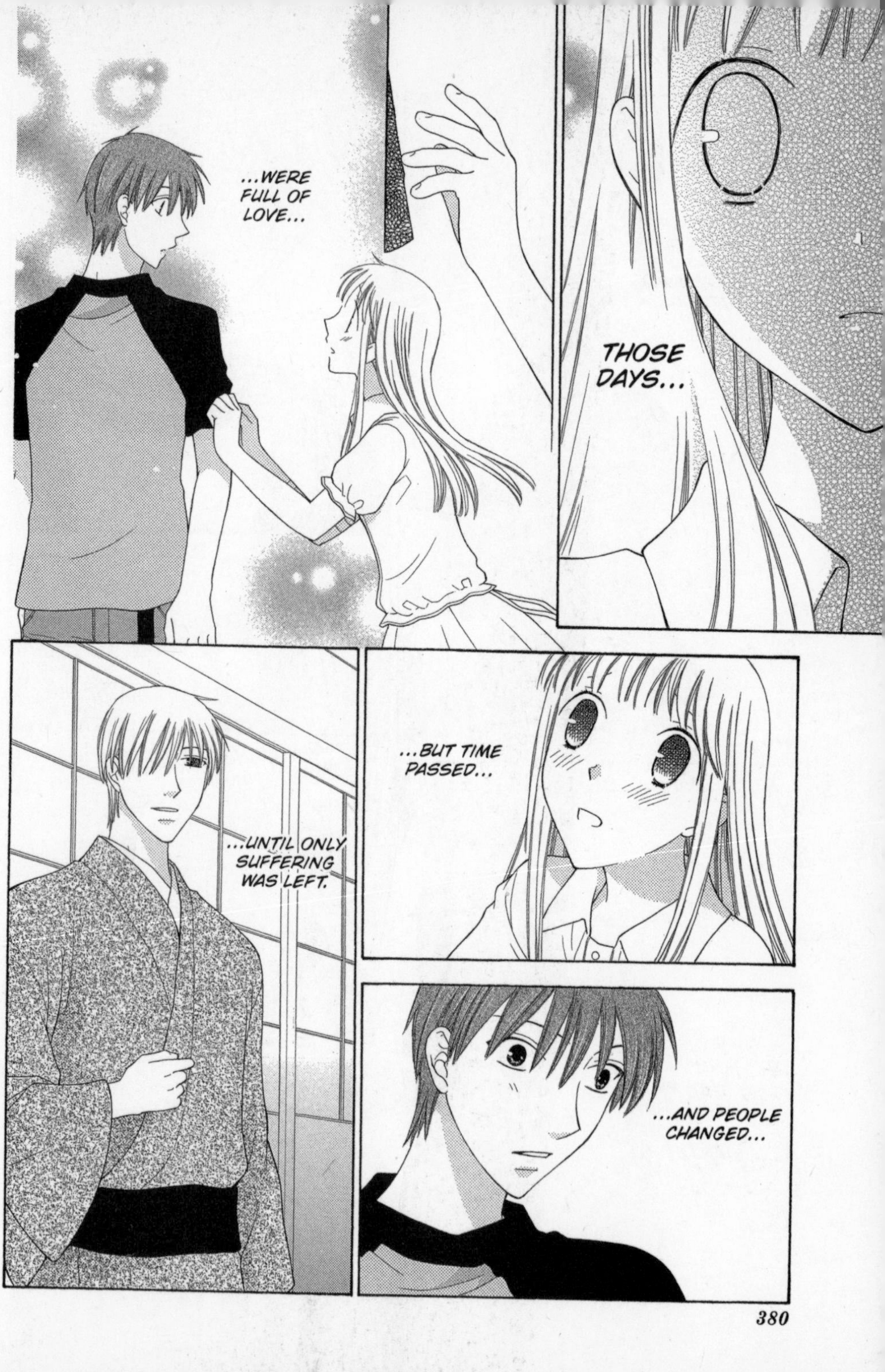
THOSE DAYS...
...WERE FULL OF LOVE...
...BUT TIME PASSED...
...AND PEOPLE CHANGED...
...UNTIL ONLY SUFFERING WAS LEFT.

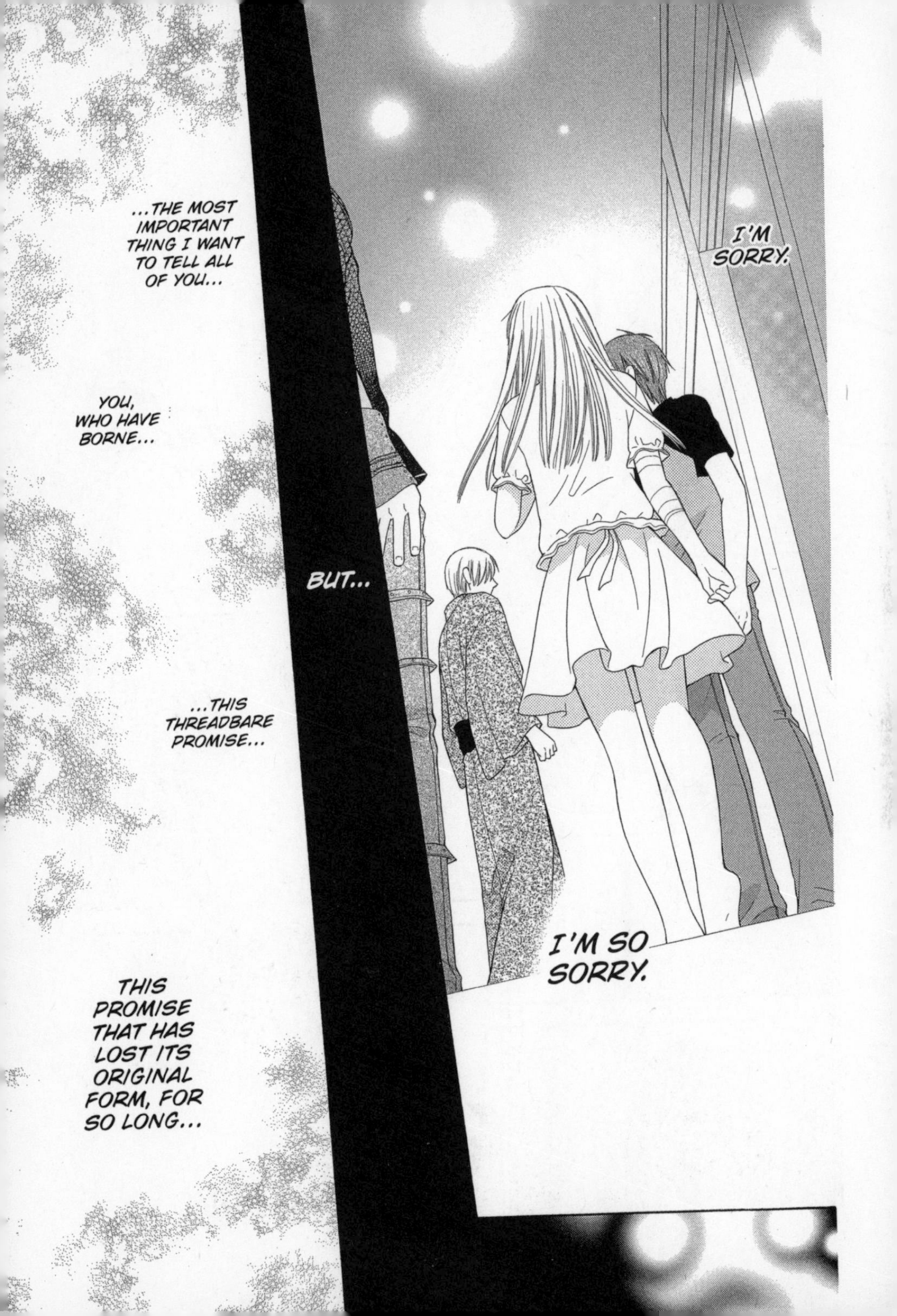
I'M SORRY.
BUT...
I'M SO SORRY.
...THE MOST IMPORTANT THING I WANT TO TELL ALL OF YOU...
YOU, WHO HAVE BORNE...
...THIS THREADBARE PROMISE...
THIS PROMISE THAT HAS LOST ITS ORIGINAL FORM, FOR SO LONG...

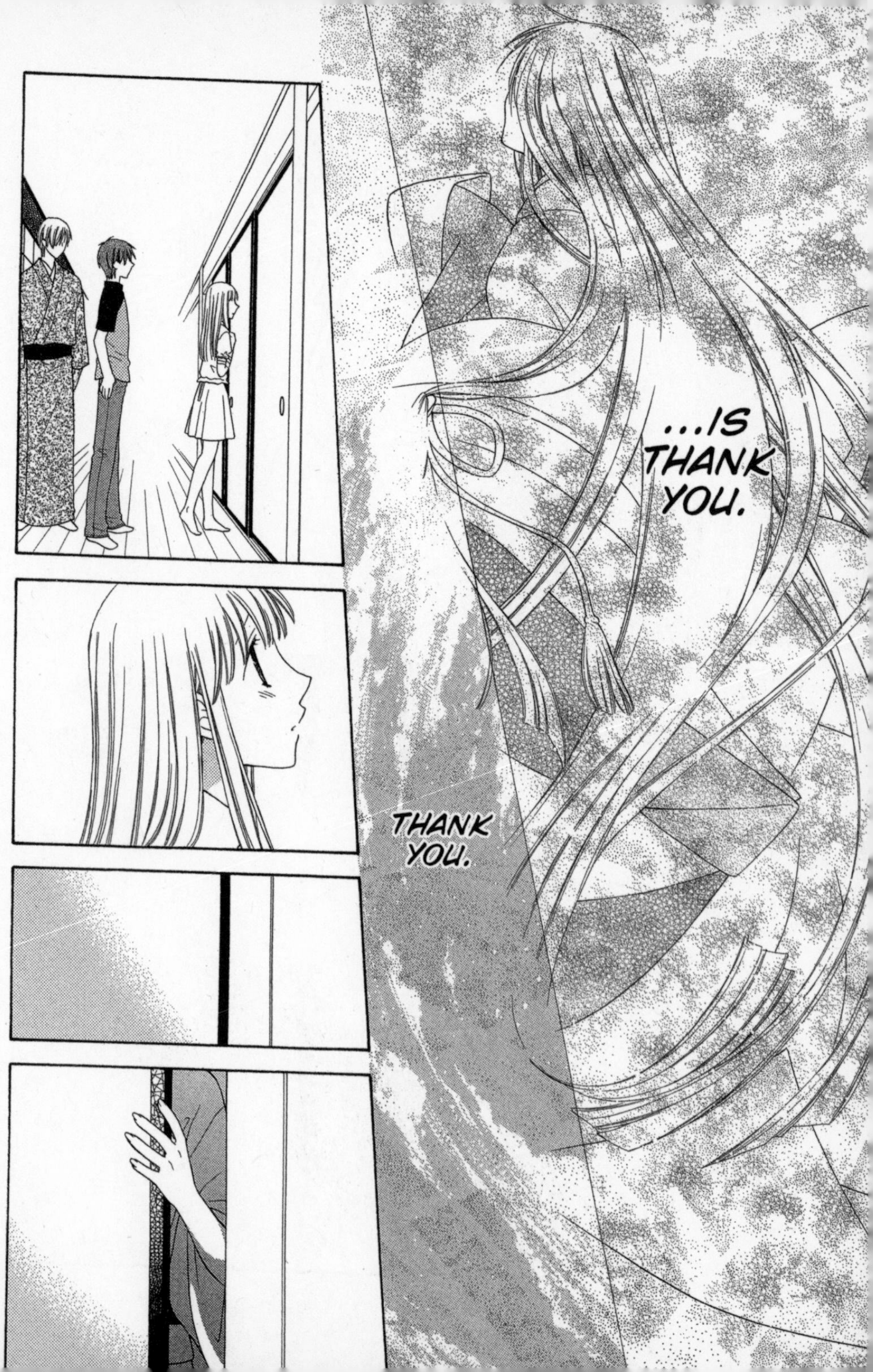
...IS THANK YOU.
THANK YOU.

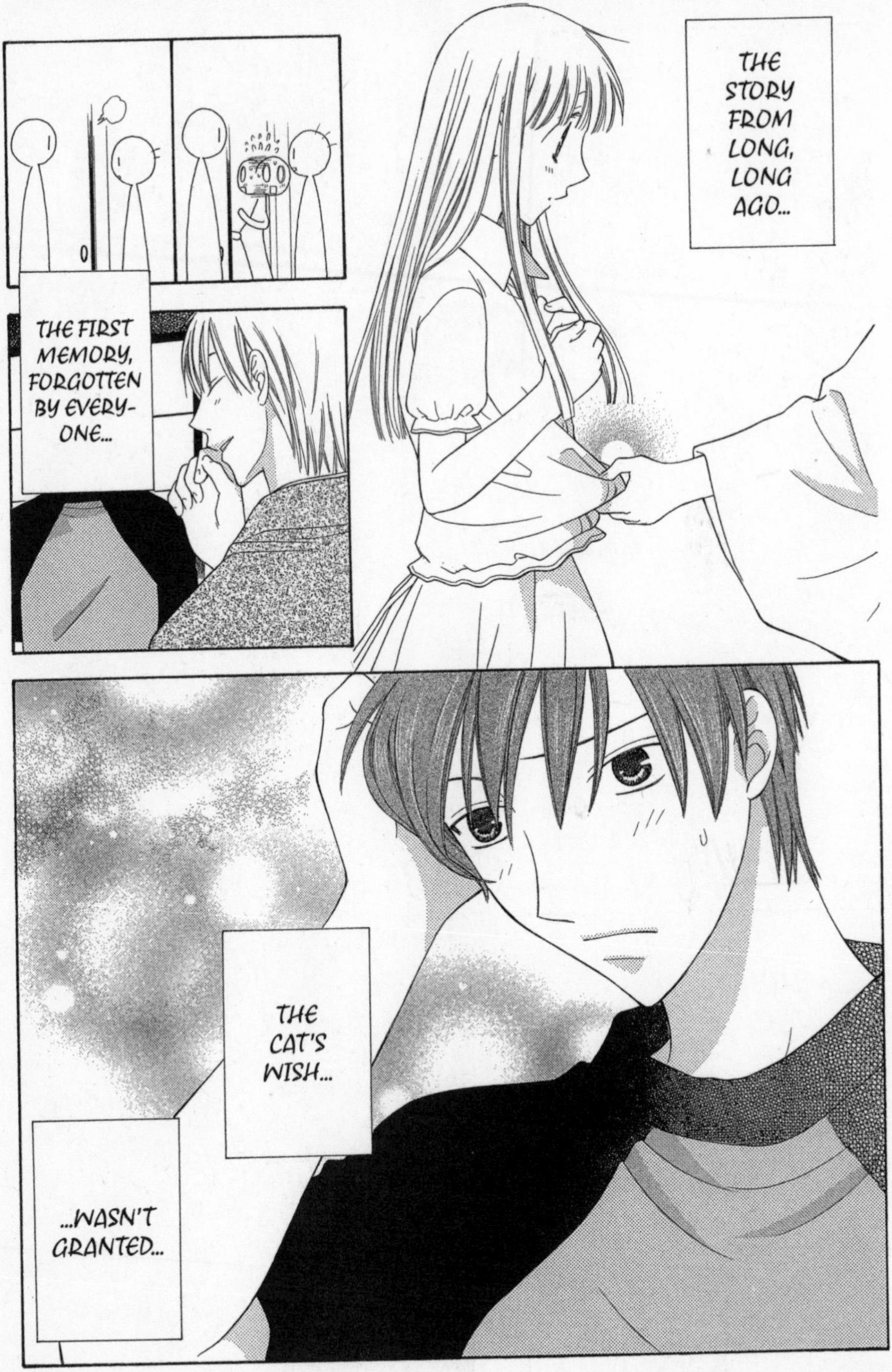
THE STORY FROM LONG, LONG AGO...
THE FIRST MEMORY, FORGOTTEN BY EVERY-ONE...
THE CAT'S WISH...
...WASN'T GRANTED...

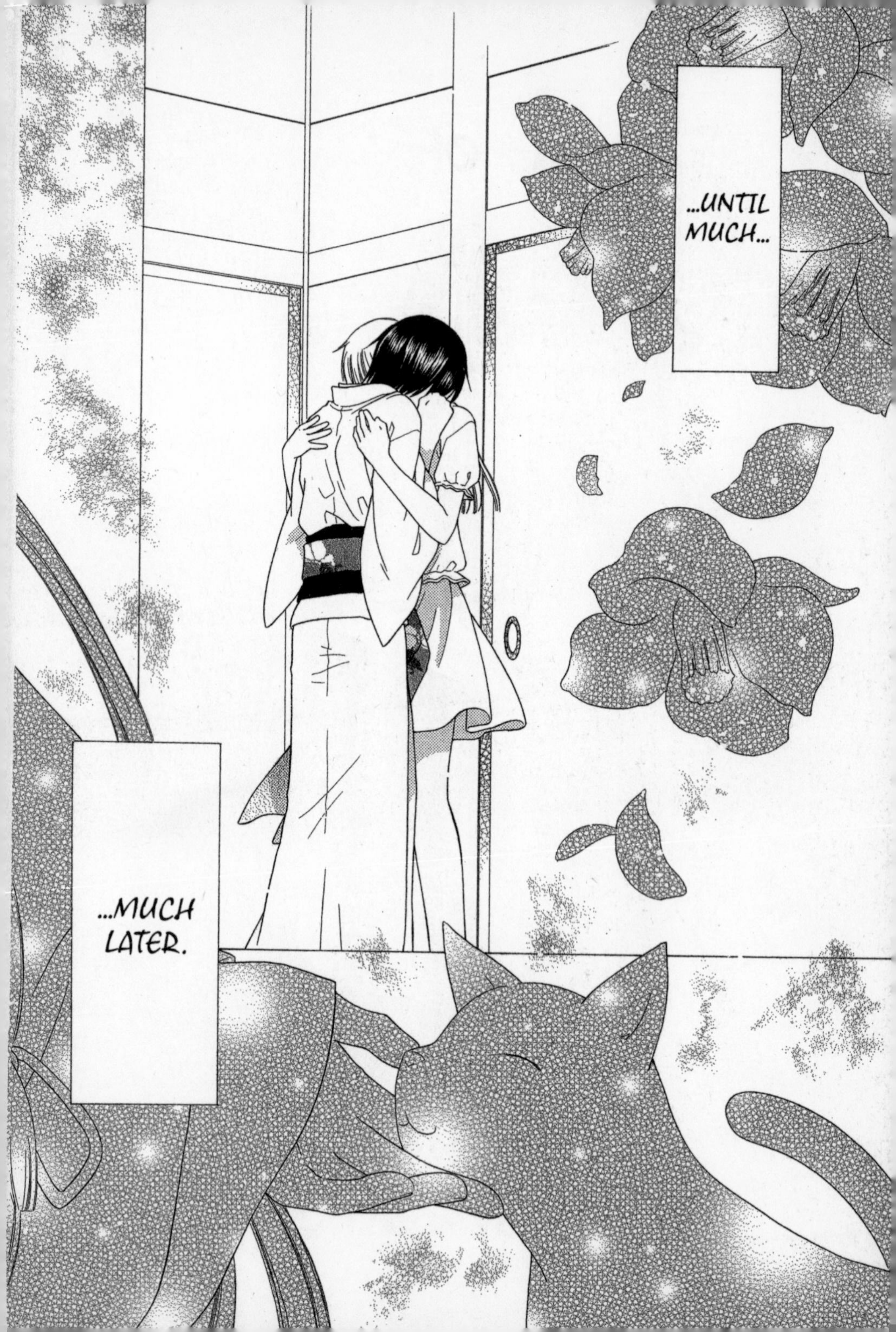
...UNTIL MUCH...
...MUCH LATER.

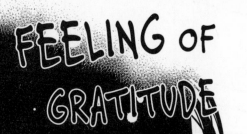

FEELING OF GRATITUDE

Even though the story is heading into the home stretch at this point, for some reason the afterword art has a menacing air...I didn't mean anything by it. (LOL) It looks like Ren-san hasn't softened at all!...

There's only one volume of these collector's editions to go. I hope you stay to watch over the remainder of the characters' journeys.

Thank you for picking up this collector's edition!

高屋奈月。
NATSUKI TAKAYA

TRANSLATION NOTES

COMMON HONORIFICS

no honorific: Indicates familiarity or closeness; if used without permission or reason, addressing someone in this manner would constitute an insult.

-san: The Japanese equivalent of Mr./Mrs./Miss. If a situation calls for politeness, this is the fail-safe honorific.

-sama: Conveys great respect; may also indicate that the social status of the speaker is lower than that of the addressee.

-kun: Used most often when referring to boys, this indicates affection or familiarity. Occasionally used by older men among their peers, but it may also be used by anyone referring to a person of lower standing.

-chan: An affectionate honorific indicating familiarity used mostly in reference to girls; also used in reference to cute persons or animals of either gender.

-senpai: A suffix used to address upperclassmen or more experienced coworkers.

-kouhai: A suffix used to address underclassmen or less experienced coworkers.

-sensei: A respectful term for teachers, artists, or high-level professionals.

Page 147
Death poem: An East Asian genre of poetry in which a person who is near death reflects on their mortality and writes a poem to encapsulate those feelings.

Page 175
"Good job!": Kakeru is saying *otsukaresan* in Japanese, a common, handy phrase that encompasses the meaning of "good job" but can be more literally read as "you must be tired (because you worked so hard)." This is one of the times when the happy-go-lucky Kakeru reveals his hidden emotional depths; he knows Yuki has been having a rough time of it, what with Tohru being in the hospital, even if Yuki doesn't show it much on the outside.

Fruits Basket

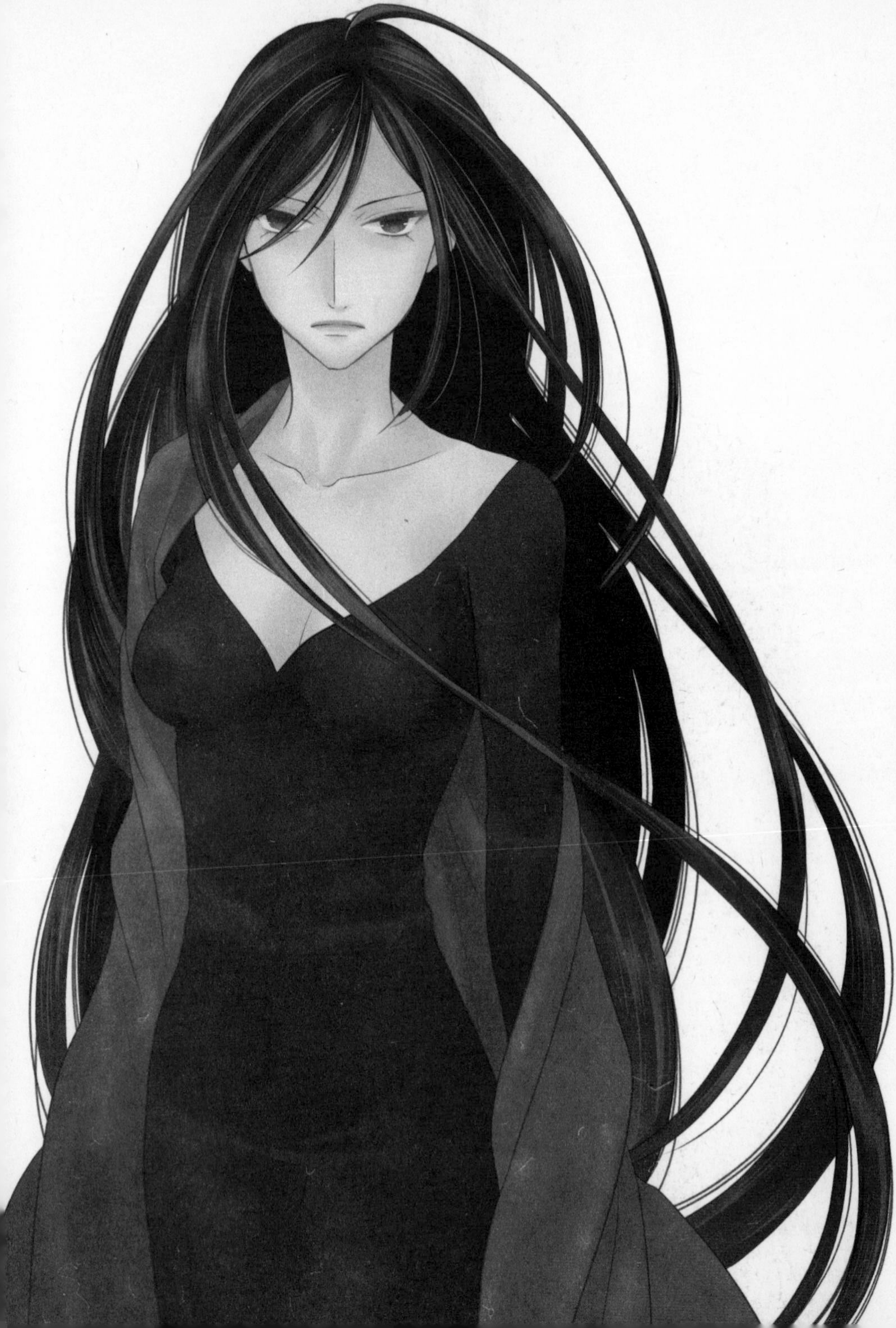

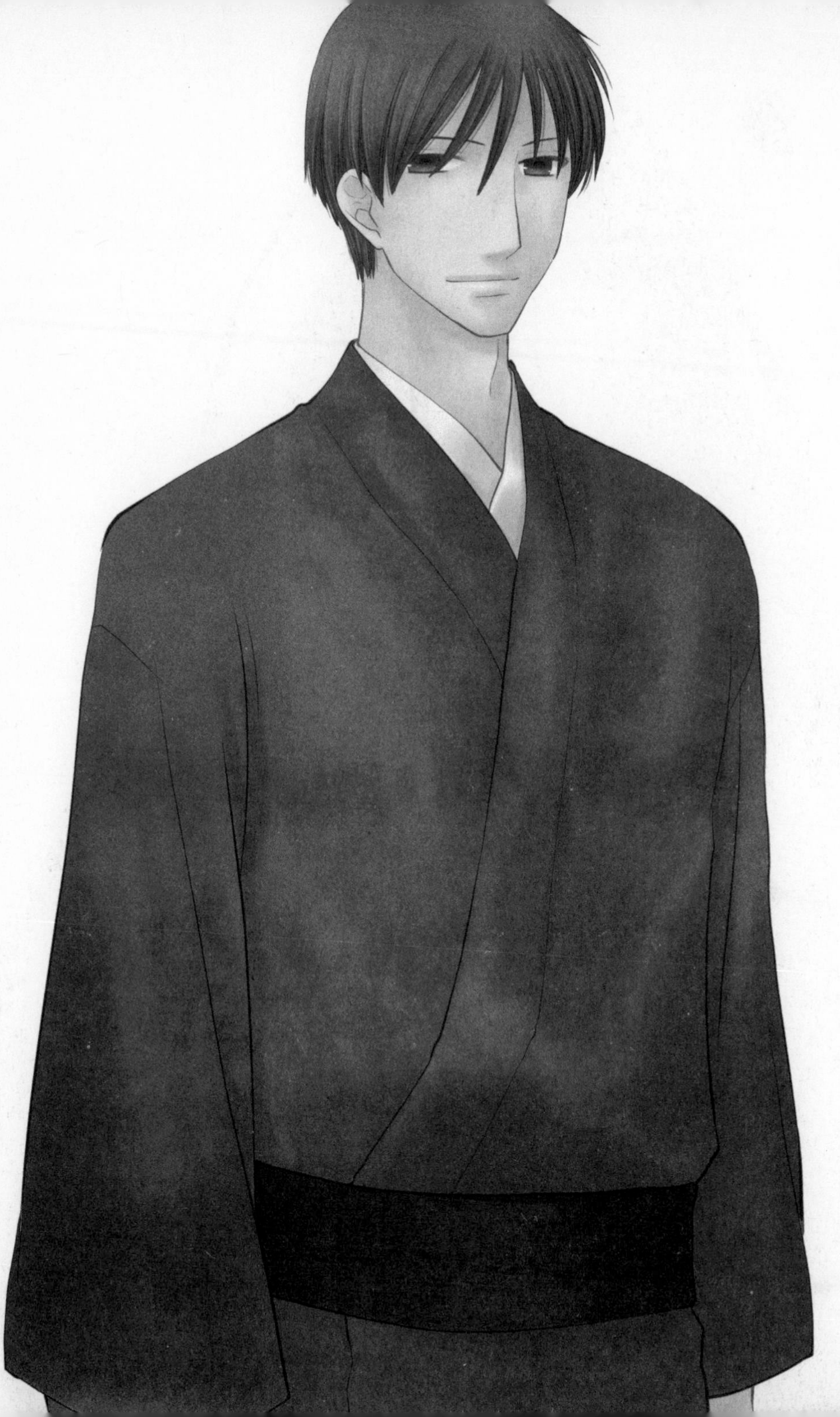

Love Natsuki Takaya?
Don't forget to check out her other works
also available from Yen Press!

Volumes 1–3,
available now.

Volumes 1–2,
available now.

COLLECTOR'S EDITION

Fruits Basket

COLLECTOR'S EDITION

Fruits Basket

NATSUKI TAKAYA

Translation: Sheldon Drzka • Lettering: Lys Blakeslee

Fruits Basket Collector's Edition, Vol. 11 by Natsuki Takaya
© Natsuki Takaya 2016
All rights reserved.
First published in Japan in 2016 by HAKUSENSHA, INC., Tokyo.
English language translation rights in U.S.A., Canada and U.K. arranged with
HAKUSENSHA, INC., Tokyo through Tuttle-Mori Agency, Inc., Tokyo.

English translation © 2017 by Yen Press, LLC

Yen Press
1290 Avenue of the Americas
New York, NY 10104

Visit us at yenpress.com
facebook.com/yenpress
twitter.com/yenpress
yenpress.tumblr.com
instagram.com/yenpress

First Yen Press Edition: March 2017

Yen Press is an imprint of Yen Press, LLC.
The Yen Press name and logo are trademarks of Yen Press, LLC.

The publisher is not responsible for websites (or their content) that are not owned by the publisher.

Library of Congress Control Number: 2016932692

ISBN: 978-0-316-50168-2

10 9 8 7 6 5 4 3 2 1

BVG

Printed in the United States of America